Perception, Action, and Consciousness

Perception, Action, and Consciousness

Sensorimotor Dynamics and Two Visual Systems

Edited by

Nivedita Gangopadhyay
Michael Madary
Finn Spicer

OXFORD
UNIVERSITY PRESS

Great Clarendon Street, Oxford OX2 6DP

Oxford University Press is a department of the University of Oxford.
It furthers the University's objective of excellence in research, scholarship,
and education by publishing worldwide in

Oxford New York

Athens Auckland Bangkok Bogotá Buenos AiresCalcutta
CapeTown Chennai Dar es Salaam Delhi Florence Hong Kong Istanbul
Karachi Kuala Lumpur Madrid Melbourne Mexico City Mumbai
Nairobi Paris São Paulo Singapore Taipei Tokyo Toronto Warsaw
with associated companies in Berlin Ibadan

Oxford is a registered trade mark of Oxford University Press
in the UK and in certain other countries

Published in the United States by
Oxford University Press Inc., New York

© Oxford University Press, 2010

The moral rights of the authors have been asserted

Database right Oxford University Press (maker)

First published 2010

British Library Cataloguing in Publication Data

Data available

Library of Congress Cataloguing in Publication Data

Data available

ISBN 978–0–19–955111–8

10 9 8 7 6 5 4 3 2 1

Typeset in Minion
by Glyph International, Bangalore, India
Printed in Great Britain
on acid-free paper by
CPI Antony Rowe, Chippenham, Wiltshire

Whilst every effort has been made to ensure that the contents of this book are as complete,
accurate, and up-to-date as possible at the date of writing, Oxford University Press
is not able to give any guarantee or assurance that such is the case. Readers are urged
to take appropriately qualified medical advice in all cases. The information in this book is
intended to be useful to the general reader, but should not be used as a means of
self-diagnosis or for the prescription of medication.

Dedication

This volume is dedicated to the memory of
Professor Susan Hurley (1954–2007).

Acknowledgement

This work was supported by the AHRC (grant number AH/E511139/1) and forms a part of the CONTACT (Consciousness in Interaction) Project. The CONTACT project is a part of the ESF Eurocores Consciousness in the Natural and Cultural Context (CNCC) scheme.

Contents

List of Contributors

Dana H. Ballard
Computer Science and Psychology,
The University of Texas at Austin,
Austin, USA

Angela Bartolo
URECA,
Univ Lille Nord de France,
Villeneuve d'Ascq
Cedex, France

Annabelle Blangero
Espace et Action – ImpAct,
Université Claude Bernard,
Bron, France

Andy Clark
Professor of Logic and Metaphysics,
School of Philosophy, Psychology, and
Language Sciences,
University of Edinburgh,
Edinburgh, UK

Yonn Coello
URECA,
Univ Lille Nord de France,
Villeneuve d'Ascq
Cedex, France

Yvonne Delevoye-Turrell
URECA,
Univ Lille Nord de France,
Villeneuve d'Ascq
Cedex, France

Nivedita Gangopadhyay
Postdoctoral Research Fellow,
Center for Subjectivity Research,
University of Copenhagen,
Copenhagen, Denmark

Melvyn A. Goodale
Centre for Brain and Mind,
The University of Western Ontario,
Ontario, Canada

Pierre Jacob
Director of research CNRS,
Institut Jean Nicod,
Paris, France

Julian Kiverstein
School of Philosophy, Psychology, and
Language Sciences,
University of Edinburgh,
Edinburgh, UK

Michael Madary
Department of Philosophy,
Tulane University,
New Orleans, USA

Flavia Mancini
University of Milano-Bicocca,
Department of Psychology and IRCCS
Istituto Auxologico Italiano,
Neuropsychological Laboratory,
Milan, Italy

Mohan Matthen
Department of Philosophy,
University of Toronto,
Toronto, Canada

Dean R. Melmoth
Applied Vision Research Centre,
Department of Optometry and Visual Science,
City University,
London, UK

A. David Milner
Emeritus Professor of Cognitive Neuroscience,
Durham University,
Durham, UK

Michael J. Morgan
Applied Vision Research Centre,
Department of Optometry and Visual Science,
City University,
London, UK

Alva Noë
Department of Philosophy
University of California at Berkeley
Berkeley, USA

J. Kevin O'Regan
Laboratoire,
Psychologie de la Perception,
Université Paris Descartes and CNRS,
Paris, France

Hisaaki Ota
Department of Rehabilitation,
Sapporo Medical University Hospital,
Chuo-ku, Sapporo, Japan

Laure Pisella
Espace et Action – ImpAct,
Université Claude Bernard,
Bron, France

Yves Rossetti
Espace et Action – ImpAct,
Université Claude Bernard,
Bron, France &
Mouvement et Handicap, Hospices
Civils de Lyon & Inserm
Hôpital Henry Gabrielle,
St Genis Laval, France

Susanna Schellenberg
Research School of Social Sciences,
The Australian National University and
Department of Philosophy,
Rutgers University
New Jersey, USA

Finn Spicer
Department of Philosophy,
University of Bristol,
Bristol, UK

Marc S. Tibber
Applied Vision Research Centre,
Department of Optometry and Visual Science,
City University,
London, UK

Giuseppe Vallar
University of Milano-Bicocca,
Department of Psychology and IRCCS
Istituto Auxologico Italiano,
Neuropsychological Laboratory,
Milan, Italy

Alain Vighetto
Hôpital Neurologique,
Hospices Civils de Lyon,
Bron, France
& Espace et Action – ImpAct,
Université Claude Bernard,
Bron, France

Frederique de Vignemont
CNRS Researcher,
Department of Philosophy,
New York University,
New York, USA

Robert A. Wilson
Department of Philosophy,
University of Alberta,
Edmonton, Canada

Abbreviations

dPM	dorsal premotor cortex
EBC	experience-based control
EBS	experience-based selection
fMRI	functional magnetic resonance imaging
IT	infero-temporal cortex
mIPS	medial bank of intraparietal cortex
IPS	intraparietal sulcus
JND	just noticeable difference
MGA	maximum grip aperture
OA	optic ataxia
POJ	parieto-occipital junction
RFI	rod-and-frame illusion
STI	simultaneous tilt illusion
SPL	superior parietal lobule
TVSS	tactile visual sensory substitution
USN	unilateral spatial neglect
VEPs	visual evoked potentials
rTMS	Transcranial Magnetic Stimulation

CHAPTER 1

Perception, action, and consciousness

N. Gangopadhyay, M. Madary, and F. Spicer

1.1. Introduction

In the last couple of decades the cognitive sciences and the philosophy of mind have witnessed growing challenges to a basic assumption about the nature of mind and cognitive states. A grounding premise of early cognitive science was the hypothesis that perception arises by the experiencing subject acting as a passive recipient of sensory stimuli. Acceptance of this assumption conferred to the subject of experience a considerably passive role in the generation of experiential states. It was deemed possible to study cognition and perception by abstracting away from the details of the embodiment and situatedness of the experiencing subject. David Marr's (1982) theory of vision is an extremely influential example of such an approach and became the meta-theory for classical information-processing theories of perception and cognition (Kosslyn and Maljkovic, 1990, Palmer, 1999). However, there have always been a few dissenting voices pointing out the limitations of a conception of experience as the output of a purely abstract computational level of description (e.g. Gibson, 1966, 1979; Turvey et al., 1981, Varela et al., 1991) but it is only recently that there has emerged an identifiable research paradigm which takes the ideas of embodiment and situatedness as fundamental to understanding the nature of cognition and consciousness.[1]

Perceptual experience, in particular, presents one of the cognitive domains where the new paradigm has found its greatest support (Hurley, 2001). The new paradigm encourages a radical rethinking of the nature of perceptual states and the subject of experience. However, even among theories which agree that perception nontrivially involves an embodied and situated subject there are major disagreements regarding the exact nature of perceptual experience. It is a fact that the embodied perceiver is situated in a relation of dynamic sensorimotor engagement with her environment. However, how far do sensorimotor dynamics enter the content of perceptual experience? Is it possible to acknowledge dynamic sensorimotor interaction as a major causal factor in perceptual experience while at the same time viewing perception and action as two distinct domains of our cognitive life?

The chapters in this volume discuss the relation between perception and action from a variety of interdisciplinary perspectives ranging from theoretical discussion of concepts to reporting original empirical data from recent studies. Along with presenting diverse ways of relating perception and action, the contributions in this volume take a range of positions with respect to the view that perception is an achievement by an agent acting in a complex environment. Another related issue is

---

[1] For a review of the development of the embodied and situated cognition approaches see Anderson (2003) and Gallagher (in press).

whether or not sensorimotor dynamics of agent-environment interactions constitute an essential ingredient in perceptual experience.

Much of this volume is devoted to a particular debate within the general research on action and perception. The volume brings together two apparently opposing positions: the action-oriented theories of visual perception, on the one hand, and the dual-visual systems hypothesis on the other. Action-oriented theories champion the role of sensorimotor dynamics in perceptual awareness and the dual-visual systems hypothesis favours a functional dichotomy between perception and action. At least on the surface, these two approaches to visual perception are in conflict. The action-oriented approach emphasizes the interdependence of action and perception, while the dual-visual systems hypothesis suggests that action and perception are functionally distinct.

In this introduction we shall present the general issues discussed in the chapters and bring out the various themes that have emerged from the discussions of the relations between perception and action. They include, but are not limited to, the following topics:

- What is action in perception?
- Does empirical evidence support the functional dichotomy between perception and action?
- What constitutes the content of perceptual experience?
- Bringing together the competing views on the interaction between perception and action.

Before entering into the central issues, let us start with a summary of the two competing approaches to perception addressed in this volume, namely, the dual-visual systems views and the action-oriented theories. One of the earliest discussions of the dual-visual systems view is presented by Trevarthen (1968) who proposed that 'vision of space' and 'vision of object identity' are subserved by anatomically distinct brain mechanisms. Schneider (1969) describes two visual pathways in the mammalian brain enabling the location of objects and the identification of objects respectively. The two visual systems view received further attention with Ungerleider and Mishkin's (1982) neurophysiological evidence for 'what' and 'where' streams in the primate visual system, streams which process different aspects of the visual world. In recent times one of the most influential and elaborate discussion of the dual-visual systems hypothesis is presented by the cognitive neuroscientists M.A. Goodale and A.D. Milner (Goodale and Milner, 1992; Milner and Goodale, 1995; Goodale and Milner, 2004; Milner and Goodale, this volume). Motivated mostly by cases of cortical damage in humans, they describe the functions of the two visual streams as 'vision for perception' and 'vision for action', respectively. Vision for perception is suggested to be subserved by processing in the ventral stream, which projects from the primary visual cortex to the inferior temporal cortex. Vision for action, on the other hand, is thought to be subserved by the dorsal stream, which projects from the primary visual cortex to the posterior parietal cortex. Vision for perception is involved in recognition and identification of objects and events whereas vision for action is involved in the programming and online control of visuo-motor actions such as reaching and grasping. The evidence for a functional dichotomy between vision for perception and vision for action mainly comes from claims of double-dissociation observed between the conditions exhibited by visual form agnosic and optic ataxic patients (Milner and Goodale, 1995, this volume). A second source of evidence is derived from studies suggesting that visuo-motor actions such as grasping are immune to illusions, e.g. the size-contrast studies by Aglioti et al., (1995), whereas perceptual awareness easily falls prey to them.

The neuroscientific analysis of the two visual streams has generated interdisciplinary interest and is defended and elaborated by philosophical and psychological literature in the field. Jacob and Jeannerod (2003) adopt the functional dichotomy between vision for perception and vision for action in their philosophical and psychological study of the two visual systems model. They propose that the same visual information undergoes two distinct types of processing depending on whether the information is used for guiding motor acts or for enabling perceptual beliefs. They label the first type of processing 'pragmatic processing' of visual information and the second type of processing 'semantic processing' of visual information. Matthen (2005, this volume) presents a philosophical study of the functional difference between the two visual streams. He argues that one type of visual stream subserves 'descriptive vision', which is imagistic characterizations of objects allowing storage and recall, and the other type of visual stream underlies 'motion-guiding vision', which is visual information enabling fine motor control for visuo-motor tasks.

Theories of visual perception adhering to a dual-visual systems model vary on finer details, especially concerning how the two visual streams interact, and we shall bring out some of their differences in the course of this introduction. However, they are united in their claim that the boundaries between perception and action are rather tight. On the one hand, perceptual awareness proceeds via a type of processing of visual information that does not require coding in terms of the perceiver's ability to act, and on the other hand conscious visual experience does not enter the control of visuo-motor actions; a significant amount of our goal-directed engagement with the world can proceed independently of conscious awareness.

Challenging the rigid boundaries between perception and action are theories which champion the idea of perceptual experience as an achievement by an active perceiver. According to this school of thought, perception and action are interdependent processes and being a perceiver is, at some level of description, inseparable from being an agent. This group of theories presents an emerging research paradigm which we shall call 'action-oriented' approaches to perception. The most discussed and elaborately defended action-oriented approach in recent philosophy of mind and cognitive science is the sensorimotor theory of perception (O'Regan and Noë, 2001; Noë, 2004; Hurley, 2008). The theory has been described under a variety of names such as the sensorimotor theory of visual consciousness (O'Regan and Noë, 2001), enactivism (Noë, 2004), and actionism (Noë, this volume). Hurley (1998) presents one of the pioneering accounts of an action-oriented theory of perception in contemporary philosophy of mind and cognitive science. In her bid to unify perceptual awareness (and consciousness in general) and action Hurley (1998) writes,

> The idea of having a *perspective* or point of view is part of our concept of what it is to be conscious. Unity is a basic feature of the perspectival aspect of consciousness. But so is agency. At the personal level, having a perspective means that what you experience and perceive depends systematically on what you do, as well as vice versa.
>
> (Hurley, 1998: 86)

Adopting a somewhat similar approach,[2] the sensorimotor theory of O'Regan and Noë (2001) and Noë (2004) defends an action-oriented theory of perceptual awareness by maintaining that perceptual content is a function of the implicit sensorimotor knowledge exercised by an active perceiver by way of exploring the environment. The action-oriented theories include neuroscientific accounts which argue against the dual-visual systems view by claiming that the functional dissociation between vision for perception and vision for action is not one that easily allows strict anatomical mapping onto specific brain regions (Rossetti et al., this volume, Vallar and Mancini, this volume). However, there is considerable difference of opinion among the action-oriented approaches regarding the role of action in perception and indeed regarding how we are to understand the notion of action in the first place. Section 1.2 addresses this issue focussing on the internal debates between the action-oriented approaches represented in this volume and between the action-oriented approaches and theories supporting a dual-visual systems view. Section 1.3 discusses the debate centring on the empirical evidence for the functional dichotomy between perception and action. Section 1.4 focuses on the various theories and issues regarding the content of perceptual experience and Section 1.5 brings together the competing views on the interaction between perception and action.

---

[2] For importance differences between Hurley's (1998, 2008) account of the relation between perception and action and that defended by O'Regan and Noë, (2001) and (Noë 2004) see Gangopadhyay and Kiverstein (2009).

1.2. **What is action in perception?**

There is considerable ambiguity among the action-oriented theories regarding the notion of action in perception. The sensorimotor theorists write,

> ... seeing is an exploratory activity mediated by the mastery of the sensorimotor contingencies. That is seeing is a skill-based activity of environmental exploration. Visual experience is not something that happens *in* individuals. It is something they *do*.
>
> (Noë and O'Regan, 2002: 567)

Faced by recent challenges (e.g. Block, 2005; Clark, 2006), the sensorimotor theorists have put forth an account of what they have in mind when they say perception is something that a perceiver does. Noë clarifies his position on incorporating action as a necessary element in perception by drawing a distinction between action and movement (real-time sensorimotor behaviour). In his actionist view of perception, perceptual experience is active in the sense of requiring the exercise of the skilful perceiver's implicit knowledge of the sensorimotor laws governing the relation between movement and change of stimuli. In Noë's theory perception is *not* active, '... in the sense that it requires that one move. What is required is that one understand the relevance of movement to action. What is required is that one knows what would happen if one were to move. Perception is active, according to the actionist, in the same way that thought is active'[3] (Noë, this volume). O'Regan (this volume) upholds a similar position arguing that nothing in the sensorimotor theory requires action in the sense of real-time ongoing movement as constituting perceptual content at any given time. What is necessary for perception to be active is the skilful perceiver's access to and exercise of her implicit knowledge of how perceptual content could vary as a function of her movement or the movement of the object.

Schellenberg's (this volume) proposal of how perceivers grasp the intrinsic properties of objects finds a place in the action-oriented camp. Her 'capacity view', however, proposes to be an alternative to actionism and similar sensorimotor approaches. Schellenberg contends that while sensorimotor approaches usually ground their theories on token actions (past, present, future, or counterfactual) the capacity view builds up on the perceiver's practical knowledge that the object of perception can be perceived from other spatial perspectives. In spite of the apparent disagreement between the sensorimotor views and the capacity view, they seem to be unanimous in claiming that the way to link perception and action is not by referring to *movements*, that is, the actual execution of sensorimotor behaviour.

Psychological and neuroscientific action-oriented theories of perception have proposed a more radical relation between perception and action in a manner avoided by both the sensorimotor theory and the capacity view. A number of cognitive neuroscientists connect action, in the sense of ongoing sensorimotor behaviour, and perception by offering evidence to show that the two share common neural processing areas. Rossetti et al. (this volume) focus on specific instances of visuo-motor behaviour to argue against a double-dissociation between perception and action. The double-dissociation is claimed to be supported by studies on optic ataxia and visual agnosia and forms the

---

[3] This marks a point of departure between the sensorimotor theory proposed by O'Regan and Noë (2001) and subsequently defended by Noë (2004, this volume) and Hurley's action-oriented theory of perception (1998, 2001, 2008). Hurley contends that real-time physical interaction with the environment is necessary for furnishing the content of experience. She writes,

> Perhaps the received tradition has focussed too much on the internal aspects of perception and ignored the external aspects. But we can correct this bias and take on board the role of movement in making information available, without going to the opposite extreme of denying that the brain processes information at all.... The right response to Gibson is ecumenical: both movement through real environments by whole organisms and brain activity play essential roles in extracting information from the environment and enabling a creature to have a perceptual perspective.
>
> (Hurley 2001: 20)

basis of the dual-visual systems hypothesis (Milner and Goodale, this volume). Rossetti et al., contend that a careful examination of cases of optic ataxia reveals that not all aspects of visuo-motor behaviour are controlled by the dorsal stream but share common processing areas with perception. Perception and action do not belong to water-tight cognitive domains as they share common processing areas, such as the areas between the ventral and the dorsal streams, and thereby enable visuo-motor behaviour by their ongoing dynamics. Therefore, a tight coupling between perception and action is justifiable on the basis of the sensorimotor (and neural) dynamics underlying the execution of certain visuo-motor actions or real-time movements. A similar line of thought is expressed by Vallar and Mancini (this volume) in their study of the neurofunctional streams underlying the neglect syndrome. Establishing action-oriented views of perception by referring to visuo-motor behaviour is an avenue explored by a considerable amount of literature in the field. Although only some of the action-oriented approaches in this volume make a brief reference to it, analysing the nature of the specific types of sensorimotor behaviour which are executed as part of the process of seeing, for example saccadic eye movements, also offers promising ways of linking perception and action.[4] This is not to say that there must be an isomorphism between perceptual content and token movements. Instead, the evidence indicates that ongoing sensorimotor dynamics impose a real-time constraint on perceptual content.

Noë (this volume) offers a taxonomy of four distinct ways of relating perception and action. These are: (1) actionism, which claims that exercise of implicit sensorimotor knowledge constitutes perceptual content, (2) 'the movement view', which states that actual motor movement is necessary for perceptual experience, (3) 'seeing is for acting', which proposes that the role of perceptual awareness is to subserve action, (4) the dual-visual systems view, which maintains that perception and action are two autonomous domains. An analysis of these different ways of relating perception and action reveals that 'action' is used in at least the following different senses by various theories. First, according to the sensorimotor view, 'action' stands for the exercise of implicit sensorimotor knowledge which may, but does not necessarily, include reference to the actual ongoing sensorimotor behaviour. This view maintains that it is possible to link perception and action without falling back on the real-time sensorimotor behaviour of the perceiver. Second, 'action' in what Noë dubs the 'movement view' can be spelt out as including real-time sensorimotor behaviour. In this view it is not only the perceiver's possession of implicit sensorimotor knowledge but also her exercise of that knowledge in the form of engaging in real-time sensorimotor behaviour which yields the sensorimotor dynamics necessary for coupling perception and action. In this view the nature of perceptual experience remains unexplained without reference to actual motor movements. Third, in the 'seeing is for acting' view 'action' stands for everyday motor behaviour as discussed, for example, by Gibson (1966, 1979). This view maintains that the content of perceptual experience is made up of the perception of potential movements with regard to the object. This view has close affinities with the sensorimotor theory of perception in highlighting the role of sensorimotor knowledge in perceptual content. However, the sensorimotor theorists do not claim that the only purpose of perceptual experience is the guidance of motor movements. Finally, in the dual-visual systems view, 'action' refers to at least three distinct elements in motor behaviour, namely, planning the motor movement in accordance with the goal to be achieved, programming the required parameters for executing the movement, and the online control of the movement (Milner and Goodale, this volume). The dual-visual systems theorists argue that the role of conscious perception is limited only to the first (the planning stage) of these three elements in action or motor movement. In this view, conscious perceptual experience and action come together in planning motor movements but conscious perception and action part ways in the later stages of programming and online control of motor behaviour.

---

[4] See Findlay and Gilchrist (2003) for one of the most influential accounts of how motor movements can constitute perception.

It is apparent that 'action' in both action-oriented approaches and dual-visual systems views covers a wide range of elements involved in an embodied agent's ongoing interactions with the environment, from highly complex cognitive components like planning and decision-making to the fine-grained control of motor behaviour. Such wide range, and at times ambiguous, uses of the term 'action' (e.g. referring to either motor movements or sensorimotor knowledge), further complicates the debate between the action-oriented and dual-visual systems accounts. For instance, consider the following issue on which the two camps disagree: How direct is the route between perception and action? While actionism (Noë, this volume) argues that action directly enters the picture in the form of the perceiver's implicit sensorimotor knowledge, in the absence of which there would be a corresponding absence of perceptual content, the dual-visual systems hypothesis advanced by Milner and Goodale (this volume) maintains that the relation between perception and action is only 'indirect and flexible … in which cognitive operations such as memory and planning play a crucial role'. As the dual-visual systems view does allow some interaction between perception and action at the cognitively demanding stage of action planning, Noë contends that far from being an opposing view to the dual-systems view, actionism is in fact a necessary building block for a strong dual-systems account. Noë argues that actionism and the dual-visual systems view are not in conflict because by 'action' actionism refers to the complex cognitive level of the perceiver's implicit understanding of sensorimotor laws, rather than to the fine-grained ongoing sensorimotor behaviour. Thus the way to secure the interaction between perception and action is in terms of the higher level cognitive component in the form of sensorimotor knowledge.

However, actionism's proposal of securing the interaction between perception and action in terms of the perceiver's implicit sensorimotor knowledge is rivalled by dual-visual systems views which offer their own explanation of how the two distinct domains of perception and action interact in everyday life. Focussing on the real-time execution of visuo-motor behaviour, Jacob and de Vignemont (this volume) contend that what really guides visuo-motor action in everyday life is not necessarily conscious perception but rather the unconscious pragmatic processing of visual information. They claim that perceptual experience involving object recognition is a function of processing in an allocentric frame of reference whereas visuo-motor actions require coding in egocentric frames. While proponents of this account object to a tight coupling between perception and action, this account has some affinities with the action-oriented account presented by Schellenberg (this volume). In Schellenberg's 'capacity view' perception of intrinsic properties of objects requires transcending an egocentric frame of reference by exercising the spatial know-how of the possibility of other spatial perspectives on the object.

Does the strategy of chalking out different frames of reference for the coding of perception and action really resolve the issue of their interaction? Schellenberg admits that it is an open empirical question as to how spatial know-how of different perspectives actually combines ego-centric and allocentric frames. In the account proposed by Jacob and de Vignemont it remains to be discussed how far the outputs of the two visual streams are available to consciousness, especially whether egocentric coding by the dorsal stream is totally encapsulated from conscious perceptual experience. Clark (this volume) raises concern on this issue and proposes that conscious experience could be best conceived of as a multifaceted phenomenon and points out that a major challenge facing any account of perception is that there is to-date no established criteria by which to assess what counts as conscious experience. This point shall be taken up for further discussion in the context of the various proposals of the interaction between the two visual streams (Section 1.5).

The disagreements between action-oriented approaches and the dual-visual systems views are also importantly based on the interpretation of the empirical evidence cited in favour of the dual-visual systems hypothesis. In particular, the debate builds upon two main sources of empirical evidence. These are: (1) the claims of double-dissociation between the conditions exhibited by a visual agnosic patient such as D. F. (Goodale and Milner, 1992) and those found in patients with optic ataxia and (2) the interpretation of studies which suggest that visuo-motor actions like grasping etc. are impervious to illusions which affect conscious visual experience (Aglioti et al., 1995). Action-oriented views of perceptual experience question the extent to which these studies establish perception and action as mutually encapsulated domains. The following section takes up the debate between action-oriented approaches and dual-systems views on the issue of empirical evidence for the functional dichotomy between perception and action.

1.3. Debates on empirical evidence for the functional dichotomy between perception and action

The dual-systems view of vision for action and vision for perception is based on the anatomically distinct cortical pathways of visual processing, namely, the dorsal and the ventral stream. From this anatomical fact Milner and Goodale (1995, Goodale and Milner, 1992) develop their model of the functional dichotomy between perception and action deriving support from two main sources. First they claim to find a double-dissociation between the conditions exhibited by D.F., the visual form agnosic patient and the conditions observed in cases of optic ataxia. The second source of evidence comes from studies which indicate that certain visual illusions (e.g. Aglioti et al., 1995), deceive conscious perception but not visually guided grasping.

Milner and Goodale propose that there is significant evidence for establishing a double-dissociation between visual form agnosia and optic ataxia, the former arising due to impairment in the ventral processing stream and the latter due to impairments in the dorsal processing stream. What does a double-dissociation signify? Double-dissociation is a tool often employed by cognitive neuroscientists to demonstrate that specific structures or systems are responsible for specific functions. Identifying specific brain systems as solely responsible for specific functions by the method of double-dissociation has been criticized (Passingham et al., 2002; Pisella et al., 2006) but is nonetheless widely used as a method of localizing cognitive functions to specific brain structures. The aim of the present discussion is not to assess the methodological merit of double-dissociation in attributing cognitive functions to brain systems but mainly to raise two issues. First, has a double-dissociation actually been established between the conditions observed in visual agnosic patients and those found in optic ataxic ones? Second, what are the implications of the debate surrounding the evidence of double-dissociation between visual agnosia and optic ataxia on the relation between perception and action?

Milner and Goodale's (1995) hypothesis regarding the functional dichotomy between perception and action was based on a series of studies conducted on the visual form agnosic patient D.F. who showed a striking contrast in her performance in visuo-motor tasks and in perceptual judgement tasks involving the same stimuli. For example, D.F. can accurately carry out the visuo-motor task of passing her hand or a hand-held plaque through a slot in a disc which is placed at different orientations in front of her but she is unable to report (including manual report) the orientation of the slot. Milner and Goodale (1995) argue that the remarkable disparity in D.F.'s performance in visuo-motor and perceptual judgement tasks is evidence for the functional dichotomy between perception and action subserved by anatomically distinct cortical pathways. To further establish the hypothesis of functional dichotomy between perception and action, Milner and Goodale (this volume) claim that a double-dissociation is clearly observed between visual form agnosia and optic ataxia in the context of demonstrating the effect of delay introduced between presentation of stimuli and a pointing response. The task assesses spatial processing in peripheral vision in both visual agnosic patient D.F. and optic ataxic patient A.T. With the introduction of the delay D.F.'s performance deteriorated while that of A.T. improved. Milner and Goodale argue that the results indicate that with the introduction of the delay there is demand on D.F.'s impaired ventral processing which leads to the corresponding drop in performance accuracy. Similarly, the delay engages A.T.'s intact ventral processing thereby improving performance. On the other hand, without the delay D.F. successfully completes the task by relying on her unimpaired dorsal processing whereas A.T.'s performance is poor because of her impaired dorsal processing. Moreover, Milner and Goodale maintain that double-dissociation is also reported in central vision between patients with optic ataxia and visual agnosic patient D.F. when they were tested for grasping accuracy and perceiving the dimension of the objects.

Optic ataxic patients revealed deficits in scaling grip aperture but not in perceiving the dimensions of the objects whereas D.F. showed the opposite pattern of impairment.

Rossetti et al. (this volume) challenge Milner and Goodale's claims of double-dissociation between optic ataxia and visual agnosia. They argue that the double-dissociation lacks sufficient evidence in a number of ways. They contend that the tasks may not have been performed in identical conditions in visual agnosia and optic ataxia patients. While D.F.'s reaching performance has mainly been studied for central vision, studies with optic ataxic patients is focussed on peripheral vision. Rossetti et al., propose that the possibility of optic ataxic patients having intact reaching abilities in central vision cannot be ruled out in which case there would be no double-dissociation.

Also, the double-dissociation is challenged on the ground that there is a difference in the lesions reported in visual agnosia patient D.F. and optic ataxic patients. The former reveals bilateral lesion whereas the latter usually manifest unilateral lesions. Rossetti et al., propose that the lack of sufficient evidence for double-dissociation between visual agnosia and optic ataxia casts a general doubt on whether or not the dorsal stream is solely involved in action. They suggest that it may be more appropriate to conceive of the function of the dorsal stream as subserving peripheral vision rather than vision for action. They contend that the data for double-dissociation supports a dissociation between processes in peripheral and central vision rather than between vision for action and vision for perception. They conclude that the double-dissociations on which the dual-visual systems hypothesis is built do not support a strict separation between perception and action.

Milner and Goodale (this volume) concede that the available data on double-dissociations between visual form agnosia patient D.F. and optic ataxic patients is not beyond doubt and does indicate some incompleteness. Nonetheless, they defend their model of the functional dichotomy between perception and action against Rossetti et al.'s criticism with the following point: even if the conditions found in visual form agnosic patient D.F. and optic ataxic patients do not, to date, conclusively establish a strong double-dissociation between visual agnosia and optic ataxia, this does not imply that the functions of the dorsal and the ventral streams cannot be doubly dissociated. Crucially, Milner and Goodale point out that optic ataxics show a deficit in reaching in peripheral *as well as* central vision.

If a double-dissociation were to be established between the functions of the dorsal and the ventral streams, could it be taken as conclusive evidence for the proposed functional dichotomy between perception and action? For example, consider the recent studies by Schenk (2006) which offer an alternative explanation of D.F.'s impairment. In a series of studies Schenk explored the possibility that D.F. retains her abilities to make perceptual judgments when the object is coded in an egocentric frame of reference. Schenk reports the following results: (1) there is no significant difference in D.F.'s performance and that of controls in egocentric motor tasks. (2) D.F. is seriously impaired in any allocentric task, motor, or perceptual, and (3) D.F. is better at egocentric perceptual tasks than at any allocentric task. Schenk's studies raise a puzzle for the functional dichotomy between perception and action based on the functions of the ventral and dorsal streams. D.F. has impairments in her ventral processing, but why does she perform poorly in an allocentric *motor* task which in the dual-visual systems model is subserved by the dorsal stream? Moreover, if vision for perception and vision for action neatly map onto processing in the ventral and dorsal streams respectively then how is it that D.F.'s performance in egocentric perceptual tasks is better than that in her allocentric motor task despite her impairment in ventral processing? Schenk proposes that D.F.'s impairment does not justify the hypothesis of separate processing for perception and action but rather that she is unable to encode spatial information in an allocentric frame irrespective of the nature of the task (motor or perceptual).

Milner and Goodale (this volume) discuss the puzzle raised by Schenk's studies and reply that the studies do not test what they have in mind while discussing vision for action. The tasks in which D.F. performs poorly are not motor tasks in any sense but are simply a form of reporting a perceptual judgement. Given that she has impaired ventral processing it is not surprising that she performs below average on a variety of perceptual judgment reporting tasks. Jacob and de Vignemont (this volume) provide a detailed theoretical justification for the line of response offered by Milner and Goodale arguing that the tasks in which D.F.'s impairment is revealed in Schenk's studies do not probe visuo-motor processing but her ability to report perceptual judgment. However, if D.F. manages to perform well in egocentric perceptual tasks, how far is it reasonable to conclude that perceptual experience is subserved by processing in the ventral stream? Speculations of such nature fuel the further debate of whether or not processing for action seeps into conscious awareness to make a considerable difference in the quality of our perceptual experience. This point will be further discussed in the following section.

The second source of evidence in favour of a functional dichotomy between perception and action comes from studies demonstrating that visuo-motor processing is significantly immune to visual illusions which deceive conscious experience (Aglioti et al., 1995). However, controversy surrounds the issue of absolute and consistent immunity of visuo-motor processing to illusions which affect perceptual awareness. Melmoth et al. (this volume) present an original study examining the effect of the Poggendorf illusion on both perceptual experience and the visuo-motor response of pointing. Their study reveals that the visuo-motor response is significantly affected by the illusory stimuli which also affect perceptual judgement. Milner and Goodale (this volume) discuss the possible reasons for visuo-motor actions being occasionally affected by illusory stimuli. They argue that the role of the dorsal stream in visuo-motor tasks is best revealed only under very specialized conditions. One such condition would be highly practiced skilful actions directed at targets that are directly visible and do not require drawing from memory or perceptual representations encoded by the ventral stream. However, this seems to narrow down the highly specialized role of dorsal stream in action to a rather small repertoire of visuo-motor behaviour. How far does such limited role of dorsal stream processing in action support the broad functional dichotomy between perception and action? Rossetti et al. (this volume) offer an alternative explanation of why certain cases of visuo-motor behaviour are immune to visual illusions. Optic ataxic patient I.G., studied by Rossetti et al., exhibits patterns of response similar to controls in visuo-motor tasks with illusory stimuli. The authors infer that I.G.'s performance points towards the possibility of visuo-motor behaviour being controlled by systems other than the dorsal stream, for example, by the inferior parietal lobule. Vallar and Mancini (this volume) draw parallels from their study of the neglect syndrome to support the claim that visuo-motor behaviours can be planned and executed independently of the dorsal stream and possibly via the route suggested by Rossetti et al.

The debates surrounding the issue of strong empirical evidence in favour of a strict functional dichotomy between vision for perception and vision for action brings to the fore further and deeper issues. First, it becomes clear that—far from being a homogenous phenomenon—action covers a wide range of visuo-motor behaviours. In addition, it is debatable whether action, as a whole, is fully controlled by the dorsal stream or whether explaining some actions necessarily implies blurring the dichotomy between perception and action. Second, the complexity of the nature of visuo-motor responses as well as that of perceptual judgements may necessitate a more complex model than that proposed by the dual-visual systems account. In the following section we shall look at the nature and content of perceptual experience to discuss its degree of immunity from processing which subserves action.

1.4. **The content of perceptual experience**

The empirical literature on the dual-visual systems pays considerable attention to the nature of visuo-motor actions. They are understood as the product of automatic processing by the largely unconscious dorsal stream. However, when it comes to the tricky problem of conscious awareness, the empirical literature on the dual-visual systems views enters the realm of philosophical theories. In this section we shall discuss the nature and content of perceptual experience and its relation to processes subserving action.

As previously discussed in the context of the notion of action in perception, action-oriented theories of perception maintain that perceptual awareness is largely inclusive of processes that subserve action. Thus, for instance, actionism (Noë, this volume) defends the view that the perceiver's knowledge of the lawful relations between movement and change of stimuli constitutes the content of perceptual experience. In the absence of such knowledge there is corresponding absence of perceptual content. While Noë dedicates his chapter to the discussion of the notion of action in perception and the compatibility of actionism with the dual-visual systems view, Kiverstein (this volume) takes up the issue of how sensorimotor knowledge contributes to perceptual experience. Kiverstein maintains that perception, which is characterized by the feeling of seeing the whole of three-dimensional objects and details of the scene, is enabled by the perceiver's exercise of sensorimotor knowledge by way of forming sensorimotor expectations. Many such expectations may never reach consciousness but nonetheless constitute the content of perception as the 'background of experience'. Kiverstein defends the constitutive role of sub-personal sensorimotor expectations in perceptual content by arguing that the sensorimotor expectations are a necessary constitutive element in perceptual experience as long as the skilful perceiver has a sense that such expectations, although not reaching full-blown consciousness, are potentially available to be accessed. The role of sensorimotor expectations in Kiverstein's account is also extended to explain how perceivers grasp the intrinsic properties of objects. Intrinsic properties of perceptual objects are not apprehended from any particular spatial viewpoint adopted under any particular viewing conditions. They exceed the foreground of experience in the same way as in the case of the three-dimensionality of objects and the feeling of perceiving a detailed visual scene. It is sensorimotor expectations alone that furnish the perceiver with a sense of the object's intrinsic properties. Thus in Kiverstein's view the content of perceptual experience, far from being encapsulated from the perceiver's ability to act, is constituted by those very capacities. The content of perceptual experience is sensorimotor in nature.

Now compare this view with Schellenberg's (this volume) account of an action-oriented approach to perception. Schellenberg is of the opinion that perceptual experience presents the perceiver with two kinds of properties, situation-dependent properties and intrinsic properties. Perception of intrinsic properties is epistemically dependent on perception of situation-dependent properties. Grasping the intrinsic properties of objects requires abstracting away from the perceiver's current point of view. However, such abstraction does not lead the perceiver to draw on her knowledge of how the perception of the object would co-vary with movements because the perceiver's self-location, from which the abstraction proceeds, can be secured merely by her capacity to act and does not rely on sensorimotor expectations. Representation of intrinsic properties simply requires that the perceiver has the practical knowledge that the object is perceivable from other view-points which are similarly conceived of as spatial positions from which perceivers can both perceive and act on objects. In Schellenberg's account the content of perceptual experience is in no way constituted by sensorimotor knowledge or expectations, neither for situation-dependent properties nor for intrinsic ones. Yet the content of perception is not impervious to action. It relies on the perceiver's ability of self-location which is constituted by her capacity to act. Is there any reason to prefer either of these accounts of action-oriented perceptual content over the other? We take up this question in the following section in the context of discussing the interaction between the two visual streams and ultimately between perception and action.

Matthen (this volume) offers an account of perceptual content which is influenced by the hypothesis of the functional dichotomy between perception and action, but nonetheless champions the idea that our ability to interact with the object of perception ushers in a non-trivial difference in the qualitative feel of the experiential state. Matthen centres the discussion on the notion of 'feeling of presence' and asks why and how it is that our normal scene vision carries with it a distinct cognitive feeling, the feeling of presence, which marks a sharp contrast between it and pictorial vision.

The issue is as follows: given the similarity of the retinal image how does the perceiver distinguish between an actually present and a depicted object? Matthen introduces the distinction between 'descriptive vision' and 'motion-guiding vision' to provide an account of the feeling of presence accompanying the perception of real objects. Descriptive vision enables the perceiver to characterize, store and recall objects whereas motion-guiding vision is deployed in the precise control of motor movements. Descriptive vision corresponds to Milner and Goodale's (1995, this volume) concept of vision for perception and motion-guiding vision resembles vision for action. Matthen contends that visual consciousness is largely a matter of descriptive vision whereas motion-guiding vision may never enter consciousness due to its being totally or almost automatic. Importantly, though, motion-guiding vision is what secures the feeling of presence accompanying our normal scene vision and the perception of real, rather than depicted, objects. Only real objects engage the perceiver's motion-guiding vision by presenting the possibilities of interaction with the object. Thus although descriptive vision is the key element in visual consciousness, motion-guiding vision is responsible for the cognitive feeling which plays the decisive role in grasping the nature of the perceptual object. In Matthen's view, the content of perceptual experience is constituted by descriptive vision, but the nature of the cognitive feeling of the perceptual state is fixed by the possibilities of interaction with the object. Matthen's account offers a way in which an indirect relationship between perception and action is established by analysing the phenomenological characteristics of a perceptual state. The content of perception is not based on action, but the distinct 'feel' accompanying a perceptual state is decided by the possibilities of interaction offered by the perceptual object.

Clark (this volume) discusses some recent challenges to the dual-visual systems views and the implications these might have on the claim that the content of visual experience is exclusively determined by the operations of the ventral stream. The first of these challenges comes from the studies by Schenk (2006) which have been discussed in the preceding section. A second source of worry is that a theoretical analysis of the nature of visual experience reveals that visual experience may prove to be too heterogeneous to be attributed in its totality to particular brain mechanisms or to be understood in all its nuances as enabled by any particular cognitive process.

Consider, for instance, the phenomenological nature of the impairment observed in visual form agnosia patient D.F. Milner and Goodale (1995, this volume) construe the impairment observed in D.F. as a lack of phenomenal awareness of the shape of visual objects presented to her. However, Wallhagen (2007) offers an alternative conception of the impairment observed in D.F. He argues that instead of lacking phenomenal awareness of shapes, D.F.'s impairment can coherently be described as her failing to conceptualize and report these elements which are perceptually experienced by her. Thus, rather than impaired visual experience, D.F. has impaired *reporting* of her perceptual experience. This interpretation comes at a price for the dual-visual systems model. It implies that the ventral stream may no longer underlie all aspects of visual experience. If D.F. does have visual awareness of shape in spite of her severely impaired ventral processing then it is considerably difficult to rule out processing in other visual streams including the dorsal as playing a role in perceptual awareness. The deeper problem underlying Wallhagen's interpretation of D.F.'s impairment is how to understand conscious experience in the first place. When are we justified in attributing conscious experience to a perceiver? Clark (this volume) offers an answer by appealing to the notion of action while at the same time suggesting a defence of the basic functional dichotomy between dorsal and ventral stream processing. He contends that in order for a perceiver to claim ownership over a conscious experience the information delivered by it must be 'poised for the control of rational action'. He further suggests that ventral stream information qualifies as conscious experience by satisfying this requirement. A considerable amount of dorsal stream processing, on the other hand, yields information that is not available to the perceiver as a rational agent in the guidance of action and consequently does not count as an element in conscious experience. Thus even if one abandons the criterion of reportability for conscious experience all is not lost. However, Clark goes further to propose that conscious experience itself need not be, and in fact most probably is not, a unitary entity. The 'Mere Motley' model of conscious experience which presents consciousness as complex, jumbled, and at times highly dissociable, capacities comprising multiple layers and streams of processing may just be the best available description of conscious experience. In this picture, action enters the content of perceptual experience only in an indirect way. The content of perceptual experience gains its status from being poised for rational action although much of the processing for the control and online guidance of action escapes the perceiver's awareness.

Jacob and de Vignemont (this volume) take up the puzzle of unreportable visual experience to offer an account of the nature of perceptual content that is consistent with the dual-visual systems hypothesis, which attributes the contents of conscious experience to the processing in the ventral stream. Taking up the challenge presented by Wallhagen's alternative interpretation of the nature of D.F.'s impairment, Jacob and de Vignemont argue that Wallhagen's conjecture at best leads to a stalemate in the debate of the nature of D.F.'s impairment. Wallhagen's arguments raise serious doubts about the lack of phenomenal awareness of shape in D.F. but they do not conclusively demonstrate its presence as a part of D.F.'s perceptual experience. Ascribing phenomenal awareness of shape to D.F. may require grounding her perceptual awareness of shape on the visuo-motor processing in the dorsal stream. However, Jacob and de Vignemont contend that mere processing by the dorsal stream may not suffice for the information to be a part of perceptual content. Visuo-motor processing by the dorsal stream may not play an automatic role in enabling the perception of full blown visual features of objects (such as their shapes) but rather compute features of objects that are immediately relevant for the task at hand. Jacob and de Vignemont argue that experimental evidence strongly indicates that D.F.'s success in visuo-motor tasks relies on her computing the width rather than the shape of objects. For example, she performs at chance when presented with a square and a rectangle of equal width. So does the processing by the dorsal stream enter into perceptual content? This would require the distinct unbound features of an object relevant for visuo-motor tasks, as processed by the dorsal stream, to be found in conscious experience and for the dorsal stream to have access to an iconic memory buffer. Jacob and de Vignemont's treatment of perceptual content makes it highly unlikely for information at the service of action to directly constitute perceptual experience. The point will be discussed in detail in the following section on the interaction between the two visual systems.

Action-oriented views of perception counteract claims regarding the nature of perceptual content as distant and at best indirectly linked to action. Some action-oriented accounts argue that a major attraction of their approach lies in the methodological remedies they offer for central issues in consciousness studies. O'Regan (this volume) defends an action-oriented approach to perception which generalizes to a broad theory of consciousness. Sensory experience presents us with puzzling features which philosophers and cognitive scientists have sought to explain for decades. Sensory experiences are ineffable, have certain structures, and are generally accompanied by something it is like to undergo the experience in question. Does adopting a functional dichotomy between perception and action take us any closer to accounting for these puzzling features of sensory experience? O'Regan contends that these essential characteristics of a sensory state are due to the perceiver's mastery of the sensorimotor laws of interaction with the environment. Abandoning the contribution of action in enabling perceptual content leads to a sort of radical neuro-reductionism with no explanatory advantage. O'Regan argues that the hard problem of consciousness remains unresolved on a 'passive' view of perception where perceptual experience proceeds by the perceiver passively receiving the sensory stimuli which are then somehow organized into meaningful perceptual experience by sub-personal neural mechanisms. In the passive view of perception an explanatory gap between the phenomenological aspect and the physical mechanism persists because there is nothing intrinsic about neural mechanisms that can account for the particular feel accompanying a perceptual state. On the other hand, the perceiver's particular sensorimotor mode of engaging with the environment when undergoing a sensory experience offers an objective and verifiable characterization of the puzzling phenomenological features of sensory experience. It is in virtue of being directly enabled by sensorimotor processes of interaction with the environment that conscious experience acquires its familiar phenomenology.

The discussion of the nature of perceptual content in action-oriented and dual-visual systems views allows us to form certain hypotheses about the nature of interaction between the two visual systems as well as about the nature of the interaction between perception and action. Let us now see how we can tackle the tricky issue of bringing together these two major components of our cognitive life.

1.5. Bringing it all together: interaction between perception and action

The goal of the conference on Perception, Action and Consciousness, which resulted in this volume, was to encourage dialogue between what appeared to be two opposing schools of thought on the nature of perception and cognition in general. Action-oriented approaches strongly defend perception as an achievement by an active perceiver whereas dual-visual systems theories are in favour of maintaining a functional dichotomy between perception and action. However, it is a fact that in normal everyday cognitive behaviour the two visual streams, the ventral and the dorsal, interact. In the remaining part of the introduction we shall explore the issue of interaction between the two visual streams and discuss whether or not an account of the interaction also leads to a resolution of the debate between the two schools of thought.

One way in which the action-oriented approaches have sought to reconcile their approach with the dual-visual systems views is by suggesting that in dual-visual system theories one must make use of an action-oriented theory of perception in order to account for the interaction between the two streams. Noë (this volume) offers a reconciliation of actionism with the existence of the dual-visual systems by arguing that conscious perception influences visuo-motor behaviour not only in the planning of the latter but in the general guidance of this behaviour as well. This claim finds support, for example, in the case of optic ataxics who appear to perform normally in everyday activities. The evidence of fine online adjustment to visuo-motor behaviour proceeding without the agent's awareness could be seen as a challenge to the idea of perception as an active engagement of the perceiver with the environment. However, Noë argues that this evidence is not incompatible with action-oriented theories: the role of the agent's awareness can well be limited to fixing the target of action without interfering with the low-level parameters of online adjustment of the visuo-motor behaviour. What is crucial for securing an adequate account of the interaction between the two visual streams is abandoning a 'picture-theory' of perception where perceptual awareness merely registers the visual scene in an allocentric frame without encoding the possibilities of interaction with the perceived objects.

Kiverstein (this volume) frames the issue of interaction between the two visual streams in terms of the 'communication problem'. How is it possible to establish communication between two systems which, if the functional dichotomy proposed by dual-visual systems theories is correct, encode information in different frames of reference? The solution proposed by Kiverstein's sensorimotor theory of consciousness is to conceive of the contents of perceptual experience as encoded in an egocentric frame of reference. Crucially, this frame of reference represents the possibilities of entering into sensorimotor engagement with an object as the object of both perception and action. While Kiverstein resolves the communication problem between perception and action by proposing egocentric coding for both, Schellenberg's (this volume) capacity view argues that allocentric encoding for perceptual awareness needs to be preserved if the theory is to explain the perception of intrinsic properties of objects. A challenge for Schellenberg is that representing the possibilities of action in terms of the perceiver's spatial know-how involves egocentric encoding. Schellenberg's view leads to the issue of how appreciating different perspectives by way of apprehending the intrinsic properties of objects allows for egocentric and allocentric encoding to fuse together. While Schellenberg leaves it an open-empirical question, studies by Delevoye-Turrell et al. (this volume) provide an empirical approach to solving the puzzle of combining different frames of reference in perception and action by invoking the role of motor-imagery in perceptual judgements. Delevoye-Turrell et al., argue that spatial know-how is not a uni-modal cognitive ability but that spatial know-how requires fusing perceptual information about the location of the object with action representations of possible visuo-motor interactions with it. Insofar as motor representations contribute to the visual judgement of what is reachable, or possible targets of visuo-motor behaviour, egocentric encoding does appear to make up part of perceptual content concerning our spatial know-how.

In disagreement with the action-oriented approaches, the dual-visual systems theories deny it is necessary to introduce elements of action into perceptual awareness in order to account for the interaction between the two visual streams. One of the strongest resistances to an action-oriented conception of perception is offered by Jacob and Jeannerod (2003) and taken up by Jacob and de Vignemont (this volume). Jacob and Jeannerod (2003) present one of the earliest objections to an over-simplistic dichotomy between the functions of the ventral and the dorsal visual streams. They propose a hierarchical model where the one and the same stimulus can undergo two different types of processing along several levels of complexity. The pragmatic processing of visual information by the dorsal stream at first delivers visuo-motor representations as a low-level component and the processing gradually increases in complexity till it delivers input for more conceptually demanding aspects of visuo-motor behaviour such as skilful use of tools, planning future actions, etc. On the other hand, semantic processing of the visual stimuli by the ventral stream similarly proceeds in several layers with the lower levels processing for non-conceptual outputs which gradually increase in complexity to inform the perceiver's complex perceptual judgements.

According to Jacob and Jeannerod (2003), however, the output of processing by the ventral stream does not interact with motor intentions. Thus perception and action remain distinct as cognitive operations but this does not prevent the theory from accounting for aspects of our visuo-motor behaviour of which we are aware. Instead of offering an account of a simple interaction between two broadly characterized visual systems, Jacob and Jeannerod (2003) and Jacob and de Vignemont (this volume) aim to explain the peculiarities of visual perception and visuo-motor behaviour by postulating a complex hierarchy for each of two distinct types of processing. These two types of processing usually work in tandem but the impairment in one does not affect the essential nature of the output delivered by the other. Thus perception and action usually interact but are not co-constitutive. Clark (this volume) tackles the issue of interaction between the two visual streams in a similar fashion by arguing in favour of a complex and non-homogenous conception of conscious experience itself. In Clark's account the interaction between the two streams of visual processing and between perception and action is required only at an 'agent-level' description. The interaction is established in terms of content, visuo-motor or perceptual, which is poised for being accessed for rational action. Perception and action usually interact causally, but the interaction is indirect and flexible allowing ample room for conscious experience to proceed without motor input from action guiding systems and vice versa.

While the theoretical approaches of the dual-visual systems views have provided conceptual analyses of the notions of perception and action for breaching the gap between the two, the proponents of the dual-visual systems' functional dichotomy offer a sequence of refinements of their views which build up on the complexity of the underlying anatomy. They maintain that the links between perception and action are indirect but the two usually interact on the basis of sharing a common retinotopic area in the primary visual cortex. The functional interaction between vision for perception and vision for action is explained via cognitive operations of memory and action planning. The quest for a common cortical system for integrating the functions of the dorsal and the ventral visual streams has occupied neuroscientific studies of the dual-visual systems for decades. Milner and Goodale's (1995) proposal of the strict functional dichotomy between the dorsal and the ventral visual streams added more fuel to this quest with many claiming it to be an oversimplification of the anatomical and functional bases of perception and action which is unable to accommodate a considerable volume of empirical literature in the field (Viviani, 2002; Rizzolatti and Matelli, 2003; Pisella et al., 2006; Gallese, 2007).

Does an account of neurophysiological interaction between the two visual streams sway the debate in favour of action-oriented theories of perception? While Milner and Goodale (this volume) maintain that a complex account of the functional and anatomical interactions between the two visual streams would nonetheless preserve the basic hypothesis of the functional dichotomy of perception and action, neuroscientific accounts which have attempted to explain the interaction between the two visual systems often argue that preserving a strict functional dichotomy may well be impossible. Consider, for example, Gallese's use of evidence from lesion studies and single neuron studies for establishing a case in favour of multiple pathways subserving perception and action (Gallese, 2007). These multiple pathways make at least certain categories of visual perception, for example, spatial perception and perception of action, reliant on processing for action. In place of a broad dichotomy between the ventral and the dorsal visual streams, Gallese defends the view that visual processing is in fact conducted along three streams, the ventral stream, the ventro-dorsal stream, and the dorso-dorsal stream. The ventro-dorsal stream, which involves projections from the inferior parietal lobe to the pre-frontal and pre-motor areas, serves as the main interaction zone for the ventral and dorsal streams where the coupling between perception and action is seen in one of its most robust forms.

Similarly, from their claims of incomplete dissociation between perception and action Rossetti et al. (this volume) hypothesize the existence of multiple pathways that make it highly improbable for perception and action to proceed as independent phenomena, not only in normal subjects but also in case of visual agnosics and optic ataxics. One of the likely reasons why a neat double-dissociation between visual agnosia and optic ataxia is yet to be established to date is because the neural structures underlying our capacities of perception and action are too intertwined to allow either to proceed totally unaffected when there is an impairment in the other. As a possible solution to the issue of interaction between the two visual streams, Rossetti et al., highlight the role of the areas lying between the ventral and the dorsal stream with special focus on structures like the inferior parietal lobe which seem to be involved in the control of action outside the dorsal stream. In a similar vein, the neuroscientific analyses by Vallar and Mancini (this volume) suggest that the dual-visual systems only partially capture the essential elements in perception and action. They highlight the role of what they term the 'dorso-ventral stream'. Vallar and Mancini discuss in detail the role of the dorso-ventral stream in both visual and motor spatial awareness. They argue that the phenomenon of unilateral spatial neglect offers a challenge to the simple dichotomy of dorsal and ventral streams because the phenomenon cannot be attributed exclusively to impairment in either. Milner and Goodale (1995) consider unilateral spatial neglect to result from impairment in the ventral stream but Vallar and Mancini argue against this conclusion on grounds that the impaired and preserved characteristics in neglect syndrome differ significantly from those of visual agnosia. Unilateral spatial neglect indicates the role of the dorso-ventral stream in combining perceptual and motor elements leading to perceptual awareness of space as well the execution of motor behaviour directed at objects situated in the perceived space.

What are we to conclude from the above neuroscientific claims of the interaction between the dorsal and the ventral streams involving structures that appear to subserve the crucial functions for both perception and action? If these claims are taken at face value then perception and action appear to be coupled, anatomically and functionally, especially at low levels of description.

Such coupling between perception and action is often invoked for explanatory advantage when it comes to accounting for higher level cognition as well as for consciousness in general. In the previous section we saw how O'Regan's sensorimotor theory of perception proposes a methodological remedy for explaining the qualitative character consciousness. Other theories have also pointed out tricky methodological issues in studying conscious experience in general within the framework of a rigid functional dichotomy between perception and action. For example, Ballard (this volume) argues against the view that conscious experience can be localized within a system that seems to be relatively impervious to processing for action by considering the question: why are we conscious? Ballard compares the role of consciousness to the process of debugging a program run on a computer. He contends that consciousness shares the same neural hardware as that of 'zombie' systems, as can be seen for example in case of the activity of mirror neurons. Furthermore, the use of the same neural hardware for both consciousness and 'zombie' programs indicates that conscious experience relies on the same neural systems that are deployed in everyday interaction between the agent and the world. Interestingly, Milner and Goodale (1998) emphasize that the reason why perception evolved is '… to provide distal sensory control of the many different movements that organisms make'. Ballard's proposal of the role of consciousness may not be in direct conflict with Milner and Goodale's hypothesis about the reason for the evolution of perceptual abilities. Ballard's main contention against the dual-visual systems view lies in the latter's attempt to localize conscious experience within a particular neural system that has at best indirect and highly flexible connections to systems responsible for the control of the organism's real-time behaviour and survival.

In the context of discussing the role of conscious visual experience in guiding action, Wilson (this volume) argues that such a role of conscious experience requires attributing to the body and the environment of the perceiver a constitutive role in enabling perceptual experience. According to Wilson, visual systems which have primarily evolved for the guidance of action are best understood as involving 'exploitative representations' or representations that rely on the body's structure and sensorimotor engagement with the environment. Wilson suggests that the consideration of a constitutive role of the body and its sensorimotor interaction with the environment in enabling perception makes a theory better able to account for basic elements involved in perception such as saccadic eye movements. Viewing vision as proceeding by dynamic feedback loops which cross the boundaries of skin and skull enables us to understand more fully the action-guiding nature of vision as well as the nature of vision as an extended cognitive system.[5]

The fact that perception and action interact in the everyday life of an organism situated in a complex environment is not disputed by any of the views that are discussed in this volume. The question is: how tight does the coupling between perception and action have to be in order to account for our perceptual awareness and motor behaviours? Action-oriented approaches to perception, both theoretical and empirical, have pointed out the inadequacies of a framework that views perception and action as only rather loosely connected in accounting for a significant amount of empirical studies in the field as well as for everyday perceptual experience and motor behaviour. On the other hand, the dual-visual systems theories have pointed out that postulating an inflexible and strongly co-dependent relation between perception and action does not go a long way in accounting for observed dissociations between the two and the existence of specialized functions. Unravelling the various components of perception and action reveals that there are lessons to be learnt from both camps. While not necessarily inseparable in all their nuances, the interaction between perception and action may turn out to be more than a marriage of convenience.

1.6. Conclusion

This volume results from the last international and interdisciplinary conference convened by the late Susan Hurley months before she passed away after her long and courageous battle with cancer. The conference on Perception, Action, and Consciousness: Sensorimotor Dynamics and Two-Visual Systems was organized as part of the CONTACT project funded by the Arts and Humanities Research Council under the European Science Foundation Eurocores Consciousness in Natural and Cultural Contexts (CNCC) scheme (grant number AH/E511139/1 of the AHRC). The goal was to bring together leading researchers in philosophy, psychology, neuroscience, and artificial intelligence in order to discuss the relation between perception and action, specifically whether perception required action or whether perceptual awareness was merely a matter of passively representing the visual world. Hurley's work in philosophy of mind and cognitive sciences covers an incredibly wide range of topics such as embodied cognition, the nature of consciousness, theories of imitation, theories of

---

[5] Readers may be familiar with Clark's similar suggestion that some cognitive systems are extended (Clark and Chalmers 1998, Clark, 2008). Wilson's claim of vision as constituting an extended cognitive system differs from Clark's. The constitutive relationship between perception and action served by feedback loops motivates Wilson's proposal of an extended cognitive system. In contrast, Clark's proposal of the extended mind is motivated by the 'parity principle'. The parity principle maintains that if external structures function as part of a process which if conducted exclusively by internal neural mechanisms would be considered as a cognitive process, then those external structures too constitute the cognitive process. Thus, unlike Wilson's hypothesis of vision as an instance of an extended cognitive system involving feedback loops, Clark's defence of the extended mind hypothesis does not rely on a tight coupling between perception and action.

perception, and social cognition to name a few. A common note running through Hurley's treatment of these diverse topics is her rigorous defence of the essentially active nature of our cognitive life. She repeatedly challenged the orthodox view of the mind which she dubbed the 'classical sandwich' because it conceives of the mind or cognition as sandwiched between the separate modules of perception and action; the former carries the input from the world to the mind and the latter carries the output from the mind to the world. In the decade between the publication of her two major works *Consciousness in Action* (1998) and 'The Shared Circuits Model' (2008) Hurley's approach was one of gradually unifying her views on social cognition with her thesis of the active nature of perception which eventually culminated in the framework of the shared circuits model where consciousness of oneself and of others arises from the dynamic perception-action coupling constituting the very core of our engagement with the world.

The dialogue between the two approaches, the action-oriented views of perception and the dual-visual system theories, presented in this volume brings out wider theoretical issues that underlie the research paradigm of cognitive sciences and philosophy of mind. These issues require critical deliberations and interdisciplinary efforts for laying the foundations of future research in the domain. For example, an important implication of the action-oriented views is that the notion of embodiment, which is crucial for understanding the notion of agency, must be wide enough to include the whole organism rather than just the brain. Consequently, some action-oriented approaches, for example the sensorimotor theories, tend to view the search for the neural correlates of consciousness with suspicion (Noë and Thompson, 2004). However, if the separation between perception and action is accepted as unavoidable for a systematic account of consciousness, such a separation implies that perceptual experience can be understood, at least to a nontrivial extent if not in its totality, by brain mechanisms dedicated to the generation of internal representations. The conference brought together leading exponents of the two approaches, renowned scholars offering a dynamic and interdisciplinary perspective of a number of fundamental issues in cognitive sciences and philosophy of mind, and aimed to take up modern challenges to classical issues from two powerful emerging perspectives while pointing out the direction of the current and future research in the domain.

The volume has been organized into six sections. The first section discusses methodological issues in a scientific study of consciousness with special focus on the role of sensorimotor dynamics (Ballard, O'Regan, Clark). The second section takes up an exposition of the two visual systems hypothesis along with discussions of empirical evidence (Milner and Goodale, Melmoth et al.). The third section discusses conceptual issues relating to the notion of agency and object perception. It includes works inspired by the dual-visual systems model (Matthen, Jacob and de Vignemont), and a work that offers a different take on an action-oriented approach to perceptual experience (Schellenberg). The fourth section presents studies in cognitive neuroscience that throw new light on the two-visual systems hypothesis (Rossetti et al., Vallar and Mancini, Delevoye-Turrell et al.). The fifth section addresses the role of action and sensorimotor knowledge from the perspective of the sensorimotor theories of perception and presents new developments in the sensorimotor theorists' conceptualization of the relation between perception and action (Noë, Kiverstein). In addition, Noë pays special attention to the relation between his action-oriented account of perception and the dual-visual systems hypothesis. The sixth and final section raises fundamental issues about the embodied situated agent and questions the traditional boundaries of the agent's embodiment (Wilson).

References

Aglioti, S., Goodale, M.A., and DeSouza, J.F.X. (1995). Size-contrast illusions deceive the eye but not the hand. *Current Biology*; **5**: 679–85.

Anderson, M.L. (2003). Embodied cognition: a field guide. *Artificial Intelligence*; **149**: 91–130.

Block, N. (2005). Review of action in perception. *Journal of Philosophy*; **102**: 259–72.

Clark, A. and Chalmers, D. (1998). The extended mind. *Analysis*; **58**(1): 7–19.

Clark, A. (2006). Vision as dance? Three challenges for sensorimotor contingency theory. *Psyche*; **12**(1): 1–10.

—— (2008). *Supersizing the mind: embodiment, action, and cognitive extension*. Oxford: Oxford University Press.

Findlay, J.M. and Gilchrist, I.D. (2003). *Active vision: the psychology of looking and seeing*. Oxford: Oxford University Press.

Gallagher, S. (in press). Philosophical antecedents to situated cognition. In *Cambridge handbook of situated cognition*. (eds Robbins, P. and Aydede, M.), Cambridge: Cambridge University Press.

Gallese, V. (2007). The 'Conscious' dorsal stream: embodied simulation and its role in space and action conscious awareness. *Psyche*; 13/1 (archived electronic journal: http://psyche.cs.monash.edu.au/).

Gangopadhyay, N. and Kiverstein, J. (2009). Enactivism and the unity of perception and action. *Topoi*; 28(1): 63–73.

Gibson, J.J. (1966). *The senses considered as perceptual systems*. Boston: Houghton Mifflin.

—— (1979). *The ecological approach to visual perception*. Boston: Houghton Mifflin.

Goodale, M.A. and Milner, A.D. (1992). Separate visual pathways for perception and action. *Trends in Neurosciences*; **15**: 20–5.

—— (2004). *Sight unseen: an exploration of consciousness and unconscious vision*. Oxford: Oxford University Press.

Hurley, S. (1998). *Consciousness in action*. Cambridge, MA: Harvard University Press.

—— (2001). Perception and action: alternative views. *Synthese*; 129: 3–40.

—— (2008). The shared circuits model: how control, mirroring, and simulation can enable imitation and mind-reading. *Behavioral and Brain Sciences*; 31(1): 1–22.

Jacob, P. and Jeannerod, M. (2003). *Ways of seeing, the scope and limits of visual cognition*. Oxford: Oxford University Press.

Kosslyn, S.M. and Maljkovic, V. (1990). Marr's meta-theory revisited. *Concepts in Neuroscience*; 1(2): 239–51.

Marr, D. (1982). *Vision: acomputational investigation into the human representation and processing of visual information*. San Francisco: W.H. Freeman.

Matthen, M. (2005). *Seeing, doing and knowing*. Oxford: Oxford University Press.

Milner, A.D. and Goodale, M.A. (1995). *The visual brain in action*. Oxford: Oxford University Press.

—— (1998). Précis of the visual brain in action. *Psyche*; 4(12): (archived electronic journal: http://psyche.cs.monash.edu.au/v4/psyche-4-12-milner.html).

Noë, A. (2004). *Action in perception*. Cambridge: MIT Press.

Noë, A. and O'Regan, J.K. (2002). On the brain basis of perceptual consciousness. In *Vision and mind: selective readings in the philosophy of perception*. (eds Noë, A. and Thompson, E.), pp. 567–98. Cambridge, MA: The MIT Press.

O'Regan, K. and Noë, A. (2001). A sensorimotor account of vision anvisual consciousness. *Behavioral and Brain Sciences*; 24(5): 883–917.

Palmer, S. (1999). *Vision science: photons to phenomenology*. Cambridge, MA: MIT Press.

Passingham, R.E., Stephan, K.E., and Kotter, R. (2002). The anatomical basis of functional localisation in the cortex. *Nature Reviews Neuroscience*; **3**: 606–16.

Pisella, L., Binkofski, F., Lasek, K., Toni, I., and Rossetti, Y. (2006). No double-dissociation between optic ataxia and visual agnosia: multiple sub-streams for multiple visuo-manual integrations. *Neuropsychologia*; 44: 2734–48.

Rizzolatti, G. and Matelli, M. (2003). Two different streams form the dorsal visual system: anatomy and functions. *Experimental Brain Research*; **153**: 146–57.

Trevarthen, C.B. (1968). Two mechanisms of vision in primates. *Psychological Research*; 31(4): 299–337.

Turvey, M., Shaw, R.E., Reed, E.S., and Mace, W.M. (1981). Ecological laws of perceiving and acting: in reply to Fodor and Pylyshyn. *Cognition*; 9: 237–304.

Schenk, T. (2006). An allocentric rather than perceptual deficit in patient D.F. *Nature Neuroscience*; 9(11): 1369–70.

Schneider, G.E. (1969). Two visual systems: brain mechanisms for localization and discrimination are dissociated by tectal and cortical lesions. *Science*; **163**: 895–902.

Ungerleider, L.G. and Mishkin, M. (1982). Two cortical visual systems. In *Analysis of visual behavior*. (eds Ingle, D.J. Goodale, M.A., and. Mansfield, R.J.W), pp. 549–86. Cambridge, MA: MIT Press.

Varela, F.J., Thompson, E., and Rosch, E. (1991). *The embodied mind*. Cambridge, MA: The MIT Press.

Viviani, P. (2002). Motor-perceptual interactions: assessing the conceptual implications of some known phenomena. In *Common mechanisms in perception and action: attention and performance*. (eds Prinz, W. and Hommel, B.), Vol. XIX. pp. 406–42. Oxford: Oxford University Press.

Wallhagen, M. (2007). Consciousness and action: does cognitive science support (mild) epiphenomenalism? *The British Journal for the Philosophy of Science*; 58(3): 539–61.

PART 1

Consciousness and sensorimotor dynamics: methodological issues

CHAPTER 2

Computational consciousness

Dana H. Ballard

Abstract

One distinguishing feature of consciousness is the ability to simulate possible futures, complete with populations of other minds and their motives. Technically, this ability places demands on the brain, which on an evolutionary scale developed structures more suitable for acting in the near term based on concrete stimuli. Thus, important insights as to the nature of consciousness can be obtained by considering how it could be implemented within these structures. Exploring the technical requirements of such an implementation results in constraints on how consciousness could appear in the brain's neural substrate. The crucial questions turn on not so much as to *where* consciousness is located, but as to *what* the component functions are that, taken together, are requisite for consciousness.

2.1. Why are we conscious?

We all have a feeling of consciousness that we can talk about and share with others. When we are alone most of us hear a compelling 'voice' in our heads articulating our thoughts, and if you are good at mental imagery, you can have a compelling sensation of different images of people, places, and all kinds of things. Such shared sensation has led philosophers and neuroscientists to search for the *mechanisms behind the sensation of consciousness*, the newest effort being by Noë (2009). However, despite all efforts to uncover the 'feeling of what happens', or pin down a quale, progress has been modest, to say the least.

Since, arguably, consciousness must reside in the brain, one thought is that progress might be speeded up if it could be isolated to a specific place therein, or at least excluded from a place. Crick and Koch declared famously that V1, the cortical area receiving visual input from the thalamus, was not conscious (Crick and Koch, 1995), perhaps bringing hope to their acolytes as V1 is a very large cortical area, and therefore the search area would be reduced. More recently Milner and Goodale have made a more positive assertion, claiming that consciousness might reside in the temporal cortex, but not the dorsal cortex (Milner and Goodale, 1995; 2006). The thrust of this chapter is to argue that this conjecture cannot be true, using two primary lines of reasoning. The first is fairly basic: a large body of experimental data simply does not support this claim. The second is more speculative and rests on claims as to the role of consciousness.

This second line presupposes that a helpful question might be: why are we conscious? If there was an answer to that question, then the mechanisms that support it could be cast in a different, possibly more constructive, light. This is the tack we take, but with a computational focus. We lay out a précis of human brain function from that perspective and then describe consciousness as an important component. The slowness of neural circuitry means that most of the brain is memory and that primarily behaviours involve memory retrievals. Consciousness is a necessary feature for the brain's process of analysing, storing, and acting on unexpected data.

Any student of consciousness has to take note of Damasio's *Descartes' Error*. In that groundbreaking treatise (Damasio, 1994), the emotions are described as a way of promoting fast decisions in a brain with slow neural circuitry. Picking behavioural programs amounts to choosing among pre-stored ratings gleaned from uses of the body's emotional state. Neurotransmitters do this and the emotions felt by the conscious self are the signature that this has happened. So neurotransmitters select among unconscious programs. However, from Wegner's experiments, we argue that consciousness is just a program too (Wegner, 2002), and very appropriately described as including as its signature 'an emotion of authorship'. For many programs the brain selects, the author/world distinction does not have to be made explicit: but for consciousness, it does. We explore the impact of this in the computational support that would be needed to implement this function (throughout this chapter, computation and program are used with their standard definitions in computer science).

2.2. Trying to put consciousness in its place

One idea is that consciousness might have a specific place in the brain, a kind of consciousness 'pineal gland', but a brief survey of experimental results can easily disabuse us of this notion. Let us start with Milner's patient HM who, when operated on to transect his hippocampus, lost the ability for new permanent memories. Since the 1960s when this was done, countless additional studies have confirmed this basic result: the hippocampus and the amygdala form a neural complex that is responsible for abstracting experiences that will be committed to long-term memory. Without these components this consolidation does not happen. One would not say that patients with hippocampal damage are not conscious (among other things they can converse in the present about their past and remember prior events they experienced with friends), but these conversations and other new events cannot be committed to permanent memory. The patients are obviously conscious, but their ability to encode new memories is gone and consequently the ability to 'know' about these new memories and consciously discourse about them disappears as well. Long-term memories are coded in the brain's cortex, which is organized into specific areas that contribute to specific functions. The role of these areas begs to be misinterpreted by functional magnetic resonance imaging (fMRI) which uses a differential measure of oxygenated blood flow to pinpoint cortical areas that are more active in certain tasks relative to a control, but what we can say safely is that different areas have roles in facilitating the neural activity all over the brain that leads to a reportable percept. A specific example will make this clear.

Patients can suffer damage to their parietal cortex in a way that leads to a deficit in object-centered locations. In eating food from a plate these patients will eat the food in either the left or right half of the plate (depending on whether the damage is in the right or left hemisphere), leaving the other half untouched. This is remarkable as the damage is not a visual field deficit, since the patients can move their eyes and will have directed their gaze at the missing pieces. However, apparently when the act of eating is engaged this information is not available. The patients are just not conscious of the 'missing' part of their visual field. These patients' deficit is particularly challenging to the idea that the temporal cortex is the site of consciousness, as it is the dorsal cortex that is damaged. Before the damage they are conscious of their full visual field and can discourse about objects anywhere in it; afterwards they are unaware of objects in the damaged object-centred field. Numerous other examples can be included here with the same result: consciousness is an add-on to the function of a specific part of the brain and when that part is damaged, the related part of consciousness is damaged also.

The main weight of the argument for the temporal-cortex-site-of-consciousness hypothesis is that, according to experiments conducted on the single patient DF, these areas are separate and dissociated. DF could post a card in a tilted slot aperture, putatively the exclusive job of the dorsal cortex, but was unable to make a judgment of the aperture's orientation with respect to a standard, putatively the exclusive job of the temporal cortex. Could it be that in the case of the parietal patients the dorsal cortex serves as a kind of switch? The argument might be that the temporal cortex remains the separate site of consciousness, but it does not receive its desired input in these cases. Enthusiasm for this line of argumentation has come from experiments that show that normal subjects who saw the Ebbinghaus illusion—a circle surrounded by larger circles looks smaller than the same circle surrounded by smaller circles—yet reached for the central circle with the correct grasp aperture. So, apparently, the dorsal cortex is unaffected by the illusion. However, Brenner and Smeets (1996) show that, while the grasp for a similar illusion is corrected, the lifting force anticipates the illusory size of an object, showing that the effects of the illusion are used in the grip calculation.

The backdrop for thinking of the cortex as having distinct areas has long-standing support from anatomical and physiological evidence, particularly fRMI studies, and, given all this evidence, it is easy to exaggerate their spatio-temporal separateness. Imagine the brain as a place in which cortical areas are analogous to French medieval villages where axonal spikes are carried back and forth between them on horseback. However, this illusion is quickly dispelled upon realizing that the fMRI measurements between test and control conditions reveal differences of just 1–3 percentage points; 97–99% of the activity is common to both conditions. Furthermore spikes travel at relatively high velocities and can communicate between areas in just a few tens of milliseconds. The point is that, realistically, any two different cortical areas are intimately part of any computation that they are both involved in.

The central claim from these observations is that any attempt to put consciousness in a neural 'place' is unlikely to succeed. The arguments for not assigning awareness to just one of the dorsal and temporal corticies can be made for any comparable set of cortical areas and indeed for the rest of the forebrain. The forebrain (amygdala, hippocampus, cortex, basal ganglia, and thalamus) is our mammalian heritage wherein any damage to one of its subsystems produces very predictable deficits in awareness. In this respect, consciousness is like the Cheshire cat in that when a piece of forebrain fails, a facility associated with that piece, that can impact consciousness in a predictable way, vanishes with it. Thus the experience of consciousness, which we perceive as a unity, below our conscious level is very much a composition of a disunity, comprised of well-defined capabilities, linked to cooperating forebrain subsystems.

2.3. **Consciousness meets computation**

If consciousness is to be considered as a program, then we should introduce computation and say a bit about programs, and in particular how programs are organized. In the 1950s when computers began their transition from special purpose one-off curiosities to mainstream platforms that handled scientific and business calculations, the idea that the brain was some kind of computer surfaced, but was not greeted with much enthusiasm in research communities beyond promoters of 'expert systems' (Anderson, 1983; Newell, 1990). The idea of computation being central to the brain was very much a metaphor that competed with other physics-based notions such as the hologram.

Nowadays the situation is reversed and information-based computational theory is seen as the most plausible scientific program in understanding brain function. The computational framework has sensitized us to the fact that most of the brain is about memories. The slow neural circuitry, over one million times slower than silicon, means that at a basic level behavioural responses have to have been pre-computed and looked up by a fast indexing technique. Before Google, we might have been skeptical that this was possible, but now we know that, in a way analogous to web-crawling and indexing, the brain works over its lifetime continually to sort its behavioural programs so that they can be brought to bear rapidly on the situation at hand.

One indication of the acceptance of computation for understanding brain functions was the endorsement of Nature Neuroscience's special issue devoted to brain computation (e.g. Hinton, 2005). This enthusiasm is a product of many modeling breakthroughs whereby complex phenomena have simple explanations once the framework of computation is introduced. Let us review two examples.

How are the memory circuits formed? A computational answer for the peripheral visual circuitry has found wide acceptance, which views those areas as constructing a code for natural images. Any good code should represent the image to be coded, but computational models have introduced a special spin: the image should indeed be coded, but a desirable property of the code is that its neural substrate should use an economical signalling strategy. Neurons signal in discrete spikes and half of the metabolic cost is in spike generation, so codes that use fewer spikes and thus save energy are to be preferred. Stunningly, when created in computational simulations, those codes appear very similar to the experimental observations from neural recordings (Olshausen and Field, 1997; Rao and Ballard, 1999). This implies that the brain has refined Occam's razor. Simple codes are preferred, but simplicity must balance the accuracy of the code against the complexity of its description.

How are memory circuits used? The visual codes that we have just been talking about allow the description of visual data but they do not include a prescription for what to do with those data. For that we must turn to further research that used trained monkeys as subjects. In primates the eyes have pronounced foveas, so that the resolution at the point of gaze is greatly increased over the periphery. In humans the factor is one hundred. As a consequence, almost all the time, primate eyes use rapid ballistic movements (saccades) to orient the high-resolution gaze-point over interesting visual targets. However, programming this gaze-change takes about a quarter of a second. Monkeys are instructed to hold their gaze at a fixed point while looking at a computer monitor. Two line segments appear and the monkey must make a saccade to the end of the segment that happens to be connected to the gaze-point.

The experiment takes advantage of the fact that the neurons in the early visual periphery are sensitive to small, precise photometric edge segments at specific retinotopic locations. The hypothesis being tested is that the monkey finds the end-point by mentally tracing the line segment from the fixation point to its end. The experimenters record from a neuron that is coding a point on this route and find that its spike-rate increases, consistent with the tracing hypothesis (Roelfsema et al., 2003).

The above examples are united by their use of computation as the core concept that guides the interpretation of any data, yet describe experiments that span two separate abstractions. When studying memory formation, the use of the memory is postponed; and when studying the use of memory, the existence of the memory is assumed. Keep in mind that these two abstractions are just two of several that must be assumed to handle the richness of human brain computation. Table 2.1 shows

Table 2.1 A proposal for the brain's use of computational hierarchies. In the task of making a sandwich different sub-tasks are described at different levels of abstraction

Level	Computational model
Operating System	Schedule all behaviours; trade-off debugging and runtime behaviours 'if all the operations are succeeding, stay in runtime mode'
Debugging	Analyse unusual events using off-line mode: 'why isn't the jelly sticking to the knife?'
Runtime	Pick a suite of behaviours to handle the current situation: 'take the lid off the jelly jar'; 'pick up the knife'
Behaviour	Sensory-motor coordinated actions: 'insert the knife into the jar and gingerly bend and remove it'
Routines	Task-specific tests of the environment: 'locate the purple jelly surface'
Calibration	Encode environmental statistics in specific circuits; filling-in phenomena: colour-constant neural circuitry
Neural	Models of specific neurons in circuits; excitation and inhibition
Synapses	Models of a neuron's components; roles for different neural transmitters; neural spike signalling; basic units of memory

a more complete candidate computational hierarchy. What about consciousness? Could it be the sole *deus ex machina* that escapes a computational description? Computation is not an all-powerful theory, and has well-understood limitations, but all of these concern mathematical infinities and are unlikely limitations for a satisfying animal brain. The odds-on bet is that when consciousness is understood at some mechanical level, that level will be isomorphic with computation. Furthermore, as some kind of program, it must fit into the computational hierarchy.

2.4. Abstraction hierarchies

As Newell pointed out, any complex system that has admitted of a description has incorporated the use of the notion of hierarchy and the brain is unlikely to be an exception (Newell, 1990). Hierarchies have two prominent properties:

1. As the description becomes more abstract its components necessarily run slower than those of the lower level and take up more physical space.

2. The more abstract description omits details from the lower level.

A ready example from silicon is that of digital circuitry. The dependence of current on voltage across a gate is continuous, but digital circuitry abstracts that into two levels. The speed of such circuitry is governed by the time it takes for the levels to change between one level and another. Here the continuous voltage value is abstracted away into a binary code. In a similar way computational models of the brain differ at different levels as the primitives at each level are correspondingly different again. Just like silicon computing, brain computation has to be organized into hierarchical levels, each of which groups primitives from the level below into equivalences. The average cortical neuron receives input from two to ten thousand other neurons and yet at any moment summarizes those inputs into a single spike or silence. Higher levels make similar kinds of abstractions. So a key question is: If consciousness is a program, how does that program project into the various computational abstraction levels?

Searle, arguing against artificial intelligence models, and by extension computation, use a now-famous example of the Chinese Room. A person who knows nothing of Chinese is in a room where Chinese sentences in characters appear at an input slot. While the person knows nothing of Chinese, he or she has access to a set of instructions in English that are of the form 'if you see these characters output these characters'. Supposedly the person is a model for the computer, mimicking linguistic behaviour but understanding nothing. Here is where the trouble starts: Is the person in the room actually a human or a computer (or a neuron)? Depending on how one answers this question there are different logical consequences and therein lies the difficulty.

The danger of confusing abstractions is easier to understand if we change venues for a moment and talk about computers and their abstractions. One can program in MATLAB, assembly language, or microcode, but each language is cast at a different level of abstraction and each involves a different level of familiarity with the underlying computer that runs the programs. MATLAB requires no knowledge of the machine at all, whereas assembly language requires an elemental model of basic random access architectures and microcode requires an intimate knowledge of a particular machine's low-level hardware instruction set. The point of these levels is that they cannot be mixed. Once an abstraction level is picked one must stay within it: MATLAB and microcode cannot be mixed.

What seems so clear when couched in silicon computational terms somehow does not always survive the translation into philosophical arguments about human computation. To return to our example, Searle's attempt to gain purchase depends on transits across abstraction boundaries. Is the occupant in the room a human or computer? It has to be one or the other; to not insist on a choice leads to what I would term the abstraction con, which comes up repeatedly in discussions about consciousness. Consider Escher's famous drawing of hands drawing each other. Is it just a drawing, or is it really a picture of something that could happen? Perhaps when nobody is looking, the hands behave like the Addams Family's Thing and take a few pencil strokes. But let us not allow this kind of magical thinking to displace the magical thinking, aka the *abstraction con*, upon which the drawing's kick depends: 'It's a pair of hands' oscillating across the abstraction boundary separating this idea from 'It's a drawing of hands'.

Let us return to consciousness and consider how consciousness is represented in an abstraction hierarchy. Could it be that: (A) consciousness is an abstraction that appears at a given level but has no discernible trace at the level below? The alternatives are that: (B) consciousness is only manifested at lower levels; or else (C) it has a trace that spans all levels. Most researchers would choose at least option (A) given our phenomenological experience of hearing our own internal directive voice, but there is obviously also enthusiasm for option (C). Koch for one has advocated a search for the neural correlate of consciousness (Koch, 2003). Of course unless one is a dualist there will be a sense in which the answer must be (C). But the cautionary note from the example of silicon computation is that one needs to understand the various abstraction levels in their own terms as well as the process of translating between them. Failing to keep them separate and mixing abstraction levels only results in confusion. This assertion can be seen as in sympathy with Lamme's view (Lamme, 2006). He points out that the various claims as to consciousness can seem confusing if they do not respect basic neural organizations. Our extension is that those organizations should be organized into computational hierarchies, because the brain is doing computations and hierarchies are the only way we know of organizing complex computational systems.

However, given that the current state of knowledge of the brain provides only an outline of plausible abstraction hierarchies, this leaves an enormous amount of work to do. At this point we will content ourselves by elaborating the differences between what we have termed in Table 2.1 the 'Runtime' level and the 'Debugging' level, the latter being the level where the contents of consciousness are most evident.

2.5. **Will work for dopamine?**

Although what we are calling the debugging level of abstraction will be the most important for understanding consciousness, to appreciate this level it is important to understand the abstraction level beneath it. How are programs established in the first place? We know a bit about the programs themselves in that, in broad outline, the cortex stores elaborate states of the world and the basal ganglia sequence through those states and trigger actions. While silicon computing sequences through stares at an incredibly high 2 gigahertz rate, the basal ganglia probably work at about 0.3 hertz, or a billion times slower than silicon. Of course, the bandwidth of the cortex in terms of its parallel processing more than makes up for the slowness. We also know a bit about how programs are formed in that the job of the amygdala is to filter out what is important and the job of the hippocampus is to 'slice and dice' those components into pieces that are compatible with what the cortex and basal ganglia have stored. So although we cannot say too much about the details, the big picture of what programs are is sketched.

Given that we have programs, who (or rather what) is the programmer? Answering this question requires understanding what programs do for us and that is, in a word, prediction. Ultimately we need to be able to reproduce successfully and, along the way, to survive and the way to do that is to be able to predict the future. One hugely important way to do that is to save what has happened in the past along with its value so that if the situation recurs one can estimate its outcome and value before its conclusion. The past is prolog.

In this process it helps to keep in mind that the brain's programs are not literal parts of the external world, but internal models of that world. Ramachandran and Sacks have described cases beautifully, where, owing to some kind of brain or body injury, that model is divorced from the true picture of the world, but the brain's conscious owner is unaware of the schism (Ramachandran and Blakeslee, 1999; Sacks, 1985). The point is that these cases of brain injury tell us about the healthy brain's structure, which is one of building and maintaining representations of the world and programs for extracting reward from it. This last point needs elaboration, for although we act in the world to successfully survive and reproduce and along the way achieve measurable rewards in terms of behaviours that satisfy us in one way or another, to accomplish all this the brain's models need 'pretend' or secondary rewards. The main neurotransmitter that signals secondary reward is known to be dopamine (Schultz, 2002), which in honour of Europe's common currency, we will term the 'neuro.' Its power is very much experienced by cocaine addicts who engage in destructive behaviours that trigger dopamine release. In fact most addictions can be conceived in terms of behavioural shortcuts to dopamine release. Most of us are calibrated, in the sense that we can engage in socially acceptable behaviours that the brain can translate into dopamine reward estimates. How can one choose between behaviours A and B? Simple: the brain can retrieve their dopamine estimates and pick the most rewarding.

Up to this point we have described the featured non-persona of philosophers and B movies, the zombie. The zombie brain has an enormous raft of programs that negotiate with the hypothalamus to be valued in neuros. With this common currency the brain can pick the most valuable for execution; no conscious thought required.

What is the zombie state? Almost all car drivers have experienced it. One drives miles of a familiar route, gets distracted and then at some point is conscious of the driving venue as well as conscious of remembering nothing about a large part of the trip wherein one was guiding the car, obeying traffic lights avoiding pedestrians etc. Perhaps you were engrossed in conversation with a passenger while you were following a familiar route, not the one you needed to follow for the particular passenger. During this period, for the driving behaviour, the zombie programs were running. There was no need for any special monitoring because the states that were directing behaviour had pre-coded expectations of consequences that were constantly being met; it is only when this does not happen that something non-zombie have to be done. Of course in philosophy there always seems to be someone on the other side of the fence. Searle, again:

> It is true, for example, that when I am driving my car 'on automatic pilot' I am not paying much attention to the details of the road and the traffic. But it is simply not true that I am totally unconscious of these phenomena. If I were, there would be a car crash.
>
> (Searle, 1990, p. 635)

This was written before the 2005 DARPA Grand Challenge that had five vehicles complete a complicated desert trail loop autonomously. Hopefully we can all agree that those vehicles were not conscious. The point is that the vehicles are essentially limited to zombie driving and did not crash.

Wallace (2007) captures the zombie state brilliantly in his essay 'How Tracy Austin broke my heart', where he asserts that professional athletes have difficulty describing their feats precisely because the descriptions *are no longer accessible* when the over-learned skills are compressed in the zombie brain:

> The real secret behind top athlete's genius, then, may be as esoteric and obvious and dull and profound as silence itself. The real, many-veiled answer to the question of just what goes through a great player's mind as he stands at the center of hostile crowd-noise and lines up at the free-throw that will decide the game might well be: *nothing at all* … there's a cruel paradox involved. It may well be that we spectators, who are not divinely gifted as athletes, are the only ones able truly to see articulate, and animate the experience of the gift we are denied. And that those who receive and act out the gift of athletic genius must, perforce, be blind and dumb about it—and not because blindness and dumbness are the price of the gift, but because they are its essence.
>
> (Wallace, 2007, pp. 154–5)

Make our inner zombie the athlete and our consciousness self the spectator and you have one of the best compact descriptions of the relationship between the two. Wallace also highlights another point. The zombie is usually disparaged as inferior, but the metaphor shows its true relevance: Zombie skills are those that have been honed to near perfection through experience. The 2005 DARPA Grand Challenge shows that, while the detailed programs that the brain might use for its

Runtime abstraction level have yet to be pinned down satisfactorily in the neural substrate, the computation that does the job is fairly well understood and is the subject of standard texts e.g. (Bishop, 2008; Thrun et al., 2005).

2.6. What is consciousness for?

Zombie programs depend on their model of the world being a very good fit; all the contingencies that can occur have been seen a significant amount of times and their responses are coded. Thus the search for alternatives has been done and remembered. However, before that happens, as models are being constructed, the statistics of the model need to be gathered. This is the role of consciousness. The best analogy for this is the process of debugging a program on a silicon computer. Once a program has been debugged it can be used in a zombie state where it is not tampered with further, but before that state is reached, the programmer must stop the program, try alternate versions of it, and test them to see if they behave according to expectations. Like consciousness, this process is much slower and has substantial off-line portions of time.

However an important contrast is that, unlike debugging, there is no programmer in the human consciousness, just a neural search program that is trying to fit a model to data. In this fitting process, it is central to distinguish between effects that the human agent produces and effects that the rest of the world produces. For this point we return to one of the best characterizations of consciousness, that of Wegner (2002). In his famous I Spy experiment, the interval of time between when subjects think of an action and when they do it is manipulated. When asked to rate their actions on a 14-point scale from 'I caused it' to 'It just happened,' subjects rate the period that has the thought preceding the action by a half a second as the most causal. Wegner's stunning suggestion is that the act of consciousness itself is just one more model that the brain uses, and its 'fit' depends on the temporal relationship between the brain's machinery and the body's actions in the external world. Wegner characterizes the result of a good fit between the two as 'an illusion of authorship', to which I would add: produced and required by the neural program in its search process.

The search process of consciousness has a special and remarkable technical problem to deal with and that is that it must share the same neural hardware as the zombie programs. This was brought to light by measurements of the firing patterns of cortical 'mirror cells' (Rizzolatti and Sinigaglia, 2008). Rizzolatti et al., discovered when recording from a monkey's cortex in motor area F5, that the cells would respond when the monkey picked up a raisin but also when another monkey did so or when the experimenter did so. The profound implication of this is that there is finally concrete evidence that the monkey (and by extension humans) use one set of neural 'hardware' for representing all these different events. What this suggests is that a large part of the experience of consciousness may be generated by mental simulation using the same neural circuitry that is used for everyday action, a point made much earlier by Merleau-Ponty (1962) and amplified recently by Barsalou (1999).

Searching by simulation using existing knowledge has a lot of advantages, the principal one being that, in the act of exploring the effect of changing one variable, the rest of the program can be used as is since it is already in place. Thus the search process can systematically try out slightly different variations of the simulation program without extensive re-programming of all the components. However this comes with an attendant disadvantage and that is that some 'bookkeeping' must be done to keep track of what is simulation and what is reality. To go back to Rizzolatti's example, the monkey's brain must somehow keep track of the difference between the experimenter doing the action (Debugging mode) or the monkey itself doing the action (Runtime mode).

2.7. Understanding the brain's ability of 'tagging'

The computational role for consciousness is to be the mechanism that does this bookkeeping, but this point requires quite a bit of elaboration. Let us call this ability 'tagging' in the sense that we can tag the actions of the brain according to the particular agent whose activities are being represented. We use the ability to tag in different ways:

1. We may need to reflect on the past or the future. In these cases the same brain hardware handles the visual perception of past and future, but, as they are not in the present, they must be tagged.

2. We may need to reflect on another's motives. In this case the other person must be simulated on our brain hardware, but of course is not us and must be tagged to keep the distinction apparent.

3. Of course it gets complicated if we have to consider what another person is thinking that we are thinking or when we must imagine the other person's future actions, but the overall ability still rests on tagging or the bookkeeping to record that the brain's activity is a simulation of reality, not reality itself.

4. Multiple personality disorders are a failure of the tagging system. Often in order to protect itself from the consequences of remembering early abuse, the brain will adopt an alternate personality that did not experience it. In this case the tagging is dropped to protect the user.

We can appreciate the usefulness of tagging with an analogy to program debugging. When a computer program is running it is in the 'zombie' state where it sequences through a set of instructions until the end of the program. However, when something goes wrong the programmer interrupts this sequence, slows down the execution and interrogates the values of particular variables, seeking to explain an unexpected part of the execution. In the analogy, the programmer is the conscious homunculus (Humphreys, 1992). In Runtime mode the zombie executes mindlessly a set of responses to coded states of the world and in doing so its programs get translated into all the more concrete models of the neural substrate. In Debugging mode identical neural hardware is used and most of the operations are indistinguishable from their Runtime mode instantiations, with one huge exception: the system 'knows,' i.e. it has the machinery to understand that, for portions of the Debugging mode program, it is simulating the results. What can complicate the matter even further is that Debugging mode may only be required for small portions of a large sequence.

The above observations have a huge implication for understanding consciousness through psychological experiments. Since the conscious mode (Debugging) is utilizing the same underlying neural substrate as the unconscious mode (Runtime), the former is actually being used as a probe to discover information about the various neural circuits rather than necessarily revealing information about itself, a point also made by Block (2007).

2.8. Conclusion

Our principal thesis has been that much previous work has concentrated on finding a mechanistic explanation of how it feels to be conscious and, specifically, in trying to trace that feeling to the neural substrate. While it might be possible to do this, it also might be an extremely difficult task, equivalent to questioning the value of the mass of a proton. Why is it the specific value that it is? In the same way, consciousness, to work, may have to produce a signature, which distinguishes the agent from the surround. Why it produces the feeling that it does as opposed to another may not be an answerable question, however compelling it is to ask it. Ramachandran cannot resist and makes it one of his central unanswered questions about consciousness, phrasing it another way: How can we distinguish the consciousness that we readily accept that others have (which he terms third person consciousness) from the consciousness that we have (first person consciousness)? The difficulty in resolving this distinction can be appreciated by recalling the all-important respect for abstraction boundaries in our discourse. Thinking about another's consciousness is at a more abstract level than living our runtime (zombie) existence. In the same way, if we want to characterize our own consciousness, we have to 'tag' it so that now we are effectively debugging ourselves as a third person simulation. To simultaneously engage the runtime environment and experience our own consciousness requires that we blur an abstraction boundary, which we have declared taboo. Of course taboos can be violated, and even celebrated, as they are in Hofstadter (2007). By violating an abstraction boundary one can create an aptly named 'strange loop', where one ends up unexpectedly at a lower level of abstraction, with the result that strange things happen. The issue is not that you cannot do these things, but, from a computational standpoint, you should not do them.

The question of why consciousness exists may have a ready answer when compared to its useful partner, the unconscious. Unconscious programs represent repeated and reliable interactions between the agent and the world that can be coded invariantly for each case. Consciousness is used to direct the search for new programs, and in that search it becomes essential to distinguish the agent from the surround. In a strong sense this chapter has advanced nothing particularly new. Others, notably Clark (2007), have drawn the distinction between consciousness and the zombie state. However the emphasis here is to stress that since the neural hardware must be shared between the two states, consciousness must be handled at a higher level of abstraction that incorporates a bookkeeping strategy that I have termed tagging. Wegner, Damasio, and Hymphreys have also pioneered the development of the chapter's core ideas. Hopefully, its main value might be in steering the quest for understanding consciousness towards more accessible computational questions.

Acknowledgements

This chapter was made possible by support from NIH Grants RR009283 and MH060624.

References

Anderson, J. (1983). *The architecture of cognition*. Mahwah, NJ: Harvard University Press.

Barsalou, L.W. (1999). Perceptions of perceptual symbols. *Behavioral and Brain Sciences*; **22**: 637.

Bishop, C.M. (2008). *Pattern recognition and machine learning*. New York: Springer.

Block, N. (2007). Consciousness, accessibility, and the mesh between psychology and neuroscience. *Behavioral and Brain Sciences*; **30**: 481–99.

Brenner, E. and Smeets, J.B.J. (1996). Size illusion influences how we lift but not how we grasp an object. *Experimental Brain Research*; **111**: 473–6.

Clark, A. (2007). What reaching teaches: consciousness, control, and the inner zombie. *British Journal for the Philosophy of Science*; **58**: 563–94.

Crick, F. and Koch, C. (1995). Are we aware of neural activity in primary visual cortex? *Nature*; **375**: 121–3.

Damasio, A.R. (1994). *Descartes' error: emotion, reason and the human brain*. Hanover: Harper.

Hinton, G.E. (2005). Computation by neural networks. *Nature Neuroscience*; **3**: 1170.

Hofstadter, D. (2007). *I am a strange loop*. New York: Basic Books.

Humphreys, N. (1992). *A history of the mind*. New York: Springer.

Koch, C. (2003). *The quest for consciousness*. Colorado: Roberts.

Lamme, V. (2006). Towards a true neural stance on consciousness. *Trends in Cognitive Sciences*; **10**: 494–500.

Merleau-Ponty, M. (1962). translated by Smith, C. *Phenomenology of perception*. London: Routledge & Kegan Paul.

Milner, A.D. and Goodale, M.A. (1995). *The visual brain in action*. Oxford: Oxford University Press.

—— (2006). Epilogue: twelve years on, *The visual brain in action*. (Second edition). Oxford: Oxford University Press.

Newell, A. (1990). *Unified theories of cognition*. Mahwah, NJ: Harvard University Press.

Noë, A. (2009). *Out of our heads: why you are not your brain, and other lessons from the biology of consciousness*. New York: Farrar, Straus and Giroux.

Olshausen, B.A. and Field, D.J. (1997). Sparse coding with an overcomplete basis set: a strategy employed by v1? *Vision Research*; **37**: 3311–25.

Ramachandran, V.S. and Blakeslee, S. (1999). *Phantoms in the brain: probing the mysteries of the human mind*. London: HarperCollins.

Rao, R.P.N. and Ballard, D.H. (1999). Predictive coding in the visual cortex: a functional interpretation of some extra-classical receptive field effects. *Nature Neuroscience*; **2**: 79–87.

Rizzolatti, G. and Sinigaglia, C. (2008). *Mirrors in the brain*. Oxford: Oxford University Press.

Roelfsema, P.R., Khayat, P.S., and Spekreijse, H. (2003). Subtask sequencing in the primary visual cortex. *Proceedings of the National Academy of Sciences USA*; **100**: 5467–72.

Sacks, O. (1985). *The man who mistook his wife for a hat*. London: Simon and Schuster.

Schultz, W. (2002). Getting formal with dopamine and reward. *Neuron*; **36**: 241–63.

Searle, J. (1990). Who is computing with the brain? *Behavioral and Brain Sciences*; **13**: 632–42.

Thrun, S., Burgard, W., and Fox, D. (2005). *Probabilistic robotics*. Cambridge, MA: MIT Press.

Wallace, D.F. (2007). *Consider the lobster*. New York: Abacus.

Wegner, D. (2002). *The illusion of conscious will*. Cambridge, MA: MIT Press.

CHAPTER 3

Explaining what people say about sensory qualia

J. Kevin O'Regan

Abstract

This paper discusses three problematic aspects of sensory experiences, namely, their ineffability, structure and 'what it's like' to undergo the experiences. It argues that these features of sensory experiences seem to admit of no explanation in terms of brain mechanisms. However, the sensorimotor account of phenomenal consciousness provides a satisfactory account of these puzzling features of sensory experience by proposing that the experienced "feel" of a sensation derives from the laws of dependency that govern an observer's current active engagement with the environment. Thus the sensorimotor view provides a natural way of describing and explaining sensory feels in terms of the objective laws that govern our sensorimotor interactions with the world. The claim is supported by empirical evidence derived from studies on sensory substitution, colour perception and change blindness. The sensorimotor approach, as presented in this paper, emphasises the distinction between two steps involved in an account of conscious experience, namely, i) characterising the quality of sensory feels as enabled by the quality of the sensorimotor interaction involved and ii) determining the requirements for an agent to be conscious of this quality.

3.1. Introduction

There is an argument promulgated by certain philosophers (notably Dennett, 1988, 1991), claiming that from a logical and philosophical point of view the notion of 'qualia' makes no sense. On the other hand, other philosophers (e.g. Nagel, 1974; Peacocke, 1983; Block, 1990) say that qualia must exist since otherwise there would be 'nothing it's like' to have sensations: we humans would merely be empty vessels making movements and interacting with our environments, but there would be no inside 'feel' to anything.

Independent of this debate there are things people usually say about their sensory experiences that relate to the notion of qualia. People say that they cannot completely describe the 'raw', basic, ultimate aspects of their sensations (e.g. the redness of red) to others (this is usually termed 'ineffability'). They say that even if they cannot describe these aspects, they can be compared and contrasted (I shall say they have 'structure'). And people say that there is 'something it's like' to have these raw sensory experiences (they have 'sensory presence'). Whether or not qualia should be taken to exist from a philosophers' point of view, these three things that people say about their sensory experiences need to be explained.

In this chapter I show how, under the 'sensorimotor' view of phenomenal consciousness (O'Regan and Noë, 2001) and further developed by O'Regan, Myin and Noë (2005, 2006) we can understand what we might mean when we say these things, independently of whether qualia actually exist. This angle on how the sensorimotor view can be applied was not stressed in my original papers.

In addition to providing an explanation for some puzzling features of sensory experience, the sensorimotor view has the additional advantage that it makes new empirical predictions and opens new theoretical horizons.

Because I want to remain neutral about whether qualia exist, I shall be defining the term 'raw feel'.[1] I shall be trying to find a definition which is such that if you believe qualia exist then you could take raw feel to be equal to qualia. If you do not think qualia exist, then you should take raw feel to be what people say about the most basic aspects of their sensory experiences. Raw feel may be part of what Block (1995) calls 'phenomenal consciousness'.

After defining raw feel below, I shall detail the three aspects of raw feel which are problematic for philosophy or science, and go on to show how the sensorimotor approach provides an explanation for them. I shall then look at some empirical consequences of conceiving raw feel in sensorimotor terms. At the end of the chapter I shall consider what it means to consciously feel.

Suppose I consciously see a red patch of colour: I have the feel of red. What exactly is this feel? What do I *experience* when I feel the feel of red? Let us peel away the components of this feel of red until we get to the core, 'raw' component.

One aspect of the feel of red is the cognitive state that red puts me into. This state might involve mental associations with roses, ketchup, blood, red traffic and brake lights, and might include knowledge about how red is related to other colours: for example that it's similar to pink and quite different from green. There are also the thoughts and linguistic utterances that seeing redness might provoke, and the changes it might cause in my knowledge, my plans, opinions, or desires.

Another component of the feel of red is the learnt bodily reactions that redness may engender, such as habits that I have established and that are associated with red: for example pressing on the brake when I see red brake lights.

Yet another aspect of the feel of red may be the physiological states or tendencies it creates. Certainly such states are found in the case of jealousy, love, and hate, which involve certain, often ill-defined, urges to do things or to modify the present situation. Similarly, emotions like fear, anger, and shame, and states like hunger and thirst may involve reactions of the autonomic nervous system, and may be accompanied by drives to engage in certain particular activities. Thus it may be that even colour sensations may involve physiological states or tendencies. For example, red may be a colour that excites you, whereas blue may calm you down.

However, all these components of red seem not to constitute the 'raw' feel of red itself. They seem to be extra components, add-ons, or products of some more basic thing, namely the primal, raw feel of red, which is at the core of what happens when I look at a red patch of colour. Arguably, it is the raw feel which is the cause of the other components. It is the raw feel of the redness of the traffic light that engenders my recognition of the redness and my urge to press on the brake.

3.2. Three problematic aspects of 'raw feel'

In the following sections I discuss three common intuitions about 'raw feel', namely their ineffability, structure, and 'what it's like', and discuss how they are problematic from a philosophic or neuroscientific point of view.

3.2.1. Ineffability

One of the first things people say about raw feel is that their raw feels are private and ultimately impossible to communicate to anyone else. For example: how can I ever know whether red looks the same to me as it does to you?

---

[1] Herbert Feigl has also used the term raw feel in a technical sense, and Kirk (1994) uses 'raw feeling'. I'm not sure of the relation to my use.

This 'ineffability' of raw feel has led philosophers to conclude that special theoretical apparatus might be needed to understand it. Ineffability is a first critical aspect of raw feel that we would like to account for.

3.2.2. Structure and why it is problematic for neurophysiology

A second thing people will say about raw feels is that they differ among each other. There is red, green, pink, black. There is the sound of a tractor, of a violin, of middle C, of the wind in the willows, there is the smell of a rose, and the scratch of an itch.

Furthermore, there may be structure in the differences. One aspect of the structure arises through the fact that certain feels can be compared and others not. For example, red and pink can be compared. We say they belong to the same sensory modality. But red and the sound of a bell cannot reasonably be compared. We say they are in different sensory modalities.

Another aspect of the structure is the fact that when (within a sensory modality) comparisons are possible, the comparisons can sometimes be described in terms of dimensions. An example of a linear dimension is intensity of sound, that goes from no sound to very strong sound. An example of a circular dimension is colour hue, which goes around from red to orange to yellow to green to blue to purple and back to red again. In some cases, such as smell, taste, or musical timbre, the dimensions may be difficult to pin down, or there may be a large number of them (in smell, up to 30 dimensions may be necessary—cf. Madany Mamlouk and Martinetz, 2004).

Structure poses problems for neurophysiological accounts. Here I will discuss the problems encountered by an account in terms of 'neural correlates', and by another neurophysiological account based on the idea of 'isomorphism'.

Take the example of colour. At the very first level of processing in the retina, information about colour is coded in three 'opponent' channels: the Blue–Yellow and Red–Green channels measure the equilibrium between blue and yellow and between red and green. There is also a light–dark channel measuring the equilibrium between black and white.

Information in the opponent channels gets transmitted via the optic nerve into the brain, through the lateral geniculate nucleus up into area V1, where it is then relayed to a multitude of other brain areas, and in particular to area V4 which is sometimes thought to be particularly concerned with colour sensation (see Gegenfurtner and Kipers, 2003, for a review and a critique of this claim). What is it in these pathways or in the higher areas that explains the nature of the raw feel of red and green and the difference between them?

It is not hard to imagine how differences in the activity in the Blue–Yellow and Red–Green channels could create differences related to what I have called the 'extra' aspects of the feel of red and green. Thus, we can imagine easily that the neuronal circuits responsible for the feel of red activate cognitive states like those responsible for the memory of strawberries and red traffic lights. We can imagine that red sensitive channels are linked to learned habits linking red sensory input to muscular output, like pressing the brake. We can imagine physiological states that are caused by red and green stimulation, and that such states affect our tendencies to act in different ways. But what about the 'core' aspect of the sensations of red and green: the 'raw feel'? How could brain mechanisms such as activation in the opponent channels generate these?

There can be no way of answering this question satisfactorily. It constitutes an instance of what Chalmers (1995) called the 'hard problem': For imagine we had actually hit upon what we thought was an explanation. Suppose that it was, say, the fact that the red-producing group of neurons generated one particular frequency of oscillations in wide-ranging cortical areas, and that the green-producing neurons generated a different frequency.

Then we could ask, why are things that way? Why does this particular frequency of oscillation produce the raw feel of red, and that frequency the raw feel of green? Couldn't it be the other way round? We could look further to see what was special about these frequencies. Perhaps we would find that the red producing frequencies favoured metabolism of a certain neurotransmitter, whereas the green producing frequencies favoured metabolism of a different neurotransmitter. Is that sufficient? No, for we would still have to explain why these particular neurotransmitters generated the particular raw feels that they do. Clearly, no matter how far we go in the search for mechanisms that generate raw feel, as noted by Dennett (1991), we will always end up being forced to ask an additional question about why things are this way rather than that. There is what Levine (1983) calls an 'explanatory gap'. We would not have any difficulty if we were simply interested in understanding how the neurotransmitters determined the extra components associated with red and green by influencing brain states and potential behaviours and bodily states, but we would not be able to explain the way they determined the raw feel itself. Any account in terms of 'neural correlates' will come up against this problem.

A possible way to partially escape this situation has been proposed by some scientists (e.g. Palmer, 1999) and philosophers (Hayek, 1953; Hardin, 1988; Clark, 1993) The idea is to give up trying to explain why raw feels are the way they are, and instead concentrate on explaining why the differences and similarities between the raw feels are the way they are. For example, there might be a set of brain states corresponding to colour sensations, such that the structure of the similarities and differences between the different states can be mapped on to the similarities and differences between colour sensations. Palmer (1999) has suggested that such an 'isomorphism' between the structure of brain states and the structure of colour sensations would provide at least part of an explanation of colour sensations.

However, this is not the case. As a concrete example, suppose some brain state produced the raw feel of red and furthermore, that brain states near that state produced feels that perceptually are very near to red. Suppose this happened in a lawful way that corresponded to people's judgments about the experienced proximity of red to other colours. The trouble is, what is meant by saying a brain state is 'near' another brain state? Brain states are activities of ensembles of neurons and there is no single way of saying this brain state is 'closer to' or 'further from' another brain state. In particular, if there is some way of ordering the brain states so that their similarities correspond to perceptual judgments about similarities between colours, then the question remains of why it is this way of ordering the brain states, rather than that, which predicts sensory judgments. A justification still needs to be given for the choice of metric used to compare brain states. This point even applies in the simplest of all cases, namely the case of intensity. Suppose the perceived intensity of a sound correlated perfectly with the logarithm of spiking frequency in a particular brain mechanism. Then we can always ask: why exactly that particular law? Why the logarithm instead of a power law or any other law? Spiking frequency is just a code used by the brain, and to explain the feel of intensity satisfactorily, we need an explanation for why the link between the code and the phenomenology is what it is (c.f. Teller's [1984] notion of 'linking proposition').

So, to summarize more generally about neural circuits and the structure of the qualities of raw feel: finding neural correlates that are necessary and sufficient to generate a particular raw feel would be very interesting, but it would not explain adequately what we would really like to know, namely how these brain structures make the feel the way it is, and how they make it similar or different to other feels.

Even discovering an isomorphism between perceptual judgments and certain associated brain states, though interesting (and in fact inevitable in any scientific explanation of how the brain determines feel), is not sufficient as an explanation of raw feel. The underlying problem is that there is no way of making a link between feel and physical mechanisms. Neural firing rates, or any physically definable phenomenon in the brain are incommensurate with raw feels.

So the fact that it is generally accepted that the qualities of raw feels have structure is a second critical aspect of feels we need to explain.

3.2.3. Sensory presence, and why it is problematic for neurophysiology

We now come to what philosophers consider to be perhaps the most mysterious thing about raw sensory feels, namely that, using Nagel's term (1974), raw sensory feels 'feel like something', rather than feeling like nothing.

Another term that has been used to qualify the particular nature of sensory feels is 'presence'. This term was used in the phenomenological tradition of Bergson, Heidegger, Husserl and Merleau-Ponty (see Natsoulas, 1997 and 1999 for a recent approach; see also Matthen, Chapter 7) and has recently become a key concept in virtual reality (see e.g. Ijsselsteijn, 2002). There are similarities and differences in the usages of the different authors, but the notion of 'presence' may be quite close to the notion of 'feeling like something'.

The trouble is, what do these terms really mean? Certainly they are evocative: for example, we all believe that there is 'nothing it's like' for a mere machine to capture a video image of red, whereas we as people really experience redness. The redness is 'present' to us, whereas for the machine it is just information that can be used for actions.

In order to make progress we need an operational definition of what it means for there to be 'something it's like' to have a sensory experience, or for an experience to have 'presence'. Since we can never be sure that everybody means the same thing, it will be useful to invent a new term and try to define it clearly. I shall use the term 'sensory presence' which seems to be close to what we want in referring to the 'what it's like' or presence of sensory experience. The strategy I will use will be to contrast mental states which we can agree have sensory presence with experiences which do not possess it, or which possess it to a lesser degree. I shall consider autonomic physiological states and thoughts, and consider again how neurophysiological explanations must fail to account for the difference in sensory presence of these states as compared to raw sensory feels.

3.2.3.1. Autonomic functions

Consider the fact that your brain is continually monitoring the level of oxygen, carbon dioxide, and sugar in your blood. It is keeping your heartbeat steady and controlling other bodily functions like your liver and kidneys. All these activities involve biological sensors that register the way different systems are functioning in your body. These sensors signal their measurements via neural circuits and are processed by the brain. And yet this autonomic neural processing has a very different status than the redness of the light: essentially whereas you feel the redness, you do not feel any of the goings-on that determine internal functions like the oxygen level in your blood. The redness of the light is perceptually present to you, whereas states measured by the majority of sensors in your body also cause brain activity but generate no such sensory presence.

Why should brain processes involved in processing input from certain sensors (namely the eyes, the ears, etc.), give rise to a felt sensation, whereas other brain processes, deriving from other sensors (namely those measuring blood oxygen levels etc.) do not give rise to a felt sensation? The answer that comes to mind is that autonomic systems like those that detect and control blood oxygen are simply not connected to the areas that govern conscious sensation.

At first this seems to make sense, but it is not a satisfactory explanation, because it merely pushes the question one step deeper: why do those areas that govern conscious sensation produce the conscious sensation? Supposing we had produced an explanation: say, that there is something special about the wiring, the neurons or the interactions this area has with other brain areas. Then just as was the case to explain the structure of sensory experiences, we can always ask, when this special thing is activated, why does conscious sensation ensue? Any argument based on brain functions is again going to encounter the infinite regress in which we can always ask the question: 'and then what happens?' (Dennett, 1991, cf. also Chalmers's [1995] 'hard problem'). We need a different way of looking at the question of why some neural processes are accompanied by a sensory 'presence' and others are not.

3.2.3.2. Thoughts

Another case we can examine as regards the degree to which we want to attribute to it the notion of 'sensory presence' concerns mental activities like thinking, imagining, remembering, and deciding. I will call all these 'thoughts', for short. As in the situation for sensory inputs, you are aware of your thoughts, in the sense that you know that you are thinking about or imagining something, and you can, to a large degree, control your thoughts, but thoughts don't have the same, specifically sensory presence as sensory experiences. Indeed I suggest that as concerns the sensory aspect of what they feel like, thoughts are more like blood oxygen levels than like sensory experiences.

Of course thoughts are *about* things and so come with mental associations: the thought of red might be associated with blood and red traffic lights and red cough drops, but the thought of red does not *itself* have a red quality or indeed any sensory quality at all. Thoughts may also come with physical manifestations: the thought of an upcoming examination might make me feel nervous. However, any such nervousness is a consequence of the thought, not a quality of the thought itself. People sometimes say they have painful or pleasurable thoughts, but what they mean is that the content of the thoughts are painful or pleasurable. The thoughts themselves have no sensory quality.

There has been some debate about whether thoughts should be considered as having phenomenal quality—for example G. Strawson (1994; also Horgan and Tienson, 2002) consider that they do. Ultimately this is a matter of what we mean by phenomenal quality, but I think no one can dispute that thoughts do not have the same kind of 'sensory' quality that sensory experiences have. When I say that there is nothing it's like to have thoughts, or that there is a sense in which they have no presence, what I mean is that they do not possess the particular 'sensory' presence of sensory experiences.

So now we can ask: why? What is it about the brain mechanisms that cause thoughts which makes them fail to have the sensory presence that sensory experiences have? Again, as was the case for autonomic functions (and for the structure of sensory experiences), any explanation in terms of particular properties of brain mechanisms will lead to an infinite regress.

To conclude: an operational definition of what we mean by raw feels having sensory presence is to note that this statement is being made in contrast with brain processes that govern autonomic bodily functions, and in contrast with thoughts or imaginings: neither of these impose themselves on us with the same sensory presence as sensory feels; for neither of these is there, in a sensory way, 'something it's like' to have them. And we also note that appealing to brain mechanisms to explain these differences provides no help. Thus 'sensory presence' is mystery number three concerning raw feel.

3.3. **The sensorimotor approach to feel: step one, the quality of feel**

I have pinpointed three things that most people will say about raw feel: ineffability, structure, and sensory presence. The problem is that these things seem to admit of no explanation in terms of brain mechanisms. I shall now show how the sensorimotor approach provides a way of thinking that accounts naturally for these things.

The sensorimotor approach involves two steps (in earlier papers on the sensorimotor approach, I had not sufficiently stressed this distinction between the two steps). The first step involves characterizing the quality of sensory feels. The claim will be that the quality of a feel is the *quality of the sensorimotor interaction involved.* The second step concerns what is required for an agent to be conscious of this quality—conscious in the sense of 'access conscious': We shall see at the end of this chapter what this involves exactly.

Most of the work of the sensorimotor approach, and the part that elucidates the three problems of ineffability, structure, and presence, depends on the first step, and it is this that I shall be detailing in the next sections. To understand the idea, I want to consider a case which is not a prototypical case of sensory feel, but which, when extended to more typical sensory feels provides the key to a solution. It is the case of the tactile sensation of softness.[2]

Imagine a person squeezing a sponge and experiencing the feel of softness. What brain mechanism might generate the softness feel? Clearly the question is ill-posed: The word 'generate' is inapplicable. Asking what generates the softness feel is the wrong kind of question to ask about softness, because softness is not the kind of thing that can be generated. The reason is that softness is not a thing, it is a quality: namely the quality of the interaction you have with a soft object like a sponge. The experienced

---

[2] I thank Erik Myin for coming up with this excellent example.

quality of softness consists in a particular fact about the sensorimotor interaction you are having, namely the fact that when you press on the sponge, it squishes.

Now we can consider how, by taking this view of what softness is and applying it to sensory feels in general, we can solve the three mysteries of ineffability, structure of qualities, and sensory presence. It will become clear that the reason the new view provides a solution is that we are no longer looking in the brain for something that generates feel. Instead we are identifying qualities of feel with qualities of modes of interaction with the world.

3.3.1. How the sensorimotor approach explains ineffability

Obviously when you squish a sponge there are all sorts of muscles that you use, different parts of your fingers are involved, and there are all sorts of precise ways that the sponge squishes under your pressure. It's inconceivable for you to have cognitive access to all these details. It's like executing a skiing manoeuvre, or whistling: you don't know what you do with your various muscles, you *just do it*.

The precise laws of the sensorimotor interaction are thus ineffable i.e. they are not cognitively available to you, nor can you describe them to other people.

Applying this idea to feels in general, we can understand that the ineffability of feels is a natural consequence of thinking about feels in terms of ways of interacting with the environment. Feels are qualities of the sensorimotor interactions which we are engaged in currently. We do not have cognitive access to each and every aspect of these interactions. As an example, the particular muscle bundles we use to move our eyes or sniff or move our head are involved in feeling the feels of seeing, smelling, and hearing, but usually we cannot know what they are.

The sponge analogy thus accounts naturally for the ineffability of feels.

3.3.2. How the sensorimotor approach explains structure

Consider now how the sponge analogy deals with the second mystery of feel, namely the fact that feels are sometimes comparable and sometimes not, and that when they are comparable, they can sometimes be compared along different kinds of dimensions.

Take sponge-squishing as compared to, say, whistling. There is little objectively in common between the modes of interaction constituted by sponge-squishing and by whistling. They are not comparable.

On the other hand the feels can be compared within the gamut of variations of sponge-squishing and within the gamut of ways of whistling. In the case of sponge-squishing for example, some things are easy to squish, and other things are hard to squish. There is a continuous dimension of softness. Furthermore, it is part of the laws that define what we mean by softness, that 'hardness' is the opposite of what we mean by softness. It is thus simply a matter of fact, deriving from the very definitions of hard and soft, that there should be a continuous dimension going from very soft to very hard.

So here we have examples that are reminiscent of what we noticed about raw feels. Sometimes comparisons are nonsensical: just as between sponge-squishing and whistling, nothing very much can be said about the comparison between the feel of seeing and that of hearing or of touch. And sometimes comparisons can be made: just as within touch there is a clear relation between hard and soft, within seeing, comparisons can be made, e.g. between bright and dim, or between red and pink.

Thus, if we take the view that the qualities of feel are qualities of sensorimotor interactions, the existence of a complex structure defining how these qualities can be compared and contrasted is a natural consequence.

Furthermore this structure derives from objective physical facts concerning the modes of interaction involved. For example, the reason softness and hardness can be compared, but softness and whistling cannot be compared is that objectively, the modes of interaction we engage in have precisely this structure. In the cases of sensory experiences like seeing, hearing, touching, tasting and smelling, the claim is that their structure is also an objective consequence of (indeed it is constituted by the structure of) the modes of interaction that we engage in when we have the associated sensory experiences. To illustrate this claim I shall be showing later how it can work to explain the structure of colour.

Note that if we considered that the differences in structure in feels were caused by neural mechanisms, we would have to explain why the neural mechanisms generate the particular structure of feels that they do. Even if we managed to find some brain mechanisms that were isomorphic to the observed structure in feels, then we would have to explain the particular choice of classification scheme or metric that we used in order to make the isomorphism apparent.

However, in the sensorimotor view we escape from this problem, since we do not consider that brain mechanisms are generating the feel. They are merely enabling an interaction, and it is this interaction that constitutes the experience of feeling. It is the quality of the interaction, that is, the laws that describe its structure, that constitute the quality of the feel.

Thus, in the sensorimotor approach, the similarities and differences between feels are no longer described in terms of neural similarities and differences for which we have no natural way of choosing a classification or metric. We no longer need to ask whether we should take this or that similarity measure among the many possible ways of comparing neural states—whether we should, for example, take neural firing rate or its logarithm or inverse. Instead, similarities and differences in feels are described in terms of the metrics or classifications that humans already use every day to describe the way they interact with the world (e.g. an object is softer when it cedes more under your pressure).

Brain mechanisms do of course play a role in the account of feel in terms of an interaction with the environment. The brain mechanisms enable the particular interactions that take place when we experience something. Interestingly, once we have found objective descriptions of the sensorimotor interactions that constitute a sensory experience, then perforce we will find brain mechanisms that enable them. To the extent that there are objective differences and similarities in the sensorimotor interactions, there will necessarily be corresponding differences and similarities in the brain mechanisms. Thus there will necessarily be an isomorphism between the brain mechanisms and the quality of the feel. And there is the risk that having discovered such an isomorphism or correlation, one might naïvely be misled into thinking that somehow it was the brain mechanism that 'generated' or was the cause of the associated feel, but this would be wrong. Taking that stance would lead immediately to the classic infinite regress underlying the explanatory gap, since one would have to explain why the brain mechanism did what it did.

However, the problem is obviated when we take the sensorimotor view according to which the quality of a feel is not generated by anything, but rather is constituted by the laws that describe our sensorimotor interaction.

3.3.3. How the sensorimotor view explains sensory presence

Now I come to the question of sensory presence, or why people say that there's 'something it's like' to have a feel. I had suggested that an operational way to understand what is meant by this statement is to make the contrast with autonomic processes in the nervous system, and thoughts, since these are brain processes that lack the 'sensory presence' of a real sensory experience. Even if we wish to argue that there is 'something it's like' to think, or to digest, or even simply to exist, whatever 'it's like' is not the same as the 'what-it's-like' of having a real sensory presence. The sensorimotor approach provides a natural way of accounting for such differences by appealing to three concepts: bodiliness, insubordinateness, and grabbiness.

Let us take again the example of sponge-squishing. What is it about sponge-squishing that gives that activity a real sensory presence? Obviously sponge-squishing involves actually engaging in an interaction with the world. But why should actually engaging in an interaction with the world give this impression of realness and presence?

I suggest the answer has to do with the fact that the degree of voluntary control we exercise when we have a sensory feel is only partial. When we have what we call a sensory feel, we have a certain degree of voluntary control over what we are doing. We can exercise this control by modifying sensory input through movements of our body (I call this 'bodiliness'). However the control is partial, because sensory input derives from the outside world and the outside world escapes our control to a certain extent (I call this 'insubordinateness'). Finally a third factor is 'grabbiness', namely the fact that the outside world has the capacity to grab our cognitive resources. Let us look at these three aspects in more detail.

a. *Bodiliness:* When you are interacting with the world, body motions generally cause systematic changes in sensory input. In the visual modality this is clearly the case: moving your eyes causes dramatic changes of the retinal image. In the case of touch, we note that touch is an exploratory sense, since only by moving our hand, for example, can we recognize an object accurately. Even for passive touch, when someone touches you, if you then voluntarily remove or shift the body part being touched, there will be a change in sensory input.

For hearing, moving the body modifies auditory input by changing the amplitude of the sound impinging on the ears, and in the case of rotation of the head, by changing the relative delay between signals coming into the two ears. The complicated shape of the earlobes creates micro-reflections that change with head orientation and are also important factors in sound localization and identification. Thus, moving the body is a way of testing whether a sound comes from the outside world. When you have a ringing in your ears, you identify the sensation as not coming from the outside world because turning your head doesn't change the sound.

Recent research on smell has also shown that humans, like other animals, can use body and head movements to monitor the delays and differences between the smells coming into the two nostrils in order to follow scents (Schneider and Schmidt, 1967; Porter et al., 2007; Sobel et al., 1998). More fundamentally, we know that we are really smelling and not just imagining it, when we can confirm that sniffing, and moving our body (in particular our head) changes the signal coming from our olfactory receptors.

All these examples show that susceptibility of sensory input to voluntary body motion is an essential feature of what it is like to be experiencing external-world stimulation. It is perhaps actually a logical consequence of the fact that what we mean by the outside world is what is delimited by our body. In all cases, moving the body and the eyes is a way of checking whether a sensation comes from the world. If no change occurs when we move, then what we are experiencing probably does not originate from the outside world.

We can now understand why it is that information provided by sensors involved in autonomic functioning, on the one hand, and neural activity involved in thinking, remembering, imagining, and other reflective activities, on the other hand, are not accompanied by a sensation of sensory presence: it is (partly) because they have no bodiliness. Voluntarily moving your body only has an indirect effect on autonomic body parameters like blood oxygen, carbon dioxide and sugar levels, and on functioning of internal organs. Moving your body has no direct effect on thought processes.[3]

b. *Insubordinatenes:* Whereas dependence on voluntary bodily motion is an essential feature of sensory input originating in the outside world, not all changes in sensory input from the outside world are caused by our voluntary body motions. The outside world has a life of its own: objects move, sounds change, smells appear and disappear, with the consequence that we are not complete masters of the changes that the world causes in our sensory input. This insubordinateness of the world is another factor that characterizes 'real' sensory inputs and distinguishes them from our own thoughts and imaginings. Thoughts and imaginings are entirely the property of our

---

[3] The case of 'epistemic actions' (e.g. the Tetris player mentioned by Clark and Chalmers, 1998) do not contradict this, since the body motions modify thoughts only indirectly through the way they change our perceptual perspective.

own minds. They are under our voluntary control, they are predictable and completely controlled by us and so we do not perceive them as corresponding to real-world events.[4]

c. *Grabbiness:* Grabbiness consists of the fact that sensory input signals have the power, in certain circumstances, to deflect our cognitive ressources and grab them incontrovertibly so that it is difficult for us to attend to anything else voluntarily. One kind of signal that has this property is so-called 'transients', that is, sudden changes in sensory input. For example, a bright flash in peripheral vision, a sudden loud noise, a sudden poke, punch, or tickle, grabs our attention, provokes an immediate orienting reflex, and causes our cognitive processing to be deviated towards the source of the change. In some sensory modalities certain kinds of non-transient stimulation can also grab our attention. For example, in hearing, very loud continuous sounds can prevent one from thinking properly. In touch, stimulations signalling tissue damage like burns and aches can grab our attention. In smell, certain pungent or obnoxious odours have the property that we cannot avoid paying attention to them.

I suggest that grabbiness is a general property of sensory systems,[5] and is not shared by other brain systems. In particular, consider the brain systems that deal with autonomic functions like keeping blood pressure stable, holding blood sugar levels constant, adjusting breathing, digesting, and keeping a host of other body functions working properly. These systems do not have the faculty of interrupting cognitive processing. This I would claim is part of the reason we do not directly 'feel' our internal vital functions as having a sensory quality (e.g. why blood sugar level does not appear to us as having the quality of a sensory experience like seeing or hearing).

Or consider thoughts: thoughts do not grab your attention like loud noises, pungent smells or intolerable pain. Except in pathological cases, you are not possessed by thoughts, you possess them.

3.3.3.1. Summary on sensory presence

To summarize why raw sensory feels feel like something rather than feeling like nothing, that is, why they have 'sensory presence': experiencing a raw sensory feel involves engaging with the real world. Doing so involves having control, but not complete control of this engagement: control derives from *bodiliness*, that is, the fact that voluntary bodily changes provoke systematic variations in sensory input. But control is not complete because our sensory input is not exclusively determined by these bodily motions: the real world is *insubordinate* and has a life of its own that creates variations in our sensory input that we cannot cause through our voluntary body motion. A final way in which our engagement with the real world escapes our control derives from *grabbiness*: the fact that our sensory input systems are wired up to be able to grab our cognitive resources incontrovertibly in certain circumstances, making us tributary to the outside world.

3.3.3.2. Why the sensorimotor approach works better than the neural correlate approach

Note the advantage of considering feels to be modes of interaction with the environment. If we thought feels were generated in the brain, we would have to go looking in the brain for something special about the neural mechanisms involved that generates the feels. We would have to postulate some kind of special neurons, special circuitry or chemical basis that provide the feeling of 'presence'

---

[4] A borderline case is hallucinations and dreams. Though they are also not real, they often do seem real to us. Perhaps part of the reason for this is precisely that they are not completely under our voluntary control.

[5] It would be interesting to find a special class of nerve projections from sensory areas in the brain to the frontal areas of the cortex where the higher cognitive processing is done. These special circuits could provide a kind of 'interrupt' command that causes normal cognitive functioning to stop and orient towards the source of the interrupting signal. Such circuits would only be present for sensory channels, and not for systems in the brain that control our autonomic functions.

or 'what it's like'. And then, as explained in previous sections, we would be led into an infinite regress, because once we had found the special neurons, we could always then ask what exactly it was that made them special.

However, if experiencing a sensory feel involves engaging in a particular mode of interaction with the environment, then since you are doing something, there will be laws that characterize the particular mode of interaction you are involved in. These laws constitute the quality of the feel. Thus by the very sensorimotor definition of feel, if you are having a feel, there must be something it is like for you to have it. What's more, if the interaction you are having involves using your sensory apparatus to get information about the outside world, then the interaction will have the hallmark of sensory feels: because of the bodiliness and grabbiness of sensory channels, and because of the external world's inherent insubordination to your will, the control the brain exercises over the interaction will only be partial. This partial control corresponds to the quality of 'sensory presence' possessed by sensory stimulation. Such sensory presence is not possessed by mental activities like thoughts or imaginings (here control is complete), nor by autonomic control systems that keep the body functioning normally (here we have no voluntary control).

3.3.4. The role of action

The role of action in the sensorimotor approach is often misunderstood. If we take feel to be defined as the quality of an interaction with the environment, then because the notion of interaction necessarily implies action, feel also necessarily implies action. However this statement should not be taken to mean that experiencing a feel at a given moment necessarily requires an action to be occurring at that moment. Saying that feel implies action should be understood to mean that in order to have a feel, action must potentially play a role (Noë, 2004 has also commented on the role of action in perception; c.f. also Noë, Chapter 13).

As an analogy, consider the dancer poised instantaneously mid-dance, the acrobat poised at the top of a jump, the mountain explorer resting at the base camp. What we mean by being engaged in an activity does not require that one should be continuously acting, only that one's current situation should be part of and should fit correctly into a potential activity.

Take as an example the feel of touch on my arm. Feeling touch on my arm is: being poised to verify that my current situation is part of what happens normally when I am being touched on my arm. In particular, if I move, there will be a change in tactile input. More precisely such a change will occur if I move my arm, but not if I move my foot. It is contingencies such as this that are constituent of a stimulation in the tactile modality, and more particularly, with a stimulation on the arm rather than on the foot.

So when I receive tactile stimulation on my arm, even without me moving at all, comparison mechanisms in the brain will register that such input has been received before, and that when this had previously been the case, such input was also associated with systematic changes that occurred when I moved, and more precisely, when I moved my arm and not other parts of my body. For this reason, I will perceive the sensation as a tactile sensation, and more precisely, as coming from my arm, and not from other parts of my body. And this will be the case even without me moving.

An interesting prediction is made from this approach. It is that sensory input that has never in the past been observed to be systematically modifiable by voluntary body motions should not be experienced as being of a sensory nature. This may provide part of the explanation of why we do not experience feels in our visceral organs: we generally cannot make movements voluntarily that modify the neural signals they provide.

The proposal that visceral organs should not be perceived as being the location of sensations is compatible with the phenomenon of 'referred pain', where damage to internal organs is perceived as originating in superficial body locations that share nerve pathways with them. Best known among types of referred pain is the pain associated with myocardial ischemia (heart attack) which can be felt in the upper chest, arm, or even hand or jaw, and appendicitis which begins as a pain near the navel. In neither case is the pain felt at the actual visceral location of the malfunction.

We do however sometimes have aches inside our body, such as stomach aches, headaches, and toothaches. How can this be accounted for? Under the approach I am suggesting, this can only occur in cases when body motion does actually modify the sensory signals. It is true that shaking the head when one has a headache modifies the pain, and that the location of the pain may perhaps be assimilated to similar sensations on the surface of the scalp that occur when one receives stimulation there. Similarly, pressing on the stomach or tooth can modify stomach and toothache, thereby providing information as to the location of the sensation. Interestingly, and compatible with the suggestions being made here, a toothache in a tooth in the lower jaw is sometimes incorrectly attributed to the tooth in the upper jaw that generally is in contact with it, and vice versa.

3.4. **Empirical evidence**

Experiencing a raw sensory feel involves engaging with the real world in a sensorimotor interaction. The laws that govern such an interaction constitute the quality of the associated raw feel. Raw feels are ineffable because they are skills that we engage in, and like all skills they are not completely accessible to cognitive analysis. Raw feels have structure because the sensorimotor interactions that constitute them are governed by the complex constraints of our sensory and motor apparatus, as well as by the constraints of the real world. In contradistinction to thoughts and autonomic processes in our central nervous systems, raw feels have sensory presence or 'what it's like-ness' by virtue of the fact that sensorimotor engagement with the world involves having control, but not complete control of this engagement: control derives from *bodiliness*, that is, the fact that voluntary bodily changes provoke systematic variations in sensory input. But control is not complete because our sensory input is not determined exclusively by these bodily motions. The real world is *insubordinate* and has a life of its own: it creates variations in our sensory input that we cannot cause through our voluntary body motion. A final way in which our engagement with the real world escapes our control derives from *grabbiness*: the fact that our sensory input systems are wired up to be able to grab our cognitive resources incontrovertibly in certain circumstances, making us tributary to the outside world.

The sensorimotor approach has an advantage over neural correlate approaches to the nature of raw feel. The view in terms of neural correlates must always appeal to some linking hypothesis that connects feel to neural mechanisms, and justification for the choice of such linking hypotheses is not forthcoming. The sensorimotor view on the other hand provides a natural way of describing and explaining sensory feels in terms of the objective laws that govern our sensorimotor interactions with the world.

In addition to this logical or philosophical advantage, the sensorimotor approach provides a way of thinking about feel that generates interesting avenues of empirical research. In particular several empirical results provide converging evidence in favour of the way the sensorimotor approach accounts for what people say about the quality of sensory feels.

3.4.1. **Sensory substitution**

A first result concerns the perceived quality of sensory feels in different sensory modalities: why are they the way they are, and why are the similarities and differences structured in a certain way? The sensorimotor approach provides a natural answer in terms of the different sensory interactions you engage in. For each sensory modality there exist laws of sensorimotor interaction that characterize that modality. When you see, for example, and you close your eyes, there is a large change in sensory input, whereas closing your eyes has no effect on sensory input when you hear. When you see, moving your eyes produces a particular kind of flow field on your retinas, whereas when you hear, moving your eyes has no effect.

A very interesting prediction ensues from these ideas. If what determines the sensory quality of a sensory modality is not some characteristic of the neural channel involved, but the laws that sensory input obeys when you move, then it should be possible to get the impression of seeing, for example, through channels other than the visual channel, provided that the laws being obeyed are visual-type laws.

This is exactly what happens in *sensory substitution*. The classic example is the work of Bach-y-Rita (1972), who equipped blind (or blindfolded) persons with an array of tactile vibrators that the persons wore on their abdomen, and which created a vibratory 'image' of information registered by a video camera held by the person. Despite the device's very poor resolution (20 by 20 vibrators) compared to the 150 million receptors in normal human vision, users reported that they had an impression of 'seeing', provided they were allowed to wield the camera actively.

Such devices have proven cumbersome in the past, but with today's technical advances there is renewed interest in developing them (for a review, see Bach-y-Rita and Kercel, 2003). Particularly successful devices have been constructed to compensate for vestibular deficits and substitution of vision with hearing. Nevertheless, the intrinsic limitations of the skin or the ear as an input channel prevent obtaining the same resolution as with the eyes. It is therefore understandable that the feel experienced by users of such devices should be far from what a normal sighted person experiences (see Auvray et al., 2007a and b and Auvray and Myin, 2009, for examples of studies to investigate these issues).

3.4.2. The case of colour

As already explained, most neuroscientists consider that colour experience is generated by neural activation in colour opponent channels in the visual system. But this idea, though appealing, has the usual 'explanatory gap' difficulty, since it immediately raises the question of exactly what in the channels causes the accompanying feels.

The idea is also questioned by empirical results (Jameson and D'Andrade 1997). If it were true, then one would expect that what people experience as 'pure' colours (what colour scientists call 'unique hues') should correspond to maximal activations in the corresponding channels. For example, the maximum activation of the opponent red–green channel in the red direction should provoke a sensation of pure red, and maximum activation in the green direction should provoke a sensation of pure green. Similar statements should be true for maximum activation in the blue–yellow channel.

However these predictions are not born out. To experience a sensation of pure blue, activation of the blue–yellow channel in the blue direction is not sufficient: some activation of the red–green channel in the green direction is needed. Similarly, to get a sensation of pure yellow, activation of the blue–yellow channel in the yellow direction is not sufficient: some activation of the RG channel in the red direction is needed (Chichilnisky and Wandell, 1999; Valberg, 2001; Knoblauch and Shevell, 2001).

Another problem with the classic view comes from Berlin and Kay's (1969) and Kay and Regier's (2003) classic anthropological data on naming coloured surfaces (also Regier, Kay, and Cook, 2005). In a sample of informants from 110 unrelated cultures throughout the world, these authors observed that there is a regular structure to the way their informants named the colours. Certain particular surfaces stood out from all the others in that they were systematically given names across all the different cultures. The first four of these special or 'focal' surfaces were precisely 'red', 'yellow', 'green', and 'blue'. Unfortunately however, although the link with the red–green and blue–yellow opponent system seems tempting, the precise structure of the data and the precise colours hues of red, yellow, green, and blue judged to be focal have not been explained by appeal to neurophysiological opponency.

On the other hand by taking the sensorimotor approach to feel, both the unique hues and the naming data can be explained satisfactorily. The idea is to say that the 'feel' of colour is constituted by a quality of our interaction with coloured surfaces. Under this view, suggested by Broackes (1992), colour is the law describing how a surface changes incoming light. Such laws have been described by physicists, who use the notion of 'reflectance function' to characterize how each incoming wavelength of light is absorbed or reflected by the surface. But this characterization does not correspond to the biological reality of our sensory systems, which cannot register light energy in individual wavelengths, but only in the wide bands of wavelength absorbed by our particular photoreceptors. For that reason Philipona and O'Regan (2006) defined a 'biological reflectance function' which corresponds to the reflectance function as registered by human photoreceptors. When this function is examined for different surfaces, it is found that those surfaces that are named frequently across multiple cultures are precisely those surfaces that have a 'singular' biological reflectance function. By 'singular' is meant the fact that, mathematically, the function has a simpler behaviour than is usually the case. To be more precise, a biological reflectance function usually maps the three-dimensional space of possible photoreceptor values corresponding to incoming light, into another three-dimensional space of photoreceptor values corresponding to reflected light. But when the function is singular the reflected light is projected into a smaller space, namely either a one-dimensional space (the case for red, blue, and green) or a two-dimensional space (the case for yellow).

Philipona and O'Regan found that when they looked at the singularity of the different surfaces used in the Kay and Regier world colour survey, there were four strongly singular surfaces, and they were almost exactly those surfaces that were most often given a name in the Kay and Regier data. The precision of the agreement observed is very striking, and strongly supports the idea that the sensorimotor approach to surface colour is on the right track (see Figs 3.1 and 3.2). Philipona and O'Regan

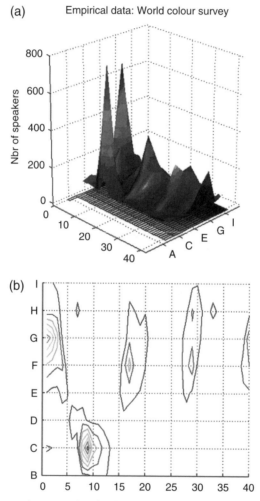

Fig. 3.1 (a, b) Histogram and contour plot showing the number of speakers in Kay and Regier's (2003) 110-culture survey of colour naming, who had a name for the colours in the selection of Munsell chips labelled A-I and 0-40 shown in the ground plane of the top graph. Strong peaks are visible at G1 and C9 corresponding to red and yellow. Weaker peaks at F17 and F29 or H29 correspond to green and blue. The iso-contours for the top 10% of these data are re-plotted as red, yellow, green, and blue coloured surfaces in Figure 3.2b for comparison with our singularity data. (See Plate 1)

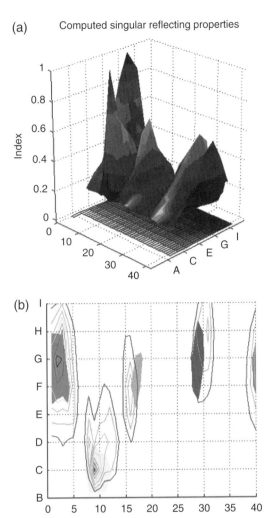

Fig. 3.2 (a, b) The degree of singularity (singularity index) of the 3×3 matrices representing the linear mapping between incoming and outgoing human cone photoreceptor absorptions for the same Munsell chips as in Figure 3.1a, as calculated by Philipona and O'Regan from known physical data for Munsell reflectances and cone absorption spectra. The peaks of singularity shown in the contour plot fall very close to the coloured surfaces corresponding to the top 10% of the Kay and Regier data, and replotted from Figure 3.1b. This shows that the colours that tend to be given names across many cultures are very close to those that change incoming light in a 'simpler' fashion (see text). Adapted from Philipona and O'Regan (2006). (See Plate 2)

extended the approach to coloured lights by assuming that lights are perceived as though they are coloured surfaces illuminated by standard white light. Predictions for 'unique hues' made in this way account for existing data better than neurophysiological approaches, accurately predicting the curious facts mentioned above about how to obtain the sensations of pure blue and pure yellow.

3.4.3. Spatial and temporal presence and continuity of the visual world: Change blindness

When we look at a visual scene, we have the impression of seeing everything in it, simultaneously and in an occurrent, ongoing fashion. According to the traditional view of seeing, this 'present' quality of visual experience arises because an internal representation of the scene has been created and is 'active' in the brain.

Under the sensorimotor view, the idea is that we store very little information about the scene internally. Instead, we access the information in the world when we need it: as suggested by O'Regan (1992), the world serves as a sort of 'outside memory'. The impression of seeing 'everything' and of doing so in a continual fashion derives from the immediate accessibility of the information at the slightest flick of attention or the eye, and not from the existence of the information in an internal brain representation.

In this way of obtaining the sensation of continuity, the grabbiness of the visual sensory modality plays a reinforcing role. This is because if anything should change in the scene, the visual transients produced in the visual channels create an automatic, incontrovertible alerting reaction which orients our attention to the change location. When there are no such transients, our conviction that everything is still there is upheld.

These ideas make the curious prediction that if we could make changes in the visual scene without the change provoking a visual transient, observers would still go on seeing what was originally there, and not see the change: unless of course they were attending explicitly to the item that changed.

This is exactly the manipulation achieved in the experimental paradigm of change blindness. In one variant of this paradigm, a large change is made in a picture, but it is made so slowly that no visual transients occur that can attract the observer's attention to the changed location. In the better known 'flicker' and 'mudsplash' paradigms, a change is made in a scene, but the change is accompanied by other, large and sudden changes which also create visual transients. These act as decoys which prevent attention going to the location of the change of interest.[6]

Results in a large literature using these paradigms (see reviews by Simons and Levin, 1997 and Simons and Rensink, 2005[7]) demonstrate very clearly that observers tend not to see the changes, confirming the prediction and providing converging evidence for the sensorimotor approach.

3.5. The sensorimotor approach to feel: step two, consciously experiencing

Up until now I have been discussing the first step of the sensorimotor approach, which was concerned with the quality of sensory experience. The approach claims that experienced sensory quality is constituted by the (physically objective) sensorimotor laws that underlie the interaction. But whereas this characterizes the quality of the experience, we still need to define what makes a sensory experience conscious.

For this we require the second step in the sensorimotor approach. The claim here is simply that a sensory experience becomes conscious when a person has a certain form of access (namely 'conscious access') to the fact that the person is engaging in a sensorimotor interaction.

To understand this, note first that when we say we are conscious of something, there is an implicit presupposition that there is indeed a 'we' to be conscious. But who or what is this 'we'? This question is essentially the question of the self.

Discussion of the nature and origin of the notion of the self is an active subject today. Philosophers are trying to decide what precise components the notion of self boils down to. Developmental psychologists and psycholinguists are trying to ascertain how the notion of self develops in the maturing child; cognitive anthropologists look at whether the notion is different in different

---

[6] Demonstrations can be seen on http://nivea.psycho.univ-paris5.fr

[7] Note that this last article has been interpreted incorrectly by Block (2008) as rejecting the view that our internal representations are sparse.

human societies; cognitive ethologists study which species possess the notion; and social psychologists investigate how the self is determined by an individual's social environment.[8]

Unlike the question of raw feel, for which there seemed to be an explanatory gap, the problem of the self (which is certainly not one problem but many problems, with organismic, cognitive and social aspects) is being approached today using the idea that brains are computational devices with the capacity to abstract, to generalize, and in the case of humans, to use language. The social aspect of the notion of 'I', with its self-validating and self-referring properties, could emerge from social interactions of agents with brains having such computational faculties.

I shall take it on faith that a conclusion from this literature is that while the problem of the self is very complex, it is nevertheless amenable to a scientific approach. Let us then consider that we have a scientific way of dealing with the notion of 'we' in the phrase 'we are conscious of X'. The next thing to do is to look at what is meant by the word 'conscious'.

Again here the philosophers have raised tremendous debates, but there seems to be agreement that one main use of the notion of 'being conscious of X' is amenable to a scientific account, namely the notion of 'access consciousness' (see Carruthers, 2009 for a review). An agent is access conscious of X when it is ready or 'poised' to make use of X in its decision-making processes (Kirk, 1994; Dretske, 1995; Tye, 1995), and (some philosophers require) also in its rational behaviour (Block 1995). The fact of being poised in this way to make use of X might additionally have to be the object of some kind of higher order representation (Armstrong, 1984; Lycan, 1996; Rosenthal, 2005; Carruthers, 2005).

From the psychologists' point of view, the notion of being access conscious of X has been taken to correspond to the idea of attending to, or devoting one's processing resources to X in such a way that X becomes globally available to a wide variety of behavioural capacities. The idea is an old one, suggested by Baars (1988) in his 'global workspace' theory, and taken up more recently in neuroanatomical terms by, for example, Dehaene and Naccache (2001).

The issues involved in defining access consciousness constitute an immense literature, but as was the case for the notion of self, the consensus is that access consciousness is a notion that can be defined functionally. There is therefore general agreement that a reasonable, scientific account can be given for it.

The second step of the sensorimotor account thus involves saying that 'we are conscious of a sensory experience' when 'we' (as defined in cognitive and social terms) become 'access conscious' (as defined in one of the functionally defined forms referred to above) of the fact that we are engaging in the sensorimotor interaction which constitutes that experience.

3.5.1. Consciously experiencing a sensory feel

In sum then, we are now in a position to functionally characterize what is meant by consciously experiencing a sensory feel.

The essential idea (or what I have been calling step one of the sensorimotor approach) is the claim that experiencing a sensory feel involves engaging in a sensorimotor interaction with the environment. The experienced quality of the feel is constituted by the laws that physically, objectively, describe this interaction. By virtue of the fact that the interaction is essentially a sensorimotor skill, the laws that describe it will escape complete description. This yields the ineffable quality of sensory feels.

---

[8] For a bibliography on different approaches to the self see the website maintained by Shaun Gallagher: http://www.philosophy.ucf.edu/pi/. See also a special issue of Annals of the New York Academy of Sciences in Vol. 1001, 2003. See also (Vierkant, 2003) for a review. There is also a rich literature on the self within psychoanalysis.

The fact that nevertheless the laws that characterize the interaction will be constrained by the physics and biology of the situation will result in objective similarities and differences between the interaction and other interactions. This yields the fact that the qualities of different sensory feels will fall into what may be a complex structure of objective similarities and differences.

Finally, if the laws of interaction are characterized objectively by bodiliness, insubordinateness, and grabbiness, then the experienced quality will have the property which is the hallmark of sensory feels, namely sensory presence. Said another way, there will seem to be 'something it's like' to have the feel, in contrast to autonomic body functions and thought processes, for which this is not true—at least in the sense I am using the term 'sensory presence' or 'what it's like'.

Step two of the approach is, then, to say that if an agent has sufficient cognitive capacities and is sufficiently integrated into a social environment to have a notion of self, and if this agent is suitably poised to cognitively access the fact that it is engaging in the sensorimotor interaction, then the agent is consciously experiencing the associated feel.

Have I explained qualia? I have expressly avoided the word 'qualia' in this treatment, on the grounds that qualia are such a contentious topic. Instead I have used the notion of raw feel, giving it what I hoped was a definition as close as possible to qualia but corresponding to a plausible version of what people say everyday about the most basic aspects of their sensations. There is little doubt that the man in the street believes that at the basis of every feel there is a 'raw' component that is producing its behavioural effects: for example, the raw feel of pain is what produces avoidance reactions, and not the opposite: the man in the street rejects the Jamesian or behaviouristic idea that being in pain is just the sum total of pain-like behavioural manifestations.

Thus, whether or not raw feels exist, people talk about them as though they did. Furthermore, people claim that they have certain properties, and among these the problematic ones (for philosophers) have been those of ineffability, structure in their qualities, and, most important, 'presence' or 'what it's like'. The sensorimotor approach provides an account of why people say their raw feels have these properties, even if certain philosophers might want to claim that qualia do not exist.

What is the relation between this approach and Dennett's (1991) eliminativist view of qualia? The difference between the two views is that, as explained in the introduction, the sensorimotor view remains neutral[9] on whether or not qualia exist, and simply tries to explain what people will tend to say about them (or at least, about 'raw feels', if qualia do not exist). Because it provides a natural explanation (in terms of physical and biological laws) of the qualities of these raw sensory feels (their ineffability, their structure, and their 'presence' or 'what it's like'), and because it opens new empirical research programmes and generates testable hypotheses such as those summarized here about sensory substitution, change blindness, and colour, the sensorimotor view is more scientifically productive than the eliminatist view.

Acknowledgements

I acknowledge warmly the help of Erik Myin in commenting on an earlier version of this chapter, the help of the participants at the December 2008 CONTACT workshop in Bristol in helping clarify some of the ideas here, and of the editors of the book in making final suggestions for improvement.

References

Armstrong, D. (1984). Consciousness and causality. In *Consciousness and causality*, (eds Armstrong, D. and Malcolm, N.), Oxford: Blackwell.

Auvray, M. and Myin, E. (2009). Perception with compensatory devices: from sensory substitution to sensorimotor extension. *Cognitive Science*; **33**(6): 1036–1058.

---

[9] The point that the sensorimotor view is neutral on whether qualia exist, and only attempts to account for what people say about qualia, was not stressed in previous presentations of the sensorimotor approach.

Auvray, M., Hanneton, S., and O'Regan, J.K. (2007a). Learning to perceive with a visuo-auditory substitution system: localisation and object recognition with 'The vOICe'. *Perception*; **36**(3): 416–30.

Auvray, M., Philipona, D., O'Regan, J.K., and Spence, C. (2007b). The perception of space and form recognition in a simulated environment: the case of minimalist sensory-substitution devices. *Perception*; **36**(12): 1736–51.

Baars, B. (1988). *A cognitive theory of consciousness*. Cambridge: Cambridge University Press.

Bach-y-Rita, P. (1972). *Brain mechanisms in sensory substitution*. New York: Academic Press.

Bach-y-Rita, P. and Kercel, S.W. (2003). Sensory substitution and the human-machine interface. *Trends in Cognitive Sciences*; **7**(12): 541–6.

Berlin, B. and Kay, P. (1969). *Basic colour terms: their universality and evolution*. Berkeley. University of California Press.

Bornstein, M.H. (1975). Qualities of colour vision in infancy. *Journal of Experimental Child Psychology*; **19**: 401–19.

Block, N. (1990). Inverted earth. In *Philosophical perspectives*, (ed. Tomberlin, J.); **4**: 53–79.

—— (1995). On a confusion about a function of consciousness. *Behavioural and Brain Sciences*; **18**(2): 227–47.

—— (2008). Consciousness, accessibility, and the mesh between psychology and neuroscience. *Behavioural and Brain Sciences*; **30**(5–6): 481–99.

Broackes, J. (1992). The autonomy of color. In *Reduction, explanation and realism*, (eds Lennon, K. and Charles, D.), pp. 421–65. Oxford: Oxford University Press.

Carruthers, P. (2005). *Consciousness: essays from a higher-order perspective*. Oxford: Oxford University Press.

—— (2009). Higher-order theories of consciousness. In *The Stanford encyclopedia of philosophy*, (ed. Zalta, E.N.). Available at: http://plato.stanford.edu/archives/spr2009/entries/consciousness-higher/.

Chalmers, D.J. (1995). Facing up to the problem of consciousness. *Journal of Consciousness Studies*; **2**(3): 200–19.

Chichilisky, E. and Wandell, B.A. (1999). Trichromatic opponent colour classification. *Vision Research*; **39**: 3444–58.

Clark, A. (1993). *Sensory qualities*. Oxford: Clarendon Press.

Clark, A. and Chalmers, D. (1998). The extended mind. *Analysis*; **58**(1): 7–19.

Dennett, D.C. (1991). *Consciousness explained*. Boston, Mass: Little, Brown and Co.

Dehaene, S. and Naccache, L. (2001). Towards a cognitive neuroscience of consciousness: basic evidence and a workspace framework. *Cognition*; **79**: 1–37.

Dretske, F. (1995). *Naturalizing the mind*. Cambridge, Mass: MIT Press.

Gegenfurtner, K.R. and Kipers, D.C. (2003). Colour vision. *Annual Review of Neuroscience*; **26**: 181–206.

Hardin, C.L. (1988). *Colour for philosophers: Unweaving the rainbow*. Indianapolis: Hackett Publishing Company.

Hayek, F.A. (1953). *The sensory order*. Chicago: University of Chicago Press.

Horgan, T.E. and Tienson, J.L. (2002). The intentionality of phenomenology and the phenomenology of intentionality. In *Philosophy of mind: classical and contemporary readings*, (ed. Chalmers, D.), pp. 520–33.

Ijsselsteijn, W.A. (2002). Elements of a multi-level theory of presence: phenomenology, mental processing and neural correlates. *Proceedings of PRESENCE 2002*, Universidade Fernando Pessoa, Porto, Portugal, Oct. 9–11, pp. 245–59.

Jameson, K. and D'Andrade, R.G. (1997). It's not really red, green, yellow, blue: an inquiry into perceptual colour space. In *Color categories in thought and language*. (eds Hardin, C.L. and Maffi, L.), pp. 295–319. Cambridge: Cambridge University Press.

Kay, P. and Regier, T. (2003). Resolving the question of colour naming universals. *Proceedings of the National Academy of Sciences*; **100**(15): 9085–9.

Kirk, R. (1994). *Raw feeling*. Oxford: Oxford University Press.

Knoblauch, K. and Shevell, S.K. (2003). Relating cone signals to colour appearance: failure of monotonicity in yellow/blue. *Visual Neuroscience*; **18**: 901–06.

Levine, J. (1983). Materialism and qualia: the explanatory gap. *Pacific Philosophical Quarterly*; **64**: 354–61.

Lycan, W. (1996). *Consciousness and experience*. Cambridge, Mass: MIT Press.

Madany Mamlouk, A. and Martinetz, T. (2004). On the dimensions of the olfactory perception space. *Neurocomputing*; **58–60**: 1019–25.

Metzinger, T. (2003). *Being no one: the self-model theory of subjectivity*. Cambridge, Mass.: Bradford Books, MIT Press.

Nagel, T. (1974). What is it like to be a Bat? *Philosophical Review*; **83**: 435–56.

Natsoulas, T. (1997). The presence of environmental objects to perceptual consciousness: a difference it makes for psychological functioning. *American Journal of Psychology*; **110**(4): 507–26.

—— (1999). A rediscovery of presence. *Journal of Mind and Behaviour*; **20**(1): 117–42.

Noë, A. (2004). *Action in perception*. Cambridge, Mass: MIT Press.

O'Regan, J.K. (1992). Solving the 'real' mysteries of visual perception: the world as an outside memory. *Canadian Journal of Psychology*; **46**(3): 461–88.

O'Regan, J.K. and Noë, A. (2001). A sensorimotor account of vision and visual consciousness. *Behavioural and Brain Sciences*; **24**(5): 883–917.

O'Regan, J.K., Myin, E., and Noë, A. (2005). Phenomenal consciousness explained (better) in terms of bodiliness and grabbiness. *Phenomenology and the Cognitive Sciences*; **4**(4): 369–87.

—— (2006). Skill, corporality and alerting capacity in an account of sensory consciousness. *Progress in Brain Research*; **150**: 55–68.

Palmer, S.E. (1999). Colour, consciousness and the isomorphism constraint. *Behavioural and Brain Science*; **22**(6): 923–43; discussion 944–89.

Peacocke, C. (1983). *Sense and content.* Oxford: Oxford University Press.

Porter, J., Craven, B., Khan, R.M., Chang, S., Kang, I., Judkewitz, B. et al. (2007). Mechanisms of scent-tracking in humans. *Nature Neuroscience*; **10**(1): 27–9.

Regier, T., Kay, P., and Cook, R.S. (2005). Focal colours are universal after all. *Proceedings of the National Academy of Sciences*; **102**(23): 8386–91.

Rosenthal, D. (2005). *Consciousness and mind.* Oxford: Oxford University Press.

Schneider, R.A. and Schmidt, C.E. (1967). Dependency of olfactory localization on non-olfactory cues. *Physiology & Behaviour*; **2**(3): 305–09.

Simons, D.J. and Levin, D.T. (1997). Change blindness. *Trends in Cognitive Sciences*; **1**(7): 261–7.

Simons, D.J. and Rensink, R.A. (2005). Change blindness: past, present, and future. *Trends in Cognitive Sciences*; **9**(1): 16–20.

Sobel, N., Prabhakaran, V., Desmond, J.E., Glover, G.H., Goode, R.L., Sullivan, E. V., et al. (1998). Sniffing and smelling: separate subsystems in the human olfactory cortex. *Nature*; **392**(6673): 282–6.

Strawson, G. (1994). *Mental reality.* Cambridge, Mass: MIT Press.

Teller, D.Y. (1984). Linking propositions. *Vision Research*; **24**(10): 1233–46.

Tye, M. (1995). *Ten problems of consciousness.* Cambridge, Mass: MIT Press.

Valberg, A. (2001). Unique hues: an old problem for a new generation. *Vision Research*; **41**: 1645–57.

Vierkant, T. (2003). *Is the self real?* Münster: LIT Verlag.

CHAPTER 4

Perception, action, and experience: unravelling the golden braid*

Andy Clark

Abstract

Much of our human mental life looks to involve a seamless unfolding of perception, action and experience: a golden braid in which each element twines intimately with the rest. We see the very world we act in and we act in the world we see. But more than this, visual experience presents us with the world in a way apt for the control and fine guidance of action. Or so it seems. Milner and Goodale's ((1995) (2006)) influential work on the dual visual systems hypothesis casts doubt on certain versions of this intuitive vision. It does so by prising apart the twining strands of conscious visual perception and the fine control of visuomotor action. Such a bold proposal is of major interest both to cognitive science and philosophy. In what follows I first clarify the major claims that the bold proposal involves, then examine three sets of worries and objections. The first set concerns some important matters of detail. The second set concerns a certain kind of conceptual or philosophical worry to the effect that the perception/action model equates visual experience itself unfairly with what are in fact certain *elements* within visual experience. The third set concerns the very idea of conscious experience as a well-defined conceptual or experimental target.

4.1 A bold proposal: vision for perception, vision for action

Milner and Goodale's (1995) bold proposal offers a certain functional gloss on the anatomical complexity of the visual system. This gloss takes as its starting point the existence of two major

* This is an expanded version of a paper originally published in a 2009 special edition of *Neuropsychologia* **47**, 1460–1468 (edited by Robert McIntosh and Thomas Schenk). Thanks to Robert McIntosh, Tim Bayne, Thomas Schenk, Michael Tye, Matthew Nudds, Mog Stapleton, Julian Kiverstein, Simon Garrod, Steve Draper, Liz Irvine, John Henderson, Ned Block, and Tillmann Vierkant for stimulating exchanges on these topics. Thanks too to the two referees, to all the participants in the *Perception, Action and Consciousness: Sensorimotor Dynamics and Dual Vision* conference held at Bristol in July 2007, and to all the members of the Edinburgh Philosophy, Psychology and Informatics Reading Group for stimulating discussions. This paper was prepared thanks to support from the AHRC, under the ESF Eurocores CNCC scheme, for the CONTACT (Consciousness in Interaction) project, AH/E511139/1.

processing streams (the ventral and the dorsal) projecting from early visual areas to the rest of the human brain. Famously, Ungerleider and Mishkin (1982) depicted these as the 'what' and 'where' streams, each specialized to perceive different aspects of the visual world. In this view, both streams contributed contents (though different ones) to human visual experience. Milner and Goodale (1995) described and defended an alternative functional gloss, according to which one stream supports 'vision-for-action' and the other 'vision-for-perception'. Thus the dorsal stream, projecting to the posterior parietal cortex, is said to support the kinds of visuomotor transformation in which visual input leads to fluent actions such as reaching and grasping, while the ventral stream, projecting to the temporal lobe, seems to be especially implicated in the recognition and identification of objects and events. Milner and Goodale (1995) and Goodale and Milner (2004) further suggest that the dorsal stream computes 'vision-for-action' in a way that is fast, transient, and unconscious, and that the ventral stream computes 'vision-for-perception' in a way that is slower, more enduring, and at least sometimes conscious. The contents of conscious visual experience, for Milner and Goodale, are thus associated strongly with the coding and processing operations carried out by the ventral stream.

To illustrate the way these two streams are then meant to interact, Goodale and Milner (2004) develop an analogy with tele-assistance approaches to the control of distant robots in distant or hostile environments. Here, a conscious human operator and a non-conscious semi-intelligent distal robot combine forces so as to perform actions in some environment (e.g. in the control of a Mars rover, where the human operator reviews images on a screen in Texas, flagging items of interest that the robot can locate and retrieve using its own onboard sensory systems and sensorimotor routines. Such approaches are contrasted with tele-operation solutions, in which the conscious human operator controls all the spatial and temporal aspects of the robots movements (perhaps via a joystick or a set of sensors that allow the operators' own arm and hand movements to be relayed to the robot). The tele-assistance analogy thus identifies the role of the conscious human operator with the role of the ventral stream (working in concert with stored memory and various 'executive control' systems). The task of this coalition, the analogy suggests, is to identify objects and to select types of action that are appropriate given the agent's current goals, background knowledge, and currently attended perceptual input. The task of the dorsal stream (and associated structures) is then to turn these high-level specifications into metrically accurate, egocentrically specified forms of world-engaging action. The dorsal stream (plus associated structures) thus plays the non-conscious robotic Mars Rover to the ventral coalition's conscious human operator, such that:

> Both systems have to work together in the production of purposive behavior-one system to select the goal object from the visual array, the other to carry out the required metrical computations for the goal-directed action.

> (Goodale and Milner, 2004: 100)

This picture of the distinct but interlocking contributions of the two visual streams explains some of the coarse dissociations and psychophysical effects described in the literature. In particular, this account of the division of labour offers a neat explanation of the differing pattern of deficits seen in patients with lesions affecting one or other of the two streams. Thus ventrally compromised patients (such as D.F.) display severe impairments in recognizing shapes, orientations, and objects. Not only can D.F. not recognize most everyday objects, or faces, she cannot distinguish between squares, rectangles, triangles, and circles. In the famous 'mailbox' task, D.F. was pretty well at chance for turning a handheld card to match the perceived orientation of a posting slot. Yet asked to actually post the card through the slot she was almost indistinguishable from normal controls (see Milner and Goodale, 1995: 128–33). On an intuitive model, D.F.'s apparent lack of conscious visual awareness of features such as shape and orientation might suggest that she has (for whatever reason) simply failed to compute the very information needed to guide the relevant visuomotor actions. Yet her fluent performance belies this. The dual streams/tele-assistance model accounts for this, since the visual information required to support the world-engaging action is computed independently (though on the basis of the same retinal input) of the information required to support conscious identification.[1]

Moving to the case of normal, unimpaired subjects, the same story neatly accounts for work by Aglioti et al. (1995). In this work, the experimenters set up a graspable version of the famous Ebbinghaus or 'Titchener Circles' visual illusion in which two central circles are presented surrounded by a ring of other circles. In one case, the surrounding circles are larger than the central one. In the other, they are smaller. This leads to the well-known illusion in which subjects misjudge the relative size of the two central circles. Such mistaken estimates of relative size do not, however, affect subjects' abilities (in the physical, poker chip version) to form precision grips that perfectly anticipate the true size of the centre discs. The explanation, according to Goodale and Milner (2004: 88–9) is that the conscious scene is computed by the ventral stream in ways that make a variety of assumptions on the basis of visual cues (e.g. attempting to preserve size constancy by treating the smaller circles as probably further away than the larger ones). The dorsal stream, by contrast, uses only the kinds of information that are metrically reliable and exploit specific opportunities for elegant, fast, metrically accurate diagnosis. For example, the dorsal stream may make great use of binocular depth information. These differences in processing, combined with the quasi-independent modes of operation of the two streams, account for the illusion's ability to impact conscious visual experience while leaving our visuomotor engagements intact.

More recently, a similar effect has been shown using the so-called 'hollow face illusion'. In this illusion a concave model of a human face appears convex, due to the influence of top-down knowledge concerning normal human faces. This suggests it is a purely ventral stream based illusion. Kroliczak et al. (2006) showed that in a task where subjects were asked to flick small targets off the actually hollow (though visually convex) face, the flicking movements found the real (non-illusory) locations of the targets. According to Milner and Goodale:

> This demonstrates that the visuomotor system can use bottom-up sensory inputs … to guide movements to the veridical locations of targets in the real world, even when the perceived positions of the targets are influenced, or even reversed, by top-down processing.
>
> (Milner and Goodale, 2006: 245)

Such demonstrations, and the more general issue of perception-action dissociations and visual illusions, have spawned a large and complex literature devoted to the search for counter-examples, alternative explanations, exceptions, refinements, and additional support (for some useful reviews, see Carey, 2001; Clark, 2001; Goodale and Westwood, 2004).[2]

Aspects of the dual visual systems picture are supported by a large and impressively varied body of evidence including a swathe of neuroimaging experiments (e.g. Le et al., 2002; James et al., 2003),

---

[1] Conversely, optic ataxics, with dorsal stream lesions, are adept at visually identifying objects that they cannot fluidly reach and grasp. Optic ataxics 'have little trouble seeing [i.e. identifying] objects in a visual scene, but a lot of trouble reaching for objects they can see. It is as though they cannot use the spatial information inherent in any visual scene' (Gazzaniga, 1998: 109).

[2] For example, it has been shown that some visual illusions do affect visuomotor engagement. Importantly, however, this seems to be the case only when the illusion is rooted in very early stages of visual processing (in primary visual cortex) and is thus 'passed on' to both streams when they subsequently diverge (Dyde and Milner, 2002; Milner and Dyde, 2003). This is, of course, fully compatible with the strong dual systems view. Moreover, several other perceptual illusions have subsequently been shown to affect conscious experience without impacting visumotor acts of grasp scaling and reaching including the Ponzo ('railway lines') and Müller-Lyer illusions (see Goodale and Milner, 2004: 89). In such cases, motor effects *are* observed when delays are introduced between viewing the illusion and producing the motor response. But this is as predicted by the model, which treats time-delayed actions as 'pantomimed' in that they cannot rely on the here-and-now computations of the dorsal stream and are instead driven by the illusion-prone deliverances of the ventral stream (see Milner and Goodale, 1995: 170–3).

a wide variety of single cell recordings and other experimental interventions in monkeys (Taira et al., 1990; Sakata 2003), and psychophysical experiments involving normal human subjects (Bridgeman et al., 1979; Goodale et al., 1986; Fecteau et al., 2001; and, as we just saw, Aglioti et al., 1995). More generally, it may be observed that the online control of motor action requires the extraction and use of radically different kinds of information (from the incoming visual signal) than do the tasks of recognition, recall, and reasoning. The former requires a constantly updated, (multiple) egocentrically-specified, exquisitely distance and orientation sensitive encoding of the visual array. The latter requires the computation of object-constancy (objects don't change their identity every time they move in space) and the recognition of items by category and significance irrespective of the fine detail of location, viewpoint, and retinal image size. A computationally efficient coding for either task thus looks to preclude the use of the very same encoding for the other (Milner and Goodale, 1995: 25–66). Different uses of visual information impose quite different computational demands on the brain, so there are compelling computational and information-processing considerations that speak in favour of a dual (or at any rate, multiple) visual systems architecture. But just how all this in turn lines up with issues concerning conscious and non-conscious vision remains open to question, as we shall see.

4.2. Complications

The very strongest claim in this area, that the contents of conscious visual experience are determined *exclusively* by the coding and processing operations carried out by the ventral stream, now looks to be empirically suspect.[3] Schenk and Milner (2006) show that form discrimination, in the visual form agnosic D.F., can be improved if she engages in a concurrent visuomotor task. Specifically, when asked to name the shape of a visually presented object while reaching for the object, performance on the naming task was significantly improved. Further experiments ruled out the suggestion that this effect is due to D.F. using proprioceptive or efferent cues, suggesting instead that she is able directly to access shape-relevant information (in fact, it turns out to be information about width) being processed by the dorsal stream. This means that D.F.'s shape judgements can be influenced by ongoing dorsal stream activity. Does this mean that processing in the dorsal stream can contribute to the contents of D.F.'s visual experience? It is not clear. For the possibility remains that the dorsal influence provides only some kind of elusive, non-visual cue. As the authors put it:

> … better 'discrimination' does not necessarily imply better 'perception', and instead D.F. could have been employing some indefinable 'implicit' cues of the kind that enable blindsight patients to perform above chance in discrimination tasks.

> (Schenk and Milner, 2006: 1502)

It has also been suggested (Matthen, 2005) that dorsal processing may contribute a kind of non-specific 'feeling of presence' to our contact with the visual scene. To bring this idea into focus, it helps first to distinguish, following Matthen, 'descriptive' from 'motion-guiding' vision. Descriptive vision, as Matthen uses the term, corresponds rather closely to the kind of vision supported by ventral stream coding. It is the kind of vision that supports sensory classification, allowing us to experience the scene as composed of objects and elements that might be classified as similar or different in sensory (visual) respects. Descriptive vision is thus, as we might say, 'epistemically pregnant': it presents the visual world in ways that are apt for reasoning about that world (see Clark, 2001). Matthen contrasts descriptive vision and 'motion-guiding vision', identifying the latter as supported

---

[3] In addition, some aspects of *online object engagement* may require ongoing ventral stream effort (grip force [Jackson and Shaw], functionally informed grips [Goodale and Milner, 2004], complex object engagements [McIntosh et al., 2004]).

by both non-cortical routes and the dorsal (cortical) stream. According to Matthen (*op cit* p. 296) 'the link between motion-guiding vision and bodily motion is direct; it is not routed through consciousness'. Conscious seeing may, of course, provide the information that leads us to choose a certain target and a certain type of action. But it does not provide moment-by-moment guidance of fine visuomotor action. This picture thus comports nicely with Milner and Goodale's view concerning the non-conscious nature of the processing and control operations carried out by the dorsal stream. Nonetheless, Matthen suggests, there is at least one way in which that picture may be incomplete. For it fails to recognize the dorsal processing origins of the 'feeling of presence' that accompanies many of our visual encounters with the world. The idea here is that the kinds of metrically accurate depth and location information computed by the dorsal stream allow us to feel that we are really in the presence of, say, a cup and not merely seeing a two-dimensional drawing or photograph of a cup. This feeling of presence (which can be at least partially duped by some kinds of two dimensional depiction) is said to form a genuine part of our visual experience. Even though it is not part of 'descriptive vision', it 'makes a difference to the quality of one's visual awareness of an object' (*op cit* p.301).

Rizzolatti and Matelli (2003), and Gallese (2007), suggest that the dorsal/ventral distinction itself is too coarse-grained, and should be replaced by a tripartite distinction between dorso–dorsal, ventro–dorsal, and ventral streams (for the anatomical details, see Gallese (*op cit* sections 2–4). The dorso–dorsal stream is said to support fast, non-conscious visuomotor transformations, just as envisaged by Milner and Goodale, while the ventral stream, again as Milner and Goodale suggest, supports object identification and classification. However, the ventro–dorsal stream, though itself anatomically part of the dorsal stream, nonetheless contributes, these authors suggest, to the determination of conscious experience. One major way it does so, it is argued, is by supporting the conscious visual experience of others' intentional actions. Such a suggestion gains plausibility if one way in which we come to grasp the nature and goals of others' observed actions is by activating our own motor systems, perhaps under the influence of mirror system (Rizzolatti et al., 1996) processing. The ventrodorsal stream is also said to be essential for the conscious visual awareness of space as an arena for our own motor activity, as when we see objects as reachable, or as manipulable in such and such ways. Holding both these strands together is the guiding idea that parieto pre-motor circuits support various forms of 'embodied simulation' (Gallese, 2005) such that 'side-by-side with the sensory description of the observed phenomena, the motor schemata associated with these actions, or objects, are evoked in the observer' (Gallese, 2007: 14). These active motor schemas are said to be the mechanism by which 'conscious awareness of actions and spatial locations are generated' (*op cit*).

In this section we have scouted what are perhaps best seen as a series of complications: refinements and additions to the strong dual visual systems view. Though outstanding questions remain,[4] accommodating these refinements and additions leaves intact many of the central tenets of the account. Other challenges, however, go deeper than this, some of them threatening even the claims concerning the non-conscious status of the basic (dorso–dorsal) visuomotor transformation itself. It is to these challenges that we now turn.

4.3. **The 'Narrow Vision of Conscious Vision' worry**

Milner and Goodale's bold proposal is, as we have already begun to see, subject to an interesting and important (though initially somewhat elusive) kind of worry. We can dub it the 'Narrow Vision of Conscious Vision' worry. The worry takes many shapes and forms, some of them more plausible, and some of them less elusive, (and some both), than others. What they all have in common is the

---

[4] One residual issue hereabouts, which I won't attempt to resolve in this treatment, concerns the nature of these projected additional elements of conscious experience. Is the 'feeling of presence' truly part of my visual experience? Is the width information available to D.F. for form discrimination really given to her as some (perhaps weak or indeterminate?) form of *visual* experience? Does the meaningfulness of a visually presented action really belong to the visual experience itself?

thought that the bold proposal illicitly identifies conscious visual experience with one or more of the components, forms, or styles, of conscious visual experience. That is to say, conscious visual experience may involve many different 'things', supported by many different processing streams and neural coalitions, and it would be a mistake to identify conscious vision with just one of them.

An analogy[5] may be helpful here. Visual and auditory experiences are different phenomena, and depend on different mechanisms and forms of internal processing. In the light of this mundane fact, we would be wrong to identify what we experience perceptually (in general) with what we experience *visually*. Correlatively, we would be wrong simply to identify the mechanisms of perceptual experience with the mechanisms of visual experience. Now suppose that within the realm of visual experience itself there exist multiple quite different varieties of experiential phenomena, each supported by different types or forms of mechanism and processing. Suppose too that one or more such elements turn out to depend preferentially, just as Milner and Goodale suggest, upon processing in the ventral visual stream. Still it would not follow that conscious visual experience itself (in all its varieties) depends preferentially upon processing in that stream. To do so would be to fall prey to what I am calling a 'Narrow Vision of Conscious Vision' error.

Here are two (distinct but related) versions of the 'narrow vision' worry drawn from the recent philosophical and cognitive neuroscientific literature:

4.3.1. Comparing like with like

Jeannerod and Jacob (2005) make a strong case that simple comparisons between the contributions of the dorsal and ventral streams are misleading insofar as they fail to control for three factors. The factors concern direction of fit, direction of causation, and level of processing. Let's take the first "two first. The underlying model here is the philosophical distinction (Anscombe, 1957; Searle, 1983) between states that are belief-like and states that are desire-like. Beliefs have a mind-to-world direction of fit, and a world-to-mind direction of causation. That is, a belief is a mental state that aims to fit the way the world is (thus, it exhibits a mind-to-world direction of fit). One good way to ensure that kind of fit is for it to be *caused* by the way the world is (thus also exhibiting world-to-mind direction of causation). Desires, by contrast describe ways the world should be (they exhibit world-to-mind direction of fit), and they may function so as to help bring it about that the world be that way (thus displaying a mind-to-world direction of causation). Notice, then, that different attitudes (belief versus desire) are here distinguished in part in terms of their direction of fit. Thus an agent may be said to be in states that share content (e.g. that the shops be open) with differences in attitude (one may believe it, another hope it, another fear it).

Apart from this question about direction of fit, there is a question concerning nature and level of processing. Thus, consider next the various ways an active agent may need to use visually presented information. The information may be used to ensure that they know how things are out in the world. Jeannerod and Jacob (*op cit* p.3) call this the 'semantic processing of visual information'. Or (or in addition) it may be used to help act upon, and alter, that world. They call this the 'pragmatic processing of visual information'. Semantic processing has a belief-like profile, exhibiting a mind-to-world direction of fit and a world-to-mind direction of causation. Pragmatic processing has a more desire-like profile,[6] exhibiting a world-to-mind direction of fit and a mind-to-world direction of causation. Moreover, each kind of processing involves many levels of abstraction. Early stages of semantic processing yield representations with 'pictorial non-conceptual contents' (for present purposes, we can think of these as essentially 'iconic', non-propositionally structured contents, in

---

[5] This analogy was originally suggested to me by an anonymous referee for Clark (2007).

[6] The actual story is a little more complex, since 'pragmatic' visuomotor representations are said (*op cit* p.3) to have a hybrid direction of fit, insofar as they also provide motor intentions with information about what actions the world affords.

the sense of Coltheart [1983], but see Clark [2001] for further discussion). Later stages yield representations whose contents are more structured and highly processed, presenting a world of objects, relations, and attributes, in ways apt to inform processes of explicit reasoning and planning. Similarly, early stages of pragmatic processing are said to represent basic geometrical properties (width, as it figures in the Schenk and Milner results discussed in section 4.2, would be one such property) of objects in ways apt for the guidance of actions such as fluent reaching and grasping, while later stages yield more abstract, or 'conceptual' representations. Crucially, according to Jeannerod and Jacob:

> The scope of pragmatic processing … is not limited to the visuomotor transformation, since pragmatic processing is involved in conceptually more complex operations like evaluating the feasibility of an action, anticipating its consequences, planning further steps, and learning the skilled use of tools by observation.
> (Jeannerod and Jacob, 2005: 5)

The upshot is that:

> The visuomotor transformation is but a first, lower level component, of the human 'pragmatic processing' of objects. [We should] contrast this lower level pragmatic processing with a higher level of pragmatic processing of objects involved in the skilled use and manipulation of complex cultural tools and artifacts.
> (Jacob and Jeannerod, 2003: xviii)

These higher levels of pragmatic processing reach, the authors argue, all the way up to representations with consciously accessible contents, as in the case where we experience motor imagery involving the manipulation of these complex tools and artifacts. Such uses go well beyond simple grasping and involve the retrieval of what Jacob and Jeannerod (2003: 216) call 'stored scripts' for the manipulation and use of cultural objects. At this point, the authors argue 'the distinction between action and perception loses much of its significance' (Jacob and Jeannerod, 2003: 253).

Let's return now to Milner and Goodale's bold proposal. The deepest worry raised by Jeannerod and Jacob may be put like this: we should be wary of conclusions (concerning the functional roles of the dorsal and ventral streams, and the alignments of those roles with conscious visual experience) that do not compare like with like. In particular, we should be wary of conclusions reached by comparing *early levels of pragmatic processing* with *later levels of semantic processing*. Early stages of pragmatic processing (those devoted to the basic visuomotor transform) involve representations with little or no conceptual content, and these are indeed not the kind of content that normally figure in our own experience. However, early levels of semantic processing, which fall short of identifying or classifying objects, are similarly silent, phenomenally speaking. While later stages of both semantic and pragmatic processing involve contents that are not silent; that are present to phenomenal awareness. If we keep the nature and levels of processing matched, what we find are thus not differences in phenomenal status but rather differences in direction of causation and of fit. That is to say, we find that there are indeed (at least[7]) two distinct roles that visual information may be serving in the agent economy, but neither role lines up exclusively with conscious visual experience.

---

[7] Jeannerod and Jacob go on to suggest a further decomposition of function within the parietal lobe/dorsal pathway, with varying admixtures of directions of fit and causation associated with the various functions. The superior partietal lobule, they suggest, is concerned with visuomotor processing, while the right inferior parietal lobule deals with the perception of spatial relationships, and the left inferior lobule with representations of goal-directed actions. Both these latter roles, they argue, are plausibly associated with certain contents of conscious visual experience.

4.3.2. **Directive content?**

What about the basic visuomotor transformation itself? Here, Jeannerod and Jacob seem to accept that the processing (that is involved in transforming visual input into fluent acts of basic reaching and grasping, for example) fails to reach or inform conscious visual experience, but even this may be called into question.

Thus consider once again the case of D.F., the ventrally compromised carbon monoxide poisoned subject studied by Milner and Goodale. In an interesting paper, Wallhagen (2007) suggests that D.F. may really experience visually presented shape, but be unable to report that experience due to some problem with bringing her experience 'under concepts'. The idea is that the intact dorsal stream processing associated with the basic visuomotor transformation has its own attendant phenomenology, and that it is this attendant phenomenology that explains D.F.'s remarkably fluent visuomotor behaviour. Thus D.F. sees (experiences visually) shapes and orientations, but when asked to *report* on what she sees, she is unable (due to her compromised ventral processing) to do so. Not only can she not report what she sees, in a real sense she does not *know* what she sees. Just as a non-human animal, lacking the concept of 'chair', might well visually experience a chair yet not in any sense know it is experiencing a chair, so too D.F. might experience a world of oriented lines, shapes, and forms but not know (neither recognize nor be able to report) that she is doing so. According to Wallhagen:

> Aspects of form may well be phenomenally present to D.F., she may well consciously sense, and hence represent, the shapes, sizes, and orientations of things, even if she cannot properly conceptualize these aspects of form.
>
> (Wallhagen, 2007: 550)

O'Regan and Noë (2001) seem tempted by a similar thought. They describe D.F. as a case of 'partial awareness' in which 'she is unable to describe what she sees but is otherwise able to use it for the purpose of guiding action' (*op cit* p.969).

These views are potentially more radical than that defended by Jeannerod and Jacob, since they call into question the identification (accepted by Jeannerod and Jacob) of conscious perceptual contents with the more highly conceptualized products of later stages of (both semantic and pragmatic) processing. One immediate problem is that these less highly processed (more 'unconceptualized') contents, if they are indeed consciously experienced, will nonetheless be hard if not impossible to bring into focus for report and description. For whenever we do so, we in effect move up the processing ladder, calling on our grasp of the scene as a structured, attended entity populated by nameable objects, shapes, and relations. But for the moment, let's bracket that worry and try to put a little more flesh on the suggestion itself.

One way to think about this kind of proposal is developed further by Nudds (2007). Nudds, like Jeannerod and Jacob, urges us to distinguish between two kinds of content that visual perceptual experiences may possess. He dubs these the 'presentational' and the 'directive' contents of visual experience. Presentational contents correspond to what Matthen (2005) termed 'descriptive vision' and what Jeannerod and Jacob (2005) termed 'semantic processing': they are contents that depict how things are in the world. Directive contents correspond to what Matthen termed 'motion-guiding vision' and what Jeannerod and Jacob called 'pragmatic processing': they are concerned with how to guide actions so as to bring about desired results. Nudds' suggestion, rather like that of Wallhagen, is that these contents figure in visual experience and help to determine the shape and nature of our world-engaging activity. It is this latter claim that marks the point of departure from both Milner and Goodale's model and (at least for the basic visuomotor transformation) that of Jeannerod and Jacob.[8]

---

[8] Similarly Matthen's comments on the 'feeling of presence' are probably best seen as a kind of restricted version of Nudds' claim (restricted insofar as the only contribution the directive contents make to experience is, on Matthen's account, the addition of that sense of presence).

Why should we believe that directive contents, associated with basic visuomotor transformations, form part of our conscious visual experience? Nudds' reasoning is appreciated best in contrast to a more standard model that depicts consciously visually guided action as guided by conscious intentions (e.g. Peacocke, 1992). On this model visual experience presents a world relative to which I may form an intention (e.g. to pick up the coffee cup I see over there) that then determines the action. Such a model is consistent with (though it does not commit you to) the tele-assistance image favoured by Milner and Goodale (see section 4.1), for it leaves room for the detailed kinematics of the action to be determined by something other than the content of the visual experience (which need only allow us to form apt intentions). Such a model, Nudds argues, is inadequate to explain visually guided action. Instead, Nudds argues that there is a distinctive kinematics (as Milner and Goodale showed) to reaching and grasping performed while in visual contact with the scene. Remove the contact and the kinematics alter. This alteration (and this is crucial for his argument) is not accounted for exhaustively by an agent's intentions (e.g. to pick up the cup, or even, moving to the higher levels of pragmatic processing, to use the screwdriver so as to screw in the screw), which may often be the same in both cases. Whereas Milner and Goodale depict these further precise kinematic details as determined by a non-conscious stream of low-level pragmatic processing, Nudds thinks this fails fully to capture the phenomenon. The reason he gives is that the precise way we perform the action seems to be something for which *we* (the agent, rather than just some subsystem of the agent's brain) are responsible. The precise way the action unfolds is, he suggests, something *we* do. That I tie my shoelaces *like this* is not something that just happens to me, or that I just find myself doing. The explanation, Nudds claims, is that (for example) the detailed lace-tying kinematics are driven by conscious but directive contents actually given in visual experience. Nonetheless we will not necessarily be well-placed to *report* on those contents, and it will not 'seem like' anything very specific to be guided by them. This is because both reporting and (more generally) knowing what we are experiencing depend on content-monitoring capacities informed by the other ('presentational') dimensions of conscious visual content.

This is perhaps the most difficult suggestion we will examine in the present treatment. On this model, D.F. (to take one striking example) may have visual experiences with rich conscious directive contents that help explain her successful and often self-initiated behaviours[9] even though [she] 'will not be under the impression that anything is any way, nor have any basis for judging that anything is any way' (Nudds, 2007: 15). This also opens up an alternative interpretation of the Aglioti et al. experiments rehearsed in section 4.1. For on Nudds' account, visual experience guides *both* the action (the well-calibrated grasp) and the illusion-prone verbal response, but it is the directive content of the experience that guides the visuomotor action and the presentational or descriptive content that guides the verbal response. Both the judgment and the action are thus guided by (different forms of) visual experience.[10] Moreover there is no inconsistency in the content of visual experience here, since these different kinds of content share no 'common currency' in which to frame a disagreement.

4.4. **The argument from agency**

In this section I aim to challenge the claim that these directive contents (both in D.F. and in neurally uncompromised subjects) are depicted properly as forming part of our conscious visual experience. As already noted, however, we cannot challenge such a claim simply by pointing to the agent's honest

---

[9] It is worth noting here that D.F. retains descriptive visual experience of colour and texture, and thus knows when there is an object out there, and what kind of surface (shiny, dull etc.) it has. This is what is usually taken to explain her ability to self-initiate actions, and thus already distinguishes her quite sharply (in terms of practical action) from blindsight patients.

[10] Tim Bayne (personal communication) suggests that the directive content described by Nudds, insofar as it is indeed consciously experienced, may be best thought of as 'motor intentional' rather than genuinely visual. This is an interesting suggestion, but one that I shall not pursue in the present context.

reports, since these will only reveal what is present or absent to descriptive vision. What we can do, however, is attempt to gain some leverage from a simple, but I think plausible, observation. The observation (which may of course be doubted, as we'll see later) is that conscious experience must always be the experience *of* some agent. The putative directive contents of visual experience, being available only for one kind of purpose, and then only in highly transient form (i.e. only while in actual contact with the visual scene), seem to fail to meet this requirement. They are more like encapsulated pockets of processing than genuine contents of visual (or any) experience. In very much this vein Gareth Evans once argued that an informational state may underpin a conscious experience only if it (the informational state) is in some sense input to a reasoning subject. According to Evans, to count as a conscious experience an informational state must serve

> ... as the input to a thinking, concept-applying and reasoning system: so that the subject's thoughts, plans, and deliberations are also systematically dependent on the informational properties of the input. When there is such a link we can say that the person, rather than some part of his or her brain, receives and processes the information.
>
> (Evans, 1982: 158)

I think this is almost right. However, the real point here is (or should be) quite independent of Evans' appeal to the subject as concept-using. What matters, rather, is that the information must be available to the agent qua 'reasoning subject', where this may be unpacked in many different ways, not all of them requiring full-blown concept-use on the part of the agent (see, e.g. Hurley, 1997; Bermúdez and McPherson, 1998). As long as an animal can form (nonconceptualized) goals, and can become directly and non-inferentially aware of specific environmental opportunities that allow, or that block, the fulfillment of those (limited) goals and projects, then transduced information can be, or fail to be, input to this kind of minimal reasoning subject (for more on this slightly less demanding conception, see Dretske [2006], Hurley [1998], Clark [2007]). A positive suggestion[11] thus emerges according to which conscious perceptual experience occurs when, and only when, information is poised, however briefly, for direct and non-inferential use in the guidance of (at least minimal) rational action. By contrast, the sensory transduction of visual information can sometimes (as in the case of blindsight) simply channel information so as to guide response, without providing the agent herself with any reasons, justifications, or rationales, for her action (see Campbell [2002], Dretske [2006]). In such cases, behaviour whose success depends on that very information will (all other things being equal) surprise the agent herself. In such cases, information is transduced, impacts behaviour, but is never poised so as to provide me with a reason (visible to myself as an agent) for my actions or choices. At other times, however, something about the form or nature of the processing poises specific items of transduced information in a way apt (if my attention is so directed) to provide me with reasons or motivations for my own actions and choices, to provide what Dretske (2006: 168) calls 'justifying reasons' for my actions. Importantly, it may be that even elements that we don't yet attend to or notice in our own visual experience can be thus poised, as might elements that are not yet fully conceptualized. In this way, as Fodor (2007) notes, even the contents of 'iconic' encodings may provide justifying reasons for a subsequent act or judgment.

For present purposes, what matters is that even these kinds of (weak but important) links between experience and agency do not seem to be present in the case of (merely) directive contents. Nudds himself comments, as we saw, that 'since directive content doesn't present an object as being some way, in having a visual experience with directive content the subject will not be under the impression that anything is any way, nor have any basis for judging that anything is any way' (Nudds, 2007). As a result, this information will not be available for use in any form of practical reasoning, and will not provide the agent herself with any reasons (visible to herself) for her own actions. However, such

---

[11] Versions of this suggestion are found in Evans (1982), Marcel (1983), Milner and Goodale (1995), Goodale and Milner (2004), Hurley (1998), Clark (2001), Jacob and Jeannerod (2003), Dretske (2006), and Clark (2007).

total fractionation of the putative conscious content from what the agent knows or (more generally) has reason to do, seems in conflict (I suggest) with the image of genuine experience being experience *of* the agent.

4.5. **The most radical challenges**

Block (2007) asks a question that reaches to the very roots of current scientific attempts to study conscious experience. He asks how we can know whether some content actually forms part of our conscious experience. The answer, he notes, is only straightforward as long as we take reportability of content (e.g. the broadcasting of content to a 'global workspace'[12]) as a requirement of conscious presence.

Suppose we don't. Suppose we ask, instead, whether conscious experience might go beyond that which we can access or report? A natural worry is that such a question is simply unanswerable. Block's response to this (in part) is to appeal to work by Sperling (1960) and Landman et al. (2003), arguing that these studies suggest that 'in a certain sense phenomenal consciousness overflows cognitive accessibility' (Block, 2007: 481). In the Sperling experiments[13] subjects are briefly (50 ms) shown a 3×3 grid of letters, such as:

T D A
S R N
F Z B

The stimulus grid is removed after 50 ms. Many subjects then claim to have had, and to have briefly retained, a conscious experience of all the letters, even though they could report reliably (in the so-called 'full report' condition) only about four of them. It may seem that there is no way to test empirically whether the subjects actually *saw* (properly saw, in distinct individual detail) more letters than they can *report*. However, Sperling then tested subjects in a further 'partial report' condition. This showed that if asked rapidly instead for the letters in any given row (the top, middle, or bottom) subjects could respond quite accurately, regardless of which row was chosen. What this (at least taken in the context of the subjects' own experiential reports) suggests to Block (and see also Dretske, 2006; Fodor, 2007) is that detailed and consciously encoded information about each and every letter was temporarily available to drive report and noticing (if attention were to be so directed rapidly) even though the subsequent selection of some letters to thus report renders the rest unavailable. That is to say, the initial experience contained more phenomenal information than (perhaps for reasons having to do with limitations on working memory) any full report can display subsequently.

In more recent studies (Landman et al., 2003) subjects were shown eight oriented rectangles for half a second, then a gray screen, then the array of eight but were informed that one rectangle may have changed orientation. Subjects were able to keep track of the orientation of about four rectangles from the group of eight (so their 'capacity measure' was four). Yet, much like the Sperling subjects, many of them reported seeing the specific orientation of all eight rectangles. Once again, a partial report condition seems to bear out the subjects' claim. If the experimenter adds a pointer on the gray screen to ask the orientation question of any given rectangle, subjects can track almost all

---

[12] Thus according to 'global workspace' theory (Barrs, 1988; 1997; Dehaene et al., 1998; Dennett, 2001; Metzinger, 2003 etc) information becomes conscious when it is poised for dissemination to many cortical areas (perhaps via long-range white matter pathways linking cortical areas—see Dehaene and Naccache, 2001). Information poised for such widespread dissemination (information 'in the global workspace') will ipso facto be poised for the control of an open-ended variety of rational responses, including report where available, so the global workspace model can be seen as providing one mechanism by means of which a strong link to personal-level agency may be implemented in the brain.

[13] These experiments are also discussed in Dretske (2006) and Fodor (2007).

the rectangles (they display a capacity measure up to six or seven). The explanation once again, according to Block, is that the initial phenomenal experience contains more information than the full report condition can display.[14]

With these results in mind, Block's (2007) strategy is then to display a neuroscientific story concerning strong back-of-the-head neural coalitions (involving pockets of recurrent processing. See Lamme, 2006) that nonetheless just fail to win a winner-take-all competition for broadcast to the 'global workspace' (recall note 11) and hence for reportability. Such a story (which I shall not attempt properly to rehearse here) is meant to make sense of the claim that in these (and in many other) cases phenomenal consciousness 'overflows' cognitive accessibility and thus that we can (and do) have experiences even in cases where we lack the kind of access that would yield some form of report that such and such an experience had occurred.

The point I want to note is that this argument (which is actually a form of inference to the best explanation) takes as its starting point the assertion that the *only grounds* we have for treating the just-losing coalitions as non-conscious is the unreportability of the putative perceptual experiences. But perhaps this is premature. Underlying the appeal to reportability is, I suggest, a deeper and perhaps more compelling access-oriented concern. It is the concern, raised in the previous section, that any putative conscious experience should be the experience *of an agent*.

Can we really make sense of the image of free-floating experiences, of little isolated islets of experience that are not even potentially more widely available to act as fodder for a creature's rational choices and considered actions? Evans' insight was that the notions of conscious experience and reasoned agency (here construed very broadly) are intertwined deeply: that there are non-negotiable links between what is given in conscious awareness and the enabled sweep of deliberate actions and choices available to a reasoning subject. One way to begin to flesh this out (see Dretske, 2006, for example) is, as we saw, to depict conscious perceptual experience as providing an agent with self-transparent reasons for her own actions.

Such a story opens up a different way of interpreting the Sperling and the Landman et al. results. In these cases subjects report registering all the items phenomenally because information concerning each item was, at that moment, available to be deployed in the service of deliberate, reasoned, goal-directed action. Responses selected on the basis of this information would meet the key condition of being self-transparently grounded in the agent's perceptual connection to the world (for more on this idea, see Clark, 2001). Such momentary potentiality is not undermined by the (interesting and important) fact that the selection of a few items to actually play that role then precludes the selection of the rest.

Contrariwise, Block argues that a subject such as G.K. (Rees et al., 2000 and 2002) suffering from visuospatial extinction may be having an experience of a face and yet it be impossible for him, qua agent, to know anything of this experience. This is because Block takes G.K.'s phenomenal experience to consist in recurrent processing in the fusiform face area. My suggestion, following Evans' would be that G.K. can be experiencing a face consciously only if the information given in the putative experience is poised at least momentarily in a way that makes it apt for use (though it need not actually be used) in the agent's personal level reasoning, planning and for the deliberate and goal-driven selection action. In that way, the link to agency is maintained. Recurrent processing in the fusiform area will no doubt prove to be among the many conditions necessary (but not sufficient) for realizing a state that plays this distinctive causal role. Block's just-losing coalitions fail to trigger winning frontal coalitions and hence fail to be in a position to contribute their contents in this manner to the full sweep of the agent's deliberate acts and choices. It is this fact (rather than the related but admittedly more superficial and unreliable indicator of mere non-reportability) that should motivate our treating the contents of the just-losing coalitions as non-conscious.

---

[14] For some interesting worries, see Byrne, Hilbert and Siegel (2008).

Such a story, it should be clear, remains consistent with Milner and Goodale's claim that the contents of our basic visuomotor transformations do not form part of our conscious visual experience. For they too fail to meet the conditions required to ascribe the experience *to* a specific agent. Isolated or 'free-floating' conscious experiences, if this line of reasoning is correct, have no place in either the scientific or the philosophical image of mind and its place in nature.

4.6. Phenomenal pockets and integrated agency

I have argued that (on pain of being unacceptably 'free-floating') conscious experience must be in some sense available to (be the experience of) an agent, where that means being poised to guide an open-ended (or at least, large enough, given the creature's perhaps limited needs and cognitive capacities) set of agent-level goals and purposes, and to support an open-ended (or at least large enough, given the creature's perhaps limited needs and cognitive capacities) set of agent-level plans and projects. To use my earlier shorthand for this, the information provided by the experience must thus be poised for the control of rational action: action that the agent can thus know, directly and non-inferentially, to be justified by her own perceptual contact with the world (for more on this notion of justified response, see Dretske, 2006). Information thus poised may perhaps fall short, under special conditions, of guaranteeing, even in linguistically fluent animals, full reportability (the role of working memory limitations in the Sperling experiment might provide one such condition). But attended, sufficiently highly processed, ventral stream supported contents certainly meet the condition, while much (though, as pointed out by Gallese and by Jeannerod and Jacob, probably not all) of the content computed by the dorsal stream does not. Call this the 'agent-level integration picture' of conscious perceptual experience.

An alternative view that is rapidly gaining currency, however, is that even this somewhat more modest appeal, requiring as it does that the contents of conscious perceptual experience be poised for the widespread control of rational action and response, distorts the true phenomenal facts. It does so, the critics argue, by conflating conscious perceptual experience with (roughly speaking) *top-down attended* perceptual experience. Thus Koch and Tsuchiya (2007) argue that consciousness and top-down attention are distinct phenomena with distinct neural signatures. For example, we can become conscious of the gist of a scene without any targeting of top-down attention (Li et al., 2002; Reddy et al., 2006). Contrariwise, we can attend to objects that escape our perceptual awareness. One such case occurs when we experience after-effects whose occurrence can be shown to require attention to objects or states of affairs (such as the orientation of gratings) of which the subject is unaware (He et al., 1996; Montaser-Kouhsari and Rajimehr, 2004). Similarly, arousing nude images have been shown to attract attention even when techniques such as flash suppression prevent the subject from becoming aware of their presence in the visual field (Jiang et al., 2006). From data such as these Koch and Tsuchiya conclude that:

> top-down attention and consciousness are distinct phenomena that need not occur together and that can be manipulated using distinct paradigms
>
> and that:
>
> untangling their tight relationship is necessary for the scientific elucidation of consciousness and its material substrate.
>
> (Koch and Tsuchiya, 2007: 16)

In a related vein, Lamme (2006) argues that to take the bulk of current neuroscientific evidence seriously is to reject the identification of conscious experience with reportable contents. For reportability, Lamme argues, is inextricably tied up with a number of cognitive functions that (he claims) are distinct from conscious experience itself. These include (*op cit* p.499) attention, working memory, episodic memory, inner speech etc. These functions are involved when we come to know that we are experiencing such and such. But in general, there is a gap between what states we are actually in and what states we know or believe ourselves to be in. If this is true for conscious experience too, reliance on report and noticing are misleading tools for the study of experience itself. Lamme's dramatic positive suggestion then is that there is phenomenal experience whenever there is recurrent processing in the brain. Wherever there is recurrent processing, Lamme suggests, there is both an inclination to induce synaptic plasticity, and some kind of accompanying phenomenal experience. I shall not attempt to display the reasoning behind this strong claim here, but merely note that if this is correct, one initially counter-intuitive consequence is that there may be much more (and more varied) phenomenal experience present in a single human agent at a moment in time than we ourselves would ever suspect. This is, of course, exactly the position defended by Block. It is much stronger than the claim made by Dretske, which was simply that we may often phenomenally experience X without noticing or tending to report that we are experiencing X. For the unnoticed experiences, on Dretske's model, must at least involve coding information in such a way that it could easily have become noticed, were the agent's attention so directed. As I read Lamme and Block, however, no such constraint is to be applied. Instead, there may be fully isolated pockets of phenomenal experience (e.g. where there is recurrent processing inside a Fodorian module: see Fodor, 1983). This yields what Bayne (ms) describes nicely as a 'quilted model of conscious experience', with the many individually isolated pockets of the quilt each capable of enclosing a sufficient mechanism (given as backdrop the wider context of the overall functioning system) for various forms of phenomenal experience.

Initally, it might seem absurd to suppose that genuine features of our own phenomenal experience should thus escape notice and report completely and irrevocably. But the idea gains in plausibility, or so it seems to me, when viewed in the light of Eric Schwitzgebel's fascinating series of publications showing the remarkable unreliability of simple ('naïve') introspection when it comes to deciding what does and does not form part of our current conscious experience. Thus Schwitzgebel and Gordon (2000) show in compelling detail that humans use echolocation to solve certain perceptual problems, that this echolocation forms part of conscious perceptual experience, and yet that subjects are typically wildly mistaken about their own experiences in this regard. This kind of argument reaches a kind of climax in Schwitzgebel (2008), where our self-knowledge concerning our own experience is shown to be unstable and contested in ways that suggest it must be faulty and untrustworthy in a depressingly wide variety of cases ranging from emotional experience to peripheral vision, to the phenomenology (or lack of it) of thought itself. If this is correct, the possibility that we may also be host to multiple isolated pockets of phenomenal experience (ones that escape our normal noticing and report) begins to seem less strange, in proportion to our lack of general awareness of our own phenomenal states!

It now begins to seem as if our grip on what it *means* for something to form part of our current conscious experience is tenuous at best. It is a grip compromised by our own congenital inability to know what we are experiencing without turning attention to it, or attempting to recollect it at a later moment, or introspecting upon it right now. Each such act alters the set of cognitive mechanisms in play, yet to eschew reliance on such methods *tout court* is to leave us with no anchor points at all. It leaves us with no means by which to decide, for example, what subsets of behaviour and response to look for in other (e.g. non-verbal, non-human, or impaired) cases. In other words, it seems we must make some antecedent decisions to get the experimental ball rolling, but that these decisions themselves cannot be checked because the experiments that do so must be interpreted according to some closely related, equally unverified, set of assumptions. From this one might conclude that there are facts here that are terminally resistant to scientific resolution. A better conclusion, it seems to me, is that there are no such finer-grained facts here at all.[15]

---

[15] Schwitzgebel's position (personal communication) is that although he can see how the arguments might be taken this way, he himself finds it compelling that there must be a clean fact of the matter concerning, e.g. the richness, or lack of it, of ongoing visual experience, and that this will be so even if that fact turns out to be permanently resistant to scientific resolution.

Take, for example, the currently extremely 'live' question of the phenomenal status of currently unattended visual stuff. Is such unattended stuff phenomenally experienced at the time, or is it at best poised to feed phenomenal experience (or perhaps merely to inform memory) at some later moment? Wright (2006) argues, convincingly it seems to me, that this question is unanswerable in the present state of the science. But more importantly, he also suggests that the question itself is relatively scientifically uninteresting. What matters, Wright argues, is getting a firm grip on what contribution is made by various systems and sub-systems, and how those contributions enable us to maintain fluent contact with, and interact successfully with, the world. In getting such a grip, we are not forced to resolve questions concerning the phenomenal status of unattended visual stuff.

The final view that I want to display, then, is one that we may call the Mere Motley model of conscious perceptual experience. According to this model the phrase 'conscious visual experience' is just a rough and ready label for a typically integrated, but potentially highly dissociable, complex of capacities. Some of these involve recall and report, some involve attention and noticing, others (if Block and Lamme are right) involve only various forms of recurrent-processing amplified neural activity. Such a model would be an instance of what Sloman (2007) calls a 'labyrinthine' theory according to which visual experience is itself highly structured and multiply layered, such that different combinations of the many bits of the labyrinth determine different (often dissociable) aspects and nuances of what we have come to think of as 'our visual experience'. Much the same picture, again based upon theoretical apparatus and insights from work in artificial intelligence and robotics, is endorsed in Ballard (2007). Conscious visual experience, if such views are correct, is not understood usefully via the metaphor of a single inner light that is either on or off (compare this to one leading voice) but consists instead in a motley swathe of surprisingly dissociable elements and effects, relative to which pressing the simple binary question ('is conscious visual experience occurring or not?') is just a recipe for trouble and confusion. The most famous defence of such a view is probably Dennett's (1991) 'multiple drafts' model of conscious experience, according to which the only real facts hereabouts concern the ways the system would respond to various kinds of probe made at various points in the ongoing cycle of processing. But the essential core of the view (which I take to be the assertion of motley processing with no simple facts of the matter concerning the presence or absence of conscious experience in many cases) may be developed in many different ways.

4.7. Conclusions: still revealing after all these years?

In the light of all this, what is most clearly right and important in the strong dual visual systems model is the claim that ventral stream processing (along with some of the highest levels of what Jeannerod and Jacob call 'pragmatic processing) determine preferentially what might be called our 'reflective take on our own visual experience'. That is to say, such processing is involved preferentially in the way our own visual experience presents itself *to us*: to rational, reflective agents motivated by a variety of plans, goals, and projects. Step outside that self-reflective arena, however, and the landscape changes dramatically. If experience, or some varieties of experience, outrun report, and dissociate from processes of top-down attention and consolidation into agent-memory (perhaps occurring simply courtesy of recurrent processing in encapsulated pockets of the cognitive economy) then all bets are off. Worse still, we may be forced to embrace what I have called a Mere Motley model of conscious experience, according to which there is simply no answer to questions concerning (for example) the phenomenal status ('seen or unseen') of what Wright (2006) calls 'unattended visual stuff'. Instead, 'visual experience' would depend on a messy, multi-faceted web of processing that links us variously to the world: a web of processing that we probe in various ways and on various time-scales, some of which inevitably recruit processing in ways tied up with report, memory, attention, and noticing, and others that do not.

Milner and Goodale have done more than just about anyone else to bring these foundational issues into focus, involving neuroscientists, cognitive psychologists, AI researchers, philosophers, and many others in what has become one of the most exciting, important, and productive debates in recent decades. On those increasingly elusive questions concerning the nature and neural underpinnings of conscious visual experience itself, the jury (it seems to me) remains out. But whatever the outcome, there is no doubting the value and impact of the dual visual systems model itself: still revealing after all these years.

References

Aglioti, S., Goodale, M., and DeSouza, J.F.X. (1995). Size contrast illusions deceive the eye but not the hand. *Current Biology*; 5: 679–685.

Anscombe, G.E. (1957). *Intention*. Oxford: Blackwell.

Baars, B.J. (1988). *A cognitive theory of consciousness*. Cambridge: Cambridge University Press.

—— (1997). *In the theater of consciousness: the workspace of the mind*. Oxford: Oxford University Press.

Bach, K. (1978). A representational theory of action. *Philosophical Studies*; 34: 361–79.

Ballard, D. (2007). 'Putting Consciousness in its Place' presented at the 'Perception, Action and Consciousness: Sensorimotor Dynamics and Dual Vision' Conference, Bristol July 2007.

Bayne, T. (ms). 'Deconstructing the Global Workspace'.

Bermúdez, J. and Macpherson, F. (1998). Nonconceptual content and the nature of perceptual experience. *Electronic Journal of Analytical Philosophy* 6 Archived at: http://ejap.louisiana.edu/archives.html.

Block, N. (2007). Consciousness, accessibility, and the mesh between psychology and neuroscience. *Behavioral and Brain Sciences*; 30(5–6): 481–499.

Bridgeman, B., Lewis, S., Heit, G., and Nagle, M. (1979). Relation between cognitive and motor-oriented systems of visual position perception. *Journal of Experimental Psychology (Human Perception)*; 5: 692–700.

Byrne, A., Hilbert, D., and Siegel, S. (2008). Do we see more than we can access? Commentary on Block, 'Consciousness, accessibility, and the mesh between psychology and neuroscience'. *Behavioral and Brain Sciences*; 30(5–6): 501–502.

Campbell, J. (2002). *Reference and consciousness*. Oxford: Oxford University Press.

Carey, D. (2001). Do action systems resist visual illusions? *Trends in Cognitive Sciences*; 5(3): 109–113.

Clark, A. (2001). Visual experience and motor action: are the bonds too tight? *Philosophical Review;* 110(4): 495–519.

—— (2007). What reaching teaches: consciousness, control, and the inner zombie. *British Journal for the Philosophy of Science*; 58: 563–594.

Coltheart, M. (1983). Iconic memory. *Philosophical Transactions of the Royal Society*; B302: 283–294.

Dehaene, S. and Naccache, L. (2001). Towards a cognitive neuroscience of consciousness: basic evidence and a workspace framework. *Cognition*; 79: 1–37.

Dehaene, S., Changeux, J.P., Naccache, L., Sackur, J., and Sergent, C (2006). Conscious, preconscious, and subliminal processing: a testable taxonomy. *Trends in Cognitive Sciences*; 10(5): 204–210.

Dehaene, S., Kerszberg, M., and Changeux, J.-P. (1998). A neuronal model of a global workspace in effortful cognitive tasks. *Proceedings of the National Academy of Science*; 95: 14529–14534.

Dennett, D. (1991). *Consciousness explained*. New York: Little Brown.

—— (2001). Are we explaining consciousness yet? *Cognition*; 79: 221–237.

Dretske, F. (2006). Perception without awareness. *In Perceptual experience,* (eds Gendler, T. and Hawthorne, J.), pp. 147–180. New York: Oxford University Press.

Dyde, R.T. and Milner, A.D. (2002). Two illusions of perceived orientation: one fools all of the people some of the time; the other fools all of the people all of the time. *Experimental Brain Research*; 144: pp. 518–527.

Evans, G. (1982). *The varieties of reference*. (ed. McDowell, J.). Oxford: Oxford University Press.

Fecteau, J.H., Chua, R., Franks, I., and Enns, J.T. (2001). Visual awareness and the on-line modification of action. *Canadian Journal of Experimental Psychology*; 55: 104–110.

Fodor, J. (1983). *The modularity of mind*. Cambridge, MA: MIT Press.

—— (2007). *The revenge of the given*. In *Contemporary debates in philosophy of mind*, (eds McLaughlin, B.P. and Cohen, J.D.). Oxford: Blackwell.

Gallese, V. (2007). The 'conscious' dorsal stream: embodied simulation and its role in space and action conscious awareness. *Psyche*; 13/1: (archived electronic journal: http://psyche.cs.monash.edu.au/)

—— (2005). Embodied simulation: from neurons to phenomenal experience. *Phenomenology and the Cognitive Sciences;* 4: 23–48.

Gazzaniga, M. (1998). *The mind's past*. Berkeley: University of California Press.

Goodale, M.A., Pelisson, D., and Prablanc, C. (1986). Large adjustments in visually guided reaching do not depend on vision of the hand or target displacement. *Nature*; 320: 748–750.

Goodale, M.A. and Milner, A.D. (2004). *Sight unseen: an exploration of conscious and unconscious vision*. Oxford: Oxford University Press.

Goodale, M.A. and Westwood, D. (2004). An evolving view of duplex vision: separate but interacting cortical pathways for perception and action. *Current Opinion in Neurobiology*; 14: 203–221.

He, S. et al. (1996). Attentional resolution and the locus of visual awareness. *Nature*; 383: 334–337.

Hurley, S. (1998). *Consciousness in action*. Cambridge, MA: Harvard University Press.

—— (1997). Non-conceptual self-consciousness and agency: perspective and access. *Communication and Cognition* **vol. 30**, (Part 1 of Special Issue: Approaching Consciousness) Nr. 3/4, 207–248.

James, T.W., Culham, J., Humphrey, G.K., Milner, A.D., and Goodale, M.A. (2003). Ventral occipital lesions impair object recognition but not object-directed grasping: an fMRI study. *Brain*; **126**: 2463–2475.

Jeannerod, M. and Jacob, P. (2005). Visual cognition. a new look at the two visual systems model. *Neuropsychologia*; **43**: 301–312.

Jiang, Y. et al. (2006). A gender-and sexual orientation-dependent spatial attentional effect of invisible images. *Proceedings of the National Academy of Sciences* U.S.A., DOI: 10.1073/pnas.0605678103. Available at: http://www.pnas.org.

Kelly, S. (ms). Merleau-Ponty on the body: the logic of motor intentionality.

Kent, B. (1978). A representational theory of action. *Philosophical Studies*; **34**: 361–379.

Koch, C. and Tsuchiya, N. (2006). Attention and consciousness: two distinct brain processes. *Trends in Cognitive Sciences*; **11**(1): 16–21.

Kouider, S., Dehaene, S., Jobert, A., and Le Bihan, D. (2007). Cerebral bases of subliminal and supraliminal priming during reading. *Cerebral Cortex*; **17**: 2019–2029.

Kroliczak, G., Heard, P.F., Goodale, M.A., and Gregory R.L. (2006). Dissociation of perception and action unmasked by the hollow-face illusion. *Brain Research*; **1080**(1): 1–16.

Lamme, V. (2006). Towards a true neural stance on consciousness. *Trends in Cognitive Sciences*; **10**(11): 494–500.

Landman, R., Spekreijse, H., and Lamme, V.A.F. (2003). Large capacity storage of integrated objects before change blindness. *Vision Research*; **43**: 149–164.

Le, S., Cardebat, D., Boulanouar, K., Henaff, M.A., Michel, F., Milner, A.D., et al. (2002). Seeing, since childhood, without ventral stream: a behavioural study. *Brain*; **125**: 58–74.

Legrand, D. (2006). The bodily self: the sensori-motor roots of pre-reflexive self-consciousness. *Phenomenology and the Cognitive Sciences*; **5**: 89–118.

Li, F.F. et al. (2002). Rapid natural scene categorization in the near absence of attention. *Proceedings of the National Academy of Sciences U. S. A*; **99**: 9596–9601.

Marcel, A.J. (1983). Conscious and unconscious perception: an approach to the relations between phenomenal experience and perceptual processes. *Cognitive Psychology*; **15**: 238–300.

Matthen, M. (2005). *Seeing, doing and knowing*. Oxford: Oxford University Press.

McIntosh, R.D., Dijkerman, H.C., Mon-Williams, M., and Milner, A.D. (2004). Grasping what is graspable: evidence from visual form agnosia. *Cortex*; **40**(4–5): 695–702.

Metzinger, T. (2003). *Being no one: the self-model theory of subjectivity*. Cambridge, MA: MIT Press.

Milner, A.D. and Goodale, M.A. (2006). Epilogue: twelve years on. In *The visual brain in action (2nd Edition)*, (eds Milner, A.D. and Goodale, M.A.) pp. 207–252. Oxford: Oxford University Press.

Milner, A. D. and Dyde, R. (2003). Why do some perceptual illusions affect visually guided action, when others don't? *Trends in Cognitive Sciences*; **7**: 10–11.

Milner, A.D. and Goodale, M.A. (1995). *The visual brain in action*. Oxford: Oxford University Press.

Montaser-Kouhsari, L. and Rajimehr, R. (2004). Attentional modulation of adaptation to illusory lines. *Journal of Vision*; **4**: 434–444.

Nudds, M. (2007). Seeing how to move: visually guided action and the 'directive' content of visual experience. Draft manuscript available at http://homepages.ed.ac.uk/mnudds/papers/shtm.pD.F.

O'Regan, J.K. and Noë, A. (2001). A sensorimotor approach to vision and visual consciousness. *Behavioral and Brain Sciences*; **24**(5): 939–973.

Peacocke, C. (1992). *A study of concepts*. Cambridge, MA: MIT Press.

Reddy, L. et al. (2006). Face identification in the near-absence of focal attention. *Vision Research*; **46**: 2336–2343.

Rees, G., Wojciulik., E., Clarke, K., Husain, M., Frith, C., and Driver, J. (2002). Neural correlates of conscious and unconscious vision in parietal extinction. *Neurocase*; **8**: 387–393.

Rizzolatti, G., Fadiga, L., Gallese, V., and Fogassi, L. (1996). Premotor cortex and the recognition of motor actions. *Cognitive Brain Research*; **3**: 131–141.

Rizzolatti, G. and Matelli, M. (2003). Two different streams form the dorsal visual system: anatomy and functions. *Experimental Brain Research*; **153**(2): 146–157.

Sakata, H. (2003). The role of the parietal cortex in grasping. *Advances in Neurology*; **93**: 121–139.

Schenk, T. and Milner, A.D. (2006). Concurrent visuomotor behaviour improves form discrimination in a patient with visual form agnosia. *European Journal of Neuroscience*; **24**: 1495–1503.

Schwitzgebel, E. (2008). The unreliability of naïve introspection. *Philosophical Review*; **117**: 245–273.

Schwitzgebel, E. and Gordon, M.S. (2000). How well do we know our own conscious experience? The case of human echolocation. *Philosophical Topics*; **28**: 235–246.

Searle, J.R. (1983). *Intentionality, an essay in the philosophy of mind*. Cambridge: Cambridge University Press.

Sloman, A. (2007). Consciousness in a multi-layered multi-functional mind, poster presented at the 'Perception, Action and Consciousness: Sensorimotor Dynamics and Dual Vision' Conference, Bristol July 2007 and available at: http://www.cs.bham.ac.uk/research/projects/cogaff/talks/#pac07.

Sperling, G. (1960). The information available in brief visual presentations. *Psychological Monographs*; **74**.

Taira, M., Mine, S., Georgopoulos, A.P., Murata, A., and Sakata, H. (1990). Parietal cortex neurons of the monkey related to the visual guidance of hand movement. *Experimental Brain Research*; **83**: 29–36.

Tse, P.U., Martinez-Conde, S., Schlegel, A.A., and Macknik, S.L. (2005). Visibility, visual awareness and visual masking of simple unattended targets are confined to areas in the occipital cortex beyond human V1/V2. *Proceedings of the National Academy of Sciences*; **102**(17): 178–183.

Ungerleider, L. and Mishkin, M. (1982). Two cortical visual streams. In *Analysis of visual behavior*, (eds Ingle. D., Goodale. M.A., and Mansfield, R.), pp. 549–586. Cambridge MA: MIT Press.

Wallhagen, M. (2007). Consciousness and action: does cognitive science support (mild) epiphenomenalism? *British Journal for the Philosophy of Science;* **58**(3): 539–561.

Wright, W. (2006). Visual stuff and active vision. *Philosophical Psychology*; **19**: 129.

PART 2
The two-visual systems hypothesis

CHAPTER 5

Cortical visual systems for perception and action*

A. David Milner and Melvyn A. Goodale

Abstract

The model proposed by the authors, of two cortical systems providing 'vision for action' and 'vision for perception' respectively, has implications, explicit or implicit, for the neural correlates of visual phenomenology. In the present article some essential concepts inherent in the model are summarized, and certain clarifications and refinements are offered. Some illustrations are given of recent experiments by ourselves and others that have prompted us to sharpen these concepts. Our hope in writing our book in 1995 was to provide a theoretical framework that would stimulate research in the field. Conversely, well-designed empirical contributions conceived within the framework of the model are the only way for us to progress along the route towards a fully fleshed-out specification of its workings.

5.1. Introduction

In 1992, we proposed a model of cortical visual processing that made a distinction between vision for perception and vision for action (Goodale and Milner, 1992; Milner and Goodale, 1993), which we expanded and developed in a later book (Milner and Goodale, 1995, 2006). Our aim in writing that book was to propose a new way of looking at the functional organization of the two broad cortical pathways of visual processing, the ventral and dorsal streams, each of which arise from the same early visual areas (Ungerleider and Mishkin, 1982; Morel and Bullier, 1990; Baizer *et al.*, 1991; Young, 1992). The essence of our proposal was that the differences in function between the two streams could be best understood not so much in terms of their visual inputs, but more in terms of the output systems the two streams serve. Both streams process information about the structure of objects and about their spatial locations, and both are subject to the modulatory influences of attentional selection. However, the two streams, we argued, process and transmit visual information in quite different ways, in order to guide their respective outputs effectively. The ventral stream transforms

---

* This is a revised and extended version of an article previously published by the authors in *Neuropsychologia*; (2008) **46**: 774–85.

its inputs into perceptual representations that embody the enduring characteristics of objects and their spatial relations. These representations enable us to parse the scene, and to think about objects and events in the visual world. In contrast, the dorsal stream's job is to mediate the visual control of skilled actions, such as reaching and grasping, directed at objects in the world. To do this, the dorsal stream needs to register visual information about the goal object on a moment-to-moment basis, transforming this information into the appropriate coordinates for the effector(s) being used.

The model has developed and crystallized steadily over the years since it was first formulated. At the same time, it has been challenged by a number of authors. In certain instances, these challenges seem to have been predicated on an imprecise reading of some of the more subtle details of the model. Indeed, some comments appear to reflect a misinterpretation of the fundamental distinction we were trying to make between what we called 'vision for perception' and 'vision for action'. Our intention in this chapter is to clarify our use of these and other terms, and also to give a fuller account of the processing characteristics for these two kinds of vision. Our concern, in other words, is with clarification and disambiguation. In making our points we will nonetheless touch upon some recent studies by ourselves and others that bear directly on the theoretical and metatheoretical issues raised.

5.2. Theory and terminology

5.2.1. Perception and action

When we first set out our account of the division of labour between the ventral and dorsal visual pathways in the cerebral cortex, our distinction between vision for perception and vision for action was intended to capture the idea that visual information is transformed in different ways for different *purposes*. We recognized fully, however, that the words 'perception' and 'action' are not scientific terms, and can mean different things to different people. Indeed these words have been used by psychologists and philosophers for centuries to convey a range of different ideas and concepts, not all of which are co-extensive with our particular usage. Such differences in usage continue to exist, and have sometimes led to a misunderstanding of exactly what we had in mind when developing our proposal. For this reason we made an effort to spell out as clearly as we could what we meant by vision for perception and vision for action, although we generally did this ostensively, rather than by providing formal definitions. In clarifying here what we were trying to say, we do not wish to imply that our usage, and only ours, is correct: simply that it needs to be distinguished from those adopted by some other writers.

So, what do we mean by 'perception'? Here we feel that we have allied ourselves with most experimental psychologists working in the mainstream tradition, as exemplified in the classic textbooks of Gregory (1997) and Bruce et al. (2003). What we are referring to primarily is the phenomenology of seeing—that is, the visual experience we have about the current stimulus array. Such a perceptual experience, in most cases, can be translated into a subjective report—at least in principle. This usage of the term 'perception' is standard in the field of psychophysics, where reporting what one sees in visual detection and discrimination tasks forms the usual dependent measure. At the same time, however, we concede that the concept needs to be extended to include 'unconscious' or 'preconscious' perception of objects and events, which refer to mental representations that potentially *could* reach phenomenal awareness, e.g., with slightly different stimulus parameters (cf. Dehaene et al., 2006). This kind of unconscious perception would be exemplified by cases of masking or inattention (normal or neurological), insofar as the unreportable stimuli can be shown to influence later cognitive operations. Unconscious perceptual information can have measurable priming effects on subsequent cognitive tasks both in healthy subjects (e.g. Dehaene et al., 1998; Merikle and Joordens, 1997) and in patients with spatial neglect where the information has been presented to the unattended side of the visual field (Berti and Rizzolatti, 1992; Schweinberger and Stief, 2001). Our point here is that this notion of unconscious perception is a natural extension of the normal sense of the word 'perception', even though the word 'perception' gains its everyday meaning from the phenomenology of perception.

Most psychologists would accept the notion that perceptual processing does not always manifest itself as phenomenology, despite believing that the mental representations of conscious and unconscious percepts, and presumably their neural correlates, are essentially similar in nature. There is much theoretical speculation about what distinguishes conscious from unconscious percepts, but for our purposes both can be seen as gaining their content from common mechanisms in the ventral stream.

Where we depart from the traditional view of perception is in terms of what happens next. Most people (including most scientists and philosophers) have made the commonsense assumption that the mental representations that underlie perception provide not only the foundations for visual cognition, but also *ipso facto* the visual metrics required for action (see Clark, 2001). Our model differs from this traditional view in a crucial way. We agree that perception represents our visual experience of the world, but not that it provides the direct foundation for action. This is not to say, of course, that perception cannot influence action. Indeed, perception would never have evolved unless it had adaptive value, since natural selection can act only on traits that make a difference to behaviour. Our point is that the link between perception and action is an indirect and flexible one, in which cognitive operations such as memory and planning play a crucial role.

So what do we mean by 'action' and what are the roles of the two visual streams in the guidance of action? The traditional behavioural and neuroscientific literature on motor control tends not to make a clear distinction between 'actions' and 'movements'. To use the theory-laden term derived from behaviorism, both are simply 'responses', but of course this way of thinking obscures the fact that what typically defines a piece of behaviour as being such-and-such an action (e.g. reaching to grasp a coffee cup), is the intended *effect* of that action, rather than its precise motor characteristics. Furthermore any given action invariably requires more than one movement, and indeed can be accomplished by a wide variety of *different sets* of constituent movements. A knee-jerk response to tapping the patellar tendon may be a single movement, but it is not an action.

5.2.2. **Planning versus programming**

In our view it is important to distinguish three aspects of any action: first, the *planning* as to what type of action is required to accomplish the goal; second, the pre-movement *programming* of the motor parameters required to implement that decision; and third, the *online control* of these movements during their execution. According to our model, the contribution of the perceptual mechanisms in the ventral stream relates only to the first of these elements, while visual processing in the dorsal stream is responsible for governing the second and third. Specifically, we propose that the ventral stream uses semantic and pragmatic information about possible and actual goal objects to select an appropriate course of action to deal with those objects. However, the subsequent *implementation* of whatever action is chosen is the job of the dorsal stream. This stream plays no role in selecting appropriate actions, but is critical for the detailed specification and online control of the constituent movements that form the action, making use of metrical visual information in the 'here and now' that will map directly onto the action. In other words, both streams contribute to action, but in quite different ways.

The role of the ventral stream in action, then, is to provide visual information to enable the identification of a goal object such as a coffee cup, and to enable other cognitive systems to plan the action of picking up that cup. This would include the selection of the class of hand postures appropriate to the particular task at hand (whether that be taking a sip of coffee, for example, or placing the cup in the dishwasher). However, action planning of this sort is quite abstract, and the final movements that constitute the action could take many different forms. It is the dorsal stream's job to use the current visual information about the size, shape, and disposition of the object in egocentric coordinates (in the case of the coffee cup, with respect to the hand) to programme and control the skilled movements needed to carry out the action. This, then, is the specialized meaning we give to 'vision for action': not the use of visual information for abstract planning, but rather its use in the detailed programming and real-time control at the level of elementary movements. To achieve this, the dorsal stream does not use the high-level perceptual representations of the object constructed by the ventral stream, but instead relies on current bottom-up information from the retina to specify the required movement parameters, such as the trajectory of the reach and the required grip aperture needed to grasp the target object.

In sharp contrast, some writers, such as Glover (2004), have convolved action planning with the detailed programming of the constituent movements of an action: for them all of this is just 'planning'. As Glover puts it, 'planning is responsible for: selecting the target; for all movement parameters relating to nonspatial target characteristics; for the initial determination of the movement parameters relating to spatial target characteristics... for determining the timing of movements ... and for the selection of macroscopic (i.e., postural) aspects of the movement' (Glover, 2004, p. 4). Thus, in terms of our model, Glover has obscured an important distinction. He goes on to argue, in agreement with Rossetti et al. (2003), that the role of the dorsal stream is restricted to the online control of movement execution and is not involved in the initial specification of the movement parameters that determine the mechanics of an action.

Undeniably, there is good evidence for a dorsal-stream role in online control during the course of an action. In particular, this aspect of reaching may be disrupted selectively by transcranial magnetic stimulation administered over the human dorsal stream (Desmurget et al., 1999), and is impaired severely in patients with bilateral 'optic ataxia' caused by damage to the dorsal stream (Pisella et al., 2000; Gréa et al., 2002). However, separate research has also shown that these very same patients with optic ataxia head off in the wrong direction right from the start when trying to reach towards visual targets (Milner et al., 2003). This cannot be explained by faulty online visual control. In addition, when reaching out to grasp objects of different sizes, these patients show deficits in pre-calibrating their grip aperture (Jakobson et al., 1991; 1994), a parameter that is determined largely before movement onset (Jeannerod and Biguer, 1982; Jeannerod, 1984; Jakobson and Goodale, 1991). Again this cannot be explained by faulty online visual control. Complementary evidence comes from the patient D.F., who has bilateral lesions to object recognition areas in the ventral stream (Milner et al., 1991; James et al., 2003). Despite the fact that D.F. is unable to discriminate or identify (whether verbally or through her actions)[1] the dimensions and orientation of objects, she has no difficulty in making accurately calibrated grasping movements with respect to those objects, presumably because her relatively unscathed dorsal stream is able to control her performance of such movements. Thus, although her severely damaged ventral stream may cause D.F. to select the *wrong* action (e.g. Carey et al., 1996, see below), her action once selected proceeds flawlessly. In short, the weight of current evidence bears out our working assumption that the dorsal stream plays a crucial role in the motor programming of actions (i.e. in the pre-specification of movement parameters), as well as in their online control.

Conversely, while the dorsal stream plays the leading role in such motor programming, there is complementary evidence that supports a ventral-stream role in the *planning* of action (in the normal sense of that term). For example, van Doorn et al. (2007) have shown recently that healthy subjects are vulnerable to the Müller-Lyer illusion, not only when making perceptual estimates of the length of a rod, but also when choosing the kind of grip (one-handed versus two-handed) necessary to pick the rod up end to end. Yet the same subjects showed no illusion in programming their actual grip size (in agreement with several previous studies—see section 5.4 below). These data cannot be explained without making a sharp distinction between the visual processes that guide action selection and those that govern motor programming. Whether or not we choose to use the metaphor of 'planning' to

---

[1] It has been suggested by Wallhagen (2007) that reportability provides an insufficient criterion for establishing a failure to perceive. In particular, he argues that D.F. might perceive size, shape, and orientation 'non-conceptually', that is without being able to report on those perceptions, or otherwise act cognitively upon them (e.g. by making a choice between objects). It remains unclear, however, whether such a claim could ever be tested empirically, since cognitively driven responses of one kind or another offer the only objective yardstick available to us for investigating perception in the sense we are using the term. Wallhagen's proposal is discussed critically elsewhere by Clark (2007, 2009, and Chapter 4 this volume) and Jacob and de Vignemont (Chapter 8, this volume).

refer to both of these aspects of action (cf. Glover, 2004), their separability shows that they are not functionally *identical* with the other.

Van Doorn *et al.*'s data accord well, of course, with many earlier observations on patient D.F., whose ventral-stream shape-processing system is destroyed (James *et al.*, 2003). For example, D.F. would often make errors in selecting the correct part of an everyday object to grasp, despite then grasping it with perfect skill (Carey *et al.*, 1996). In a recent study, D.F. (and a second patient with bilateral ventral-stream damage, S.B.) proved to be quite unable to anticipate which wrist posture to adopt when reaching out to pick up a 6-cm block endwise that was presented in various different orientations (Dijkerman *et al.*, 2009). Unlike healthy subjects, who make a consistent switch from a 'thumb-left' (clockwise) to a 'thumb-right' (anti-clockwise) grasp whenever the orientation of the object exceeds about 110° with respect to the mid-sagittal plane, D.F. and S.B. seem quite unable to tailor their hand posture according its likely 'end-state comfort' (Rosenbaum *et al.*, 1993). All of this evidence tells us unequivocally that the distinction between the planning and programming of actions is a crucial one to preserve.

The visual information used by the dorsal stream for programming and online control is not, according to the model, truly *perceptual* in nature. According to our definitions, therefore, it cannot provide visual phenomenology, even in principle. In other words, although we may be fully aware of the *actions* we perform, the visual information used to programme and control those actions can never be experienced (for recent empirical evidence that this is the case, see McIntosh *et al.*, 2004a; Schenk *et al.*, 2005; Milner, 2008; Striemer *et al.*, 2009). We maintain that the nature of both dorsal-stream vision and blindsight stand in sharp contrast to visual processing in the ventral stream, *even when the latter fails to reach awareness*. Perceptual representations—conscious or unconscious—are, according to our model, restricted to the ventral stream.

5.3. **Ambiguities in inferring function from behaviour**

5.3.1. **Tasks versus processes**

As Weiskrantz (1997) wryly observed, '*There is no such creature in psychology as a pure task, nor will there ever be*' (p. 42). It is axiomatic in psychology that no task, however cleverly devised, ever provides a pure measure of a given mental or neural process. Behaviour (and indeed the brain) is far too complex for that ever to be possible. There is, accordingly, no such thing as a pure 'visuomotor task' nor a pure 'perceptual task'. Even when we perform an apparently simple task like reaching or grasping, we cannot help but simultaneously perceive the goal object quite clearly, as well as also our hand reaching out towards it. Indeed, as we have indicated above, in most normal circumstances, our actions will be visually co-determined by complementary processing in both dorsal and ventral streams. This of course is an important reason why the kind of dual processing model that we have advocated is difficult to test using healthy subjects and non-invasive experimental paradigms. At first sight, it might be expected that when one system is severely disabled, whether through damage or through temporary interference, then a given task might get closer towards that elusive task-process correspondence, by effectively removing a large subset of alternative processing possibilities. For example, we can argue that we are witnessing a 'purer' form of visuomotor processing, less contaminated by perceptual influences, when our ventral-stream damaged patient D.F. performs a simple act of prehension.

Even here, however, inferences have to be made with great caution. For example, when D.F. is given a 'perceptual' task (e.g. one requiring the identification or comparison of geometric shapes), do the correct responses she sometimes makes necessarily reflect accurate or successful *perception* in the sense we have defined it above? Can we even infer that she is treating the task as a perceptual task at all, in the normal sense? Clearly not. It is notable that D.F.'s response latencies are invariably very long, and she will often confess that she is 'guessing'. When supplementary information such as colour or visual texture are absent in such 'perceptual' testing, her most successful efforts are often attributable to *non*-perceptual ways of solving the problem she is faced with. For example, Murphy *et al.* (1996) showed that when D.F. was asked to pick up a square when faced with both an oblong and a square block, she performed above chance, even though in a verbal discrimination she did not. Close examination of video recordings of her grasp revealed that when she was incorrectly reaching towards the rectangle, she would sometimes correct herself midstream and grasp the square instead. It appeared that she was using sensory feedback (or perhaps efference copy) to help her make the correct decision. In other words, she was using information derived from *performing an action* to improve performance on a 'perceptual' task. In this regard, it is interesting to note that D.F. always felt that she was guessing—and that her performance remained far from perfect. A later observation by Dijkerman and Milner (1997) demonstrated another strategy in D.F.: she was able to perform above chance in copying lines of different orientation in a simple drawing task, but only when she was allowed either to draw 'in the air' over the stimulus line first, or at least allowed the time to form a motor image of herself doing so. She was not able to form a *visual* image of the line, but could imagine herself drawing over it with the pencil. In other words, we see here a second example of D.F.'s ability to use *vision for action* in order to help her perform an ostensibly 'perceptual' task. Recent data suggest that D.F. can use internal cross-cueing in the size domain as well (Schenk and Milner, 2006). In this study D.F. did significantly better at guessing whether a shape was a square or a rectangle when performing a concurrent grasping (but not a simple pointing) action towards the shape. A further control condition, however, showed that the visuomotor cueing benefited only *width* discrimination (i.e. not shape discrimination *per se*). Thus the transmitted information was restricted to the dimension determining the calibration of grasping, suggesting again a visuomotor, rather than a visual, source of the signal. Anecdotal observations suggest that D.F. adopts non-perceptual strategies on a regular basis in dealing with the everyday world; sometimes knowingly, but often not. She does this in circumstances where a healthy person would depend on their perception unhesitatingly, and where it is all too easy to assume, mistakenly, that D.F. is doing the same.

5.3.2. A recent illustration of the problem

These observations bear on a recent paper by Thomas Schenk (2006) who argues that the dissociations we have reported in D.F. are not between vision for perception and vision for action, but rather between what he calls allocentric and egocentric processing. Schenk bases this claim on the results of an experiment that used a 2×2 design in which D.F. was tested for her ability to use allocentric or egocentric spatial processing in both 'perceptual' and 'action' tasks. Not surprisingly, D.F. did poorly on an allocentric perceptual task in which she was asked to report verbally which of two targets was closer to a visual fixation point (see Fig. 5.1a). Again not surprisingly, she did as well as normal subjects on an egocentric action task in which she was simply asked to point to a target (see Fig. 5.1d). Both of these cells of the 2×2 design accord with previous studies and conform straightforwardly with our model. However, Schenk went on to show that D.F.'s performance on the perceptual task improved when her finger was placed on the fixation point (see Fig. 5.1b). He argued that this was because the task was now an egocentric one in which she was being asked to judge which of two targets was closer to her finger, rather than which was closer to an external reference point. In the light of the findings by Murphy *et al.* (1996) and Dijkerman and Milner (1997), however, this result could be equally well explained within the terms of our model. D.F. needed only to imagine making pointing movements to each stimulus in order to help her make a judgement as to which of the two was closer. Thus, unlike a healthy control subject, who would have made a perceptual judgement automatically, D.F., on this interpretation, would have used a *non*-perceptual strategy to solve the task.[2]

Finally, Schenk showed that D.F. failed on what he characterized as an allocentric 'action' task, in which she was asked to reproduce the position of the target with respect to the reference point by

---

[2] This may explain why D.F. performed at the bottom end of the normal range on this task—in striking contrast to her performance on the egocentric action task (Fig. 5.1d) in which she did as well as the very best control subject.

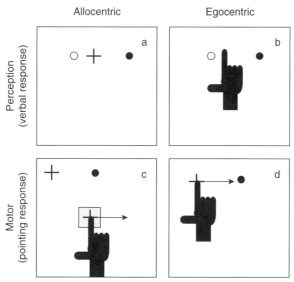

Fig. 5.1 A diagrammatic representation of the tasks used by Schenk (2006). (a) The 'allocentric perception' task. Patient D.F. was asked to make a verbal judgement as to which of two stimuli was closer to a reference point located between them. (b) The 'egocentric perception' task. Here the patient was asked to make a similar judgement, but this time her forefinger was located at the reference point. (c) The 'allocentric motor' task, in which the patient was asked to make a pointing response from an arbitrary start point to mime the location of the test stimulus with respect to the reference point. (d) The 'egocentric motor' task, in which the patient was asked to make a direct pointing response from a start location to a target stimulus. Figure reproduced in modified form from Schenk (2006), with permission.

moving her finger a matching distance from a designated start point (Fig. 5.1c). In our terms, however, this task would not test vision for action, since it is not a task in which the critical visual information maps directly on to the response, guiding it in the 'here and now'. What D.F. was really being asked to do, we would argue, is to reproduce what she perceives, using an arbitrary response (cf. Milner *et al.*, 1991; Goodale *et al.*, 1991). In other words, she was making a *manual report* on her perceptual judgement, similar in essence to the verbal report she used in the allocentric perceptual task. Both 'allocentric' tasks were, in our terms, tests of spatial perception, and thus it is not surprising that D.F. did poorly on them both. For a complementary discussion of the issues raised by Schenk (2006) and Schenk and Milner (2006), the reader is referred to the chapter by Jacob and de Vignemont (Chapter 8).

Schenk's (2006) report illustrates starkly the importance of distinguishing carefully between process and task. The fact that a task involves action does not mean that the performance of this task would engage vision for action in the sense that we use that phrase. Conversely, asking D.F. or any other patient with neurological damage to perform a perceptual task does not guarantee that she will use perception to solve it.

5.4. **Metrics and frames of reference for perception and action**

It has always been central to our argument that the two separate streams of visual processing evolved because perception and action require quite different transformations of the visual signals. To be able to grasp an object successfully, for example, it is essential that the brain compute the actual physical size of the object, and its orientation and position with respect to the observer (i.e. in egocentric coordinates). We also argued that the time at which these computations are performed is equally critical. Observers and goal objects rarely stay in a static relationship with one another for long, and as a consequence the egocentric coordinates of a target object can change radically from moment to moment. For these reasons, it is essential that the required coordinates for action be computed in an egocentric framework at the very moment the movements are to be performed.

Perceptual processing needs to proceed in a quite different way. Vision for perception does not need to compute the absolute size of objects, nor to compute their egocentric locations with respect to the observer. In fact, such computations would be counter-productive. It would be better to encode the size, orientation, and location of objects relative to the other, preferably larger and immobile, objects that are present. Such a scene-based frame of reference permits a perceptual representation of objects that transcends particular viewpoints, while preserving information about spatial relationships (as well as relative size and orientation) as the observer moves around. The products of perception also need to be available over an indefinite time scale, to allow us to recognize objects (and their interrelationships) from one occasion to the next by combining current input with stored information. Such perceptual mechanisms thereby allow us to escape the present and to use visual information from the past to inform our actions.

5.4.1. Illusion and action

These considerations led us to predict that normal observers would show, under appropriate conditions, clear differences between perceptual reports and object-directed actions when interacting with pictorial illusions, particularly size-contrast illusions. This counter-intuitive prediction was based initially on the simple assumption that the perceptual system could not avoid computing the size of a target object in relation to the size of neighbouring objects, whereas visuomotor networks need to compute the true size of the object. This prediction was confirmed in a study by Aglioti *et al.* (1995) which showed that the scaling of grip aperture in-flight was remarkably insensitive to the Ebbinghaus illusion, in which a target disc surrounded by smaller circles appears to be larger than the same disc surrounded by larger circles. In short, maximum grip aperture was scaled to the real (not the apparent) size of the target disc.

This initial demonstration that grasping is refractory to size-contrast illusions triggered a good deal of interest among researchers studying vision and motor control. Many investigators have replicated the dissociation between perception and action, while others have not (for review, see Goodale, 2008). Needless to say, the fact that actions such as grasping *are* sometimes sensitive to illusory displays does not refute the idea of two visual systems, which is based securely on a large body of evidence ranging from neuroimaging to neurophysiology. Indeed, in the light of our earlier discussion, one should not be surprised that perception can affect our motor behaviour. The real surprise, at least for traditional monolithic accounts of vision, is that there are numerous unassailable instances in which visually guided action is genuinely unaffected by perceptual illusions. Nevertheless, if the perception/action model is to be credible as an explanation of those instances where action is immune to visual illusions, it also has to be able to offer alternative accounts of why it is that sometimes action is *not* immune to illusory distortions.

5.4.2. Why would illusions sometimes affect action?

5.4.2.1. Motor factors

In thinking about this experimental literature, it is important to note first that not all experiments that appear to show an effect of perceptual illusions on action are truly doing so. Once more a major problem arises from the impurity of the measures that are used in the laboratory, in this case to assay the visual calibration of grasp kinematics during an act of prehension. The hand does indeed open more widely for larger than for smaller objects, other things being equal; but other things are not always equal. The size of one's anticipatory hand grip is not a pure and unadulterated measure of visuomotor calibration. One notable factor that appears to be at work in the case of experiments using the Ebbinghaus display is the very presence of neighbouring stimulus items when grasping movements are made. The problem is that these stimuli (i.e. the annulus of circles that surround the target disc in these experiments) may influence the movements that are made for purely *non-perceptual* reasons. One important factor at work here is that the visuomotor system appears to treat these flanking stimuli as potential obstacles to the grasping movement (Haffenden and Goodale, 2000; Haffenden *et al.*, 2001; Gilster *et al.*, 2006). Recent experiments by de Grave *et al.* (2005), for example, have shown that simply shifting the location of the individual circles within the surrounding annulus can affect maximum grip aperture, presumably because the fingers would be more likely to 'collide' with the circles in some positions than in others. If the direction of this purely *visuomotor* effect on grip aperture coincides with what would be expected from the perceptual illusion, then the investigator may well conclude erroneously that the action programming is sensitive to the illusion.

Grip aperture may be affected by such 'obstacle avoidance' behaviour in the case of the Muller-Lyer illusion as well (Biegstraaten *et al.*, 2007). These authors contrasted peak grip aperture, the standard measure of visual guidance in size-illusion experiments, with an alternative measure of size processing, namely the velocity of grip closure just before contact. Biegstraaten and her colleagues suggest that the latter measure may provide a purer assay of vision for action in the size domain than grip aperture. They found that when subjects grasped a bar placed on the shaft of a Muller-Lyer figure, the figure influenced peak grip aperture to some degree (as others have found), but did not influence the velocity of grip closure as one would expect if size processing was truly affected by the illusion. The authors conclude that there is no reason to believe that perceived size guides the way that we reach and grasp an object.

Independent studies have confirmed that the proximity of potential obstacles has a systematic effect on grip size during reaching, not only in healthy subjects (Mon-Williams *et al.*, 2001) but in patient D.F. as well (Rice *et al.*, 2006). This latter fact suggests that the dorsal stream, which is functionally intact in D.F. (James *et al.*, 2003) governs these obstacle-avoidance behaviours. This inference is strongly supported by the observation by Schindler and colleagues (2004) that patients with dorsal-stream damage fail completely to take into account the positions of potential obstacles in programming the trajectory of target-directed movements (Schindler *et al.*, 2004). It is worth noting that in other pictorial illusions, such as the Ponzo or Diagonal illusions, where the presence of potential 'obstacles' is less of a problem, investigators have typically found that grip aperture is quite immune to the effects of the illusory display (e.g. Brenner and Smeets, 1996; Jackson and Shaw, 2000; Stöttinger and Perner, 2006).

5.4.2.2. Equating attention for perception and action

Even so, some authors have argued that the perceptual tasks and the action tasks in many of these experiments have not been adequately matched for attentional demands, and that when such demands are matched across both kinds of tasks, grasping can be shown to be as sensitive to size-contrast illusions as psychophysical judgements (e.g. Franz *et al.*, 2000). Although this explanation, at least on the face of it, seems reasonable, it cannot explain why Aglioti *et al.* (1995) and Haffenden and Goodale (1998) found that when the relative sizes of the two target objects in the Ebbinghaus display were adjusted so that they appeared to be perceptually identical, the grip aperture that participants used to pick up the two targets continued to reflect the physical difference in their size.

Franz and colleagues' attentional explanation also cannot explain the results of a recent study by Ganel and colleagues that used a version of the Ponzo illusion in which a real difference in size was pitted against a perceived difference in size in the opposite direction (Ganel *et al.*, 2008b). In the typical Ponzo illusion, when two objects of equal size are presented at different ends of the display, the object placed at the converging end is usually perceived as longer than the one presented at the diverging end. In Ganel *et al.*'s experiment, however, the two target objects were always different in length. On each trial, participants were instructed to pick up either the shorter target objects or the longer one. Critically, on a large subset of trials, the target that was perceived to be the longer one was actually physically shorter (see Fig. 5.2). This meant that on those trials, when participants picked up the object they perceived to be the shorter of the two, they were actually picking up the longer one (and vice versa). Nevertheless, as Fig. 5.3 shows, even though participants believed that the shorter object was

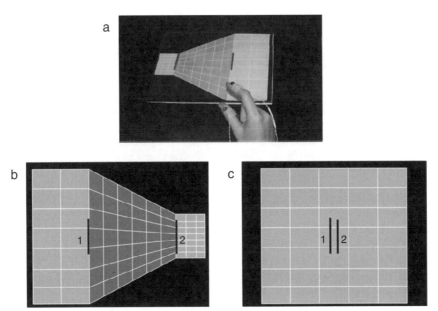

Fig. 5.2 The experiment of Ganel and colleagues (2008b). (a) Subjects were asked to grasp one of two objects presented on a background board, which (despite its 3-D appearance in this picture) lay flat on the table. The distance between the fingers was measured throughout the grasping action by means of infra-red markers attached to each participant's index finger and thumb. (b) The arrangement of objects on critical incongruent trials, in which real length and perceived length were pitted against one another. In this example, object 1 is typically perceived as shorter than object 2 because of the illusory context, although it is actually longer. (c) The real difference in size becomes apparent when the two objects are placed next to one another on a non-illusory control background. Figure reproduced from Ganel et al. (2008b), with permission.

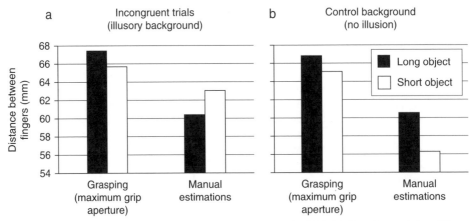

Fig. 5.3 Results of the experiment by Ganel and colleagues (2008b). (a) Experimental data (illusory background). Subjects opened their handgrip appropriately for the true length while *grasping* the objects (left), despite the fact that they judged the shorter object as longer and vice-versa (right) when making *manual estimates* of length. (b) Control data (plain background). Subjects now opened their handgrip appropriately in both the grasping and perceptual estimation tasks.
Figure reproduced from Ganel et al. (2008b), with permission.

the longer one (or vice versa), the in-flight aperture between the finger and thumb of their grasping hand reflected the real, not the illusory size of the target objects. In other words, on the same trials in which participants erroneously decided that one object was the longer (or shorter) of the two, the anticipatory opening between their fingers reflected the real direction and magnitude of size differences between the two objects. When, in a separate experiment, participants were asked to estimate the size of the objects by opening their index finger and thumb a matching amount, their manual estimates now reflected the illusory not the real difference in size between the target objects. Across the two experiments then, the real and apparent differences in the size of the objects had opposite effects on action (grasping) and perception (manual estimations). Overall, these results underscore once more the profound difference in the way visual information is transformed for action and for perception. Importantly too, the results are difficult to reconcile with any argument suggesting that grip aperture is sensitive to illusions, and that the absence of an effect found in many studies is simply a consequence of differences in the task demands (Franz *et al.*, 2000).

5.4.2.3. Temporal factors

According to our two visual systems model, vision for action works only in real time and is not normally engaged unless the target object is visible during the programming phase, that is when bottom-up visual information is being converted into the appropriate motor commands. When there is a delay between stimulus offset and the initiation of the grasping movement, the programming of the grip would be driven by a memory of the target object that was derived originally from a perceptual representation of the scene, created moments earlier by mechanisms in the ventral stream (Goodale *et al.*, 1994a; Fischer, 2001; Hu *et al.*, 1999). Striking support for such a restriction of dorsal-stream coding to the 'here and now' was reported by Goodale *et al.* (1994a) in a study of patient D.F., who has visual form agnosia due to ventral-stream damage (see section 5.2.1 above). Subjects were shown an object, whose size varied from trial to trial, which was then withdrawn. After five seconds they were asked to make a 'pantomimed' grasping movement, as if the object were still present. Healthy subjects still scaled their grip size reliably in proportion to the size of the object they had been shown. D.F., in sharp contrast, showed no such scaling, despite of course tailoring her grip perfectly to the size of an object during normal 'real-time' grasping. Unlike normal subjects, D.F. was apparently quite unable to use a working-memory based representation of the object's geometry to guide her grasping actions, presumably because she had not *perceived* that geometry in the first place.

This 'here and now' property of dorsal-stream visual coding clearly implies that visually guided actions could only ever be immune to visual illusions when made directly to a currently visible object. In contrast we would predict that memory-guided grasping *would* be affected by the illusory display, because the stored information about the target's dimensions would reflect the earlier perception of the illusion. As it turns out, a range of studies has shown that this is exactly the case (Gentilucci *et al.*, 1996; Hu and Goodale, 2000; Westwood and Goodale, 2003; Westwood *et al.*, 2000). These findings not only confirm the dissociation between perception and action, but also provide strong support for the idea that the dorsal 'action' stream operates only in real time (while actions that are driven by remembered targets are dependent on earlier ventral-stream processing). It is worth noting that these results could not have been predicted, nor are they easily explained, by alternative accounts that are predicated on a single visual representation that drives both perception and action.

5.4.2.4. The locus of the illusion

Less obviously, perhaps, our model does not predict that actions demonstrably driven by the dorsal stream will be immune to *all* visual illusions. Dyde and Milner (2002) pointed out that illusions which arise from early visual cortical areas, before the two streams diverge, should affect both perceptual judgements and the calibration of actions, whereas illusions that arise during later stages of processing within the ventral stream should affect only perception. To test this idea, they selected two

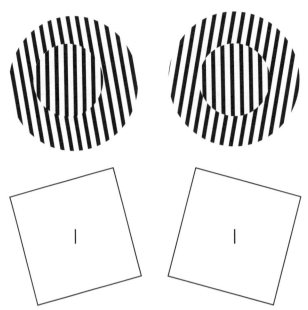

Fig. 5.4 Two illusions of visual orientation. The simultaneous tilt illusion (STI, top) is thought to be caused by local interactions between neurons sensitive to slightly different orientations lying within neighbouring columns of the primary visual cortex. The rod-and-frame illusion (RFI, bottom), in contrast, appears to have a 'higher-level' locus, bringing about a large-scale recalibration of the spatial frame of reference. It has been found that the RFI does not cause an illusory distortion of the visuomotor act of 'posting', presumably because it affects processing only within the ventral stream. The STI, however, affects both perception and action equally, presumably because its 'early' locus results in a distortion of the visual input to both ventral and dorsal streams.

illusions of orientation, equally powerful in their effects but very different in their likely neural origins. They chose the simultaneous tilt illusion (STI: see Fig. 5.4, top), specifically because it is thought to be generated through local neuronal interactions in early cortical visual areas V1 and/or V2 (Morgan and Casco, 1990). They contrasted this with the rod-and-frame illusion (RFI: see Fig. 5.4, bottom), because this illusion specifically could not be explained by such local interactions within retinotopic areas, since it involves distant interactions between a very large frame and a rod located centrally within that frame (e.g. Di Lorenzo and Rock, 1982). In other words the RFI is likely to arise much later, at some stage of the perceptual system where spatially remote effects can operate. As predicted, Dyde and Milner found that the STI affected action and perception equally, whereas the RFI affected only perception.[3]

Another illusion thought to arise at an early stage of the cortical visual system is the Poggendorf illusion (e.g. Morgan, 1999), and this illusion, like the STI, also gives rise to illusory effects on action as well as on perceptual judgements (see chapter by Melmoth *et al.*, Chapter 6). Findings like these illustrate the potential pitfalls that can beset investigators attempting to demonstrate (or not) a dissociation between perception and action using visual illusions. It is an essential prerequisite to consider where in the brain a given illusion is likely to arise.

---

[3] Crajé, van der Kamp and Steenbergen (2008) have recently reported that the RFI directly influences the type of grip (thumb-right versus thumb-left) that is selected in a grasping task (see section 5.2.2 above). This finding supports our assumption that the RFI is mediated by ventral-stream mechanisms.

5.4.2.5. The nature of the action

Another less obvious potential pitfall is related not to the selection of the display but rather to the nature of the actual movements that are required to perform the task. Not all movements will be mediated by the 'encapsulated' visuomotor networks in the dorsal stream. The more unpractised and novel the action, the more likely it is to require a good deal of cognitive supervision and thereby to be influenced by perceptual processing. The first time you use chopsticks, for example, you are vividly aware of what you are doing and you monitor your movements quite consciously, something you do not do when using your fingers, or even a fork, to pick up food. Presumably, this conscious monitoring of unpractised movements depends upon information provided by the perceptual networks in the ventral stream. As a consequence, ventral-stream processing can intrude into the visual guidance of these movements (for related discussions, see van der Kamp *et al.*, 2008; Milner and Goodale, 2008). Once the action is well-practised and becomes automatized, however, it seems that control of the constituent movements is passed to visuomotor networks in the dorsal stream, which then play the dominant visual role (for recent fMRI evidence in support of this conceptualization, see Grol *et al.*, 2006). One might predict therefore that if awkward or unfamiliar hand postures are used to grasp a target object, grip aperture would now be sensitive to pictorial illusions. Gonzalez *et al.* (2008) explored this possibility by directly comparing the sensitivity of skilled versus awkward grasping movements, directed at the same targets presented against the same backdrop of a Ponzo illusion, predicting that the skilled but not the unskilled actions would escape the effects of the illusion. Some subjects were required to use a normal precision grip (with the thumb and index finger), while other subjects used a much more awkward grip (with the thumb and ring finger). The results were clear and unambiguous. Even though the illusion had no effect on grip scaling in subjects who used a precision grasp, it had a large and significant effect on grip scaling in the subjects who used an awkward grasp. This result provides some confirmation of the idea that awkward actions, which require the use of more deliberate cognitive control, are more likely to rely on the same perceptual processing participants use to make conscious judgments about the size of objects in illusory displays. Interestingly, after three days of practice with the awkward grasp, grip scaling became no longer sensitive to the illusion, presumably because the action had become more automatized and thus controlled by the dorsal stream.

These results suggest strongly that in experiments designed to investigate possible differences between vision for action and vision for perception, one should be careful to ensure that the recording methods used to measure the actions do not interfere with the 'automaticity' of the constituent movements. It may be no accident that those laboratories where effects of pictorial illusions on grip scaling have been regularly reported have used quite intrusive recording devices to measure grip aperture (e.g. Franz *et al.*, 2000; 2003; cf. also Radoeva *et al.*, 2005). It is notable that the interpretations favoured by Franz and colleagues, which infer a common visual foundation for both perception and action, are quite unable to accommodate the results of Gonzalez and colleagues (2008). Other experiments by Gonzalez *et al.* (2006) have shown that precision grasping with the right hand is much more resistant to the effects of pictorial illusions such as the Ebbinghaus and Ponzo than precision grasping with the left hand. This again suggests that skill is a major factor in determining whether or not an action will escape the influence of perceptual illusions.[4]

Taken together, these findings highlight the importance of paying close attention to the nature of the task and the nature of the required response when using visual illusions to tease apart the workings of vision for action and vision for perception. Only highly practised actions with the right hand operating in real time and directed at visible targets presented in the context of high-level illusions are likely

---

[4] It should be mentioned, however, that there are other factors at work as well. It turns out that left-handers show a similar right-hand advantage. That is, their right- but not their left-hand grasping movements are immune to the effects of illusions. This latter finding suggests that there may be a special relationship between the left hemisphere and the right hand for the visuomotor control of precision grasping (Gonzalez *et al.* 2006).

to escape the intrusion of ventral-stream perceptual control. Only under these conditions will the specialized role of the dorsal stream in visuomotor control be fully revealed.

5.4.3. The coding of visual information for action

There is recent evidence that the way in which dorsal-stream mechanisms compute the size of goal objects for action does not obey the same fundamental psychophysical principles that are classically known to govern perception (Ganel *et al.*, 2008a). It turns out that when people pick up objects that vary in length, they do not exhibit the typical increase in their just noticeable difference (JND) as the size of the objects increases. Instead, the JND remains constant over a broad range of object sizes. Of course, when the same individuals are asked to make perceptual judgements of these objects, the JND increases with size just as Weber's Law (Baird and Noma, 1978) predicts it should. This would suggest that the computation of absolute size by the dorsal stream is not subject to the familiar non-linear transformations that characterize perception and is instead linked in a fundamental way to the actual size of the object.

Although all these findings are consistent with the idea that visually guided action and visual perception make use of different metrics and frames of reference, there is another account that can also handle the difference in sensitivity to size-contrast illusions, as well as this recent demonstration that grasping is refractory to Weber's Law. According to this explanation, put forward by Smeets and Brenner (1999; 2001), the trajectories of the two digits in a precision grasp are programmed independently with respect to the goal object. In other words, the visuomotor system does not compute the *size* of the object but instead computes the two locations on the surface of object where the finger and thumb will be placed. Thus, because size is irrelevant to the planning of these trajectories, the size-contrast illusion has no effect on grip aperture, the scaling of which is simply an epiphenomenon of the independent finger trajectories. Through similar logic, their account can also handle the finding that JNDs for grasping do not increase with object size.

Although Smeets and Brenner's account has been challenged (Mon-Williams and Tresilian, 2001), it has to be acknowledged that their digit-control model offers a parsimonious explanation for the lack of an effect of illusions on grasping and the apparent violation of Weber's Law. Nevertheless, there are some observations that cannot be accommodated by their model. For example, as discussed earlier, if a delay is introduced between viewing the target and initiating the grasp, the scaling of the anticipatory grip aperture is much more likely to be sensitive to size-contrast illusions (Westwood *et al.*, 2000; Westwood and Goodale, 2003; Fischer, 2001; Hu and Goodale, 2000). Similarly, delayed grasping also obeys Weber's Law; i.e. now the JNDs for grasping increase with object size just as they do for perceptual judgements (Ganel *et al.*, 2008a). These results cannot be explained by the Smeets and Brenner model without conceding that (with delay) grip-scaling is no longer a consequence of programming individual digit trajectories, but reflects instead the perceived size of the target object. Similarly, their model cannot easily explain why grip scaling is sensitive to illusions when people use unpractised finger postures and/or their left hand. Smeets and Brenner would have to argue that individual control over the digits occurs only after practice.

It is fair to say that at this point the difference between a modified Smeets and Brenner model and our own begins to blur. Both accounts posit that real-time control of skilled grasping depends on visuomotor transformations that are quite distinct from those involved in the control of delayed or unpractised grasping movements. The difference in the two accounts turns on the precise nature of the control exercised over skilled movements performed in real time. The important point for present purposes is that even if Smeets and Brenner are correct that the trajectories of the individual digits are programmed individually on the basis of spatial information that ignores the size of the object, this would not obviate the idea of two visual systems—one for perceiving the world and one for controlling our movements in that world. Indeed, the virtue of the two-visual-systems proposal is that it accounts not only for the dissociations outlined above between the control of action and psychophysical report in normal observers in a number of different settings, but it also accounts for a broad range of neuropsychological, neurophysiological, and neuroimaging data. To take just one example, even a modified version of the Smeets and Brenner model cannot easily account for the observation discussed earlier (section 5.3.1) that D.F. can use action-related information about object size (presumably from her intact dorsal stream) to improve her performance when asked to make judgments regarding the length of an object that she is about to pick up (Schenk and Milner, 2006).

A more general point implicit in the above discussions merits explicit consideration here: the question as to what parts of the visual array are analysed by each system. In our initial writings we over-simplified the contrast between the two systems by implying that the dorsal stream is concerned only with processing the target of an action, while arguing that the ventral stream takes obligatory account of the spatial context in which the target is embedded. Even a brief reflection on the nature of visuo-motor control, however, suffices to establish that this cannot be correct. First, we know from the long history of the topic that online visual feedback from the hand is an important factor in the control of reaching and grasping (Jeannerod 1988; 1997). This visual information has to be processed some-where, with the dorsal stream being the obvious candidate. Second, our actions typically do not take place in an empty space, where the only visible external object (other than perhaps a fixation point) is the target of our action. (A Martian might be excused for thinking that this was the case, given the impoverished arrays used in 99% of experimental studies on reaching and grasping in psychology and neuroscience.) Our actions need to take other, non-target, objects into account, and again the dorsal stream is the obvious candidate to take on this role.

As already mentioned, there is good empirical evidence now for the role of the dorsal stream in the guidance of our reaches with respect to non-target objects in the immediate environment. Thus the patients I.G. and A.T. with bilateral optic ataxia both show a total abolition of the normal lawful shifts in reach trajectory that are associated with shifts in location of a left or right non-target object that could pose the risk of collision (Schindler *et al.*, 2004). In a recent study we tested a patient with unilateral left parietal damage (M.H.), who shows a rare pattern of optic ataxia in which only pointing with his right arm to targets in the right visual field is impaired. Strikingly, M.H. shows a highly selective deficit on Schindler *et al.*'s task—only ignoring potential obstacles on his right, and only doing that when he is reaching with his right hand (Rice *et al.*, 2008). This identical pattern of deficits in pointing and obstacle avoidance suggests that the two may both be mediated by the same dorsal-stream subsystem. A nice further parallel with the processing of visual target information for pointing is provided by the observation that patient M.H. shows quite normal obstacle avoidance behaviour with respect to the right-side object when tested in a delayed version of the reaching task (Rice *et al.*, 2008). Presumably, just as in delayed pointing or grasping, the ventral stream is recruited to code the spatial array in readiness for making the delayed reach (see section 5.5 below), enabling M.H. to perform normally.

In contrast to these deficits after dorsal stream damage, most spatial neglect patients tested in a similar obstacle avoidance task show no impairment at all, despite failing to take account of the left object when asked to make an explicit bisection response between the two objects (McIntosh *et al.*, 2004b). Likewise patients D.F. and S.B. with visual form agnosia both show obstacle avoidance behaviour within the normal range (Rice *et al.*, 2006). Furthermore, Striemer *et al.* (2009) have shown recently that a patient with a dense hemianopia following an occipital lesion could avoid obstacles placed in his blind field, even though he never reported seeing these obstacles. This patient, in other words, showed clear evidence of 'blindsight for obstacles' (rather like the famous monkey 'Helen', studied by Humphrey, 1974). We have argued that most blindsight phenomena may be explicable on the basis that while both visual streams receive inputs from primary visual cortex (V1), the dorsal stream also receives inputs through a separate subcortical route that bypasses V1 (Milner and Goodale, 1995). Thus the damaged V1 in Striemer *et al.*'s patient would have prevented the obstacles from reaching visual awareness via the ventral stream, but not from reaching the dorsal-stream mechanisms that control obstacle avoidance.

Taken together, this body of data argues strongly that the processing of non-target objects that might pose a threat of collision depends heavily on dorsal stream circuitry. At the same time however, it must be recognized that just as in the processing of visuomotor *targets*, the ventral stream can play a role as well, and not only when a delayed response is being made. The ventral stream's role may assume particular importance when the potential obstacles need to be analysed for their semantic or material properties, such as their fragility or noxiousness. Under such circumstances, the subtle adjustments to reach and grasp parameters that appear to be mediated by the dorsal stream are overshadowed by gross diversions of the reaching hand and a slowing of the movements made (Mon-Williams et al., 2001).

Online visual processing of hand location during manual reaching and grasping is also likely to depend on dorsal-stream mechanisms, though direct evidence for this is not yet available from patients with optic ataxia. Nonetheless, neurons have been found in the reach-related region of the dorsal stream that code this feedback information in monkeys (Battaglia-Meyer et al., 2001). It will be of some interest to examine using fMRI whether in humans too the homologous reach-related region mediates the use of visual feedback from the hand during reaching. This could be done by comparing closed-loop reaching (i.e. under conditions when the hand is in view during reaching) with open-loop (when the hand is not visible).

In summary, then, although both streams need to focus on a selected target object in performing their primary visual roles, neither does this to the exclusion of other visual information present on the retina. The ways in which non-target information is dealt with, however, are qualitatively different in the two cases. In the case of the ventral stream, the visual coding of the target object is *itself* inherently scene-based—that is its metrics are fundamentally determined by the surrounding array. In the case of the dorsal stream this is not so: indeed the coding of the target has to be as far as possible absolute, and needs to be referred to an egocentric rather than a scene-based framework. Non-target visual information needs to impact dorsal stream processing dynamically, thereby influencing the moment-to-moment kinematics of the action. It seems likely that this happens without the visual coding of target information being itself modulated: in other words that both target and non-target information each modulates motor control directly and quasi-independently.

5.5. **Double dissociations**

The model we have developed was inspired by, and to some extent depends on, a set of partial or complete double dissociations that have been observed between patients like D.F., who has ventral stream damage, and patients with optic ataxia, who have damage to the dorsal stream. Such evidence, of course, is necessarily imperfect, due to such factors as imprecise correspondences between lesion locations and functional brain systems, and the effects of neural and behavioural compensation following brain damage.

5.5.1. **Optic ataxia and the dorsal stream**

An example of the former difficulty is that one of the patients most studied in recent research on optic ataxia has lesions that extend into neighbouring territory well beyond the dorsal stream, including large parts of area 39 in the inferior parietal lobule (patient A.T.: Jeannerod et al., 1994). Inevitably, this means that she does not have a fully intact perceptual apparatus, since the right inferior parietal region plays a critical role in integrating the various perceptual analyses carried out in the ventral stream (Jeannerod and Jacob, 2005; Milner and Goodale, 2006; Husain and Nachev, 2007). She does, however, have a rather complete disruption of the dorsal stream, as evidenced by the fact that her visuomotor difficulties extend beyond the classical domain of visually guided reaching, to include a disorder of grip formation during midline object grasping (Jeannerod et al., 1994). A similar disorder of grasping objects presented in central vision has been reported in other patients (Jeannerod, 1986; Jakobson et al., 1991). In contrast, patient IG (Milner et al., 2001; Rossetti et al., 2005) has a much more circumscribed lesion, largely restricted to occipitoparietal and posterior parietal areas, and her deficits are correspondingly less extensive. For example, although she has a severe impairment of grip calibration during real-time grasping for objects placed at five degrees eccentricity (Milner et al., 2001; 2003), anecdotal evidence (Rossetti, personal communication) suggests that this does not extend to central vision. It is even possible that I.G.'s poor grip scaling at peripheral locations is entirely secondary to her pronounced misreaching at such locations, as seems to be the case in the unilateral optic ataxia patient, M.H. (Cavina-Pratesi *et al.*, 2009).

Of course, 'optic ataxia' is defined traditionally (after Bálint, 1909) as pathologically inaccurate *reaching or pointing in visual space*, without any reference to other domains of possible visuomotor impairment. As mentioned above, nonetheless, associated problems in orienting and shaping the hand during grasping have often been documented in patients with optic ataxia (Perenin and Vighetto, 1988; Jeannerod *et al.*, 1994; Jakobson *et al.*, 1991; Milner *et al.*, 2001). Our assumption has been that these associated impairments are the result of damage to dorsal-stream areas concerned with the processing of shape, size, and orientation for the calibration of grasping, *as well as* those concerned with processing visual location for the control of reaching. Of course, it is entirely to be expected that some patients with optic ataxia will have subtotal dorsal-stream lesions, and that some aspects of visuomotor control will consequently remain unaffected.

It is now well established that different aspects of visuomotor control are concentrated in different parts of the superior occipito-parietal region: reaching in posterior parts, saccadic eye movements in the lateral intraparietal sulcus (LIP: Shikata *et al.*, 2008), and grasping in the anterior intraparietal region (Binkofski *et al.*, 1999; Culham *et al.*, 2003, 2006). In other words, we would predict that some patients with lesions located posteriorly within and around the intraparietal sulcus (IPS) will have visuomotor deficits that are limited to the visuospatial domain (Cavina-Pratesi *et al.*, 2009), whereas those whose lesions extend more anteriorly will have grasp-related deficits, with or without misreaching. Indeed Binkofski *et al.* (1998) described several patients with impaired grasping who were *not* diagnosed as having optic ataxia. The area of common damage in these patients with impaired grasping was located in the anterior region of the IPS. Clearly, patients like these, whose dorsal stream damage impairs the visual processing of geometric object properties for the purpose of guiding grasping, would permit far more suitable comparisons with D.F. than do patients with optic ataxia *sensu strictu*, whose visuomotor problems lie primarily in the spatial control of reaching movements. D.F.'s problem, after all, is visual *form* agnosia.

5.5.2. The need to compare like with like

Comparable caveats need to be made concerning patients who have ventral-stream damage. The lesions of patient D.F. (like the dorsal-stream lesions of the patients of Binkofski *et al.* [1998], but unlike patient A.T.) are very clearly subtotal, though there seems to be a functionally complete destruction of the area most concerned with object-form perception, area LO (James *et al.*, 2003). The evidence suggests that areas concerned with spatial processing in the ventral stream, including the parahippocampal place area, are somewhat spared in D.F. (Steeves, Humphrey, Culham, Menon, Milner, and Goodale, 2004).[5] Clearly, this being so, there will be only restricted possibilities for observing dissociations in the spatial domain between patient D.F. and patients with optic ataxia, in whom the primary diagnostic criterion is a failure to point or reach accurately in space towards visual targets. For the same reason, there will be only restricted possibilities for observing dissociations in the shape domain between patient D.F. and patients with pure optic ataxia.

Given these considerations one would not expect that strict and absolute double dissociations between the two kinds of patients would exist, and this incompleteness has been documented by Rossetti and colleagues (Rossetti *et al.*, 2003; Pisella *et al.*, 2006; Rossetti *et al.*, Chapter 10, this volume). It is a fundamental error, however, to infer, as Rossetti and colleagues do, that because visual form agnosia and optic ataxia do not mirror each other exactly, therefore the functions of the *dorsal and ventral streams* do not mirror each other. It is important to compare like with like when asking whether evidence from brain damaged patients supports or does not support our perception/action model.

---

[5] Even the so-called 'fusiform face area' (Kanwisher *et al.*, 1997) appears to be intact in D.F. Yet she does suffer from prosopagnosia, seemingly because of damage to more posterior ventral stream areas concerned with face processing (Steeves *et al.*, 2006; 2009).

Even within their own terms, Rossetti and colleagues overstate their case grossly, claiming as they do that *no* clear double dissociations have yet been established between D.F. and patients with optic ataxia. Indeed they have suggested that until additional testing is carried out one cannot exclude the possibility that the division of labour between the ventral and dorsal streams might be better characterized as a difference between central and peripheral vision rather than as a difference between vision for perception and vision for action. In truth the neuropsychological evidence in favour of the perception-action model is much stronger than Rossetti and his colleagues have presented it to be. Indeed, despite the difficulties, several convincing examples do exist of double dissociations between visual form agnosia and optic ataxia. For present purposes we summarize just two of them: the first in the spatial domain, and the second in the non-spatial domain. These dissociations co-exist with the undeniable difference in emphasis on central vs. peripheral coding between the two streams, but are perfectly consistent with it. We would contend, in fact, that this difference in visual field emphasis makes a great deal of sense within our perception-action framework.

5.5.3. Evidence for double dissociations

Rossetti and colleagues are correct, of course, in pointing out that the reaching deficits in most, though not all, optic ataxia patients are clearest for stimuli in the visual periphery. When these patients are tested in central vision, they often do much better, though even here they are not entirely normal (e.g. patient A.T.: see Milner *et al.*, 1999b). A critical point, however, is that when a delay is interposed between the presentation of the stimulus and the signal to respond, optic ataxic patients show a significant improvement in their pointing accuracy (Milner *et al.*, 1999b; Himmelbach and Karnath, 2005; Revol *et al.*, 2003). Milner *et al.* (1999b) argued that this improvement occurred because patient A.T. would now use a memory of the stimulus location, based on perceptual processing carried out at the time of stimulation by her relatively intact ventral stream (see section 5.4.2.3 above). In support of their interpretation, they cited experimental data on patient D.F. that demonstrated a directly opposite pattern of results (Milner *et al.*, 1999a). Thus when D.F. was asked to point towards peripheral targets in real time, her accuracy was excellent, but the dependence of that preserved ability on dorsal-stream processing was revealed by the fact that when a delay was introduced between the stimulus and response, D.F.'s pointing became highly inaccurate, with errors now more than twice as large as those of control subjects. Milner *et al.* (1999b) concluded that the delayed task required participation of ventral stream systems, which are compromised in D.F. but presumably largely spared in their patient with optic ataxia (A.T.). In a collaborative review, a similar argument, citing the identical evidence, was made later by Milner *et al.* (2003). Clearly, despite the contrary picture later painted by Pisella and colleagues (2006), these data show a very clear double dissociation of abilities and deficits following damage to the dorsal and ventral stream. The contrasting patterns of performance in the two patients are shown in Fig. 5.5, re-plotted for purposes of direct comparison.[6]

The above double dissociation between damage to the two streams refers to spatial processing in peripheral vision, but similar dissociations are just as evident in central vision, and in the domain of object processing. Thus, several patients with optic ataxia have been reported to show clear deficits in scaling their grip aperture to objects presented directly in central vision, even though whenever they were tested for their ability to perceive the dimensions of the same objects they did quite well (Binkofski *et al.*, 1998; Jakobson *et al.*, 1991; Jeannerod, 1986; Jeannerod *et al.*, 1994; Goodale and Wolf, 2009). In addition, Goodale *et al.* (1994b) showed that a patient with optic ataxia was unable to use vision to guide her fingers to stable grasp points on the circumference of irregularly shaped objects placed in central vision—even though she was well able to distinguish between them. Quite the opposite pattern of results was evident in the visual form agnosia patient D.F., who could grasp accurately but could not discriminate between the different target objects nor estimate their size manually

---

[6] As can be seen in Fig. 5.5, the delayed reaching accuracy of optic ataxia patients still does not improve to the level seen in healthy control subjects, perhaps because of attentional deficits in these patients. This fact does not detract from the striking double dissociation between the patient groups.

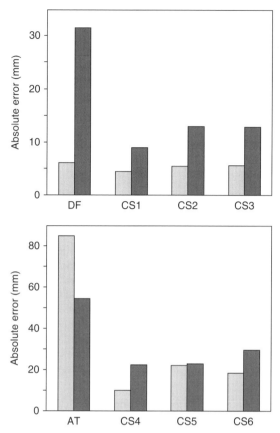

Fig. 5.5 Pointing to a peripheral visual target in a patient with visual form agnosia (D.F.), as contrasted with the performance of a patient with optic ataxia (patient A.T.). Data are presented in both an immediate pointing condition (light grey bars) and a delayed testing condition, in which the patient had to wait several seconds before responding (dark grey bars). The two graphs are taken from two separate experiments, each of which included three age-matched healthy controls (who were therefore rather younger in the D.F. experiment). The y-axis shows the resultant absolute errors in millimetres in both studies. The data are re-plotted from Milner *et al.* (1999a) and (1999b), respectively, with permission.

(Goodale *et al.*, 1991; 1994b; Carey *et al.*, 1996). It is particularly surprising that this second strong double dissociation (see Figure 5.6 for illustrative data), like that described above for pointing to peripheral targets, was overlooked in the recent paper by Pisella *et al.* (2006). Those authors even entitle their article 'No double dissociation between optic ataxia and visual agnosia'. The existence of these two clear double dissociations in the published literature belies that assertion.

It is worth reiterating that the dissociations predicted by the Milner/Goodale model are *dissociations between the results of damage to the dorsal stream and damage to the ventral stream*, not between two particular syndromes (optic ataxia and visual form agnosia). Such complete dissociations are seen clearly in experiments with non-human primates, where selective near-total destruction of one stream or the other can be made, as in the classic studies of 'inferior temporal cortex' and 'posterior parietal cortex' (e.g. Milner and Goodale, 2006, chapters 4 and 5). No such neat experiments can be replicated in humans; but if they could, then the theory would certainly imply a much more comprehensive set of double dissociations than we see between optic ataxia and visual form agnosia.

The existence of some clear double dissociations between optic ataxia and visual form agnosia (despite the fact that the former is primarily a visuospatial disorder and the latter primarily a disorder of shape processing) provide strong evidence in support of our proposal that the two visual streams

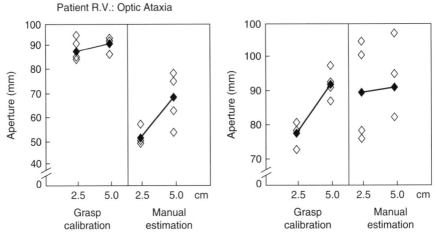

Fig. 5.6 Grip calibration in a patient with visual form agnosia (D.F.) as contrasted with the performance of a patient with optic ataxia (patient R.V.). For both experiments, the stimuli were presented centrally, and the patient was asked either to reach out and pick up the object using a finger-thumb precision grip (left panel in each case), or to mime its width using finger and thumb (right panel in each case). The y-axis shows the maximum separation of markers attached to the tips of forefinger and thumb during reaching to grasp, or at asymptote when the patient had arrived at her judgement, respectively. Data are plotted in each graph for rectangular blocks of 2.5 and 5.0 cm width respectively. Open shapes show data points from individual trials, and closed shapes the mean of these individual scores. The data for D.F. are re-plotted from Goodale et al. (1991), with permission.

are specialized for different ends, namely for perception and for action. However, this proposed division of labour is entirely compatible with the known differences in the extent to which the visual fields are represented in the two streams. In fact, these differences in coding can be regarded as an integral part of the functional specialization of the streams. Already at the level of primary visual cortex, there is a pronounced cortical magnification of central vision. This becomes exaggerated further in the ventral stream, while if anything somewhat reduced in the dorsal stream (for review, see Brown et al., 2005). This over-emphasis on central vision in the ventral stream is just what one might expect in a system whose job it is to construct a rich and detailed representation of the world. The ventral stream exploits the high resolution and wavelength selectivity that characterize processing in the fovea, and is much less concerned with the low-resolution information from the periphery. The ventral stream's need for a constant updating of such detailed information entails that gaze must move constantly from one part of the world to another, bringing the processing power of the fovea to bear on the stimulus array (Findlay and Gilchrist, 2003). Thus the role of peripheral stimuli in the ventral stream is a supporting one, helping only to provide a coarse contextual framework for perception. Matters are quite different in the dorsal stream, where the peripheral field is relatively well represented. Indeed some dorsal-stream areas, such as the parieto-occipital area (PO), show almost no cortical magnification at all, with a large amount of neural tissue devoted to processing inputs from the peripheral visual fields (Colby et al., 1988). This broad representation of the visual field in the dorsal pathway is presumably necessary for the efficient visual control of behaviour in which the effector (such as the hand) and the controlling stimuli (such as potential obstacles) are often present in the visual periphery.

As mentioned earlier in this section, optic ataxia patients show an improvement in reaching when a delay is imposed, suggesting that they are able to make use of a relatively intact ventral stream. Over time, these patients may well learn to rely more on the cognitive control offered by the ventral stream than on the depleted automatic control available from the impaired dorsal stream—even when acting in real time. In other words, in order to perform what used to be a skilled act, they may revert to the kind of *unskilled* strategy that we all use when beginning to master a novel visuomotor act (like using chopsticks: see section 5.4). Indeed, in a limiting case, if the dorsal stream were totally destroyed, the patient would have to rely entirely on whatever control the ventral stream could provide. However, this kind of compensation would necessarily be far more effective in central vision, since that enjoys a much stronger representation in the ventral than in the dorsal stream. This reasoning provides a possible explanation for some cases of central 'sparing' during real-time reaching in optic ataxia patients (e.g. Milner *et al.*, 1999b). Of course, when a delay is imposed on the response, so that the damaged dorsal stream can no longer be engaged at all, the ventral stream must necessarily deal with signals from the periphery as well. Despite its not being well-equipped to do this, the ventral stream may still be able to guide reaching to peripheral targets better than a badly damaged dorsal stream, thereby causing the typical improvement in pointing accuracy seen with delay. If, on the other hand, the ventral stream is already dealing with central targets even during real-time pointing, then we would not expect a delay to have any beneficial effect on accuracy, and indeed a slight deterioration has been reported (Milner *et al.*, 1999b).

5.6. **Concluding comments**

Our intention in writing this chapter was to revisit some of the issues and concepts that may not have been made fully clear in our original exposition of the model, or which have developed to some degree in subsequent versions of it. We hope that in doing so we have made our ideas more explicit, and thereby cast light upon some recent controversies in the area. At the same time, by specifying the ideas behind the model in more detail, we hope that we have helped to clear the way for more definitive experiments to be designed that will extend, and undoubtedly modify, the model in the future.

Acknowledgements

The authors are grateful to the Medical Research Council, Leverhulme Trust, and Canadian Institutes of Health Research for financial support, and to Thomas Schenk for his comments on an early draft of this manuscript.

References

Aglioti, S., Goodale, M.A., DeSouza, J.F.X. (1995). Size-contrast illusions deceive the eye but not the hand. *Current Biology*; 5: 679–85.

Baird, J.C. and Noma, E. (1978). *Fundamentals of scaling and psychophysics.* New York: Wiley.

Baizer, J.S., Ungerleider, L.G., and Desimone, R. (1991). Organization of visual inputs to the inferior temporal and posterior parietal cortex in macaques. *Journal of Neuroscience*; 11: 168–90.

Balint, R. (1909). Seelenlähmung des 'Schauens', optische Ataxie, räumliche Störung der Aufmerksamkeit. *Monatsschrift für Psychiatrie und Neurologie*; 25: 51–81.

Battaglia-Mayer, A., Ferraina, S., Genovesio, A., Marconi, B., Squatrito, S., Molinari, M., et al. (2001). Eye-hand coordination during reaching. II. An analysis of the relationships between visuomanual signals in parietal cortex and parieto-frontal association projections. *Cerebral Cortex*; 11: 528–44.

Berti, A. and Rizzolatti, G. (1992). Visual processing without awareness: evidence from unilateral neglect. *Journal of Cognitive Neuroscience*; 4: 345–51.

Biegstraaten, M., de Grave, D.D., Brenner, E., and Smeets, J.B. (2007). Grasping the Muller-Lyer illusion: not a change in perceived length. *Experimental Brain Research*; 176: 497–503.

Binkofski, F., Dohle, C., Posse, S., Stephan, K.M., Hefter, H., Seitz, R.J., et al. (1998). Human anterior intraparietal area subserves prehension. A combined lesion and functional MRI activation study. *Neurology*; 50: 1253–9.

Brenner, E. and Smeets, J.B.J. (1996). Size illusion influences how we lift but not how we grasp an object. *Experimental Brain Research*; 111: 473–6.

Brown, L.E., Halpert, B.A., and Goodale, M.A. (2005). Peripheral vision for perception and action. *Experimental Brain Research*; 165: 97–106.

Bruce, V., Green, P.R., and Georgeson, M.A. (2003). *Visual perception: physiology, psychology and ecology, Fourth edition.* Hove and London: Psychology Press.

Carey, D.P., Harvey, M., and Milner, A.D. (1996). Visuomotor sensitivity for shape and orientation in a patient with visual form agnosia. *Neuropsychologia*; 34: 329–38.

Cavina Pratesi, C., Ietswaart, M., Humphreys, G.W., and Milner, A.D. (2009). Impaired grasping in a patient with optic ataxia: Primary visuomotor deficit or secondary consequence of misreaching? *Neuropsychologia*; **48**: 226–234.

Clark, A. (2001). Visual experience and motor action: are the bonds too tight? *Philosophical Review*; **110**: 495–519.

—— (2007). What reaching teaches: consciousness, control, and the inner zombie. *British Journal for the Philosophy of Science*; **58**: 563–94.

—— (2009). Perception, action, and experience: unraveling the golden braid. *Neuropsychologia*; **47**: 1460–8.

Colby, C.L., Gattas, R., Olson, C.R., and Gross, C.G. (1988). Topographic organization of cortical afferents to extrastriate visual area PO in the macaque: a dual tracer study. *Journal of Comparative Neurology*; **269**: 392–413.

Crajé, C., van der Kamp, J., and Steenbergen, B. (2008). The effect of the 'rod-and-frame' illusion on grip planning in a sequential object manipulation task. *Experimental Brain Research*; **185**: 53–62.

de Grave, D.D., Biegstraaten, M., Smeets, J.B., and Brenner, E. (2005). Effects of the Ebbinghaus figure on grasping are not only due to misjudged size. *Experimental Brain Research*; **163**: 58–64.

Dehaene, S., Naccache, L., Le Clec'H, G., Koechlin, E., Mueller, M., Dehaene-Lambertz, G., et al. (1998). Imaging unconscious semantic priming. *Nature*; **395**: 597–600.

Dehaene, S., Changeux, J.P., Naccache, L., Sackur, J., and Sergent, C. (2006). Conscious, preconscious, and subliminal processing: a testable taxonomy. *Trends in Cognitive Sciences*; **10**: 204–11.

Desmurget, M., Epstein, C.M., Turner, R.S., Prablanc, C., Alexander, G.E., and Grafton, S.T. (1999). Role of the posterior parietal cortex in updating reaching movements to a visual target. *Nature Neuroscience*; **2**: 563–7.

Di Lorenzo, J.R. and Rock, I. (1982). The rod and frame effect as a function of righting of the frame. *Journal of Experimental Psychology Human Perception and Performance*; **8**: 536–46.

Dijkerman, H.C. and Milner, A.D. (1997). Copying without perceiving: motor imagery in visual form agnosia. *Neuroreport*; **8**: 729–32.

Dijkerman, H.C., McIntosh, R.D., Schindler, I., Nijboer, T.C.W., and Milner, A.D. (2009). Choosing between alternative wrist postures: action planning needs perception. *Neuropsychologia*; **47**: 1476–82.

Dyde, R.T. and Milner, A.D. (2002). Two illusions of perceived orientation: one fools all of the people some of the time, but the other fools all of the people all of the time. *Experimental Brain Research*; **144**: 518–27.

Findlay, J.M. and Gilchrist, I.D. (2003). *Active vision*. Oxford: Oxford University Press.

Fischer, M.H. (2001). How sensitive is hand transport to illusory context effects? *Experimental Brain Research*; **136**: 224–30.

Franz, V.H., Gegenfurtner, K.R., Bülthoff, H.H., and Fahle, M. (2000). Grasping visual illusions: no evidence for a dissociation between perception and action. *Psychological Science*; **11**: 20–5.

Franz, V.H., Bulthoff, H.H., and Fahle, M. (2003). Grasp effects of the Ebbinghaus illusion: obstacle avoidance is not the explanation. *Experimental Brain Research*; **149**: 470–7.

Ganel, T., Chajut, E., and Algom, D. (2008a). Visual coding for action violates fundamental psychophysical principles. *Current Biology*; **18**: R599–R601.

Ganel, T., Tanzer, M., and Goodale, M.A. (2008b). A double dissociation between action and perception in the context of visual illusions: opposite effects of real and illusory size. *Psychological Science*; **19**: 221–5.

Gentilucci, M., Chieffi, S., Daprati, E., Saetti, M.C., and Toni, I. (1996). Visual illusion and action. *Neuropsychologia*; **34**: 369–76.

Gilster, R., Kuhtz-Buschbeck, J.P., Wiesner, C.D., and Ferstl, R. (2006). Grasp effects of the Ebbinghaus illusion are ambiguous. *Experimental Brain Research*; **171**: 416–20.

Glover, S. (2004). Separate visual representations in the planning and control of action. *Behavioral and Brain Sciences*; **27**: 3–78.

Gonzalez, C.L.R., Ganel, T., and Goodale, M.A. (2006). Hemispheric specialization for the visual control of action is independent of handedness. *Journal of Neurophysiology*; **95**: 3496–501.

Gonzalez, C.L.R., Ganel, T., Whitwell, R.L., Morrissey, B., and Goodale, M.A. (2008). Practice makes perfect, but only with the right hand: Sensitivity to perceptual illusions with awkard grasps decreases with practice in the right but not the left hand. *Neuropsychologia*; **46**: 624–31.

Goodale, M.A. (2008). Action without perception in human vision. *Cognitive Neuropsychology*; **25**: 891–919.

—— (1992). Separate visual pathways for perception and action. *Trends in Neurosciences*; **15**: 20–5.

Goodale, M.A. and Milner, A.D. (2004). *Sight unseen: an exploration of conscious and unconscious vision*. Oxford: Oxford University Press.

Goodale, M.A. and Wolf, M.E. (2009). *Vision for action. In Computation, cognition, and Pylyshyn*, (eds Dedrick, D. and Trick, L.), pp. 101–38. Cambridge: MIT Press.

Goodale, M.A., Milner, A.D., Jakobson, L.S., and Carey, D.P. (1991). A neurological dissociation between perceiving objects and grasping them. *Nature*; **349**: 154–6.

Goodale, M.A., Jakobson, L.S., and Keillor, J.M. (1994). Differences in the visual control of pantomimed and natural grasping movements. *Neuropsychologia*; **32**: 1159–78.

Goodale, M.A., Meenan, J.P., Bülthoff, H.H., Nicolle, D.A., Murphy, K.J., and Racicot, C.I. (1994b). Separate neural pathways for the visual analysis of object shape in perception and prehension. *Current Biology*; **4**: 604–10.

Gréa, H., Pisella, L., Rossetti, Y., Desmurget, M., Tilikete, C., Grafton, S., et al. (2002). A lesion of the posterior parietal cortex disrupts on-line adjustments during aiming movements. *Neuropsychologia*; **40**: 2471–80.

Gregory, R.L. (1997). *Eye and brain: the psychology of seeing, Fifth edition*. Oxford: Oxford University Press.

Grol, M.J., de Lange, F.P., Verstraten, F.A., Passingham, R.E., and Toni, I. (2006). Cerebral changes during performance of overlearned arbitrary visuomotor associations. *Journal of Neuroscience*; **26**: 117–25.

Haffenden, A.M. and Goodale, M.A. (2000). Independent effects of pictorial displays on perception and action. *Vision Research*; **40**: 1597–607.

Haffenden, A.M., Schiff, K.C., and Goodale, M.A. (2001). The dissociation between perception and action in the Ebbinghaus illusion: nonillusory effects of pictorial cues on grasp. *Current Biology*; **11**: 177–81.

Himmelbach, M. and Karnath, H.O. (2005). Dorsal and ventral stream interaction: contributions from optic ataxia. *Journal of Cognitive Neuroscience*; **17**: 632–40.

Hu, Y., Eagleson, R., and Goodale, M.A. (1999). The effects of delay on the kinematics of grasping. *Experimental Brain Research*; **126**: 109–16.

Hu, Y. and Goodale, M.A. (2000). Grasping after a delay shifts size-scaling from absolute to relative metrics. *Journal of Cognitive Neuroscience*; **12**: 856–68.

Humphrey, N.K. (1974). Vision in a monkey without striate cortex: a case study. *Perception*; **3**: 241–55.

Husain, M. and Nachev, P. (2007). Space and the parietal cortex. *Trends in Cognitive Sciences*; **11**: 30–6.

Jackson, S.R. and Shaw, A. (2000). The Ponzo illusion affects grip-force but not grip-aperture scaling during prehension movements. *Journal of Experimental Psychology Human Perception and Performance*; **26**: 418–23.

Jakobson, L.S., Archibald, Y.M., Carey, D.P., and Goodale, M.A. (1991). A kinematic analysis of reaching and grasping movements in a patient recovering from optic ataxia. *Neuropsychologia*; **29**: 803–09.

Jakobson, L.S. and Goodale, M.A. (1991). Factors affecting higher-order movement planning: a kinematic analysis of human prehension. *Experimental Brain Research*; **86**: 199–208.

James, T.W., Culham, J., Humphrey, G.K., Milner, A.D., and Goodale, M.A. (2003). Ventral occipital lesions impair object recognition but not object-directed grasping: a fMRI study. *Brain*; **126**: 2463–75.

Jeannerod, M. (1984). The timing of natural prehension movements. *Journal of Motor Behavior*; **16**: 235–54.

—— (1986). The formation of finger grip during prehension: a cortically mediated visuomotor pattern. *Behavioural Brain Research*; **19**: 99–116.

—— (1988). *The neural and behavioural organization of goal-directed movements*. Oxford: Oxford University Press.

—— (1997). *The cognitive neuroscience of action*. Oxford: Blackwell.

Jeannerod, M. and Biguer, B. (1982). Visuomotor mechanisms in reaching within extrapersonal space. In *Analysis of visual behavior*, (eds Ingle, D.J., Goodale, M.A., and Mansfield, R.J.W.), pp. 387–409. Cambridge, MA: MIT Press.

Jeannerod, M. and Jacob, P. (2005). Visual cognition: a new look at the two-visual systems model. *Neuropsychologia*; **43**: 301–12.

Jeannerod, M., Decety, J., and Michel, F. (1994). Impairment of grasping movements following bilateral posterior parietal lesion. *Neuropsychologia*; **32**: 369–80.

Kanwisher, N., McDermott, J., and Chun, M.M. (1997). The fusiform face area: a module in human extrastriate cortex specialized for face perception. *Journal of Neuroscience*; **17**: 4302–11.

McIntosh, R.D., McClements, K.I., Schindler, I., Cassidy, T.P., Birchall, D., and Milner, A.D. (2004a). Avoidance of obstacles in the absence of visual awareness. *Proceedings of the Royal Society of London B*; **271**: 15–20.

McIntosh, R.D., McClements, K.I., Dijkerman, H.C., Birchall, D., and Milner, A.D. (2004b). Preserved obstacle avoidance during reaching in patients with left visual neglect. *Neuropsychologia*; **42**: 1107–17.

Merikle, P.M. and Joordens, S. (1997). Parallels between perception without attention and perception without awareness. *Consciousness and Cognition*; **6**: 219–36.

Milner, A.D. (2008). Conscious and unconscious visual processing in the human brain. In *Frontiers in consciousness research*, (eds Weiskrantz, L. and Davies, M.). Oxford: Oxford University Press.

Milner, A.D. and Goodale, M.A. (1993). Visual pathways to perception and action. *Progress in Brain Research*; **95**: 317–37.

—— (1995). *The visual brain in action*. Oxford: Oxford University Press.

—— (2006). *The visual brain in action, Second edition*. Oxford: Oxford University Press.

—— (2008). The two visual streams: in the right ballpark? *International Journal of Sport Psychology*; **39**: 131–5.

Milner, A.D., Perrett, D.I., Johnston, R.S., Benson, P.J., Jordan, T.R., Heeley, D.W., et al. (1991). Perception and action in visual form agnosia. *Brain*; **114**: 405–28.

Milner, A.D., Dijkerman, H.C., and Carey, D.P. (1999a). Visuospatial processing in a pure case of visual-form agnosia. In *The hippocampal and parietal foundations of spatial cognition*, (eds Burgess, N., Jeffery, K. J. and O'Keefe, J.), pp. 443–66. Oxford: Oxford University Press.

Milner, A.D., Paulignan, Y., Dijkerman, H.C., Michel, F., and Jeannerod, M. (1999b). A paradoxical improvement of optic ataxia with delay: new evidence for two separate neural systems for visual localization. *Proceedings of the Royal Society of London, B*; **266**: 2225–30.

Milner, A.D., Dijkerman, H.C., Pisella, L., McIntosh, R.D., Tilikete, C., Vighetto, A., et al. (2001). Grasping the past: delay can improve visuomotor performance. *Current Biology*; **11**: 1896–901.

Milner, A.D., Dijkerman, H.C., McIntosh, R.D., Rossetti, Y., and Pisella, L. (2003). Delayed reaching and grasping in patients with optic ataxia. *Progress in Brain Research*; **142**: 225–42.

Mon-Williams, M., Tresilian, J.R., Coppard, V.L., and Carson, R. G. (2001). The effect of obstacle position on reach-to-grasp movements. *Experimental Brain Research*; **137**: 497–501.

Morel, A. and Bullier, J. (1990). Anatomical segregation of two cortical visual pathways in the macaque monkey. *Visual Neuroscience*; **4**: 555–78.

Morgan, M.J. (1999). The Poggendorff illusion: a bias in the estimation of the orientation of virtual lines by second-stage filters. *Vision Research*; **39**: 2361–80.

Morgan, M.J. and Casco, C. (1990). Spatial filtering and spatial primitives in early vision: an explanation of the Zollner-Judd class of geometrical illusion. *Proceedings of the Royal Society of London B Biol Sci*; **242**: 1–10.

Murphy, K.J., Racicot, C.I., and Goodale, M.A. (1996). The use of visuomotor cues as a strategy for making perceptual judgments in a patient with visual form agnosia. *Neuropsychology*; **10**: 396–401.

Perenin, M.-T. and Vighetto, A. (1988). Optic ataxia: a specific disruption in visuomotor mechanisms. I. Different aspects of the deficit in reaching for objects. *Brain*; **111**: 643–74.

Pisella, L., Gréa, H., Tilikete, C., Vighetto, A., Desmurget, M., Rode, G., et al. (2000). An 'automatic pilot' for the hand in human posterior parietal cortex: toward reinterpreting optic ataxia. *Nature Neuroscience*; **3**: 729–36.

Pisella, L., Binkofski, F., Lasek, K., Toni, I., and Rossetti, Y. (2006). No double-dissociation between optic ataxia and visual agnosia: multiple sub-streams for multiple visuo-manual integrations. *Neuropsychologia*; **44**: 2734–48.

Radoeva, P.D., Cohen, J.D., Corballis, P.M., Lukovits, T.G., and Koleva, S.G. (2005). Hemispheric asymmetry in a dissociation between the visuomotor and visuoperceptual streams. *Neuropsychologia*; **43**: 1763–73.

Revol, P., Rossetti, Y., Vighetto, A., Rode, G., Boisson, D., and Pisella, L. (2003). Pointing errors in immediate and delayed conditions in unilateral optic ataxia. *Spatial Vision*; **16**: 347–64.

Rice, N.J., McIntosh, R.D., Schindler, I., Mon-Williams, M., Démonet, J.-F., and Milner, A.D. (2006). Intact automatic avoidance of obstacles in patients with visual form agnosia. *Experimental Brain Research*; **174**: 176–88.

Rice, N.J., Edwards, M.G., Schindler, I., Punt, T.D., McIntosh, R. D., Humphreys, G.W., et al. (2008). Delay improves the obstacle avoidance deficit in optic ataxia. *Neuropsychologia*; **46**: 1549–57.

Rosenbaum, D.A., Vaughan, J., Jorgensen, J., Barnes, H.J., and Stewart, E. (1993). Plans for object manipulation. In *Attention and performance XIV: synergies in experimental psychology, artificial intelligence, and cognitive neuroscience*, (eds Meyer, D.E. and Kornblum, S.), pp. 803–20. Cambridge, MA: MIT Press.

Rossetti, Y., Pisella, L., and Vighetto, A. (2003). Optic ataxia revisited: visually guided action versus immediate visuomotor control. *Experimental Brain Research*; **153**: 171–9.

Rossetti, Y., McIntosh, R.D., Revol, P., Pisella, L., Rode, G., Danckert, J., et al. (2005). Visually guided reaching: bilateral posterior parietal lesions cause a switch from fast visuomotor to slow cognitive control. *Neuropsychologia*; **43**: 162–77.

Schenk, T. (2006). An allocentric rather than perceptual deficit in patient *D.F. Nature Neuroscience*; **9**: 1369–70.

Schenk, T. and Milner, A.D. (2006). Concurrent visuomotor behaviour improves form discrimination in a patient with visual form agnosia. *European Journal of Neuroscience*; **24**: 1495–503.

Schenk, T., Schindler, I., McIntosh, R.D., and Milner, A.D. (2005). The use of visual feedback is independent of visual awareness: evidence from visual extinction. *Experimental Brain Research*; **167**: 95–102.

Schindler, I., Rice, N.J., McIntosh, R.D., Rossetti, Y., Vighetto, A., and Milner, A.D. (2004). Automatic avoidance of obstacles is a dorsal stream function: evidence from optic ataxia. *Nature Neuroscience*; **7**: 779–84.

Schweinberger, S.R. and Stief, V. (2001). Implicit perception in patients with visual neglect: lexical specificity in repetition priming. *Neuropsychologia*; **39**: 420–9.

Shikata, E., McNamara, A., Sprenger, A., Hamzei, F., Glauche, V., Büchel, C., et al. (2008). Localization of human intraparietal areas AIP, CIP, and LIP using surface orientation and saccadic eye movement tasks. *Human Brain Mapping*; **29**: 411–21.

Smeets, J.B. and Brenner, E. (1999). A new view on grasping. *Motor Control*; **3**: 237–71.

—— (2001). Independent movements of the digits in grasping. *Experimental Brain Research*; **139**: 92–100.

Steeves, J.K.E., Culham, J.C., Duchaine, B.C., Cavina Pratesi, C., Valyear, K.F., Schindler, I., et al. (2006). The fusiform face area is not sufficient for face recognition: evidence from a patient with dense prosopagnosia and no occipital face area. *Neuropsychologia*; **44**: 594–609.

Steeves, J., Dricot, L., Goltz, H.C., Sorger, B., Peters, J., Milner, A.D., Goodale, M.A., Goebel, R., and Rossion, B. (2009). Abnormal face identity coding in the middle fusiform gyrus of two brain-damaged prosopagnosic patients. *Neuropsychologia*; **74**: 2584–92.

Stöttinger, E. and Perner, J. (2006). Dissociating size representation for action and for conscious judgment: grasping visual illusions without apparent obstacles. *Consciousness and Cognition*; **15**: 269–84.

Striemer, C.L., Chapman, C.S., and Goodale, M.A. (2009). 'Real-time' obstacle avoidance in the absence of primary visual cortex. *Proceedings of the National Academy of Science*; **106**: 15996–6001.

Trevarthen, C.B. (1968). Two mechanisms of vision in primates. *Psychologische Forschung*; **31**: 299–337.

Ungerleider, L.G. and Mishkin, M. (1982). Two cortical visual systems. In *Analysis of visual behavior*, (eds Ingle, D.J. Goodale, M.A. and Mansfield, R.J.W.), pp. 549–86. Cambridge, MA: MIT Press.

van der Kamp, J., Rivas, F., van Doorn, H., and Savelsbergh, G. (2008). Ventral and dorsal contributions in visual anticipation in fast ball sports. *International Journal of Sport Psychology*; **39**: 100–30.

van Doorn, H., van der Kamp, J., and Savelsbergh, G.J.P. (2007). Grasping the Müller-Lyer illusion: the contributions of vision for perception in action. *Neuropsychologia*; **45**: 1939–47.

Wallhagen, M. (2007). Consciousness and action: does cognitive science support (mild) epiphenomenalism? *British Journal for the Philosophy of Science*; **58**: 539–61.

Weiskrantz, L. (1997). *Consciousness lost and found: a neuropsychological exploration*. Oxford: Oxford University Press.

Westwood, D.A. and Goodale, M.A. (2003). Perceptual illusion and the real-time control of action. *Spatial Vision*; **16**: 243–54.

Westwood, D.A., Heath, M., and Roy, E.A. (2000). The effect of a pictorial illusion on closed-loop and open-loop prehension. *Experimental Brain Research*; **134**: 456–63.

Young, M.P. (1992). Objective analysis of the topological organization of the primate cortical visual system. *Nature*; **358**: 152–5.

CHAPTER 6

Hermann Lotze's Theory of 'Local Sign': evidence from pointing responses in an illusory figure

Dean R. Melmoth, Marc S. Tibber, and Michael J. Morgan

Abstract

Hermann Lotze's Theory of 'Local Signs' (*Localzeichen*) proposed that our visual sense of the position of objects in the visual scene uses the same mechanism as that required to move the eyes and hands. An alternative is that perceptual and motor responses depend on different neural substrates. We have tested whether perceptual and motor 'pointing' responses are similarly affected by a well-known perceptual bias, the Pogendorff illusion. The two-stream hypothesis of visual perception (Goodale and Milner, 1992; Goodale et al., 1994; Milner and Goodale, 1995; Hu and Goodale, 2000) suggests that illusions will not affect motor responses since they are mediated by the dorsal stream which operates via egocentric (absolute) metrics, whilst the allocentric (relative) metrics used for perception by the ventral stream are systematically biased by such illusions. This prediction has received some support from size-contrast illusions, but pointing responses have received much less attention. We find that perceptual and motor pointing responses are significantly affected in the same direction by the Poggendorff effect, except that the motor biases are somewhat greater. Our results support Lotze's conjecture of a unified representation of spatial position for perception and action, rather than the two-stream model.

6.1. Introduction

Hermann Lotze (1817–1881) thought with unusual clarity about the encoding of spatial position in vision and the role of topographic maps (Morgan, 2003; 2008). An object in external space stimulates a specific position on the retina, but this is not sufficient in itself to explain the sense of visual direction; some method of making the information explicit is required. The same applies to topographic maps of spatial information in the cortex. Initially, Lotze proposed some special quality in each nerve fibre that encoded its spatial position (this was the original meaning of 'local sign'). Later, he changed his mind and proposed that special machinery could translate position in a topographic map into motor responses. We know that such neural machinery exists, because we can move our eyes effortlessly and rapidly to bring an object in peripheral vision onto the fovea. Lotze proposed that whatever mechanisms are involved in this also underlie our *perception* of visual direction.

Lotze's conjecture, and behavioural theories of perception in general, have not found much favour in modern neuroscience. The trend towards modularity has eclipsed efforts to find a common underlying mechanism for perception and action. The recently influential two-stream hypothesis of visual perception (Goodale and Milner, 1992; Goodale et al., 1994; Milner and Goodale, 1995; Hu and Goodale, 2000) has suggested that motor responses are associated with a reflexive, unconscious dorsal cortical stream of processing, while conscious perception is associated with a ventral stream. Evidence for this dissociation has come from visual illusions, which were predicted to affect perception, but not action. In particular, the hypothesis predicts that size-contrast illusions will not affect motor responses since they are mediated by the dorsal stream which operates via egocentric (absolute) metrics, while the allocentric (relative) metrics used for perception by the ventral stream are systematically biased by such illusions. Studies have revealed dissociations consistent with this hypothesis, whereby subjects make accurate motor responses to illusory stimuli, despite perceptual responses that are biased in accordance with the illusion (Aglioti et al., 1995; Haffenden and Goodale, 1998; Westwood et al., 2000a; 2000b; Haffenden et al., 2001; Servos et al., 2000; Mack et al., 1985). However, there are also reports of motor and perceptual responses being affected approximately equally by visual illusions (Franz et al., 2001; Gentilucci et al., 1996; Predebon, 2004; van Donkelaar, 1999; Daprati and Gentilucci, 1997; Franz, 2003; Franz et al., 2003; Elliott and Lee, 1995; Meegan et al., 2004; de Grave et al., 2004) which have been used to argue in favour of a single representation for both perceptual and motor responses (Franz et al., 2003).

In contrast to work on size illusions, little has been done on visual direction. Indeed, despite considerable recent progress in the understanding of basic visual processes such as colour and motion perception, we know surprisingly little about the mechanisms of basic visual geometry. Consider the very simple task of deciding whether a vertical line points at a dot or not; or to put this more formally, whether a dot is collinear with the points on a straight line. To make this into a task where we can measure accuracy, we require the observer to decide whether the dot is displaced clockwise or anticlockwise of the vertical line defined by the pointer, over a series of trials where the actual position of the dot relative to the line is varied. Observers perform this task with high accuracy. No matter what the separation of the tip of the line from the dot, observers can report reliably the direction of shift when the position of the dot is rotated +/− 1° from the vertical. They are similarly accurate when the line is horizontal, although less so with oblique lines.

If we had pencil and paper available we could decide whether a line and dot were collinear by the active process of *extrapolation*. But how does the visual system do the task, without making an overt movement? It might be thought that the task is the same as that of deciding whether a line or grating is tilted from the vertical, and that it could depend, therefore, on the oriented receptive fields in visual cortex described originally by Hubel and Wiesel (1959). However, there is a strong consensus that this cannot be the case. Accurate extrapolation can occur over distances much larger than receptive fields in V1. The fact that performance with widely separated targets is relatively unimpaired when patches of different spatial frequency (Toet, 1988), orientation (Kooi, 1991), colour (Kooi, 1991), or contrast polarity (Levi and Waugh, 1996; Morgan, 1991, Fig. 4.12) are used, or when irrelevant 'distracters' are placed between the targets (Morgan 1990) suggests that simple linear filters alone are not capable of carrying out the computation of extrapolation.

Visual extrapolation suffers from several well-documented biases, the most remarkable of which is the so-called 'Poggendorff Illusion' (Fig. 6.1). We wondered whether a motor extrapolation response would show a similar bias. The only study we are aware of that examined a motor version of the Poggendorff effect reported an approximately equal impact of the illusion upon both response modes (Predebon, 2004). However, the motor response in this experiment was not a natural ballistic pointing movement, but a form of manual estimation and was also performed open-loop (i.e. from memory without visual feedback). We used a task in which the observer performed a pointing response as rapidly as possible after stimulus onset, and we compared the dynamics of the response to those of pointing towards an explicit, non-illusory target.

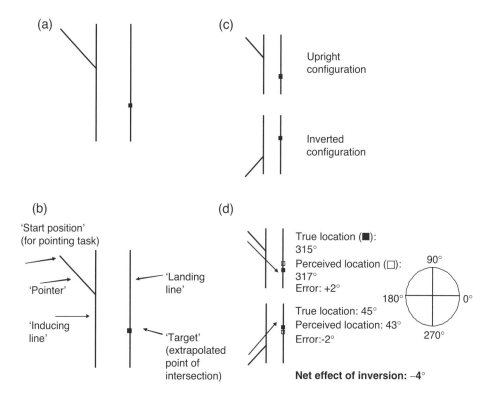

Fig. 6.1 (a): Experimental stimulus in upright configuration. The black dot shows the true point of intersection if the oblique pointer is extrapolated to meet the vertical landing line. The Poggendorff effect creates the illusion that the extrapolated intersection is too low. (b): Terminology used to describe each component of the stimulus. (c): The two configurations used in the experiments. (d): By presenting both upright and inverted stimuli and noting the difference between the two, it is possible to observe the net effect attributable to the illusion, irrespective of any inherent cross-condition bias.

6.2. Materials and methods

6.2.1. Subjects

Seven subjects with a median age of 28.2 years participated. All subjects were right-handed and had normal or corrected-to-normal vision. Procedures were in accordance with the Declaration of Helsinki and, apart from the authors, all subjects were naïve as to the purpose of the experiment.

6.2.2. Stimuli

Stimuli were presented on a vertically oriented Protouch 17-inch TFT flat-screen display, via a PC fitted with a VSG graphics card (Cambridge Research Systems Ltd., Rochester, UK) running custom-written scripts for MATLAB (MathWorks Ltd., Cambridge, UK). On-screen pixel size was 0.36 mm and average background luminance was 55 cd/m^2, while average luminance of the stimulus components was 130 cd/m^2. Inducing and landing lines measured 25.4 cm × 0.07 cm with a 7.3 cm separation in the parallel conditions. The oblique pointer was 5.1 cm long, angled at 315° or 45° relative to the landing line to top-down or bottom-up conditions, respectively. See Fig. 6.1 for details. A randomized angular jitter of +/− 5° was added to prevent stereotyped responses or learning effects and the on-screen position of the entire stimulus configuration was spatially jittered from trial to trial.

6.2.3. Procedure

Subjects were seated at a comfortable reaching distance from the screen (approximately 50 cm). For perceptual tasks, subjects initiated the measurement via their keyboard and the stimulus appeared. A small 8×8 pixel target marker was positioned randomly on the landing line below its true intersection with the extrapolated oblique pointer. Using the keyboard, subjects moved this on-screen marker to where they believed the intersection to be, at which point they pressed another key to log their response. The marker was then randomly re-positioned—this time *above* the true point of intersection—and another measurement was taken. The average of these two measurements was taken as the response for that trial and therefore each measurement consisted of two responses (one starting from below and one from above). Stimuli were presented randomly either upright or inverted (50% of trials each) and either with or without the inducing line present (50% of trials each) with five repeats of each condition, giving a total of 40 responses. Responses were not time-constrained.

For the motor task a small lightweight infra-red reflective marker was attached to the nail of the right index finger. At the beginning of a trial, a small 8×8 pixel starting point was displayed on the screen and subjects placed their fingertip on it. Its position was jittered from trial to trial, but it always marked the origin of the yet unseen pointer line. When the experimenter initiated the presentation, the stimulus appeared and subjects had to make a rapid ballistic movement, pointing to the extrapolated intersection of the pointer line and the landing line. Subjects were instructed to move as soon as the stimulus appeared, and the angle of the pointer was jittered around the 315°/45° angle to prevent stereotyped movements or pre-planning of trajectories. Pointing was closed-loop (i.e. under visual guidance, and no feedback was given regarding accuracy of responses). After the corresponding cue to begin, the pointing movements stimuli appeared onscreen for 750 ms, which provided enough time for subjects to complete their programmed movement, but meant the stimulus had disappeared before they could look back to the pointer to evaluate or adjust their finger position. For comparison to a simple pointing response without calibration, on half of trials the true point of intersection was marked explicitly with an 8×8 pixel cursor on the landing line and subjects simply pointed to it. Responses in trials without the explicit marker (i.e. when subjects had to extrapolate themselves) were measured relative to the average pointing position with the explicit marker in the corresponding condition. Again, stimuli were presented either upright or inverted. Thus, with both orientations; with and without the intersection marked; with and without the inducing line present; with five repeats for each condition, a total of 40 measurements were taken. Movements were recorded using Qualysis ProReflex (Sweden) motion capture cameras, with a resolution of >0.4 mm.

Subjects' responses (on-screen cursor position for perceptual task or finger-tip position for motor task) were converted to an angular errors relative to the true trajectory from start position to extrapolated intersection: 315° and 45° (plus jitter) for the upright and inverted configuration, respectively. See Fig. 6.1 for details.

6.3. Results

6.3.1. Effect of the Poggendorff illusion on perceptual judgements

Figures 6.2a and 6.2b shows mean biases in the perceptual task for the upright and inverted stimulus configuration respectively. Filled squares indicate the true extrapolated intersection; unfilled squares indicate average subject settings—distances are not to scale. Since the Poggendorff effect is an illusion of misalignment or misangulation (Hotopf and Hibberd, 1989; Ninio and O'Regan, 1999), we report the bias in degrees of angle relative to the true trajectory from the start position at the distal end of the pointer to its intersection with the landing line: 315° and 45° for the upright and inverted configurations, respectively (see Fig. 6.1c). This is to allow direct comparison with pointing trajectories. To ensure that any bias was not simply artefactual to a given orientation, stimuli were presented both upright and inverted. The 'net inversion effect' therefore gives the angular bias for the inverted configuration *relative to that for the upright configuration*, quantifying the Poggendorff effect independently of any underlying systematic bias (see Fig. 6.1d). Clearly, subjects succumbed to the

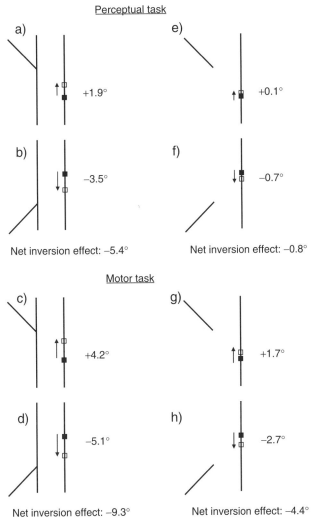

Perceptual task

a) +1.9°

b) −3.5°

Net inversion effect: −5.4°

e) +0.1°

f) −0.7°

Net inversion effect: −0.8°

Motor task

c) +4.2°

d) −5.1°

Net inversion effect: −9.3°

g) +1.7°

h) −2.7°

Net inversion effect: −4.4°

Fig. 6.2 Pictorial representations of the stimuli for each condition along with the true extrapolated intersection of the pointer and landing line (filled squares) and the mean subject response (unfilled squares). Distances are not to scale. Figs. 2a-d show upright and inverted stimulus configurations of the full Poggendorff stimulus for perceptual and motor (pointing) response modes.Figs. 2e-h show upright and inverted stimulus configuration for the 'pointer-and-landing-line-only' condition in which the Poggendorff inducing line (and thus the acute angle it forms with the pointer) is removed.

Poggendorff illusion, displaying average angular errors in the perceptual task of +1.9° and −3.5° for the upright and inverted stimulus configurations, respectively, i.e. a net inversion effect of −5.4°. The asymmetry of the biases in the two orientations shows that using only the upright stimulus configuration would produce an underestimation of the magnitude of the Poggendorff effect.

6.3.2. **Effect of the Poggendorff illusion on motor responses**

The Poggendorff effect was also manifest in motor responses—a closed-loop ballistic pointing task— with average angular trajectory errors of +4.2° and −5.1° for the upright and inverted configurations, respectively (Figs 6.2c and 6.2d), yielding a net inversion effect of −9.3°. Thus, surprisingly, motor response bias to the Poggendorff stimulus was actually *greater* than perceptual bias [$t_{(1,6)} = -4.05$, $p < 0.01$]. Figures 6.2e, 6.2f, 6.2g, and 6.2h reveal the source of this additional bias.

6.3.3. A motor-specific bias in the pointer-only condition

To determine baseline performance in the absence of the acute angle formed between inducing line and oblique pointer, which is the presumed origin of the Poggendorff illusion, stimuli were presented without the inducing line on half of the trials. Figures 6.2e and 6.2f show that in these 'pointer-only' conditions perceptual estimates of the extrapolated intersection were near veridical: +0.1° error for the upright stimulus and −0.7° for the inverted stimulus, giving a net inversion effect of just −0.8°. These very small perceptual biases were not significantly different from each other. Small perceptual biases known to operate on isolated and/or co-linear oblique lines include the Zehender effect, horizontal assimilation and vertical–horizontal extent illusions. However, for a stimulus consisting of an oblique line with a second vertical line, presented in a single orientation analogous to our 'inverted' configuration, Weintraub and Krantz (1971) reported a bias of just −0.8°. This is very close to our value of −0.7° for the corresponding condition. In contrast to perceptual responses, Figs 6.2g and 6.2h show that in the pointer-only conditions motor response biases were +1.7° and −2.7° for the upright and inverted configurations respectively, yielding a net inversion effect of −4.4°. This is substantially and significantly greater than the corresponding perceptual bias ($t_{(1,6)} = -5.82$, $p < 0.01$). Since this bias occurs without the Poggendorff-inducing parallel, we will refer to this bias as the 'landing line bias'.

Figure 6.3a summarizes mean net inversion effects for each condition, i.e. for motor and perceptual tasks, with and without the Poggendorff-inducing line. Figure 6.3b shows individual data. The diagonal line indicates equal magnitude of bias for motor and perceptual responses. The fact that all data points fall below this line shows that motor biases were greater than perceptual biases. The smaller magnitude of the landing line bias in the pointer-only condition compared to the full Poggendorff stimuli is clear from the relative location of the triangle and square symbols respectively. Net inversion effects were entered into a two-factor (response mode, stimulus type) analysis of variance which confirmed a significant effect of the Poggendorff-inducing line, with greater biases when the inducing line was present compared to 'pointer-only' conditions [$F_{(1,6)} = 27.1, p < 0.01$]; and a significant effect of response mode, with motor biases being greater than perceptual biases [$F_{(1,6)} = 33.1, p < 0.01$]. Analysis of standard deviations revealed that while motor responses were more variable than perceptual responses [$F_{(1,6)} = 100.4, p < 0.001$], the addition of the Poggendorff-inducing line did not affect standard deviations within each response mode [$F_{(1,6)} = 3.51$, n.s.], indicating that the Poggendorff effect systematically biased both response modes without increasing variability (Tibber et al., 2008).

6.3.4. A shared bias for motor and perceptual responses from the acute angle

Comparison of each pointer-only condition (Figs 6.2e, 6.2f, 6.2g, and 6.2h) with its corresponding full Poggendorff stimulus (Figs 6.2a, 6.2b, 6.2c, and 6.2d) shows that introducing the inducing line adds a fairly consistent 2–3° of additional bias on top of whatever landing line bias is already present in the pointer-only condition. Indeed, the magnitude of the bias difference between the pointer-only and full Poggendorff conditions was almost identical for both perceptual and motor tasks (−4.7° and −4.9°, respectively; $t_{(1,6)} = 0.1678$, n.s.), indicating that once the greater baseline landing line bias in motor responses for the pointer-only condition was taken into account, the subsequent effect of adding the Poggendorff inducing line was similar across response modes. Note that the difference in the net inversion effect of approximately 5° represents the sum of the upright and inverted differences of 2–3° shown in Fig. 6.2. This finding was supported further by the absence of any interaction between response mode and stimulus type in the ANOVA [$F_{(1,6)} = 0.033$, n.s.]. This common additional bias for motor and perceptual responses is consistent with a shared mechanism.

Figure 6.4 shows representative velocity profiles of pointing movements and average values for key kinematic measures, with and without the Poggendorff-inducing line and/or an explicit target.

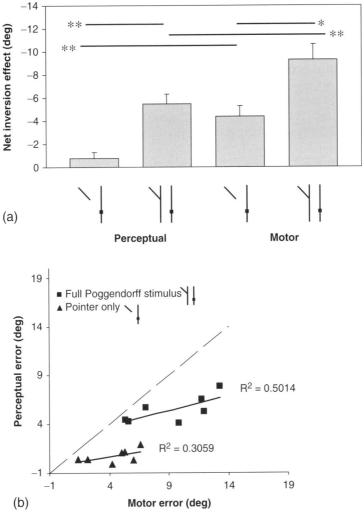

Fig. 6.3 (a): Mean net inversion effects (bias for inverted stimulus relative to bias to upright stimulus) for each response mode—perceptual or motor—and each stimulus condition—with and without Poggendorff inducing line. Note that y-axis increases negatively. The pictorial representations below are for illustrative purposes to clarify the condition, and show the upright configuration of the stimulus; the data in the bar chart depict the difference in bias between these upright configurations and their corresponding inverted configurations (see Figure 2). A two-factor ANOVA confirmed significant main effects of stimulus type whereby biases were larger with the Poggendorff inducing line than with just the pointer [F(1,8) = 227, p<0.0001] and of response mode, whereby biases were larger for motor responses than perceptual response [F(1,8) = 6.12, p<0.05]. (b): Net inversion effects for each subject. The diagonal line depicts equal bias for perceptual and motor responses. The fact that every subject falls below the line shows that motor biases were always greater.

Paired *t*-tests revealed few significant differences between inducer and no inducer conditions (when no target was present), indicating that the addition of the Poggendorff-inducing line had no effect upon kinematic measures of planning (e.g. latency of movement onset; peak velocity) or execution (e.g. movement time; length of deceleration phase). The single (highly) significant difference

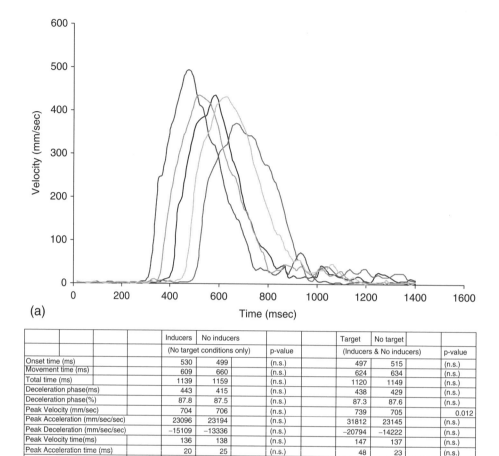

(a)

				Inducers	No inducers			Target	No target		
				(No target conditions only)		p-value		(Inducers & No inducers)		p-value	
Onset time (ms)				530	499	(n.s.)		497	515	(n.s.)	
Movement time (ms)				609	660	(n.s.)		624	634	(n.s.)	
Total time (ms)				1139	1159	(n.s.)		1120	1149	(n.s.)	
Deceleration phase(ms)				443	415	(n.s.)		438	429	(n.s.)	
Deceleration phase(%)				87.8	87.5	(n.s.)		87.3	87.6	(n.s.)	
Peak Velocity (mm/sec)				704	706	(n.s.)		739	705	0.012	
Peak Acceleration (mm/sec/sec)				23096	23194	(n.s.)		31812	23145	(n.s.)	
Peak Deceleration (mm/sec/sec)				−15109	−13336	(n.s.)		−20794	−14222	(n.s.)	
Peak Velocity time(ms)				136	138	(n.s.)		147	137	(n.s.)	
Peak Acceleration time (ms)				20	25	(n.s.)		48	23	(n.s.)	
Peak Deceleration time (ms)				296	351	(n.s.)		314	323	(n.s.)	
Total distance moved (mm)				141.7	147.4	0.005		152	145	0.000	

(b)

Fig. 6.4 Representative samples of velocity profiles for pointing movements and average values of key kinematic variables, along with p-values of paired t-tests.

was in the total distance that the finger was moved, which is an alternative kinematic verification of the angular end-point bias already reported: i.e. given that subjects always moved the same horizontal distance to the landing line, this shorter distance comes from not moving far enough down the landing line. Thus, pointing movements to Poggendorff stimuli were indistinguishable from normal pointing movements, except for the systematic end-point bias. The same is true for the target vs. no target conditions: when the target was not present, subjects moved their finger a shorter total distance. A well-known correlate of programmed reaching distance is peak velocity and accordingly this measure also shows a significant (though slight) decrease in the no-target conditions. Since no preview of the reach trajectory was given and since onset times were no different whether a target was present or not, this confirms that reach distance programming was performed in real-time during the onset latency after the stimulus appeared, strongly implicating dorsal stream mechanisms.

6.4. **Discussion**

Our data show that a manual pointing response is affected strongly by a bias that also affects the perceived perceptual position of an object. Why does a motor response in this case show the illusion, while in the case of illusions of size contrast, the illusion is apparently confined to perception? A specific suggestion by Franz et al. (2008) is that size illusions in certain conditions are resistant to a perceptual illusion because the subject can use online visual feedback to make their response accurate. When online feedback cannot be used, the illusion will persist. Our data are consistent with this suggestion, since in the absence of an explicit target, subjects had no opportunity to use feedback.

An alternative interpretation, more in line with the dual-stream hypothesis, is that the perceptual and motor biases arise from a common process before the split into action and perceptual streams. If an illusion manifests itself early in the visual system then both the dorsal and ventral streams will inherit the bias (Milner and Dyde, 2003) and since the Poggendorff illusion may manifest itself early, perhaps due to expansion of the acute angle due to lateral inhibition of orientation detectors (Blakemore et al., 1970); 'bowing' of the transversal pointer (Wenderoth, 1980), or blurring of second stage filters in V2 (Morgan, 1999), such a shared inheritance could explain an equal bias of both motor and perceptual responses. The common bias of the Poggendorff effect upon perception and action, which added a consistent 2–3° of bias on top of whatever landing line bias was already present in the pointer-only condition (Fig. 6.2), supports the notion that angular illusions of this type arise before the division into dorsal and ventral processing streams, possibly in V1 or V2.

We suggest, in conclusion, that the jury should stay out on the question of dual vs. single streams for the processing of visual extrapolation. The data do not at present rule out the attractive idea that perceptual extrapolation is an active process using covert motor mechanisms. We are pursing this idea currently by extending our paradigm to saccadic eye movements, and by seeing whether eye movements and perceptual extrapolation share common resources in a dual-task paradigm (Tibber et al., 2009).

Acknowledgement

The preliminary results reported in this chapter form part of a more extensive experiment now published in: Melmoth, D., Grant, S., Tibber, M., and Morgan M.J (2009). The poggendorfff illusion affects manual pointing as well as perceptual judgements. *Neuropsychologia*; **47**: 3217–24.

References

Aglioti, S., DeSouza, J.F.X., and Goodale, M.A. (1995). Size-contrast illusion deceives the eye but not the hand. *Current Biology*; **5**: 679–85.

Blakemore, C., Carpenter, R.H.S., and Georgeson, M.A. (1970). Lateral inhibition between orientation detectors in the human visual system. *Nature*; **228**(5266): 37–9.

Daprati, E. and Gentilucci, M. (1997). Grasping an illusion. *Neuropsychologia*; **35**: 1577–82.

de Grave, D.D., Brenner, E., and Smeets, J.B. (2004). Illusions as a tool to study the coding of pointing movements. *Experimental Brain Research*; **155**: 56–62.

Elliott, D. and Lee, T. (1995). The role of target information on manual aiming bias. *Psychological Research*; **58**: 2–9.

Franz, V.H., Hesse, C., and Collath, S. (2008). Visual illusions, delayed grasping and memory: no shift from dorsal to ventral control. *Neuropsychologia*, doi:10.1016/j.neuropsychologia.2008.08.029

Franz, V.H., Fahle, M., Bulthoff, H.H., and Gegenfurtner, K.R. (2001). Effects of visual illusion on grasping. *Journal of Experimental Psychology Human*; **27**: 1124–44.

Franz, V.H. (2003). Manual size estimation: a neuropsychological measure of perception. *Experimental Brain Research*; **151**: 471–7.

Franz, V.H., Bülthoff, H.H., and Fahle M. (2003). Grasp effects of the Ebbinghaus illusion: obstacle avoidance is not the explanation. *Experimental Brain Research*; **149**: 470–7.

Gentilucci, M., Chieffi, S., Deprati, E., Saetti, M.C., and Toni I. (1996). Visual illusion and action. *Neuropsychologia*; **34**: 369–76.

Goodale, M.A. and Milner, A.D. (1992). Separate visual pathways for perception and action. *Trends in Neurosciences*; **15**: 20–5.

Goodale, M.A., Jakobson, L.S., and Keillor, J.M. (1994). Differences in the visual control of pantomimed and natural grasping movements. *Neuropsychologia*; **32**: 1159–78.

Haffenden, A.M. and Goodale, M.A. (1998). The effect of pictorial illusion on prehension and perception. *Journal of Cognitive Neuroscience*; **10**(1): 122–36.

Haffenden, A.M., Schiff, K.C., and Goodale, M.A. (2001). The dissociation between perception and action in the Ebbinghaus illusion: nonillusory effects of pictorial cues on grasp. *Current Biology*; 11: 177–81.

Hotopf, W.H.N. and Hibberd, M.C. (1989). The role of angles in the inducing misalignment in the Poggendorff figure. *The Quarterly Journal of Experimental Psychology A*; 41A(2): 355–83.

Hu Y. and Goodale, M.A. (2000). Grasping after a delay shifts size-scaling from absolute to relative metrics. *Journal of Cognitive Neuroscience*; 12: 856–68.

Hubel, D.H. and Wiesel, T.N. (1959). Receptive fields of single neurons in the cat's striate cortex. *The Journal of Physiology*; 148: 574–91.

Kooi, F.L., De Valois, R.L., and Switkes, E. (1991). Spatial localization across channels. *Vision Research*; 31(9): 1627–31.

Levi, D.M. and Waugh, S.J. (1996). Position acuity with opposite-contrast polarity features: evidence for a nonlinear collector mechanism for position acuity? *Vision Research*; 1, 36(4): 573–88.

Mack, A., Heuer, F., Villardi, K., and Chambers, D. (1985). The dissociation of position and extent in Müller-Lyer figures. *Perception and Psychophysics*; 37: 335–44.

Meegan, D.V., Glazebrook, C.M., Dhillon, V.P., Tremblay, L., Welsh, T.N., and Elliot, D. (2003). The Muller–Lyer illusion affects the planning and control of manual aiming movements. *Experimental Brain Research*; 155: 37–47.

Milner, A.D. and Dyde, R. (2003). Why do some perceptual illusions affect visually guided action, when others don't? *Trends in Cognitive Sciences*; 7: 10–11.

Milner, A.D. and Goodale, M.A. (1995). *The visual brain in action.* Oxford: Oxford University Press.

Morgan, M.J. (1977, reprinted 2008). *Molyneux's question: vision, touch and the philosophy of perception.* Cambridge: Cambridge University Press.

Morgan, M.J., Ward, R.M., and Hole, G.J. (1990). Evidence for positional coding in hyperacuity. *Journal of the Optical Society of America A*; 7(2): 297–304.

Morgan, M.J. (1991). Hyperacuity. In *Spatial vision* (ed. Regan, D.M.), pp. 87–113 London: Macmillan.

—— (1999). The Poggendorff illusion: a bias in the estimation of the orientation of virtual lines by second-stage filters. *Vision Research*; 39: 2361–80.

—— (2003). *The space between our ears.* London: Weidenfeld & Nicholson.

Ninio, J. and O'Regan, J.K. (1999). Characterisation of the misalignment and misangulation components in the Poggendorff and corner-Poggendorff illusions. *Perception*; 28: 949–64.

Predebon, J. (2004). Influence of the Poggendorff illusion on manual pointing. *Perceptual and Motor Skill*; 98(1): 47–52.

Servos, P., Carnahan, H., and Fedwick, J. (2000). The visuomotor system resists the horizontal-vertical illusion. *Journal of Motor Behaviour*; 32(4): 400–04.

Tibber, M.S., Melmoth, D.R., and Morgan, M.J. (2008). Biases and sensitivities in the Poggendorff effect when driven by subjective contours. *Investigative Ophthalmology and Visual Science*; 49(1): 474–8.

Toet, A. and Koenderink, J.J. (1998). Differential spatial displacement discrimination thresholds for Gabor patches. *Vision Research*; 28(1): 133–43.

van Donkelaar, P. (1999). Pointing movements are affected by size-contrast illusions. *Experimental Brain Research*; 125: 517–20.

Weintraub, D.J. and Krantz, D.H. (1971). The Poggendorff illusion: amputations, rotations, and other perturbations. *Perception and Psychophysics*; 10: 257–64.

Wenderoth, P. (1980). Alignment errors in Poggendorff-like displays when the variable segment is a dot, a dot series, or a line. *Perception and Psychophysics*; 27: 505–18.

Westwood, D.A., Chapman, C.D., and Roy, E.A. (2000a). Pantomimed actions may be controlled by the ventral visual stream. *Experimental Brain Research*; 130: 545–8.

Westwood, D.A., Heath, M., and Roy, E.A. (2000b). The effect of a pictorial illusion on closed-loop and open-loop prehension. *Experimental Brain Research*; 134: 456–63.

PART 3

Understanding agency and object perception

CHAPTER 7

Two visual systems and the feeling of presence

Mohan Matthen

Abstract

Vision subserves two kinds of function. First, it classifies objects for creating and updating the databases that help an organism keep track of the state of the world. Second, it contributes to the guidance of the organism's body as it interacts with its surroundings. Call the former 'descriptive' vision, and the second 'motion-guiding'. Motion-guiding vision generally operates by directly controlling the limbs in the execution of bodily action, whether voluntary or involuntary. The data that it deploys are agent-centred and relative to an organism's momentary position. Consequently, these data are not in a form that can be reused on later occasions. In other words, motion-guiding data do not constitute appropriate entries into a database concerning the state of the world. Thus, the specific content is cloaked from consciousness, which is mostly concerned with data that can be recalled and reused. I shall argue, however, that motion-guiding vision does, nonetheless, contribute to awareness of our surroundings. Specifically, it does so by putting an organism into a position of being able to make contact with objects in its surroundings. I shall argue that such action-enabling connections with environmental objects constitute a *indexical or demonstrative* form of conscious content, which is different from the descriptive content provided by descriptive vision. It provides an organism with the feeling that the objects in its environment are *present* to it. In this respect, it is different from the kind of consciousness that is involved in pictorial vision, mental imagery, dreams, and episodic memory.

7.1. Introduction

When I look down at my hands right now, it looks as if they are working on a black computer keyboard. There is something about my visual state that makes it seem as if the keyboard is really there, and that it is really black. My visual state would be inaccurate, or false, if this were not the case.

When I am relaxing in an armchair, I can close my eyes and summon up a fairly detailed and vivid image of my hands on a black keyboard. This state of visual imaging is different from my present visual state. It does *not* make it seem as if the keyboard is really there, or that it ever was, or that it is really black. I could just as well summon up an image of my hands playing a piano: I know I never did play the piano, hence, it is immaterial, as far as the veracity of this image is concerned, what colour the keys are. (Here and in what follows, I shall use 'visual state' to mean states that arise from looking—visual imaging does not fall under this term as I am using it here.)

What is the difference between these two states? Why does the keyboard have (as I shall say) a *feeling of presence* in my present visual state, but not in the state of visual imaging? In this chapter, I employ the Two Visual Systems theory to offer a partial answer to this question. Although this answer addresses only one aspect of the feeling of presence, which very likely traces to many different cognitive processes, it reveals something important about how the two visual streams function. The problem that I want to tackle in this chapter concerns the origin and semantic significance of the feeling of presence. It might well be that this feeling attaches to a scene only when that scene has been identified as really there (and not just depicted). Thus, the visual system might have to solve the problem of whether what is seen is real *before* it attaches the Feeling of Presence to things it determines to be real. My problem, though, is not so much the conditions under which the visual system certifies something as present and real, or the method by which the visual system proceeds to such certification. My problem is rather the *meaning* of the feeling of presence. What exactly is it?

7.2. Content-directed attitudes

A. Visual experience tells the viewing subject something descriptive about her surroundings. For instance:

I know by looking that *somebody on my left is looking at me and extending his hand.*

Two caveats:

    a. The italicized portion of the displayed sentence above—the part after 'that'—expresses in English a *part* of what vision tells me about the world. No sentence will express *all* of what vision tells me in a normal scene.

    b. Vision tells me this in its own expressive medium, i.e. in visual qualia, not in English[1] (The fact that visual imagery is involved will turn out to be important in what follows).

I shall call this descriptive component of a visual state its *content.*

B. Generalizing from the above: visual states are *content-directed attitudes.* That is, they can be expressed in the following form:

Subject + attitude + content.

The example given above can be analysed in the following way:

I (subject) + see (attitude) + [that + somebody on my left is looking at me and extending his hand] (content).

Here are some other content-directed attitudes:

Anand (subject) + believes (attitude) + [that + it will rain tomorrow] (content).

Kwame (subject) + hopes (attitude) + [that + it will be a pleasant summer] (content).

Anand's belief and Kwame's hope are *propositional* attitudes: these have been discussed extensively in the philosophical literature. Here, I emphasize that they are a species of content-directed attitudes. Treating visual states under this rubric allows us to bring certain well-known tools of philosophical analysis to bear on them.

C. Certain propositional attitudes, such as *belief*, present their content as *actual.* Belief above is an example: Anand's belief embodies his commitment that tomorrow will actually be rainy; it

---

[1] Vision is restricted with regard to what it can tell you. People sometimes say things like: 'I see that you like to drive fast.' What they mean is that they infer from what vision tells them (as well as other sources of information) that you have this tendency. My claim here is that there are things that vision tells you directly, without the need for such inference on your part.

purports to Anand the actuality of rain tomorrow; it would be false if it didn't rain tomorrow. *Hope*, by contrast, does not represent its content as actual: Kwame's state does not purport that summer *will* be pleasant, and so his hope would not be false if summer turned out not to be pleasant; indeed, hope is not (for just this reason) properly considered true or false.[2] Let's call attitudes *actuality-committing* (or just *committing*) if (like belief) they represent their propositional complements, or content, as being true.

D. Committing and non-committing attitudes can share content. Koko can both believe and hope the same content: for instance, that she will soon be able to afford to give her mother an expensive present. Her belief is committing but her hope is not. Since these mental states share the same content, the difference between them—that one is committing and the other is not—must trace to the nature of the attitude. This implies that committment pertains to attitude. Hope attaches non-committing force to the content, while belief attaches committing force to it. (Of course, attitude carries more than commitment or its contradictory: hoping that summer will be pleasant is not the same as imagining it. Neither of these attitudes is committing, but they are different.)

E. Seeing is committing in the sense given above: visual states purport to describe what is really there, and they are false or inaccurate if the description they offer is not actually the case. Equally, it is obvious that *visual imaging* is not committing: visually imaging does not purport actuality. It follows from D. that this is a difference of force pertaining to attitude. In this chapter, I shall try to show that the Two Visual Systems theory can account for this difference of force between seeing and visual imaging.

7.3. Cognitive feelings

A mental state is *sub-personal* if it is generated by the brain without the full control of the subject's rational faculties of assessment and choice. Perceptual states and emotions are sub-personal; complex, well-articulated beliefs and rational plans, by contrast, are normally under the the subject's full control. It is clear why belief is committing. To believe a proposition is to assess it as true. But how do sub-personal states such as perception, memory, and emotion get their attitudinal character? The subject is not in control of the process by which these states are generated; she is aware only of the end result. What is it about states like these that constitutes their attitude? This is the question taken up in the present section.

Having established some general approaches to the topic, I'll return in the following section to the question about seeing.

A. States of *episodic* memory are characterized by what one might call a *feeling of pastness*; this distinguishes them from states of semantic memory, for example. You probably remember some incident in your childhood when you were in trouble with your teacher (T). You can recall the classroom in which it occurred, the teacher's look and voice, your own feelings, and so on. You may also remember some journey you took with your family at roughly the same time (J).

1. The *content* of these memory states, T and J, is very different, but both are presented as having occurred *in the past*.

2. The content of each of these memory states is an *image*. For present purposes, this may be construed as follows: *the content of the states is spatio-temporally formatted*. Every item presented in the content is presented as spatially located relative to every other item presented,

---

[2] Of course, it is either true or false that Kwame hopes that summer will be pleasant: the point is that his hoping this does not imply that summer will in fact be pleasant.

and if the image is temporally extended, then the same holds for temporal location.[3] (Note, however, that presented items need not be located relative to the observer of the image: sometimes they are, sometimes they are not.)

3. Images of past events do not contain any element that differentiates them from images concerning the present or future. Pastness is amodal: it is not a *visual* idea, nor does it belong to any other sensory modality. In fact, a remembered image is ideally the *same* as that which was *sensed* when the remembered incident actually occurred. This implies that it can't have a *component* that marks it as past.

4. That the imagistic content of episodic memory is presented as being past is, therefore, not a matter of what the image contains, but something about how the image is entertained. In other words, the imagistic content of T and J are entertained in a way that gives them their past-positing quality.

5. Though the feeling of pastness is not part of the content of these memory states, it has representational significance. For there is obviously a semantic difference between 'I was in trouble with my teacher' (*Past* T), and 'I am in trouble with my teacher' (*Present* T)—and this exactly is the difference between your episodic memory of T and the imagistic experience of T that you suffered at the time it occurred. The feeling of pastness characteristic of episodic memory states represents the tense in *Past* T.

6. The feeling of pastness differentiates episodic memories from *semantic* memories. You remember that (P): Paris is the capital of France. There is nothing past-like about P, and also nothing imagistic. In the first place, it is a present fact that you remember in this case, not a past one. (You can even remember a future fact in this way: that you have a meeting with your doctor tomorrow.) Moreover, you do not remember the occasion when you learned this—and even if you did, this would be a different memory state than regarding P. Your memory of P is *semantic* memory; semantic memory is characteristically not imbued with a feeling of pastness, while episodic memory is.[4]

These characteristics of the feeling of pastness point to a neglected, yet extremely important, feature of mental states whose content is 'imagistic' in the manner of perceptual states, namely that *some semantically significant material gets into the content-directed attitude itself*. Episodic memory can be expressed as follows:

Subject + episodically remembers (attitude) + sensory image (content)

The point that I want to make is that the feeling of pastness is a characteristic of the *attitude*, not of the content.

Now, the difference between *believing* T and *believing* past-T finds its way into belief *content*. For in the case of belief or *semantic* memory, we can present a past tense belief equivalently in one of two ways:

$$X \text{ believes that } [\text{Past } (S \text{ is}_{\text{UNTENSED}} F)]$$
$$X \text{ believes that } [S \text{ was } F].$$

---

[3] Note that on this construal, the proposition 'Rome is 800 km south of Paris' is an image. Though it shows that spatiotemporal coding is not sufficient for something to be an image, I am not bothered too much by this in the present context. The criterion of spatiotemporal coding is interesting only when a large number of things is presented. However, one could add the requirement that images are analogue representations. (See Dretske, 1981, chapter 6, for analogue representation.)

[4] Of course, semantic memory has a connection to the past: your belief in P rests in some way on some past incident, the occasion of learning. My point is that remembering this occasion is in no way a part of the memory that P.

In both pastness, the pastness is part of content—the manner of believing is the same in both cases, though the structure of what is believed is different. But since the content of episodic memory is an *image*, the above styles of presentation are ruled out. Thus, we get:

$$X \text{ remembers}_{\text{PAST}}: S \text{ is}_{\text{UNTENSED}} F.$$

The feeling of pastness is not a judgement that we make about a stored image. Experiencing an episodic memory is not like going through a photo-album and using one's written records and discursive powers to write a date below each picture. The feeling of pastness is generated sub-personally. Episodic memory is, in and of itself, an experience of an image as in the past.

The separateness of content and pastness attached to content is attested also by stories such as that of a painter, Franco Magnani, related by Daniel Schacter (1996, 28–31). Magnani suffered a strong fever accompanied by delirium, and after that began to dream of his childhood village of Pontito in Italy. His dreams had a 'hallucinatory intensity with a wealth of minute detail', says Schacter. Magnani later captured some of his dream images in paintings, and it was confirmed that these paintings are accurate: in fact, they contain a multiplicity of perspectives characteristic of painting but impossible to reproduce in photographs (e.g. an accurately placed flowerbed impossible to see from the perspective portrayed) suggesting that the dreams incorporated movement around the scene.

Now, vivid dreams do not present themselves as memories but as current experiences. Thus, Magnani's dreams seem to present content that is in fact remembered under a non-memorial attitude—a shuffling of content and attitude that proves their independence. Further, the fact that these dreams occurred after delirious episodes suggests that they are the result of brain damage. Thus, one might conclude that content and attitude are generated separately. This in turn is confirmed by studies that show that patients with damage to the prefrontal cortex show a diminished capacity to remember the episodes in which they learned facts that they remember (Wheeler, 2000). Normally, we all repress the sources of our knowledge (do you remember learning that 2×6 is 12?). These lesions, however, magnify the dissociation: patients forget where they learned lists and captioned pictures in just a week, though they had no trouble remembering the lists themselves.

B. Here is another example, somewhat different in structure. Patients who suffer from Capgras syndrome think that people who live with them—their spouses, for instance—are impostors. This is not a matter of failing to register the look of their spouses' faces. These unfortunate patients know that the person they see *resembles* their spouses, and will even acknowledge that they resemble them exactly. Moreover, they do not suppose that people other than their spouses—their medical attendants, for example—are impersonating their spouses.

In the case of selective deficits such as this one, cognitive neuroscientists infer that some component of normal brain function is damaged. Capgras syndrome shows that the normal human visual capacity to recognize other humans does not merely consist in recognizing that one face resembles another (Capgras syndrome is specifically visual: patients do not think that the telephone voice of their spouse is that of an impostor). Face-recognition has two logically independent components:

(This person looks like x to the nth degree) AND (This person is x).[5]

Let's say that when we realize that somebody is x we recognize them *properly*, and that when we realize that they look like x, we 'register the face-similarity metric'. In Capgras syndrome, the face-similarity metric is dissociated from recognition proper.[6]

---

[5] Clearly, it is consistent to think that somebody resembles x but is not x. It is also consistent to think that somebody does not look like x (as one remembers x), but is actually x.

[6] When two normally associated cognitive capacities are asymmetrically damaged in patients with lesion-induced deficits, neuroscientists infer that the brain processes responsible for these capacities are sufficiently separate in location that the lesion compromises one while sparing the other. In fact, the face-similarity metric and the arousal response are *double dissociated*—though they are normally associated with one another, each

Now, the fact that the face-similarity metric is in place shows that the problem in Capgras syndrome cannot be visual. A number of neuroscientists (H.D. Ellis and A.W. Young [1990], V.S. Ramachandran [Ramachandran and Blakeslee, 1998, chapter 8], and Max Coltheart [2005 and elsewhere]) have suggested that what is damaged in Capgras patients is an autonomic affective response. Normally, one responds strongly to people one knows intimately, because of the wealth of associations and expectations that these people trigger. Capgras patients are faced with the troubling experience of seeing somebody who looks just like their spouse, but of not experiencing a strong emotional response to them. To 'explain' their own reaction, Coltheart says, they arrive at the belief that the person in question is *not* their spouse. Ramachandran takes a similar view. The view is that the delusion has a 'cognitive' or inferential component.

I want to stay detached from the 'explanation' hypothesis, focussing only on the claim that there is no appropriate level of emotional arousal in these patients. I said that since the face recognition metric is in place, the visual image must be the same. So, the difference must lie in the attitudes. Let's say, therefore, that the visual state of a Capgras patient, C, is a content-directed attitude of the following form:

$$C + R + \text{visual image of spouse.}$$

Let's say that before the onset of the affliction, C was in a different kind of state:

$$C + R' + \text{visual image of spouse.}$$

If Ramachandran and Coltheart are right, the actual difference between the attitudes is one of emotional arousal. This would imply that this emotional difference has a semantic significance beyond itself. In Capgras patients, emotional non-arousal *means* that the person being viewed is not (though she looks like) the patient's spouse.

In normal people, the arousal component of face-recognition is cognitively penetrable by evidence that the person is not the same as the one whom she remembers. Imagine somebody who has the *experience* of recognizing her lover NN, but is presented with strong evidence (driver's licence; phone call from the absent NN professing to be hundreds of miles away, etc.) that it is in fact NN's twin sister MN. Then, perhaps, the arousal component weakens, and the state no longer has the feel of NN-recognition. This would mimic the state in which Capgras patients find themselves. The person *looks like* their spouse, but does not elicit the appropriate level of response. Consequently, their experience does not have the feel of recognition. (This is, in addition, deeply disturbing to them since the person who looks like their spouse seems to have taken their spouse's place in their homes, etc.) This is the non-imagistic difference between a resemblance-experience (such as the one that Capgras patients suffer, and also the MN-experience above) and a recognition-experience. This difference carries semantic significance, but it is not part of the imagistic content.

C. One other example of a cognitive feeling may be mentioned briefly; this time imagistic content is not involved. Antonio Damasio (1995) notes that some patients who suffer lesions of the ventromedial portion of the prefrontal cortex are unable to formulate a plan of action and carry it through to execution, and suffer, moreover, a lack of emotional affect. However, when only this portion of the brain is damaged, it appears that many forms of rational processing are spared, including those that lead to the social and moral assessment of hypothetical scenarios. Thus, it appears, the lack of decisiveness is associated not with the inability to assess a situation, but from a disengagement of motivation. Conversely, there are many lesions of dorsolateral prefrontal cortex which result

---

is spared in some patients in which the other is damaged. For in addition to Capgras patients whose face-similarity metric is spared, there are patients with acquired prosopagnosia—a face-similarity metric deficit associated with lesions in the fusiform gyrus—who respond non-visually to their spouses. (See Bergeron and Matthen, 2006 for a review of modularity inferences from dissociations.)

in deficits of rational processing but not necessarily in flatness or lack of emotional response (Milner, 1964). In summary:

	Emotional Affect/ Decisiveness	Rational Assessment of Social/Moral Scenarios
(Some) ventromedial lesions (Damasio 1995)	Impaired	Spared
(Some) dorsolateral lesions (Milner 1964)	Spared	Impaired

Consider a proposition such as: *It is good to give money to charity.* There are people (with ventromedial lesions) who are able to reason to such conclusions, but are either too distracted by other projects or just plain disinclined to act upon them. They are motivationally flat. Consider, on the other hand, motivationally potent states that are not associated with the endorsement of an *It is good to* proposition—irrational anger or inappropriately louche behaviour are often examples of this. There are people (with dorsolateral lesions) who will display such behaviour to an abnormal extent, though they have no inclination rationally to endorse propositions that would justify such behaviour.

As noted with the earlier examples, these are merely exaggerated versions of failures of rationality we all fall into from time to time. Having read Peter Singer, I have resolved time and time again to give 5% of my income to charity (less than he recommends, by the way). Time and again, I fail to do so. On the other hand, I am sometimes irritated inappropriately with people who commit minor offenses against taste and propriety, such as taking up more of an airplane armrest than they are entitled to, or honking their horn at me when I not doing anything illegal, though I have never succeeded in rationalizing such feelings. (In fact, I believe strongly that it would be good to be unaffected by such behaviour.) Such lapses of practical rationality seem to indicate (as Aristotle long ago realized) that the knowledge that something is good (or bad) is often causally neither sufficient nor necessary to be motivated to pursue (or avoid) it.

What is the difference between two men, both of whom judge that it is good to give money to charity, but only one of whom actually does so? Is it that the donor has an additional belief—for instance, the belief that his own preferences would be better served if he gave money? No, because it is notorious that even this additional belief will not necessarily secure the action. Additional *content* does not fix the problem. Nor is the donor marked by an additional *desire*—I really *want* to give 5% of my income to charity; I just never end up doing so. The lesion evidence cited by Damasio suggests a special form of processing that enables the translation of moral belief into moral action. Perhaps the moral belief has to be entertained in a certain way for it to result in reasoned action; perhaps, this results in a *feeling of motivation*, a manner of entertaining the content of these moral beliefs that gives them greater motivational force. The lesion evidence mentioned above gives some credence to the speculation that parts of the brain other than those involved in forming the content itself are involved in attaching to that content a certain motivationally relevant attitude. Independently of the credibility of this suggestion, my treatment of this example illustrates how the content-attitude distinction helps set up the phenomenon.

In this section, we have seen that mental states can be represented as an attitude taken up by an subject with respect to a certain content, which may be a proposition or an image. Both differences of content and differences of attitude make a difference to the semantic significance of the mental state. I have attempted to illustrate, by reference to three examples, the kinds of evidence we can appeal to in order to show that differences of attitude are involved, as opposed to differences of content. In these examples, I have suggested further that the parts of the brain that are involved in forming content, on one hand, and determining attitude, on the other may be distinct. In the following section, I deploy these ideas in examining how the two visual systems contribute to the feeling of presence.

7.4. **The 'Feeling of Presence'**

Definition: A cognitive feeling *C* is a subpersonally generated, phenomenologically accessible feature of a mental state *S* that imparts to *S* semantic or practical import different from that of another state *S'*, though *S* and *S'* have the same *content*. The difference of import between *S* and *S'* is accounted for by construing the feeling as a propositional operator (or *neustic* as R. M. Hare called it in 1952) that operates on the content of *S*.

The attitudinal forces identified in the preceding section are instances of cognitive feelings. My aim in the rest of this chapter is to characterize a cognitive feeling that accompanies ordinary visual states: the Feeling of Presence.

Traditionally, philosophers influenced by empiricism have given a rather impoverished account of the representational content of visual experience—their account has often been that we experience nothing but the distribution of colour and brightness across a two-dimensional field. More recently, many philosophers have found themselves dissatisfied with this account. In vision we experience a *scene* consisting of discrete objects and their properties, including location. In addition, we see a great variety of overlapping objects: not only material objects, but shadows, patches of light, films, stains, vapours, three-dimensional regions of illumination or darkness, reflections, and more. As far as visual properties are concerned, we directly see shapes, motion, and faces (as the evidence alluded to in section I above shows). The idea of vision presenting only coloured patches arrayed in a two-dimensional field is now being abandoned: increasingly, it is widely acknowledged that we see visual objects in three-dimensional locations, and, moreover, that where there are no objects to see, we do not see anything—we do not see unfilled visual field places. For instance, I simply don't see anything in between me and my computer screen.[7]

My claim is that normal (or 'real life') scene vision—the vision that one enjoys in a normal every-day setting, looking out of window or around a room, for instance—carries a cognitive feeling that I call *the Feeling of Presence*. As with the cognitive feelings discussed in the preceding section, I shall try to bring out the significance of the Feeling of Presence by contrasting scene vision with a case in which the content can be quite similar: pictorial vision. I shall argue that, despite the similarity of content, the representational (or 'semantic') significance of normal scene vision is very different from that of the contrast case. Normal scene vision is actuality-committing; pictorial vision is not. I account for this difference by a difference of attitudinal force, marked by the Feeling of Presence. The difference is *not* one of content, but just as in the examples discussed earlier, it is one of attitudinal force. Some philosophers have, as we shall see, attributed the difference to one of content, but I shall argue that as a result they get committed to vision having non-imagistic content—which is a problem for them.

When we look at a picture, we see: (i) the picture itself, a two-dimensional surface bearing coloured marks; and at the same time (ii) depicted three-dimensional objects *in* the picture. The case that I wish to use as a contrast for normal scene vision concerns the second—the scenes and objects we see *in* pictures. Seeing an object in a picture is phenomenologically very different from seeing it in real life, or normally. For, as I just mentioned, pictorial vision is not actuality-committing, while real-life vision is. Yet these two kinds of object-vision can be imagistically very similar. Since the similarities between real-life and pictorial images can be increased asymptotically without making the objects seen in pictures seem present, it would be a mistake to try to pin the difference between the two kinds of vision on whatever differences may exist. This contrast will help us understand

---

7 One person who disagrees with this last claim is Roy Sorensen (2008). He thinks that we see holes, and he has suggested to me in conversation that we might by the same token see gaps between objects. I agree that we see holes. However, I would contend that holes are features of objects, whereas gaps are not. So there is a difference.

something important about normal scene vision. (I don't think it makes much difference whether we consider stills or movies here, but I'll concentrate for the most part on stills.)[8]

There are, of course, many differences between seeing objects in real life and seeing them in pictures. One of these differences is particularly diagnostic for my approach. The real life objects you see seem connected to you in space; the objects you see in pictures do not. Imagine a picture (or a flat screen TV) on the wall, representing people you know sitting in a room. Contrast this with a window in the wall through which you can view people sitting in the room next door. The two scenes could be the same. Of course, the scene in the picture will never *exactly* resemble the scene through the window. Nonetheless: no matter how close the picture comes with respect to the projection it throws on your retina, there will be a sharp difference between the two visual experiences. When you view the pictured scene, the people look disconnected from you spatially. When you view the scene through the window, they do not. There is nothing about the picture that tells you where the people are, or even if they are anywhere.

Think of a picture of objects and people you recognize: a picture of people around a dinner table, or a still-life of edible fruit. Where are these things? You may *know*, of course, because you may recognize the room or the occasion. But putting this aside, the picture by itself offers no help. When you actually look at the same scene, the answer is obvious: the people are *there*. You know how to get to them: you know where they are relative to yourself; you can assign them egocentric coordinates. In the case of depicted objects, they could be anywhere, indeed they could be nowhere. You have no idea how to get to depicted objects—the picture simply does not and cannot give you the information; it does not even purport to do so. Nor are they at any definite distance away; they don't appear to get closer when you walk up to the picture. Objects in the picture stand in spatial relations to each other, but pictorial vision does not present them as spatially connected to real objects. Of course, you know where the *picture* is, and how to get to *it*, but this is a different matter. The picture is a real-life object that you see in a real life way. It 'feels present', to put it in the language I have been using, but objects *in* the picture have no location relative to you, the viewer.

Of course, there are pictures that, viewed from a certain angle, seem to offer a real-life view of the objects in them—*trompes l'oeil* as they are called. When pictures deceive you in this manner, the objects in them seem to be in the same space as you. When they do not deceive you, you may admire the fidelity with which they represent seen objects, but those objects do not seem to occupy the same space as you. Consider a wall-painting that looks from a certain angle to be a window through which you can see trees, water, sky. This picture fools you when and only when these objects seem to be outside and beyond the wall. When your perspective on the painting makes it obvious that it is just a painting, the trees look life-like, but located nowhere in your space. The Feeling of Presence, which defines normal scene vision, is, among other things, a visual feeling of spatial connection. Pictorial vision is characterized by a feeling of spatial disconnection.

This is where we are. First, there is a phenomenological difference between real-life seeing and pictorial seeing: real-life seeing is actuality-committing; pictorial seeing is not. Second, the difference does not seem to be a matter of image-similarity, since it survives increases in the latter. Lastly, there is a further associated phenomenological difference in that real-life seeing gives the subject a felt spatial connection to seen objects, but pictorial seeing does not.

7.5. Diagnosing the 'Feeling of Presence'

One theoretical problem that arises with respect to seeing-in-pictures is how the visual system is able to differentiate between a depicted object and an object which is actually present. This is something

---

[8] Of course, one can be fooled by a picture. Usually, this is a matter of context: for instance, the boundaries of the picture have to be hidden. The claim that I am making here is only that the difference between pictorial images and images in real vision cannot account for the major differences between pictorial seeing and real-life seeing.

of a puzzle, given the similarity between the retinal image thrown by the picture and that which would be thrown if things were as depicted. Here is what is difficult to understand: why does this similarity not induce an illusion? Why does *greater* fidelity not induce a *greater* temptation to take the depicted for the real? There are a number of relevant factors here, though I shall be arguing that they do not tell the whole story, because they are all differences of degree and as such they do not answer the questions asked in the preceding paragraph.

In the first place, there is a duality of seeing in the case of pictures, as mentioned earlier. When we look at a picture, we see two things: a surface with coloured marks or lights (the physical picture itself) and a depicted scene. Obviously, looking at a real scene (with no pictures in it) is nothing like this. There are none of the indications of coloured dyes on paper, no brush strokes, no glossiness or other texture of the paper or canvas, etc. This difference is relevant to knowing that the picture is a picture and the real scene is not. However, if we increase or decrease the visibility of these character-istics of physical pictures, it makes little difference to pictorial seeing. Venetian art of the fifteenth century began the trend in Western art to be up-front with painterly technique: this simply does not decrease the propensity of the viewer to see objects in pictures. Conversely, one is able by all sorts of techniques to reduce the visibility of physical-pictures to near-zero: these do not generally give one the illusion of real-life object-seeing.

Secondly, depicted objects give size and distance cues that conflict with one another. A picture can be very large or very small—and it is confusing how a building could throw a tiny image, or a face a gigantic one, and yet seem no particular distance away. The face shown on a postage stamp doesn't seem as far away as a face would have to be in order to throw so small an image; in fact, it does not seem to be at *any* particular distance away from you, the viewer. The person on the stamp does not seem any further away than a person portrayed by a large oil-painting. And the puzzle runs deeper than this, for when one walks away from or closer to a picture that hangs on the wall, the scene it depicts does not seem that much closer or further away. This strange disconnection marks depicted objects off from real ones. The question, though, is this: does this disconnection come from pictorial seeing or vice versa?

Finally, when we move, the perspective that we have on a depicted object does not change. Bring to mind (or to your computer screen, via Google Images) Peter Paul Rubens' painting of Samson asleep with his head on Delilah's lap, his hair being cut by a servant whose work is illuminated by a candle held by an old woman. In the background are several people looking at the action through an open door. Now if this were a real scene, then as one moved to the right, the visual angles and occlu-sion relations would change. Samson's head would partially hide Delilah's bare breast; the old woman's anxious face would be occluded by Delilah; more spectators would come into view through the door, and some that you now see would go out of sight. Nothing of this sort happens. Everybody and everything stays the same in relation to everybody and everything else. No previously hidden side is revealed as one moves in such a way as would shift one's perspective. Your curiosity about the back of Samson's head, or Delilah's other ear, remains unsatisfied.

As I have been suggesting, these differences between real-life seeing and pictorial seeing is that while they figure unquestionably in the diagnostics employed by the visual system, they do not immediately throw light on the Feeling of Presence. Consider for instance the duality of seeing: it implies, of course, the distinctness of pictorial objects and the objects that are pictures. This might lead one to reason along the following lines.

> Rubens' brush-strokes are *there*, related *so* to me. Delilah cannot be in the same place as the brush-strokes—she does not look as if she has brush-strokes on her face. So she must be somewhere else. But where? Not in my space: for my space is already fully occupied (by empty as well as filled spaces). This is the content of depicted-Delilah seeming to be in a disconnected space.

This is clearly rather weak reasoning. When you look at a picture, you flip-flop between looking at the picture itself and looking at the things it depicts: it's notoriously difficult, if not impossible, to attend to the surface features of the painting at the same time as you look at the things depicted. It is not quite clear why the depicted scene should not appear arrayed in front of you at one pole of the flip-flop. Why should it not be present when you are attending to it, as opposed to the brush-strokes, etc., and absent when the reverse is true? Of course, there is the unresponsiveness of your perspective on the scene as you move around, and maybe this is relevant too—but how does all of this fit into a coherent account of the Feeling of Presence?

Susanna Siegel (2006) has a deep and insightful discussion of a problem closely related to the one that I have just conducted. She notes that in the case of normal scene-vision:

> visual experiences ... inherit their truth-value from the truth-value of their contents. If the content of an experience is true, then the experience itself is veridical; if the content of an experience is false, then the experience is falsidical. (361–2)

To paraphrase:

> If visual experience V is as of situation S, then if S is true/false, V is correspondingly veridical/falsidical.

I'll call this condition the *Inheritance of Truth-Valuation* condition—notice that this condition is equivalent to what I have called 'actuality-commitment'. Normal scene vision satisfies the condition. However, this is not true of all visual experience. Pictorial vision and visual imaging are not veridical or falsidical at all, regardless of the truth of their content. I am trying to explain this difference, and so is Siegel. [9]

Now, Siegel is concerned with a different contrast case than mine. I have been contrasting normal scene-vision with seeing objects in pictures. Siegel, on the other hand, contrasts normal object-seeing with cases where the objects you 'see' are merely subjective. Her two lead cases are, first, the 'stars' you 'see' when you hit your head or stand up too quickly, and second, the strange case of an invariant doll-view.

In the first of these cases, the 'stars' in no way seem real. These 'stars' do not exhibit the requisite independence from yourself: when you turn around and face the other way, they are still in front of you; when you move, they do not appear to stay where they were in objective space but do stay the same way relative to you (in other words: their allocentric coordinates do not stay the same, but their egocentric coordinates do); when you close your eyes, they do not disappear. [10] Suppose you were hit on the head just when you were enjoying a real scene in which there were similar holographically projected green dancing dots. The 'stars' that result from the blow to your head do not seem to be added, as it were, to those that are present in the real scene. You experience not just one scene, but two disconnected sets of objects: one real and out there, the other subjective and 'in the head'.

In the second case, Siegel imagines looking at a doll, and its suddenly losing its independence from you. Whereas previously it would appear further left in your visual field when you turn your head right, it now 'moves with movements of your head as if you were wearing a helmet with an imperceptible arm extending from the front, keeping the doll in your field of view'. Regardless of how you move, you retain the same view of the doll. Even when you close your eyes, your view of the doll persists the same. Siegel contends quite plausibly that after a while the doll would cease to look as if it is an object that exists independently of yourself as viewer. 'Overall', she writes, 'your experience of the doll comes to operate much like the experience of "seeing stars" from being hit on the head' (370).

---

[9] Siegel (2006) and I arrived at these problems independently: the Feeling of Presence is discussed in Matthen (2005), chapter 13.

[10] Seigel consistently places 'sees' and 'stars' in scare quotes when she is talking about this subjective phenomenon, and I will follow her in this.

Siegel identifies two conditions that, according to her, form a part of the content of *ordinary* object-seeing. In modified form,[11] they are:

(Subject-Independence) If I were to change my perspective on the object, then the object would not thereby seem to change its dimensions or move. (E.g., my computer screen does not seem to move or get larger as I move my head toward it.)

(Perspectival Connectedness) If I were to change my perspective on the object, my view of the object and of its relations to other objects that I see would change as a result of this change.

Siegel contends that these conditions are part of how we see objects in real-life vision: Subject-Independence and Perspectival Connectedness are among the 'expectations ... found at the level of visual experience', she says (*op cit.* pp. 358–9). In the experiences of the doll and of 'seeing stars', she says, these expectations are *not* built into content. And this, according to her, is the difference between these two kinds of seeing—real-life or objective seeing, and the visual experience of objects that look to be unreal or subjective. The 'stars' look subjective because these conditions fail in the 'seeing stars' experience. Presumably, then, the Inheritance of Truth-Valuation fails for these cases because the failure of the above conditions marks the visual experiences as not purporting to be about the real world.

I agree with the main thrust of Siegel's analysis. In the cases just discussed, the 'stars' and the doll are indeed seen as not belonging to the real external world. They appear, rather, to be subjective. But I do not agree that this is a difference of *content*. Rather, it is a difference of cognitive feeling. One argument to support this contention is the same as the one I gave before for the case of episodic memory. The content of these visual experiences is imagistic i.e. it is just like an ordinary visual experience, except insofar as it does not purport to present a real situation. It is not clear how a visual image of what is real could differ from one of a visually similar scene that is not real. Therefore the difference is not a difference of content. Nevertheless, there is a semantic difference: the visual images that one has when one figuratively 'sees stars' after being knocked on the head do not present themselves as truth-assessible; the visual images that one has when one actually sees stars do so present themselves. Since this semantic difference cannot be traced to a difference of content, contrary to what Siegel contends, they must be traced to a difference of attitudinal force. The Feeling of Presence is supposed to be a difference of force.

The veridicality of 'seeing stars' is *not* inherited from the truth-value of the content of this experience. That is, the experience of seeing stars is not false because there happen not to be any such objects in your vicinity. Why? Because the experience of 'seeing stars' does not purport to tell you that there are such objects near about you. It does not have the feel of an experience that is informative about the real world. I have just argued that this cannot be a matter of what is contained in the content. Therefore, it has to be a matter of how the content is asserted, a matter of content-directed attitude, not content. For suppose that Subject-Independence and Perspectival Connectedness *were* part of the content of ordinary seeing, as Siegel contends. Suppose that, contrary to argument that I have given, these conditions could somehow be presented visually—imagistically, that is. What would then prevent us from merely imagining Subject-Independence and Perspectival Connectedness? Can't every visual quality be imagined, anticipated, and episodically remembered?

Here is a further important point. Siegel's two conditions come apart in the case of seeing objects in pictures. Perspectival Connectedness fails in this kind of seeing, since walking around a picture does not affect occlusion relations or which side of objects you see. However, Subject-Independence continues in place: the dimensions and position of objects do not appear to change when the viewer's

---

[11] Siegel's formulations are fine for her case, but I am not sure how exactly they should be applied to the pictorial case, to which I will return in a moment. I don't want to take time discussing this rather peripheral question— my formulations are a bit less specific, but they preserve the spirit of Siegel's conditions, and they too are plausibly represented in the doll case.

position changes. Yet, depicted objects do not appear real: seeing objects in pictures is not like seeing them in real life.[12] The same holds of the distant objects: in the limit case (think of heavenly objects, for example) Perspectival Connectedness fails, and in the case of far-away terrestrial objects are concerned, it fails with respect to relatively small movements such as we can complete in a few seconds. However, Subject-Independence holds with respect to distant objects.

In Siegel's case of 'seeing stars' after being hit on the head, the stars one 'sees' are green and dancing just in case one's experience of them is as of green and dancing stars. There is nothing independent to measure the stars against, and vision does not represent them as having this independence. Siegel's point about the doll is that as it fails Perspectival Connectedness, vision gradually ceases to represent *it* too as having this kind of independence from the subject's own experience. The case of pictorial seeing is different: here, the failure of Perspectival Connectedness does not lead to vision failing to represent depicted objects as independent of the subject. Vision represents depicted objects as not really present; nonetheless, it represents them as independent of the subject.

7.6. The feeling of presence and the two visual systems

I want now to offer my own account of the Feeling of Presence.

Recently, evidence has accumulated for the existence of two kinds of visual system. Originally, researchers concentrated on the difference between thalamic and tectal vision—visual data-streams that run to the cortex via the lateral geniculate nucleus, and those that run through the superior colliculus to the mid-brain (Schneider, 1969). More recently, the discussion has been about two cortical data-streams (Goodale and Milner, 2004), one that runs from the primary visual cortex to the infero-temporal cortex (the so-called 'ventral stream') and one that runs from the primary visual cortex to the posterior parietal cortex (the 'dorsal stream').

I am not concerned with the precise anatomical details of these data-streams here. My concern is rather with a broad functional difference and the (double) dissociability of these functions. The basic point is that one kind of visual data-stream provides the perceiver with imagistic *characterizations* of objects in her visual field. For instance:

- that objects are of such and such a colour and shape;
- that they are moving slowly or quickly in this or that direction;
- in the case of inanimate objects, that they are constructed of long/short/round/square (etc.) parts in such and such and such a configuration;
- in the case of humans, information about their faces that is useful for subsequent identification; and so on.

Such characterizations of objects are storable and recallable; and they influence future behaviour via memory functions such as conditioning, habituation, sensitization, and priming. Typically, they are at least potentially conscious—visual awareness is precisely consciousness of objects under the above characterization. I shall group such visual functions together under the term *descriptive vision*.

A second kind of data-stream provides the perceiver with information for bodily guidance at a level of fine motor control of which the perceiver is not usually (or ever) aware. For example:

- that objects are oriented thus for the purposes of grip alignment when reaching to pick them up or manipulate them;

---

[12] Listening to music through earphones provides another example where perspectival connectedness fails but some sort of subject-independence is preserved, however the latter is exactly to be formulated. For when one listens through earphones, the sound appears to be located in and around one's skull, but when one moves one's head, it stays pasted to one's skull. Yet the music does seem subject-independent (however that is to be understood).

- that some sudden change is occurring in the visual periphery, so that vision and attention can be directed towards it by means of an attentional saccade;
- that the light is bright or dark, so that the aperture of the pupil can be adjusted; and so on.

Such characterizations of objects are not stored in order to influence future behaviour and they are generally not recallable. Nor do the differences among objects thus characterized enter into consciousness: the actions thus guided are not undertaken because of visual states of which we are consciously aware. I shall group such visual functions together under the term *motion-guiding vision*.

It is important to reiterate and emphasize before we continue that I do not intend the terms 'descriptive vision' and 'motion-guiding vision' to be co-extensive with the terms 'ventral stream vision' and 'dorsal stream vision'. As I said earlier, the visual systems that Schneider differentiated were thalamic and tectal—a quite different distinction anatomically. What is of importance to the philosopher is not the anatomical characterization of these functions, but rather the question of whether there can be motion-guiding vision in the absence of descriptive vision. Given certain kinds of blindsight, this question can be answered in the affirmative, but the question of whether there is dorsal stream vision in the absence of ventral stream vision can be and is disputed (for instance, by Yves Rosetti in this volume).[13]

It is a crucial fact about these visual functions that they are doubly dissociable. Famously, there are patients, who, because of lesions in the parietal cortex, lack the ability to manipulate objects effectively, even though they perform well when they attempt to describe these objects. Similarly, there are patients who, because of lesions in the temporal lobes claim not to be able to see very much, and perform poorly when asked to describe objects, but are quite good—sometimes extraordinarily good, as in the case of the famous DF (a patient studied by Goodale and Milner)—at manipulating objects, negotiating uneven terrain, and so on. This is a double dissociation between one kind of motion-guiding vision and one kind of descriptive vision—with regard to each function, some patients are more or less impaired with respect to it, while the other is spare—and though it is somewhat controversial exactly where the functional and anatomical divisions between these visual systems lie, it is by now extremely well established that some such division exists. In what follows, this is all that I need.

Thanks to motion-guiding vision, we have the feeling that we are able to manipulate objects in our immediate vicinity, and reach out to them. This is centrally relevant to our ability to communicate by pointing to objects. When I point at an object, I am utilizing my visually guided ability to reach for it, get to it, and come into contact with it. You understand my gesture in part because of your own ability to interact with the object in these ways. Thus, motion-guiding vision is involved in our ability to locate objects relative to ourselves.

Motion-guiding vision locates objects in egocentric terms: it gives us information not so much about objective spatial location, but about location relative to our own bodies and our own motions. When we walk towards or around an object, the object does not seem to change its spatial location—this is thanks to the contribution of descriptive vision. From the point of view of bodily motion, however, the object does change its coordinates: it is located differently with respect to which of the perceiver's hands is best for touching it, how far the perceiver will have to reach or walk in order to do so, etc.

Now, motion-guiding vision—i.e. the sum of the visual data-streams that guide object-manipulation—is known to engage only those objects with which one is able to make contact by reaching, or with a tool such as a stick. Motion-guiding vision does not engage far-away objects. What it does is to assign perceiver-relative coordinates to objects that are close by—it calibrates objects in what we may call *near-space*; the outer boundaries of near-space are no more than, say, ten feet away from

---

[13] Athanasios Raftopoulos (forthcoming) is critical of some of my views (Matthen, 2005, chapter 13) precisely because he thinks I overplay the distinctness of ventral and dorsal stream processing—but I was explicit that I have no attachment to this distinction at all, except insofar as it inspired the distinction between descriptive and motion-guiding vision.

the perceiver. Once near-space has been calibrated, the more objective spatial coordinates provided by *descriptive* vision can be converted into egocentric coordinates. Nearby objects are connected to far-away objects by visible paths: the fineness of visible detail and angular dimensions of seen objects varies down these paths in predictable ways; these and other clues help us locate objects in *far-space* relative to ourselves.[14] Motion-guiding vision is thus the anchor for interacting with objects in the space that surrounds us, whether near or far—directly in the case of near-by objects, and indirectly with far away objects.

Depicted objects do not engage motion-guiding vision either directly or indirectly. Normal object-seeing involves a simultaneous engagement of both kinds of vision, and feedback from each to the other. Thus, normal seeing involves the assignment of egocentric coordinates to seen objects as well as the assignment of allocentric (or objective) coordinates to them. However, pictorial seeing involves only descriptive vision. Depicted objects cannot be located relative to the perceiver's near-space. Thus, they stand in spatial relations to one another, but not in determinate spatial relations relative to objects that are in near-space. But, I have argued, the visual guidance of our interactions with objects depends crucially on the engagement between motion-guiding vision and objects in near-space. Thus, the visual system affords us no guidance concerning interaction with depicted objects.[15]

To summarize:

Depicted objects cannot visually be located relative to the perceiver. Although we are able to perceive spatial relations within pictures, there is no continuity between near space and depicted space. There is an abrupt cut-off at the surface of the picture. Consequently, we cannot see where these objects are relative to ourselves. We can, of course, point at an object in a picture ('*That's* Delilah, not the old woman with a candle'), but this is different from pointing at an object in real life. When we point at a depicted object, we do so without indicating where it is, perhaps it is a form of deferred ostension—we point at the coloured patches that depict the object, and secure reference to the object through their intervention.

This leads me to a thesis regarding normal object-seeing.

The Feeling of Presence is a matter of objects being visually locatable relative to the perceiver. Perspectival Connectedness is not the essential condition, since it fails also with respect to distant objects, which feel as if they are present.

7.7. **Visual experience and demonstratives**

Visual experience has a demonstrative element, I now want to argue, and this is constitutive of the Feeling of Presence. More explicitly, the ability to interact with objects by locating them in egocentric space is indicative of a demonstrative element in visual content, and the Feeling of Presence is a consequence of this demonstrative element.

First, let us define demonstratives. To do so, we need the prior notion of indexicals. You say 'I am tired'; I say 'I am tired'. Though the same words, with the same meaning, were uttered by you

---

[14] At the conference, there were questions about whether the heavenly bodies (i.e. stars) possessed the Feeling of Presence. I take it that they do, because there are visual paths between objects in near space and the stars. But this requires a special sense of visual path, in which there is *no* visual path between nearby objects and the 'stars' that one sees after a blow to the head. I take it that when objects fail of Siegel's Subject-Independence test, they are presented as not being located in the viewer's space.

[15] I do not mean to deny the possibility of learned visual interactions. For instance, surgeons can snip objects revealed to them by images on a television screen by small cameras, and Andy Clark has pointed out to me (at the conference) that there are fake interactions in three-dimensional video simulations.

and by me, we spoke about different persons—what I said was about me; what you said was about you. How can this be?

The classic answer is due to David Kaplan (1988). 'I' is an *indexical*: one component of its meaning is what Kaplan calls *character*. The reference of an indexical is determined by *context*. Context consists, minimally, of a speaker, a place, and a time. The reference of 'I' is the speaker; that of 'here' is the place; that of 'now' is the time—each of these relative to the context of utterance. In the example considered in the preceding paragraph, the context of my utterance is different from that of yours. That is why the referent of 'I' is different.

A *demonstrative* is a term the reference of which is determined by context (speaker, time, place), as well as a specific kind of relationship that obtains between the elements of the context and other things. 'That' is an example of such a term. Its referent is determined not just by the speaker, place, and time, but also by some kind of gesture, such as pointing, performed by the speaker. You understand my saying 'that' by understanding first that I am the speaker relative to whom the term should be evaluated, and by grasping the relatum of my gesture towards some object.

One important property of a demonstrative is that the pointing gesture associated with it operates independently of the speaker's beliefs. Suppose I point and say 'That dog'. Imagine that I believe that there is one dog in front of me and one behind me and that I am pointing to the one in front. By the normal rules of pointing, I would have been pointing at the dog in front of me, had there been one, and I intend to point to the dog I think is there. As things really are, however, the 'dog' in front of me is a reflection in a mirror of the dog behind me. And the rules of pointing dictate that when I say 'that dog' and point at a reflection, then I refer to the dog itself (not the reflection). Thus, by the rules, I am pointing at the dog behind me, though I *think* (falsely) that I am pointing to a dog in front of me. My contention is that in such a case my beliefs do not determine what I refer to; rather, the rules do. The demonstrative does not refer to a particular dog because of what I believe about that dog. Rather, it refers to that dog, because the pointing gesture is sensitive to where the dog really is (regardless of my beliefs) and to changes in where it is—if the dog were to move, the pointing gesture would have to be modified appropriately.

A demonstrative, then, is a term D such that

i. the reference of D is determined by context, an associated description, and a certain relationship R between the speaker (in that context) and some object, and such that

ii. the speaker's own beliefs about this relationship R do *not* play any role in determining the reference of D, and

iii. the relationship R is sensitive to the location of the object demonstrated.

The demonstrative element in visual experience is to be understood by analogy with that in language. You are sitting in a darkened room looking at an illuminated blue sphere S_1; I am sitting in a darkened room thousands of miles away looking at an exactly similar sphere S_2. Though we have qualitatively similar experiences, your experience is about S_1, while mine is about S_2. What makes this so? Clearly not the imagistic content of our visual experiences, for they are the same.

One kind of answer to this question sheds no light on the significance of the visual state to the perceiver. H.P. Grice (1961) argued that S_1 is the object of your visual experience (not S_2), because S_1 (not S_2) caused it, and the same is true *mutatis mutandis* of S_2 and my experience. True, but this tells us nothing about the significance of each visual state for the perceiver—given that our visual experiences are qualitatively similar, the question is: how can your experience afford you a capacity with regard to S_1 that my experience does not give me, and how does mine give me a corresponding capacity with regard to S_2 that is not available to you? Grice's distinction does not answer this question; indeed, no merely relational fact about a perceiver can explain how he comes to have a substantive capacity. The kind of answer that I am interested in adumbrating here consists of identifying some intrinsic fact about a visual experience that makes the experience informative about one object rather than another. Thus, I will take it that a visual experience is about S_1 rather than about S_2 only if this experience enhances the perceiver's capacities with respect to S_1, but not with respect to S_2.

Now, one difference between our visual states is that the motion-guiding component of your visual state enables you to interact with S_1 in a specific way, while mine enables me to interact with S_2. Changes in S_1 result in your body being differently poised with respect to it were you to try to grasp or move towards it; changes in S_2 do not have this result. Let us call this the *visual-interaction-relative-to-S_1* relation, or $I(S_1)$ for short. Note that this relation is not merely a matter of the perceiver being affected by S_1; it is that the perceiver is capable, in virtue of $I(S_1)$, of acting on S_1, and of adjusting his or her own orientation to respond to changes in S_1's position.

My claim is that $I(S_1)$ constitutes a demonstrative relationship between the visual perceiver and a certain object in his or her visual field. It picks out a visual object that with which this perceiver is able to interact in virtue of his or her visual state.

There is also evidence that motion-guiding vision calculates spatial coordinates for pictured objects *differently* from descriptive vision. For it appears that motion-guiding vision is immune to size-contrast illusions such as the Ebbinghaus illusion (Haffenden and Goodale, 2000). When a perceiver is presented with identical circular objects, one surrounded by a halo of very small circles, and the other by very large circles, the former looks much larger. However, when the perceiver reaches for these same targets, he does so without error. Yet, size contrast illusions are part of what serve as cues of distance in pictures. So it seems that motion-guiding vision is insensitive to the size and distance of objects in pictures.

Moreover, the visual-interaction relation operates *independently* of descriptive vision. For this reason, the perceiver's ability to interact with a visual object is independent of any visual description that he can provide. Suppose that you misperceive the colour and position of an object in your visual field. There is evidence that motion-guiding vision will not necessarily be deceived in tandem with these errors of perception. Thus, taking both components of the visual system into account, the visual experience consists first in engaging with an object by virtue of a non-descriptive relation, and second in ascribing certain visual features to the object. Seen in this way, the visual state carries a message of the form 'That is F' for some visual feature F.

The perceiver stands in no such relationship with respect to depicted objects. I have argued already that the perceiver is unable to locate these objects relative to his own limbs. The Feeling of Presence arises, then, out of an informationally rich demonstrative relationship between visual experience and visual object.

One last point: the Feeling of Presence has now been tied to the ability to locate an object in space in such a way as to be able to interact with it. If this is correct, then a visual experience, for example of a blue sphere, includes as components: first a demonstrative element that identifies the object; and secondly a description of the object so identified as possessing certain visual features—it is presented as a blue sphere. Normal visual experience is thus quite determinate with respect to truth conditions: a definite object has to have determinate properties in order for the experience to be veridical—the object and properties identified by the content of the experience. With respect to pictures, by contrast, the content of the experience concerns an indeterminate object in an indeterminate location. The state of affairs in the real world is irrelevant to pictorial experience, which therefore does not inherit its truth value from the truth value of the content.

7.8. Summary

Visual experiences have imagistic content. Real existence cannot be asserted by imagistic content. Normal scene-vision, however, does assert real existence. Hence, there is a semantically significant component of visual experience that is distinct from its imagistic content. This is the Feeling of Presence. My conjecture is that the Feeling of Presence arises out of a visually guided but non-descriptive (i.e. non-conscious, unstored, unrecallable) capacity for bodily interaction with external objects.

References

Bergeron, V. and Matthen, M. (2006). Assembling the emotions. In (ed. Faucher, L. and Tappolet, C.), *The Modularity of Emotions Canadian Journal of Philosophy*; supp.**32**: 185–212

Coltheart, M. (2005). Conscious experience and delusional belief. *Philosophy, Psychiatry, and Psychology*; **12**: 153–7.

Dretske, F.I. (1981). *Knowledge and the flow of information*. Cambridge, MA: MIT Press.

Ellis, H.D. and Young, A.W. (1990). Accounting for delusional misidentifications. *British Journal of Psychiatry*; **157**: 239–48.

Goodale, M.A. and Milner, D. (2004). *Sight unseen: an exploration of conscious and unconscious vision*. Oxford: Oxford University Press.

Grice, H.P. (1961). The causal theory of perception. *Proceedings of the Aristotelian Society*; supp.**35**: 121–52.

Kaplan, D. (1988). Demonstratives. In *Themes from Kaplan*, (ed. Almog, J., Perry, J., and Wettstein, H.), pp. 491–563. New York: Oxford University Press.

Matthen, M. (2005). *Seeing, doing, and knowing: a philosophical theory of sense perception*. Oxford: Clarendon Press.

Milner, B. (1964). Some effects of frontal lobectomy in man. In *The frontal granular cortex and behavior*, (eds Warren, J. and Akert, K.), pp. 313–31. New York: McGraw-Hill.

Raftopoulos, A. (forthcoming). Reference, perception, and attention. *Philosophical Studies*. DOI 10.1007/s11098-008-9213-5.

Ramachandran, V.S. and Blakeslee, S. (1998). *Phantoms of the brain: probing the mysteries of the human mind*. New York: William Morrow.

Schacter, D.L. (1996). *Searching for memory: the brain, the mind, and the past*. New York: Basic Books.

Schneider, G. (1969). Two visual systems. *Science*; **163**: 895–902.

Siegel, S. (2006). Subject and object in the contents of visual experience. *Philosophical Review*; **115**: 355–88.

Sorensen, R. (2008). *Seeing dark things: the philosophy of shadows*. New York: Oxford University Press.

Wheeler, M.A. (2000). Episodic memory and autonoetic awareness. In *The oxford handbook of memory*, (ed. Tulving, E. and Craik, F.), pp. 597–608. Oxford: Oxford University Press.

CHAPTER 8

Spatial coordinates and phenomenology in the two visual systems model

Pierre Jacob and Frédérique de Vignemont

Abstract

The 'two-visual' systems hypothesis (Goodale and Milner, 1992; Milner and Goodale, 1995) has recently come under attack regarding its proposed functional dichotomy between vision-for-action and vision-for-perception as well as for the limited interaction it allows between visual awareness and processing in the dorsal stream. Schenk (2006) questions the rigid functional dichotomy between vision-for-perception and vision-for-action arguing that the dual model of vision is best accounted for in terms of a dissociation between egocentric and allocentric spatial coordinate systems. Wallhagen (2007) argues that there is no evidence to claim that the processing in the dorsal stream cannot underlie visual awareness. This paper offers a response to both challenges and disentangles the contribution of two separable factors to the two-visual systems model, namely, (i) how spatial information is coded and (ii) the relation between consciousness and processing in the ventral and dorsal streams respectively.

8.1. Introduction

What is known as the 'two-visual systems model' of human vision was first presented by Goodale and Milner (1992). The core of the model involves three complementary ingredients: (i) the functional distinction between *vision-for-action* and *vision-for-perception*; (ii) the mapping of the functional distinction onto the anatomical segregation between the dorsal stream and the ventral stream of the human visual system; (iii) the restrictive link between visual awareness and vision-for-perception at the expense of vision-for-action.

One of the crucial pieces of empirical evidence on which advocates of the two-visual systems model have relied is the close investigation of visual form apperceptive agnosic patient D.F., who is deeply impaired in the visual recognition of the shape, size, and orientation of visual stimuli, but who can grasp objects accurately. Advocates of the two-visual systems model (e.g. Goodale and Milner, 2004) have argued recently that the dissociation between impaired visual perception and spared visuo-motor capacities exemplified by D.F. is an attenuated version of the dissociation exemplified by blindsight patients.

Recently, claims (i) and (iii) of the two-visual systems model have been challenged. According to Schenk (2006), the dual model of vision is best accounted for in terms of a dissociation between egocentric and allocentric spatial coordinate systems. He argues that D.F. is impaired, not in perceptual tasks per se, but in either visuo-motor or perceptual tasks that require making use of spatial information coded in allocentric coordinates. According to Wallhagen (2007), the evidence does not show that the dorsal stream cannot underlie visual awareness. He argues that D.F. might well have visual phenomenal experience of the shapes of objects, but she might be unable to form perceptual judgments about the shapes of objects because she fails to conceptualize the content of her visual experience. Since, arguably, there are many cases to which the distinction between visual phenomenal experience and perceptual judgment applies (e.g. in change blindness experiments, in split-brain patients, and in neglect patients), Wallhagen's (2007) conjecture raises an important challenge.

In this chapter, we offer a response to both challenges. In the process, we try to clarify the functional role of two parameters of the two-visual systems model: first, visual perception and visually guided action use different frames of reference for coding relevant spatial information. Secondly, their respective outputs are not equally available to consciousness. In section 8.2, we review the evidence in favour of the dual model of vision. In section 8.3, we analyse the complex links between visually guided action, visual perception, egocentric coordinates, and allocentric coordinates. In section 8.4, we contrast two possible criteria of conscious experience: namely, 'reportable' information and information stored in an 'iconic buffer'. In section 8.5, we argue that D.F.'s visuo-motor computation of aspects of shape is unlikely to make her visually aware of the shapes of objects on which she acts efficiently.

8.2. **The evidence for the dual model of vision**

Contrary to common sense and much philosophy of perception, human vision is not a unitary psychological activity, whose single purpose is to yield a unified conscious picture of the visible features of the world. As shown by a variety of empirical evidence ranging from electrophysiological recordings in non-human primates, the examination of brain-lesioned human patients and psychophysical experiments in healthy human participants, one and the same visual stimulus can be processed differently according to the task.[1]

Ungerleider and Mishkin (1982) first reported a double dissociation between the results of lesions respectively in the ventral and the dorsal pathways of the cortical visual system of macaque monkeys. They found that animals with a lesion in the dorsal pathway were impaired in their ability to localize an object with respect to a landmark, but were still able to recognize the shape, colours, and texture of objects. Conversely, they found that animals with a lesion in the ventral pathway were impaired in the recognition of the shape, colours, and texture of objects, but were still able to localize an object with respect to a landmark.[2] In brain-lesioned human patients, Goodale and Milner (1992) reported a double dissociation between optic ataxic and visual form agnosic patients.[3] Optic ataxic patients, who suffer from a lesion in the dorsal pathway (but whose ventral stream is intact), are still able to recognize the size, shape and orientation of visually presented targets, but impaired in reaching and grasping them. Conversely, visual form agnosic patients, who suffer from a lesion in the ventral pathway (but whose dorsal stream is intact), are impaired in the recognition of the size, shape and

---

[1] The scope of the functional duality between perceptual and visuo-motor processing must be restricted to the visual processing of objects that can be either enumerated or manipulated with one's hand.

[2] On the basis of this dissociation, Ungerleider and Mishkin (1982) labelled the ventral stream the *What*-system and the dorsal stream the *Where*-system.

[3] For experimental evidence challenging the view that visual form agnosic patients and optic ataxic patients exemplify a double dissociation, cf. the chapter by Rossetti et al. (Chapter 10); and for a reply, cf. Milner and Goodale (2008).

orientation of visually presented objects. However, their preserved visuo-motor transformation enables them to reach and grasp visual targets (Goodale and Milner, 1992; Milner and Goodale, 1995; Goodale and Milner, 2004; James et al., 2003). For example, patient D.F. was presented with a set of so-called Efron rectangles, all of which with the same surface area, some of which were squares and others had various elongated shapes. When asked for same/different judgments, she was at chance when the pair of shapes was minimally different. She was also at chance when required to match the width of such simple geometrical forms by scaling the distance between her thumb and index finger. As noticed by Milner and Goodale (1995, p. 200), it is significant that D.F.'s impaired perceptual judgments of shape were tested using a manual, non-verbal report, because it shows that D.F.'s perceptual impairment cannot be caused by a dissociation between visual processing and language processing. By contrast, measurement of her maximum grip aperture (MGA) in visuo-motor tasks of grasping revealed an excellent correlation with the physical width of rectangular blocks. Furthermore, when grasping objects with curved shapes between her thumb and index finger, unlike a patient with optic ataxia, D.F. turned out to select the correct points on the objects' surface on which to apply her thumb and index finger (Goodale et al., 1991; Milner et al., 1991; Milner and Goodale, 1995; Goodale and Milner, 2004).[4]

Further evidence for the dual model of vision has been provided by the psychophysical investigation of the responses of healthy human subjects to illusory displays, such as the Müller-Lyer illusion, the Ponzo illusion, the Titchener (or Ebbinghaus) illusion, or the hollow face illusion. Many such behavioural studies have revealed a subtle dissociation between perceptual judgments and visuo-motor responses. For example, in the hollow face illusion, participants perceive a three-dimensional concave (or hollow) mask as a convex (or protruding) face. If asked to slowly point to a small target attached to the hollow mask, participants directed their finger movements to the illusory location of the target. However, if asked to quickly flick the target off the face (as if it were a small insect), they directed their finger movements to the actual or veridical location of the target (cf. Kroliczak et al., 2006). Similarly, when presented with a Titchener disk illusory display, participants judge that the diameter of a disk is larger when the disk is surrounded by an annulus of smaller circles than when it is surrounded by an annulus of larger circles. But when participants are asked to grasp the central disk, measurement of their maximum grip aperture shows that the visuo-motor computation of the size of the diameter of the disk is not affected by the illusion to the same extent (Haffenden and Goodale, 1998; Haffenden et al., 2001).

Such dissociations in both neuropsychological patients and healthy individuals show the existence of two independent types of visual processing of one and the same stimulus. Either type of visual processing can be selectively impaired, but only one of the two is sensitive to the mechanisms generating size-contrast illusions. The distinction between visuo-motor processing and perceptual processing has been mapped onto the anatomical segregation between the dorsal and the ventral streams (Goodale and Milner, 1992; Milner and Goodale, 1995). Roughly speaking, the dorsal stream projects primary visual areas onto the superior parietal lobe (SPL), which sends further projections to the primary motor cortex via the dorsal premotor cortex (dPM). The ventral stream projects primary visual areas onto the infero-temporal cortex (IT).[5] The anatomical segregation between the dorsal and the ventral streams, however, leaves a number of computational and functional parameters involved in the documented dissociations unsettled.

What is the difference between visually formed perceptual judgments and visuo-motor representations? Recent discussions have stressed three major functional distinctions: (i) the first is the distinction between vision-for-perception and vision-for-action (Goodale and Milner, 1992;

---

[4] In his chapter (Chapter 13), Noë emphasizes the limits of patient D.F.'s visuo-motor processing of the shapes of objects, particularly with respect to the object's function.

[5] Gallese (2007) argues for a tripartite model including a dorso-dorsal stream, a ventral-dorsal stream, and a ventral stream.

Milner and Goodale, 1995) or (in slightly different terms) between the semantic and the pragmatic processing of visual information (Jacob and Jeannerod, 2003; Jeannerod and Jacob, 2005); (ii) the second is the distinction between coding spatial information about a stimulus in allocentric and in egocentric coordinates (Milner and Goodale, 1995; Jacob and Jeannerod, 2003; Schenk, 2006); (iii) the third is the distinction between conscious and unconscious processing (Milner and Goodale, 1995; Jacob and Jeannerod, 2003; Pisella et al., 2000). However, it is not entirely clear how these three contrasts are supposed to interact. In the following sections, we shall focus on the last pair of distinctions and address two joint questions. First, we shall try to determine in what way patient D.F.'s spared dorsal stream enables her to code spatial information about the target on which she acts successfully. Secondly, we shall ask to what extent activity in her spared dorsal stream makes D.F. visually aware of the shapes of objects on which she acts successfully.[6]

8.3. Coding spatial information and the two-visual systems model

The functional duality between visual perception and the visual control of actions was first advanced by Goodale and Milner (1992). Whereas segregating an object from both its background and competitors is a *perceptual* process (Shoemaker, 1994), grasping and pointing to an object are *visuo-motor* processes. The action/perception functional distinction has since been embraced under various labels by several authors. For example, Jeannerod (1993, 1997), Jacob and Jeannerod (2003), and Jeannerod and Jacob (2005) have generalized the action/perception model of visual processing into the distinction between pragmatic and semantic processing of visual information. The pragmatic processing of visual information is at the service of promoting an agent's intention by guiding her motor acts (at the various levels of complexity in the representation underlying the hierarchical organization of her action). The semantic processing of visual information is at the service of the elaboration of an agent's beliefs (and knowledge) about her surroundings. Furthermore, Jacob and Jeannerod (2003), Jacob (2005), and Jeannerod and Jacob (2005) have hypothesized that, unlike visual percepts, visuo-motor representations serve motor intentions and have a hybrid direction of fit: they have both a world-to-mind and a mind-to-world direction of fit. In Matthen's (2005) terminology, the action/perception distinction is captured by the distinction between 'motion-guiding' and 'descriptive vision'.

8.3.1. Types of action and the two-visual systems model

For the purpose of understanding the varieties of visual processing, the distinction between perception and action is an unacceptable oversimplification. On the one hand, slowing down or speeding up the timing of a visually guided action makes a difference to which anatomical pathway is likely to underlie the act. For example, visual form agnosic patients with a lesion in the ventral stream are able to produce fast, immediate, and accurate pointing actions towards a target, but they are significantly impaired if there is a delay between the extinction of the stimulus and the onset of the pointing gesture. Conversely, optic ataxic patients with a lesion in the dorsal stream are impaired when requested to produce a fast, immediate, and automatic pointing gesture towards a target, but their performance improves if there is a delay between the extinction of the stimulus and the onset of their pointing gesture (Milner and Goodale, 1995; Milner and Goodale, 2008; Jacob and Jeannerod, 2003; Pisella et al., 2000; Rossetti et al., 2005).[7]

---

[6] In addressing both questions, we assume, on the basis of the brain-imaging work reported by James et al. (2003), that the spared parts (if any) of her ventral stream are not doing any work.

[7] As showed by Kroliczak et al. (2006), the same contrast is exemplified in healthy subjects who are asked to point towards a target on a hollow mask.

On the other hand, it would be a mistake to assume that every hand (or finger) action standing in some relation to a visual object is guided by a visuo-motor representation of a target. Some hand actions instead count as perceptual reports. For instance, scaling the distance between thumb and index finger can be involved in either a visuo-motor task of grasping or in reporting a perceptual judgment. Interestingly, the underlying processes are very different. According to Jeannerod (1997, p. 35), in a visuo-motor task of grasping, but not in a manual report, grip formation (i.e. finger shaping) starts during reaching (i.e. transportation of the hand at the object's location): 'preshaping involves a progressive opening of the grip with straightening of the fingers, followed by a closure of the grip until it matches object size'. Maximum grip aperture, which is much wider than, but significantly correlated with, the physical size of the target, occurs at 60% to 70% of the reaching phase. This process can unfold in 'open loop' conditions in which participants have no visual access to their own hand movement and cannot, as in the context of a manual report, visually compare the distance between their thumb and index finger to the size of the target. Indeed, it was a great surprise to discover that whereas patient D.F. was able to accurately scale her finger grip to the physical size of a target in a visuo-motor task of grasping, she turned out to be at chance when asked to scale the distance between her thumb and index finger to provide a manual estimation of the size. Similarly, healthy subjects scale their finger grip accurately when asked to grasp an illusory Titchener disk, but when asked to judge the diameter of the disk, measurement of the distance between their thumb and index finger shows that their estimation of the diameter of the disk is illusory.

On the one hand, an agent could not grasp accurately a target unless she coded the target's position in egocentric coordinates centred on her own body. On the other hand, the size-contrast illusion prompted by the perception of a Titchener disk surrounded by an annulus of circles (either smaller or larger than it) arises from the automatic comparison between the diameter of the central disk and the diameter of the surrounding circles. These results suggest that whether an agent codes the spatial position of an object in egocentric coordinates (centred on her own body) or in allocentric coordinates (centred on an item of the visual array) matters to the accuracy of the movement whereby she scales the distance between her thumb and index finger. In short, visual awareness of shape and size seems to be dissociated from accuracy of grip (cf. Haffenden and Goodale, 1998; Haffenden et al., 2001).

8.3.2. Egocentric and allocentric frames of reference

The notion of a frame of reference was first defined as 'a locus or set of loci with respect to which spatial position is defined' (Pick and Lockman, 1981, p. 40). The spatial location of an object can be encoded in relation to either the agent's own spatial position or the spatial position of some other object independent of the agent. The former frame of reference centred on the agent is egocentric, whereas the latter frame of reference, which depends neither on the presence of the agent nor on her location, is allocentric.

In a task of reaching and grasping an object, the visuo-motor system must compute the absolute (non-relative) size, shape, and orientation of the target and represent its location in an egocentric frame of reference centred on the agent's body.[8] In fact, it must update the representation of the location of the target relative to the agent, as the action unfolds, by converting the representation of the location of the target from eye-centred coordinates, to head-centred coordinates, to torso-centred coordinates, and finally to hand- or finger-centred coordinates.[9]

---

[8] By 'absolute size', we mean that the visuo-motor system does *not* compute the size of the target relative to surrounding objects present in the visual array.

[9] Coding a target's spatial position in egocentric coordinates is also necessary for pointing when pointing is a visuo-motor behavior, i.e. when it involves making contact with the target as opposed to producing an ostensive communicative gesture (either as an imperative request or to draw someone else's attention to some target).

By contrast, perceptual judgments exhibit more flexibility: some perceptual judgments use an egocentric frame of reference; others use an allocentric frame of reference. In particular, perceptual judgments about the spatial position of an object can either use an egocentric or an allocentric frame of reference. For example, one can judge (or form the belief) that an apple is on one's right. One can also form the judgment that the apple is on the plate. In the former case, the perceptual judgment uses spatial information coded in an egocentric frame of reference. In the latter case, it uses spatial information coded in an allocentric frame of reference. Now, as emphasized by advocates of the two-visual systems model, perceptual judgments about the size, shape, and colour of objects often require the use of an allocentric (or scene-based) frame of reference centred on items of the visual array (Milner and Goodale, 1995; Jacob and Jeannerod, 2003). The reason is that visually based perceptual judgments of size are typically comparative: in a perceptual task, one automatically sees some things as smaller (or larger) than others.[10] This is why perceptual judgments of e.g. relative sizes or shapes, unlike visually guided actions, are notoriously open to visual illusions. Insofar as a perceptual judgment about an object's shape involves a correlative judgment about its size, if the latter is comparative, so is the former.[11] (For a discussion of this claim, see Bermudez, 2007 and Schröder, 2007. For a reply see Jacob and Jeannerod, 2007b.) Furthermore a goal of perceptual processing is to enable recognition (or identification) of an object over time by linking new visually processed information to older information already stored in memory. Observers never occupy exactly the same spatial standpoint relative to an object twice. Nor are illumination conditions twice ever exactly the same. Thus, recognition of objects over time is best served by an object-dependent and viewer-independent representation.

8.3.4. How does D.F. code spatial information?

Previous investigation has showed that patient D.F.'s spared dorsal stream enables her to grasp a target successfully, and, we suggest, to code its spatial position in egocentric coordinates centred on her hand and fingers. However, D.F.'s spared dorsal stream does not enable her to make perceptual judgments about the size and shape of visually presented objects. As we just argued, unlike perceptual judgments of relative size and shape (which require the use of allocentric coordinates), perceptual judgments about the spatial location of a visual object can be made using either an allocentric or an egocentric frame of reference. So, the question arises whether D.F.'s spared dorsal stream might enable her to make perceptual judgments about the spatial position of a visual object coded in an egocentric frame of reference. This question has been explored in a set of interesting experiments by Schenk (2006). These 2 × 2 experiments were designed to dissociate the contrast between perceptual and visuo-motor processing from the contrast between coding the spatial position of an object in respectively an allocentric and an egocentric frame of reference (see Fig. 5.1, p. 77).

In the so-called 'allocentric perceptual' task, two dots (one white and one black) were presented at various distances to the left and right of a cross. Participants were asked to judge which of the two dots was closer to the cross (see Fig. 5.1a). In the 'egocentric perceptual task', the cross was replaced by the participant's felt (but unseen) fingertip. The participants' task was to judge which of the two visible dots was closer to the fingertip—using proprioceptive information about the finger's position (see Fig. 5.1b). In the 'allocentric motor task', a dot was displayed to the right of a cross (at various distances) and participants were asked to point their index finger to an invisible target whose distance

---

[10] Hence the illusory perceptual judgments in e.g. Titchener illusions.

[11] A perceptual judgment about the location of an object can make use of spatial information coded in some egocentric frame of reference. But if one is to form a perceptual judgment about the relative size and/or shape of an object (i.e. its size and/or shape relative to the size and/or shape of some other neighbouring object), then the spatial positions (relative to one another) of the objects, whose attributes are being visually compared, must be coded in some allocentric frame of reference.

relative to the starting position of their finger was identical to the distance between the dot and the cross (see Fig. 5.1c). In the 'egocentric motor' task, a target dot was presented to the right of the starting position of the participant's index finger and the participant's task was to move his finger from its starting position to the target (see Fig. 5.1d).

As predicted by the action/perception dual model, Schenk (2006) found that there was no significant difference between D.F. and controls in the egocentric motor task (1d), whereas D.F. was deeply impaired in the allocentric perceptual task (1b). The results are more puzzling for the egocentric perceptual task and the allocentric motor task. Despite the fact that the task was perceptual, Schenk (2006) found that D.F. was significantly better in the egocentric perceptual task (Fig. 5.1b) than in both allocentric tasks (Fig. 5.1a) and (Fig. 5.1c). Furthermore, despite the fact that the task was motor, she was deeply impaired in the allocentric motor task (Fig. 5.1c). On the basis of the fact that D.F.'s performances in both egocentric tasks (Fig. 5.1b)–(5.1d) are better than her performances in both allocentric tasks (Fig. 5.1a)–(5.1c), Schenk (2006) argues that the dissociation exemplified by D.F. is not between perceptual and visuo-motor processing, but instead between the ability to code spatial information in respectively allocentric and egocentric coordinates.

Schenk's (2006) argument for the view that D.F.'s impairment is better conceptualized as 'an allocentric than a perceptual deficit' is weakened by two putative confounds. First, it is really unclear that the process probed by allocentric motor task (Fig. 5.1c) should be conceived as a visuo-motor process. Instead, as noticed by Milner and Goodale (2008, p. 778), what D.F. is requested to do in this task (Fig. 5.1c) is to provide a non-verbal *manual report* of her perceptual judgment about the distance between the cross and the dot. On this account, D.F.'s failure is not evidence of a visuo-motor deficit, but a failure of perceptual judgment tested via a manual report. If so, then D.F.'s failure in this task (Fig. 5.1c) jointly shows that she cannot code the position of a dot relative to a cross in an allocentric frame of reference and that her perceptual judgment about the distance between the cross and the dot (as revealed by her manual report) is severely impaired (as predicted by the action/perception dual model).

Nor is it clear which mental process is being probed in the egocentric perceptual task (Fig. 5.1b) in either healthy controls or in D.F. Arguably, for healthy participants, task (Fig. 5.1b) counts as a perceptual task leading to a perceptual judgment about which of two dots is further away from the participant's fingertip. Schenk (2006) assumes that healthy participants code the position of each dot in an egocentric frame of reference centred on their fingertip. However, contrary to Schenk's (2006) assumption, it is unclear whether healthy participants solve the task by making use of spatial information about the positions of the dots in an egocentric or an allocentric frame of reference. The experiment has not ruled out the possibility that healthy participants, who can feel it but can't see it, code the spatial position of their fingertip relative to each dot in an allocentric frame of reference centred on each dot. If so, then it is misleading to describe the task as a perceptual *egocentric* task. Furthermore, as has been suggested by Milner and Goodale (2008, p. 777), the experiment does not rule out the possibility that D.F. solves the task by using motor imagery, e.g. by imagining pointing her index finger to each dot. If so, then the process whereby D.F. solves task (Fig. 5.1b) is *not* a perceptual process.

Schenk (2006, p. 1370) argues further that D.F.'s 'normal' performance in egocentric perceptual task (1b) casts doubt on Jacob and Jeannerod's (2003, chapter 6) claim that making a perceptual judgment about an object's visual attribute (e.g. size, shape, orientation) requires coding the object's spatial position in an allocentric frame of reference. First of all, it is worth observing, as Milner and Goodale (2008, p. 777) have, that D.F.'s performance in this task (Fig. 5.1b), although better than her own performance in this task (Fig. 5.1c), is significantly worse than both the performance of average controls in task (Fig. 5.1b) and her own performance in the egocentric visuo-motor task (Fig. 5.1d), in which she is as good as the best controls. On the assumption that task (Fig. 5.1b) probes a perceptual process in either healthy controls or D.F., the relevant perceptual judgment is about a dot's spatial location (or position), not about an object's size, shape, or orientation. Secondly, it is open to doubt whether in the egocentric perceptual task (Fig. 5.1b) controls code the positions of dots in an egocentric frame of reference and also whether the process whereby D.F. solves this task (Fig. 5.1b) is a perceptual process. If so, then it is at least questionable whether Schenk's results in task (Fig. 5.1b) are inconsistent with Jacob and Jeannerod's (2003) thesis.

In summary, D.F.'s spared dorsal stream enables her to code the location of target of pointing in egocentric coordinates centred on her index finger. Her spared dorsal stream does not enable D.F. to code spatial information about an object in an allocentric frame of reference centred on another item present in the visual array. This is why she fails to make a perceptual judgment about whether a white dot is further away from a cross than a black dot. This is also why she fails to match the distance between a cross and a dot by moving her finger, which of course requires her to make a perceptual judgment about the distance between the cross and the dot. Finally, the evidence reported by Schenk is compatible with the possibility that D.F.'s spared dorsal stream enables her to decide which of two dots is closer to her fingertip by means of a two-step heuristic involving (i) coding the distance between each dot and her finger tip in egocentric coordinates centred on her (felt) fingertip and (ii) imagining moving her finger to each dot.

8.4. **Conscious experiences and reportability**

We said earlier that the distinction between vision-for-perception and vision-for-action has been tied by advocates of the two-visual systems model to two further distinctions, one of which we just addressed. The second is the distinction between conscious and unconscious processing, to which we now turn. According to Clark's (2001) thesis of 'experience-based selection' (EBS), vision-for-perception enables an agent to select a relevant target present in the visual array by discriminating it from both the background and potential competitors. Once the target has been selected perceptually, vision-for-action takes over the control and guidance of the fine-tuning of the hand movement towards the target. Clark (2001, p. 496) further rejects what he calls the thesis of 'experience-based control' (EBC) i.e. the assumption that:

> conscious visual experience presents the world to the subject in a richly textured way, a way that presents fine detail (detail that may, perhaps, exceed our conceptual or propositional grasp) and that is, in virtue of this richness, especially apt for, and typically utilized in, the control and guidance of fine-tuned, real world activity.

Joint acceptance of EBS and rejection of EBC entail that visually guided actions are not based on conscious visual representations. On this view, the dorsal pathway is, in Pisella et al.'s (2000) terms, an 'automatic pilot'. If so, then agnosic patient D.F. has no conscious experience of the very properties (e.g. size and shape) of stimuli that she can efficiently process for the purpose of accurate grasp. This is why D.F.'s residual visuo-motor capacities have been compared to those of blindsight patients and her impairment has been described as a lack of visual awareness (or consciousness) of the shape, size, and orientation of objects (Goodale and Milner, 2004, p. 71). Weiskrantz (1997, p. 138) has further characterized 'the dorsal route [subserving] visual action as [...] in a sense, blindsight without blindness'.

In a recent provocative paper, however, Wallhagen (2007) has challenged Clark's (2001) endorsement of EBS and his correlative rejection of EBC on the grounds that it has the unacceptable metaphysical epiphenomenalist consequence that conscious psychological states lack causal efficacy in the production of an agent's behaviour. Wallhagen's goal is to protect the role of conscious experience in the causation of an agent's behaviour by reinterpreting the purported evidence for epiphenomenalism. Wallhagen claims that D.F. has preserved conscious visual experiences. In his view, the evidence has not ruled out the possibility that the dorsal stream could underlie some conscious experiences. Wallhagen's argument for this challenging claim is based on an interesting criticism of the reportability criterion of consciousness to which we presently turn. Wallhagen's suggestion is that, although D.F. might not be able to report her visual experience of the shapes of objects that she is able to grasp accurately, nonetheless she might enjoy some visual experience of the objects' shapes. So Wallhagen's suggestion involves a criticism of the reportability criterion of consciousness.

8.4.1. **The reportability criterion**

The reportability criterion of consciousness has been endorsed by philosophers and scientists, including those who subscribe to the so-called 'global workspace model of consciousness'.[12] In fact, this model combines two separable theses: (i) a global workspace model of *reportability*; together with (ii) acceptance of the *reportability* criterion of *consciousness*. According to the global workspace model of reportability, what makes the content of a representation reportable is its being broadcast to a wide range of brain areas or equivalently its being made globally available (or accessible) to a wide variety of consuming cognitive mechanisms (attention, working memory, planning, and reasoning). For example, as emphasized by the global workspace model of reportability, unless the content of a subject's representation were being made available to the subject's attention and working memory, the subject would fail to report it. According to the reportability criterion of consciousness, not unless a subject could report the content of a representation could the represented content count as *conscious*.

The workspace model of reportability and the reportability criterion of consciousness are clearly dissociable. For example, Block (2005, 2007, 2008) argues strongly against the reportability criterion of phenomenal consciousness, but he does accept the evidence for the workspace model of reportability or accessibility.[13] There are both grounds for and grounds against the reportability criterion of consciousness. What drives some philosophers and scientists towards the reportability criterion of phenomenal consciousness are two related worries: a verificationist epistemic worry about the intractability of consciousness to scientific investigation, and a worry about the introspective sense of ownership of experience.

If the phenomenal character of one's conscious experience is unreportable (verbally or otherwise), then the risk is that it is bound to escape the scope of objective scientific investigation.[14] The second worry is that if the phenomenal character of one's conscious experience is divorced from reportability, then conscious experience will not be of any relevance for the subject. Suppose that the phenomenology (or phenomenal character) of one's visual experience of e.g. a red tomato outstrips the conceptual content of one's belief that the relevant tomato is red (by virtue of being richer, more fine-grained and more detailed). Suppose also that all one can report (verbally or otherwise) is what one believes and that what one believes depends on one's cognitive (i.e. conceptual) resources. Suppose finally that the phenomenal character of one's conscious experience is partly or fully inaccessible to one's own cognitive resources. If so, then one could have a conscious experience and not believe it, i.e. not be aware of it. If so, then the phenomenal character of one's conscious experience would correspondingly not matter to anyone: it would make no difference to anyone. Furthermore, if a conscious experience is both inaccessible to scientific investigation and to oneself,

---

[12] For a defence of the global workspace model, cf. Dehaene and Naccache (2001), Dehaene and Changeux (2004), Dehaene et al. (2006), Naccache and Dehaene (2007). They argue that what secures the reportability of the content of a visual representation is the existence of long-distance neuronal connections between the visual occipito-temporal areas and parietal and frontal areas. Dennett (2001) offers a nice philosophical gloss in terms of the fame theory of consciousness.

[13] What makes a process unreportable (verbally or otherwise) by a subject is presumably that it is cognitively inaccessible to the subject's attention and working memory. If so, then cognitive accessibility (to attention and working memory) is a necessary condition of reportability.

[14] As Dehaene and Changeux (2004) write, for example: '... we shall deliberately limit ourselves, in this review, to only one aspect of consciousness, the notion of *conscious access* [...] we emphasize *reportability* as a key property of conscious representations [...] Our view [...] is that conscious access is one of the few empirically tractable problems presently accessible to an authentic scientific investigation.' See also Dennett (2001). For a reply, see Block (2007).

then one might have a conscious experience and nobody might know anything about it.[15] Hence, the reportability criterion seems to be a useful tool to dispel both the verificationist and the introspective worries.

8.4.2. Unreported conscious experiences

However, what casts doubt on the reportability criterion is the empirical evidence for the existence of unreported conscious experiences suggested by the examination of neglect patients and by experiments on change blindness. There are no doubt cases where a person rightly believes that, although her visuo-motor behaviour shows that she does process some visual information about a stimulus, nonetheless she is visually unaware of it. Blindsight patients, whose condition results from a lesion in the primary visual areas, seem to be such a case (cf. Weiskrantz, 1997). However, there also seem to be cases where a person is visually aware of something but fails to acknowledge it: she sees something and believes that she does not. If such cases exist, then they show that people may have visual experiences that they cannot report because they fail to turn their visual experience into a perceptual judgment. Such cases have been reported and, as we shall argue shortly, the scientific evidence about these cases does not support the application of the reportability criterion of consciousness.

Arguably, among the necessary conditions for forming the introspective belief that one saw (or visually experienced) property F of stimulus s is that one forms the perceptual judgment that F is being exemplified by s. Arguably, one could not judge that s is F unless one possessed and deployed some concept of property F. Nor could one believe that one saw F unless one possessed and deployed the concept SEE. But now it clearly seems like an unacceptably strong necessary condition for one to visually experience F that one deploys the concept SEE. Similarly, it seems too strong to require that not unless one deploys the concept F could one visually experience an F. For example, it seems overly strong to require that not unless one recognizes or identifies an object's geometrical shape by applying to it the concept *octagonal* could one visually experience an octagonal object. Therefore, a subject can lack the introspective belief that she visually experienced some stimulus s or some property F (e.g. *octagonal*) of stimulus s because of an attentional or a memory failure, and yet she can have the experience in question.[16]

We start with patients with unilateral spatial *neglect* and/or *extinction*, whose impairment results from a lesion in the right inferior parietal lobe. Unlike blindsight patients, patients with unilateral extinction in their contralesional left hemispace may detect an isolated stimulus on their left, but, if they are presented with two *competing* stimuli, the stimulus located more towards the ipsilesional side of the lesion 'extinguishes' its competitor located more towards the contralesional side. As Driver and Vuilleumier (2001) emphasize, extinction reveals that neglect patients have a deep impairment in allocating *attentional* resources to competing stimuli according to their respective positions in the patient's hemispace. For instance, Mattingley et al. (1997) report an experiment in which a parietal patient was presented with bilateral stimuli consisting of partially occluded four black circles that could either give rise to an illusory Kanizsa square or not. Mattingley et al. (1997) found that the extinction was significantly less severe when the stimulus gave rise to the subjective experience of an illusory common surface than when it did not (even though the experience of illusory contours

---

[15] Something like this worry seems behind Levine's (2007) claim that 'the idea of phenomenal consciousness totally divorced from any access by the subject does not really seem like any kind of consciousness at all.' For some replies, see Block (2007) and Dretske (1993), who endorses explicitly the view that one might have a conscious experience and not be conscious of it, hence not know it.

[16] Such cases are used by Dretske (2006) as evidence against what he calls the 'subjective test of consciousness' ($_sTa$) and by Block (2007) who argues that the neural machinery underlying cognitive accessibility is not a constitutive part of the neural machinery underlying visual phenomenology. Block's (2007) distinction between phenomenal and access consciousness can be more or less mapped onto Dretske's (2006) distinction between object-awareness and fact-awareness.

required visual filling-in). The contrast between the two conditions is the contrast between attending either to a *single* object spread over both sides of the patient's visual field or to *four* competing distinct entities. In the first condition, the stimuli are transformed into constituents of a *single* object (e.g. one Kanizsa square). In the second condition, the stimuli compete for the patient's perceptual attention in the neglected hemispace and competition produces extinction on the left side. Thus, the patient's ability to report her visual experience of the stimuli in her neglected visual field depends on whether the task requires her to allocate her attention to one object or more (cf. Fig. 8.1).

Driver and Vuilleumier (2001, p. 54) report a remarkable attentional modulation of extinction according to the requirements of the task. When presented with objects of different shapes in one, two, or possibly four distinct locations and asked to report their location, the patient extinguished left-sided stimuli in bilateral displays. But when shown the *same* stimuli and asked to *enumerate* them (i.e. one, two, or four), the same patient had no difficulty reporting 'two' or 'four' shapes in bilateral displays. In the first localization task, the stimuli compete for the patient's attention and competition produces extinction in the left side of the patient's visual field. In the second enumeration task, it is likely that the patient exploits a subitizing procedure which enables her to extract the cardinality of a small set by processing preattentively distinct elements as members of a *single* set (cf. Fig. 8.2). If so, then it is likely that the patient's preattentive visual experience of the very same stimuli on her left side is the same in both conditions. Arguably, a switch in the patient's allocation of attention is likely to modify aspects of the phenomenal character (e.g. the intensity) of his or her visual experience. However, it does not seem plausible to assume that a switch in the patient's allocation of attention

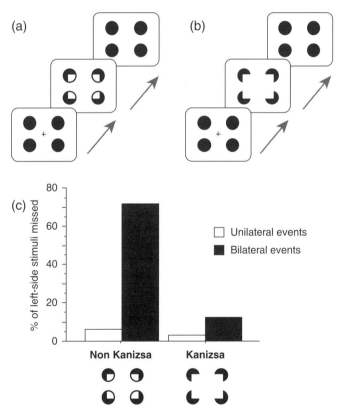

Fig. 8.1 A neglect patient was showed either bilateral or unilateral presentations of either (b) a Kanizsa white square of (a) four partially occluded black circles. (c) shows much lower extinction of bilateral presentations of Kanizsa square than bilateral presentations of non-Kanizsa stimuli. (From Driver and Vuilleumier, 2001. Reprinted with the permission of Cognition.)

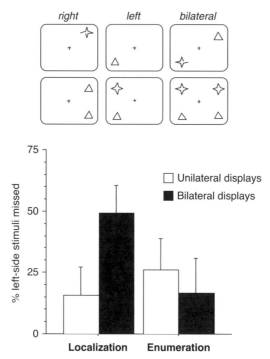

Fig. 8.2 Three right parietal patients were showed visual stimuli in one, two, or four possible locations across hemifields. When asked to report where the shapes appeared (i.e. on the left, right, or both sides), the patients consistently extinguished left-sided stimuli in bilateral displays. However, when shown the same stimuli but now asked to enumerate them (i.e. one, two, or four), the patients had no difficulty reporting 'two' or 'four' shapes in bilateral displays: extinction was eliminated. (From Driver and Vuilleumier, 2001. Reprinted with the permission of Cognition.)

creates (or *generates*) her visual experience. To say that a modulation of attention may alter the character of one's visual experience is not to say that it can *create* it *ex nihilo*. As Block (2007a), Dretske (2006), and Lamme (2006) have argued, failures of attention are consistent with the existence of visual experience in the neglected part of the visual field.

We now turn to instances of so-called *change blindness*, i.e. an experimentally demonstrated phenomenon whereby healthy participants turn out to neglect a significant change in their visual environment. The interpretation of *change blindness* is controversial. Some take it to show that healthy participants believe that they are visually aware of more than they really are (Dennett, 1991, 2001; O'Regan and Noë, 2001; Dehaene et al., 2006). Others take it to show that healthy participants are visually aware of more than they think they are. On this latter view, what subjects believe they are visually aware of results from what they can attend to, judge and report, and not from what they are visually aware of, and what they are visually aware of can be richer and more fine-grained than what they can attend to, judge and report (Block, 2007, 2008; Dretske, 2004, 2006; Simons and Rensink, 2005). Lamme (2003) and Landman et al. (2003) report an experiment that combines features of both the change blindness paradigm and Sperling's (1960) paradigm (for extended discussion, see also Block, 2007). Healthy participants are presented for 500 ms with a circular array of eight rectangles each of which is either horizontally or vertically oriented. Then the array is occluded by a grey screen for a duration varying from 200 ms to 1500 ms. Finally, subjects are presented with a new circular array of eight rectangles either horizontally or vertically oriented. Participants are required to say whether or not the orientation of a particular cued rectangle in the new array is the same as it was in the previous array. In condition (a), the cue appears at the end when participants are asked to judge. Participants respond correctly only 60% of the time (a result in accordance with experiments on change blindness). In condition (b), the cue appears during the initial presentation of the array at the beginning. Not surprisingly, participants' responses are almost 100% correct. The most interesting condition is the last one. In condition (c), the cue is superimposed on the grey screen during the interval between the two array presentations (cf. Fig. 8.3). When the relevant rectangle is cued after removal of the stimulus, participants' performance is almost as good as in condition (b), in which the relevant rectangle is cued while it is visible. As Lamme (2003, pp. 13–14)

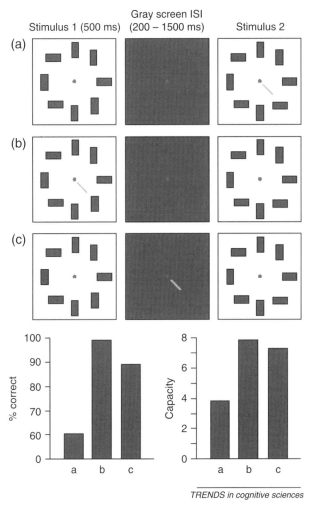

TRENDS in cognitive sciences

Fig. 8.3 Subjects see Stimulus 1, followed by a grey screen inter-stimulus interval (ISI), after which they see Stimulus 2. Subjects are then asked whether the cued item (indicated by the orange segment) has changed or not. In (a) it has changed orientation. Subjects perform poorly at this task (60% correct, lower left histogram). Performance can be converted into a 'capacity' measure (lower right histogram) indicating how many items the subject had available (in working memory) for change detection: in this case, approximately four items. When the relevant item is cued in advance (b), subjects perform almost 100% correct (resulting in a virtual capacity of all eight objects). However, when subjects are cued (c) after the removal of Stimulus 1, but before the onset of Stimulus 2, they perform almost as well and seem to have stored information about almost all objects. (From Lamme, 2003. Reprinted with the permission of Trends in Cognitive Sciences.)

observes, cueing a visible item in an array before the change protects against change blindness. Remarkably, this experiment demonstrates that cueing an item before the change, but after removal of the stimulus, also protects (almost as efficiently) against change blindness.

There are two main theoretical options to account for the experimental results reported by either Sperling (1960) or Lamme (2003) and Landman et al. (2003), according to whether or not one accepts the distinction between the content of a visual experience and the content of a perceptual judgment. If one rejects the distinction, then arguably participants' visual experience is generated by attentional processes triggered by the cue. On this view, participants' visual experience (i.e. perceptual judgment) would occur after the cue. However, if one accepts the distinction, then participants' visual experience (unlike their perceptual judgment) may pre-exist to the cue, which acts as a selective mechanism. Rightly in our view, Block (2007, 2008), Lamme (2003), Landman et al. (2003), and Landman and Sligte (2007) choose the latter option.

8.4.3. Iconic buffer and working memory

Both Block (2007, 2008) and Lamme (2003) argue against the reportability criterion of consciousness on the basis of a distinction between two short-term memory systems. The first is an 'iconic' (visual or sensory) memory system with higher storage capacity but shorter persistence, in which all (or almost all) of the items in the first array can be stored for at least 1500 ms. The second 'working memory' system has a longer persistence but a maximum storage capacity of about four items, which have been submitted to attentional processes. They hypothesize that being stored in the working memory system is a necessary condition for being reportable. After an item stored in the iconic memory system has been cued, it is transferred from the iconic to the working memory system for report.[17]

As Block (2008, pp. 307–09) points out, it is likely that information about the orientation of the cued rectangle (in the Landman et al., 2003 experiment) is stored in the iconic memory system *before* being cued. What the cue does is merely to trigger attention to the represented cued item. Attention in turn triggers a process of information transfer from iconic to working memory. Transfer is a selective process of elimination in which some of the information present in iconic memory is being *erased*. On the alternative view, until cueing occurs, no (or little) information about the orientation of the rectangle to be cued would be encoded. The representation of the orientation of the cued rectangle would thus be generated by the creative process following the occurrence of the cue.[18]

To recap, storing information about orientation in the iconic buffer may secure visual experience, but being encoded in the iconic buffer is not sufficient for report. The information needs to be stored in working memory for judgment and report. Arguably to achieve a coherent description of the results of Landman et al.'s (2003) experiment on change blindness, it seems necessary to assume that in condition c), healthy subjects are able to store in the iconic buffer the content of their visual phenomenal experience of the orientation of the rectangle *before* it is cued. After the non-visible rectangle has been cued (i.e. after the rectangle is occluded by the grey screen), information about the orientation of the cued rectangle becomes accessible for report by being transferred into working memory. On this account, a subject's failure to report the orientation of a rectangle entails that the subject failed to make a judgment about the orientation of the rectangle, but it does not entail that the subject failed to have a visual experience of the orientation of the rectangle. What recommends this account is that on the alternative account, the subject would not form a visual representation of the orientation of the rectangle until the cue occurs, i.e. until the rectangle becomes invisible!

One of the two goals of this chapter has been to assess Wallhagen's (2007) argument for the thesis that, contrary to the standard interpretation offered by advocates of the two-visual systems model,

---

[17] For a similar account of Sperling's (1960) experiment, cf. Dretske (2006) and Fodor (2007).

[18] Block's (2007, 2008) further view is that the iconic memory system is a repository for rich visual phenomenology.

apperceptive agnosic patient D.F. might be visually conscious of the sizes and shapes of objects which she can grasp successfully. One major premise in Wallhagen's (2007) argument is the rejection of the reportability criterion of consciousness. In this section, we have examined independent empirical evidence that does support Wallhagen's (2007) rejection of the reportability criterion of consciousness. Nonetheless, as we shall argue in the following section, we think that the evidence about D.F. fails to support Wallhagen's contention that she is visually aware of shape.

8.5. **Is D.F. visually aware of shape?**

We can now turn to the question: does activity in D.F.'s spared dorsal stream make her visually aware of the shape of objects on which she acts efficiently? As Milner and Goodale (1995, p. 200) recognize, what the evidence shows is that D.F. exemplifies a dissociation between visuo-motor processing of size and shape and perceptual report of size and shape. Clearly, D.F.'s impaired ability to report reflects her inability to make perceptual judgments about size and shape. Given our previous description of the results of change blindness, it is still an open possibility that activity in the dorsal stream underlying visuo-motor computations makes D.F. visually aware of size and shape.

8.5.1. **What does failure to report show?**

As Milner (1995) and Milner and Goodale (1995: 200) acknowledge, D.F. is

> unable to demonstrate any recognition of different shapes no matter what form of perceptual report is required, including forced-choice responding [...] it could be argued that the best available characterization of the dissociations we have observed is one between perceptual report (by whatever means) and visuo-motor guidance.

D.F. is able to compute an object's size, shape, and orientation in a visuo-motor format for the purpose of grasping it, but according to the reportability criterion of consciousness, she would be visually aware of an object's size, shape, and orientation only if she were able to report manually (or otherwise) her perceptual judgment about an object's size, shape, and orientation, which she is not. As argued in section 8.3, the dissociation between spared visuo-motor processing and impaired perceptual processing of an object's shape exemplified by patient D.F. is a crucial piece of evidence for the claim that activity of the dorsal stream does not underlie visual awareness. Indeed, the dissociation exemplified by visual form apperceptive agnosic patient D.F. has been linked explicitly by Milner and Goodale (1995, p. 200) and Goodale and Milner (2004, pp. 70–1) to similar dissociations exemplified by blindsight patients, who, unlike neglect patients, are recognized widely to lack visual experience.

The inference leading from the fact that D.F. fails to make accurate perceptual judgment about shape to the conclusion that she lacks visual awareness of shape is precisely the target of Wallhagen's (2007) criticism. As Wallhagen (2007) correctly points out, as such, this inference seems to rely on the reportability criterion of consciousness. As we pointed out in section 8.4, there are grounds for rejecting the reportability criterion of consciousness. If this criterion fails, then it is conceivable that D.F. could fail to make accurate judgments of shape and still be visually aware of shape. In Wallhagen's (2007, pp. 18–19) challenging view, the experimental evidence shows only that D.F. is severely impaired in tasks requiring her to make a manual *report* about an object's shape, size, and orientation. The reason D.F. cannot report (manually or otherwise) the shape, size, and orientation of an object is that she cannot make a perceptual judgment about an object's shape, size, and orientation, which she cannot do because her problem is, as Wallhagen (ibid.) puts it:

> a conceptual one: she cannot identify shapes, sizes and orientations, she cannot 'bring them under concepts' [...] However, [...] it does not follow that she is not aware, in a non-conceptual way, of the shapes, sizes, and orientations of things [...] Aspects of form may well be phenomenally present to D.F

Wallhagen (2007, pp. 18–19) argues that, as the experimental evidence shows, D.F.'s intact dorsal stream enables her to grasp objects efficiently, which, he argues, she could not do unless she was visually aware of the shape, size, and orientation of the grasped object. As Clark (2008, 1464) notes, though in different philosophical jargon, Wallhagen's (2007) diagnosis of D.F.'s impairment is reminiscent of O'Regan and Noë's (2001, p. 969) characterization of D.F.'s condition as one of 'partial awareness' whereby 'she is unable to describe what she sees but is otherwise able to use it for the purpose of guiding action' (see Goodale, 2001, for a rebuttal).

In a nutshell, from the fact that D.F. fails to form accurate judgments about shape, it does not logically follow that she is not visually aware of shape; but it does not logically follow either that she is visually aware of the shape. Blindsight patients exhibit visuo-motor capacities but they lack visual awareness of the stimuli onto which they can act. Suppose we apply Wallhagen's (2007) use of the argument against the reportability criterion to healthy subjects whose visual perceptual capacities give rise to visual awareness. In the presence of a Titchener disk surrounded by an annulus of circles either larger or smaller than it, for example, healthy subjects are visually aware of the illusory size of the diameter of a Titchener disk, in accordance with their illusory perceptual belief or judgment (as revealed by their manual report). They also visually compute the non-illusory size of the diameter of the disk when they accurately grasp it (as revealed by their maximum grip aperture), but this does *not* make them visually aware of the non-illusory size of the diameter of the disk. Participants give no evidence that they experience a cognitive dissonance: they do not seem to have contradictory beliefs about the size of the diameter of the central disk. If so, then the visuo-motor processing that leads to the veridical size of the target does not give rise to a belief. It seems as if the content of the visuo-motor representation (if any) does not make its way to the agent's consciousness. Only a manual report of a perceptual judgment is evidence of what a subject both believes and is visually aware.

Now the question raised by Wallhagen's (2007) critique of the application of the reportability criterion of consciousness to patient D.F. can be decomposed into two sub-questions: first, does the activity of D.F.'s spared dorsal stream enable her to compute the shape (or contour) of objects that she can grasp? Secondly, does the output of the visuo-motor computation of the properties of objects that enable her to grasp them make her visually aware of these properties?

8.5.2. Can D.F. compute shape per se?

A recent series of experiments on D.F. reported by Schenk and Milner (2006) are relevant to the first question, i.e. whether D.F.'s spared dorsal stream enable her to compute the shape of objects on which she acts efficiently. Schenk and Milner (2006) ran a series of five experiments designed to explore the parameters involved in D.F.'s representation of an object's shape. In experiment 1, D.F. was showed either a square or a rectangle with the same area and different widths (the rectangle being the wider of the two). D.F.'s task was to name the shape. As in previous experiments, in this task, D.F. was at chance. However, when D.F. was asked to grasp the target object with her right hand while calling out the object's shape during the action (experiment 2) or just before she started her hand movement (experiment 3), her recognition of the object's shape was significantly above chance.[19] This positive effect was lost when D.F. was asked to name the object's shape while pointing to the object (experiment 4). Only grasping, not motor activity in general, enhances D.F.'s ability to recognize an object's shape. So far, the results show that performing a task of grasping considerably helps D.F. make a perceptual judgment about an object's shape. On this basis, one might conclude, as Wallhagen does, that D.F. has a conscious visual experience of shape.

---

[19] The result of experiment 3 rules out the putative contribution of proprioceptive information, haptic information, or efferent information about her maximum grip aperture to D.F.'s recognition of an object's shape in experiment 2.

However, Schenk and Milner (2006) performed a last experiment where D.F. was showed objects of identical width and different shapes: either a rectangle or a square (experiment 5). Like in experiment 2, she was asked to grasp the target object with her right hand while calling out the object's shape during the action. In this condition, D.F.'s ability to discriminate between the two shapes was at chance. The contrast with the previous results shows that the relevant parameter in both D.F.'s perceptual judgment and her visuo-motor act is the object's *width*, not its shape proper.

Furthermore, Schenk and Milner (2006) report that, in experiment 3, D.F.'s verbal reports about the object's shape (produced before the onset of her act of grasping) are significantly better than her motor discriminations as revealed by measurements of her maximum grip aperture (MGA). They also report that D.F.'s actual verbal reports (in experiment 3) are significantly better than they would be if they strictly reflected her motor responses as revealed by measurement of her MGA. Now, these two further results raise the following puzzle: the computation of the object's width (presumably performed by D.F.'s intact dorsal stream) is available for both grasping the object and verbally reporting its shape. The puzzle is: why is verbal report more accurate than grasping? Why does processing of width information during the preparation of grasping better serve D.F.'s verbal response than her MGA?

This is puzzling for two reasons. First, earlier evidence seemed to suggest that when showed Efron rectangles, D.F. was significantly better at grasping them than at discriminating them verbally. Secondly, in experiment 3, the route from width information to accurate grasping (grip calibration or motor discrimination) seems more direct than the route from width information to verbal report of shape. Arguably, accurate grip formation just consists in width discrimination, but verbal discrimination (between a square and a rectangle of different widths) requires combining width discrimination with the knowledge that the rectangle is wider than the square. A possible solution to the puzzle is that in experiments 2 and 3, verbal report and motor discrimination compete for access to width information. But in experiment 3 (unlike experiment 2), D.F. is requested to make the verbal judgment *before* starting her motor act. In other words, the former dominates the latter in the competition. If so, then verbal report gains access to width information at the expense of motor discrimination. This might explain the surprising fact that D.F.'s verbal judgments are more accurate than her motor discriminations in Schenk and Milner's (2006) experiment 3.

8.5.3. Visuo-motor computation and phenomenal awareness of width

Schenk and Milner's (2006) experiments show that performing a visuo-motor task of grasping helps significantly D.F. in making a verbal judgment about an object's shape. We suggest that D.F. can make accurate use of visual information about features of the shape of a target when she codes the location of the target in egocentric coordinates centred on her fingers. However, as we argued above, two distinct issues arise: (a) which features of shape does D.F. make use of?; and (b) is she visually aware of the features of shape she makes accurate use of?

Schenk and Milner's (2006) experiment 5 helps us solve question (a): she makes use of width, not shape (or contour) per se. Why? Because when a square and a rectangle are equal in width, she is at chance. Milner and Goodale (2008, p. 777) rightly argue that 'the visuo-motor cueing benefited only width discrimination [...], not shape discrimination per se'. In other words, D.F.'s spared dorsal stream enables her to compute accurately width information, not shape information per se. In order to accurately grasp a target, D.F. must combine information about the target's width and the target's location coded in an egocentric frame of reference centred on her fingers. Furthermore, experiment 3 shows that there can be competition between (verbal or manual) report and grip formation for access to width information. In experiment 3, when she was required to make a verbal report before the onset of her motor act, her grip formation turned out to be less reliable than her verbal judgment. Arguably, after being first used as a cue for making a verbal report about the object's shape, width information might have been degraded when later combined with information about the location of the target coded in an egocentric frame of reference centred on D.F.'s fingers. It thus seems as if D.F.

can compute width information (relevant to grasping), not shape information per se, and use the former as a cue for making *guesses* about an object's shape (in restricted conditions).[20]

Let us now turn to the second question: is D.F. visually aware of the features of an object's shape (e.g. width) that enable her to grasp objects? Three pieces of evidence are relevant to investigating the second question. First of all, as the brain-imaging study conducted by James et al. (2003) show, unlike healthy participants, D.F. showed no difference in activity in her lateral occipital cortex (area LO of the ventral stream) for the contrast between scrambled line drawings and line drawings of common objects. This suggests that activity in D.F.'s spared dorsal stream underlying the visuo-motor computation of parameters relevant for grasping is not sufficient for making her visually aware of features of shape.[21]

Secondly, the results from Schenk and Milner's (2006) experiments show that D.F. computes width, not shape per se. Let us suppose that the width and length of a two-dimensional object are features of the object that must be bound together by the visual system to generate a representation the object's shape. One possibility is that the lesion in D.F.'s ventral stream impairs the process whereby in healthy subjects the visual system binds together the width and the length to generate a visual representation of the overall shape or contour of a two-dimensional object. If so, then the question arises whether D.F. is visually aware of width per se.

Thirdly, in section 8.4, on the basis of Landman et al.'s (2003) change blindness experiment, we argued that storing information about the orientation of a rectangle in working memory is necessary for reportable judgment, but not for phenomenal awareness. Following Block (2007) and Landman and Sligte (2007), we hypothesized that it is necessary and sufficient for phenomenal awareness of orientation that information about orientation be stored in the iconic buffer—a sensory memory system with larger storing capacity and shorter persistence than working memory. If we extend this hypothetical condition to D.F.'s visual awareness of width, then it is a necessary and sufficient condition for D.F.'s visual awareness of width that she can store width information in an iconic buffer.

Given these three pieces of empirical evidence, the question whether D.F. is visually aware of the width of objects that she grasps successfully can be reduced to two further empirical questions: (i) can one be visually aware of unbound features of shape (e.g. width)? Or instead does one's visual awareness of the features of an object's shape result from their being bound together into a full shape?; and (ii) can activity of D.F.'s spared dorsal stream store representations of features of shape in iconic memory? If the answer to either question is negative, then it is unlikely that D.F. is visually aware of the width of objects.

8.6. Conclusion

In this chapter, we have disentangled the contribution of two separable factors to the two-visual systems model of vision: how spatial information is coded and whether visual information reaches consciousness. We have claimed that visuo-motor processing (or vision-for-action) must code spatial information in egocentric coordinates. By contrast, perceptual judgment is more flexible: judgments about the spatial position of a visual object can make use of either an egocentric or an allocentric frame of reference. But making a comparative judgment about the relative size of an item (in relation to the size of another item) in a visual array requires localizing the spatial position of the first item in an allocentric frame of reference centred on the visual scene. We have also suggested that an agent may be visually unaware of the shape of an object if she codes its spatial position in egocentric coordinates centred on her fingers (as D.F. must in a task of grasping). Clearly, on the reportability

---

[20] Visual form agnosic patient S.B. examined by Dijkerman et al. (2004) seems slightly better than patient D.F. at discriminating features of shape.

[21] Preserved islands in her ventral stream seem involved, however, in D.F.'s sensitivity to, and visual phenomenal awareness of, colours (cf. James et al., 2003; Goodale and Milner, 2004).

criterion of consciousness, D.F. counts as visually unaware of the shape of objects. But we also argued against the reportability criterion of consciousness. Finally, we argued in favour of the following conditional claim: if D.F.'s spared dorsal stream does not enable her either to bind the width and the length of a visual object or to store in iconic memory information about bound or unbound width, then it is unlikely that she is visually aware of features of shape (e.g. the width) of objects.[22]

References

Bermudez, J. (2007). From two visual systems to two forms of content? Comments on Pierre Jacob and Marc Jeannerod, *Ways of Seeing: The Scope and Limits of Visual Cognition. Psyche*; **13**(2): April 2007. Available at: http://psyche.cs.monash.edu.au/

Block, N. (2005). Two neural correlates of consciousness. *Trends in Cognitive Sciences*; **9**(2): 46–52.

—— (2007). Consciousness, accessibility and the mesh between psychology and neuroscience. *Behavioral and Brain Sciences*; **30**: 481–548.

—— (2008). Phenomenal and access consciousness. *Proceedings of the Aristotelian Society*; **cviii**: 289–317.

Clark, A. (2001). Visual experience and motor action: are the bonds too tight? *Philosophical Review*; **110**: 495–519.

—— (2007). What reaching teaches. *British Journal for the Philosophy of Science*; **58**: 563–594.

—— (2008). Perception, action, and experience: unraveling the golden braid. *Neuropsychologia*; **47**: 1460–1468.

Dehaene, S. and Changeux, J.P. (2004). Neural mechanisms for access to consciousness. In *The cognitive neurosciences III*, (ed. Gazzaniga, M.), pp. 1145–58. Cambridge, MA: MIT Press.

Dehaene, S. and Naccache, L. (2001). Towards a cognitive neuroscience of consciousness: basic evidence and a workspace framework. *Cognition*; **79**(1–2): 1–37.

Dehaene, S., Changeux, J.P., Naccache, L., Sackur, J., and Sergent, C. (2006). Conscious, preconscious, and subliminal processing: a testable taxonomy. *Trends in Cognitive Sciences*; **10**: 204–211.

Dennett, D.C. (1991). *Consciousness explained*. London: Allen Lane, The Penguin Press.

—— (2001). Are we explaining consciousness yet? *Cognition*; **79**(1–2): 221–237.

Dijkerman, H.C, Lê, S., Démonet, J-F., and Milner, A.D. (2004). Visuo-motor performance in a patient with visual agnosia due to an early lesion. *Cognitive Brain Research*; **20**(1): 12–25.

Dretske, F. (1981). *Knowledge and the flow of information*. Cambridge, MA: MIT Press.

—— (1993). Conscious experience. In *Perception, knowledge and belief*, (ed. F. Dretske, F.), Cambridge: Cambridge University Press.

—— (2000). *Perception, knowledge and belief*. Cambridge: Cambridge University Press.

—— (2004). Change blindness. *Philosophical Studies*; **120**: 1–18.

—— (2006). Perception without awareness. In *Perceptual experience*, (eds Gendler, T.S. and Hawthorne, J.), pp. 147–180. Oxford: Oxford University Press.

Driver, J. and Vuilleumier, P. (2001). Perceptual awareness and its loss to unilateral neglect and extinction, *Cognition*; **79**(1–2): 39–88.

Fodor, J.A. (2007). The revenge of the given. In *Contemporary debates in philosophy of mind*, (eds McLaughlin, B.P. and Cohen, J.D.), pp. 105–116. Oxford: Blackwell.

Gallese, V. (2007). The 'conscious' dorsal stream: embodied simulation and its role in space and action conscious awareness. *Psyche*; **13**(1). Available at: http://psyche.cs.monash.edu.au/.

Goodale, M.A. (2001). Real action in a virtual world. *Behavioral and Brain Sciences*; **24**: 984–985.

—— (2007). Duplex vision: separate cortical pathways for conscious perception and the control of action. In *The Blackwell companion to consciousness*, (eds Velmans, M. and Schneider, S.)Vpp. 616–627. Oxford: Blackwell.

Goodale, M.A. and Milner, D.M. (1992). Separate visual pathways for perception and action. *Trends in Neuroscience*; **15**(1): 20–25.

—— (2004). *Sight unseen: explorations in conscious and unconscious vision*. Oxford: Oxford University Press.

Goodale, M.A., Milner, A.D., Jakobson I.S., and Carey, D.P. (1991). A Neurological dissociation between perceiving objects and grasping them. *Nature*; **349**: 154–156.

Haffenden, A.M. and Goodale, M. (1998). The effect of pictorial illusion on prehension and perception. *Journal of Cognitive Neuroscience*; **10**(1): 122–136.

---

[22] Thanks to Anne Tüscher and Jérôme Dokic for useful conversations about the topic of this chapter. We are also grateful to the editors of this volume for their useful comments on the first draft of this chapter, and especially to Nivedita Gangopadhyay, not only for her comments, but also for her crucial role in both the organization of the Bristol Conference and the publication of this volume as well.

Haffenden, A.M., Schiff, K.C., and Goodale, M.A. (2001). The dissociation between perception and action in the Ebbinghaus illusion: non-illusory effects of pictorial cues on grasp. *Current Biology*; **11**: 177–181.

Jacob, P. (2005). Grasping and perceiving objects. In *Cognition and the brain, the philosophy and neuroscience movement*, (eds Brook, A. and Atkins, K.), pp. 241–283. Cambridge: Cambridge University Press.

Jacob, P. and Jeannerod, M. (2003). *Ways of seeing, the scope and limits of visual cognition*. Oxford: Oxford University Press.

—— (2007a). Précis of ways of seeing. *Psyche*; 13(2): April 2007. Available at: http://psyche.cs.monash.edu.au/.

—— (2007b). Replies to our critics. *Psyche*; 13(2): April 2007.Available at: http://psyche.cs.monash.edu.au/.

James, W.T., Culham, H., Humphrey, G.K., Milner A.D., and Goodale, M.A (2003). Ventral occipital lesions impair object recognition but not object-directed grasping: an fMRI study. *Brain*; **126**: 2463–2475.

Jeannerod, M. (1997). *The cognitive neuroscience of action*. Oxford: Blackwell.

Jeannerod, M. and Jacob, P. (2005). Visual cognition: a new look at the two-visual systems model. *Neuropsychologia*; **43**: 301–312.

Keysers, C. and Perrett, D. (2004). Demystifying social cognition. *Trends in Cognitive Sciences*; 8(11): 501–507.

Lamme, V.A.F. (2003). Why visual attention and awareness are different. *Trends in Cognitive Sciences*; 7: 12–18.

—— (2006). The true neural correlates of conscioussness. *Trends in Cognitive Sciences*; 10(11): 494–501.

Lamme, V.A.F. and Landman, R. (2001). Attention sheds on light on the origins of phenomenal experience. *Behavioral and Brain Sciences*; **24**: 993.

Landman, R., Spekreijse, H., and Lamme, V.A.F. (2003). Large capacity storage of integrated objects before change blindness. *Vision Research*; **43**(2): 149–164.

Landman, R. and Sligte, I.G. (2007). Can we equate iconic memory with visual awareness? *Behavioral and Brain Sciences*; **30**: 512–513.

Levine, J. (2007). Two kinds of access. *Behavioral and Brain Sciences*; **30**: 514–515.

Mahon, B.Z. and Caramazza, A. (2005). *Cognitive Neuropsychology*; **22**(3/4): 480–494.

Matthen, M. (2005). *Seeing, doing and knowing*. Oxford: Oxford University Press.

Mattingley, J.B., Davis, G., and Driver, J. (1997). Preattentive filling-in of visual surfaces in parietal extinction. *Science*; **275**(5300): 671–674.

Milner, D.M. (1995). Cerebral correlates of visual awareness. *Neuropsychologia*; **33**(9): 1117–1130.

Milner, D.M. and Goodale, M.A. (1995). *The visual brain in action*. Oxford: Oxford University Press.

—— (2008). Two visual systems reviewed. *Neuropsychologia*; **46**: 774–785.

Milner, A.D., Perrett, D.I., Johnston, R.S., Benson, P.J., Jordan, T.R., Heeley, D.W. et al. (1991). Perception and action in 'visual form agnosia'. *Brain*; **114**: 05–428.

Naccache, L. and Dehaene, S. (2007). Reportability and illusions of phenomenality in the light of the global neuronal workspace model. *Behavioral and Brain Sciences*; **30**: 518–520.

O'Regan J.K. and Noë, A. (2001). A sensorimotor account of vision and visual consciousness. *Behavioral and Brain Sciences*; **24**: 939–1031.

Palmer, S.E. (1999). *Vision science: photons to phenomenology*. Cambridge, MS: MIT Press.

Pisella L., Gréa H., Tilikete C., Vighetto A., Desmurget M., Rode G. et al. (2000). An 'automatic pilot' for the hand in human posterior parietal cortex: toward a reinterpretion of optic ataxia. *Nature Neuroscience*; **3**(7): 729–736.

Rees, G., Wojciulik, E., Clarke, K., Husain, M., Frith, C., and Driver, J. (2002). Neural correlates of conscious and unconscious vision in parietal extinction. *Neurocase*; **8**: 387–393.

Schenk, T. (2006). An allocentric rather than perceptual deficit in patient D.F. *Nature Neuroscience*; **9**(11): 1369–1370.

Schenk, T. and Milner, D.M. (2006). Concurrent visuo-motor behaviour improves form discrimination in a patient with visual form agnosia. *European Journal of Neuroscience*; **24**: 1495–1503.

Schröder, T. (2007). Two ways of seeing *Ways of Seeing*. *Dialogue*; **20**(46:2): 341–343.

Shoemaker, S. (1994). Self-knowledge and inner sense: the Royce Lectures. *Philosophy and Phenomenological Research*; **54**: 249–314.

Simons, D.J. and Rensink, R.A. (2005). Change blindness: past, present, and future. *Trends in Cognitive Sciences*; **9**(1): 16–20.

Sperling, G. (1960). The information available in brief visual presentations. In *Essential sources in the scientific study of consciousness*, (eds Baars, B.J., Banks, W.P., and Newman, J.B.), pp. 325–356. Cambridge, MA: MIT Press.

Sperry, R.W. (1968). Hemisphere Deconnection and unity in conscious awareness. In *Essential sources in the scientific study of consciousness*, (eds Baars, B.J., Banks, W.P., and Newman, J.B.), pp. 161–174. Cambridge, MA: MIT Press.

Ungerleider, L. and Mishkin, M. (1982). Two cortical visual systems. In *Analysis of visual behaviour*, (eds Ingle, D.J., Goodale, M.A., and Mansfield, R.J.W.), pp. 549–586. Cambridge, MA: MIT Press.

Wallhagen, M. (2007). Consciousness and action: does cognitive science support (mild) epiphenomenalism? *The British Journal for the Philosophy of Science*; **58**(3):539–561.

Weiskrantz, L. (1997). *Consciousness lost and found*. Oxford: Oxford University Press.

CHAPTER 9

Perceptual experience and the capacity to act

Susanna Schellenberg

Abstract

This paper develops and defends the capacity view, that is, the view that the ability to perceive the perspective-independent or intrinsic properties of objects depends on the perceiver's capacity to act. More specifically, I argue that self-location and spatial know-how are jointly necessary to perceive the intrinsic spatial properties of objects. Representing one's location allows one to abstract from one's particular vantage point to perceive the perspective-independent properties of objects. Spatial know-how allows one to perceive objects as the kind of things that are perceivable from points of view other than one's own and thus to perceive them as three-dimensional space occupiers.

9.1. Introduction

When we see an object, we see it from a particular point of view. As a consequence, the question arises as to how we can perceive the perspective-independent spatial properties of objects, such as their shape and size. In this paper, I will address this question. In section 9.2, I will present the idea that there is an epistemic dependence between perceiving situation-dependent properties and perceiving perspective-independent or more generally intrinsic properties. In sections 9.3 and 9.4, I will argue that the ability to perceive the intrinsic spatial properties of objects depends on the capacity to act. I will call this view *the capacity view*. More specifically, I will argue that the ability to perceive the intrinsic spatial properties of objects depends on representing one's location in relation to perceived objects, on the one hand, and having a practical understanding of space, on the other. Representing one's location in relation to perceived objects allows one to abstract from one's particular vantage point. Having a practical understanding of space allows one to perceive objects as the kind of things that are perceivable from points of view other than one's own. As I will argue, abstracting from one's particular vantage point and perceiving objects as the kind of things that are perceivable from points of view other than one's own are jointly necessary to perceive intrinsic spatial properties. In section 9.5, I will contrast the capacity view with a number of alternative views.

9.2. **The epistemic primacy of situation-dependent properties**

What is the relationship between the way objects are presented given one's point of view and the way we perceive objects to be? In the history of philosophy, the way objects are presented given one's point of view has, traditionally, been either ignored or understood in terms of mind-dependent appearance properties, such as phenomenal properties or visual field properties. In contrast to both traditions, I am proposing to understand the way objects are presented in terms of external, mind-independent properties. More specifically, I am proposing to understand the way objects are presented in terms of what I have elsewhere called situation-dependent properties.[1] Situation-dependent properties are ontologically dependent on and exclusively sensitive to intrinsic properties of the environment (such as the intrinsic shape and colour reflectance properties of objects) and situational features (such as the perceiver's location and the lighting conditions). In this sense, situation-dependent properties are functions of intrinsic properties and situational features.

So situation-dependent properties are not only mind-independent, but moreover independent of any properties of the relevant perceiver other than the perceiver's location. When I speak of a perceiver, I mean any being that is capable of being sensorily responsive to at least some properties in its environment. One can imagine perceivers whose sensory organs are extended spatially such that they can perceive an object from several angles simultaneously. The way the sensory organs are extended spatially depends on the particular kind of perceiver, but it is a necessary feature of perception that subjects perceive from somewhere at some time. As a consequence, objects are always perceived subject to situational features.

A few examples will elucidate the notion of situation-dependent properties. Consider the colour of the wall to my right. The intrinsic white colour property of the wall manifests itself in a certain way given the lighting conditions. The corners are presented as darker than the part of the wall that is in sunlight. The way the colour of the wall is presented just is the colour situation-dependent property of the wall. So the colour situation-dependent property of the wall is a function of the intrinsic white colour property of the wall and the current lighting conditions. If the intrinsic colour property is conceived of as a reflectance property, then the correlating situation-dependent property will be a wavelength emittence property.

Similarly, take the table to my left. It is presented in a certain way given my location: its shape is presented in an egocentric frame of reference, which in turn means that the object and its parts are presented as standing in specific spatial relations to my location. One side is closer to my location than the other; one part faces away from me; the length of the side closer to my location is presented as longer than the length of the side further away from my location. Any perceiver occupying the same location would, ceteris paribus, be presented with the table in the very same way. The way the table is presented to a location is, on the suggested view, an external and mind-independent, albeit situation-dependent property of the world.

It will be helpful to contrast situation-dependent properties with Shoemaker's (2001, 2006) appearance properties, Noë's (2004) P-properties, and Lewis's (1986) centred worlds. Shoemaker introduces appearance properties to reconcile an intentionalist account of phenomenal character with the possibility of spectrum-inverted subjects that are not misrepresenting. The main difference between situation-dependent properties and Shoemaker's appearance properties is that the latter but not the former are analysed in terms of how things appear to a subject, situation-dependent properties are not analysed in terms of how things appear to subjects. As Shoemaker puts it, an appearance property 'is such that something one sees has it just in case it appears to one to have it' (2006, p. 465). Insofar as these appearance properties are analysed in terms of how things appear to a subject, they are at least in part mind-dependent. So while appearance properties are relative to the sensory capacities of

---

[1] For a development and defence of situation-dependent properties, see Schellenberg, 2008. Among others, Peacocke (1983), Lycan (1995a,b), and Shoemaker (2001, 2006) treat the ways objects are presented in terms of mind-dependent properties or objects.

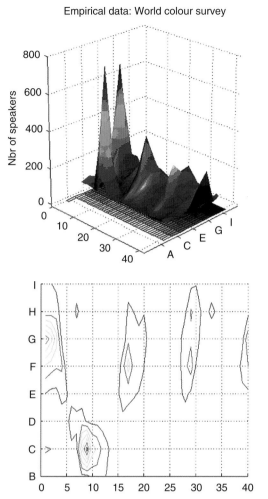

Plate 1 Histogram and contour plot showing the number of speakers in Kay and Regier's (2003) 110-culture survey of colour naming, who had a name for the colours in the selection of Munsell chips labelled A-I and 0-40 shown in the ground plane of the top graph. Strong peaks are visible at G1 and C9 corresponding to red and yellow. Weaker peaks at F17 and F29 or H29 correspond to green and blue. The iso-contours for the top 10% of these data are re-plotted as red, yellow, green, and blue coloured surfaces in the bottom right graph. (See Fig. 3.1(a, b))

Computed singular reflecting properties

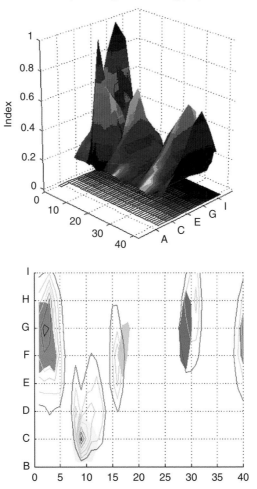

Plate 2 The degree of singularity (singularity index) of the 3×3 matrices representing the linear mapping between incoming and outgoing human cone photoreceptor absorptions for the same Munsell chips, as calculated by Philipona and O'Regan from known physical data for Munsell reflectances and cone absorption spectra. The peaks of singularity shown in the contour plot fall very close to the coloured surfaces corresponding to the top 10% of the Kay and Regier data. This shows that the colours that tend to be given names across many cultures are very close to those that change incoming light in a 'simpler' fashion (see text). Adapted from Philipona and O'Regan (2006). (See Fig. 3.2(a, b))

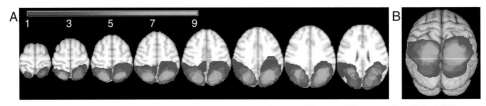

Plate 3 A: Slices representation of the lesion overlay (from z=26 to z=68, step of z=6, in MNI space). The brighter the region, the more of the patient's lesion it contains, going from 0 to 8. B: three-dimensional render of the lesion overlay, posterior view of the brain. MRIcron (http://www. sph.sc.edu/comd/rorden/mricron/) was used to draw, overlay and map the lesions From Pisella et al., in revision. (See Fig. 10.5)

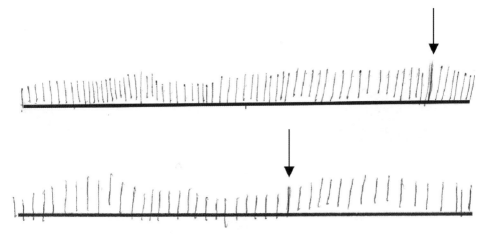

Plate 4 Segmentation and Line Bisection. Two lines segmented, and subsequently bisected, (red marks, indicated by black arrows) by two right-brain-damaged patients with left USN, who exhibit a rightward bisection error (reprinted with permission of the British Psychological Society from Gallace et al., 2008, Figure 3). (See Fig. 11.2)

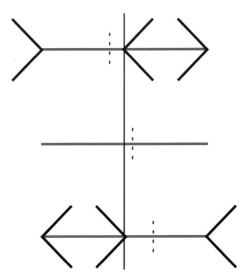

Plate 5 The Brentano- Müller-Lyer Illusion. (A)The Brentano or combined form of the Müller-Lyer illusion. The to-be-bisected segment is red, and the outward/inward projecting fins are black. The filled vertical line indicates the physical centre of the horizontal red segment. The short dashed line indicates the bisection error committed by one right-brain-damaged patient with left USN. In the baseline condition (central stimulus) the patient makes a rightward error, indicating left USN. With illusory stimuli, the bisection point is displaced leftwards (upper stimulus), or rightwards (lower stimulus), according to the side of the horizontal segment expanded by the fins (modified from Daini et al., 2002). (See Fig. 11.3)

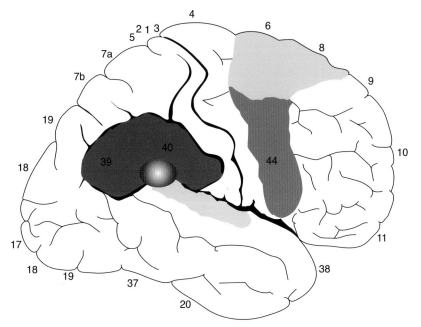

Plate 6 The Anatomy of USN.
(A) Cortical lesion sites associated with USN. Most anatomo-clinical correlation studies show that the lesion responsible for USN involves the right inferior parietal lobule (BA 39 and BA 40, red area), and the temporo-parietal junction (black-grey area). USN after right frontal damage is less frequent, and usually associated with lesions to the frontal premotor cortex, particularly to its more ventral parts (BA 44, and ventral BA 6, blue area). Lesions may involve the white matter fibre bundles, that connect the posterior parietal region and the temporo-parietal junction with the frontal premotor cortex. USN may be associated also with damage to the more dorsal and medial regions of the frontal premotor cortex, and to the superior temporal gyrus (azure areas) (reprinted with permission of Elsevier from Halligan et al., 2003, Figure 3). (See Fig. 11.4)

a potential perceiver, no reference to a perceiver (or even a potential perceiver) is necessary to specify the situation-dependent properties of an object. In this sense situation-dependent properties are mind-independent properties in a way that appearance properties are not. Moreover, a situation-dependent property is a property that a perceived object can have without any experiencing subject (actual, potential, present, or past) being conscious of it having the property. Situation-dependent properties are properties that objects actually have, given the situational features, regardless of what any potential perceiver could pick up given its sensory capacities. It should be noted that recognizing situation-dependent properties does not stand in conflict with recognizing Shoemaker's appearance properties or any other kind of mind-dependent properties. If one acknowledges situation-dependent properties alongside mind-dependent, appearance properties, then the mind-dependent properties will stand in representation relations both to intrinsic properties and to situation-dependent properties.[2]

Noë (2004) understands P-shapes as projections on a plane perpendicular to the subject's line of sight. Although he insists that they are objective, mind-independent properties, he analyses them in terms of how things look to perceivers, more specifically in terms of what he calls phenomenal objectivism and in terms of the psychological notion of a visual field.[3] In this respect, they are of the very same kind of properties that Gibson's (1950) visual field properties, Peacocke's (1983) sensations, and Shoemaker's (2001, 2006) appearance properties. Similarly, Matthen (2005, Chapter 7, this volume) defends a notion of properties that are analysed in terms of how things look to perceivers. According to Matthen, a surface is presented as it is (colour-wise) in part because of a property it has, its colour, and in part because of the condition it is in. In contrast to any such properties and sensations, situation-dependent properties are not analysed in terms of how things look. They are analysed exclusively in terms of external mind-independent properties and features of the environment. So, they are not psychological properties of the visual field. Furthermore, in contrast to Noë's P-shapes, situation-dependent shape properties are not two-dimensional geometrical projections, but are rather, like intrinsic shape properties, three-dimensional features.

While situation-dependent properties are very different from Shoemaker's appearance properties and Noë's P-properties, they are closely related to Lewis's notion of centred worlds. Indeed with certain qualifications, *spatial* situation-dependent properties could be understood as what constitutes a centred world, that is, in terms of centred properties. The qualifications pertain to how centred worlds are understood. If centred worlds are understood such that the subject's mind-dependent point of view affects the metaphysical nature of the centred world, then spatial situation-dependent properties cannot be understood in terms of what constitutes a centred world. If, however, centred worlds are understood such that only external, mind-independent features determine their nature, then situation-dependent properties can be understood as elements of a centred world. The distinction between a centred and an uncentred world is, however, only helpful to bring out the contrast between intrinsic spatial properties and the correlating situation-dependent properties. It is not helpful to bring out the contrast between intrinsic colours and the correlating situation-dependent properties. For the situational features that determine the way a certain colour is presented in a situation will be part of both the centred and the uncentred world. While the situational features relevant for perceiving spatial properties are centre-relative (for instance, the distance from the perceiver and the orientation relative to the perceiver), the situational features relevant for perceiving colour properties are not (for instance, the lighting conditions). Therefore, the framework of centred worlds is not helpful to analyse the distinction between intrinsic colour properties and their correlating situation-dependent properties, or properties the nature of which is similar to that of colour properties.

---

[2] For a detailed discussion of Shoemaker's appearance properties, see my 2008, pp. 71–3. See also Egan (2006).

[3] Noë (2004) argues that analysing what it is for something to *be coloured* in terms of what it is for something to *look coloured* is compatible with the idea that colours are mind-independent. However, insofar as such an account treats colours in terms of experiences of colour, they are just a version of the view that colours are mind-dependent properties. For a defence of this thesis, see Allen (2007).

In light of the notion of situation-dependent properties, we can address how perception of intrinsic properties relates to perception of situation-dependent properties. The question of how we can perceive intrinsic spatial properties arises because there is a primacy to situation-dependent properties over intrinsic properties in perception. We perceive intrinsic properties in virtue of perceiving situation-dependent properties. Moreover, we perceive an object's intrinsic properties precisely because of the way the object is presented. We perceive a table to remain constant in size as we move away from it precisely because it is presented as smaller. And we perceive the intrinsic shape property of the table precisely because of the way the shape is presented in our egocentric frame of reference. Similarly, we perceive a uniformly white wall to be uniformly white precisely because it is presented the way white walls are presented in the very lighting conditions under which we are perceiving it.

Just what does it mean to say that there is a primacy of situation-dependent properties over intrinsic properties? No one denies that if a subject sees an actual-world object, then *the object* causally affects *the subject*. Arguably, what is causally relevant is what I call the situation-dependent properties of the object. This is not to deny that typically our perceptual reports concern perceivable intrinsic properties rather than situation-dependent properties. The reason for this fact is largely psychological. While situation-dependent properties may be salient for navigation, the properties of our environment that remain constant regardless of our location and regardless of the current lighting conditions are typically more interesting in the context of perceptual reports. But the fact that intrinsic properties rather than situation-dependent properties are typically in the foreground of cognitive high-level perceptual awareness does not imply that they are causally or epistemically primary. It is important to distinguish between what is *causally* primary, what is in the foreground of *consciousness*, and what is *epistemically* primary.

Regardless of how one stands on the question of a causal primacy or a primacy in consciousness, there is, I will argue, an epistemic primacy of situation-dependent properties over intrinsic properties.[4] More specifically, I will argue that perceptual knowledge of intrinsic properties is epistemically dependent on representations of the relevant situation-dependent properties. I will call this thesis the *epistemic dependence thesis*. Consider Peacocke's (1983) two same-sized trees, one located nearer to the perceiving subject than the other. The nearer tree is presented as larger than the tree that is further away. This difference in size with regard to the tree's situation-dependent properties is one element on the basis of which the subject gains perceptual knowledge that the trees are the same size. The subject has experiential evidence that the two trees are the same size. This evidence is, however, parasitic on her evidence that the nearer tree is presented as larger than the tree that is further away from her. Both layers of evidence are liable to defeat. However, if evidence for the situation-dependent properties is defeated, the subject's evidence for the intrinsic properties is defeated, but not vice versa. In other words, evidence that undercuts a subject's justification that an object has the situation-dependent property F, would undercut the subject's perceptual justification that the object has the intrinsic property G, but not vice versa. So, evidence for intrinsic properties is dependent on evidence for situation-dependent properties. Another way of expressing the same point is that evidence of situation-dependent properties is what Pryor calls a 'justification-making condition' for perceptual knowledge of intrinsic properties (2005, p. 182). If this is right, then evidence of the way objects are presented is the basis for perceptual knowledge of intrinsic properties.

---

[4] Cohen (forthcoming) develops a computational analysis of the relation between the causal and epistemic dependency of perception of intrinsic properties on perception of situation-dependent properties, building on the epistemic dependency thesis developed in Schellengberg (2008). It would lead too far afield to discuss Cohen's account here. I will reserve this task for a future occasion. For the purposes of this chapter, I will remain neutral on whether the epistemic dependence of perception of intrinsic properties on perception of situation-dependent properties implies or presupposes a causal dependence.

The epistemic dependence thesis is a direct consequence of the spatio-temporal nature of perception. If one necessarily perceives objects from a particular location at a particular time, then perceptual knowledge of the intrinsic properties of objects must be dependent on representations of the ways objects are presented. It is important to note that for a subject to have perceptual knowledge of intrinsic properties it is not necessary that she have *knowledge* of the relevant situation-dependent properties. The epistemic dependency thesis is weaker: evidence of situation-dependent properties is the basis for perceptual knowledge of intrinsic properties. Evidence of situation-dependent properties can (but need not) constitute knowledge. It is important to note also that the relation of epistemic dependence need not imply that subjects arrive at perceptual knowledge of intrinsic properties by an *inference*.[5] Indeed, the thesis that evidence for *p* defeats evidence for *q*, has no implications for the means by which evidence for *q* is arrived at.

The epistemic dependence thesis needs to be clarified in one final respect. A subject can have *evidence of* situation-dependent properties without the relevant situation-dependent properties being salient in her consciousness, or without her being in any significant way aware of situation-dependent properties.[6] As mentioned earlier, human perceivers are typically primarily aware of intrinsic properties rather than situation-dependent properties. However, what we are primarily aware of and what is epistemically primary can come apart. In an extreme case, properties can play an epistemic role, while playing only a marginal phenomenological role, if any.

9.3. **Self-location and the capacity to act**

I have argued that perception of intrinsic properties is epistemically dependent on perception of situation-dependent properties. What makes it possible to perceive the intrinsic shape and size of objects given the fact that there is such a primacy to situation-dependent properties? There is a sense in which we perceive intrinsic spatial properties of objects in abstraction from the vantage point we happen to have on these objects. So let's call the condition that needs to be met to perceive intrinsic spatial properties *the abstraction-condition*. I will argue that a subject's perception is not limited to the ways objects are presented in her egocentric frame of reference since: (1) she represents her location in relation to the perceived object, which allows her to abstract from her particular vantage point; and (2) she has a practical understanding of space that allows her to see objects as the kind of things that are perceivable from points of view other than her own. I will address these two theses in turn and then show how they are related.

If we accept that how things are presented to a subject's location is a relational property, then the subject's vantage point must play a role in perceptual content insofar as it forms the point of origin of an egocentric frame of reference.[7] I will argue that subjects represent their location as the point of origin of their perceptions and actions. More precisely, the idea is that subjects represent their location as the location from which they both perceive objects and would act in relation to objects were they to act.

What is the relevant location that is represented? The relevant location is determined by the axes of our egocentric frame of reference, which in turn are determined by our dispositions to act that

---

[5] For further discussion, see McDowell (1994).

[6] For a defence of the thesis that a subject can have evidence without being aware of this evidence, see Bergmann (2006). The terminology here is messy. One can understand awareness such that a subject can be aware of *p* although she thinks and reports that she is not aware of *p*. The fact that she is aware of *p* will reveal itself, for instance in her behaviour. The qualification 'in any significant way' is supposed to exclude such cases of awareness.

[7] Peacocke (1999) can be read as defending this idea.

bring about a practical understanding of basic spatial directions. More specifically, the idea is that the axes of our egocentric frame of reference is determined by the spatial locations from which possible movements originate and the directions of the relevant movements. So the axes are not determined simply by the space we occupy, but rather by the possibilities for action that we have, given the way we occupy that space. When I see an object as within reach and in front of me, the axes are not determined simply by the position of my body, but rather by how I would move my body given the position of my body. The represented location is determined by the axes of this egocentric frame of reference.

It will be helpful to contrast the thesis that perceivers of intrinsic spatial properties necessarily represent their location with the more contentious thesis that perceivers are necessarily aware of their location or indeed self-aware. While human perceivers may sometimes be self-aware or have awareness of their location in relation to perceived objects, the thesis that perceivers of intrinsic spatial properties necessarily represent their location in relation to the perceived objects, does not by itself imply or amount to any kind of self-awareness. It does not even imply awareness of one's location. Representing one's location may, however, be understood as a kind of proto self-awareness. However, I am not arguing that subjects need to be aware of themselves as perceiving, nor am I arguing that subjects need be aware of their location in order to represent their location. While we may often have either of these two forms of awareness when perceiving, such awareness is not, I am arguing, *necessary* for something as cognitively minimal as perceiving the intrinsic spatial properties of objects. It may be that self-awareness is necessary for perceptual judgment, but I am not concerned here with perceptual judgment. My concern is with mere perception. Insofar as infants and non-rational animals can perceive, self-awareness is cognitively too demanding a requirement for mere perception.

The way in which self-location figures in perception of intrinsic spatial properties can be clarified by making explicit its indirect and monadic nature. The representation of one's location is indirect: one represents one's location indirectly insofar as one represents it by perceiving an object. Moreover, the thesis that one perceives objects in relation to one's location does not imply that one perceives objects to *one's* right or to *one's* left. It implies only that one perceives objects to the right or to the left. One represents objects as standing in egocentrically specified spatial relations without necessarily having either awareness of one's location or awareness of oneself as standing in spatial relations to those objects. In this sense, representation of one's location is monadic: we can endorse the thesis that perception involves a relationship between the perceiver and the perceived objects while acknowledging that the perceiver need not be aware of one side of the relationship.[8] So the suggestion is not that a subject consciously computes her position in space by reflecting on her spatial relation to objects. When a cat perceives a chair it might not see it *as* a chair, but it sees something that is located in a certain relation to itself and something onto which it can jump. Through perception it gauges the distance it must jump to land on the chair. Its location in relation to the chair must figure in its perception for it to be able to flex its muscles so as to land on the chair. I do not mean to assume anything about cat-perception. What is at issue does not depend on whether cats can perceive intrinsic spatial properties. The point is only to show that the representation of the perceiver's location is understood practically in a way that is not only unproblematic to ascribe to cats, but moreover necessary to ascribe to cats to explain what cats do. I have argued that the thesis that one represents one's location in relation to objects does not require awareness of oneself as standing in spatial relation to those objects. It requires, rather, that one represent one's location in a dual mode: the point of origin of perception presents itself as the point of origin for

---

[8] For the distinction between monadic and relational spatial representations, see Campbell (1994, p. 119). For an excellent discussion of relational properties that can appear as monadic properties, see Gupta (1999).

bodily movement. One occupies *one* position from which one *both* perceives and would act were one to act.

Why should perception alone or possible action alone be insufficient to represent one's location? I will address this question in detail in the following section. For now, it will suffice to say that the frame of reference of action and perception changes as the spatial relations between oneself and the perceived objects change, and these changes allow one to represent one's location in relation to these objects. Through changes in perception brought about by changes in the spatial relations to objects, one can triangulate back to one's location. If this is right, then perception alone or action alone cannot be sufficient to gain the self-location necessary for perception. These considerations bring out not only how self-location comes about, but also what is represented. One represents one's location as the vantage point of perception and the location from which changes in perception are registered, which are brought about through changes in the spatial relations to perceived objects.

The thesis that perception depends on action has received significant attention recently.[9] However, typically the action-dependency thesis is understood such that it is committed to the contentious thesis that perception is either dependent on token actions, or, alternatively, it turns out that perception is not actually dependent on action, but just on movement, where this movement may be induced by something or someone other than the relevant perceiver. However, If the action-dependency thesis amounts to the thesis that either past or current token actions are necessary in every single event of perception, then it cannot be right.[10]

In what sense does the view presented endorse the thesis that perception depends on action? I will argue that having the *capacity* to act is what is necessary to meet the abstraction-condition. More specifically, I will argue that the ability to represent one's location depends on the capacity to act. However, this capacity need not ever be actualized. As a consequence, perception does *not* depend on token actions. So on the presented view, the connections between perception and action are not so tight as to exclude the possibility that someone, who is not physically able to initiate movements, can perceive intrinsic spatial properties. As I will show in the rest of this section, the thesis that perception depends on the capacity to act does not amount to the thesis that perception depends on token actions, while being stronger than the thesis that being moved in relation to objects is sufficient to perceive intrinsic spatial properties. To show how, it will be helpful to take a closer look at the notion of capacities in play.

Following the Aristotelian distinction between first and second potentialities as well as first and second actualities of capacities (*De Anima* II.5, 417a22–30), we can distinguish between an English speaker's innate capacity to speak a language (first potentiality); her capacity to speak English when she is sleeping (second potentiality or first actuality); and her capacity to speak English when she is talking English (second actuality). In light of this distinction, we can say that representing one's location requires first actuality, but not second actuality of one's capacity to act. This implies that were one (for whatever reason) not able to move in a particular moment (and thus lack second actuality, but not first actuality of one's capacity to act), this would not challenge one's ability to perceive the intrinsic spatial properties of objects. The reason is that one's inability to move in any given moment does not affect one's capacity to act. More specifically, it would not affect one's capacity to know what it would mean to act in relation to perceived objects. One would just lack the ability to act on

[9] See, among others, Gibson (1979), Baldwin (1998), Hurley (1998), Kelly (2001, 2004), Thompson and Varela (2001), Noë (2004, forthcoming), Briscoe (2008), and Kiverstein (2010) (Chapter 14, this volume). The action-dependency thesis can be thought of as a particular interpretation of the thesis that the mind is extended. The thesis was first introduced by Clark and Chalmers (1998). It has since been developed in detail by Clark (2001a, 2008), though it is important to note that Clark endorses the more modest extended cognition thesis rather than the extended mind thesis.

[10] I discuss the problems that any view faces according to which perception is dependent on token actions in Section 9.5.

this knowledge. In this sense, representing one's location requires that one have first actuality, but not second actuality of one's capacity to act.

Recognizing the notion of the first actuality of a capacity allows one to hold on to the action-dependency thesis without being committed to the implausible requirement that token actions are necessary in every event of perception. Certainly a subject who is temporarily unable to act can represent the location from which she perceives and from which she would act were she able to act. It cannot be necessary that one, say, actually reach out to an object that one perceives as within reach. The notion of first actualities of capacities makes room for a notion of a capacity without requiring that this capacity be acted on. Although it cannot be necessary that one actually reach out to an object that one perceives as within reach, one must know what it would be to reach out to an object that one perceives as within reach. More generally, one must *know* what it would be to act in relation to a perceived object.

With this notion in hand, we can cut a path between two unattractive routes: that perception depends on actual token actions; and that being moved in relation to objects is sufficient to perceive their intrinsic spatial properties. It cannot be right that we need to act in every particular situation of perception, but the alternative is not that being moved in relation to objects is sufficient for perception of intrinsic spatial properties. I am taking a middle route, one that involves the capacity to act. The kind of action that perception depends on is not actual self-activated movement, but rather potential self-activated movement. The relevant capacity to act is knowledge of what it would be to act. As the Aristotelian distinction between first and second actuality of capacities allows us to see, this is knowledge that one can have even if one is not able to act on one's capacity. Given the central role of capacities in the view I have presented, it is fitting to call it *the capacity view*. In the following section, I will specify the details of this view by arguing that the ability to perceive the intrinsic spatial properties of objects depends jointly on representing one's location in relation to perceived objects and having a practical understanding of space. While representing one's location in relation to perceived objects allows one to abstract from one's particular vantage point, having a practical understanding of space allows one to perceive objects as the kind of things that are perceivable from points of view other than one's own.

9.4. **Space and the capacity to act**

So far I have argued that a necessary condition for perceiving intrinsic spatial properties is that one abstract from one's point of view so as to transcend one's egocentric frame of reference. I argued that abstracting from one's point of view requires representing one's location. The most cognitively minimal way of doing so is to represent one's location as the location from which one both perceives objects and would act in relation to the objects were one to act. I developed this idea in terms of capacities to act. So, I have argued that perception depends on the capacity to act.

While this condition is necessary to perceive intrinsic spatial properties, it is by no means sufficient. In this section, I will develop the idea that representing one's location allows one to gain a conception of space, which makes it possible to perceive objects as perceivable from different locations. By doing so, I will go some way towards elaborating what more is required to perceive intrinsic properties. The basic idea is that a practical conception of space is necessary to perceive the intrinsic spatial properties of objects. As I will argue, this practical conception of space can be understood as a kind of spatial know-how—a kind of know-how that is unproblematic to ascribe to non-rational animals. I will argue that perceiving intrinsic spatial properties requires perceiving objects as perceivable from locations other than the one that one happens to occupy. This idea does not require that a subject have knowledge of what objects look like from other locations. In this respect, the idea is radically different from any view according to which perception involves sensorimotor patterns that in turn involve assumptions or indeed knowledge of how objects look from other perspectives. It requires only that a subject must have spatial know-how that involves understanding that there are different possible perspectives on any three-dimensional space-occupier.

The idea of spatial know-how can be spelled out more precisely by introducing the notion of an alter-ego vantage point.[11] An alter-ego vantage point is a location that the perceiver understands as a possible alternative vantage point. The notion is connected closely to the familiar notion of an allocentric frame of reference. An allocentric frame of reference is a frame of reference that is centred on a point in space distinct from the one that the perceiver is occupying. An alter-ego vantage point is a particular way of understanding the location on which an allocentric frame of reference is centred. It is a location that the perceiver understands as a possible point of view. In light of the notion of an alter-ego vantage point, we can formulate the idea of spatial know-how more precisely. Perceiving intrinsic spatial properties requires entertaining alter-ego points of view on the object.[12]

It is important that allocentric frames of reference are engaged, since the information provided in an allocentric frame of reference is only available to us through a potential egocentric frame of reference.[13] In order to show why, it is necessary to consider in more detail the nature of the egocentric organization of perception. Determining the egocentric frame of reference for *movement* is straightforward. It is determined by the direction of the movement and the relevant bodily parts. The coordinates of the movements involved in walking are very different from the coordinates of the movements involved in writing. In the one case, they are centred on the main axis of the body; in the other case, they are centred on the hand. This might lead one to think that the frame of reference of visual perception is centred on the eyes, but this cannot be right. The position of one's body in relation to a perceived object is at least as important as the position of one's eyes. When we turn our head to the left we do not perceive the objects to the left of our body as in front of ourselves. If this is right, then the coordinates of perception cannot be centred simply on our eyes.

What else is involved? One conceivable answer is to say that the axes of the egocentric frame of reference are determined by minimal spatial concepts, such as up, down, left, right, with the centre identified as here. However, one might object that this suggestion implies that only creatures that have the concept of, say, left can perceive objects as being to their left. There are good reasons not to limit perception to creatures that have conceptual skills. One can, however, avert this objection, while holding on to the basic idea of the suggestion. The spatial locations from which possible movements originate and the directions of the relevant movements are crucial for determining the coordinates of perception. The axes of our egocentric frame of reference are determined by our dispositions to act that bring about a practical conception of basic spatial directions. Such dispositions to act are a particular kind of a capacity to act. The practical conception of basic spatial directions that we have in virtue of having such disposition to act is a kind of spatial know-how.[14] The idea

---

[11] I owe this label to Grush (2001).

[12] The question of how allocentric and egocentric frames of reference are combined in alter-ego points of view is an open empirical question. For an overview of competing explanations, see Paillard (1991) as well as Klatzky (1998). For a discussion of the neural mapping from egocentric to allocentric spatial frames of reference, see Goodale and Anderson (1998). For a discussion of the same issue with regard to cognitive processing, see Iachini and Ruggiero (2006). Finally, for a discussion of the mapping of allocentric and egocentric frames of reference in a computational model of spatial development, see Hiraki et al. (1998). Grush (2001, in particular section 2.3) provides a philosophical interpretation of this literature.

[13] It is conceivable that a creature that is able to navigate in space has neither alter-ego vantage points nor egocentric frames of reference. Indeed, there are creatures that navigate in space by relating to a fixed point in their environment, for instance the South or North Pole. So they navigate in space by relating only to an allocentric frame of reference. Maguire et al. (1998) describe this model of spatial navigation as the slope-centroid model. Although a creature can *navigate* in space in such an allocentric frame of reference, the information provided in the allocentric frame of reference is arguably not meaningful to the creature because it is not connected to its egocentric frame of reference.

[14] For a discussion of dispositions to act, see Mumford (1998, 1999). Following Ryle (1949), I am using 'know-how' as a means to express a practical, non-intellectual conception that non-rational beings could have. Ryle's conception of know-how has been criticized by Carr (1979) and more recently by Stanley and

of spatial know-how is related to Evans's (1982) thought that an understanding of spatial directions is not related simply to the place we occupy, but rather is related to the possibilities for action that one has given the way one occupies that space. So the reference of 'up' is not determined only by the position of my head, but rather by how I would move my body given the position of my body.

Now, one could say that having such spatial know-how just is having basic spatial concepts. It is unproblematic to think of spatial know-how in terms of spatial concepts as long as one recognizes that the spatial concepts are not what enable spatially oriented movement and actions. The direction of explanation goes the other way. One has spatial concepts only insofar as these concepts are grounded in one's dispositions to act. If having such dispositions to act amounts to having basic spatial concepts, then it must be acknowledged that any creature that has the relevant dispositions to act will possess the relevant basic spatial concepts. Alternatively, one might argue that one can have the relevant dispositions to act without possessing the basic spatial concepts that these dispositions ground. Only some creatures, for instance those capable of linguistic thought, will possess basic spatial concepts in virtue of having the relevant dispositions to act. For the present purposes, we can remain neutral on this issue. The important point is that these dispositions to act allow one to have the spatial know-how that can be expressed with spatial concepts.

I have argued that the coordinates of perception are determined by our dispositions to act on perceived objects. In light of these considerations, we can see more clearly why allocentric frames of reference are not sufficient to meet the abstraction-condition. We can gain the spatial information that is structured in an allocentric frame of reference only because we understand that were we to occupy the location on which the allocentric frame of reference is centred, our dispositions to act on the perceived object would change. If this is right, then the location on which the allocentric frame of reference is centred must be an alter-ego vantage point, that is, a location that one understands as a potential viewpoint. So I have argued that perceiving the intrinsic spatial properties of objects requires that an object be perceived as perceivable from points of view other than the one that the subject happens to occupy. In order to perceive objects as perceivable from other points of view, one must be able to move from egocentric to allocentric frames of reference. These allocentric frames of reference must be engaged insofar as one understands them as possible vantage points on the perceived object. The alter-ego points of view are thus tied to egocentric frames of reference insofar as they involve remapping the dispositions to act in relation to a perceived object.

9.5. Capacities to act in context

I have argued that perceiving the intrinsic spatial properties of objects requires having a conception that the object *is perceivable* from viewpoints other than one's own. It will be helpful to contrast the suggested view with three alternative ways of meeting the abstraction-condition. The first alternative is that perceiving the intrinsic spatial properties of objects requires having a conception of *the way an object looks* from viewpoints other than one's own. The second alternative is that perceiving the intrinsic spatial properties requires having a conception that the object *is perceived* from viewpoints other than one's own. The third alternative is that subjects who have the ability to perceive intrinsic spatial properties have a *concept of three-dimensional space* or alternatively a *concept of objects as three-dimensional space occupiers* that allows them to transcend their egocentric frame of reference. I will consider these three alternatives in turn.

On the first alternative option, perceiving inherent spatial properties requires having knowledge of what objects look like from points of view other than one's own. This is the idea that Hurley (1998)

Williamson (2001). In short, the criticism is that 'know-how' expresses the same relation as 'know-that'. Addressing this criticism would only affect the wording of my argument. My argument does not depend on the terminology. For a critical discussion of Stanley and Williamson's argument and a defense of a concept of know-how, see Hornsby (2004). Her concern is with semantic know-how, but a parallel argument can be given for spatial know-how.

and Noë's (2004) sensorimotor theory is based on. On this view, perception of, say, a round plate is constituted by (implicit) sensorimotor knowledge of the form: if one were to move to the right, the sensory stimulation caused by the plate would change thus, namely in the characteristic way that the sensory stimulation caused by circular objects varies as one's spatial relation to the perceived object changes. Grasping such practical conditionals connecting action and perception is what allows one to perceive the intrinsic shape of the object.

The main difference between the capacity view and sensorimotor theories is that the latter is committed to perception being dependent on either past, present, actual, or counterfactual token actions.[15] In order to elaborate on this difference, it will be helpful to distinguish two possible versions of sensorimotor theories. If the requirement is simply that our perceptions be integrated in sensori-motor patterns allowing us to anticipate how our perceptions would change were our spatial relations to the perceived objects to change, then it is not obvious why it would not be sufficient that either our body be moved in relation to perceived objects or objects be moved in relation to our bodies. There is no reason why perception should require self-movement. The response to this objection depends on the details of the notion of sensorimotor knowledge at issue. A *modest* version of the sensorimotor thesis stops short at the thesis that perception involves practical knowledge of the *effects* of move-ment on perception. On such a modest version of the sensorimotor thesis, it would be sufficient to be a sentient statue in order to have the relevant sensorimotor knowledge; that is, it would be suffi-cient that either our body be moved in relation to perceived objects or objects be moved in relation to our bodies. So this modest version of the sensorimotor thesis does not, in fact, support the thesis that perception depends on action. Noë and Hurley can both avoid this objection easily, for they both defend what we can call the *radical* version of the sensorimotor thesis.

According to the radical version, sensorimotor knowledge can only be acquired through token actions. Noë argues that 'only through *self*-movement can one *test* and so *learn* the relevant patterns of sensorimotor dependence' (2004, p. 13). According to the radical version, the ability to self-activate movement is necessary for perception. So, in contrast to the modest version, the radical version supports the thesis that perception depends on action. However, the radical version presupposes the problematic idea that perceiving an object's intrinsic shape requires that one grasp or know the senso-rimotor profile of the shape-type that the object exemplifies. So perceiving a round object requires that one grasp or know the sensorimotor profile of round objects. If one has not been acquainted with an object exemplifying the same or sufficiently similar spatial properties, then one cannot have the relevant sensorimotor knowledge to perceive the object. Typically, no doubt, one learns the token shapes of particular objects through perception. But *contra* Noë, it cannot be right that one can only perceive the shape of a particular object once one has learnt the patterns of sensorimotor dependence for the relevant shape-type. The idea that one learns to perceive shape-types is odd in light of our capacity to perceive the spatial properties of objects without previously having seen an object exemplifying the same spatial properties.[16] In contrast to such an approach, I have argued

---

[15] In the most recent formulation of his view (Chapter 13, this volume), Noë denies that he is committed to the thesis that token actions are necessary for perception. However, arguably even in this modified version of his view, past or counterfactual token actions are necessary for the sensorimotor connections to have any force. For a detailed discussion of this set of issues, see Schellenberg (2007). For a critical discussion of sensorimotor theories, see also Clark (2001b).

[16] Noë acknowledges that 'as we get to more complicated forms, such as animal bodies, plants, and so forth, the mathematics needed to determine the sensorimotor profile of an object gets more complicated'. But he holds on to the thesis that sensorimotor knowledge is necessary for specific shape-types by asserting that 'our visual perceptual skills, however, are that sophisticated, encompassing these complex (but ultimately manageable) relationships' (2004, p. 78). A related issue is how we perceive the hidden sides of objects. For discussion, see Madary (in press). The capacity view offers an account of perceiving intrinsic properties that does not rely on any kind of expectation of what the hidden sides of objects look like. This is not to deny that we often have such expectations. The crucial point is that in the capacity view, perception of intrinsic properties in no way depends on having such expectations.

that perception depends on the capacity to act. The thesis that perception depends on the capacity to act does not amount to the thesis that perception depends on token actions, while being stronger than the thesis that being moved in relation to objects is sufficient to perceive intrinsic spatial properties.

A related, second difference between the capacity view and sensorimotor theories is that while sensorimotor theories arguably cannot accommodate the dual-stream systems hypothesis, the capacity view is neutral on this hypothesis.[17] The capacity view is neutral since it does not imply that perception is dependent on token actions—be they past, present, actual, or counterfactual.

A third difference concerns the role of the different ways objects look from different perspectives in perceiving the intrinsic spatial properties of objects. According to sensorimotor theories, grasping practical conditionals connecting action and perception is what allows one to perceive the intrinsic shape of the object. Such practical conditionals provide us with (implicit) knowledge that were one to move, say, to the right of a perceived plate, the sensory stimulation caused by the plate would change thus and so, namely in the characteristic way that the sensory stimulation caused by circular objects varies as one's spatial relation to the perceived object changes. On such an account, expectations or knowledge of what objects look like from other locations constitutes perceptual experience. As a consequence, perceptual experience of objects is not limited to the information projected onto one's retina. This approach implies that perception of intrinsic spatial properties requires at least two encounters with objects—either past, present, actual, or counterfactual—and that these encounters must be unified into the perception of an object.

Sensorimotor views rely essentially on practical conditionals of the form if I were to move to the right, then my perception would change in this and that way. Grasping such practical conditionals necessarily involves expectations or knowledge of how the relevant object looks like from other perspectives. In contrast, on the capacity view, perception of intrinsic spatial properties does not involve any expectations or knowledge of what objects look like from other perspectives. It relies only on practical knowledge *that* objects can be perceived from other locations. As a consequence, the capacity view posits that perception of intrinsic spatial properties is not made possible by conjoining different ways objects look to a unified whole. The idea is rather that we perceive intrinsic spatial properties by perceiving objects as perceivable from different possible locations. So, according to the capacity view, perception of intrinsic spatial properties does not depend on subjects having two encounters with an object (either past, present, actual, or counterfactual). Just one encounter is required. Perceiving the intrinsic spatial properties of an object is integrated in the perspective-dependent aspect of perception.

Finally, the capacity view contrasts from sensorimotor theories in that it does not require appeal to the specific ways objects look from points of view other than that which one occupies. The requirement for perceiving intrinsic spatial properties is more flexible: perception requires only spatial know-how. Such spatial know-how involves knowledge of the possibility of other vantage points on the perceived object.

On the second alternative way of meeting the abstraction condition, perceiving inherent spatial properties requires practical knowledge that objects are perceived from points of view other than that which one occupies. Kelly (2001, 2004) defends a version of this view building on ideas of Merleau-Ponty (1945, p. 68). Such an approach avoids the problem of having knowledge of what objects look like from other locations and unifying this knowledge into the perception of an object. However, it leads to the problem of how the different possible actual viewpoints can be unified into the perception of the object. So while the sensorimotor thesis that perception necessarily involves knowledge or expectations of what an object looks like from viewpoints other than one's own leads to the problem

---

[17] For the classic presentation of the dual-visual systems hypothesis, see Milner and Goodale (1995); for an excellent analysis of the dual-visual systems hypothesis, see Clark's article in this volume (Chapter 4). Goodale (2001), Block (2005), and Matthen (2005) argue that the dual-visual systems hypothesis challenges the plausibility of any sensorimotor theory. For a response to this criticism, see Noë's article in this volume (Chapter 13).

of how these different appearances of the object are unified into the perception of the object. Kelly's thesis that perception involves knowledge that the object is perceived from other points of view leads to the problem of how the different actual points of view are unified into the perception of the object. Insofar as on the capacity view, the necessary conditions for perception of intrinsic spatial properties are more minimal, it can avoid the problems of either of these two approaches. On the capacity view, the necessary condition for perceiving the intrinsic spatial properties of objects is that the perceiver has a conception that the object *is perceivable* from viewpoints other than one's own. As I argued in section 9.4, perceiving objects as perceivable from other points of view amounts to having spatial know-how.

The third alternative option has it that subjects who have the ability to perceive intrinsic spatial properties have a *concept of three-dimensional space* or alternatively a *concept of objects as three-dimensional space occupiers* that allows them to transcend their egocentric frame of reference. An approach that relies on any such idea can be traced back to Kant. The problem with any such approach is that it over-intellectualizes perception. The very concept of space and the very concept of objects as three-dimensional space-occupiers are arguably grounded in perception. This is just to say that one has the concept of objects as solid, three-dimensional space-occupiers only because one's perception is structured in a certain way. If the aim is to bring out what this structure is, then presupposing that perception is so structured would beg the question. Moreover, it is far from obvious that a concept of objects or a concept of space is necessary to perceive intrinsic spatial properties. It is important to acknowledge that perceptual experience is a primitive cognitive skill. In contrast to approaches that rely on any presupposition that perceivers have a concept of space or a concept of objects, I have developed a view that brings out the minimal requirements for perception of intrinsic spatial properties.

9.6. Conclusion

I have argued that self-location and spatial know-how are jointly necessary to perceive the intrinsic spatial properties of objects. Action has played a role in both the idea of self-location and spatial know-how. Actual token actions or indeed token movements are, however, not necessary for either self-location or spatial know-how. In contrast to any thesis according to which perception depends on past, current, actual, or counterfactual token actions, I have argued that perception depends on the capacity to act. More specifically, I argued first that perceiving the intrinsic spatial properties of objects requires abstracting from one's particular perspective in a way that allows one to perceive the perspective-independent spatial properties of objects. I argued that the best way to meet the abstraction-condition is to recognize that we represent our location in relation to perceived objects as the point of origin of perception and action. By representing one's location one can abstract from the particular vantage point one happens to have and perceive the perspective-independent spatial properties of objects. More precisely the thesis is that one represents one's location as the position from which one both perceives objects and would act in relation to objects were one to act. I spelled out this thesis by arguing that perception is dependent on the capacity to act and identified this capacity as a kind of know-how, namely knowledge of what it would be to act. So I argued that self-location does not require token actions or even token movements, but rather the capacity to act.

In section 9.4, I developed this view by arguing that perceiving intrinsic spatial properties requires perceiving objects as perceivable from locations other than the one that one happens to occupy. Perceiving objects as perceivable from other locations in turn requires moving from egocentric to allocentric frames of reference. I argued that these allocentric frames of reference must be engaged insofar as one understands them as different possible vantage points on the perceived object. The axes of our egocentric frame of reference are determined by our dispositions to act that bring about a practical conception of basic spatial directions. The practical conception of basic spatial directions that we have in virtue of having such disposition to act is a kind of spatial know-how. What is necessary for spatial know-how is only knowledge that one's *dispositions* to act would change were one to occupy a different location in relation to a perceived object. Such dispositions to act are a particular kind of a capacity to act. So again, the idea does not depend on token actions, but rather on the capacity to act.

References

Allen, K. (2007). The mind-independence of colour. *European Journal of Philosophy*; **15**: 147–58.
Aristotle. *De Anima*. In *The complete works of Aristotle*, (Trans. Smith, J.A., ed. Barnes, J.), pp. 641–92. Princeton: Princeton University Press.
Baldwin, T. (1998). Objectivity, causality, and agency. In *The body and the self*. (ed. Bermúdez, J.L.), pp. 107–25. Cambridge, MA: The MIT Press.
Bergmann, M. (2006). *Justification without awareness*. New York: Oxford University Press.
Block, N. (2005). Review of Alva Noë, *Action in Perception*. *The Journal of Philosophy*; **102**: 259–72.
Briscoe, R. (2008). Egocentric spatial representation in action and perception. *Philosophy and Phenomenological Research*; **79**(2): 423–60.
Campbell, J. (1994). *Past, space and self*. Cambridge MA: The MIT Press.
Carr, D. (1979). The logic of knowing how and ability. *Mind*; **88**: 394–409.
Clark, A. (2008). *Supersizing the mind: embodiment, action, and cognitive extension*. Oxford: Oxford University Press.
—— (2001a). Reasons, robots and the extended mind. *Mind and Language*; **16**: 121–45.
—— (2001b). Visual experience and motor action: are the bonds too tight? *The Philosophical Review*; **110**: 445–519.
Clark, A. and Chalmers, D. (1998). The extended mind. *Analysis*; **58**: 7–11.
Cohen, J. (forthcoming). Perception and computation. *Philosophical Issues*.
Egan, A. (2006). Appearance properties? *Noûs*; **40**: 495–521.
Evans, G. (1982). *Varieties of reference*. Oxford: Clarendon Press.
Gibson, J.J. (1950). *The perception of the visual world*. Boston: Houghton Mifflin.
—— (1979). *The ecological approach to visual perception*. Boston: Houghton Mifflin.
Goodale, M. (2001). Real action in a virtual world: commentary on O'Regan & Noë. *Behavioral and Brain Sciences*; **24**: 984–5.
Goodale, M. and Andersen, R. (1998). Frames of reference for perception and action in the human visual system. *Neuroscience and Biobehavioral Reviews*; **22**: 161–72.
Grush, R. (2001). Self, world and space: on the meaning and mechanisms of egocentric and allocentric spatial representation. *Brain and Mind*; **1**: 59–92.
Gupta, A. (1999). Meaning and misconceptions. In *Language, logic, and concepts: essays in memory of John Macnamara*, (eds Jackendoff, R., Bloom, P., and Wynn, K.), pp. 15–41. MA: The MIT Press.
Hiraki, K., Sashima, A., and Phillips, S. (1998). From egocentric to allocentric spatial behavior: a computational model of spatial development. *Adaptive Behavior*; **6**: 371–91.
Hornsby, J. (2004). Semantic knowledge and practical knowledge. *Supplement to the Proceedings of the Aristotelian Society*; **79**: 107–30.
Hurley, S. (1998). *Consciousness in action*. Cambridge, MA: Harvard University Press.
Iachini, T. and Ruggiero, G. (2006). Egocentric and allocentric spatial frames of reference: a direct measure. *Cognitive Processing*; **7**: 126–7.
Kelly, S. (2004). Seeing things in Merleau-Ponty. In *The Cambridge companion to Merleau-Ponty*, (eds Carman, T. and Hansen, M.), pp. 74–110. Cambridge: Cambridge University Press.
—— (2001). The non-conceptual content of perceptual experience: situation dependence and fineness of grain. *Philosophy and Phenomenological Research*; **62**: 601–08.
Klatzky, R. (1998). Allocentric and egocentric spatial representations: definitions, distinctions, and interconnections. In *Spatial cognition: an interdisciplinary approach to representation and processing of spatial knowledge*, (eds Freska, C., Hebel, H., and Wender, K.F.). pp. 1–17. Berlin: Springer.
Lewis, D. (1986). *On the plurality of worlds*. Oxford: Blackwell.
Lycan, W. (1995a). Layered perceptual representation. In *Philosophical issues* 7, (ed. Villanueva, E.), pp. 81–100. Atascadero: Ridgeview Publishing.
Lycan, W. (1995b). Replies to Tomberlin, Tye, Stalnaker and Block. In *Philosophical issues*, 7, (ed. Villanueva, E.), pp. 127–42. Atascadero: Ridgeview Publishing.
Madary, M. (in press). Husserl on Perceptual Constancy, *European Journal of Philosophy*.
Maguire, E.A., Burgess, N. Donnett, J.G., Frackowiak, R.S.J., Frith, C.D., and O'Keefe, J. (1998). Knowing where and getting there: a human navigation network. *Science*; **280**(5365): 921–4.
Matthen, M. (2005). *Seeing, doing and knowing: a philosophical theory of sense perception*. Oxford: Clarendon Press.
McDowell, J. (1994). The content of perceptual experience. *The Philosophical Quarterly*; **44**: 190–205.
Milner, A.D. and Goodale, M.A. (1995). *The visual brain in action*. Oxford: Oxford University Press.

Mumford, S. (1999). Intentionality and the physical: a new theory of disposition ascription. *The Philosophical Quarterly*; **195**: 215–25.

—— (1998). *Dispositions*. Oxford: Oxford University Press.

Noë, A. (2004). *Action in perception*. Cambridge, MA: The MIT Press.

Paillard, J. (1991). Motor and representational framing of space. In *Brain and space*, (ed. Paillard, J.), pp.163–82. Oxford: Oxford University Press.

Peacocke, C. (1999). *Being known*. Oxford: Clarendon Press.

—— (1983). *Sense and content*. Oxford: Clarendon Press.

Pryor, J. (2005). There is immediate justification. In *Contemporary debates in epistemology*, (eds Sosa, E. and Steup, M.), pp. 181–201. Oxford: Blackwell.

Ryle, G. (1949). *The concept of mind*. Chicago: The University of Chicago Press.

Schellenberg, S. (2008). The situation-dependency of perception. *The Journal of Philosophy*; **105**: 55–84.

—— (2007). Action and self-location in perception. *Mind*; **116**: 603–32.

Shoemaker, S. (2006). On the way things appear. In *Perceptual experience*, (eds Gendler, T. and Hawthorne, J.), pp. 461–80. New York: Oxford.

—— (2001). Introspection and phenomenal character. *Philosophical Topics*; **28**: 247–73.

Stanley, J. and Williamson, T. (2001). Knowing how. *The Journal of Philosophy*; **98**: 411–44.

Thompson, E. (2007). *Mind in life: biology, phenomenology, and the sciences of mind*. Cambridge, MA: Harvard University Press.

Thompson, E. and Varela F. (2001). Radical embodiment: neural dynamics and consciousness. *Trends in Cognitive Sciences*; **5**: 418–25.

PART 4

Perception and action: studies in cognitive neuroscience

Why does the perception-action functional dichotomy not match the ventral-dorsal streams anatomical segregation: optic ataxia and the function of the dorsal stream

Yves Rossetti, Hisaaki Ota, Annabelle Blangero,
Alain Vighetto, and Laure Pisella

Abstract

A main issue in the debate centring on the relation between perception and action is the following: how much of our actions can be performed independently from perception? An answer to this question seems to be provided in the field of motor neuroscience. Accordingly, the main paradigms in the field have tried to investigate residual visuo-motor abilities in patients with visual deficits (e.g. visually guided reach-to-grasp in cortical blindness (blindsight) or visual form agnosia), or to delineate specific visual deficits that would be specific to the action system and not affect perceptual responses (e.g. optic ataxia). This chapter is aimed at reassessing the conclusions which can be drawn from the investigation of optic ataxia through a review of the recent developments made in relation to this neurological condition. It argues that a general oversimplification of the dual-visual systems hypothesis (Milner and Goodale 1995) has led to the popular interpretation that 'dorsal = action' and challenges the claims of a neat double dissociation between the conditions observed in optic ataxia and visual agnosia, and in turn between perception and action.

10.1. Introduction

Introspective assessment of the relationship between perception and action first suggests that they belong to a serial process in which perception has to precede action. A closer examination also reveals that there are instances in everyday life when motor responses appear to be independent from perception. The serial view seems to fit the general organization of voluntary actions, whereas the dissociated view seems to fit the specific case of reflex and automated motor responses. Therefore, the most important question in the field is to determine where the boundary between these two cases can be outlined. This question has been stimulated by the finding that the unfolding of simple voluntary movements can be controlled by autonomous pilots (Pélisson et al., 1986; Pisella et al., 2000; Rossetti and Pisella, 2003). The whole debate about the dual stream theory of the visual system seems to focus on a related question: how much of our actions can be performed independently from perception? It is interesting to observe that although the original question has been raised in the field of visual neuroscience, the answer to this question seems to be provided in the field of motor neuroscience. Accordingly the main paradigms in the field have tried to investigate residual visuo-motor abilities in patients with visual deficits (e.g. visually guided reach-to-grasp in cortical blindness (blindsight) or visual form agnosia), or to delineate specific visual deficits that would be specific to the action system and not affect perceptual responses (e.g. optic ataxia [OA]). This chapter is aimed at reassessing the conclusions which can be drawn from the investigation of optic ataxia through a review of the recent developments made in relation to this neurological condition.

Over the last 40 years, dual stream accounts of the visual brain first focused on anatomical distinctions, either between subcortical and cortical structures, or between the dorsal and ventral cortical visual streams (for historical reviews, see Jeannerod and Rossetti, 1993; Rossetti et al., 2000; Rossetti and Pisella, 2002; Danckert and Rossetti, 2005). Initially, a 'what?' vs. 'where?' dissociation depicted the putative function of these different streams (Schneider, 1969; Ungerleider and Mishkin, 1982). However, most subsequent theoretical formulations have emphasised a dissociation between reporting ('conscious', 'explicit', 'perceptual') and describing ('What?', 'semantic') the visual stimulus, and performing simple automatic motor responses (unconscious', 'implicit', 'visuo-motor', 'pragmatic', 'How?') to the visual stimulus. When human neuropsychology has been taken into consideration, the output of the two streams has been emphasized (Goodale and Milner, 1992; Jeannerod and Rossetti, 1993; Milner and Goodale, 1995). In parallel to this neurophysiological approach a psychophysical school also tackled the issue of perception–action relationships (e.g. Bridgeman et al., 1981, 1997; Bridgeman, 2000; Paillard, 1987, 1991). A large body of psychophysical data contrasting visual and visuo-motor functions became fertile ground for speculating on the neural basis of perception–action dissociations (e.g. Rossetti, 1998; Bridgeman, 2000). One of these distinctions has been largely widespread and clearly dominates the field of cognitive neuroscience: the two visual stream theory proposed by Milner and Goodale (1992, 1995) associated an occipito-temporal—ventral visual pathway with vision-for-perception, and an occipito-parietal—dorsal visual pathway with vision-for-action. The core argument for the perception/action reading of the ventral/dorsal anatomical pathways heralded by Milner and Goodale (1992, 1995, 2008) was the contrast between visual agnosia and optic ataxia, two neurological conditions encountered following brain damage to the main projection areas from the visual cortex.

Optic ataxia was described by Bálint (1909) in the early twentieth century and studied mostly in the 1960s, with the notable exception of Jeannerod (1986) and Vighetto and Perenin in the 1980s (Vighetto, 1980; Vighetto and Perenin, 1981; Perenin and Vighetto, 1988; for review see Pisella et al., 2008). The basic features of optic ataxia are a deficit for reaching to a visual target in peripheral vision associated with the absence of intrinsic visual (the patient can see, and describe the visual world), motor (the patient can move the two arms freely), and proprioceptive (the patient can match joint angles between the two arms) deficits (Garcin et al., 1967; Perenin and Vighetto, 1988). Typical patients exhibit a major pointing/grasping deficit when they use the contralesional hand to reach in the contralesional visual field, which is frequently associated with moderate deficits when the contralesional hand reaches in the healthy visual field (isolated hand effect) and when the healthy hand reaches in the contralesional visual field (isolated field effect) (Fig. 10.1).

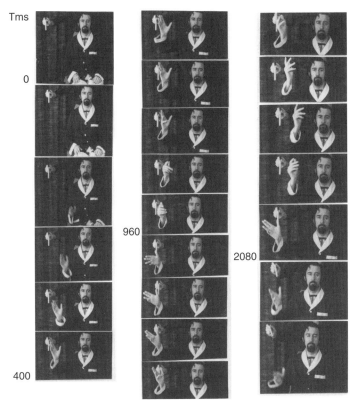

Fig. 10.1 Images of a reaching movement made by patient presenting with right optic ataxia. Time is indicated in ms. Note that the patient is fixating straight-ahead (the camera) and reaching in peripheral vision. A full movement (including finger closure) is realized to an erroneous location in space. Then, surprisingly, the patient wanders in space as if blind and he finally gives up on this trial. (From Vighetto, 1980).

At the time of the first theoretical elaboration of the two visual streams, the most influential paper on optic ataxia was the group study by Perenin and Vighetto (1988), in which 11 patients had been investigated, and in which quantitative descriptions were provided for the first time. Thanks to the rise in popularity of Milner and Goodale's theory (1992, 1995, 2008), the scientific interest in optic ataxia has risen considerably, and a new era of investigation has begun since the late 1990s.

In contrast to optic ataxia, which is often described as a symptom associated with a fairly circum-scribed cortical area, a variety of visual agnosias can be distinguished following lesions to the temporal lobe (Devinsky et al., 2008). The originality of Milner and Goodale was to focus their attention on a single case (Milner et al., 1991; Goodale et al., 1991), D.F., who was to become the source of an incredible number of studies. D.F. presented with a bilateral lesion of the occipito-temporal junction and a severe visual form agnosia. Although she could not recognize objects, the extraordinary finding that she could nevertheless reach and grasp simple objects accurately, has provided the decisive element for the dissociation from optic ataxia. Indeed, D.F. appeared capable of performing just the kind of visual reaching task that patients with optic ataxia were impaired at, and the latter group did not exhibit D.F.'s obvious visual recognition deficits. Some aspects of visuo-motor behaviour seem to be impaired specifically in optic ataxia, and in turn some aspects of visual perception seem to be impaired specifically in visual agnosia. Based on these observations, several authors argued that there was a double dissociation between the two conditions and hence between perception and action (Milner and Goodale, 1995; Rossetti, 1998). See Table 10.1.

Table 10.1 The 'Classical' View. The shaded boxes highlight the main features of the two neurological conditions. These features have been used to argue for a double-dissociation between visual agnosia and optic ataxia

	Visual Ataxia	Optic Ataxia
Perception	Impaired	Intact
Action	Intact	impaired

Building on the recent wave of studies on optic ataxia and visual agnosia patients, we have recently returned to this theoretical point, and have argued that there is not, in fact, unequivocal evidence for a double dissociation between these two conditions (Pisella et al., 2006. See Table 10.2).

Definitions of double dissociation imply that patient with lesion A is impaired specifically for task X whereas patient with lesion B is impaired specifically for task Z, and not vice versa (see Rossetti and Revonsuo, 2000). There are four ways in which the evidence for such a double dissociation is lacking. First, to argue for a double dissociation between two cases one must make sure that the tasks to be compared have been performed in identical conditions in the two patients. Specifically, optic ataxia reaching deficits are described in peripheral vision, whereas D.F.'s reaching performance had only been described in central vision. Milner and Goodale (2008) have confirmed recently the preservation of the reaching abilities of patient D.F. with visual agnosia in peripheral vision. However, the preservation of the reaching abilities of optic ataxia patients in central vision remains a fact which questions the model of the double-dissociation. A number of arguments can be made for a more general dissociation in the control of reaching movements to objects viewed centrally vs. peripherally. Second, to argue for a dissociation internal to the patient, one has to make sure that identical conditions have been used for the two tasks considered. Unfortunately, the perceptual ability of patients with optic ataxia had been analysed only in central vision, whereas their reaching deficit is largely predominant in peripheral vision. We will show in the present chapter that the perceptual ability of patient I.G. with bilateral optic ataxia is impaired in peripheral vision. Third, D.F., like most visual agnosia patients (Devinsky et al., 2008), presented with a bilateral lesion whereas optic ataxia is frequently observed following a unilateral lesion. This element suggests that different patterns of

Table 10.2 The apparent double dissociation between the two neurological conditions becomes questionable when one considers the precise experimental conditions used for the two types of patients. Reaching and grasping performances have been documented in different conditions, namely in central and/or peripheral viewing conditions. Reaching and grasping are impaired in peripheral vision whereas they remain largely preserved in central vision. Actions to peripheral targets have been only recently documented in one VA patient for pointing (Milner and Goodale, 2007). Another missing control was about visual perception of OA patients in peripheral vision. Several studies showed that it is impaired in patients with optic ataxia (Rossetti et al., 2005a, and 2005b, see Figure 7; Goodale et al., 1994; Pisella et al., 2007, 2009). Underlined text corresponds to data published following our 2006 review (Pisella et al. 2006)

Task	Visual Agnosia	Optic Ataxia
Object recognitionin peripheral vision	???	Impaired
Object recognition free=central vision	Impaired	Spared
Pointing in peripheral	Spared	Impaired
Pointing in central vision	Spared	Spared
Grasping in peripheral	???	Impaired
Grasping in central vision	Spared	Spared

functional connectivity must be attributed to the brain areas corresponding to these lesion sites. Fourth, more generally, we have proposed that different neural pathways within the parietal lobe may subserve different types of action (Pisella et al., 2006). That is, the dorsal stream is involved in action under specific conditions. This discussion will be extended with new experimental data on patient I.G.'s ability to perform non-standard visuo-motor transformations.

In the following sections, we will review and discuss the evidence supporting our contention that there is an incomplete dissociation between perception and action, following the four arguments just described. Finally, we will follow up on our proposal (Rossetti et al., 2003) that the function of the dorsal stream would be labelled more appropriately as 'peripheral vision' than as 'vision for action' (Milner and Goodale, 1995; Rossetti, 1998). We will argue that optic ataxia patients fail systematically under conditions in which the location of gaze is dissociated from the location of the visual stimulus of (perceptual or motor) interest.

10.2. Peripheral vision for action

Clinical evidence showed that most optic ataxia patients are only impaired when they reach a visual target in peripheral vision, whereas they are accurate in central vision (Garcin et al., 1967; Perenin and Vighetto, 1988). Recent quantitative investigations have confirmed this idea by measuring visuo-motor errors throughout the visual field of these patients.

10.2.1. 'Ataxie Optique' vs. 'Optische Ataxie'

Clinically, patients with pure optic ataxia (i.e. only this symptom of Bálint's syndrome) present with posterior parietal lesions and an obvious deficit for reaching for visual goals presented in their peripheral visual field. In Japan, the French *ataxie optique* is used to describe such pure cases with unilateral lesions and deficits restricted to the peripheral visual field, following the initial description of these patients by Garcin et al. (1967). The initial German term *optische Ataxie* remains specifically for patients with Bálint's syndrome consecutive to bilateral damage, including visuo-motor problems in central vision, in which case praxic (ocular and manual) and attentional (simultagnosia, unilateral neglect) aspects are difficult to disentangle from ataxic symptoms. *Optische Ataxie* and *ataxie optique* are two terms still accepted as different definitions, because they point out an important distinction between different clinical patterns. This distinction relies on the presence or absence of deficits in central vision and has been rephrased by Buxbaum and Coslett (1997, 1998) as 'foveal' and 'non-foveal' optic ataxia. In the most recent studies on visuo-motor deficits of optic ataxia patients, most experiments have only tested peripheral vision (Blangero et al., 2007, 2008; Dijkerman et al., 2005; Gaveau et al., 2008; Khan et al., 2005a; Revol et al., 2003). Those studies that tested central vision did not show any deficit (Rice et al., 2008; Himmelbach et al., 2005; Rossetti et al., 2005). This may be because, in addition to a unilateral or a bilateral lesion, the presence of concomitant symptoms of Bálint's syndrome has become an exclusion factor prior to considering central reaching deficits. Let us now review the available data on this central issue (Rossetti et al., 2003, 2005; Pisella et al., 2006; Milner and Goodale, 2008).

10.2.2. Mis-reaching specific to peripheral vision in pure optic ataxia

As pointed out earlier, patients with pure optic ataxia do not complain about visuo-motor problems in everyday life (Rossetti et al., 2003). Patients with unilateral deficit can drive a car and work (Pisella et al., 2009). Their professions include taxi driver, university finance manager, and hotline support technician for business softwares. In our experience, patients with bilateral optic ataxia also report no specific visuo-motor deficits in central vision when Bálint symptoms are limited. Second, consider the pioneering group study by Perenin and Vighetto (Vighetto, 1980; Perenin and Vighetto, 1988), which provided the key publication that has been cited intensively for 20 years. They qualitatively examined video recordings of ten patients with unilateral OA, evaluating their ability to reach for

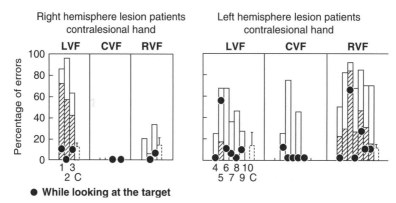

Fig. 10.2 Percentage of reaching errors produced with the contralesional hand towards the left, central, and right visual field (LVF, CVF, RVF) in ten patients with unilateral PPC lesions (three in the right and seven in the left hemisphere). The mean (and standard deviation) percentage of errors of five control subjects (C) is presented for comparison. The subjects were asked to reach an object presented by an experimenter standing in front of them while keeping the eyes fixed (histograms) or after foveating the object (circles). The dashed histograms correspond to uncorrected errors (i.e. the object was finally not reached) whereas the blank bars correspond to the percentage of errors corrected during the execution. (Adapted from Perenin and Vighetto, 1988).

and grasp objects presented in central or peripheral visual fields. Only three of them (all of whom showed associated symptoms such as hypokinesia, apraxia, Gerstmann syndrome, or neglect), exhibited reaching errors in their central visual field. However these errors could be corrected spontaneously by the patients. In contrast, most of them exhibited massive, uncorrected mis-reaching in the contralesional visual field (Figure 4 in Perenin and Vighetto, 1988, adapted here in Fig. 10. 2).

Remarkably, the errors corrected spontaneously found in the central visual field were suppressed fully (to 0% in nine of the ten patients) when patients were asked to gaze at the target objects prior to initiating their movement (Table 9.4 in Perenin and Vighetto, 1988). The only patient who showed errors after foveating the target object had a very extensive left cortical and subcortical lesion, and showed a variety of associated symptoms (hypokinesia, loss of right hand preference, ideomotor, ideational and constructional apraxia, body schema alteration, autotopoagnosia, abnormal limb posture at rest, and unilateral neglect) likely to account for this central deficit (see below). Therefore, it was very clear from this reach-to-grasp task that the OA patient's visuo-motor deficit was essentially specific to peripheral vision. No further errors were observed for a wrist-orientation 'posting' task using central vision that was also examined (comparison between Figures 4 and 5 in Perenin and Vighetto, 1988). Although no quantitative measurements were available at the time of this pioneering study, Perenin and Vighetto (1988) observed that 'the largest errors always occurred with the contralesional hand reaching in the contralesional space' (p. 655). Figure 10.3 illustrates the dramatic error difference found between free gaze (central vision) and central fixation conditions.

Finally, consider the recent quantitative assessments of reaching errors in patients with optic ataxia. The two patients who have been tested most extensively are I.G. and A.T. Typically, these two bilateral patients show an extraordinary difference between central and peripheral reaching accuracy. Initially, A.T. showed a limited deficit when grasping in central vision during the early stage of her disease, i.e. when more associate Bálint's symptoms were present (Jeannerod et al., 1994). Then the pointing accuracy of the two patients became very similar: accuracy was essentially normal in central vision and errors increased dramatically with target eccentricity (Milner et al., 1999, 2003; Rossetti et al., 2003, 2005). I.G. has also been tested in a dowel grasping task with and without object displacement. When the object remained static such that the grasping movement was guided by central vision, neither significant mis-reaching nor systematic kinematic abnormalities were revealed

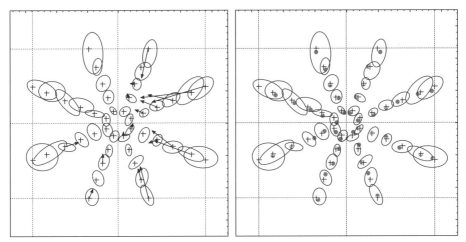

Fig. 10.3 Pointing performance of a patient with unilateral optic ataxia in central fixation (left) vs. free gaze (right) conditions. The central point is the eye fixation target. Targets were presented along eight radial lines from this position. Ellipses represent confidence ellipses of endpoints reached by healthy controls. Arrows depict individual errors of the patient that lied out of these confidences ellipses. The patient's errors in the free gaze condition all fell within the normal range. In the fixation condition large errors (up to more than 100 mm) were obtained in the right visual field of the patient.

(Gréa et al., 2002). Therefore subsequent studies of grasping in these patients used only peripheral object presentations (e.g. Milner et al., 2001, 2003).

The quantitative assessment of reaching error patterns of patients with unilateral optic ataxia has also led to more specific conclusions about the central/peripheral issue. It has been shown that pointing errors of optic ataxia patients depend on the position of the gaze (Buxbaum and Coslett, 1998; Khan et al., 2005a; Blangero et al., 2009) and does not vary with head or body position (Dijkerman et al., 2005). Moreover, depending on the severity of their disorder, optic ataxia patients tend to perform hypometric reaches (Vighetto, 1980; Perenin and Vighetto, 1988; Milner et al., 2003; Jackson et al., 2005; Rossetti et al., 2005; Blangero et al., 2010; Ota et al., 2003) or more radically show a striking attraction of their pointing onto the fixation point, i.e. 'magnetic misreaching' (Carey et al., 1997; Buxbaum and Coslett, 1998). In our experience, this magnetic mis-reaching behaviour appears to be most apparent during the early stage of recovery following a bilateral lesion.

A recent study examined the performance of seven unilateral OA patients reaching to visual targets displayed on a two-dimensional matrix. (Blangero et al., 2010; Ota et al., 2003). As shown in Fig. 10.4 error vectors produced in the contralesional field were directed systematically towards the central fixation point, and were better explained along polar coordinates centred on the gaze than along Cartesian coordinates. Based on this strongly consistent and reproducible error pattern, we conclude that a retinocentric reference frame is being used to encode the movement plan in these optic ataxia patients. Subsequently, pointing errors are highly dependent on the target eccentricity relative to the gaze position (Blangero et al., 2010; Ota et al., 2003; Rossetti et al., 2005), which provides another demonstration of the specificity of OA reaching deficits for peripheral vision. It is worth noticing that the retinocentric error vectors are characteristic of the field effect i.e. reaching errors in the contralesional visual field. Errors due to the hand effect (i.e. use of the contralesional hand) are not directed towards the gaze fixation.

10.2.3. Reaching errors in central vision explained by concomitant deficits

Jakobson et al. (1991) studied a patient recovering from Bálint's syndrome in a grasping task in central vision, and described 'subtle deficits in midline pointing and prehension' (p. 803). However, this patient still displayed 'persisting difficulties' which 'were evident in her visual-scanning ability and in visuospatial/constructional skills' (p. 804), and therefore could not be considered a case of pure optic ataxia.

In the light of the observations of Perenin and Vighetto (1988) and Jakobson et al. (1991), we suggest that patients with bilateral lesion suffering from Bálint's syndrome may be impaired in central vision due to additional visuo-spatial deficits such as simultanagnosia, which prevents the concomitant viewing of the hand and the target, resulting in reaching inaccuracy. (Moreover, patients with reaching deficits in central vision are shown to be *more* accurate when they are prevented from receiving visual feedback about the hand during the execution of the movement (open-loop condition) (Jakobson et al., 1991; Buxbaum and Coslett, 1998). This is likely to be explained by interference between visual information from the target and visual information from the hand (simultanagnosia), which is resolved in open-loop condition. In contrast, pure optic ataxia patients are *less* accurate in open-loop than in closed-loop reaching (Vighetto, 1980; Jeannerod, 1986; Rossetti et al., 2003, Figure 10.4; Blangero et al., 2007). The absence of visual feedback of the hand thus has a deleterious effect on reaching accuracy in pure OA patients. Blangero et al., (2007) proposed that this deleterious effect could be attributed to an impaired ability to determine the spatial position of the ataxic hand using proprioceptive information.

10.3. Arguments for a central/peripheral dissociation in the control of reaching

Thus far we have considered both historical clinical observations and recent empirical data emphasizing the importance of distinguishing centrally from peripherally-guided reaching when evaluating the contribution of data from OA patients to any model of parallel visual processing. Here, we will review three further lines of evidence that support the more general notion of independent processing, to some extent, of reaches to targets acquired from foveal vs. non-foveal sources.

10.3.1. The functional anatomy of the parietal lobe

A possible explanation for the dissociation between the visuo-motor behaviour in central versus peripheral vision comes from a neuroimaging study from Prado and collaborators (2005). When comparing the brain activity of subjects pointing to central vs. peripheral visual targets, they observed a main module localized in the medial part of the intraparietal sulcus (mIPS) that was involved in visually-guided action towards both central and peripheral targets. Importantly, they also showed that the parieto-occipital junction (POJ) was activated specifically in only the peripheral pointing condition. From this, the authors proposed that POJ is necessary to plan a reaching movement in peripheral vision. Notably, this area also corresponds to the region that recently has been considered responsible (when damaged) for optic ataxia by Karnath and Perenin (2005). Conversely, and consistent with the data of Prado et al. (2005), there is (to our knowledge) no case description of a reaching deficit specific to central vision.

We have also investigated this anatomical issue in our group of patients. The lesions of 11 published pure OA patients (five left, four right unilateral, and two bilateral PPC lesions) have been overlaid. The clinical descriptions of the patients used for the lesion overlap are already published in previous studies (four left and three right unilateral lesion patients from Blangero et al., 2010; one unilateral right lesion patient from Revol et al., 2003, one unilateral left lesion patient from Blangero et al., 2007; two bilateral lesion patients: Rossetti et al., 2005).

The lesions are centred in the parieto-occipital regions (Fig. 10.5). The centre of the maximum overlay zone is situated just in front of the POJ (left hemisphere: x=-24, y=-66, z=44; right hemisphere: x=30, y=-68, z=46; MNI space). Even if most of the IPS (mIPS) is included in the maximum lesion overlap, the anterior part (aIPS), identified by Binkofski et al. (1998) as responsible for grasping, is mostly spared. This observation is consistent with the fact that none of their patients with a pure aIPS lesion (Binkofski et al. 1998) showed optic ataxia (Binkofski, personal communication).

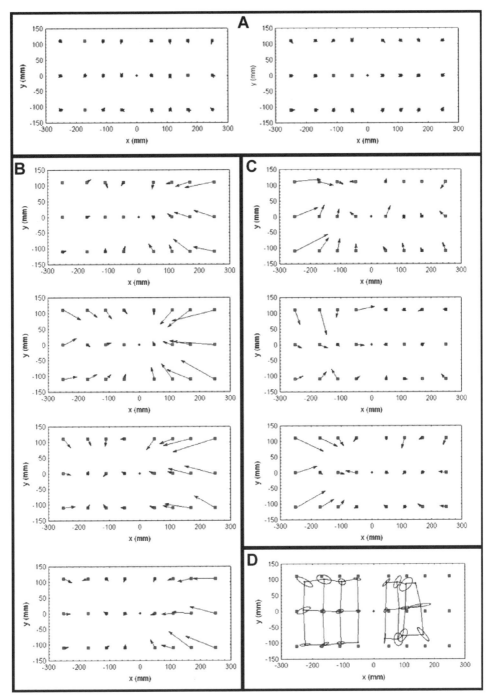

Fig. 10.4 Terminal errors observed during pointing at peripheral targets. Eye fixation is in the centre of the two-dimensional target array and 12 targets (red squares) are presented in each hemifield. Individual error vectors are depicted as arrows pointing from the target to the movement endpoint. A: Normal subject pointing with left and right hands exhibit no significant pointing errors. B: Four patients with right optic ataxia pointing with the right hand show a very systematic hypometria in their controlesional hemifield, with error vectors pointing towards the fixation point. C. Three patients with left optic ataxia pointing with their left hand show a remarkably symmetrical pattern. D. Average of patients. Between subject variability is depicted by confidence ellipses and the average points are joined by lines to emphasize the visuo-motor space contraction observed in the controlesional hemifield. (From Blangero et al. [2010]).

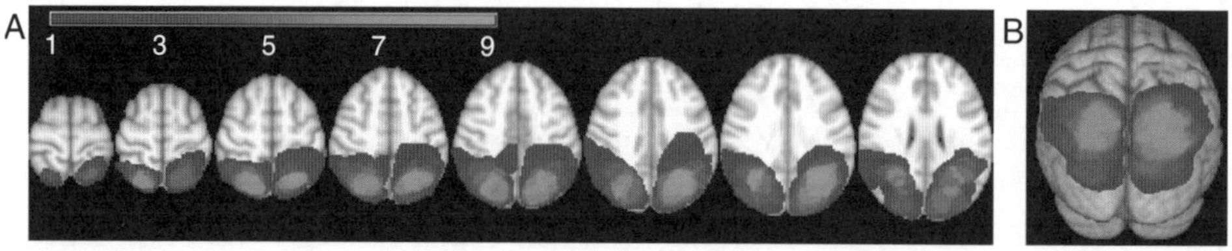

Fig. 10.5 (See Plate 3) A: Slices representation of the lesion overlay (from z=26 to z=68, step of z=6, in MNI space). The brighter the region, the more of the patient's lesion it contains, going from 0 to 8. B: three-dimensional render of the lesion overlay, posterior view of the brain. MRIcron (http://www.sph.sc.edu/comd/rorden/mricron/) was used to draw, overlay and map the lesions From Pisella et al., in revision.

The grasping deficits of the patient may then come from the lesion of the caudal part of the IPS (cIPS) which projects to AIP in the monkey or from the lesion of parieto-occipital region corresponding to the monkey area V6a which has been shown to be involved both in reaching and grasping (Fattori et al., 2004). This area, when lesioned in the monkey, produces behavioural deficits for reach-to-grasp movements, which have been related to optic ataxia in humans (Battaglini et al., 2002). These two functional monkey areas have probably been included in the human POJ through evolution. A final point concerning the anatomical basis to a central/peripheral dissociation in reach planning has to do with the visual topography of this area V6a in the monkey (Galletti et al., 1999). The fact that V6a does not exhibit the foveal magnification commonly found in cortical visual areas is an additional argument for a functional specificity to peripheral vision.

10.2.2. **Online control deficits**

Several studies have shown that patients with bilateral OA are severely impaired in their ability to update reaching trajectories in response to unpredictable target displacement either when the target is experimentally moved away after being acquired foveally (Pisella et al., 2000; Gréa et al., 2002; Rossetti and Pisella, 2003) or in peripheral vision (Rossetti et al., 2005). A deficit in the representation of a target in peripheral vision can explain this difficulty, as well as a more general problem with online movement control. Blangero and colleagues (2008) tested patient CF with unilateral optic ataxia in a target jump pointing task. The movements were made by the healthy or by the ataxic hand, and the target could jump from central vision towards either the patient's healthy or ataxic visual field. For simple pointing towards stationary targets in peripheral vision, we found a classical combination of hand and field effects in this patient. Only very few movements made by the ataxic hand could be corrected when the target jumped into the ataxic field (16.6%). In contrast, the patient performed even better than normal subjects when using his healthy hand in his healthy visual field (77.1%). The patient showed intermediate performance in the two crossed conditions (39%). Moreover, the rare movements that could be corrected in the ataxic field were those which preceded by a saccade that brought the target in central vision. These data demonstrate that central vision is necessary to direct (or re-direct) the reaching movement correctly in optic ataxia (this was also suggested by the study of eye-hand coordination in bilateral optic ataxia: Gaveau et al., 2008). Anatomically, this would again suggest that the modules subserving visuo-motor transformations for targets acquired in central vision are preserved, whereas the analogous modules for targets acquired in peripheral vision (putatively POJ)—necessary for online motor corrections—are impaired.

10.2.3. **The effect of a temporal delay**

Still another argument for a specifically peripheral deficit can be found in a series of experiments that investigated delay effects in bilateral optic ataxia (Milner et al., 1999, 2001; Rossetti et al., 2005; Himmelbach and Karnath, 2005). These studies showed a remarkable paradoxical improvement of pointing performance when a delay was introduced between target presentation and reaching response (Fig. 10.6). As shown in Milner et al. (2008) D.F. showed a dramatic increase of pointing

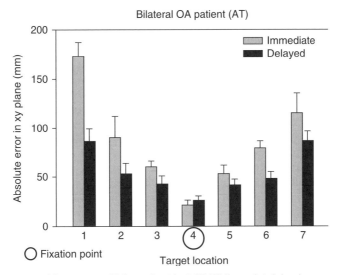

Fig. 10.6 Absolute reaching errors of bilateral patient AT. While maintaining her eyes fixed on the central target, the patient was asked to reach to visual targets as soon as she saw them (grey) or after a delay of 5s (black). We can clearly see that large errors 1) increase dramatically with target eccentricity; and 2) are reduced in the delay condition. Similar results were described in another bilateral patient by Rossetti et al., 2005. (Adapted from Milner et al., 1999).

error in delayed conditions as compared to normal performance in peripheral vision. Conversely, optic ataxia patients show only a relative reduction of pointing errors in the delayed condition, corresponding to absolute values significantly larger than controls (i.e. a partial improvement only). Unlike Milner and Goodale (Chapter 5, this volume) we believe that the evidence for a double dissociation is thus insufficient (Table 10.3). This is compatible with the view that the improvement with delay found in optic ataxia can be accounted for by an involvement of not only the ventral stream, but also intermediate pathways such as the inferior parietal cortex (e.g. Mattingley et al., 1998).

Interestingly, the positive effect of delay in optic ataxia could not be observed for central targets, and remained specific to peripheral vision (e.g. Milner et al., 1999). Interestingly, a detailed analysis of the delay effect revealed that its magnitude was proportional to target eccentricity (Fig. 10.6. See also Rossetti et al., 2005). This suggests that the lesioned brain areas responsible for optic ataxia are contributing specifically to reaching in peripheral vision. The effect of eccentricity also shows that, even for the same simple pointing action, redundant visuo-motor pathways may exist with different spatial encoding and different temporal constraints, pathways which do not involve the dorsal stream.

Table 10.3 Delayed pointing and grasping has not been tested in all combinations of central/peripheral and immediate/delayed conditions for either type of patients. The available data show that D.F. shows normal immediate performance in peripheral vision and impaired delayed performance (Milner and Goodale, 2008), but delayed performance obtained in optic ataxia is only improved and remains far from control values (Milner et al., 1999; Rossetti et al., 2005; Himmelbach and Karnath, 2005)

Tasks	Visual Agnosia	Optic Ataxia
Delayed Pointing in peripheral vision		Improved
Delayed Pointing in central vision	Improved	Spared
Delayed Grasping in peripheral vision		Improved
Delayed Grasping in central vision	Improved	

This idea will be developed further in the final section. First, however, we will review evidence for the idea that optic ataxia affects not only the *actions* based on peripheral vision, but the *perceptions* as well.

10.4. Peripheral vision for perception is affected in optic ataxia

Milner and Goodale (2008) define the function of the ventral stream as 'vision for perception', and define this label as 'the conscious experience of seeing'. We have previously put forward an alternative hypothesis about the substrate crucial for visual consciousness, in a review of hemineglect (Pisella and Mattingley, 2004), a pathology defined by a loss of consciousness for visual stimuli on the left. In hemineglect, the ventral stream is preserved fully and bilaterally. Altered visual perception in optic ataxia also provides arguments against the ventral stream being solely responsible for visual consciousness. For example, a lesion of the dorsal stream in optic ataxia patients does not affect visual perception in central vision, but it affects drastically the performance in both visual change detection, and identification in peripheral vision. In addition, the processes for covert visual attention are impaired contralesionally in pure optic ataxia. The involvement of the parietal cortex in visual attention is acknowledged (e.g. Corbetta and Schulmann, 2002) and may be a key to understanding why the dorsal stream (with its saliency map(s), see Gottlieb et al., 1998; Striemer et al., 2007; Pisella et al., 2007; Khan et al., 2008) appears crucial for 'the conscious experience of seeing'.

10.4.1. A deficit in perceptual detection of visual changes

Our first observation in an OA patient of a deficit in the perceptual detection of a visual change was unexpected. It was made during the exploration of visuo-motor reactions to target changes in location occurring in visual periphery during a memory delay (Rossetti et al., 2005). Two patients with bilateral OA (I.G. and A.T.) and aged-matched controls were shown a visual target for two seconds in the peripheral visual field. The target was then hidden for five seconds and was shown again at a congruent (80%) or an incongruent (differing by up to 20°) location. The subjects were instructed to point at it immediately after the second presentation. Results demonstrated that, contrary to healthy controls who initiated their reaches based only on the second target location, the pointing trajectory of the two patients were mostly influenced by the memorized initial target location, rather than the present 'secondary' target location. Reactions to the changed target location were manifest as trajectories averaged in space between the memorized and the present locations, or as late corrections of the trajectory in the direction of the present location (in nine of 16 trials for patient A.T. and in 13 trials for patient I.G.). This visuo-motor behaviour extended the demonstration of a deficit in processing visual information for action in real time (Milner et al., 1999; Pisella et al., 2000; Milner et al., 2001; Gréa et al., 2002). Furthermore, it revealed a deficit in change detection in peripheral vision in the two patients. Indeed, after this experiment, patient A.T. was questioned about her perception of the target jumps in the visual periphery: she reported that she never perceived that the target location changed sometimes during the delay. Patient I.G., who detected target location changes spontaneously at the beginning of the experiment, was then asked systematically whether the target changed in location during the delay. Numerous false alarms were recorded on her verbal responses, as well as numerous trajectory corrections in the stationary (congruent) trials carrying the hand further away from the true target location (also considered false alarms). Further analyses of the data compared the patient performance for visuo-motor and perceptual responses to target jumps in peripheral vision (Pisella et al., 2007). Whereas I.G. performed numerous (late) trajectory corrections for location-change trials with respect to no-change trials, her perceptual performance (d-prime=1.35) appeared to be even poorer than the visuo-motor performance (d-prime=3.9).

To investigate the perceptual impairment for detecting visual change in optic ataxia further, we examined the performance of patient I.G. (bilateral lesion of the dorsal visual stream) in change detection for not only location, but also for other visual attributes (shape, size, and orientation), in central vs. peripheral vision (20°). According to the two visual streams theory of Milner and Goodale (1995), the perceptual performance should be preserved after bilateral lesion of the dorsal stream

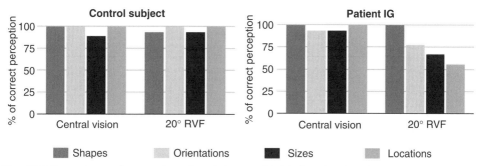

Fig. 10.7 Percentages of correct detection of changes (hits) in four visual attributes tested in blocked sessions (shape, orientation, size, and location). The patient and control subject had to respond by a button press whether the first and second images presented either in central or in peripheral (20 deg) vision were 'same' or 'different'. From Pisella et al. (2009).

(contrary to the goal-directed actions). Accordingly, the detection of visual changes was equivalent to age-matched control in central vision (significantly above chance level with percentages of correct detection of changes above 90%: Fig. 10.7). However, this was not the case in peripheral vision (20°) where the performance of I.G. decreased below 80% for the size, below 70% for the orientation, and below 60% for the location changes. More qualitative observations have been made by Perenin and Vighetto (1988, Table 9.2). Specifically, five out of five unilateral optic ataxia patients, tested for their perception of object location, exhibited a performance decrement in their contralesional field compared to their ipsilesional field. A performance decrement was also observed in three out of five patients tested for orientation perception. Peripherally guided reach performance in OA patients thus appears to reflect a gradient of visual attribute processing between the dorsal stream (processing the spatial/metric properties: Where) and the ventral stream (processing 'object' properties: What) for both action and perception purposes (model proposed in Rossetti et al., 2000; Figure 1–7 in Rossetti and Pisella 2002). The functional difference between dorsal and ventral streams in this pattern of results is thus explained by their visual inputs. Without the dorsal stream, the perceptual processing of object location in peripheral vision appeared to be the most impaired visual attribute. At the other extreme of the gradient, the change detection of shape (which can be categorized verbally) remained preserved in peripheral vision in I.G. This performance in shape processing was the only one not to diverge from the control subjects' performance, who remained equivalent in central and peripheral (20°) vision for all attributes (Fig. 10.7). Note that the optic ataxia patient RV, for whom detailed neuropsychological examination details are not available, and who showed an associated substantial lesion of the occipital cortex, also exhibited a clear deficit for shape orientation discrimination in central vision (Goodale et al., 2004; Milner and Goodale, Chapter 5, this volume).

Note that the preservation of the location change detection in central vision does not contradict our claim above that a 'jump' of a target initially acquired by the fovea would transfer its location into peripheral vision, and hence to the processing of POJ for visuo-motor transformation (online motor corrections). Indeed, a motor response consisting of pressing a button (or stopping an ongoing movement: Pisella et al., 2000) can simply be triggered by the detection of the disappearance of the visual target from the fovea, contrary to the adjustment of the motor reaching trajectory towards the new target location. Consequently, I.G. can be as fast as control subjects in producing arbitrary motor response to a target jump in central vision, but drastically delayed when implementing online visuo-motor control (Pisella et al., 2000).

10.4.2. Impaired covert attention in optic ataxia?

Striemer et al. (2007) examined the peripheral visual attention in two patients with left unilateral optic ataxia (C.F. and M.E.) with no clinical neglect and no clinical extinction. They utilized the covert orienting of visual attention task (COVAT) in which participants must fixate a central cross while attending to peripheral locations to the left and right (Posner, 1980). Previous studies examining covert attention in patients with parietal lesions without OA had demonstrated a characteristic deficit in 'disengaging' attention, such that they are abnormally slow to detect targets in contralesional space when the preceding cue appears in ipsilesional space (Posner et al., 1984; Losier and Klein, 2001). Both unilateral OA patients displayed deficits in orienting *and* reorienting attention towards contralesional space (Striemer et al., 2007). The fact that both patients exhibited slower reaction times for all targets occurring in contralesional space (even when a cue was not presented) is consistent with an overall decrease in the salience of stimuli in the ataxic field. So far there seems to be no *known case of pure OA who does not exhibit attentional deficits*. In conclusion, it seems that in order to observe normal performance in OA, having the eye at the goal of interest (central vision) is the crucial factor in the context of 'vision for perception', as we already argued for 'vision for action' (reaching).

10.4.3. Distinct cortical pathways underlying different transformation processing

Current research suggests that the parallel networks formed via reciprocal connections between premotor and parietal areas have important roles in transforming sensory information about limb and target position into movement (e.g. Battaglia-Mayer and Caminiti, 2002). These networks are heavily involved in coordinating both the reaching movement that transports the arm to an object of interest, and the grasping movements for interacting with that object once the hand has arrived at its destination. Examinations of the neural correlates of non-standard visual-to-motor transformations over the last couple of decades have begun to reveal a network of specific brain regions involved in non-standard mapping. In particular, areas of the brain thought to be vital for the learning and/or performance of these tasks include the prefrontal cortex (PF, highly connected with the infero-temporal cortex: ventral stream), the dorsal premotor cortex (PMd), and nuclei of the basal ganglia (BG) (Hadj-Bouziane et al., 2003).

Pisella et al. (2006) proposed different-but-interconnected pathways processing information related to the different types of visual-to-motor transformations/visuo-motor compatibility (see also the idea of a gradual dorsal/ventral contribution to visuo-motor transformation depending on inputs and outputs in Rossetti et al., 2000, Figure 4; and in Rossetti and Pisella, 2002, Figure 1.7). These multiple pathways would ultimately converge upon the primary motor cortex and spinal cord, which then incorporates the various dynamic factors and biomechanical details needed for final movement production (Sergio and Kalaska, 2003). While subcortical structures are not specifically drawn into the schematic, cerebellar-cortical and basal ganglia-cortical loops would probably be involved heavily in dissociated reaching production. These subcortical-cortical pathways have a well-known topographic parallel arrangement. We presume that these loops would also be separate for the different types of visuo-motor processing discussed here, mirroring the segregated cortical pathways that we have proposed.

Altogether, patients with unilateral optic ataxia typically exhibit no reaching errors in central vision. When they do, these errors are extremely marginal with respect to the large errors consistently observed in peripheral vision. We have listed arguments that suggest that optic ataxia is a basic deficit for reaching in the peripheral visual field, i.e. when eye and hand coordinates are not aligned.

10.5. Confronting visuomotor and perceptual performance with illusions

In the healthy brain a large number of studies have compared the performance of the visuomotor and the perceptual systems in the presence of illusory set-up. Overall it has been argued that visual illusions fool the perceptual responses while they may affect the visuo-motor accuracy to a lesser extent (review: Bruno et al., 2008; Goodale and Westwood, 2004). Although largely debated, this has provided another argument for a segregation of the visual brain in two main functional modules devoted to perception and action (Goodale and Haffenden, 1998; Goodale and Westwood, 2004). Interestingly, the effect of visual illusions can either be identical (Coello et al., 2003) or even higher on the visuo-motor system than on perception (Yamagishi et al., 2001). Taking advantage of this variety of pattern, Coello et al. (2007) have investigated the effects of visual illusions on the bilateral optic ataxic patient I.G. They tested the patients and normal controls on three different illusory set-up presented in the horizontal plane. First, they used the induced Roelof's effect (see Bridgeman, 2000) by which the position of a visual target is misjudged by perceptual responses whereas it is pointed accurately. Whereas previous studies used a vertical fronto parallel presentation of the off-centre frame responsible for the illusion, this experiment used a left-right presentation as in Coello et al. (2003). If, as predicted by the dual steam theory of the visual system, the immunity of the visuo-motor responses to visual illusions result from the involvement of the dorsal stream, then a patient with a bilateral lesion of the posterior parietal cortex should not exhibit this immunity and her performance would be identical in the perceptual and in the visuo-motor versions of the test. As displayed in Fig. 10.8 (left) however, I.G. showed a perfectly normal pattern of result, which implies that the immunity of the visuo-motor system to visual illusion cannot be attributed to a participation of the dorsal stream. Second, they also used the size-contrast illusion, which has been used very extensively to argue for a clear dissociation between the contribution of the dorsal and the ventral stream in the healthy brain (e.g. Goodale and Westwood, 2004). As for the induced Roelof's effect, the obvious prediction of the dual stream theory of vision is that a bilateral lesion of the PPC should lead to an identical performance for the perceptual and the visuo-motor responses. As shown in Fig. 10.8 (centre), this straight-forward prediction is again falsified by the pattern of result found in I.G.: The differential effect of the two illusory set-ups used traditionally in these experiments was even less in I.G. than in healthy controls. In addition, these authors used an additional illusory situation in which the Roelof's effect was induced in the near-far dimension. As shown by Coello et al. (2003) this specific orientation of the illusion induces an identical amount of error for both perceptual and

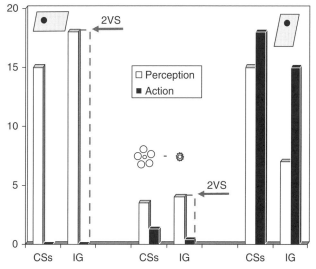

Fig. 10.8 Perceptual (white) and visuo-manual (black) performance of the bilateral patient IG and of control subjects (CSs) with three illusory set-ups. Predictions of the two visual stream theory are depicted with dashed lines with the arrows (2VS). Left: The induced Roelofs effect produced in the horizontal left-right plane. Centre: The size-contrast illusion as used in Haffenden and Goodale. Right: the induced Roelofs effect produced in the horizontal near-far plane. None of these three experiments provided evidence for a specific role of the PPC in the performance obtained with the visuo-manual responses. (from Coello et al. 2007)

visuo-motor responses. Therefore the capacity of I.G. to process the illusory set-ups could be evaluated with this experimental situation. As a matter of fact I.G. exhibited an illusory effect for both responses, which was comparable to that found in healthy subjects (see Fig. 10.8, right).

Altogether these three experiments have lead to the conclusion that the visuo-motor system that is defective in I.G. (dorsal stream) cannot be identified with the visual subsystem responsible for the relative immunity of some visual illusions. The finding that I.G. performed similarly to controls in three different illusory contexts argues against this obvious prediction and shows, that the dorsal stream does not control all aspects of visuo-motor behaviour. These results suggest that visually guided action can be planned and executed independently of the dorsal pathways, possibly through the inferior parietal lobule (e.g. Mattingley et al., 1998; see Coello et al., 2007). It does clearly call for a revision of a simplistic dual-stream model of the visual brain and underlines the need for clarifying the contribution of the areas lying between the dorsal and the ventral streams in perception and action (Pisella et al., 2006), possibly as an anatomo-functional gradient (Rossetti and Pisella, 2002).

10.6. Conclusion

The general oversimplification of the Milner and Goodale (1995) account for the visual brain in action has led to the popular interpretation that 'dorsal = action'. However, it has to be examined carefully what 'action' may refer to in this context. The fact that pure optic ataxia patients are not impaired in everyday life (see also Rossetti et al., 2003; Pisella et al., 2009) is a clear demonstration that their deficit is not a general disruption of a global action system. Rather, the specificity of optic ataxia for peripheral vision suggests that it is a subroutine level of action that is impaired. Clearly online motor corrections of simple aiming movements are impaired severely in optic ataxia, but other aspects of action should be investigated systematically. In addition, recent investigations have revealed gradually that optic ataxia is also responsible for perceptual deficits in peripheral vision, suggesting that the parieto-occipital junction (centre of lesions producing optic ataxia), may be a crucial area for representing the visual periphery *for both perception and action*. Support for this view can be found from experimental conditions in which visual and motor coordinates are dissociated (target displacement, remote visual display) and result in a deficit for optic ataxia patients. When perceptual and visuo-motor responses were compared with visual illusions, the performance found in bilateral optic ataxia was very similar to healthy subjects. This result confirmed that other pathways than just the dorsal and the ventral stream are strongly involved in visuo-motor control (see section 4, Pisella et al., 2006). The main task of future investigations in the field will be to assess how many anatomical pathways contribute to the organization of visuo-motor responses and to what extent distinct anatomical pathways can be associated with functionally specific processes.

Acknowledgements

The authors wish to thank M. Jean-Louis Borach for his contribution to illustrations and Michelle Soulier for her contribution to manuscript formatting.

References

Bálint, R. (1909). Seelenlähmung des Schauens, optische Ataxie, raümliche Störung der Aufmerksamkeit. *Monatsschrift für Psychiatrie und Neurologie*; **25**: 51–81.

Battaglia-Mayer, A. and Caminiti, R. (2002). Optic ataxia as a result of the breakdown of the global tuning fields of parietal neurones. *Brain*; **125**(2): 225–37.

Battaglia-Mayer, A., Ferraina, S., Genovesio, A., Marconi, B., Squatrito, S., Molinari, M. et al. (2001). Eye-hand coordination during reaching. II. An analysis of the relationships between visuomanual signals in parietal cortex and parieto-frontal association projections. *Cerebral Cortex*; **11**(6): 528–44.

Battaglini, P.P., Muzur, A., Galletti, C., Skrap, M., Brovelli, A., and Fattori, P. (2002). Effects of lesions to area V6A in monkeys. *Experimental Brain Research*; **144**(3):419–22.

Binkofski, F. and Fink, G. (2005). Apraxias. *Nervenarzt*; **76**: 493–512.

Binkofski, F., Dohle, C., Posse, S., Stephan, K. M., Hefter, H., Seitz, R. J. et al. (1998). Human anterior intraparietal area subserves prehension: a combined lesion and functional MRI activation study. *Neurology*; **50**: 1253–9.

Blangero, A., Revol, P., Delporte, L., Ota, H., Vindras, P., Rode, G. et al. (2007). Optic Ataxia is not only 'optic': impaired spatial integration of proprioceptive information. *Neuroimage*; **36**(Suppl 2): T61–T68.

Blangero, A., Gaveau, V., Luauté, J., Rode, G., Salemme, R., Boisson, D. et al. (2008). A hand and a field effect on on-line motor control in unilateral optic ataxia. *Cortex*, **44**: 560–8.

Blangero, A., Ota, H., Rossetti, Y., Fujii, T., Ohtake, H., Tabuchi, M. et al. (2010). Systematic retinotopic error vectors in unilateral optic ataxia. *Cortex*; **46**(1): 77–93.

Bridgeman B., Peery, S., and Anand, S. (1997). Interaction of cognitive and sensorimotor maps of visual space. *Percept Psychophys*; **59**(3): 456–69.

Bridgeman, B. (2000). Interactions between vision for perception and vision for behaviour. In *Beyond dissociation: interaction between dissociated implicit and explicit processing*, (eds Rossetti, Y. and Revonsuo, A.), pp. 17–39. Amsterdam: Benjamins.

Bridgeman, B., Kirch, M., and Sperling, A. (1981). Segregation of cognitive and motor aspects of visual function using induced motion. *Perception and Psychophysics*; **29**: 336–42.

Bruno, N., Bernardis, P., and Gentilucci, M. (2008). Visually guided pointing, the Müller-Lyer illusion, and the functional interpretation of the dorsal-ventral split: conclusions from 33 independent studies. *Neuroscience and Biobehavioral Reviews*; **32**(3): 423–37.

Buxbaum, L.J. and Coslett, H.B. (1997). Subtypes of optic ataxia: reframing the disconnection account. *Neurocase*; **3**: 159–66.

—— (1998). Spatio-motor representations in reaching: evidence for subtypes of optic ataxia. *Cognitive Neuropsychology*; **15**: 279–312.

Carey, D.P. (2004). Neuropsychological perspectives on sensorimotor integration: eye-hand coordination and visually-guided reaching. In *Functional neuroimaging of visual cognition: attention and performance XX*, (eds Kanwisher, N. and Duncan, J.), pp. 481–502. Oxford: Oxford University Press.

Carey, D.P., Coleman, R.J., and Della Sala, S. (1997). Magnetic misreaching. *Cortex*; **33**: 639–52.

Coello, Y., Danckert, J., Blangero, A., and Rossetti, Y. (2007). Do visual illusions probe the visual brain? Illusions in action without a dorsal visual stream. *Neuropsychologia*; **45**(8): 1849–58. Erratum in: *Neuropsychologia* 2008 **46**(1): 390–1.

Coello, Y., Richaud, S., Magne, P., and Rossetti, Y. (2003). Vision for spatial perception and vision for action: a dissociation between the left-right and near-far dimensions. *Neuropsychologia*; **41**(5): 622–33.

Corbetta, M. and Shulman, G.L. (2002). Control of goal-directed and stimulus-driven attention in the brain. *Nature Reviews Neuroscience*; **3**(3): 201–15.

Croxson, P.L., Johansen-Berg, H., Behrens, T.E., Robson, M.D., Pinsk, M.A., Gross, C.G. et al. (2005). Quantitative investigation of connections of the prefrontal cortex in the human and macaque using probabilistic diffusion tractography. *The Journal of Neuroscience*; **25**(39): 8854–66.

Danckert, J. and Rossetti, Y. (2005). Blindsight in action: what can the different sub-types of blindsight tell us about the control of visually guided actions? *Neuroscience and Biobehavioral Review*; **29**(7): 1035–46.

Deubel, H. and Schneider, W.X. (1996). Saccade target selection and object recognition: evidence for a common attentional mechanism. *Vision Research*; **36**: 1827–37.

Devinsky, O., Farah, M., and Barr, W.B. (2008). Visual agnosia. In *Handbook of clinical neurology*, (eds Goldenberg, G. and Miller, B.), 3rd Series, Vol 88, *Neuropsychology and behavioral neurology*, pp. 417–27. Edinburgh: Elsevier.

Dijkerman, H.C., McIntosh, R.D., Anema, H.A., de Haan, E.H.F., Kapelle, L.J., and Milner, A.D. (2006). Reaching errors in optic ataxia are linked to eye position rather than head or body position. *Neuropsychologia*; **44**: 2766–73.

Fattori, P., Breveglieri, R., Amoroso, K., and Galletti, C. (2004). Evidence for both reaching and grasping activity in the medial parieto-occipital cortex of the macaque. *European Journal of Neuroscience*; **20**(9): 2457–66.

Galletti, C., Fattori, P., Kutz, D.F., and Gamberini, M. (1999). Brain location and visual topography of cortical area V6A in macaque monkey. *European Journal of Neuroscience*; **11**: 575–82.

Garcin, R., Rondot, P., and de Recondo J. (1967). Ataxie optique localisée aux deux hémichamps visuels homonymes gauches. *Revue Neurologique* (Paris); **116**: 707–14.

Gaveau, V., Pélisson, D., Blangero. A., Urquizar C., Prablanc C., Vighetto A. et al. (2006). A common parietal module for saccade and reach: eye–hand coordination and saccadic control in optic ataxia. *Neuropsychologia*; **46**: 475–86.

Goodale, M.A., Milner, A.D., Jakobson, L.S., and Carey, D.P. (1991). A neurological dissociation between perceiving objects and grasping them. *Nature*; **349**(6305): 154–6.

Goodale, M.A. and Milner, A.D. (1992). Separate visual pathways for perception and action. *Trends in Neurosciences*; **15**(1): 20–5.

Goodale, M.A. and Haffenden, A. (1998). Frames of reference for perception and action in the human visual system. *Neuroscience and Biobehavioral Review*; **22**(2):161–72.

Goodale, M.A., Meenan J.P., Bülthoff H.H., Nicolle D.A., Murphy K.J., and Racicot C.I. (1994). Separate neural pathways for the visual analysis of object shape in perception and prehension. *Current Biology*; **4**(7): 604–10.

Goodale, M.A. and Westwood, D.A. (2004). An evolving view of duplex vision: separate but interacting cortical pathways for perception and action. *Current Opinion in Neurobiology*; **14**(2): 203–11.

Gottlieb, J.P., Kusunoki, M., and Goldberg, M.E. (1998). The representation of visual salience in monkey parietal cortex. *Nature*; **391**: 481–4.

Gréa, H., Pisella, L., Rossetti, Y., Desmurget, M., Tilikete, C., Prablanc, C. et al. (2002). A lesion of the posterior parietal cortex disrupts on-line adjustments during aiming movements. *Neuropsychologia*; **40**: 2471–80.

Hadj-Bouziane, F., Meunier, M., and Boussaoud, D. (2003). Conditional visuo-motor learning in primates: a key role for the basal ganglia. *Journal of Physiology – Paris*; **97**(4–6): 567–79.

Himmelbach, M. and Karnath, H.O. (2005). Dorsal and ventral stream interaction: contributions from optic ataxia. *Journal of Cognitive Neuroscience*; **17**: 632–40.

Jackson, S.R., Newport, R., Mort, D., and Husain, M. (2005). Where the eye looks, the hand follows; limb-dependent magnetic misreaching in optic ataxia. *Current Biology*; **15**: 42–6.

Jakobson, L.S., Archibald, Y.M., Carey, D.P., and Goodale, M.A. (1991). A kinematic analysis of reaching and grasping movements in a patient recovering from optic ataxia. *Neuropsychologia*; **29**: 803–09.

Jeannerod, M. and Rossetti, Y. (1993). Visuo-motor coordination as a dissociable function: experimental and clinical evidence. In *Visual perceptual defects*, (ed. Kennard, C.), pp. 439–60. Baillère's Clinical Neurology, International Practise and Research Vol 2, no 2. London: Ballière Tindall.

Jeannerod, M. (1986). Mechanisms of visuo-motor coordination: a study in normals and brain-damaged subjects. *Neuropsychologia*; **24**: 41–78.

Jeannerod, M., Decety, J., and Michel, F. (1994). Impairment of grasping movements following bilateral posterior parietal lesion. *Neuropsychologia*; **32**: 369–80.

Karnath, H.O. and Perenin, M.T. (2005). Cortical control of visually guided reaching: evidence from patients with optic ataxia. *Cerebral Cortex*; **15**: 1561–9.

Blangero, A., Rossetti, Y., Salemme, R., Luauté, J., Deubel, H. et al. (2009). Parietal damage dissociates saccade planning from presaccadic perceptual facilitation. *Cerebral Cortex*; **19**(2): 383–7.

Khan, A.Z., Pisella, L., Rossetti, Y., Vighetto, A., and Crawford, J.D. (2005b). Impairement of gaze-centered updating of reach targets in bilateral parietal-occipital damaged patients. *Cerebral Cortex*; **15**(10): 1547–60.

Khan, A.Z., Pisella, L., Vighetto, A., Cotton, F., Luauté, J., Boisson, D. et al. (2005a). Optic ataxia errors depend on remapped, not viewed, target location. *Nature Neuroscience*; **8**: 418–20.

Losier, B.J. and Klein, R.M. (2001). A review of the evidence for a disengage deficit following parietal lobe damage. *Neuroscience and Biobehavioural Review*; **25**: 1–13.

Mattingley, J.B., Husain, M., Rorden, C., Kennard, C., and Driver, J. (1998). Motor role of human inferior parietal lobe revealed in unilateral neglect patients. *Nature*; **12** 392(6672): 179–82.

Michel, F. and Hénaff, M.A. (2004). Seeing without the occipito-parietal cortex: simultagnosia as a shrinkage of the attentional visual field. *Behavioural Neurology*; **15**: 3–13.

Milner, A.D., Perrett, D.I., Johnston, R.S., Benson, P.J., Jordan, T.R., Heeley, D.W. et al. (1991). Perception and action in 'visual form agnosia'. *Brain;* **114**: 405–28.

Milner, A.D. and Goodale, M.A. (1995). *The visual brain in action*. Oxford: Oxford University Press.

Milner, A.D., Paulignan, Y., Dijkerman, H.C., Michel, F., and Jeannerod, M. (1999). A paradoxical improvement of misreaching in optic ataxia: new evidence for two separate neural systems for visual localization. *Proceedings Biological Sciences*; **266**: 2225–9.

Milner, A.D. and Goodale, M.A. (2008). Two visual systems re-viewed. *Neuropsychologia*; **46**: 774–85.

Milner, A.D., Dijkerman, H.C., McIntosh, R.D., Rossetti, Y., and Pisella, L. (2003). Delayed reaching and grasping in patients with optic ataxia. *Progress in Brain Research*; **142**: 225–42.

Milner, A.D., Dijkerman, H.C., Pisella, L., McIntosh, R.D., Tilikete, C., Vighetto, A., et al. (2001). Grasping the past. Delay can improve visuo-motor performance. *Current Biology*; **11**: 1896–901.

Neggers, S.F. and Bekkering, H. (2000). Ocular gaze is anchored to the target of an ongoing pointing movement. *Journal of Neurophysiology*; **83**(2): 639–51.

Neggers, S.F. and Bekkering, H. (2001). Gaze anchoring to a pointing target is present during the entire pointing movement and is driven by a non-visual signal. *Journal of Neurophysiology*; **86**(2): 961–70.

Ota, H., Pisella, L., Rode, G., Jacquin-Courtois, S., Luauté, J., Boisson, D. et al. (2003). Spatial miscomputation in optic ataxia. Poster presented at TENNET XIV, Montreal.

Paillard, J. (1987). Cognitive versus sensorimotor encoding of spatial information. In *Cognitive processes and spatial orientation in animal and man*, (eds Ellen, P. and Thinus-Blanc), pp. 43–77. Dordrecht: Nijhoff Publications.

—— (1991). Motor and representational framing of space. In *Brain and space*, (ed. Paillard, J.), pp. 163–81. Oxford: Oxford University Press.

Pélisson, D., Prablanc, C., Goodale, M.A., and Jeannerod, M. (1986). Visual control of reaching movements without vision of the limb. II. Evidence of fast unconscious processes correcting the trajectory of the hand to the final position of a double-step stimulus. *Experimental Brain Research*; **62**(2): 303–11.

Perenin, M.T. and Vighetto, A. (1988). Optic ataxia: a specific disruption in visuomotor mechanisms. I. Different aspects of the deficit in reaching for objects. *Brain*; **111**: 643–74.

Pisella, L. and Mattingley, J.B. (2004). The contribution of spatial remapping impairments to unilateral visual neglect. *Neuroscience and Biobehavioral Reviews*; **28**(2): 181–200.

Pisella, L., Binkofski, F., Lasek, K., Toni, I., and Rossetti, Y. (2006). No double-dissociation between optic ataxia and visual agnosia: multiple sub-streams for mutiple visuo-manual integrations. *Neuropsychologia*; **44**: 2734–48.

Pisella, L., Gréa, H., Tilikete, C., Vighetto, A., Desmurget, M., Rode, G. et al. (2000). An automatic pilot for the hand in the human posterior parietal cortex toward a reinterpretation of optic ataxia. *Nature Neuroscience*; 3: 729–36.

Pisella, L., Ota, H., Vighetto, A., and Rossetti, Y. (2008). Optic ataxia and Bálint syndrome: neurological and neurophysiological prospects. In *Handbook of clinical neurology*, (eds Goldenberg, G. and Miller, B.), 3rd Series, Vol 88, Neuropsychology and Behavioral Neurology, pp. 393–416 (Elsevier).

Pisella, L., Rossetti, Y., and Arzi, M. (1998). The timing of color and location processing in the motor context. *Experimental Brain Research*; **121**(3): 270–6.

Pisella, L., Striemer, C., Blangero, A., Gaveau, V., Revol, P., Salemme, R. et al. (2007). Perceptual deficits in optic ataxia? In *Attention and performance XXI: sensorimotor foundations of higher cognition*, (eds Haggard, P., Rossetti, Y., Kawato, M.), pp. 47–71. Oxford: Oxford University Press.

Pisella, L., Sergio, L., Blangero, A., Torchin, L., Vighetto, A., and Rossetti, Y. (2009). Contributions of the dorsal stream to perception and action. *Neuropsychologia*; **47**(14): 3033–44.

Posner, M.I. (1980). Orienting of attention. *Quarterly Journal of Experimental Psychology*; **32**: 3–25.

Posner, M.I., Walker, J.A., Friedrich, F.J., and Rafal, R.D. (1984). Effects of parietal injury on covert orienting of attention. *The Journal of Neuroscience*; **4**: 1863–74.

Prado, J., Clavagnier, S., Otzenberger, H., Scheiber, C., Kennedy, H., and Perenin, M.T. (2005). Two cortical systems for reaching in central and peripheral vision. *Neuron*; **48**: 849–58.

Revol, P., Rossetti, Y., Vighetto, A., and Pisella, L. (2003). Pointing errors in immediate and delayed conditions in unilateral optic ataxia. *Spatial Vision*; **16**: 347–64.

Rice, N., Edwards, M., Schindler, I., Punt, T., McIntosh, R., Humphreys, G. et al. (2008). Delay abolishes the obstacle avoidance deficit in unilateral optic ataxia. *Neuropsychologia*; **46**(5): 1549–57.

Rossetti, Y. and Pisella, L. (2003). Mediate responses as direct evidence for intention: neuropsychology of not to-, not now- and not there- tasks. In *Taking action: cognitive neuroscience perspectives on the problem of intentional acts*, (ed. Johnson-Frey, S.H.), pp. 67–105. Cambridge, MA: The MIT Press.

—— (2002). Several 'vision for action' systems: a guide to dissociating and integrating dorsal and ventral functions. In *Attention and performance XIX; common mechanisms in perception and action*, (eds Prinz, W. and Hommel, B.), pp. 62–119. Oxford: Oxford University Press.

Rossetti, Y. and Revonsuo, A. (2000). *Beyond dissociation: interaction between dissociated implicit and explicit processing*. Amsterdam: Benjamins.

Rossetti, Y. (1998). Implicit short-lived motor representation of space in brain-damaged and healthy subjects. *Consciousness and Cognition*; **7**: 520–58.

Rossetti, Y., Pisella, L., and Pélisson, D. (2000). Eye blindness and hand sight: temporal constraints and visuo-motor network. *Visual Cognition*; **7**(6): 785–809.

Rossetti, Y., Revol, P., McIntosh, R., Pisella, L., Rode, G., Danckert, J. et al. (2005). Visually guided reaching: bilateral posterior parietal lesions cause a switch from fast visuo-motor to slow cognitive control. *Neuropsychologia*; **43**: 162–77.

Rossetti, Y., Vighetto, A., and Pisella, L. (2003). Optic ataxia revisited: immediate motor control versus visually guided action. *Experimental Brain Research*; **153**: 171–9.

Rushworth, M.F., Behrens, T.E., and Johansen-Berg, H. (2006). Connection patterns distinguish 3 regions of human parietal cortex. *Cerebral Cortex*; **16**(10): 1418–30.

Schneider, G.E. (1969). Two visual systems. *Science*; **163**: 895–902.

Sergio, L.E. and Kalaska, J.F. (2003). Systematic changes in motor cortex cell activity with arm posture during directional isometric force generation. *Journal of Neurophysiology*; **89**(1): 212–28.

Silver, M.A., Ress, D., and Heeger, D.J. (2005). Topographic maps of visual spatial attention in human parietal cortex. *Journal of Neurophysiology*; **94**(2): 1358–71.

Striemer, C., Blangero, A., Rossetti, Y., Boisson, D., Rode, G., Vighetto, A. et al. (2007). Deficits in peripheral visual attention in patients with optic ataxia. *Neuroreport*; **18**(11): 1171–5.

Ungerleider, L. and Mishkin, M. (1982). Two cortical visual systems. In *Analysis of motor behaviour*, (eds Ingle, D.J. Goodale, M.A., and Mansfield, R.J.W.), pp. 549–86. Cambridge MD: The MIT Press.

Vighetto, A. and Perenin, M.T. (1981). Optic ataxia: analysis of eye and hand responses in pointing at visual targets. *Revue Neurologique* (Paris); **137**: 357–72.

Vighetto, A. (1980). Etude neuropsychologique et psychophysique de l'ataxie optique. PhD dissertation. Université Claude Bernard Lyon I.

Yamagishi, N., Anderson, S.J., Ashida, H. (2001). Evidence for dissociation between the perceptual and visuo-motor systems in humans. *Proceedings Biological Sciences*; **7**, 268(1470): 973–7.

CHAPTER 11

Mapping the neglect syndrome onto neurofunctional streams

Giuseppe Vallar and Flavia Mancini

Abstract

The syndrome of unilateral spatial neglect (USN) is currently conceived of as a multifarious deficit. This reflects, in turn, the multi-component structure of spatial representational/attentional processes, that are not monolithic in nature. A main dimension of the USN syndrome is along the premotor vs. perceptual distinction. The impairment of some USN patients may be confined to the planning and execution of movements towards the contralesional, neglected, side of space. A main aspect of the disorder may be characterized, however, in terms of the defective perceptual awareness of contralesional events, that may be, nevertheless, processed implicitly. Such an implicit processing ranges from semantic priming, lexical effects in reading, to preserved sensory illusions. From the neuropsychological vantage-point of USN, we take the view that the two visual streams dichotomy, both in the original version of Ungerleider and Mishkin (1982), and in the development by Milner and Goodale (1995, this volume), captures only partially the neural loops concerned with perception and action in the visual domain. The USN syndrome suggests the existence of a neural system supporting perceptual awareness in spatial reference frames, for vision, and for other sensory modalities, as well as goal-directed, intentional, action in the space surrounding us (Rizzolatti et al., 1997). A third, dorsal-ventral, stream, including the inferior parietal lobule, and the ventral premotor cortex (Gallese, 2007; Rizzolatti and Matelli, 2003), may constitute the neural underpinnings of spatial awareness for perception and action.

11.1. The neglect syndrome and multiple visual streams

The dichotomy and the (controversial) relationships between perception and action have a long story (see, for instance, the case of perceptual learning in Gibson, 1969, pp. 53–74). Leaving aside the distinction between primary sensory and motor neural systems, established in the nineteenth century (see Boring, 1950, pp. 61–79), it was only in the early 1980s that perceptual and action-related processing streams were associated with discrete neural pathways and circuits. Ungerleider and Mishkin (1982) suggested, in the domain of vision, a distinction between an occipitotemporal ventral pathway for identifying objects (the 'what' processing stream), and an occipitoparietal pathway for perceiving the spatial relationships among objects and localizing them (the 'where' processing stream) (see also Haxby et al., 1991). This distinction was primarily perceptual, even though a role of the dorsal stream in guiding movements towards objects was suggested successively (e.g. Courtney et al., 1996). Ten years later, Goodale and Milner (1992; Milner and Goodale, 2006. See also Milner and Goodale, 1995) reinterpreted and developed Ungerleider and Mishkin's two visual streams account. Particularly, the proposal of Goodale and Milner was that the dorsal stream plays a critical role in the real time control of action, while the perceptual role of the ventral stream in object identification, originally suggested by Ungerleider and Mishkin (1982), was maintained. The neuropsychological implications of the 'ventral' vs. 'dorsal' distinction were immediately clear, and are illustrated by the following examples, quoted by Haxby et al. (1991). Patients with posterior parietal lesions may exhibit spatial deficits of visual localization and reaching (see Ratcliff and Davies-Jones, 1972, for a localization in the superior parietal lobule of the responsible lesions, see also Newcombe et al., 1987, patient #1 VRD). Patients with temporal lobe damage, by contrast, may show an impairment characterized by a deficit of face recognition, with a preserved performance in spatial tasks, such as cube counting and stylus maze learning (Newcombe et al., 1987, patient #2 J S). In Goodale and Milner's account (1992; Milner and Goodale, 1995, 2006; Goodale, 2008) the neuropsychological counterparts of damage to the dorsal ('vision for action') and to the ventral ('vision for perception') streams are the syndromes of 'optic ataxia' (OA) and 'visual agnosia' (VA). In the following, we consider the clinical characteristics of these two syndromes, and their relationships with USN.

a. *The syndrome of 'USN'.* USN does not have a definite anatomical counterpart in the two visual streams anatomo-functional model of visual processing. It is, in fact, considered tangentially in the context of the dorso-ventral distinction. For instance, Milner and Goodale (Chapter 5, this volume) mention USN as relevant to the effect that sensory information may be processed unconsciously. The USN syndrome (Vallar, 1998; Bisiach and Vallar, 2000; Halligan et al., 2003; Husain, 2008) is, however, relevant to any dorso-ventral distinction, since these patients exhibit a unilateral deficit of spatial awareness, which includes a main 'perceptual' component, but also an 'action' ('premotor') impairment.

b. *USN vs. VA.* The 'perceptual' impairments of patients with USN differ from VA in at least two important respects. First, patients with VA fail to identify objects, and may be impaired at discriminating features such as their dimension and orientation (see Milner and Goodale, Chapter 5, this volume). By contrast, as we shall show in this chapter, the main deficit of patients with USN concerns perceptual awareness of sensory events occurring in the side of space contralateral to the side of the lesion (contralesional, hence the term 'unilateral' neglect). Contralesional objects are typically undetected by patients with USN. Secondly, 'neglected' information is nevertheless processed in depth, outside perceptual awareness (Berti, 2002). This unconscious processing by patients with USN has been revealed by a variety of paradigms, provided no explicit report and localization is required. In VA the evidence suggesting processing of perceptual features of objects concerns visuo-motor paradigms such as grasping, putatively recruiting the unimpaired 'dorsal' stream (see Milner and Goodale, Chapter 5, this volume).

c. *USN vs. OA.* OA is a deficit of reaching to a visual target in peripheral vision, with no associated visual, motor and proprioceptive impairments. Patients with OA may show no evidence of USN (Rossetti et al., Chapter 10, this volume). The 'premotor' deficit of patients with USN (namely, a disproportionate difficulty to initiate or execute reaches to a contralesional target, see discussion in Coulthard et al., 2006) differs from the pattern of OA, that is characterized by errors in pointing accuracy, particularly in peripheral vision (Rossetti et al., Chapter 10, this volume).

These three syndromes differ also in their anatomical correlates. The parietal lesions of patients with USN are typically located ventrally with respect to the dorsal stream, and dorsally with respect to the ventral stream, involving the posterior inferior parietal lobule and the temporo-parietal junction (review in Halligan et al., 2003).[1]

The chapter is structured as follows: section 11.2 provides an overview of the USN syndrome as a multicomponent deficit, focusing on the distinction between its 'perceptual' and 'premotor' impairments, as well as on related evidence from the processing of visual illusions. This review of the 'perceptual' and of the 'premotor' deficits of USN allows mapping them onto the two visual streams dichotomy (Milner and Goodale, 1995; Milner and Goodale, 2006; Goodale, 2008). This analysis is accomplished in section 11.3, where the USN syndrome, and its neural correlates, are compared with the two disorders ('VA' and 'OA'), which represent the neuropsychological counterparts of 'vision-for-perception' (the 'ventral' stream), and of 'vision-for-action' (the 'dorsal' stream).

From the neuropsychological vantage-point of USN, we take the view that the two visual streams dichotomy, both in the original version of Ungerleider and Mishkin (1982), and in the development by Milner and Goodale (review in this volume), captures only partially the neural loops concerned with perception and action in the visual domain. The syndrome of USN suggests the existence of a neural system supporting perceptual awareness in spatial reference frames, for vision, and for other sensory modalities, as well as goal-directed, intentional, action in the space surrounding us (Rizzolatti et al., 1997). A third, dorsal-ventral, stream, including the inferior parietal lobule, and the ventral premotor cortex (Rizzolatti and Matelli, 2003; Gallese, 2007), may constitute the neural underpinnings of spatial awareness for perception and action. Finally, in humans, the dorsal-ventral stream is functionally asymmetric, with a main contribution from the right cerebral hemisphere (Vallar et al., 1999; Bisiach and Vallar, 2000; Galati et al., 2000; Mesulam, 2002; Bottini et al., 2005).

11.2. The syndrome of unilateral spatial neglect: a multi-component deficit

In this section we shall first summarize concisely the state of the art of USN. USN is a neuropsychological disorder, more frequent and severe after damage to the right cerebral hemisphere, whereby patients fail to report sensory events taking place in the portion of space contralateral to the side of the lesion (contralesional), and to explore through motor acts (namely, ocular movements, reaching movements, navigation through locomotion) that portion of space (Vallar, 1998; Halligan et al., 2003; Heilman et al., 2003). This clinical description incorporates a main dichotomy that characterizes the USN syndrome. The contralesional portion of space may be 'neglected', in principle, either (a) because patients fail to perceive consciously, or are not aware of, and then are unable to report, contralesional events, or (b) because they fail to set up and implement into actual movement, motor acts directed towards objects located in the contralesional part of space. This distinction between 'failure to perceive' vs. 'failure to reach for' has suggested the existence of two main components of USN: 'perceptual' vs. 'premotor' (Bisiach et al., 1990), or 'attentional' vs.' intentional' ('directional hypokinesia', see Watson et al., 1978; Heilman and Valenstein, 1979; Coslett et al., 1990). The distinction may also more generally be couched in terms of the impairment of 'input' vs. 'output' systems (Bisiach et al., 1998a).

The 'perceptual' vs. 'premotor', or, more generally, 'perception' vs. 'action', distinction is likely to have been the first successful attempt, starting from the late 1970s (Watson et al., 1978; Heilman and Valenstein, 1979; Heilman et al., 1985), at fractionating the unitary, monolithic view of USN, and, by implication, of the neuro-functional systems supporting the internal representation of space.

---

[1] The report (Karnath, 2001, Karnath et al., 2001, Committeri et al., 2007) that right-brain-damaged patients with left visual USN for peripersonal space show damage involving the superior temporal gyrus (namely, a 'ventral' region) is relevant for the dorsal vs. ventral distinction in the light of the definite behavioral differences between USN and VA.

The 'perceptual' vs. 'premotor' distinction implies that, within a given sector of space (personal, peripersonal, far i.e. beyond hand reach, and extra-personal), USN may be traced back to two differ- ent pathological factors, which operate within that sector of space. In this respect, the 'perceptual' vs. 'premotor' distinction is orthogonal to other factors, such as parts of space (i.e., USN for 'near' or 'far' space, 'personal' neglect, see Vallar and Maravita, 2009, for a discussion of these multiple repre- sentations of space), and stimulus type (e.g., neglect 'dyslexia'. See Ellis et al., 1987 and Arduino et al., 2002), 'facial' neglect (Young et al., 1990, 1992).

An assessment of the relative weight of 'perceptual' vs. 'action-related' components in bringing about USN requires first a definite disentangling of these two putative pathological factors. Secondly, the proportion of 'perceptual' vs. 'premotor' patterns of impairment in patients with USN is to be consid- ered, in order to characterize it, if at all possible, primarily as a 'perceptual' or as a 'premotor' disorder. Table 11.1 shows a taxonomy of the USN syndrome, which illustrates the 'perceptual' and 'premotor' components, as well other manifestations, that may be traced back to 'perceptual', 'premotor', or a combination of these two classes of dysfunction. However, the set of empirical data directly support- ing the existence of 'perceptual' vs. 'premotor' pathological factors, and elucidating their mecha- nisms, is more limited, and is considered in the next section.

The neuropsychological terminology concerning the premotor impairments is often confused (Mark et al., 1996; Heilman, 2004; Fink and Marshall, 2005). In this chapter, we shall use the term 'premotor' (as distinguished from 'perceptual') to denote, in general, impairments that should be traced back to the programming, initiation, and execution of movements, as well as to lateral response biases, independent of the characteristics of the stimulus. All these disorders are 'premotor' in that they cannot be traced back to a primary motor impairment.

Within 'premotor' disorders, 'directional hypokinesia' shall refer to direction-specific deficits of movement initiation, 'directional bradykinesia' to direction-specific deficits of movement execution. Patients with directional hypokinesia may be disproportionately slow in initiating goal-directed movements towards targets in the contralesional side of space, or may even fail to start them. Directional bradykinesia refers to slowness in the execution of such movements, directed towards the contralesional side, after they have been initiated. These directional deficits involve movements performed by the unaffected limbs, ipsilateral to the damaged hemisphere. Accordingly, in right- brain-damaged patients, directional disorders concern movements performed using the right limbs, ipsilateral to the side of the cerebral lesion (ipsilesional), and, therefore, unaffected by primary motor impairments.

'Motor neglect' (Heilman et al., 2003), or the *négligence motrice* of the French neurologists (Castaigne et al., 1970, 1972), shall refer to the inability to initiate and perform movements, using the contralesional limbs. Motor neglect, concerning the left, contralesional, limbs of right-brain- damaged patients needs to be distinguished from a possible concomitant motor impairment.

11.2.1. Extra-personal space: 'Perceptual' vs. 'Premotor' neglect

In this section, we shall review a number of studies that investigated the 'perceptual' and 'premotor' components of USN for extra-personal space, and attempt at elucidating the underlying pathological mechanisms, as well as their cerebral lesion correlates.

In their seminal study, Heilman and Valenstein (1979)[2] asked six right-brain-damaged patients with left USN to report a letter located to the left or to the right end of an horizontal segment, before setting its subjective mid-point (line bisection). The task was given with the lines being placed at either the right, the centre, or the left of the body midline. Performance in trials when participants were required to look to the left before bisecting the line did not differ from when they were required to look right, but was significantly better (although not fully preserved) when the line was placed to

---

[2] See also Watson (1978), for an earlier suggestion of the existence of intentional factors underlying the USN in the monkey by frontal or reticular formation lesions.

Table 11.1 A Taxonomy of the Clinical Syndrome of Unilateral Spatial Neglect (USN). 'Defective' manifestations (the better known and more extensively investigated aspect of USN) refer to 'negative' phenomena, characterized by the 'absence' of specific behavioural responses, such as the impaired exploration of the contralesional side of space, or the failure to report stimuli presented in that sector of space. 'Productive' manifestations refer to 'positive' phenomena, characterized by the 'presence' of specific behaviours. The 'input'/'output' dichotomy is listed first. Putative premotor manifestations are in italics; the so-called 'sensory' neglect is considered as a 'perceptual' manifestation of the syndrome (modified from Vallar, 2008).

A. Defective manifestations

Extra-personal space		Personal/bodily space
Dimension	**Variety**	
Input/output	Perceptual USN[a]	Hemisomatognosia[b]
	Premotor/intentional USN, directional hypokinesia/ bradykinesia[d]	Anosognosia[c] *Motor neglect*[e]
Sensory modality[f]	Visual USN (pseudo-hemianopia) Auditory USN Olfactory USN	Somatosensory USN
Sectors of space (with reference to the body)	Lateral external USN[g] Lateral internal (imaginal) USN Altitudinal[h]	
Reference frames	Egocentric USN[i] Allocentric/object-based USN	
Processing domain[j]	Facial USN Neglect dyslexia	

B. Productive manifestations

Extra-personal space	Personal/bodily space
Avoidance[k] Hyperattention, magnetic attraction towards ipsilesional targets *Perseveration*[m] *and gratuitous productions*[n]	Somatoparaphrenia[l]

Note:
[a] Defective awareness of targets in the neglected sector of space.
[b] Defective awareness of the contralesional side of the body.
[c] Defective awareness or denial of contralesional motor, somatosensory, and visual half-field deficits.
[d] Defective initiation/execution of movements of the ipsilesional limbs towards the contralesional, neglected, sector of space.
[e] Failure to move the contralesional limbs, in the absence of primary motor impairment (hemiparesis or hemiplegia).
[f] Defective awareness of sensory input in a particular sensory modality.
[g] Along a left-right axis: near, far.
[h] Along a vertical axis: upper, lower.
[i] With reference to the head, the trunk, the limbs.
[j] Material-specific forms of neglect.
[k] Active withdrawal from contralesional targets.
[l] Delusional beliefs concerning the contralesional side of the body, often disownership.
[m] The iteration of a behaviour, which is no longer appropriate, but continues steadfastly after the termination or change of the task's demands, or in the absence of the appropriate exciting stimulus.
[n] More or less complex behaviours, entirely unnecessary and unrelated to the task's demands.

the right side of the body, than to the left. Heilman and Valenstein (1979) suggested that 'directional hypokinesia' accounted for the improvement found when the stimulus was placed on the right-hand side, with respect to the mid-sagittal plane of the patients' body. Also a memory deficit may contribute to the patients' impairment when looking leftwards. Although the patients saw the left side of the line in their preserved right visual field, they could have been incapable of forming a stable trace, and had performed the line bisection task as if they had not seen the left side of the line. Later studies found that left-sided cueing may reduce left USN (reporting a left- or a right-sided flanker letter, see Riddoch and Humphreys, 1983; touching the left end point of the segment, see Ishiai et al., 2000). These positive effects of left-sided cueing, however, are ambiguous with respect to the 'perceptual' vs. 'premotor' features of the ameliorated impairment. Both such putative mechanisms of the rightward error committed by patients with left USN in line bisection may be affected by the cueing manipulation. Interestingly, Riddoch and Humphreys (1983) interpreted their findings in terms of a defective contralesional orientation of automatic attention, that could be overcome by the intact processes of voluntary attention, triggered by cueing.[3]

With reference to Table 11.1, the main component deficits of the USN syndrome, where 'perceptual' vs. 'premotor' mechanisms may be involved, comprise virtually all manifestations of the disorder, provided the premotor pathological factors are considered to include the planning and execution of arm movements, as well as of ocular movements. Premotor pathological factors may play a highly relevant role, according to the so-called 'premotor theory of attention', whereby the facilitation of perception due to attentional mechanisms is accounted by the activation of the relevant motor circuits (Rizzolatti et al., 1987; Rizzolatti and Berti, 1993. See Chambers and Mattingley, 2005, for discussion; see Umiltà, 2001, for a review).

Studies in brain-damaged patients with contralesional USN have definitely confirmed Heilman and Valenstein's (1979) original observation that the patients' inability to initiate movements directed towards the contralesional side of space is a component deficit of the USN syndrome ('directional hypokinesia'). Heilman et al. (1985) found that right-brain-damaged patients with left USN were overall slower in initiating lateral movements, and in executing them, using the unaffected right upper limb, compared with left-brain-damaged patients. Crucially, right-brain-damaged patients with left USN were slower from right to left than from left to right, showing, therefore, a directional impairment. In a series of 24 right-brain-damaged patients, Mattingley et al. (1992) found that patients with left USN ($n = 18$) were slower in initiating leftward movements in a sequential pressing task. Movement time was also slower, particularly when the sequence was performed in the left-hand side of space ('directional bradykinesia'). Right-brain-damaged patients and left-brain-damaged patients without USN did not show this directional pattern, with their performance being comparable to that of neurologically unimpaired control participants. As for the lesion correlates of these findings, right-brain-damaged patients with both anterior/subcortical and posterior lesions showed leftward 'directional hypokinesia' (i.e., slower initiation time), while only right-brain-damaged patients with anterior/subcortical damage exhibited leftward 'directional bradykinesia' (i.e., slower movement time). One left-brain-damaged patient with right USN showed rightward directional hypokinesia, but no bradykinesia. Perceptual factors, however, appear to modulate reaching performance (Behrmann and Meegan, 1998).[4]

As for ocular movements, it has long been known that right-brain-damaged patients with left USN fail to explore by means of eye-scanning movements the contralesional side of space (Chedru et al., 1973. See Ishiai, 2006, for a recent review), and to make saccades towards the left visual half-field (Girotti et al., 1983). Ocular fixations are shifted ipsilesionally in right-brain-damaged patients

---

[3] A review of the view that 'automatic' orienting of attention towards stimuli arising in the half space contralateral to the damaged hemisphere is disrupted in USN, whereas 'controlled', 'volitional', orienting can be more or less completely spared, may be found in Gainotti (1996).

[4] An extensive review of the disorders of reaching in patients with USN may be found in Coulthard et al. (2006). These reaching deficits appear largely unrelated to USN (see Rossit et al., 2009, for recent evidence), suggesting, as argued in this chapter, that the disorder is primarily perceptual in nature.

with left USN (Barton et al., 1998), with fewer fixations and shorter inspection times on the contralesional, left, side of space (Behrmann et al., 1997; Behrmann et al., 2002).

However, the studies discussed above, while showing that the initiation of leftward movements may be defective in patients with left USN, do not elucidate the precise nature of the impairment. The same line of reasoning applies to ocular exploration. Directional hypokinesia, and the ipsilesional bias of ocular exploration, may reflect a higher order perceptual impairment, whereby the representation of the contralesional side of space is corrupted, disrupting the initiation of limb movements, as well as of ocular movements towards the contralesional side (see Bisiach and Vallar, 2000, for such a representational account). Alternatively, discrete 'perceptual' and 'premotor' pathological mechanisms may contribute to shaping the manifold manifestations of the USN syndrome. The putative distinction between 'perceptual' and 'premotor' factors in USN bears some resemblance to the search for a double dissociation between the perceptual deficit of VA and the action impairment of OA (see Rossetti et al., Chapter 10, this volume).

Investigators attempted at disentangling the 'perceptual' vs. 'premotor' factors of USN through three main types of paradigms:

a. *Tasks requiring arm movements*, that introduce a contrast between the visual control of the movement of the upper limb and its initiation and execution. The 'incompatible' condition is typically compared to a 'compatible' condition, in which, as in everyday life, the visible movement matches the actual movement.

b. *Tasks selectively assessing one or the other component, with no 'incompatible' conditions* (e.g., reaching vs. naming; dissociating the spatial position of the target [to the left or to the right of the midsagittal plane of the participant's trunk] from the direction [leftward/rightward] of the movement of the upper limb).

c. *Tasks including optional choice responses*, which reveal the impairment of each component, or a combination of both (the Landmark task and its variants, that require judging the shorter/longer of the two parts of a pre-bisected segment).

11.2.1.1. Tasks requiring arm movements, with 'Incompatible' conditions

Some paradigms attempted at dissociating the 'perceptual' vs. 'premotor' components of USN by decoupling the direction of the movement of the hand from the visual control of the display. In the bisection paradigm devised by Bisiach et al. (1990) a lateral (leftward or rightward) movement of the hand brought about a movement of a pointer, setting the subjective midpoint of the line in the opposite direction, through a pulley device; this condition was contrasted with a standard bisection task, where the midpoint was directly manipulated by the participant (Fig. 11.1-A). Applying a similar logic to a cancellation task, Tegnér and Levander (1991), and Bisiach et al. (1995), decoupled the direction of the hand movement from the patient's visual control of the display through a 90° angle mirror (Fig. 11.1-B). Nico (1996) used an epidiascope, as well as a 90° angle mirror. Na et al. (1998), and Adair et al. (1998) precluded the direct view of the hand and of the target, with a TV monitor guiding performance. Under these conditions, patients saw a mirror-reversed display, so that, for instance, in a cancellation task left-sided targets were seen on the right-hand side, but, in the working physical space, they were on the left-hand side (Fig. 11.1-C). These paradigms, therefore, contrasted a 'congruent'/'compatible' condition, in which the patient saw the actual direction of the hand movement in the visual display, with a 'non-congruent'/'incompatible' condition, in which, by means of a device (a pulley, a mirror, an epidiascope, or a TV monitor), the movement of the hand took place in an opposite direction to that of the relevant visual stimulus (the midpoint of the line, the hand itself), which was seen mirror-reversed. In these paradigms, a premotor directional deficit would be characterized by the patients' inability to perform leftward movements, in both the congruent and the non-congruent conditions. By contrast, a perceptual deficit would bring about a right-sided bias, relative to the display as seen by the patient, independent of the actual direction of the hand movement.

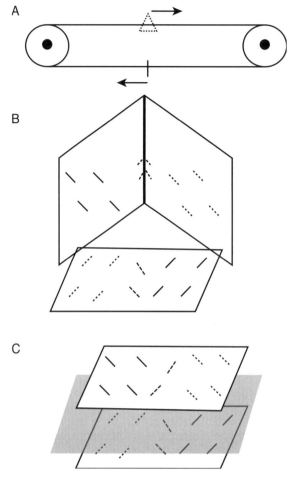

Fig. 11.1 Paradigms Used to Disentangle 'Perceptual' vs. 'Premotor' Factors in USN. *Incompatible tasks.*
In all variants of these incompatible conditions participants do not have a direct view of the display and
of their moving hand. (A) The Pulley device of Bisiach et al. (1990) for line bisection. In the incompatible
condition, when participants move the lower part of the pulley, a leftward movement displaces the
upper pointer (dashed triangle) rightwards, and vice versa. In the compatible condition participants
move the upper pointer, under visual control.
(B) The 90° Mirror device of Tegnér and Levander (1991) for target cancellation. In the incompatible
condition, through a 90° mirror participants see a reversed display, as well as mirror-reversed hand
movements. In the compatible condition no mirror is present, with the task being a canonical
cancellation test. (C) The epidiascope device of Nico (1996), and the TV apparatus of Na et al. (1998)
and of Adair et al. (1998). In Nico's paradigm, in the incompatible condition participants see a mirror-
reversed image of the target cancellation display (upper cancellation sheet in the figure), and of the
hand movements, through an epidiascope. In Na et al.'s (1998), and Adair et al.'s (1998) paradigms
participants look at a monitor connected to a video camera. In the incompatible condition the video
camera takes a mirror-reversed image of the display (upper cancellation sheet in the figure), and of the
moving hand, that is shown via the monitor.

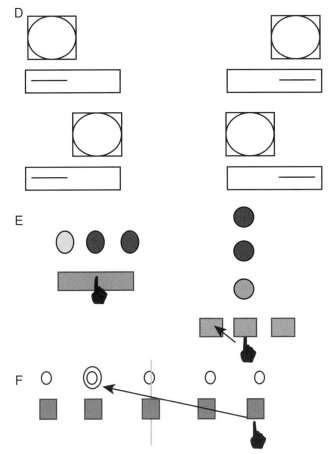

Fig. 11.1 (continued) *Compatible tasks.* Patients have a complete and direct view of the display and their moving hand. (D) In the paradigm of Coslett et al. (1990), participants see the line to-be-bisected (that can be placed to the left or to the right of the midsagittal plane of the participant's body) through a left-sided or a right-sided monitor, generating four conditions: line bisection and visual feedback in the same side of space (left or right, upper part of the D section of the figure); line bisection and visual feedback in the opposite sides of space (left-right; right-left, lower part of the D section of the figure). (E) The 'Traffic light paradigm' (Bartolomeo, 2002, 2001, 1998). In the 'perceptual' task the stimulus is lateralized (left-sided, right-sided: when one circle becomes grey participants press the spacebar of a computer keyboard). In the 'motor' task participants press the left-hand side, right-hand side, or middle keys, when the lower, upper, or middle circle becomes grey; the circle-key association can be reversed (the three sectors of the keyboard are denoted by grey rectangles). (F) The types of paradigms used by Mattingley et al. (1998), Husain et al., (2000), and Sapir et al. (2007) include conditions where left- and right-sided targets, and left-, central, and right-sided starting points give rise to leftward and rightward movements, from the left- or the right-hand side of space, towards left- or right-hand side targets. The figure shows a leftward movement towards a left-hand side target, from a right-sided starting point.

11.2.1.2. Tasks assessing one or the other component, with no 'Incompatible' conditions

Other paradigms contrasted verbal vs. manual responses (Bottini et al., 1992; Chiba et al., 2005), or space of vision vs. space of manual action (Coslett et al., 1990, see Fig. 11.1-D; Bartolomeo, 2002, see Fig. 11.1-E), without introducing, however, any incompatible condition.

Finally, some studies measured latencies of initiation movements to left-sided and right-sided targets, from left-sided, central, and right-sided spatial positions, with respect to the mid-sagittal plane of the participant's body (Mattingley et al., 1998; Husain et al., 2000; Sapir et al., 2007). Figure 11.1-F shows a schematic drawing of this paradigm. In the studies by Husain et al. (2000) the critical result was that patients with a premotor impairment were faster in initiating a movement towards a left-sided target, when the movement was in a rightward direction, rather than in a leftward direction (in this latter condition alone, in fact, perceptual and premotor impairments are confounded). A similar logic was used by Sapir et al. (2007). In right-brain-damaged patients with left 'directional hypokinesia', the latency for initiating a motor response to a left-sided target was faster when the starting position was to the left of it (and a rightward movement was required), than when the starting position was to the right (and a leftward movement was required).

Table 11.2 summarizes the results of the studies discussed in sections 11.2.1.1 and 11.2.1.2. Two main conclusions may be drawn. Notwithstanding the methodological differences between the tasks used by the different investigators, the reported studies definitely suggest that USN may be due to either 'perceptual' (i.e., 'sensory inattention', 'attentional' neglect), or 'premotor' (i.e., 'directional hypo-kinesia', 'intentional' neglect) factors, or to a variable combination of them. Second, when large series of brain-damaged patients have been examined, in a number of studies 'perceptual' pathological mechanisms appears to be more frequently involved, compared to premotor factors (Bisiach et al., 1990; Tegnér and Levander, 1991; Nico, 1996; Bartolomeo et al., 1998; Sapir et al., 2007). In some studies the difference favouring perceptual deficits is less marked (Adair et al., 1998; Na et al., 1998 for target cancellation). A few studies report a greater proportion of 'premotor neglect' (Na et al., 1998, for line bisection), or a broadly comparable rate of occurrence of the two types of USN (Bisiach et al., 1995), with also mixed patterns of impairment (Chiba et al., 2005). The conclu-sion that perceptual factors are the prevailing, though not exclusive, pathological mechanism of USN is also suggested by a study using simple reaction time in a two-step task (detection of a lateralized target, and initiation of reaching for it), in a series of 22 right-brain-damaged patients with USN and 29 right-brain-damaged patients without USN (Shimodozono et al., 2006).

A suggestion of a hemispheric asymmetry comes from a study by Bartolomeo et al. (2001). Three left-brain-damaged patients with right visuo-spatial USN (out of a series of 28 left-brain-damaged patients) exhibited slower rightward movements. This 'motor' bias ('directional hypokinesia') corre-lated with the 'perceptual' bias shown by the patients (see related evidence in Mattingley et al., 1992, from one left brain-damaged patient with right USN). These results suggest that 'premotor' patho-logical factors may be a more relevant component of USN after left, than after right, brain damage, and may be related to the well-known role of the left hemisphere in the programming of action (Schluter et al., 2001; Rushworth et al., 2003). This pattern differs from the prevailing 'perceptual' left USN associated with right brain damage, as assessed by the 'traffic light' paradigm (Bartolomeo et al., 1998).

The 'perceptual' vs. 'premotor' distinction, however, appears to be affected by experimental manipulations, such as cueing. In the study by Bisiach et al. (1995), placing the patient's hand on the side that had been neglected in a previous part of the experiment (not constrained as to the hand's starting point) resulted in a reversal of USN type (from 'ophthalmokinetic' ['perceptual'] to 'meloki-netic' ['premotor'], or vice versa, in five out of 36 patients). Finally, the same particular patient may show perceptual or premotor USN in different tasks (target cancellation vs. line bisection: Adair et al., 1998; Na et al., 1998. See also Hamilton et al., 2008, for similar observations). These findings suggest, from the perspective of USN, a multicomponent organization of perceptual and premotor systems.

11.2.1.3. Tasks including optional choice responses: the landmark task and its variants

The relative contribution of 'perceptual' and 'response' pathological factors to visual USN has been assessed also by another task, which requires participants to compare the length of the two segments of pre-bisected lines, the 'Landmark task' (see Milner et al., 1993). In the original version of this task, patients had to make a forced-choice manual judgment as to whether each line was transected nearer

Table 11.2 Studies Assessing 'Perceptual' Vs. 'Premotor' Components in Right-Brain-Damaged Patients with Left Contralesional Neglect.

Study	Task	Results (n. of patients classified PE/PM)	Lesion
Bisiach et al.[a] (1990) n=15	LB-I. (a pulley moving the bisector in the opposite direction with respect to the arm mov)	13 MIX (PE>PM), 2 MIX (PM>PE)	Patients with PM>PE:F
Coslett et al.[b] (1990) n=4	LB-C. (L/R stimulus seen through a monitor in the L/R side of space)	2 PE 2 PM	PE#3: P post-inf-T-O; PE#4: T-P-post F PM#1: F-P-BG; PM#2: F-T
Tegnér and Levander[c] (1991) n=18	TC-I. (via a 90° mirror, arm mov seen in the opposite direction)	10 PE 4 PM	PE: 9 post (P,T, or O), 1(F-T-P) PM: 3 ant-post, 1 subco
Bottini et al.[c] (1992) n=2	TC/D-C. (arm mov vs. visuo-verbal discrimination)	1 PE 1 PM	PE: T-P PM: dorsolateral F, BG
Bisiach et al.[d] (1995) n=36	See Tegnér and Levander; cued conditions added	17 PE# 19 PM#	PE§: 5 ant-subco, 10 post PM§: 11 ant-subco, 5 post
Nico[c] (1996) n=22	TC-I. (arm mov seen in the opposite direction through an epidiascope or a 90° mirror)	22 PE	No lesion information
Na et al.[e] (1998) n=10	LB-I and TC-I. (arm mov seen in the opposite direction through a TV monitor)	LB: 2 PE, 8 PM TC: 5 PE, 4 PM, 1 NC	LB-TC-PE: 1 P,1 P-T subco LB-TC-PM: 1 F, 1 F-T subco 1 F-P subco, 1 subco
Adair et al.[f] (1998) n=26	See Na et al.	LB: 14 PE, 12 PM TC: 8 PE, 10 PM, 8 NC LB-TC: 6 PE, 8 PM	LB-PE: 6 post, 1 ant, 4 ant-post LB-PM: 9 ant, 2 subco TC-PE: 3 post, 1 ant, 2 ant-post TC-PM: 8 ant LB-TC-PE: 3 post LB-TC-PM: 6 ant, 1 subco

(Continued)

Table 11.2 (Continued) Studies Assessing 'Perceptual' Vs. 'Premotor' Components in Right-Brain-Damaged Patients with Left Contralesional Neglect.

Study	Task	Results (n. of patients classified PE/PM)	Lesion
Bartolomeo et al.[g] (1998) n=14 left neglect out of 34[@]	C. SRT to L/R targets, central responses, CRT to U/L targets with l/centre/r arm mov	14 PE	PE: 4 ant-post, 6 post, 1 post-subco, 3 subco
Mattingley et al.[h] (1998) and Husain et al.[h] (2000) n=6	C. SRT to L/R targets with l/r/arm mov and L/centre/R starting position	3 PE, 3PM	PE: F PM: P
Chiba et al.[f] (2005) n=14	LB-C. (manual vs. verbal: reading a character close to the midline	4 PE, 5 PM, 5 MIX	Post (2 PE), ant-subco (1 PM), ant-post (2 PE, 4 PM, 3 MIX), subco (2 MIX)
Sapir et al.[i] (2007) n=52	C. SRT to L/R targets with l/r/arm mov and L/centre/R starting position	43 PE, 9 PM	PM (BG: ventral lat. Putamen, claustrum, F wm), anatomical analysis in 29 patients

Task C/I: compatible/incompatible. LB: line bisection. TC/D: target cancellation/discrimination. S/C-RT: simple/choice reaction time. R/L: left-/right-hand side of space; l/r: leftward/rightward; mov: movement. PE/PM/MIX/NC: perceptual/premotor/mixed/not classified deficit. F/T/P/O: frontal/temporal/parietal/occipital damage. BG: basal ganglia; subco: subcortical; post/inf/lat: posterior/inferior/lateral. The two types of neglect (i.e. PE vs. PM) were referred to as in the note:

Note:
[a] 'perceptual' vs. 'premotor';
[b] 'hemispatial inattention' vs. 'directional hypokinesia';
[c] 'perceptual' vs. 'premotor'-'directional hypokinesia';
[d] 'ophthalmokinetic' vs. 'melokinetic', with reference to the two components (eyes/limbs) putatively involved in the task;
[e] 'sensory-attentional' vs. 'motor-intentional';
[f] 'perceptual-attentional' vs. 'premotor-intentional';
[g] 'perceptual' and 'motor' biases;
[h] 'sensory' and 'motor' biases;
[i] 'attentional-perceptual' vs. 'directional hypokinesia'.
[#] As classified in the uncued condition;
[§] 'reversible' cases—where cueing reversed neglect type—were excluded from the anatomical correlation analysis;
[@] two patients out of the 34 showed a right motor bias, without evidence of visual USN in cancellation, bisection, and identification tasks.

to either its left or right end. The number of left-end responses provides an index of the extent to which patients 'saw' the left half of the line as shorter than the right, namely showed a 'perceptual' bias. In this task there are no incompatible conditions, at variance from some of the paradigms discussed previously. In Milner et al.'s study (1993), three right-brain-damaged patients showed a 'perceptual' bias. In a successive report (Harvey et al., 1995a), the prevailing pattern of impairment was again found to be 'perceptual' in nature (seven right-brain-damaged patients), with one patient pointing rightwards, and showing, therefore, a 'premotor'deficit (Ishiai et al., 1998, for converging evidence, Harvey et al., 1995b, see also Harvey and Milner, 1999). This 'perceptual' impairment cannot be traced to defective eye movements (Harvey et al., 2003).

The paradigm was used subsequently by Bisiach and colleagues, who manipulated the type of response (verbal or manual, namely: pointing to, or naming the colour of the shorter-or-longer segment of the line) (Bisiach et al., 1998a). The choice of the contralesional segment as shorter (or of the ipsilesional segment as longer) would reflect USN due to a 'perceptual' bias, the choice of the ipsilesional segment, both when patients are required to indicate the shorter, and when they are required to indicate the longer segment, would reflect USN due to 'response' bias. In one study, performed in a large series of 121 right-brain-damaged patients, Bisiach et al. (1998a) confirmed the existence of the two types of biases in their version of the Landmark task, finding positive correlations between each of the two biases ('perceptual' and 'response'), and the two landmark tasks (verbal, and manual) (see confirmatory evidence in Bisiach et al., 1998b). An analysis of the performance of the individual patients showed that, in both tasks, 'perceptual', 'response' biases, or a combination of them, could be present. A double dissociation was also found with four patients showing a 'perceptual' bias on the verbal landmark task, and a 'response' bias on the manual landmark task; two other patients exhibited the opposite pattern of impairment. These results indicate that the 'perceptual' and 'response' biases are modulated by the different types of response (i.e., manual pointing vs. naming). In general, as noted in the previous section (see the effects of cueing and the target cancellation vs. bisection difference), perceptual and premotor systems appear to be articulated into multiple components, which may be selectively impaired by brain damage.

Finally, one study (Harvey et al., 2002) compared the occurrence of 'perceptual' vs. 'premotor'/'response' biases, using modified versions of three tasks discussed previously: Nico's Overhead task (1996), Bisiach's Pulley device technique (Bisiach et al., 1990), and the Landmark task (Milner et al., 1993). The main results of the study, that included 12 right-brain-damaged-patients, may be summarized as follows: on the Overhead task four patients were classified as perceptual, and eight as premotor; on the Pulley device task five perceptual, and seven premotor (although the classification was not definite for five patients); on the Landmark task, ten perceptual, one premotor, and one unclassified. Importantly, only one out of the 12 patients exhibited a pattern of USN consistent across the three tasks (patient ER, with a right fronto-temporal ischemic lesion, and showing a perceptual USN).

Importantly, the impairments revealed by the Landmark task are independent of the main manifestations of the USN syndrome. Harvey and Milner (1999) reported two right-brain-damaged patients with left USN. One patient (LC) had a lesion involving the temporo-occipital regions, and the basal ganglia, and a left hemianopia. The other patient (MH) had a temporo-parietal damage, without visual field deficits. The two patients, about two months after stroke, showed a rightward error in line bisection, contralesional left omissions in target cancellation, and a performance suggesting a perceptual bias in the Landmark task. Twelve months after stroke onset USN had recovered remarkably, including the rightward error in line bisection, while the performance in the Landmark task was still defective.

Furthermore, Bisiach's and Milner's versions of the Landmark task, given to the same patients, do not appear to provide a consistent classification along the 'perceptual'/'premotor'—'response' dichotomy (Harvey and Olk, 2004). This suggests that even apparently minor variations of the tasks' demands involve different 'perceptual' or 'premotor'—'response' components. In Milner's task participants have to point manually to the half of a centrally pre-bisected line that, to them, appears shorter; in the motor version of Bisiach's Landmark Test participants have to judge not only centrally pre-bisected, but also asymmetrically bisected lines (see also Harvey, 2004, for review).

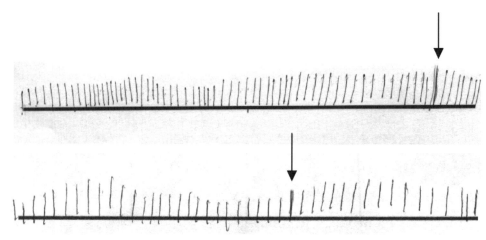

Fig. 11.2 Segmentation and Line Bisection. Two lines segmented, and subsequently bisected, (red marks, indicated by black arrows) by two right-brain-damaged patients with left USN, who exhibit a rightward bisection error (reprinted with permission of the British Psychological Society from Gallace et al., 2008, Figure 3). (See Plate 4)

11.2.1.4. The modulation of the 'Perceptual' and 'Premotor' factor in spatial neglect by 'Local' vs. 'Global' processing

A recent demonstration that the boundaries of the 'perceptual' and of the 'premotor' impairments are far from immutable comes from a recent study (Gallace et al., 2008). Right brain-damaged patients with left USN were required to set the subjective midpoint of a 16-cm horizontal line (namely, a classical line bisection task), and subsequently to segment that line into a number of smaller lines, as in the provided sample (i.e., a 2.1-cm line divided by eight vertical bars, with the distances between consecutive drawn segments being equal, approximately 0.3 cm). All patients used their unaffected right hand. The study aimed at investigating the role of 'global' vs. 'local' levels of impairment of visuo-spatial processing in shaping the performance of patients with left visual USN in line bisection tasks, rather than at exploring the distinction between 'perceptual' vs. 'premotor' components of the USN syndrome. The results are relevant to the latter distinction, however. Figure 11.2 shows the dissociation between bisection and segmentation. The subjective centre of the 16-cm line, as marked by two illustrative right-brain-damaged patients with left visual USN, was displaced rightwards, as expected (Bisiach et al., 1976; Schenkenberg et al., 1980). However, the segmentation performance was preserved entirely in most patients. Particularly, only three out of the 13 right-brain-damaged patients with left USN were impaired when required to segment the line, moving from the right end to the left end, with, therefore, evidence of left 'directional hypokinesia' (Heilman et al., 2003). The other ten patients were able to complete the segmentation task both from left to right, and from right to left, showing no evidence, in this particular task, of a 'premotor' impairment. Accordingly, also this study suggests that the inability to perform movements in a leftward direction, towards the unaffected side of space, does not represent the prevailing pattern of impairment characterizing the USN syndrome.

11.2.1.5. Visual illusions and the 'Premotor' deficits of patients with spatial neglect

Another source of related evidence comes from the investigation of the processing of illusory effects by right-brain-damaged patients with left USN (see Vallar and Daini, 2002; Vallar and Daini, 2006, for reviews). Again, as in the study discussed previously (Gallace et al., 2008), the primary aim of

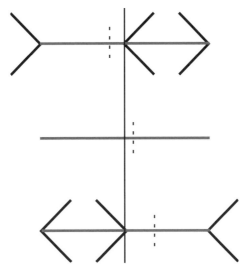

Fig. 11.3 The Brentano-Müller-Lyer illusion. (A) The Brentano or combined form of the Müller-Lyer illusion. The filled vertical line indicates the physical centre of the horizontal segment. The short dashed line indicates the bisection error committed by one right-brain-damaged patient with left USN. In the baseline condition (central stimulus) the patient makes a rightward error, indicating left USN. With illusory stimuli, the bisection point is displaced leftwards (upper stimulus), or rightwards (lower stimulus), according to the side of the horizontal segment expanded by the fins (modified from Daini et al., 2002). (See Plate 5)

these investigations does not concern the 'perceptual' vs. 'premotor' dichotomy[5], but the results are nevertheless of interest for it. When illusions of length or displacement are used,[6] and the illusory effects are assessed by a manual bisection task, a leftward displacement of the subjective midpoint involves a leftward movement, as compared with a baseline, not-illusory, condition. Left USN is characterized by a rightward bias. When the left-hand side of the stimulus is expanded illusorily, the brain-damaged patients with left USN displace leftwards the subjective centre of the line, like the neurologically unimpaired participants. This would indicate that, under certain conditions, leftward movements may take place.

A number of studies have shown that right-brain-damaged patients with left USN exhibit illusory effects with stimuli that expand the perceived extent of a horizontal line both in a rightward and in a leftward direction, namely also towards the 'neglected' side of space. These findings include the Müller-Lyer figure with unilateral fins (Mattingley et al., 1995; Olk et al., 2001), the Brentano or combined form of the Müller-Lyer illusion with bilateral fins (Vallar et al., 2000; Daini et al., 2002), the Judd illusion (Ro and Rafal, 1996; Olk et al., 2001), triangular backgrounds, related to the Müller-Lyer illusion with unilateral fins (Shulman et al., 2002), and the Oppel-Kundt illusion

---

[5] These studies elucidate the role of spatial attention in the processing of some visual illusions. Were USN patients not sensitive to illusory effects arising from the left side of space, the conclusion might be drawn that these illusions require the attentional processes impaired by USN. Alternatively, were the processing of illusions preserved in these patients, the hypothesis that the illusory effects are based on pre-attentive processing would be supported (see Umiltà, 1988 and 2001, for reviews).

[6] Variants of the Müller-Lyer figure: (a) Müller-Lyer figure with unilateral outward or inward projecting fins; (b) Brentano figure, as shown in Fig. 3-A; (c) Judd figure with outward projecting fins on one end and inward projecting fins on the other end.

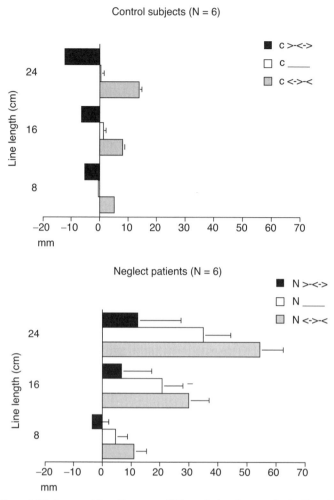

Fig. 11.3 (continued) (B) Average bisection error (SE) made by six neurologically unimpaired control participants, and six right-brain-damaged patients with left USN, with simple lines, and Brentano stimuli (leftward expansion/rightward compression, rightward expansion/leftward compression), 8, 16, and 24 cm long. Illusory effects are present in both groups, with the patients' performances being overall displaced rightwards, in line with the presence of left USN (reprinted with permission of Elsevier from Vallar et al., 2000, figure 2).

(Ricci et al., 2004; Savazzi et al., 2007). Figure 11.3-A shows the performance of one representative patient on the Brentano version of the Müller-Lyer illusion. The patient's rightward baseline error in manual line bisection, that indicates left USN, is modulated by the illusion both with a leftward, and with a rightward, illusory expansion, that displaces the perceived subjective centre of the line leftwards and rightwards, respectively (Daini et al., 2002). Figure 11.3-B shows the preserved illusory effects of a group of six right-brain-damaged patients with left USN (Vallar et al., 2000).

The preserved illusory effects in the bisection task may be contrasted with the evidence that the explicit processing of the left-sided portion of the stimuli is defective, as assessed by the verbal report of the left-sided fins (Mattingley et al., 1995), and by same-different judgments (Olk et al., 2001, Ro and Rafal, 1996), indicating that the processing of illusory configurations occurs at an 'implicit', 'pre-attentive' level (Vallar and Daini, 2006, Roche and Commins, 2009, chapter 4). As far as 'premotor' USN is concerned, however, the complete preservation of illusory effects with a leftward expansion or displacement of the horizontal line, characterized by a leftward displacement in a line bisection task, indicates that, under these conditions, leftward movements may be performed. Particularly, the 'premotor' deficit of brain-damaged patients with USN may involve goal-directed movements, which require the allocation of attentional resources (Mattingley et al., 1992, 1994, 1998). By contrast, leftward movements may be performed, provided they are not 'intentional', namely goal-directed, being instead elicited by left-sided cues, such as in the case of illusory figures, independent of spatial attention. 'Premotor' USN, similar to its 'perceptual' counterpart (Berti, 2002), may be characterized as an impairment of the setting up, programming, and initiation of movements directed towards the contralesional side of space, taking place at a level of processing entailing awareness. When leftward movements are elicited by configurations that do not involve attentional processing, such as visual illusions of length and position, the observed effects are preserved entirely.

Finally, the available anatomical evidence suggests that right-brain-damaged patients with left USN exhibit preserved illusory effects, provided the extrastriate occipital regions are not damaged, and no visual field deficits are present (Daini et al., 2002; Ricci et al., 2004; Savazzi et al., 2007). These findings are in line with a recent fMRI experiment in neurologically unimpaired participants (Weidner and Fink, 2007). A task, requiring to judge as to whether the central fin correctly bisected the horizontal line of the Brentano version of the Müller-Lyer figure, was compared to a Landmark task requiring a similar judgment on a pre-bisected simple line. For the illusory stimulus, which is of interest here, activations were found bilaterally in the lateral occipital extrastriate cortex, particularly in the inferior occipital gyrus, and also in the superior end of the right superior parietal lobule. These activated ventral (the lateral occipital extrastriate cortex) and dorsal (the right superior parietal lobule) regions (Weidner and Fink, 2007) are typically spared in patients with USN, whose lesions encroach in the inferior parietal lobule, at the temporo-parietal junction (Halligan et al., 2003), and in the fronto-parietal subcortical white matter (Bartolomeo et al., 2007). These neuropsychological (Daini et al., 2002; Ricci et al., 2004; Savazzi et al., 2007) and functional imaging (Weidner and Fink, 2007) findings, indicate that the ventral stream (with a possible, right-hemisphere based, contribution from the dorsal stream, for the Brentano version of the Müller-Lyer figure, see Weidner and Fink, 2007) constitutes the main neural bases of illusions such as the Müller-Lyer and the Oppel-Kundt.

These complementary neuropsychological and functional imaging observations also indicate that the USN syndrome cannot be interpreted in terms of damage to either the dorsal or the ventral stream. Interestingly, the single case study of patient IG, who had no USN but bilateral OA, shows that bilateral lesions of the dorsal visual stream (i.e., the superior parietal lobule, Brodmann's area (BA) 7; the upper part of the angular gyrus, BA 39; the intraparietal sulcus; the extrastriate areas, BAs 18, and 19) do not affect the processing of visual illusions (namely, the Roelofs effect, and the Titchener–Ebbinghaus illusion), as assessed by both perceptual judgments and, importantly, visuo-motor tasks. These findings suggest that, at least under the conditions assessed in that study, visually guided action can be planned and executed independent of the operation of the dorsal stream, severely damaged in the patient (Coello et al., 2007. See also Rossetti et al., Chapter 10, this volume). Rossetti et al., conclude that 'visually guided action can be planned and executed independently of the dorsal pathways, possibly through the inferior parietal lobule'. The preservation of illusory effects involving visually guided action in patients with USN, in whom the inferior parietal lobule is typically damaged, complements this statement, suggesting that the integrity of the inferior posterior parietal region is not necessary for these visuo-motor effects to take place.

11.2.1.6. Neural correlates of 'Perceptual' and 'Premotor' neglect

Taken together, the studies which made use of non-compatible conditions (Adair et al., 1998; Bisiach et al., 1990; Bisiach et al., 1995) suggest an association of the premotor pathological mechanisms of visual USN with damage involving anterior regions (frontal lobe, basal ganglia), and of the perceptual factors with damage involving posterior regions (temporo–parietal–occipital). However, a potential confound, when using non-compatible conditions, is the role of some working memory or executive components (Baddeley, 1996), which may become involved in the more difficult, non-congruent task, and have been associated with frontal lobe function (see the related discussion of Fink et al., 1999). It should be noted, however, that a similar anterior-posterior dissociation has been found in paradigms which made use of congruent conditions only (Bottini et al., 1992; Coslett et al., 1990). Patient FS, who showed left USN with a right subcortical lesion involving the basal ganglia, the internal capsule, and the frontal white matter, frequently failed to react to right-sided stimuli (presented in the preserved side of space), when he had to respond by pressing a left-sided key, using the right unaffected hand (Bisiach et al., 1985). These findings also indicate that output processes may affect visual perception.[7]

In the study by Bartolomeo et al. (1998) all 14 right-brain-damaged patients showed a 'perceptual' type of left USN in the experimental tasks (see Fig. 11.1-E). As summarized in Table 11.2, the pattern of lesions was mixed, but no patient had a lesion confined to the frontal lobe. The two patients with a rightward bias in the 'motor' task did not exhibit visual USN. Their lesions involved the superior parietal region (patients #6, and #17), and the dorsolateral frontal cortex (patient #17). This latter patient, though not included in the left USN group, showed slow responses in the 'perceptual' task and 'signs of mild neglect' (Bartolomeo et al., 1998, p. 232). The three left-brain-damaged patients with right visual USN reported by Bartolomeo et al. (2001), who showed both 'perceptual', and 'motor' biases, as assessed by the 'traffic light' paradigm (see Fig. 11.1-E), had extensive fronto-temporo-parietal lesions (two patients), and damage to the corona radiata (one patient).

The recent study by Sapir et al. (2007) used a compatible task, where the starting position of the hand (left, centre, right, with respect to the mid-sagittal plane of the body), and the position of the target (left, right, with respect to that plane) were manipulated. The anatomical analysis, performed in a subgroup of 29 out of 53 patients, six with and 23 without directional hypokinesia, showed an association of directional hypokinesia with damage involving the putamen, and the claustrum (100% of the patients), followed by the white matter underlying the frontal lobe in correspondence to the precentral gyrus, the inferior frontal gyrus, the frontal operculum, and the anterior insula (80% of the patients).

In a recent study in neurologically unimpaired participants, using the incompatible paradigm devised by Na et al. (1998), repetitive Transcranial Magnetic Stimulation (rTMS) delivered to either the right middle frontal gyrus or to the right posterior parietal cortex brought about a rightward error in line bisection, indicating a left experimentally induced USN, relative to the baseline. In the incompatible condition (where participants had a mirror-reversed view of the working space), however, only frontal rTMS interference still produced a rightward error (corresponding to a leftward deviation as seen on the monitor), suggesting a premotor impairment (Ghacibeh et al., 2007).

A notable exception to this converging pattern of results is the finding that USN patients with parietal damage were disproportionately slow in initiating leftward movements towards visual targets in the left hand-side of space; conversely, USN patients with frontal lesions did not show such an impairment (Mattingley et al., 1998; Husain et al., 2000).

The anatomo-clinical correlation data from the Landmark test are much less clear. Bisiach et al. (1998a) found that frontal damage was associated with a perceptual bias, subcortical damage with a response bias. The studies performed by Harvey, Milner, and their coworkers, reviewed earlier, do not provide any definite anatomo-clinical indication. The Landmark paradigms have been used also in neurologically unimpaired participants, who have undergone 'virtual' lesions through rTMS. A number of studies have shown that posterior parietal (Fierro et al., 2001; Fierro et al., 2000; Ellison et al., 2004), and frontal (Brighina et al., 2002) rTMS interference brings about a neglect-like

---

[7] Conversely, contralesional actions may improve the report of contralesional visual stimuli. In one left-brain-damaged patient (RH) with right extinction and mild right USN (Kitadono and Humphreys, 2009), successive pointing leftwards and then rightwards reduced errors to right-sided visual stimuli, as compared to pointing leftwards only, in single and double stimulation condition.

performance in the Landmark task. Consistently, when neurologically unimpaired participants perform a perceptual line bisection (Landmark) task (Milner et al., 1993), neural activity increases in the parietal-frontal regions, predominantly in the right hemisphere (Fink et al., 2000; Fink et al., 2001). As for the 'perceptual' vs. 'premotor' dichotomy, posterior parietal and frontal TMS gives rise to a 'perceptual' bias, with no 'response' bias being induced by rTMS on parietal and frontal sites (Brighina et al., 2002).

11.2.1.7. Interim conclusion

The anatomo-clinical correlation studies and the TMS experiments reviewed in the previous section concur to emphasize the role of 'perceptual' factors in the determinism of USN, although both 'perceptual' and 'premotor' pathological mechanisms contribute to shaping the manifold manifestations of the syndrome. Seen in this perspective, USN is mainly a 'perceptual' impairment. However, the absence of deficits of 'vision-for perception', like VA, in USN patients, points to the limitations of the account of perceptual disorders offered by the dorsal/ventral visual streams dichotomy.

The 'perceptual' vs. 'premotor' distinction is not fixed across tasks. Individual patients may show different 'perceptual' vs. 'premotor'/'response' biases, that vary according to the demands of the task. This suggests that the 'perceptual' vs. 'premotor'/'response' distinction requires a fine grain componential analysis, considering the characteristics of the stimulus, and the actions to be performed.

Finally, as for the anatomical correlates of the 'perceptual' vs. 'premotor' distinction in USN, the more definite data suggesting an association of frontal/subcortical-basal ganglia damage with 'premotor' USN, and of posterior parietal damage with 'perceptual' USN, come from paradigms involving goal-directed arm movements. The data from the Landmark task and its variants are less definite. It should be considered, however, that the Landmark task assesses a lateral bias ('response/output' vs. 'perceptual'), rather than the programming and execution of directional movements of the limbs. Furthermore, impairments in this task may be independent of the main clinical manifestations of the USN syndrome (Harvey and Milner, 1999).

11.2.2. **Personal space: 'Motor' vs. 'Sensory' neglect**

In the last two decades, it has become clear that motor and sensory impairments (hemiplegia, and hemianaesthesia) include higher order components (attentional, or intentional), related to USN, although this possibility had long been suggested by clinicians (Critchley, 1953; Friedland and Weinstein, 1977). These disorders, as well as visual half-field deficits (hemianopia), are more frequent after right brain damage than after left brain damage (Sterzi et al., 1993), indicating a possible role for USN. At variance with the 'perceptual' and 'premotor' deficits discussed earlier, 'motor' and 'somatosensory' USN, concerning the contralesional side of the body, should be distinguished from 'primary' sensory and motor disorders, due to damage of the sensorimotor cortex and of the afferent and efferent nervous pathways. At the level of the neurological clinical exam, Laplane and Degos (1983), summarizing previous work performed by Castaigne et al. (1970, 1972) define 'motor neglect' as a disturbance of spontaneous movement involving one half of the body and having the appearance of hemiplegia, yet with normal strength and dexterity, which can be proven by prompting an extraordinary effort on the part of the patient during the examination'. Motor neglect may be associated with both temporo-parietal (Castaigne et al., 1970; Triggs et al., 1994), and frontal (Castaigne et al., 1972; Laplane, 1990) lesions. Patients with motor neglect may show no associated somatosensory deficits or USN (Laplane and Degos, 1983). Somatosensory USN is a manifestation of 'sensory' neglect or 'inattention' (i.e., 'a deficit in awareness of stimuli contralateral to a lesion that does not involve sensory projection systems or the primary sensory areas to which they project'. See Heilman et al., 2003, p. 296).

Experimental evidence supporting the view that 'motor', 'visual', and 'somatosensory' deficits may be due, at least in part, to USN, comes from different sources of converging evidence. First, right-brain-damaged patients with left hemianopia (Vallar et al., 1991b; Angelelli et al., 1996), and left hemianaesthesia (Vallar et al., 1991a) may show relatively preserved early evoked potentials. The latencies of steady-state visual evoked potentials (VEPs) to contralesional stimuli have been found, however, to be systematically longer (10–30 ms) than those to ipsilesional stimuli, suggesting some defective processing of sensory input (see Di Russo et al., 2008, for a review of these studies in supplementary Tables 11.1 and 11.2). Yet, a recent study using transient VEPs found that bottom-up processing of a visual stimulus located in the neglected half-field was intact up to 130 ms from stimulus onset, with hemispheric differences being not significant for either the C1 or P1 components, representing the activity of the striate and extrastriate areas of the occipital cortex (Di Russo et al., 2008). Taken together, these results concur to suggest that the early stages of sensory processing are largely preserved in patients with USN, who, nevertheless, fail to report contralesional stimuli. These findings are consistent with the view, discussed earlier, that the deficit of USN is largely 'perceptual', rather than due to a sensory impairment (Bisiach and Vallar, 1988. For a discussion of the interpretations of USN as a 'sensory' hypotheses see Friedland and Weinstein, 1977).

Second, physiological stimulations that ameliorate a number of aspects of the USN syndrome temporarily (Vallar et al., 1997b; Rossetti and Rode, 2002; Kerkhoff, 2003) may also improve deficits of tactile (caloric vestibular stimulation, see Vallar et al., 1990. For transcutaneous nervous electrical stimulation, see Vallar et al., 1996. For prism adaptation, see Maravita et al., 2003), and proprioceptive sensation (position sense in the upper limbs, see Vallar et al., 1993a and 1995). Similarly, vestibular (Rode et al., 1992; Vallar et al., 2003), and optokinetic (Vallar et al., 1997a) stimulations may improve contralesional motor deficits temporarily in right-brain-damaged patients. These findings indicate that left-sided motor and somatosensory deficits may have a spatial component, related to the USN syndrome, and to right hemispheric damage. The view that the right hemisphere contributes to somatosensory awareness for the whole of the body, possessing a spatial representation of both the contralesional (left), and of the ipsilesional (right) side of the body (Mesulam, 2002. See Bisiach and Vallar, 2000) is supported by the finding that caloric vestibular stimulation through irrigation of the left ear canal ameliorates not only the left hemianaesthesia of right-brain-damaged patients (Vallar et al., 1990, 1993b), as discussed above, but also the right hemianaesthesia of left-brain-damaged patients (Bottini et al., 2005). These effects are mainly based on the temporary activation of right hemisphere regions (Bottini et al., 2005; Bottini et al., 2001; Bottini et al., 1994. See Dieterich, 2007, for a review of the anatomical evidence based on neuroimaging studies in humans).

Third, maneuvers that dissociate somatotopic or retinotopic frames of reference from spatial frames may ameliorate somatosensory and visual-half-field deficits temporarily in right-brain-damaged patients with left USN. Some studies manipulated the posture of the participants' hands, in order to investigate the contribution of the somatotopic, and higher-order spatial reference frames in modulating the somatosensory deficits exhibited by right-brain-damaged patients. Brain-damaged patients with USN and tactile extinction fail to report somatosensory stimuli delivered to the contralesional side of either wrist, when both sides of it are stimulated simultaneously, regardless of whether the patients' hands are positioned palm up or palm down. That is, irrespective of hand posture, patients extinguish the contralesional stimulus, with reference to the spatial, not to the sensory (somatotopic), coordinates frames (Moscovitch and Behrmann, 1994). In a similar vein, the effects of the spatial position of the participants' hands on somatosensory awareness have been explored in right-brain-damaged patients with left somatosensory deficits or extinction. The patients' accuracy in detecting stimuli delivered to the left hand (both single and associated with a simultaneous stimulus delivered to the right hand) improves when their hands are crossed over the midline, so that each hand is positioned in the opposite side of space: namely, the left hand in the right-hand side of pace, and the right hand vice versa (Smania and Aglioti, 1995; Aglioti et al., 1999; Moro et al., 2004). Taken together, these results elucidate the role of higher order, spatial pathological mechanisms in the determinism of somatosensory deficits of right-brain-damaged patients with tactile extinction or USN (Vallar, 1999). In line with these conclusions, a right-brain-damaged patient with a mild left USN and a left tactile extinction showed a reduction of neural activity in the primary somatosensory areas of the left hemisphere (left postcentral somatosensory cortex, SI, to which sensory input from the right hand is projected), when the patient's right, ipsilesional, hand was placed in the left (contralesional) side of space, as compared to when the hand was held in the right, ipsilesional, side of space, with reference to the midsagittal plane of the body's trunk. Behaviourally, the detection of touches to the right hand in a crossed position was reduced dramatically only when a simultaneous stimulation of the right elbow (placed in the right-hand side of space) was given. The fMRI responses, however, were reduced under both bilateral and unilateral tactile stimulation of the right hand in a crossed position, namely in the left-hand side of space. This may suggest that the spatial position of body parts, that is the relevant spatial reference frame, can modulate the strength of activation of early somatosensory areas in response to both single and double tactile stimulations (Valenza et al., 2004).

In the visual domain, similar results have been obtained by dissociating retinotopic vs. spatial egocentric reference frames. Right-brain-damaged patients with left visual inattention fail to report left-sided visual stimuli when looking straight ahead, or towards the left, neglected, side. However, when such patients look towards the ipsilesional side (rightwards), they become able to detect stimuli presented in the right-hand side of space, with reference to the body's midsagittal plane, but still in the left visual half-field in retinotopic reference frames (Kooistra and Heilman, 1989). Visual inattention may be independent of other manifestations of the USN syndrome (Nadeau and Heilman, 1991).

In sum, as for extra-personal space, investigations in right-brain-damaged patients with left USN suggest the existence of a distinction between 'premotor' intentional ('motor neglect'), and 'perceptual' ('sensory inattention'), higher order impairments of sensorimotor processing in the contralesional side of the body. The precise elucidation of the higher-order, spatial, nature of these disorders is made difficult by the co-occurrence of 'primary' motor and sensory deficits (Heilman et al., 2003; Halligan and Marshall, 2002; Vallar, 1999). However, electrophysiological data, studies using physiological stimulations, and the manipulation of the somatotopic and retinotopic vs. spatial (egocentric) reference frames, concur to support a 'perceptual' vs. 'premotor' distinction also as far as personal space, namely, the body, is concerned.

11.3. Mapping the 'Premotor' and 'Perceptual' components of the spatial neglect syndrome onto neurofunctional streams

11.3.1. The anatomical basis of Unilateral spatial neglect

The anatomical correlates of the USN syndrome, traditionally confined to damage to the posterior parietal regions (Critchley, 1953; Jewesbury, 1969), have progressively expanded in the last few decades to include the lateral frontal cortex, as well as subcortical structures, such as the thalamus, the basal ganglia, and white matter fibre tracts connecting the fronto-parietal regions (Vallar, 2001). Figure 11.4 summarizes the neural network supporting spatial representation and attention, whose damage may bring about the USN syndrome. In recent years, many anatomo-clinical correlation studies have been devoted to elucidating in further detail its precise correlates. This enterprise is made complex also by the fact that, as shown in Table 11.1, the syndrome is multifarious, and, typically, the vast majority of studies have assessed extra-personal visual USN. With these caveats in mind, the initial focus was on the inferior parietal lobule (supramarginal gyrus) at the temporo-parietal junction (Hécaen et al., 1956; Vallar and Perani, 1986; Vallar and Perani, 1987; Heilman and Valenstein, 1972; Heilman et al., 1994). Subsequent studies suggested a role of the posterior part of the superior temporal gyrus (Karnath, 2001; Karnath et al., 2001),[8] and of the angular gyrus of the inferior parietal lobule (Mort et al., 2003). Other relevant regions include the vascular territory of the posterior

---

[8] The relevance of the latter lesion site has been a matter of controversy, and the interested reader is referred to a number of discussion papers (Karnath and Himmelbach, 2002; Karnath et al., 2004; Mort et al., 2004).

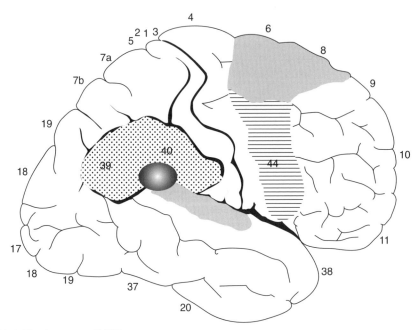

Fig. 11.4 The Anatomy of USN.
(A) Cortical lesion sites associated with USN. Most anatomo-clinical correlation studies show that
the lesion responsible for USN involves the right inferior parietal lobule (BA 39 and BA 40), and the
temporo-parietal junction. USN after right frontal damage is less frequent, and usually associated
with lesions to the frontal premotor cortex, particularly to its more ventral parts (BA 44, and ventral
BA 6). Lesions may involve the white matter fibre bundles, that connect the posterior parietal
region and the temporo-parietal junction with the frontal premotor cortex. USN may be associated
also with damage to the more dorsal and medial regions of the frontal premotor cortex, and to the
superior temporal gyrus (reprinted with permission of Elsevier from Halligan et al., 2003, Figure 3).
(See Plate 6)

cerebral artery (Vallar and Perani, 1986), with the suggestion of a relevant role for lesions of the
white matter in the occipital lobe, disrupting the connections between the parahippocampal gyrus
and the angular gyrus of the parietal lobe (Bird et al., 2006). A fronto-parietal disconnection
may play a crucial role in bringing about the USN syndrome (Leibovitch et al., 1998, 1999; Doricchi
and Tomaiuolo, 2003; Thiebaut de Schotten et al., 2005; Bartolomeo et al., 2007; Doricchi et al.,
2008, for review. See also Vallar and Perani, 1986, for early evidence). Particularly, damage to
the parietal-frontal fibres of the superior longitudinal fasciculus (Doricchi and Tomaiuolo,
2003; Leibovitch et al., 1998; Bartolomeo et al., 2007; Thiebaut de Schotten et al., 2005), and of the
inferior fronto-occipital fasciculus (Urbanski et al., 2008), may be relevant in causing USN. In
line with these suggestions (Doricchi et al., 2008, for review), a recent study (Committeri et al., 2007)
indicates that damage to a circuit including the right frontal (ventral premotor cortex, and
middle frontal gyrus), and the superior temporal regions, is associated with extra-personal visual
USN, as assessed by a battery including cancellation, bisection, reading, and perceptual tasks. By
contrast, personal USN was found to be associated to damage to the right inferior parietal regions
(supramarginal gyrus, post-central gyrus, and especially the white matter medial to these
structures).

Also damage to the subcortical grey nuclei may bring about many manifestations of the USN
syndrome. Relevant structures include the basal ganglia (particularly the putamen), and the posterior
part (pulvinar) of the thalamus (see Vallar, 2008, for review).

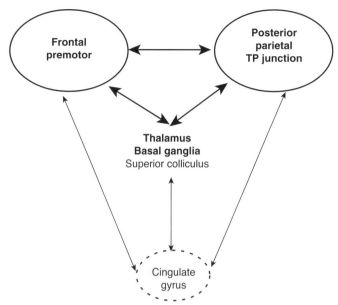

Fig. 11.4 (Continued) (B) Cortico-subcortical networks for spatial attention and representation. The premotor frontal areas, the posterior-parietal regions/temporo-parietal junction, the subcortical grey nuclei, and their connections. The main structures whose damage is most frequently associated with USN in humans are marked bold (reprinted with permission of Psychology Press from Vallar, 2008, figure 2. See also Mesulam, 2002). Finally, a few studies have considered the possible role of the specific tasks used for assessing extra-personal visual USN. One main finding is that posterior lesions are associated with disproportionate impairments in line bisection (with an ipsilesional, rightward, neglect-related error), compared to cancellation tasks, that are brought about by anterior lesions, involving the frontal lobe (Binder et al., 1992; Daini et al., 2002; Rorden et al., 2006; Golay et al., 2008. See related evidence in Doricchi and Angelelli, 1999).

11.3.2. Unilateral spatial neglect and the dorsal stream: optic ataxia

It has long been known that patients with OA have lesions more dorsal than those of patients with USN. In patients with OA, lesions spare the inferior parietal lobule, involving the superior parietal lobule (Ratcliff and Davies-Jones, 1972; Perenin and Vighetto, 1988. See Perenin, 1997, for a review). Recently, the suggestion has been made that the neural correlate of OA is damage to a set of lateral and medial parieto-occipital structures: bilaterally, the lateral cortical convexity at the occipito-parietal junction; in the left hemisphere also the junction between the occipital cortex, and the superior parietal lobule; the parietal white matter, and the precuneus, close to the occipito-parietal junction (Karnath and Perenin, 2005). These anatomical dissociations between OA and USN have a behavioral counterpart. Patients with OA, and lesions involving the superior parietal lobule, may exhibit no extinction or USN (Levine et al., 1978; Perenin and Vighetto, 1988; Coulthard et al., 2006, patient GS), while patients with left USN typically do not show OA (see Karnath et al., 1997, for an experimental study), conjuring up a double dissociation (Vallar, 2000) between the two disorders (see Coulthard et al., 2007; Himmelbach et al., 2007, for a discussion of the impairments of action control, particularly in relationship with OA, in patients with USN). Patients may also show an association of the two disorders. For instance, some evidence is provided by left-brain-damaged patients #6 and #8 of the series of ten patients with OA of Perenin and Vighetto (1988), who showed a leftward position preference in writing and drawing, using only the ipsilesional left-hand side of the sheet, with, however, no evidence of USN on bisection and cancellation tasks. In one of these patients (#6) the lesion extended to the inferior parietal lobule, particularly the angular gyrus (see Mort et al., 2003, for relevant evidence). In the other patient (#8) the lesion involved the intraparietal sulcus, as well as the deep parietal white matter, which, however, were also variably damaged in the other eight patients with OA without USN. Right-brain-damaged patient B. N. (Coulthard et al., 2006), who showed both USN and OA, had a lesion involving the precuneus, the underlying white matter, as well as fibre tracts lying below the surface of the inferior parietal lobule, the latter damage possibly accounting for the USN deficit (Doricchi and Tomaiuolo, 2003).

In sum, patients with USN may show a 'premotor' impairment, as discussed particularly in section #2.1, dissimilar from OA. The neural correlates of the two disorders are also different, with 'premotor' neglect being often associated with frontal-basal ganglia damage.

11.3.3. Unilateral spatial neglect and the ventral stream: visual agnosia

Patients with left USN, however, do not show not only 'OA', but also 'VA', that represents the hall-mark neuropsychological impairment associated with damage to the ventral stream (Milner and Goodale, 1995 and 2006. See also Rossetti et al., this volume), and is not a component deficit of the USN syndrome, as summarized in Table 11.1. The deficit that characterizes the USN syndrome is multifarious, 'perceptual' rather than 'premotor'in the majority of patients. The 'perceptual' impairment of USN patients is to be conceived as the defective access to conscious experience of contralesional events. Such information, however, is processed in all its main constituents, including semantics (e.g., priming effects, see the reviews of Berti, 2002 and McGlinchey-Berroth, 1997), and the physical extent of the stimulus, as revealed by the processing of visual illusions (Vallar and Daini, 2002; Vallar and Daini, 2006). This preserved processing may be revealed under conditions in which no explicit report (e.g., detection, identification) is required. Furthermore, some studies have shown that, under these conditions, the performance of right-brain-damaged patients with USN is not only qualitatively (i.e., patients exhibit stimulus –related effects as neuro-logically unimpaired participants do) but also quantitatively (i.e., level of accuracy) entirely preserved. Patients with left neglect dyslexia[9] show a level of performance comparable to that of neurologically unimpaired participants in lexical decision[10] (Arduino et al., 2003. See also Stenneken et al., 2008).

In sum, the pattern of 'perceptual' impairment (namely, defective perceptual awareness of contral-esional events), and of preserved function (namely, a wide range of non-conscious processing of such 'neglected' events) is definitely different from that of VA (Farah, 2004). Accordingly, considering USN as an impairment of the 'ventral stream', as conceived by Milner and Goodale (2006, p. 201), runs into difficulties. Furthermore, from a neuropsychological vantage point, the 'ventral-stream' account is admittedly incomplete (Milner and Goodale, 2006, p. 201), being also unable to account for the 'premotor' components of the syndrome, such as directional hypokinesia, that 'is not closely tied to the dorsal stream … is associated with modulatory systems on the "output" side of the brain rather than at the visuomotor interface' (Milner and Goodale, 2006, p. 200).

Similarly, the whole of the productive aspects of the USN syndrome, such as perseveration (Na et al., 1999; Rusconi et al., 2002; Nys et al., 2006; Ronchi et al., 2009) and the symptom-complex of somatoparaphrenia (namely, delusional beliefs, most often disownership, concerning the contral-esional limbs, and a variety of contralesional misperceptions in the visual and in other sensory

---

[9] Left neglect dyslexia in single word reading is characterized by errors in the left-hand side of the word (Ellis et al., 1987). The more common error types are 'substitutions' [e.g., the target word *albero* (tree) read as *pobero*, a nonword in which two initial letters have been substituted], 'omissions' [e.g., the target word *famiglia* (family) read as *miglia* (miles), a word in which two initial letters have been omitted], or, less frequently, 'additions' [e.g., the target word *luna* (moon) read as *moluna*, a nonword in which two letters have been added to the left]. The relative proportion of these error types varies across patients (Arduino et al., 2002).

modalities, see Vallar and Ronchi, 2009, for review), are largely outside the 'ventral' vs. 'dorsal' stream dichotomy. The anatomical correlates of perseveration in patients with left visual USN, that include frontal and subcortical (basal ganglia) regions (Na et al., 1999; Rusconi et al., 2002; Nys et al., 2006), suggest an impairment concerning the control of motor output (but see Bottini and Toraldo, 2003, for evidence suggesting a role of left-to-right allochiria). The neural correlates of somatopara-phrenia include an extensive fronto-parietal network, though the role of posterior (parietal, at the temporo-parietal junction) damage, and of lesions involving the insular cortex (Baier and Karnath, 2008) appear to be much relevant. Interestingly, damage to the insula (Karnath et al., 2005) has been associated to anosognosia for left hemiplegia (see also Berti et al., 2005, but with a main role of damage to the frontal premotor cortex, see Pia et al., 2004, for review), a component of the USN syndrome that also eludes the 'dorsal'/'ventral' dichotomy.

11.3.4. The 'Dorsal'/'Ventral' visual stream dichotomy and unilateral spatial neglect

The 'dorsal'/'ventral' visual stream dichotomy (Goodale, 2008; Milner and Goodale, 2006; Milner and Goodale, 1995), as useful as it is, may be too simple and rigid (Rizzolatti et al., 2007), to account for the complex function of these brain regions. Rizzolatti and colleagues have proposed, on the basis of neurophysiologic and neuroanatomic considerations, a subdivision of the dorsal stream into a dorsal-dorsal and a dorsal-ventral component, with the latter including the inferior parietal lobule and the ventral premotor cortex (Rizzolatti and Matelli, 2003; Rozzi et al., 2006; Gallese, 2007). Such a system is a candidate neural network for having the USN syndrome as a neuropsychological clinical counter-part, also encompassing the 'perceptual' vs. 'premotor' distinction, which characterizes this disorder of spatial awareness. In a somewhat similar vein, Husain and Nachev (2007) suggest a functional fractionation of the inferior parietal lobule, emphasizing the role not only of spatial, but also of non-spatial (see Husain and Rorden, 2003, for review) impairments in shaping the syndrome of USN.

Studies investigating 'viewer-based' (or 'egocentric', namely with reference to spatial frames such as the midsagittal plane of the body) vs. 'object-based' (or 'allocentric', namely with reference to, for instance, the principal axis of the object) manifestations of USN (see Walker, 1995, for a review) suggest a possible functional fractionation of the ventral posterior regions of the brain. Recent stud-ies in large series of brain-damaged patients have confirmed this distinction, using a test where patients are required to cross circles with a left-sided or a right-sided gap (Ota et al., 2001). Patients who make omissions in the contralesional side of the display, with reference to the midsagittal plane of the body, may be regarded as showing an 'egocentric' type of USN. Conversely, patients omitting to cross out circles with a left-sided, or a right-sided, gap, independent of their position on the display with reference to the midsagittal plane of the body, may be regarded as exhibiting an object-based type of USN. Patients may show either form of USN, both in the visual, and in the tactile modality, with a double dissociation between USN type and modality (Marsh and Hillis, 2008). Furthermore, object-based USN appears to be less frequent (in the series of 100 right-brain-damaged patients reported by Marsh and Hillis, 2008, over 80% of the patients showed 'egocentric' USN, in either modality). Another study from the same group, in a series of 50 patients with acute right hemi-spheric stroke, has revealed an association of left 'allocentric' USN (namely, errors on the left-hand side of individual stimuli, regardless of their location with respect to the viewer) with hypoperfusion of the right superior temporal gyrus, and of left 'egocentric' USN (errors on the left of the viewer) with hypoperfusion of the right angular gyrus of the inferior parietal lobule. Again, 'egocentric' USN was more frequent than 'allocentric' USN: 25 patients with 'egocentric' neglect, five patients with 'allocentric' USN, and one patient with a mixed deficit (Hillis et al., 2005). Finally, there is evidence that (right) 'allocentric' USN may be more frequently associated with left-brain damage: nine out of 47 left-brain-damaged patients showed right neglect, that was 'allocentric' in six, 'egocentric' in one, and mixed in two patients (Kleinman et al., 2007). These data from brain-damaged patients with USN have found some support in a recent TMS study in neurologically unimpaired participants.

Interference with neural activity in the right superior temporal gyrus disrupted visual search in an 'object-based' reference frame, while posterior parietal interference had no such effects (Schindler et al., 2008, see also Ellison et al., 2004, for related evidence). Conversely, TMS over the right posterior parietal cortex impaired detection of left-sided stimuli in a 'scene-based', 'egocentric', rather than in an 'object-based', 'allocentric' reference frame (Muggleton et al., 2006).

11.4. Conclusion

The syndrome of USN comprises many deficits that may occur in dissociated form (see Table 11.1), but the disorder is most frequently 'perceptual' in nature, though 'premotor' impairments play a definite role. The deficit is most often 'egocentric', but patients may also show 'allocentric' impairments. The main neural correlates of the USN syndrome include damage to a fronto-parietal system: the inferior parietal lobule, the temporo-parietal junction, the ventral premotor cortex and, possibly, the more posterior portions of the superior temporal gyrus (see Fig. 11.4). Specific aspects of the USN syndrome may result from damage to specific parts of this network. The inferior parietal lobule is located dorsally with respect to the occipito-temporal 'ventral' stream, ventrally with respect to the occipito-superior parietal 'dorsal' stream. The inferior parietal lobule is a component of a posterior inferior parietal-ventral premotor frontal network, concerned with perceptual awareness in spatial reference frames, and the planning of goal-directed movements towards objects in space. Spatial perceptual awareness (i.e., detection and localization) is to be distinguished from the aware processes of object identification supported by the 'ventral' stream. The planning of directional goal-directed movements towards objects in space is to be distinguished both from the online control of movement supported by the 'dorsal stream' (see Rossetti et al., this volume), and from the more abstract action selection, supported by the 'ventral' stream (see Milner and Goodale, Chapter 10, this volume).

A complex patterns of interactions between the dorsal and the ventral regions in the posterior parietal and occipital cortices is likely to take place, as suggested, for instance, by a recent electrophysiological study on line bisection judgments in neurologically unimpaired participants (Waberski et al., 2008).

Acknowledgments

This work was supported in part by PRIN Grants 2005 and 2007, and by a FAR 2007 Grant to G.V.

We are grateful to Vittorio Gallese and Corrado Sinigaglia for their helpful comments and suggestions.

References

Adair, J.C., Na, D.L., Schwartz, R.L., and Heilman, K.M. (1998). Analysis of primary and secondary influences on spatial neglect. *Brain and Cognition*; **37**: 351–67.

Agliotti, S., Smania, N., and Peru, A. (1999). Frames of reference for mapping tactile stimuli in brain-damaged patients. *Journal of Cognitive Neuroscience*; **11**: 67–79.

Angelelli, P., De Luca, M., and Spinelli, D. (1996). Early visual processing in neglect patients: a study with steady-state VEPs. *Neuropsychologia*; **34**: 1151–7.

Arduino, L.S., Burani, C., and Vallar, G. (2002). Lexical effects in left neglect dyslexia: a study in italian patients. *Cognitive Neuropsychology*; **19**: 421–44.

—— (2003). Reading aloud and lexical decision in neglect dyslexia patients: a dissociation. *Neuropsychologia*; **41**: 877–85.

Baddeley, A.D. (1996). Exploring the central executive. *Quarterly Journal of Experimental Psychology*; **49A**: 5–28.

Baier, B. and Karnath, H.-O. (2008). Tight link between our sense of limb ownership and self-awareness of actions. *Stroke*; **39**: 486–8.

Bartolomeo, P. (2002). The traffic light paradigm: a reaction time task to study laterally directed arm movements. *Brain Research Brain Research Protocols*; **9**: 32–40.

Bartolomeo, P., D'Erme, P., Perri, R., and Gainotti, G. (1998). Perception and action in hemispatial neglect. *Neuropsychologia*; **36**: 227–37.

Bartolomeo, P., Chokron, S., and Gainotti, G. (2001). Laterally directed arm movements and right unilateral neglect after left hemisphere damage. *Neuropsychologia*; **39**: 1013–21.

Bartolomeo, P., Thiebaut De Schotten, M., and Doricchi, F. (2007). Left unilateral neglect as a disconnection syndrome. *Cerebral Cortex*; **17**: 2479–90.

Barton, J. J., Behrmann, M., and Black, S. (1998). Ocular search during line bisection. The effects of hemi-neglect and hemianopia. *Brain*; **121**: 1117–31.

Behrmann, M., Watt, S., Black, S.E., and Barton, J.J. (1997). Impaired visual search in patients with unilateral neglect: an oculographic analysis. *Neuropsychologia*; **35**: 1445–58.

Behrmann, M. and Meegan, D.V. (1998). Visuomotor processing in unilateral neglect. *Consciousness and Cognition*; **7**: 381–409.

Behrmann, M., Black, S.E., Mckeeff, T.J., and Barton, J.J. (2002). Oculographic analysis of word reading in hemispatial neglect. *Physiology & Behavior*; **77**: 613–19.

Berti, A. (2002). Unconscious processing in neglect. In *The cognitive and neural bases of spatial neglect*, (eds Karnath, H.-O., Milner, A.D., and Vallar, G.), pp. 313–26. Oxford: Oxford University Press.

Berti, A., Bottini, G., Gandola, M., Pia, L., Smania N., Stracciari A., et al. (2005). Shared cortical anatomy for motor awareness and motor control. *Science*; **309**: 488–91.

Binder, J., Marshall, R., Lazar, R., Benjamin, J., and Mohr, J.P. (1992). Distinct syndromes of hemineglect. *Archives of Neurology*; **49**: 1187–94.

Bird, C.M., Malhotra, P., Parton, A., Coulthard, E., Rushworth, M.F., and Husain, M. (2006). Visual neglect after right posterior cerebral artery infarction. *Journal of Neurology Neurosurgery and Psychiatry*; **77**: 1008–12.

Bisiach, E., Capitani, E., Colombo, A., and Spinnler, H. (1976). Halving a horizontal segment: a study on hemisphere-damaged patients with cerebral focal lesions. *Schweizer Archiv für Neurologie und Psychiatrie*; **118**: 199–206.

Bisiach, E., Berti, A., and Vallar, G. (1985). Analogical and logical disorders underlying unilateral neglect of space. In *Attention and performance*, (eds Posner, M.I. and Marin, O.S.M.), pp. 239–46. Hillsdale, New Jersey: Lawrence Erlbaum.

Bisiach, E. and Vallar, G. (1988). Hemineglect in humans. In *Handbook of neuropsychology*, (eds Boller, F. and Grafman, J.), pp. 195–222. Amsterdam: Elsevier.

Bisiach, E., Geminiani, G., Berti, A., and Rusconi, M.L. (1990). Perceptual and premotor factors of unilateral neglect. *Neurology*; **40**: 1278–81.

Bisiach, E., Tegnèr, R., Làdavas, E., Rusconi, M.L., Mijovic' D., and Hjaltason, H. (1995). Dissociation of ophthalmokinetic and melokinetic attention in unilateral neglect. *Cerebral Cortex*; **5**: 439–47.

Bisiach, E., Ricci, R., Lualdi, M., and Colombo, M.R. (1998a). Perceptual and response bias in unilateral neglect: two modified versions of the Milner landmark task. *Brain and Cognition*; **37**: 369–86.

Bisiach, E., Ricci, R., and Neppi Mòdona, M. (1998b). Visual awareness and anisometry of space representation in unilateral neglect: a panoramic investigation by means of a line extension task. *Consciousness and Cognition*; **7**: 327–55.

Bisiach, E. and Vallar, G. (2000). Unilateral neglect in humans. In *Handbook of neuropsychology*, (eds Boller, F., Grafman, J., and Rizzolatti, G.), 2nd edn, pp. 459–502. Amsterdam: Elsevier Science, B.V.

Boring, E.G. (1950). *A history of experimental psychology*. Englewood Cliffs, N.J.: Prentice-Hall.

Bottini, G., Sterzi, R., and Vallar, G. (1992). Directional hypokinesia in spatial hemineglect. *Journal of Neurology Neurosurgery and Psychiatry*; **55**: 431–6.

Bottini, G., Sterzi, R., Paulesu, E., Vallar, G., Cappa, S.F., Erminio, F., et al. (1994). Identification of the central vestibular projections in man: a positron emission tomography activation study. *Experimental Brain Research*; **99**: 164–9.

Bottini, G., Karnath, H.-O., Vallar, G., Sterzi, R., Frith, C.D., Frackowiak, R.S., and Paulesu, E. (2001). Cerebral representations for egocentric space: functional-anatomical evidence from caloric vestibular stimulation and neck vibration. *Brain*; **124**: 1182–96.

Bottini, G. and Toraldo, A. (2003). The influence of contralesional targets on the cancellation of ipsilesional targets in unilateral neglect. *Brain and Cognition*; **53**: 117–20.

Bottini, G., Paulesu, E., Gandola, M., Loffredo, S., Scarpa, P., Sterzi, R., et al. (2005). Left caloric vestibular stimulation ameliorates right hemianesthesia. *Neurology*; **65**: 1278–83.

Brighina, F., Bisiach, E., Piazza, A., Oliveri, M., La Bua, V., Daniele, O., et al. (2002). Perceptual and response bias in visuospatial neglect due to frontal and parietal repetitive transcranial magnetic stimulation in normal subjects. *NeuroReport*; **13**: 2571–5.

Castaigne, P., Laplane, D., and Degos, J.-D. (1970). Trois cas de négligence motrice par lésion rétro-rolandique. *Revue Neurologique*; **122**: 234–42.

—— (1972). Trois cas de négligence motrice par lésion frontale pré-rolandique. *Revue Neurologique*; **126**: 5–15.

Chedru, F., Leblanc, M., and Lhermitte, F. (1973). Visual searching in normal and brain-damaged subjects (contribution to the study of unilateral inattention). *Cortex*; **9**: 94–111.

Chiba, Y., Yamaguchi, A., and Eto, F. (2005). A simple method to dissociate sensory-attentional and motor-intentional biases in unilateral visual neglect. *Brain and Cognition*; **58**: 269–73.

Coello, Y., Danckert, J., Blangero, A., and Rossetti, Y. (2007). Do visual illusions probe the visual brain? Illusions in action without a dorsal visual stream. *Neuropsychologia;* **45**: 1849–58.

Committeri, G., Pitzalis, S., Galati, G., Patria, F., Pelle, G., Sabatini, U., et al. (2007). Neural bases of personal and extrapersonal neglect in humans. *Brain*; **130**: 431–41.

Coslett, H.B., Bowers, D., Fitzpatrick, E., Haws, B., and Heilman, K.M. (1990). Directional hypokinesia and hemispatial inattention in neglect. *Brain*; **113**: 475–86.

Coulthard, E., Parton, A., and Husain, M. (2006). Action control in visual neglect. *Neuropsychologia*; **44**: 2717–33.

—— (2007). The modular architecture of the neglect syndrome: implications for action control in visual neglect. *Neuropsychologia*; **45**: 1982–4.

Courtney, S., Ungerleider, L., Keil, K., and Haxby, J. (1996). Object and spatial visual working memory activate separate neural systems in human cortex. *Cerebral Cortex*; **6**: 39–49.

Critchley, M. (1953). *The parietal lobes.* New York: Hafner.

Daini, R., Angelelli, P., Antonucci, G., Cappa, S.F., and Vallar, G. (2002). Exploring the syndrome of spatial unilateral neglect through an illusion of length. *Experimental Brain Research*; **144**: 224–37.

Di Russo, F., Aprile, T., Spitoni, G., and Spinelli, D. (2008). Impaired visual processing of contralesional stimuli in neglect patients: a visual-evoked potential study. *Brain*; **131**: 842–54.

Dieterich, M. (2007). Functional brain imaging: a window into the visuo-vestibular systems. *Current Opinion in Neurology*; **20**: 12–18.

Doricchi, F. and Angelelli, P. (1999). Misrepresentation of horizontal space in left unilateral neglect. Role of hemianopia. *Neurology*; **52**: 1845–52.

Doricchi, F. and Tomaiuolo, F. (2003). The anatomy of neglect without hemianopia: a key role for parietal-frontal disconnection? *NeuroReport*; **14**: 2239–43.

Doricchi, F., Thiebaut De Schotten, M., Tomaiuolo, F., and Bartolomeo, P. (2008). White matter (dis)connections and gray matter (dys)functions in visual neglect: gaining insights into the brain networks of spatial awareness. *Cortex*; **44**: 983–895.

Ellis, A.W., Flude, B.M., and Young, A.W. (1987). 'Neglect dyslexia' and the early visual processing of letters in words and nonwords. *Cognitive Neuropsychology*; **4**: 439–64.

Ellison, A., Schindler, I., Pattison, L.L., and Milner, A.D. (2004). An exploration of the role of the superior temporal gyrus in visual search and spatial perception using TMS. *Brain*; **127**: 2307–15.

Farah, M. (2004). *Visual agnosia.* Cambridge, MA: MIT Press, Bradford Books.

Fierro, B., Brighina, F., Oliveri, M., Piazza, A., La Bua, V., Buffa, D., et al. (2000). Contralateral neglect induced by right posterior parietal rTMS in healthy subjects. *NeuroReport*; **11**: 1519–21.

Fierro, B., Brighina, F., Piazza, A., Oliveri, M., and Bisiach, E. (2001). Timing of right parietal and frontal cortex activity in visuo-spatial perception: a TMS study in normal individuals. *NeuroReport*; **12**: 2605–07.

Fink, G.R., Marshall, J.C., Halligan, P.W., Frith, C.D., Driver, J., Frackowiak, R.S.J., et al. (1999). The neural consequences of conflict between intention and the senses. *Brain*; **122**: 497–512.

Fink, G.R., Marshall, J.C., Shah, N.J., Weiss, P.H., Halligan, P.W., Grosse-Ruyken, M., et al. (2000). Line bisection judgments implicate right parietal cortex and cerebellum as assessed by fMRI. *Neurology*; **54**: 1324–31.

Fink, G.R., Marshall, J.C., Weiss, P.H., and Zilles, K. (2001). The neural basis of vertical and horizontal line bisection judgments: an fMRI study of normal volunteers. *NeuroImage*; **14**: S59–67.

Fink, G.R. and Marshall, J.C. (2005). Motor aspects of unilateral neglect and related disorders. In *Higher-order motor disorders*, (eds Freund, H.J., Jeannerod, M., Hallett, M., and Leiguarda, R.), pp. 413–41. Oxford: Oxford University Press.

Friedland, R.P. and Weinstein, E.A. (1977). Hemi-inattention and hemisphere specialization: introduction and historical review. In *Advances in Neurology. Volume 18. Hemi-inattention and hemisphere specialization*, (eds Weinstein, E.A. and Friedland, R.P.), pp. 1–31. New York: Raven Press.

Gainotti, G. (1996). Lateralization of brain mechanisms underlying automatic and controlled forms of spatial orienting of attention. *Neuroscience & Biobehavioral Reviews*; **20**: 617–22.

Galati, G., Lobel, E., Vallar, G., Berthoz, A., Pizzamiglio, L., and Le Bihan, D. (2000). The neural basis of egocentric and allocentric coding of space in humans: a functional magnetic resonance study. *Experimental Brain Research*; **133**: 156–64.

Gallace, A., Imbornone, E., and Vallar, G. (2008). When the whole is more than the sum of the parts. Evidence from visuospatial neglect. *Journal of Neuropsychology*; **2**: 387–413.

Gallese, V. (2007). The 'conscious' dorsal stream: embodied simulation and its role in space and action conscious awareness. *Psyche*; **13**: 1–20.

Ghacibeh, G.A., Shenker, J.I., Winter, K.H., Triggs, W.J., and Heilman, K.M. (2007). Dissociation of neglect subtypes with transcranial magnetic stimulation. *Neurology*; **69**: 1122–7.

Gibson, E.J. (1969). *Principles of perceptual learning and development.* New York: Appleton-Century-Crofts.

Girotti, F., Casazza, M., Musicco, M., and Avanzini, G. (1983). Oculomotor disorders in cortical lesions in man: the role of unilateral neglect. *Neuropsychologia*; **21**: 543–53.

Golay, L., Schnider, A., and Ptak, R. (2008). Cortical and subcortical anatomy of chronic spatial neglect following vascular damage. *Behavioral Brain Function*; **4**: 43.

Goodale, M.A. and Milner, A.D. (1992). Separate visual pathways for perception and action. *Trends in Neuroscience*; **15**: 20–5.

Goodale, M.A. (2008). Action without perception in human vision. *Cognitive Neuropsychology*; **25**: 891–919.

Halligan, P.W., and Marshall, J.C. (2002). Primary sensory deficits after right brain damage – an attentional disorder by any other name? In *The cognitive and neural bases of spatial neglect*, (eds Karnath, H.-O., Milner, A.D., and Vallar, G.), pp. 327–30. Oxford: Oxford University Press.

Halligan, P.W., Fink, G.R., Marshall, J.C., and Vallar, G. (2003). Spatial cognition: evidence from visual neglect. *Trends in Cognitive Sciences*; **7**: 125–33.

Hamilton, R.H., Coslett, H.B., Buxbaum, L.J., Whyte, J., and Ferraro, M.K. (2008). Inconsistency of performance on neglect subtype tests following acute right hemisphere stroke. *Journal of the International Neuropsychological Society*; **14**: 23–32.

Harvey, M., Milner, A.D., and Roberts, R.C. (1995a). An investigation of hemispatial neglect using the Landmark Task. *Brain & Cognition*; **27**: 59–78.

Harvey, M., Milner, A.D., and Roberts, R.C. (1995b). Differential effects of line length on bisection judgements in hemispatial neglect. *Cortex*; **31**: 711–22.

Harvey, M. and Milner, A.D. (1999). Residual perceptual distortion in 'recovered' hemispatial neglect. *Neuropsychologia*; **37**: 745–50.

Harvey, M., Kramer-Mccaffery, T., Dow, L., Murphy, P.J., and Gilchrist, I.D. (2002). Categorisation of 'perceptual' and 'premotor' neglect patients across different tasks: is there strong evidence for a dichotomy? *Neuropsychologia*; **40**: 1387–95.

Harvey, M., Gilchrist, I.D., Olk, B., and Muir, K. (2003). Eye-movement patterns do not mediate size distortion effects in hemispatial neglect: looking without seeing. *Neuropsychologia*; **41**: 1114–21.

Harvey, M. (2004). Perceptual and premotor neglect: is there an ideal task to categorise patients? *Cortex*; **40**: 323–8.

Harvey, M. and Olk, B. (2004). Comparison of the Milner and Bisiach Landmark Tasks: can neglect patients be classified consistently? *Cortex*; **40**: 659–65.

Haxby, J.V., Grady, C.L., Horwitz, B., Ungerleider, L.G., Mishkin, M., Carson, R.E., et al. (1991). Dissociation of object and spatial visual processing pathways in human extrastriate cortex. *Proceedings of the National Academy of Sciences, USA*; **88**: 1621–5.

Heilman, K.M. and Valenstein, E. (1979). Mechanisms underlying hemispatial neglect. *Annals of Neurology*; **5**: 166–70.

Heilman, K.M., Bowers, D., Coslett, H.B., Whelan, H., and Watson, R.T. (1985). Directional hypokinesia: prolonged reaction times for leftward movements in patients with right hemisphere lesions and neglect. *Neurology*; **35**: 855–9.

Heilman, K.M., Watson, R.T., and Valenstein, E. (2003). Neglect and related disorders. In *Clinical neuropsychology*, (eds Heilman, K.M. and Valenstein, E.), 4th edn, pp. 296–346. New York: Oxford University Press.

Heilman, K.M. (2004). Intentional neglect. *Frontiers in Bioscience*; **9**: 694–705.

Hillis, A.E., Newhart, M., Heidler, J., Barker, P.B., Herskovits, E.H., and Degaonkar, M. (2005). Anatomy of spatial attention: insights from perfusion imaging and hemispatial neglect in acute stroke. *Journal of Neuroscience*; **25**: 3161–7.

Himmelbach, M., Karnath, H.-O., and Perenin, M.T. (2007). Action control is not affected by spatial neglect: a comment on Coulthard et al. *Neuropsychologia*; **45**: 1979–81.

Husain, M., Mattingley, J.B., Rorden, C., Kennard, C., and Driver, J. (2000). Distinguishing sensory and motor biases in parietal and frontal neglect. *Brain*; **123**: 1643–59.

Husain, M. and Rorden, C. (2003). Non-spatially lateralized mechanisms in hemispatial neglect. *Nature Reviews Neuroscience*; **4**: 26–36.

Husain, M. and Nachev, P. (2007). Space and the parietal cortex. *Trends in Cognitive Sciences*; **11**: 30–6.

Husain, M. (2008). Hemispatial neglect. In *Handbook of clinical neurology*, (eds Goldenberg, G. and Miller, B.L.), pp. 359–72. Amsterdam: Elsevier, B.V.

Ishiai, S., Koyama, Y., Seki, K., and Nakayama, T. (1998). What is line bisection in USN? Analysis of perceptual and motor aspects in line bisection tasks. *Brain and Cognition*; **36**: 239–52.

Ishiai, S., Koyama, Y., Seki, K., and Izawa, M. (2000). Line versus representational bisections in unilateral spatial neglect. *Journal of Neurology, Neurosurgery, and Psychiatry*; **69**: 745–50.

Ishiai, S. (2006). What do eye-fixation patterns tell us about unilateral spatial neglect? *Restorative Neurology and Neuroscience*; **24**: 261–71.

Jewesbury, E.C.O. (1969). Parietal lobe syndromes. In *Handbook of clinical neurology*, (eds Vinken, P.J. and Bruyn, G.W.), pp. 680–99. Amsterdam: North Holland.

Karnath, H.-O. (2001). New insights into the functions of the superior temporal cortex. *Nature Reviews Neuroscience*; **2**: 568–76.

Karnath, H.-O., Dick, H., and Konczak, J. (1997). Kinematics of goal-directed arm movements in neglect: control of hand in space. *Neuropsychologia*; **35**: 435–44.

Karnath, H.-O., Ferber, S., and Himmelbach, M. (2001). Spatial awareness is a function of the temporal not the posterior parietal lobe. *Nature*; **411**: 950–3.

Karnath, H.-O. and Himmelbach, M. (2002). Strategies of lesion localization. Reply to Marshall, Fink, Halligan and Vallar. *Cortex*; **38**: 258–60.

Karnath, H.-O., Fruhmann Berger, M., and Küker, W. (2004). Using SPM normalization for lesion analysis in spatial neglect. *Brain*; **127**: E10.

Karnath, H.-O. and Perenin, M.T. (2005). Cortical control of visually guided reaching: evidence from patients with optic ataxia. *Cerebral Cortex*; **15**: 1561–9.

Karnath, H.-O., Baier, B., and Nagele, T. (2005). Awareness of the functioning of one's own limbs mediated by the insular cortex? *Journal of Neuroscience*; **25**: 7134–8.

Kerkhoff, G. (2003). Modulation and rehabilitation of spatial neglect by sensory stimulation. *Progress in Brain Research*; **142**: 257–71.

Kitadono, K. and Humphreys, G.W. (2009). Sustained interactions between perception and action in visual extinction and neglect: evidence from sequential pointing. *Neuropsychologia*; **47**: 1592–9.

Kleinman, J.T., Newhart, M., Davis, C., Heidler-Gary, J., Gottesman, R.F., and Hillis, A. E. (2007). Right hemispatial neglect: frequency and characterization following acute left hemisphere stroke. *Brain and Cognition*; **64**: 50–9.

Kooistra, C.A. and Heilman, K.M. (1989). Hemispatial visual inattention masquerading as hemianopia. *Neurology*; **39**: 1125–7.

Laplane, D. and Degos, J.D. (1983). Motor neglect. *Journal of Neurology Neurosurgery and Psychiatry*; **46**: 152–8.

Laplane, D. (1990). La négligence motrice: a-t-elle un rapport avec la négligence sensorielle unilatérale? *Revue Neurologique*; **146**: 635–8.

Leibovitch, F.S., Black, S.E., Caldwell, C.B., Ebert, P.L., Ehrlich, L.E., and Szalai, J.P. (1998). Brain-behavior correlations in hemispatial neglect using CT and SPECT: The Sunnybrook Stroke Study. *Neurology*; **50**: 901–08.

Leibovitch, F.S., Black, S.E., Caldwell, C.B., Mcintosh, A.R., Ehrlich, L.E., and Szalai, J. P. (1999). Brain SPECT imaging and left hemispatial neglect covaried using partial least squares: the Sunnybrook Stroke Study. *Human Brain Mapping*; **7**: 244–53.

Levine, D.N., Kaufman, K.J., and Mohr, J.P. (1978). Inaccurate reaching associated with a superior parietal lobe tumor. *Neurology*; **28**: 555–61.

Maravita, A., Mcneil, J., Malhotra, P., Greenwood, R., Husain. M., and Driver, J. (2003). Prism adaptation can improve contralesional tactile perception in neglect. *Neurology*; **60**: 1829–31.

Mark, V.W., Heilman, K.M., and Watson, R. (1996). Motor neglect: what do we mean? *Neurology*; **46**: 1492–3.

Marsh, E.B. and Hillis, A.E. (2008). Dissociation between egocentric and allocentric visuospatial and tactile neglect in acute stroke. *Cortex*; **44**: 1215–20.

Mattingley, J.B., Bradshaw, J.L., and Phillips, J.G. (1992). Impairments of movement initiation and execution in unilateral neglect. Directional hypokinesia and bradykinesia. *Brain*; **115**: 1849–74.

Mattingley, J.B., Bradshaw, J.L., Bradshaw, J.A., and Nettleton, N.C. (1994). Recovery from directional hypokinesia and bradykinesia in unilateral neglect. *Journal of Clinical and Experimental Neuropsychology*; **16**: 861–76.

Mattingley, J.B., Bradshaw, J.L., and Bradshaw, J.A. (1995). The effects of unilateral visuospatial neglect on perception of Müller-Lyer illusory figures. *Perception*; **24**: 415–33.

Mattingley, J.B., Husain, M., Rorden, C., Kennard, C., and Driver, J. (1998). Motor role of human inferior parietal lobe revealed in unilateral neglect patients. *Nature*; **392**: 179–82.

Mcglinchey-Berroth, R. (1997). Visual information processing in hemispatial neglect. *Trends in Cognitive Sciences*; **1**: 91–7.

Mesulam, M.-M. (2002). Functional anatomy of attention and neglect: from neurons to networks. In *The cognitive and neural bases of spatial neglect*, (eds Karnath, H.-O., Milner, A.D., and Vallar, G.), pp. 33–45. Oxford: Oxford University Press.

Milner, A.D., Harvey, M., Roberts, R.C., and Forster, S.V. (1993). Line bisection errors in visual neglect: misguided action or size distortion? *Neuropsychologia*; **31**: 39–49.

Milner, A.D. and Goodale, M.A. (1995). *The visual brain in action*. Oxford: Oxford University Press.

—— (2006). *The visual brain in action*. Oxford: Oxford University Press.

Moro, V., Zampini, M., and Aglioti, S.M. (2004). Changes in spatial position of hands modify tactile extinction but not disownership of contralesional hand in two right brain-damaged patients. *Neurocase*; **10**: 437–43.

Mort, D. J., Malhotra, P., Mannan, S.K., Rorden, C., Pambakian, A., Kennard, C., et al. (2003). The anatomy of visual neglect. *Brain*; **126**: 1986–97.

Mort, D.J., Malhotra, P., Mannan, S.K., Pambakian, A., Kennard, C., and Husain, M. (2004). Using SPM normalization for lesion analysis in spatial neglect. **127**, E11.

Moscovitch, M. and Behrmann, M. (1994). Coding of spatial information in the somatosensory system: evidence from patients with neglect following parietal lobe damage. *Journal of Cognitive Neuroscience*; **6**: 151–5.

Muggleton, N.G., Postma, P., Moutsopoulou, K., Nimmo-Smith, I., Marcel, A., and Walsh, V. (2006). TMS over right posterior parietal cortex induces neglect in a scene-based frame of reference. *Neuropsychologia*; **44**: 1222–9.

Na, D.L., Adair, J.C., Williamson, D.J., Schwartz, R.L., Haws, B., and Heilman, K.M. (1998). Dissociation of sensory-attentional from motor-intentional neglect. *Journal of Neurology Neurosurgery and Psychiatry*; **64**: 331–8.

Na, D.L., Adair, J.C., Kang, Y., Chung, C.S., Lee, K.H., and Heilman, K.M. (1999). Motor perseverative behavior on a line cancellation task. *Neurology*; **52**: 1569–76.

Nadeau, S.E. and Heilman, K.M. (1991). Gaze-dependent hemianopia without hemispatial neglect. *Neurology*; **41**: 1244–50.

Newcombe, F., Ratcliff, G., and Damasio, H. (1987). Dissociable visual and spatial impairments following right posterior cerebral lesions: clinical, neuropsychological and anatomical evidence. *Neuropsychologia*; **25**: 149–61.

Nico, D. (1996). Detecting directional hypokinesia: the epidiascope technique. *Neuropsychologia*; **34**: 471–4.

Nys, G.M., Van Zandvoort, M.J., Van Der Worp, H.B., Kappelle, L.J., and De Haan, E. H.F. (2006). Neuropsychological and neuroanatomical correlates of perseverative responses in subacute stroke. *Brain*; **129**: 2148–57.

Olk, B., Harvey, M., Dow, L., and Murphy, P.J.S. (2001). Illusion processing in hemispatial neglect. *Neuropsychologia*; **39**: 611–25.

Ota, H., Fujii, T., Suzuki, K., Fukatsu, R., and Yamadori, A. (2001). Dissociation of body-centered and stimulus-centered representations in unilateral neglect. *Neurology*; **57**: 2064–9.

Perenin, M.T. (1997). Optic ataxia and unilateral neglect: clinical evidence for dissociable spatial functions in posterior parietal cortex. In *Parietal lobe contributions to orientation in 3D space*, (eds Thier, P. and Karnath, H.-O.), pp. 289–308. Heidelberg: Springer-Verlag.

Perenin, M.T. and Vighetto, A. (1988). Optic ataxia: a specific disruption in visuomotor mechanisms. I. Different aspects of the deficit in reaching for objects. *Brain*; **111**: 643–74.

Pia, L., Neppi-Modona, M., Ricci, R., and Berti, A. (2004). The anatomy of anosognosia for hemiplegia: a meta-analysis. *Cortex*; **40**: 367–77.

Ratcliff, G. and Davies-Jones, G.A.B. (1972). Defective visual localization in focal brain wounds. *Brain*; **95**: 49–60.

Ricci, R., Pia, L., and Gindri, P. (2004). Effects of illusory spatial anisometry in unilateral neglect. *Experimental Brain Research*; **154**: 226–37.

Riddoch, M.J. and Humphreys, G.W. (1983). The effect of cueing on unilateral neglect. *Neuropsychologia*; **21**: 589–99.

Rizzolatti, G., Fadiga, L., Fogassi, L., and Gallese, V. (1997). The space around us. *Science*; **277**: 190–1.

Rizzolatti, G. and Matelli, M. (2003). Two different streams form the dorsal visual system: anatomy and functions. *Experimental Brain Research*; **153**: 146–57.

Rizzolatti, G., Sinigaglia, C., and Anderson, F. (2007). *Mirrors in the brain. How our minds share actions, emotions, and experience.* Oxford: Oxford University Press.

Ro, T. and Rafal, R.D. (1996). Perception of geometric illusions in hemispatial neglect. *Neuropsychologia*; **34**: 973–8.

Roche, R.A.P. and Commins, S. (2009). Cognition beyond perception: higher processing despite spatial neglect. Discussion of: Vallar, G., Daini, R. & Antonucci, G. (2000). Processing of illusion of length in spatial hemineglect: a study of line bisection. Neuropsychologia; 38(7): 1087–97, in R. A. P. Roche and S. Commins (Eds.) *Pioneering studies in cognitive neuroscience;* pp. 46–65. New York, McGraw-Hill: Open University Press.

Rode, G., Charles, N., Perenin, M.T., Vighetto, A., Trillet, M., and Aimard, G. (1992). Partial remission of hemiplegia and somatoparaphrenia through vestibular stimulation in a case of unilateral neglect. *Cortex*; **28**: 203–08.

Ronchi, R., Posteraro, L., Fortis, P., Bricolo, E., and Vallar, G. (2009). Perseveration in left spatial neglect; drawing and cancellation tasks. *Cortex*; **45**: 300–12.

Rorden, C., Fruhmann Berger, M., and Karnath, H.-O. (2006). Disturbed line bisection is associated with posterior brain lesions. *Brain Research*; **1080**: 17–25.

Rossetti, Y. and Rode, G. (2002). Reducing spatial neglect by visual and other sensory manipulations: non-cognitive (physiological) routes to the rehabilitation of a cognitive disorder. In *The cognitive and neural bases of spatial neglect*, (eds Karnath, H.-O., Milner, A.D. and Vallar, G.), pp. 375–96. Oxford: Oxford University Press.

Rossit, S., Malhotra, P., Muir, K., Reeves, I., Duncan, G., Livingstone, K., et al. (2009). No neglect-specific deficits in reaching tasks. *Cerebral Cortex*; **19**: 2616–24.

Rozzi, S., Calzavara, R., Belmalih, A., Borra, E., Gregoriou, G.G., Matelli, M., et al. (2006). Cortical connections of the inferior parietal cortical convexity of the macaque monkey. *Cerebral Cortex*; **16**: 1389–417.

Rusconi, M.L., Maravita, A., Bottini, G., and Vallar, G. (2002). Is the intact side really intact? Perseverative responses in patients with unilateral neglect: a productive manifestation. *Neuropsychologia*; **40**: 594–604.

Rushworth, M.F., Johansen-Berg, H., Göbel, S.M., and Devlin, J.T. (2003). The left parietal and premotor cortices: motor attention and selection. *NeuroImage*; **20** Suppl. 1: S89–100.

Sapir, A., Kaplan, J.B., He, B.J., and Corbetta, M. (2007). Anatomical correlates of directional hypokinesia in patients with hemispatial neglect. *Journal of Neuroscience*; **27**: 4045–51.

Savazzi, S., Posteraro, L., Veronesi, G., and Mancini, F. (2007). Rightward and leftward bisection biases in spatial neglect: two sides of the same coin? *Brain*; **130**: 2070–84.

Schenkenberg, T., Bradford, D.C., and Ajax, E.T. (1980). Line bisection and unilateral visual neglect in patients with neurologic impairment. *Neurology*; **30**: 509–17.

Schindler, I., Ellison, A., and Milner, A.D. (2008). Contralateral visual search deficits following TMS. *Journal of Neuropsychology*; **2**: 501–08.

Schluter, N.D., Krams, M., Rushworth, M.F., and Passingham, R.E. (2001). Cerebral dominance for action in the human brain: the selection of actions. *Neuropsychologia*; **39**: 105–13.

Shimodozono, M., Matsumoto, S., Miyata, R., Etoh, S., Tsujio, S., and Kawahira, K. (2006). Perceptual, premotor and motor factors in the performance of a delayed-reaching task by subjects with unilateral spatial neglect. *Neuropsychologia*; **44**: 1752–64.

Shulman, M.B., Alexander, M.P., Mcglinchey-Berroth, R., and Milberg, W. (2002). Triangular backgrounds shift the bias of line bisection performance in hemispatial neglect. *Journal of Neurology Neurosurgery and Psychiatry*; **72**: 68–72.

Smania, N. and Aglioti, S. (1995). Sensory and spatial components of somaesthetic deficits following right brain damage. *Neurology*; **45**: 1725–30.

Stenneken, P., Van Eimeren, L., Keller I., Jacobs, A.M., and Kerkhoff, G. (2008). Task-dependent modulation of neglect dyslexia? Novel evidence from the viewing position effect. *Brain Research*; **1189**: 166–78.

Sterzi, R., Bottini, G., Celani, M.G., Righetti, E., Lamassa, M., Ricci, S., et al. (1993). Hemianopia, hemianaesthesia, and hemiplegia after left and right hemisphere damage: a hemispheric difference. *Journal of Neurology Neurosurgery and Psychiatry*; **56**: 308–10.

Tegnér, R. and Levander, M. (1991). Through a looking glass. A new technique to demonstrate directional hypokinesia in unilateral neglect. *Brain*; **114**: 1943–51.

Thiebaut De Schotten, M., Urbanski, M., Duffau, H., Volle, E., Levy R., Dubois B., et al. (2005). Direct evidence for a parietal-frontal pathway subserving spatial awareness in humans. *Science*; **309**: 2226–8.

Triggs, W.J., Gold, M., Gerstle, G., Adair, J., and Heilman, K.M. (1994). Motor neglect associated with a discrete parietal lesion. *Neurology*; **44**: 1164–6.

Umiltà, C. (1988). Orienting of attention. In *Handbook of neuropsychology*, (eds Boller, F. and Grafman, J.), pp. 175–93. Amsterdam: Elsevier Science.

—— (2001). Mechanisms of attention. In *The handbook of cognitive neuropsychology*, (ed. Rapp, B.), pp. 135–58. Philadelphia: Psychology Press.

Ungerleider, L.G. and Mishkin, M. (1982). Two cortical visual systems. In *Analysis of visual behavior*, (eds Ingle D.J., Goodale, M.A. and Mansfield, R.J.W.), pp. 549–86. Cambridge, MA: MIT Press.

Urbanski, M., Thiebaut De Schotten, M., Rodrigo, S., Catani, M., Oppenheim, C., Touzé, E., et al. (2008). Brain networks of spatial awareness: evidence from diffusion tensor imaging tractography. *Journal of Neurology Neurosurgery and Psychiatry*; **79**: 598–601.

Valenza, N., Seghier, M.L., Schwartz, S., Lazeyras, F., and Vuilleumier, P. (2004). Tactile awareness and limb position in neglect: functional magnetic resonance imaging. *Annals of Neurology*; **55**: 139–43.

Vallar, G. and Perani, D. (1986). The anatomy of unilateral neglect after right hemisphere stroke lesions. A clinical CT/Scan correlation study in man. *Neuropsychologia*; **24**: 609–22.

Vallar, G., Sterzi, R., Bottini, G., Cappa, S., and Rusconi, M.L. (1990). Temporary remission of left hemianaesthesia after vestibular stimulation. *Cortex*; **26**: 123–31.

Vallar, G., Bottini, G., Sterzi, R., Passerini, D., and Rusconi, M.L. (1991a). Hemianesthesia, sensory neglect and defective access to conscious experience. *Neurology*; **41**: 650–2.

Vallar, G., Sandroni, P., Rusconi, M.L., and Barbieri, S. (1991b). Hemianopia, hemianesthesia and spatial neglect. A study with evoked potentials. *Neurology*; **41**: 1918–22.

Vallar, G., Guariglia, C., Magnotti, L., and Pizzamiglio, L. (1995). Optokinetic stimulation affects both vertical and horizontal deficits of position sense in unilateral neglect. *Cortex*; **31**: 669–83.

Vallar, G., Rusconi, M.L., and Bernardini, B. (1996). Modulation of neglect hemianesthesia by transcutaneous electrical stimulation. *Journal of the International Neuropsychological Society*; **2**: 452–9.

Vallar, G., Guariglia, C., Nico, D., and Pizzamiglio, L. (1997a). Motor deficits and optokinetic stimulation in patients with left hemineglect. *Neurology*; **49**: 1364–70.

Vallar, G., Guariglia, C., and Rusconi, M. L. (1997b). Modulation of the neglect syndrome by sensory stimulation. In *Parietal lobe contributions to orientation in 3D space*, (eds Thier, P. and Karnath, H.-O.), pp. 555–78. Heidelberg: Springer-Verlag.

Vallar, G. (1998). Spatial hemineglect in humans. *Trends in Cognitive Sciences*; **2**: 87–97.

—— (1999). Spatial frames of reference and somatosensory processing: A neuropsychological perspective. In *The hippocampal and parietal foundations of spatial cognition*, (eds Burgess, N., Jeffery, K.J. and O'Keefe, J.), pp. 33–49. Oxford: Oxford University Press.

Vallar, G., Lobel, E., Galati, G., Berthoz, A., Pizzamiglio, L., and Le Bihan, D. (1999). A fronto-parietal system for computing the egocentric spatial frame of reference in humans. *Experimental Brain Research*; **124**: 281–6.

Vallar, G., Antonucci, G., Guariglia, C., and Pizzamiglio, L. (1993a). Deficits of position sense, unilateral neglect, and optokinetic stimulation. *Neuropsychologia*; **31**: 1191–200.

Vallar, G., Bottini, G., Rusconi, M.L., and Sterzi, R. (1993b). Exploring somatosensory hemineglect by vestibular stimulation. *Brain*; **116**: 71–86.

Vallar, G. (2000). The methodological foundations of human neuropsychology: studies in brain-damaged patients. In *Handbook of neuropsychology*, (eds Boller, F., Grafman, J., and Rizzolatti, G.), 2nd edn, pp. 305–44. Amsterdam: Elsevier.

Vallar, G., Daini, R., and Antonucci, G. (2000). Processing of illusion of length in spatial hemineglect. A study of line bisection. *Neuropsychologia*; **38**: 1087–97.

Vallar, G. (2001). Extrapersonal visual unilateral spatial neglect and its neuroanatomy. *NeuroImage*; **14**: S52–S58.

Vallar, G. and Daini, R. (2002). Illusions in neglect, illusions of neglect. In *The cognitive and neural bases of spatial neglect*, (eds Karnath, H.-O., Milner, A.D., and Vallar, G.), pp. 209–24. Oxford: Oxford University Press.

Vallar, G., Bottini, G., and Sterzi, R. (2003). Anosognosia for left-sided motor and sensory deficits, motor neglect, and sensory hemiinattention: is there a relationship? *Progress in Brain Research*; **142**: 289–301.

Vallar, G. and Daini, R. (2006). Visual perceptual processing in unilateral spatial neglect. The case of visual illusions. In *Imagery and spatial cognition: Methods, models and cognitive assessment*, (eds Vecchi, T. and Bottini, G.), pp. 337–62. Amsterdam, the Netherlands, and Philadelphia, USA: John Benjamins Publishers.

Vallar, G. (2008). Subcortical neglect. In *Neuropsychological research. A review*, (eds Märien, P. and Abutalebi, J.), pp. 307–30. Hove: Psychology Press.

Vallar, G. and Maravita, A. (2009). Personal and extra-personal spatial perception. In *Handbook of neuroscience for the behavioral sciences*, (eds Berntson, G.G. and Cacioppo, J.T.), pp. 322–36. New York: John Wiley & Sons.

Vallar, G. and Ronchi, R. (2009). Somatoparaphrenia: a body delusion. A review of the neuropsychological literature. *Experimental Brain Research*; **192**: 533–51.

Waberski, T.D., Gobbelé, R., Lamberty, K., Buchner, H., Marshall, J.C., and Fink, G.R. (2008). Timing of visuo-spatial information processing: electrical source imaging related to line bisection judgements. *Neuropsychologia*; **46**: 1201–10.

Walker, R. (1995). Spatial and object-based neglect. *Neurocase*; **1**: 371–83.

Watson, R.T., Miller, B.D., and Heilman, K.M. (1978). Nonsensory neglect. *Annals of Neurology*; **3**: 505–08.

Weidner, R. and Fink, G.R. (2007). The neural mechanisms underlying the Müller-Lyer illusion and its interaction with visuospatial judgments. *Cerebral Cortex*; **17**: 878–84.

Young, A.W., De Haan, E.H.F., Newcombe, F., and Day, D.C. (1990). Facial neglect. *Neuropsychologia*; **28**: 391–415.

Young, A.W., Hellawell, D.J., and Welch, J. (1992). Neglect and visual recognition. *Brain*; **115**: 51–71.

CHAPTER 12

Motor representations and the perception of space: perceptual judgments of the boundary of action space

Yvonne Delevoye-Turrell, Angela Bartolo, and Yonn Coello

Abstract

We present current knowledge about how the perceptual space is organized in relation to body and action representations. In particular, we will focus on the understanding of how the brain distinguishes between peripersonal and extrapersonal space. Action representations can be viewed as a component of a predictive system, which includes a neural process that simulates (through motor imagery) the dynamic behaviour of the body in relation to its environment. The function of the predictive system is to prepare the motor system for the consequences of motor execution, but also to provide the self with information on the feasibility of deployable actions. The distinction between actions that are feasible or unfeasible is, furthermore, assumed to represent the underlying principle for distinguishing peripersonal from extrapersonal spaces. Empirical data will be presented that demonstrate that (1) modifying the predicted outcome of motor acts, or (2) inhibiting motor brain areas using transcranial magnetic stimulation interferes with the perceptual judgments of what is reachable. We will also consider the case of mental pathology, with the report of data that suggest that patients with schizophrenia reveal poor ability in the use of motor representations for the delimitation of action space. Finally, we examine the functional association between motor representations, spatial cognition and the development of social interactive skills.

> Man senses distance as other animals do. His perception of space is dynamic because it is related to action—what can be done in a given space—rather than what is seen by passive viewing.
>
> Hall, E.T., 'The hidden dimension', 1966, p. 115.

12.1. Introduction

How we perceive our spatial environment in relation to our body and motor system is a topic of fundamental importance and a widely debated theoretical issue. Since Berkeley's famous essay on vision, theorists of perception have defended the idea that the experience of spatiality proceeds from an interpretation of sensory information through reference to the possibilities of action (Berkeley, 1709[1985]). A similar perspective has been defended repeatedly afterwards, by psychologists like Gibson (1979), mathematicians like Poincaré (1907), and philosophers like Bergson (1896), Husserl (1907), or Merleau-Ponty (1945). According to the latter, locations within space are not to be defined as objective positions in relation to the objective position of our body; rather they inscribe around us the variety of reaches that our limbs can produce. Space is thus not uniform but depends on our past experiences about opportunities, effects and costs of acting in a given environment, with our own body parts (Previc, 1998; Proffitt, 2006b). Nevertheless, it is not sufficient to consider perception in the context of an environment-body interacting system (Merleau-Ponty, 1945). It is also necessary to consider that possibilities of action may subtend the process of constitution of the perceived external environment. Indeed, in a social context, it seems necessary to define those spatial areas that surround our body according to the specific possibilities of functional interactions with objects and/or individuals within these areas. A near body area, for example, must be specified so as to protect our body from impending collision when moving through a crowd. The boundary of peripersonal space may also help to determine, in an implicit and natural way, the distance of comfort to set during a one-to-one conversation.

Therefore, because of the deterministic body disposition for movement, interactions with the external world must depend on our ability to discriminate objects and individuals that can be easily reached from those that are out of reach (Coello and Delevoye-Turrell, 2007). It is thus probable that the brain constructs these spaces specifically in relation to action (Previc, 1998). In this chapter, we will investigate primarily the functional distinction between peripersonal and extrapersonal space. We will define peripersonal space as the subjective area in which interactions with objects can occur at the present moment. By contrast, extrapersonal space will be defined as the subjective areas in which interactions with objects can occur only in the future, following a displacement of the body, i.e., after a translation of the area in which the objects are beyond the sphere of influence. This distinction is crucial not only for the regulation of interactions with nearby objects, but also for our social life, since social distance depends on the type of expected relationship that will be set with conspecifics (Hall, 1966). As such, the perceptually delimitation of peripersonal space will require the combination of optically specified geometry of visual scenes and objects, with current behavioural goals and the potential to achieve this goal. Consequently, the general aim of this chapter will be to defend the idea that the capacity to differentiate peripersonal from extrapersonal spaces depends essentially on our ability to anticipate the sensory and spatial consequences of deployable actions. These spaces exist only by virtue of this potentiality. Indeed, an object can be reached only if our arm is long enough to touch or grasp it. Thus, separation between reachable and non-reachable objects depends on our ability to anticipate the effort and consequences associated with actions towards those objects, and this renders possible the distinction between peripersonal and extrapersonal spaces.

In what follows, we will first present the current knowledge about how the perceptual space is organized in relation to body and action representations. We will then present a neuro-cognitive model that accounts for the dynamical properties of spatial perception, which is thought to rely on the brain's capacity to anticipate the sensory and spatial consequences of deployable actions. Recent data obtained in healthy controls will be presented that show how the manipulation of motor representations and more specifically the predicted outcome of motor action can perturb the subjects' capacity to delimitate functional spaces significantly. We will also report a study demonstrating that transient inhibition of the motor brain area using transcranial magnetic stimulation interferes with the perceptual judgments of what is reachable. Finally, in the final section, we will consider the case of mental pathology. More precisely, data will be presented that reveal problems of delimitating peripersonal space in a group of patients with schizophrenia, which suggests poor ability in using motor representations. A closing discussion will argue over possible functional associations between the creation of motor representations, the delimitation of peripersonal space, and the development of social interactive skills.

12.2. **The specification of functional spaces**

Living organisms must define the areas in which they feel secure, can easily find food, and may meet conspecifics. Necessarily, these areas are specified or perceived as a function of the capacity for the organism to move through space. Those organisms that can move with a high velocity may use a larger area for exploratory behaviour and may accept closer proximity with other organisms especially those characterized by lower displacement capacities. Thus, spatial perception and social interactions might be closely related to the capacity of action of every living organism. In the following section, we will present data from ethology studies that confirm the existence of functional spaces in animals.

12.2.1. **The origin of the concept**

The issue of spatial perception based on interaction between sensory processing and motor representation was investigated originally in ethology through the concept of flight initiation distance in animals. Based on the pioneering work by Hediger (1934), on biological social distance in animals, an optimal flight initiation distance is thought to exist in all species, which represents the distance at which the animal will initiate flight in presence of an objective threat. Hediger had, in fact, distinguished between flight initiation distance, critical distance (attack boundary), personal distance (distance separating members of non-contact species), and social distance (intraspecies communication distance). Considering that one of the basic function of the motor system in all animals is to protect the body from unwanted attack (Graziano and Cooke, 2006), the optimal escape theory (Ydenberg and Dill, 1986) predicts that an animal should begin to escape from an approaching intruder when the latter reaches a point at which the risk of being reached equals the behavioural cost of escape. This aptitude emphasizes the capacity in every animal to evaluate spatial distances according to its own motor capacities and the probability to be considered as a prey. As a consequence, flight initiation distance increases when intruders pose a greater threat and decreases when escape costs increase (Cooper et al. 2003). Flight initiation distance increases with magnitude of risk for several risk factors, including the dangerousness of the intruder (McLean and Godin, 1989; Walther, 1969), approach speed (Cooper, 1997b), directness of approach (Bulova, 1994; Burger and Gochfeld, 1990; Cooper, 1997a, 1998), location of the refuge (Bulova, 1994; Bonenfant and Kramer, 1996; Kramer and Bonenfant, 1997; Dill, 1990), availability of cover (Grant and Noakes, 1987; LaGory, 1987), and lowered body temperature that results in lower escape speed (Rand, 1964; Smith, 1997). Furthermore, flight initiation distance is shorter when food is present, when males are guarding or courting females, and when rival males are present (Cooper, 1999; Martín and Lopéz, 1999). Interestingly, animal body size is the most often cited factor accounting for interspecific behaviour. Larger species had greater flight initiation distances than smaller species (Blumstein et al. 2005). If large-bodied species are less agile than smaller bodied species (Marden, 1987; Witter et al., 1994), they should benefit from early response and flight to escape. Large species are predicted to have greater detection distances, greater flight initiation distances, and to move further following disturbance. Taken as a whole, these factors underline clearly the necessity to understand flight behaviour according to a coupling between spatial information and behavioural capacities.

The idea that spatial boundaries depend on social context and motor capacities was later extended to human social behaviour (Hall, 1966). Considering the latter, human beings belong to the family of non-contact[1] animal but need nevertheless to stay in touch with each other. A psychological

---

[1] According to Hall (1966, p. 13), contact animals are those species that huddle together and require physical contact with each other (e.g. the pig, the brown bat, the parakeet …). Horses, dogs and humans are considered non-contact species.

distance for social interactions needs thus to be specified. Many researchers noted that humans possess an invisible bubble of protective space surrounding the body, generally larger around the head, extending farthest in the direction of sight (e.g. Dosey and Meisels, 1969; Hall, 1966; Horowitz, Duff, and Stratton, 1964; Sommer, 1959). When that personal space is violated, the person steps away to reinstate the margin of safety. Personal space, therefore, is the flight zone of a human with respect to conspecifics. The size of the personal space varies depending on context. Indeed, a person who is placed in a potentially threatening context will have an expanded personal space; a person in friendly company will have a reduced personal space (Dosey and Meisels, 1969; Felipe and Sommer, 1966). Hall has described four different spaces: an intimate space (up to 0.5 m, a distance allowing physical contact with others), a personal space (up to 1.20 m, a distance allowing inter-individual communication in a non-contact situation and constituting also a protective space), a social distance (up to 4 m, a distance allowing communication with non-familiar individuals), and a public distance (further that 4 m, a distance for considering communication with groups or maintaining people out of our sphere of interest). Beyond the psychological organization of space in a social context (the proxemics perspective), individuals must also spatially structure their perceptual environment according to their own potentiality of action within a given environment.

12.2.2. Near body space, peripersonal space, extrapersonal space

At the individual level, different functional egocentric spaces need to be considered depending on the type of physical interaction expected with the external world. To protect the organism from the unwanted experience of contact with moving or stationary objects, a *near body space* is to be represented in order to constitute a safety zone for protecting the body surfaces from impending impacts (Graziano and Cooke, 2006; Makin et al. 2008). This safety area is multimodal since the same brain activations have been revealed in the presence of visual or auditory stimuli close to a body segment or a tactile stimulus delivered on it (Rizzolatti et al. 1981; Graziano and Gross, 1995). These multisensory neurons were found in monkeys studies in the premotor cortex (Rizzolatti et al., 1981), the intra-partietal sulcus (Avillac et al., 2007; Bremmer et al., 2001; Duhamel et al., 1998; Schlack et al., 2005), the parietal lobe (Duhamel et al., 1997; Graziano and Gross, 1995; Robinson and Burton, 1980), the putamen (Graziano and Gross, 1993), and the somatosensory cortex (Iriki et al., 1996; Obayashi et al., 2002) and they show spatial correspondence between their visual, auditory, and tactile receptive fields. As a consequence, these neurons respond in a non-linear way to the combined presentation of stimuli within the receptive field. These results are evidence for a multisensory integration and probably, for a binding mechanism that provides the means to integrate different sensory events within a unique and structured percept (Avillac et al., 2005; Makin et al., 2008).

In humans, the concept of a near-body space has been studied mainly in the context of multimodal sensory attention (di Pellegrino et al., 1997; Halligan and Marshall, 1991; Ladavas et al., 1998, 2001; Pavani and Castiello, 2004; Spence et al., 2000). It was shown, for instance, that stimulating the skin on the hand leads frequently to increased attention towards the stimulated site. However, stimulating the hand not only enhances attention to the location of the stimulation, but also speeds the processing of a visual stimulus presented at the vicinity of the stimulated area (Spence et al. 2000). The inverse effect was observed when a visual stimulus was presented near the cheek; it enhanced the processing of tactile stimuli in the same area (Ladavas et al. 1998). Thus, there is a spatial boundary that extends out from the body to a limit of up to ten centimetres (Colby et al. 1993). This multimodal perception of tactile and near-body stimuli may represent a shell of multimodal attentional space (Graziano and Cooke, 2006) and has revealed interesting consequences in pathology. Patients suffering from spatial neglect resulting from damage in the right hemisphere generally show biased spatial perception in the contralesional hemifield. Under certain conditions, these patients show signs of extinction, which is a syndrome characterized by the systematic unsuccessful detection of a contralesional stimulus in the presence of a concurrent stimulus presented within the hemifield ipsilateral to the lesion. Multisensory integration deficits were demonstrated by showing that extinction of a tactile stimulus applied on the contralesional side hand can be obtained by the simultaneous presentation of a visual stimulus close to the lesional side hand (di Pellegrino et al., 1997; Ladavas et al., 1998; Mattingley et al., 1997). This phenomenon of cross-modal extinction was found to be specific for near-body space, in particular peri-hand space (Farné et al., 2005). Interestingly, this observation has stimulated studies on cross-modal perception in neurologically intact subjects. Using a cross-modal congruency task, Walton and Spence (2004) showed, for instance, that the discrimination of the location of a visual target placed on the index finger or the thumb was influenced by the simultaneously vibrotactile stimulation presented on either finger. Participants responded more slowly on this visual-discrimination task when the vibrotactile distracters were incongruent with the location of the visual targets.

Beyond the near-body safety space, a *peripersonal space* can be described as an area representing the space surrounding our body and for which objects can be reached and manipulated easily. Beyond peripersonal space extends extrapersonal space in which objects cannot be reached adequately without moving towards them, and both of these spaces are thought to involve specific brain processing areas (Previc, 1998). Brain (1941) was the first to provide clinical evidence for a dissociation of near and far space. He described a case of right hemisphere glioblastoma: the patient was impaired in pointing to objects in near space without comparable difficulty for objects in far space. The opposite pattern of results was described later (Cowey et al., 1994; Halligan and Marshal, 1991). According to Brain (1941), 'although external space is finally presented to consciousness as one, estimation of "grasping distance" depends in a similar way on the association paths between the visual cortex and the hand-arm area'. This was probably the first neuropsychological report that considered motor representation as being part of the visual function. Other clinical investigations have emphasized the brain structures subtending the perception of near and far space. In this regard, studies on radial line bisection have shown that bilateral temporo-occipital lesions can be associated with a significant mis-bisection towards the body, interpreted as neglect of far space (Shelton et al., 1990). By contrast, lesions of bilateral parieto-occipital cortex have been associated with a significant mis-bisection away from the body, interpreted as neglect of near space (Mennemeier et al., 1992). In a different context, Bjoertomt et al. (2002) also probed the prevalence of the ventral and dorsal visual streams in processing near and far space using a horizontal line bisection task. The participants' task was to indicate whether the part of the line to the left or right of the transection appeared longer, while submitted to repetitive transcranial magnetic stimulation. Results showed that the magnetic stimulation of the right posterior parietal cortex and the right ventral occipital lobe selectively induced a significant shift to the right in the perceived midpoint for near- and far-space lines, respectively. According to the authors, this dissociation supports the hypothesis of a dorsal/near space-ventral/far space segregation of processing within the visual system (Milner and Goodale, 1995). From these observations, peripersonal space was then considered as the area within arm's reach (Berti et al., 2002; Coello and Delevoye-Turrell, 2007; Halligan et al., 2003; Milner and Goodale, 1995; Rizzolatti et al., 1983; Weiss et al., 2003). However, how the transition from near to far space is specified within the brain remains an open issue. It is worth noting that the transition between near and far space might be gradual, with no abrupt shift at arm's length (Longo and Lourenco, 2006), and may also not be rigid with the possibility to transiently extend near space through the use of tools (Berti and Rizzolatti, 2002; Iriki et al., 1996; Witt et al., 2005). However, whatever these qualitative accounts, this does not provide any assumption about the mechanism subserving the transition and how it can be implemented at the neural level.

Interestingly, opportunities for reaching objects seem detectable very early in children. From the onset of development, reaching behaviour appears to be determined by the appreciation of a critical distance at which objects are reachable (Clifton et al., 1991; Field, 1976; Yonas and Hartman, 1993). For instance, Rochat and his colleagues presented four- to seven-month-old children with an object presented at either within reach, at the limit of reachability, or outside the boundary of prehensile space (Rochat and Wraga, 1997). They found a marked decrease in the frequency of reach attempts for the object when it was placed near the boundary of their reachable space or out of reach. Interestingly, infants appear to calibrate their attempts to reach relative to their ability to sit independently or to lean forward with their trunk (Rochat and Goubet, 1995; Yonas and Hartman, 1993).

In the same way, children aged three years or more were found to scale their perception of what is reachable for themselves and for others (Rochat, 1995). When asked to judge what is reachable by an adult, they systematically attributed more reachability to the adult than to themselves. They show the same ability when required to make the judgement according to an imaginary posture. Thus, from very young age children are able to differentiate objects for themselves or others on the basis of either perception itself or a combination of perception and motor imagery (Rochat and Wraga, 1997).

Beyond peripersonal space extends *extrapersonal* space. Extrapersonal space represents the subjective area in which interactions with objects can occur only in the future following a transfer of the body and also the area where objects are beyond the sphere of influence. Obviously, the decision to direct the body towards a particular object depends mainly on interaction between optical information about distal layout and estimated behavioural potential and cost associated with intended actions (Proffitt, 2006a). Thus, there is a boundary in extrapersonal space that must be specified on the basis of the energy cost associated with a particular action. Though very few studies have investigated this issue, recent experiments have shown that distance perception is influenced by motor representations in many ways. For instance, objects appear farther away as the energy required to act upon them increases. Indeed, viewing a target while wearing a heavy backpack causes its distance to appear greater relative to when no backpack is worn (Proffitt, et al., 2003). The same effect was reported after adaptation to greater effort necessary to walk when performing the task on a treadmill (Proffitt et al., 2003). As a whole, these data show that extrapersonal space must also be delimited, and a perceived boundary requires anticipation about the consequences of deployable actions away from peripersonal space. However, this issue falls beyond the scope of the present chapter and would require a specific development as well as further investigations.

12.2.3. Specifying the boundary of peripersonal space

The core issue when considering peri- and extrapersonal spaces is how to specify the delimitation between the two spaces. Evaluating where the boundary of peripersonal space is perceived requires a methodology that probes the spatial organization of the external world at both the cognitive and neurophysiological levels. Classically, the critical test has consisted in placing individuals facing a horizontal surface and to present series of visual objects in various near and far locations. The participants' task is simply to provide a verbal response about whether the visual object is reachable with their arm or not. While performing the judgement task, no arm movements are allowed and the mobility of the trunk is generally restricted. When using this method, the general agreement is that the boundary of peripersonal space is perceived according to where the extremity of the stretched arm is thought to be located in space, thus providing some sign of embodied perception[2] (Coello and Delevoye-Turrell, 2007). Furthermore, presenting target information for only 150 ms was revealed to be sufficient for estimating a reach as being within one's general peripersonal workspace (Gabbard and Ammar, 2007). However, perception of what is reachable, albeit body-scaled, is often associated with biases in judgement. Previous studies have indeed revealed that people show a tendency to overestimate their reachable space. In other words, they tend to perceive an object within the reaching space, when actually it is out of reach (Bootsma et al., 1992; Carello et al., 1989; Coello and Iwanow, 2006; Fischer, 2000; Gabbard et al., 2006; Rochat, 1995; Rochat and Wraga, 1997; Robinovitch, 1998; Schwebel and Plumert, 1999). Although consistent in adults, studies have reported that overestimation is even greater in children (Gabbard et al. 2006, 2007a, 2009). This overestimation is also greater when judging approaching instead of stationary objects (Rochat and Wraga, 1997). Considering that veridical spatial information is required for planning an accurate goal-directed movement, it seems quite odd that people generally perceptually overestimate their action capacities. Several theoretical frameworks have been considered in the past, which varied

---

[2] Embodied perception is the perception of our world that depends not only on optical variables but also on the agent's physiological motor capacity and potentiality of action.

mainly by their focus upon the biomechanical, the perceptual, the cognitive, or the dynamical components of the task.

According to the *postural stability hypothesis*, the perceived boundary of reachable space depends upon one's representation of postural context and task constraints. More precisely, it was suggested that perceived reaching limit depends upon one's perceived postural limits (Carello et al., 1989; Robinovitch, 1998). This hypothesis was validated by showing that changing the postural context of a person while attempting to perceptually determine what is reachable, modified where the boundary of reachable space was perceived. For example, Robinovitch (1998) and later Gabbard et al. (2007b) demonstrated this effect by having adult participants estimating their reachable space, either sitting or standing up and leaning forward. As expected, participants overestimated their reaching capacities while seated, whereas they underestimated their reaching capacities when subjected to lower postural stability associated with the standing position. This observation seems to emphasize the ability in healthy adults to anticipate postural consequences of limb movement in relation to visual information so as to scale the location of every visual target in terms of postural demand.

Interestingly, the effect of postural constraints was not observed in infants, up to 11 years of age (Gabbard et al., 2009). Children display similar profiles for stable and less stable postures with the tendency to overestimate reachable space. This finding can be linked to the developmental trend in postural control that was noted during childhood as reaching abilities improved (van de Heide et al., 2003; Fallang et al., 2000; van der Fits et al., 1999). In agreement with this, development is characterized by concomitant decreasing postural control and increasing reaching success (Berthenthal and von Hofsten, 1998; Fontaine and Pierrault-le Bonniec, 1988; Rochat and Goubet, 1995; Samson and de Groot, 2000). This observation also suggests that judgements of estimating what is reachable continue to be refined between adolescence and adulthood. One improvement during this period concerns motor imagery abilities. Choudhury et al. (2007) found, for instance, that the duration of movement execution time correlated significantly with the duration of similar movement performed in an imagery condition. However, they also found a significant increase in the execution-imagery time correlation between adolescence and adulthood, which suggests that the developmental change was specific to generating accurate motor images due probably to the development of certain brain structures (like the parietal cortex) during this period.

For other authors, the main explanation for consistent overestimation of reachable space refers to the *whole body engagement* hypothesis (Rochat and Wraga, 1997). According to this theory, individuals generally preconceive and calibrate potential actions in multiple degrees of freedom, whereas they are generally tested in restricted postural situations that prevent natural body movements. For instance, in a one degree of freedom workspace for reaching (i.e. a situation that involves only the forearm for action), the participant may exhibit an inability to restrain simulating action with the remaining body degrees of freedom (i.e. the torso). It was observed that perceived reachability in a one degree of freedom workspace more closely approximated measured estimates for an actual multiple degrees of freedom reach (Mark et al., 1997; Rochat and Wraga, 1997). Accordingly, overestimation was interpreted as originating from people's everyday experience of reaching, which naturally requires multiple skeletal degrees of freedom (Carello et al., 1989; Fischer, 2000; Gabbard et al., 2006; Rochat and Wraga, 1997).

Because the perceived reachability includes two main factors (perceived motor ability and perceived task demands), it was suggested that both factors provide the basis for confidence, which is viewed as a cognitive aspect of motor processing (*the cognitive state hypothesis*, Gabbard et al., 2005, 2006). According to this approach, overestimation bias in perceptual judgement of what is reachable may reflect a relatively high state of confidence about motor and postural context. This would be particularly the case with more stable perceived postures. To test this hypothesis, Gabbard et al. (2005) evaluated the accuracy of reachability estimates for targets presented either along the body sagittal axis pointing straight ahead, or in the left or right visual field along a radial axis pointing towards the subject from different directions. They found that though the classical overestimation was observed when the visual stimuli were presented at midline, there was a significant reduced overestimation bias on the side visual fields (Gabbard et al. 2006). Given that the task demands were similar whatever the direction of the reachability estimates, explanations for the differential effect reported was formulated in terms of cognitive states that depend on subjective anticipated reaching constraints, perception of comfort and evaluation of postural stability.

Exploring reaching abilities or postural constraints does not represent the only factor that may account for overestimating reachable space. In previous studies, perceptual judgements were made in various visual contexts, which depending on the structure of the environment, may have influenced where objects were located in space (*the perceptual account hypothesis*, Coello and Iwanow, 2006). Indeed, it is well acknowledged that the coding of objects' position relies on the geometry of surface layout and objects as revealed in optical and oculomotor variables. As a consequence, impoverishing the optical signal generally leads to a modification of where objects are perceived in space, with a tendency for a constriction of egocentric space in function of a decrease in quantity of retinal cues (Coello and Iwanow, 2006; Tresilian et al., 1999). In the aim of testing the effect of modifying the optical and oculomotor variables on the judgement of the boundary of what is reachable, Coello and Iwanow (2006) contrasted actual reaching performances and judgement of reachability performed both in darkness and in the presence of a textured background. The analysis of motor performances showed that participants underestimated target distance in darkness but not when the target was presented against a textured background. This result confirmed that optical variables determine the perception of objects distance. The other relevant observation was that performing a perceptual judgement task in a textured rather than a dark visual scene reduced overestimation, with an estimation of the boundary of peripersonal space closely related to actual limb anthropometric characteristics. Thus, the systematic overestimation of reachable space reported in the literature should be in part explained by the test conditions: a dark visual context was often favoured thus leading to the removal of most of the ambient visual information while performing reachability estimates (i.e. Carello et al., 1989).

In conclusion, these different interpretations suggest that perceived reachability is a complex phenomenon based on several interacting factors. Action opportunities are thus context dependent and we may assume that the perceptual judgement of what is reachable does not rely only on information about anticipated postural constraints and the geometry of surface layout as revealed in optical and oculomotor variables, but also on the consequences of anticipated actions. Put in another way, the judgement of what is reachable may be dependent on how an actual reaching action is normally planned and executed (Rochat and Wraga, 1997).

12.3. A neuro-cognitive model for the delimitation of space boundaries

In support of the idea that the delimitation of the boundary of peripersonal space may depend directly on the motor processes required for motor planning and execution, we presented in a previous report a neuro-cognitive model that may account for the perceptual judgement of what is reachable on the basis of action representations and motor imagery (Coello and Delevoye-Turrell, 2007). In the next section, we briefly present this model and propose a series of three experiments that were used to further validate its use in the construction of action space.

12.3.1. An internal anticipation system for spatial cognition

Action representations can be viewed as a component of a predictive system that includes a neural process, which simulates through motor imagery the dynamic behaviour of the body in relation to the environment (Grush, 2004; Jordan, 1995; Wolpert et al., 1995). This view suggests that the presentation of a visual stimulus may evoke automatically a potential motor action, which, regardless of whether the action is subsequently executed or not, maps the spatial stimulus position in motor terms (Jeannerod, 2003). Through the general concept of internal modelling, it was suggested further that a predictive system enables optimal planning of movement (inverse model) as well as the anticipation of action outcome, limb kinematics, and parameter changes of the external world (forward model, Choudhury et al., 2007; Grush, 2004; Wolpert and Kawato, 1998). The function of the predictive system would be not only to shape and prepare the motor system for the consequence of motor execution, but also to provide the self with information on the feasibility of deployable actions (Jeannerod, 2001, 2006). Indeed, considering for instance that in a given situation expected consequences of action specify an outstretched posture, this would provide an internal signal for distinguishing reachable from not reachable objects. Such distinction between reachable and unreachable objects may then represent the underlying principle for subdividing external space into peripersonal and extrapersonal spaces (Coello and Delevoye-Turrell, 2007). The decision to execute or not an action would thus depend on the outcome of the motor anticipation process. In agreement with this, Coello and Delevoye-Turrell (2007) recently reported the case of the patient G.L. who suffered a permanent and specific loss of the large sensory myelinated fibres in all her four limbs, following several episodes of sensory polyneuropathy. Clinical investigations revealed a total loss of the senses of touch, vibration, pressure, and kinaesthesia, as well as absent tendon reflexes in the limbs. Pain and temperature sensations were preserved. Motor nerve conduction velocities and needle EMG investigation of the muscles of the arm proved normal. In an experimentally controlled task, it was observed that G.L. was impaired in performing a reachability judgement task, despite the fact that she was still able to accurately perform open-loop reaching movements and revealed no particular visual deficit. In G.L., the difficulty to anticipate sensory consequences of self-generated actions reduced her ability to delimit accurately the boundary of peripersonal space. This finding strongly supports the contribution of motor representation in the visual judgement of what is reachable.

12.3.2. Manipulating the spatial consequences of action

A straightforward method to establish the role of motor representation in the perceptual judgement of what is reachable consists in modifying the sensory consequences of action while performing a simple open-loop pointing task. In this context, we have designed an experiment that included 18 healthy right-handed participants (7 males and 11 females, 19–34 years old), who were required to execute a series of one hundred accurate pointing movements towards visual targets, that were presented at various distances (100 mm, 130 mm, and 160 mm from the maximum reachable distance, Coello et al., 2009). Before (pre-test) and after (post-test) the motor task, all participants performed a perceptual judgement task of what is reachable. Twenty-five targets were presented five times in a random order at different distances from the maximum reachable distance (± 8 mm up to ±96 mm) and participants were asked to estimate whether the target presented was reachable or not (yes–no response), but without the possibility of moving the upper limbs during the perceptual task. The crucial aspect of the study was that half of the participants received biased visual feedback (+ 3 cm in distance) about end-point accuracy during the motor task, while the other half received accurate visual feedback (see Fig. 12.1a). To analyse the effect of adapting to the biased feedback on the motor system, participants also performed a motor task at the beginning of the experiment in which there was no perturbation for the two groups (motor pre-test). This task was identical to the adaptation motor task except that participants performed only 36 movements. At the end of each motor task, participants performed 16 pointing movements towards targets placed at 115 mm and 145 mm from the maximum reachable distance, which received no feedback. No visual information about hand displacement was available during the motor tasks. Data analysis consisted in comparing radial error, i.e. error in amplitude in the pre-test and post-test for both groups and for the two tasks independently. Concerning the motor task, the introduction of biased feedback of 3 cm had the consequence of decreasing movement amplitude by 3.7 cm, as shown in Fig. 12.1b. Interestingly, none of the participants noted the presence of a bias in the feedback. Furthermore, the group that received accurate feedback showed a stable motor performance that varied by only 0.1 cm during the whole motor session. The consequence of providing accurate or biased feedback during the motor task was then tested on the perceptual judgement of what is reachable. We found that participants

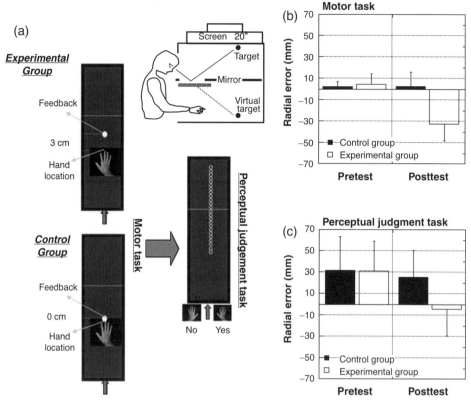

Fig. 12.1 (a) Schematic representation of the experimental apparatus and targets display in the motor and perceptual tasks. Note that the biased feedback was delivered to the experimental goup only. Radial errors (Mm) and standard deviations for the control group and the experimental group in the pre-test and post-test conditions when performing (b) The motor task and (c) The perceptual task. (Adapted from Coello et al. [2009]).

who received accurate feedback overestimated the boundary of what is reachable after having performed the adaptation motor task (2.52 cm), as this was the case before having performed this task (3.16 cm), showing thus a small difference between the two estimates (−0.64 cm). Conversely, participants that received biased feedback during the adaptation motor task perceived the boundary of what is reachable closer after (−0.41 cm) than before this task (3.11 cm, see Fig. 12.1c), with a difference (3.5 cm) that was close to the feedback bias (3 cm). Thus, modifying the spatial consequences of action by the use of a biased visual feedback had the effect of progressively reducing movement amplitude with a concomitant decrease of the distance where the boundary of what is reachable was perceived.

In this experiment, we also analysed reaction times in the perceptual task, i.e. the time required for providing the response after target presentation. This represents a crucial factor for estimating the processes involved in the perceptual estimates. Indeed, since the pioneering work by Fitts (1954) and Henry and Rogers (1960), it is acknowledged that task constraints can influence reaction time in a manual reaching response. Overall, the data suggest a fixed relationship between the spatial component of motor production and reaction time (Klapp, 1996). In agreement with Fitts's law, movement time increases as the distance of the target increases with a concomitant increase of reaction time (Munro et al., 2007). Interestingly, analysing reaction time in the reachability judgement task revealed that the time to respond increased nearly linearly until the maximum reachable distance was achieved, and at that point reaction time was maximum (see Fig. 12.2a and 2b). Reaction time decreased

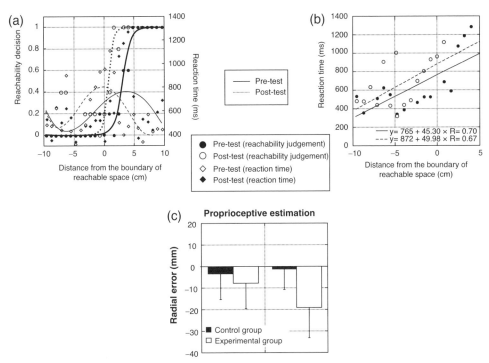

Fig. 12.2 (a) Illustration of the relationship between the logistic function (Thick Line) used to determine the boundary of what is reachable and the 4th order polynomial function (Thin Line) used to find where maximum reaction time occurred in the pretest (Plain Line) and posttest (dashed line; dots represent reachability decision according to the distance of the target and diamonds represent reaction time according to the distance of the target). Note that the distance corresponding to the 0.5 density of 'Reachable' response is very closed to the distance where maximum reaction times occurred, and both vary similarly in the posttest session when compared to the pretest session. (b) Illustration of the correlation between reaction time and target distance in the perceptual judgement task for a representative participant in the pretest (Plain Line) and posttest (Dashed Line). (c) Radial errors (mm) and standard deviations when performing the proprioceptive estimation of the location of unseen right index finger after passive displacement by the experimenter in the pretest and posttest conditions for the control group and the experimental group. (Adapted from Coello et al. [2009]).

abruptly for distances further than the boundary of reachable space. The same pattern of result was found in the pre-test and post-test, though maximum reaction time was noted for a closer target in the post-test for the experimental group. This pattern of results was thus very similar to the one reported when investigating actual motor productions. Overall, these data seem to indicate that judging what is reachable involves action representation in the form of motor imagery with temporal characteristics similar to what was reported with actual motor performance.

A complementary analysis showed that adapting to the biased visual feedback also had the consequence of modifying perceived arm length, with the subjective feeling of a shorter arm length (8 mm) after motor adaptation (see Fig. 12.2c). Perceived arm length was tested by asking subjects to indicate with their left index finger in darkness where, in space, they felt their right index finger following a passive displacement of the right arm by the experimenter. Participants indicated a position that was closer after adaptation than before, and closer than the control group, which received accurate feedback. This finding seems to indicate that manual adaptation to the biased visual feedback without direct vision of the upper limb had an impact on the internal body segment representation. The fact that the represented arm shrunk in size while adapting to the biased visual feedback provides another argument in favour of an involvement of motor representation in the estimation of what is reachable. Moreover, this may provide a framework for accounting for the egocentric displacement of the boundary of peripersonal space following visuo-motor adaptation.

This experiment provides direct evidence for a perceptual judgement of what is reachable based on motor representation and motor imagery. According to the neuro-cognitive model depicted above, we can speculate that adapting to the biased feedback had a direct consequence on the spatial content of the forward model, which contributed to predict the sensory consequences of anticipated action. However, because the present motor task led to adapt both motor efferent signal and the spatial consequences of action, it remains a possibility that the change in the perceptual decision of what is reachable came from a modification of efferent information for similar visual target, rather than a modification of expected spatial consequence of action. We tested this hypothesis in the experiment reported in the following paragraph.

12.3.3. Manipulating movement cost

In this study, we tested the consequences of sensorimotor adaptation to an inertial perturbation on the following estimate of what is reachable (Bourgeois and Coello 2009). The perturbation had the form of a 1.5 kg weight that was attached to the arm when performing the visuo-manual reaching task. In such situation, participants had to adapt the motor efferent command in order to maintain the same level of accuracy in the motor task. As a consequence of the adaptation process, the spatial outcome of the motor act remained unchanged. Three targets were used during the adaptation period and were placed at 100 mm, 130 mm, and 160 mm from the maximum reachable distance. Participants were required to perform 88 pointing movements and they were provided with accurate visual feedback about end-point location. The last 16 pointing movements were performed towards the targets placed at 115 mm and 145 mm from the maximum reachable distance, which received no feedback. The study involved 20 normal right-handed participants (8 males and 12 females, 19–40 years old), who were assigned randomly to one of the two groups used in this experiment (perturbation present or absent). All participants had normal or corrected-to-normal vision and were naive as to the purpose of the study. All participants carried out a perceptual judgement task before and after performing the motor task. As in the previous study, 25 targets were presented five times in a random order at different distances from the maximum reachable distance (± 8 mm up to ±96 mm) and participants had to judge whether the target presented was reachable or not (yes–no response), but without the possibility to move the upper limb voluntarily. To analyse the effect of adapting to the inertial load on the motor system, participants also performed a motor task at the beginning of the experiment in which there was no perturbation for the two groups (motor pre-test). This task was identical to the adaptation motor task except that participants performed only 46 movements. The last 16 pointing movements were also performed towards the targets placed at 115 mm and 145 mm from the maximum reachable distance, which received no feedback. No visual information about hand displacement was available during the motor tasks. Data analysis consisted in comparing radial error (i.e. error in amplitude in the pre-test and post-test for both groups and for the two tasks independently). In the motor task, as shown in Fig. 12.3a, the first pointing movement when carrying the weight produced an undershoot of the target (−5cm) demonstrating the lack of motor efference to overcome the inertial effect of the weight. The spatial error reduced progressively and 30 successive movements were overall necessary for the performance to improve and reach the base line (Fig. 12.3c). Interestingly, this motor adaptation had no effect on perceived arm length when tested afterwards by asking subjects to indicate with their left index finger in darkness where, in space, they felt their right index finger following a passive displacement of the arm by the experimenter (Fig. 12.3d). When considering the perceptual judgement task, we found that estimates of what is reachable were not affected by the motor adaptation to the weight, since the overestimation observed before adaptation (3.22 cm) was nearly the same than after adaptation (3.11 cm). These values were close to those observed for the control group that performed the same motor task but without carrying any weight

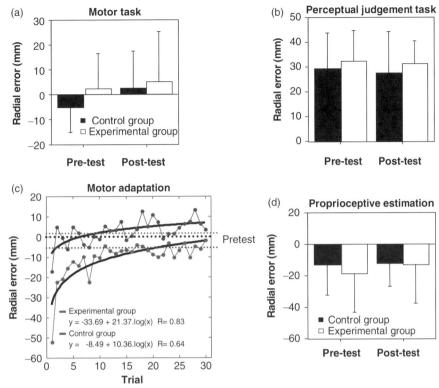

Fig. 12.3 Radial errors (mm) and standard deviations for the control group and the experimental group in the pre-test and post-test conditions when performing (a) the motor task and (b) the perceptual task. (c) Variation of radial error across the first 30 trials in the motor adaptation task for the control group and the experimental group. Note that the radial error when carrying the weight for the very first time was –5cm. (d) Radial errors (mm) and standard deviations when performing the proprioceptive estimation of the location of unseen right index finger after passive displacement by the experimenter in the pre-test and post-test conditions for the control group and the experimental group. (Adapted from Bourgeois et al. [2009]).

(2.91 cm and 2.74 cm, respectively, see Fig. 12.3b). Thus, modifying the efferent command to adapt motor response to a new inertial context but leaving the sensory consequences of action unchanged had no direct effect on where the boundary of what is reachable was perceived. Considered altogether, these data provide evidence for a perception of peripersonal space based on motor representation. Through motor imagery, participants were able to evaluate the sensory consequences of anticipated action and based their judgement on this information.

12.3.4. A neurobiological validation

Motor representations can be conceived as neural networks that overlap with the one activated during motor planning and motor execution, and also during motor imagery and even motor cognition (Jeannerod, 2006). It has been shown that this is particularly true for the motor and premotor cortices, the supplementary motor area and the posterior parietal cortex (Decety et al., 1994; Lotze et al., 1999; Gérardin et al., 2000; Hanakawa et al., 2003). Through a TMS study, it was possible to investigate whether this network was also involved in the perceptual judgement of what is reachable, providing thus neuroanatomical support for our neuro-cognitive model. The rationale was to test the involvement of motor representations in the perception of what is reachable by stimulating the motor areas while subjects performed the perceptual task (Coello et al., 2008).

It has been shown that TMS at a frequency equal to or below 1 Hz has the effect of depressing cortical excitability for a short period of time after each pulse (O'Shea and Walsh, 2007). According to the neuro-cognitive model (Coello and Delevoye-Turrell, 2007), applying a TMS pulse on the motor brain areas (i.e. motor and pre-motor cortices) was thought to perturb the perceptual judgement of what is reachable spatially (i.e. establish the boundary of what is reachable) and/or temporally (i.e. reaction times in response to reachability judgement). We decided thus to stimulate three different cortical sites at a sub-threshold intensity using a single pulse TMS: the left motor area associated with the right radial extensor carpi activation (involved in grasping movement), the left pre-motor cortex and the left temporo-occipital area used as control site, while judging perceptually what is reachable with the right hand. A perceptual right-left decision (control) task and an actual grasping movement task were also administered. In all conditions, TMS pulse was delivered 50 ms, 100 ms, 200 ms, or 300 ms after target presentation and performances were compared to the condition with no TMS.

Results showed a temporal facilitation effect in trials where TMS was applied, and this was the case in all tasks when stimulating any of the brain sites considered. The magnitude of the facilitation effect was dependent on the SOA between stimulus presentation and TMS onset. Reaction time was systematically shorter at SOA-50 ms (67 ms on average) and increased progressively until SOA-200 ms condition for the grasping task (−0.5 ms) and the reachability judgement task (−5 ms), and up to 300 ms-SOA for the right-left decision task (−7 ms). Such a facilitation effect of the TMS depending on the SOA is in agreement with previous studies that have reported similar finding when using TMS at sub-threshold intensity (Day et al., 1989; Foltys et al., 2000; Pascual-Leone et al., 1992). This effect has been interpreted as an improved processing of the visual target in the presence of multimodal congruent sensory signals (visual, auditory, and tactile) instead of a single one (visual). Another result achieved in the TMS study was that the reachability judgement task requires more elaborate processing than the right-left decision task and the grasping task, as suggested by the different reaction times in the no-stimulation condition (573 ms, 404 ms, 431 ms, respectively). However, and interestingly, solely when the TMS was applied on the motor cortex, and only while subjects were running the reachability judgement task, the facilitation effect reduced significantly for all SOAs (−34 ms on average), suggesting a role of the motor cortex in performing this task. Our claim was that determining whether an object is reachable or not requires the combination of perceptual information about object location with motor representations about possible movements towards that object. In line with our model, activating motor representations through motor imagery involves a neural network including the motor cortex which enables anticipating the final state of self-generated movements. This internal predictive model may represent the support for specifying the boundary of peripersonal space (Coello and Delevoye-Turrell, 2007).

12.4. The boundary of peripersonal space in schizophrenia

'As many psychiatrists know, patients with schizophrenia have trouble with the intimate and personal zones and cannot endure closeness to others' (Hall, 1966, p. 115). This leads to the question of a functional link between the organization of space and social behaviour. From a pure clinical perspective, therapists working with patients suffering from schizophrenia have reported their patients experiencing something that seems very similar to the flight reaction described in section A. Indeed, when approached too closely, these patients panic in much the same way as an animal recently locked up in a zoo (Hall, 1966). In describing their feelings, such patients refer to anything that happens within their 'flight initiation distance' as taking place literally inside them. That is, the boundaries of the self extend beyond the body. These experiences indicate that the realization of the self (as we know it) is associated intimately with the process of making boundaries explicit. In this section, we will present data obtained in patients with schizophrenia that suggest a functional link between a deficit in acting upon internal motor representations, on the one hand, and a problem in delimitating peripersonal space, on the other hand. We will finish this section by showing that the delimitation of peripersonal space is even more impaired in schizophrenia when patients are required to interact with people rather than with an inert object.

12.4.1. **Motor representations for voluntary action**

Schizophrenia is characterized by so-called 'positive' (e.g. hallucinations, delusions, thought disorders) and 'negative' (e.g. apathy, flattened effect) symptoms (Frith, 1992). Although genetic and environmental factors no doubt play a role in the disorder, its aetiology remains unknown (Sawa and Snyder, 2002). Recent research has suggested that many of the positive (or first rank) symptoms of the disorder (e.g. the so-called delusions of control in which patients believe external forces are controlling their thoughts or actions) can be characterized as impairments in reality monitoring or the self-monitoring of internally generated thoughts and actions. A self-monitoring deficit, which manifests itself as an inability to recognize one's thoughts or actions as their own, may also be usefully applied to the phenomenon of auditory hallucinations (i.e. the inability to recognize internal speech as self-generated). However, schizophrenia is a heterogeneous psychiatric disorder demonstrating impairments of attention, memory, and executive functions. Thus, one difficulty in assessing the hypothesis that patients with schizophrenia are characterized by impaired monitoring of their own intentions and actions is that the tasks typically used to assess this possibility also tap into the same range of cognitive functions that are impaired in theses patients. An elegant method, therefore, is to use simple motor tasks that require prediction and thus, the use of internal representations of action goals.

As described above (section 12.3), the fluent execution of motor actions requires the internal generation of a motor plan (inverse model) that is then used to prepare the motor system for the sensory consequences of self-initiated actions (forward model, Wolpert et al., 1998). For example, if we move a heavy weight up and down we have to alter the grip force we apply to compensate for the changing gravitational forces; gripping harder as we move up and less hard when we move down (Flanagan and Wing, 1997). These force changes do not lag behind our movements, as would be the case if we depended on detecting changes in sensory experiences. The force changes are made exactly in phase with the movements, indicating that the initiation of the appropriate muscle commands must be made in anticipation. Patients with schizophrenia reveal normal patterns of results when moving objects up and down (Delevoye-Turrell et al., 2002). They also show normal motor capacities when adjusting grip force in anticipation when lifting objects of various weights (Delevoye-Turrell et al., 2003). Overall, these results suggest that schizophrenia does not affect the internal generation of a forward model for low-level motor control. However, it has also been shown that grip change is delayed beyond normal as soon as sequential actions are required, e.g., when patients are asked to optimize the fluency of movement sequence (Delevoye-Turrell et al., 2007), to produce a collision by hitting something with an object they are holding (Delevoye-Turrell et al., 2003), to control efficiency levels when interacting with a moving pendulum (Bulot et al., 2007) or to decide what force level to apply in a force matching task (Shergill et al., 2005). Overall, these observations suggest that when actions are reactive, or largely automatic, the prediction system works normally in schizophrenia, but when more cognitive aspects of behaviour intervene (e.g., efficiency, decision-making) predictive adjustments are not made in an optimal fashion. As such, Frith (2005) suggested that it may be the case in schizophrenia that those motor predictions made by the forward dynamic model are only available to low-level control systems (i.e., they remain implicit). If patients with delusions of control have implicit, but not explicit knowledge of these predictions, then such positive symptoms should be more likely to occur in conjunction with intentional movements rather than more automatic ones, or when using motor representation for perceptual decision.

A good way to test this would be to demonstrate that patients with schizophrenia are able to use motor predictions made by the forward dynamic for low-level motor planning but that they fail to use it when imagining that they are performing the movement. Indeed, motor imagery also requires subjects to generate an internal representation of the intended action, and to anticipate the consequences of that action as if it has really been carried out (Anquetil and Jeannerod, 2007; Jeannerod, 2006). That is, motor imagery can accurately predict the time needed to execute a movement and engaging in an effortful motor imagery task results in many of the same physiological changes as the actual execution of that task (Carnahan et al., 1997; Decety et al., 1991; Decety and Lingren, 1991). In the following section, we will present two studies that explored motor imagery in schizophrenia.

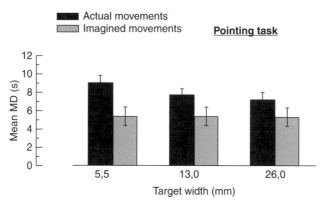

Fig. 12.4 Group mean movement duration (MD) in seconds for both actual (black) and imagined (grey) movements according to target width. Contrary to that observed in healthy controls, MD is not affected by target width for imagined movements in schizophrenic patients whereas it is for actual movements. (Adapted from Danckert et al. [2002]).

12.4.2. A deficit for actions towards imaged goals

The control of actual pointing movements conforms to a speed–accuracy trade-off function as captured by Fitts's law (1954), which states that movement duration varies as a function of movement amplitude (A) and target width (W), expressed as an index of difficulty (ID). According to this law, movement duration should increase linearly as the ID increases, which is precisely what happens both for actual and imagined movements in healthy controls (Duarte and Latash, 2007). That is, when subjects imagine making movements to targets of various sizes, imagined movement times increases as ID increases. Patients with schizophrenia show dissociation between actual and imagined movements (Danckert et al., 2002). That is, despite a normal speed–accuracy trade-off for actual movements, imagined movements were not modulated by changes in target size (see Fig. 12.4). The degree of impairment in imagined movements was not correlated with symptom profile, although the sample size was small (N=10). Thus, schizophrenia does not seem to be associated to an automatic use generation and use of forward modelling but reveals a specific deficit in the more cognitive (higher level) use of forward modelling for action monitoring.

Even if Danckert and colleagues (2002) controlled for several parameters, as, for instance the number of eye movements made in function of target size, the question remained as to whether patients with schizophrenia were performing the imagined motor task correctly. To confirm this result, we conducted an experiment for which subjects were required to move even in the imagined condition. To do so, we included 12 patients with schizophrenia and their group-matched controls. All subjects were presented with two contrasting tasks, which both consisted of experiencing a collision with a pendulum. In the producing task, subjects were asked to use a load cell to hit a pendulum in order to make it reach maximum target angles of 8°, 16°, and 32°. In the receiving task, subjects were required to hold the load cell immobile and to stop the fall of the pendulum that was released from angles of 8°, 16°, and 32° (Fig. 12.5a). All subjects performed the real collision tasks first. Second, they were instructed to take a small step back from the table on which was placed the pendulum and then, subjects performed the two tasks once again but now with the pendulum moving in the background. They were instructed to pretend controlling the collision, though no direct contact was experienced. For all trials, an accelerometer placed on the back of the subjects' hand recorded arm acceleration.

Figures 12.5b and 12.5c present the results for controls and for patients with schizophrenia respectively. As one can see, control subjects adjust grip force in relation to the forthcoming impact force, and in a similar way for both actual and imagined collision. Patients with schizophrenia scaled grip force to the magnitude of impact forces when actually performing the movements, for both the producing task (Fig. 12.5c) and the receiving task (not shown). These findings confirm previously

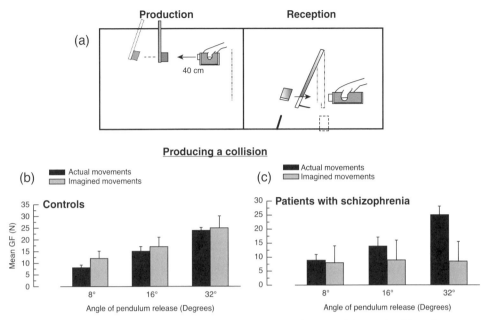

Fig. 12.5 (a) Schematic representations of the producing and the receiving tasks. Mean force developed and standard deviations measured in the collision tasks according to the height of release of the pendulum for (b) The group of healthy controls and (c) The group of patients with schizophrenia in the actual and imagined conditions.

published results of preserved capacity to scale motor parameters in schizophrenia (Carnahan et al., 1997; Delevoye-Turrell et al., 2002; Saoud et al., 2000). However, when imagining the collisions, grip force was not scaled to predicted impact forces: a constant level of grip force was applied on the load cell throughout the series. This pattern of results resembles that reported in Fig. 12.4 for the pointing task. In our case, however, we could verify in the producing task that patients were performing the imagining task correctly. Indeed, acceleration measurements provided us with the means to verify that arm kinematics was identical in actual and imagined collision tasks, and was the case for both patients and controls. Nevertheless, even if patients moved faster when imagining hitting the pendulum to 32°, and moved slower when imagining hitting the pendulum to 8°, grip force modulations kept flat.

Overall, these results suggest that patients with schizophrenia are able to use motor representations and anticipate the sensory consequences of action when an automatic planning of the movement is possible. However, patients revealed a difficulty in making use of an internal representation for imagined movements, suggesting a deficit in motor imagery. This dissociation between actual and imagined movements in schizophrenia motivates the question as to whether the brain makes use of forward modelling in the same way for actual and imagined movements. It is the case that environment-based and representation-based actions may be subsurved by different neural correlates (Keller and Koch, 2006; Passingham et al., 2000; Waszak et al., 2005). But before considering the neuro-cognitive model of representation-based actions, let us consider in this last section the implication in schizophrenia of the abnormal use of motor representations on the boundary of peripersonal space.

12.4.3. Motor representations and peripersonal space

In the previous section, we provided evidence for the use of motor representations in the perception of peripersonal space. Indeed, through motor imagery, participants seemed to have been able to evaluate the sensory consequences of anticipated action and based their judgement on this information.

What would happen to the perception of peripersonal space in patients with impairments affecting the use of motor representations? To investigate this question, we conducted a series of two experiments for which peripersonal space was evaluated in ten patients with schizophrenia and their matched controls (gender, age, IQ). Throughout the unique session, participants were tested individually in an isolated room. In the first study, subjects were seated at a table. A rod was moved in line with the subjects' midline at a constant speed of 1 cm/s, so that its end (a red diode) moved either towards the subject or away from the subject. The direction of diode displacement defined two experimental conditions and for both, subjects were asked to make reaching judgments from a seated position assuming that only arm extension was permitted. They were never allowed to truly move the hand to touch the diode.

Under the condition where the diode moved towards the subject (*approaching*), the task was to say 'stop' when they thought they could barely contact it with their fingertips by fully extending their right arms (see Fig.12.6a). Under the condition where the diode moved away from the subject (*departing*), the task was to say 'stop' as soon as they thought they could contact the diode with their fingertips, just before it appears too far. In other words, the subjects' task was to determine on each and every trial when the red diode reached the limits of peripersonal space. Carbon paper was used to note the subjects' responses without leaving a mark on the tabletop in order to prevent subjects from using landmarks on the table for their estimates. This measure is here referred to as an estimate of reachability. Two estimates from approaching objects and two estimates from departing objects (corresponding to descending and ascending object distance conditions, respectively) were obtained in individually randomized order, for seven different angles of approach. At the end of the session,

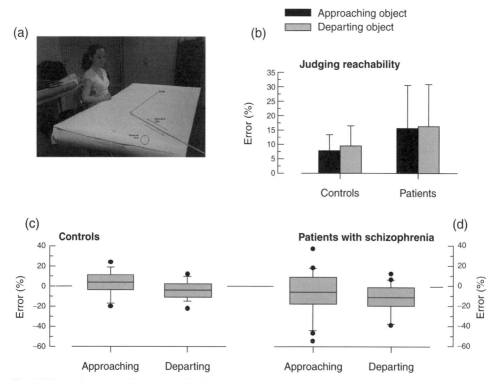

Fig. 12.6 (a) Setup used in the reachability judgement task for which no movement was permitted. (b) Means of absolute error in percentage (error bars code for standard deviation) for the groups of healthy controls and patients with schizophrenia. (c) Mean, percentiles and outliers of signed judgement errors for controls and (d) Patients with schizophrenia.

the actual reaching limits were determined by measuring the span from the outer edge of the shoulder joint (acromion) to the tip of the middle finger, to the nearest millimetre. This measure is here referred to as the actual reaching range. At the end of the experiment, participants were debriefed and asked about possible strategies to check that they had adhered to the instructions (no obvious strategies were discovered). Estimates of reachability were compared to actual reachability by computing an accuracy indicator ([true-judged]*100/true). As such, positive values corresponded to over-estimations, which were analysed through a 2(Group) × 2(Direction) repeated measures analysis of variance.

Healthy adults revealed a high accuracy level in determining the limits of reachability (Fig. 12.6b). Nevertheless, they revealed an overall tendency to overestimate actual reach, i.e. they judge the boundary of peripersonal space to be further than actual by a little less than 10% (Fig. 12.6c). This is consistent with many studies reported in the literature that used various types of protocols: reaching for pegs (Heft, 1993); reaching for objects (Bootsma et al., 1992; Carello et al., 1989; Rochat and Wraga, 1997); walking towards objects (Mark et al., 1997). Furthermore, we replicated the directional effect reported by Fisher (2003) such that approaching objects led to stronger overestimation of reachability compared to departing objects (Fig. 12.6c). Patients with schizophrenia made significantly more errors and were more variable in their estimates of reachability (Fig. 12.6b). Furthermore, they revealed a different pattern of results: in both approaching and departing conditions, patients underestimated the boundary of peripersonal space (Figure 6d). These results are in line with the previously proposed idea that the capacity to set boundary of peripersonal space are impaired in patients that had difficulties in the explicit use of motor representations.

In a second experiment, we wanted to investigate whether this abnormal boundary of functional space in schizophrenia would be similar if required to interact with a person rather than with an object. Thus, the same ten patients and controls were invited to stand up and go in the room next door, in which a second experimenter was waiting, standing with a neutral expression in the middle of the room. There were three tasks. In the first task, subjects were asked to walk towards the person and to stop as soon as they thought they could touch her, with the arm stretched out (self towards a person). In the second task, subjects were asked to walk towards the person and to stop as soon as they thought that the person could touch them, with her arm stretched out (other towards me). In the last condition, an object that was hanging from the ceiling replaced the person, and subjects were asked to walk towards the object and to stop as soon as they thought they could touch it, with the arm stretched out (self towards an object). After each trial, subjects were required to walk back to the door. Two trials for each condition was performed in semi-randomized order.

Contrary to the previous experiment, subjects were required to walk until they reached the boundary of peripersonal space. Under such condition, results revealed that all subjects were biased towards overestimation. In the group of control subjects, mean errors were of comparable magnitude across the three conditions. This suggests that whether interacting with an object or with a person, peripersonal space was evaluated with the same degree of accuracy. Furthermore, errors were in the same range of those reported in the more classic reachability experiments for which subjects are seating and the object is moved (10% errors). For the patient group, results revealed an overall greater overestimation. Nevertheless, patients and controls performed similarly in the task for which they had to move towards an object until it was reachable. However, performances were abnormal in the patient group in both person-to-person tasks. More specifically, when subjects were asked to stop at the boundary of their own peripersonal space, errors of over 20% were measured (Fig. 12.7). Errors were even larger when patients were required to stop at the limit of another person's peripersonal space (25%). Overall, these results suggest that judgments of what is reachable are normalized through action in patients with schizophrenia only when interacting with an object; movement is not sufficient to compensate for the abnormal organization of space when interaction with a person, i.e. in the case of social interactions. These preliminary results need obviously to be confirmed namely in a bigger patient group in order, among other questions, to see whether there is a correlation between symptoms and the magnitude of the errors that are here reported.

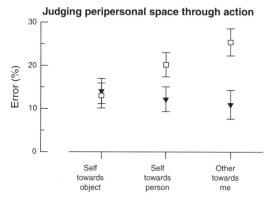

Fig. 12.7 Errors in % in estimating reachable distance when subjects were required to walk towards an object (left) or towards a person (middle and right). Results are presented for controls (triangle) and patients with schizophrenia (square). The subjects' task was to stop as soon as they judged that they could touch the object ('Self towards object'), touch the person ('Self towards person') or that the person could touch them ('Other towards me').

12.5. **Conclusion**

The data presented in this chapter underline the importance of processing visual information in relation to one's action possibilities so as to organize the surrounding world spatially and reliably. We demonstrated that the use of motor representations enables a purposeful access to objects' position in space to the extent that it refers to a series of possibilities, which constitutes a form of rationality from which the environment may be constructed, organized and thus understood. We defend the idea that it may not be sufficient to consider spatial perception only in the context of an environment-body interacting system. It is in fact essential to recognize that the possibilities of action subtend the perceptual process of the basic organization of the external world. This is similar to the sense of spatiality developed in phenomenological philosophy by authors like Heidegger, Husserl, or even Merleau-Ponty who suggested that 'locations within space are not to be defined as objective positions in relation to the objective position of our body; rather, they inscribe around us the variable reach of our intentions or of our movements' (Mearleau-Ponty, 1945). This philosophical approach thus acknowledges the role performed by potential action in the constitution of perceptual experience. In line with this perspective, we have provided in the present chapter arguments suggesting that motor representations may be viewed as a component of a predictive system that includes a neural process which simulates through motor imagery the dynamic behaviour of the body in relation to its environment. More specifically, being able to anticipate the consequences of deployable actions would represent the core and underlying mechanism that would render possible the perceptual distinction between reachable and unreachable objects. In turn, this would provide the basis for distinguishing perceptually between peripersonal and extrapersonal spaces.

Experimental results have suggested further that this predictive mechanism has probably a significant element related to spatial content. Indeed, modifying the spatial consequences of acting in peripersonal space was shown to modify how accurately the boundary of peripersonal space was perceived, which was not the case when only the cost of moving was manipulated. Thus, the possibility to project in the future the position in space of our limbs or of our body would constitute the main mechanism that would account for how we can select objects for action and then, how we can organize the external world for adequate interaction. The data reported in patients with schizophrenia further confirmed the need of motor representations for the organization of peripersonal space. Indeed, our preliminary results suggested that in pathologies affecting the capacity to use motor representations, tasks requiring specifically motor anticipation processes were impaired. This was evident in the various motor imagery tasks, in contrast to the preserved ability to perform the motor actions correctly (sequential pointing; grip force modulation for collisions). The novelty that was presented lay however, in the fact that these same patients also revealed significant difficulties in delimitating correctly the boundary of action space. Thus, the incapacity to simulate through motor imagery the dynamic behaviour of the body in relation to the environment, led these patients to have difficulties in distinguishing the boundary of their peripersonal space.

The last but not least intriguing theme that was touched upon was the fact that the motor predictive system might be influenced by the social context. Indeed, we reported that for patients who showed deficits in using motor representations, the delimitation of peripersonal space using the classic judgements task was significantly underestimated and much more variable than that observed in healthy controls. Inversely, when actively moving to place oneself on the boundary of peripersonal space during person-to-person interaction, patients significantly overestimate their action capacities. It has been suggested that people can use different ways of constructing information when forming perceptual judgements (Henderson et al., 2006). Psychologically distant events would be represented more by their essential, general, and prototypical features (high-level construals) whereas psychologically close events would be represented in terms of their incidental, specific, and unique features (low-level construals). It is thus possible that two different mechanisms are used for forming judgements about the boundary of action space, and that schizophrenia affects these two mechanisms differently. In such cases, one could hypothesise that in peripersonal (near) space, direct perception can be used (low-level motor representations) and thus, judgements towards objects positioned in near space are preserved in schizophrenia. Whenever high-level motor representations are required (interacting with positioned objects in far space, moving objects in near or far space, people in near or far space), patients with schizophrenia would be severely impaired. This hypothesis is now being conducted in our laboratories, which would enable us to test the motor theory for schizophrenia (Van Hoof, 2003). Finally, our results lead to the reflection around the idea that the contrasting accuracy in judgements of peripersonal space for objects and for conspecifics respectively, may highlight the cognitive mismatch that triggers hallucinatory experiences. In more general situations, such mismatch would lead patients to establish a greater distance between self and other in order to compensate for the pathological difficulty in distinguishing own action spaces from others.

Acknowledgements

Supported by Maison Européenne des Sciences de l'Homme et de la Société (MESHS), Région Nord Pas de Calais and University Charles De Gaulle grants, European Science Foundation, Eurocores CNCC CRP grant and ANR 'Neurosciences, Neurologie et Psychiatrie' program from the French Ministry.

References

Anquetil, T. and Jeannerod, M. (2007). Simulated actions in the first and in the third person perspectives share common representations. *Brain Research*; **1130**: 1161–125.

Avillac, M., Ben Hamed, S., and Duhamel, J-R. (2007). Multisensory integration in the ventral intraparietal area of the macaque monkey. *Journal of Neuroscience*; **27**: 1922–32.

Avillac, M., Deneve, S., Olivier, E., Pouget, A., and Duhamel, J-R. (2005). Reference frames for representing visual and tactile locations in parietal cortex. *Nature Neuroscience*; **8**: 941–9.

Bergson, H. (1896). *Matière et mémoire*. Paris: PUF.

Berkeley, G. (1709[1985]). Essai pour une nouvelle théorie de la vision. In *Trad. collective sous la direction de G. Brykman*, Œuvres, Vol. I. Paris: PUF.

Berthenthal, B. and Von Hofsten, C. (1998). Eye, head and trunk control: the foundation for manual development. *Neuroscience and Biobehavioral Reviews*; **22**: 515–20.

Berti, A. and Rizzolatti, G. (2002). Coding near and far space. In *The cognitive and neural bases of spatial neglect*, (eds Karnath, H.O., Milner, A.D., and Vallar, G.), pp. 119–29. New York: Oxford University Press.

Berti, A., Smania, N., Rabuffetti, M., Ferrarin, M., Spinazzola, L., and D'Amico, A. (2002). Coding of far and near space during walking in neglect patients. *Neuropsychology*; **16**: 390–99.

Bjoertomt, O., Cowey, A., and Walsh, V. (2002). Spatial neglect in near and far space investigated by repetitive transcranial magnetic stimulation. *Brain*; 125: 2012–22.

Blumstein, D.T., Fernandez-Juricic, E., Zollner P.A., and Garity, S. (2005). Inter-specific variation in avian responses to human disturbance. *Journal of Applied Ecology*; 42: 943–53.

Bonenfant, M. and Kramer, D.L. (1996). The influence of distance to burrow on flight initiation distance in the woodchuck. *Marmota monax. Behavioural Ecology*; 7: 299–303.

Bootsma, R.J., Bakker, F.C., van Snippenberg, F., and Tdlohreg, C.W. (1992). The effect of anxiety on perceiving the reachability of passing objects. *Ecological Psychology*; 4: 1–16.

Bourgeois, J. and Coello, Y. (2009). Role of inertial properties of the upper limb on the perception of the boundary of peripersonal space. *Psychologie Française*; 54: 225–39.

Brain, W.R. (1941). Visual disorientation with special reference to lesions of the right cerebral hemisphere. *Brain*; 64: 244–72.

Bremmer, F., Schlack, A., Duhamel, J-R, Graf, W., and Fink, G.R. (2001). Space coding in primate posterior parietal cortex. *Neuroimage*; 14: S46–51.

Bulot, V., Thomas, P., and Delevoye-Turrell, Y. (2007). A pre-reflective indicator of an impaired sense of agency in patients with Schizophrenia. *Experimental Brain Research*; 183: 115–26.

Bulova, S.J. (1994). Ecological correlates of population and individual variation in antipredator behavior of two species of desert lizards. *Copeia*; 4: 980–92.

Burger, J. and Gochfeld, M. (1990). Risk discrimination of direct versus tangential approach by basking black iguana (*Ctenosaura similis*): variation as a function of human exposure. *Journal of Comparative Psychology*; 104: 388–94.

Carello, C., Grosofsky, A., Reichel, F.D., Solomon, H.Y., and Turvey, M.T. (1989). Visually perceiving what is reachable. *Ecological Psychology*; 1: 27–54.

Carnahan, H., Aguilar, O., Malla, A., and Norman, R. (1997). An investigation into movement planning and execution deficits in individuals with schizophrenia. *Schizophrenia. Research*; 23: 213–21.

Choudhury, S., Charman, T., Bird, V., and Blakemore, S. (2007). Development of action representation during adolescence. *Neuropsychologia*; 45: 255–62.

Clifton, R.K., Rochat, P., Litovsky, R.Y., and Perris, E.E. (1991). Object representation guides infants' reaching in the dark. *Journal of Experimental Psychology: Human Perception and Performance*; 17: 323–9.

Coello, Y. and Delevoye-Turrell, Y. (2007). Embodiement, space categorisation and action. *Consciousness and Cognition*; 16: 667–83.

Coello, Y., Bartolo, A., Amiri, B., Houdayer, E., and Derambure, P. (2008). Perceiving what is reachable depends on motor representations: A study using transcranial magnetic stimulation. *Plos One*, http://www.plosone.org/article/info%3Adoi%2F10.1371%2Fjournal.pone.0002862.

Coello, Y., Bartolo, A., and Bourgeois, J. (2009). Visual perception of peripersonal space depends on motor representation: evidence from psychophysical and brain imaging studies. Paper presented at the European Conference on Visual Perception (Regensburg, 24–28 August).

Coello, Y. and Iwanow, O. (2006). Effect of structuring the workspace on cognitive and sensorimotor distance estimation: no dissociation between perception and action. *Perception and Psychophysics*; 68: 278–89.

Colby, C.L., Duhamel, J.R., and Goldberg, M.E. (1993). Ventral intraparietal area of the macaque: anatomic location and visual response properties. *Journal of Neurophysiology*; 69: 902–14.

Cooper, W.E. (1997a). Escape by a refuging prey: the broad-headed skink (*Eumeces laticeps*). *Canadian Journal of Zoology*; 75: 943–7.

—— (1997b). Threat factors affecting antipredatory behavior in the broad-headed skink (*Eumeces laticeps*): repeated approach, change in predator path, and predator's field of view. *Copeia*; 3: 613–19.

—— (1998). Direction of predator turning, a neglected cue to predation risk. *Behaviour*; 135: 55–64.

—— (1999). Tradeoffs between courtship, fighting, and antipredatory behavior by a lizard, *Eumeces laticeps*. *Behavioural Ecoligical Sociobiology*; 47: 54–9.

Cooper, W.E., Perez-Mellado, V., Baird, T., Baird, T., Caldwell, J.P., and Vitt, L.J. (2003). Effects of risk, cost, and their interaction on optimal escape by nonrefuging Bonaire whiptail lizards, Cnemidophorus murinus. *Behavioral Ecology*; 14: 288–93.

Cowey, A., Small, M., and Ellis, S. (1994). Left visuo-spatial neglect can be worse in far than in near space. *Neuropsychologia*; 32: 1059–66.

Danckert, J., Rossetti, Y., d'Amato, T., Dalery, J., and Saoud, M. (2002). Exploring imagined movements in patients with schizophrenia. *Neuroreport*; 13(5): 605–09.

Day, B.L., Rothwell, J.C., Thompson, P.D., Maertens de Noordhout, A., Nakashima, K., and Marsden, C.D. (1989). Delay in the execution of voluntary movement by electrical or magnetic brain stimulation in intact man. *Brain*; 112: 649–63.

Decety, J. and Lindgren, M. (1991). Sensation of effort and duration of mentally executed actions. *Scandinavian Journal of Psychology*; 2: 97–104.

Decety, J., Jeannerod, M., Germain, M., and Pastene, J. (1991). Vegetative response during imagined movement is proportional to mental effort. *Behavioural Brain Research*; 31: 42, 1–5.

Decety, J., Perani, D., Jeannerod, M., Bettinardi, V., and Tadary, B. (1994). Mapping motor representations with positron emission tomography. *Nature*; 371: 600–02.

Delevoye-Turrell, Y., Giersch, A., Wing, A.M., and Danion, J.M. (2007). Motor fluency deficits in the sequencing of actions in schizophrenia. *Journal of Abnormal Psychology*; 116: 56–64.

Delevoye-Turrell, Y., Giersch, A., and Danion, J.M. (2003). Abnormal sequencing of motor actions in patients with schizophrenia: evidence from grip force adjustments during object manipulation. *American Journal of Psychiatry*; **160**(1): 134–41.

Delevoye-Turrell, Y., Giersch, A., and Danion, J.-M. (2002). A deficit in the adjustment of grip force responses in schizophrenia. *NeuroReport*; **13**(12): 1537–9.

Di Pellegrino, G., Ladavas, E., and Farne, A. (1997). Seeing where your hands are. *Nature*; **388**: 730.

Dill, L.M. (1990). Distance-to-cover and the escape decisions of an African cichlid fish, *Melanochromis chipokae*. *Environmental Biology of Fishes*; **27**: 147–52.

Dosey, M.A. and Meisels, M. (1969). Personal space and self-protection. *Journal of Personal and Social Psychology*; **11**: 93–7.

Duarte, M. and Latash, M.L. (2007). Effects of postural task requirements on the speed-accuracy trade-off. *Experimental Brain Research*; **180**: 457–67.

Duhamel, J-R., Bremmer, F., BenHamed, S., and Graf, W. (1997). Spatial invariance of visual receptive fields in parietal cortex neurons. *Nature*; **389**: 845–8.

Duhamel, J-R., Colby, C.L., and Goldberg, M.E. (1998). Ventral intraparietal area of the macaque: congruent visual and somatic response properties. *Journal of Neurophysiology*; **79**: 126–36.

Fallang, B., Saugstad, O.,and Hadders-Algra, M. (2000). Goal directed reaching and postural control in supine position in healthy infants. *Behavioural Brain Research*; **115**: 9–18.

Farne, A., Dematte, M-L., and Ladavas, E. (2005). Neuropsychological evidence of modular organization of the near peripersonal space. *Neurology*; **65**: 754–8.

Felipe, N.J. and Sommer, R. (1966). Invasions of personal space. *Social Problems*; **14**: 206–14.

Field, J. (1976). Relation of young Infant's reaching behavior to stimulus distance and solidity. *Developmental Psycholgogy*; **5**: 444–8.

Fischer, M.H. (2000). Estimating reachabililty: whole-body engagement or postural stability? *Human Movement Science*; **19**: 297–318.

Fitts, P.M. (1954). The informed capacity of the human motor system in controlling the amplitude of movements. *Journal of Experimental Psychology*; **47**: 381–91.

Flanagan, J.R. and Wing, A.M. (1997). The role of internal models in motion planning and control: evidence from grip force adjustments during movements of hand-held loads. *Journal of Neuroscience*; **17**: 1519–28.

Foltys, H., Kemeny, S., Krings, T., Boroojerdi, B., Sparing, R., Thron, A. et al. (2000). The representation of the plegic hand in the motor cortex: a combined fMRI and TMS study. *NeuroReport*; **11**: 147–50.

Fontaine, R. and Pieraut-le Bonniec, G.P. (1988). Postural evolution and integration of the prehension gesture in children aged 4 to 10. *British Journal of Developmental Psychology*; **6**: 223–33.

Frith, C.D. (1992). *The cognitive neuropsychology of schizophrenia*. Hove: Lawrence Erlbaum.

—— (2005). The self in action: Lessons from delusions of control. *Consciousness and Cognition*; **14**: 752–70.

Gabbard, C, and Ammar, D. (1995). Visual cues and perceived reachability. *Brain and Cognition*; **59**: 287–291.

Gabbard, C. and Ammar, D. (2007a). Does target viewing time influence perceived reachability. *International Journal of Neuroscience*; **117**: 1331–9.

Gabbard, C., Ammar, D., and Lee, S. (2006). Perceived reachability in single- and mutilple-degree-of-freedom workspaces. *Journal of Motor Behaviour*; **38**: 423–9.

Gabbard, C., Cordova, A., and Ammar, D. (2007). Children's estimation of reach in peripersonal and extrapersonal space. *Developmental Neuropsychology*; **32**: 749–56.

Gabbard, C., Cordova, A., and Lee, S. (2007b). Examining the effects of postural constraints on estimating reach. *Journal of Motor Behavior*; **39**: 242–6.

—— (2009). Do children perceive postural constraints when estimating reach (action planning)? *Journal of Motor Behavior*; **41**: 100–05.

Gérardin, E., Sirigu, A., Lhéricy, S., Poline, J.B., and Gaymard, B. (2000). Partially overlapping neural networks for real and imagined hand movements. *Cerebral Cortex*; **10**: 1093–104.

Gibson, J.J. (1979). *The ecological approach to visual perception*. Hillsdale, N.J.: Lawrence Erlbaum Associates.

Grant, J.W. and Noakes, D.L.G. (1987). Escape behaviour and use of cover by young-of-the-year brook trout, *Salvelinus fontinalis*. *Canadian Journal of Fisheries and Aquatic Sciences*; **44**: 1390–6.

Graziano, M.S.A. and Cooke, D.F. (2006). Parieto-frontal interactions, personal space, and defensive behavior. *Neuropsychologia*; **44**: 845–59.

Graziano, M.S.A. and Gross, C.G. (1993). A bimodal map of space: somatosensory receptive fields in the macaque putamen with corresponding visual receptive fields. *Experimental Brain Research*; **97**: 96–109.

—— (1995). The representation of extrapersonal space: a possible role for bimodal, visual–tactile neurons. In *The cognitive neurosciences*, (ed. Gazzaniga, M.S.), pp. 1021–34. Cambridge, MA: MIT Press.

Grush, R. (2004). The emulation theory of representation: motor control, imagery, and perception. *Behavioral and Brain Sciences*; **27**: 377–442.

Hall, E. (1966). *The hidden dimension*. New York: Anchor books.

Halligan, P.W., Fink, G.R., Marshall, J.C., and Vallar, G. (2003). Spatial cognition: evidence from visual neglect. *Trends in Cognitive Sciences*; **7**: 125–33.

Halligan, P.W. and Marshall, J.C. (1991). Left neglect for near but not far space in man. *Nature*; **350**: 498–500.

Hanakawa, T., Immisch, I., Toma, K., Dimyan, M.A., and Van Gelderen, P. (2003). Functional properties of brain areas associated with motor execution and imagery. *Journal of Neurophysiology*; **89**: 989–1002.

Hediger, H. (1934). Zur Biologie und Psychologie der Flucht bei Tieren. *Biologisches Zentralblatt*; **54**: 21–40.

Heft, H. (1993). A methodological note on overestimates of reaching distance: distinguishing between perceptual and analytical judgments. *Ecological psychology*; **5**: 255–71.

Henderson, M.D., Fujita, K., Trope, Y., and Liberman, N. (2006). Transcending the 'Here': the effect of spatial distance on social judgment. *Journal of Personality and social Psychology*; **91**: 845–56.

Horowitz, M J, Duff, D.F., Stratton, L.O. (1964). Body buffer zone-exploration of personal space. *Archives of General Psychiatry*; **11**: 651–656.

Husserl, E. (1907/1998). Ding and Raum: Vorlesungen. Husserliana 16. In *Collected works*, vol. 7. (ed Claesges, U.), The Hague: M. Nijhoff, 1973. (trans. Rojceicz, R. *Thing and space: Lectures of 1907*). Dordrecht, Netherlands: Kluwer Academic Publishers.

Iriki, A., Tanaka, M., and Iwamura, Y. (1996). Coding of modified body schema during tool use by macaque postcentral neurones. *Neuroreport*; **7**: 2325–30.

Jeannerod, M. (2001). Neural simulation of action: a unifying mechanism for motor cognition. *Neuroimage*; **14**: S103–S109.

—— (2003). The mechanism of self-recognition in humans. *Behavioural Brain Research*; **142**: 1–15.

—— (2006). The origin of voluntary action: history of a physiological concept. *Comptes Rendus de l'Académie des Sciences-Biologies*; **329**: 354–62.

Jordan, M.I. (1995). The organization of action sequences: evidence from a relearning task. *Journal of Motor Behaviour*; **27**: 179–92.

Klapp, S.T. (1996). Reaction time analysis of central motor control. In Zelaznik H.N. (ed.) *Advances in motor learning and control* (pp 13–35). Human Kinetics, Champaign, IL.

Keller, P.E. and Koch, I. (2006). The planning and execution of short auditory sequences. *Psychological Bulletin Review*; **13**(4): 711–16.

Kramer, D.L. and Bonenfant, M. (1997). Direction of predator approach and the decision to flee to a refuge. *Animal Behaviour*; **54**: 289–95.

Ladavas, E., di Pellegrino, G., Farne, A., and Zeloni, G. (1998). Neuropsychological evidence of an integrated visuotactile representation of peripersonal space in humans. *Journal of Cognitive Neuroscience*; **10**: 581–9.

Ladavas, E., Pavani, F., and Farne, A. (2001). Auditory peripersonal space in humans: a case of auditory–tactile extinction. *Neurocase*; **7**: 97–103.

Ladavas, E., Zeloni, G., and Farne, A. (1998). Visual peripersonal space centred on the face in humans. *Brain*; **121**: 2317–26.

LaGory, K.E. (1987). The influence of habitat and group characteristics in the alarm and flight response of white-tailed deer. *Animal Behaviour*; **35**: 20–5.

Longo, M.R. and Lourenco, S.F. (2006). On the nature of near space: effects of tool use and the transition to far space. *Neuropsychologia*; **44**: 977–81.

Lotze, M., Montoya, P., Erb, M., Hülsmann, E., Flor, H., and Klose, U. (1999). Activation of cortical and cerebellar motor areas during executed and imagined hand movements: an fMRI study. *Journal of Cognitive Neuroscience*; **11**: 491–501.

Makin, T.R., Holmes, N.P., and Ehrssond, H.H. (2008). On the other hand: dummy hands and peripersonal space. *Behavioural Brain Research*; **191**: 1–10.

Marden, J.H. (1987). Maximum lift production during takeoff in flying animals. *Journal of Experimental Biology*; **130**: 235–58.

Mark, L.S., Ncmeth, K., Garciner, D., Dainoff, M.J., Paasche, J., and Duffy, M. (1997). Postural dynamics and the preferred critical boundary for visually guided reaching. *Journal of Experimental Psychology: Human Perception and Performance*; **23**: l365–79.

Martín, J. and Lopéz, P. (1999). An experimental test of the costs of antipredatory refuge use in the wall lizard, *Podarcis muralis*. *Oikos*; **84**: 499–505.

Mattingley, J.B., Driver, J., Beschin, N., and Robertson, I.H. (1997). Attentional competition between modalities: extinction between touch and vision after right hemisphere damage. *Neuropsychologia*; **35**: 867–80.

McLean, E.B. and Godin, J.G.J. (1989). Distance to cover and fleeing from predators in fish with different amounts of defensive armour. *Oikos*; **55**: 281–90.

Mennemeier, M., Wertman, E., and Heilman, K.M. (1992). Neglect of near peripersonal space: evidence for multidirectional attentional systems in humans. *Brain*; **115**: 37–50.

Merleau-Ponty, M. (1945). *Phénoménologie de la perception*. Paris: Gallimard.

Milner, A.D. and Goodale, M.A. (1995). *The visual brain in action*. Oxford: Oxford University Press.

Munro, H., Plumb, M.S., Wilson, A.D., Williams, J.H.G., Mon-Williams, M. (2007). The effect of distance on reaction time in aiming movements. *Experimental Brain Research*; **183**: 249–257.

O'Shea, J. and Walsh, V. (2007). Transcranial magnetic stimulation. *Current Biology*; **17**: 196–9.

Obayashi, S., Suhara, T., Nagai, Y., Maeda, J., Hihara, S., and Iriki, A. (2002). Macaque prefrontal activity associated with extensive tool use. *Neuroreport*; **13**: 2349–54.

Pascual-Leone, A., Brasil-Neto, J.P., Valls-Sole, J., Cohen, L.G., and Hallett, M. (1992). Simple reaction time to focal transcranial magnetic stimulation. *Brain*; **115**: 109–22.

Passingham, R.E., Toni, I., and Rushworth, M.F. (2000). Specialisation within the prefrontal cortex: the ventral prefrontal cortex and associative learning. *Experimental Brain Research*; **133**: 103–13.

Pavani, F. and Castiello, U. (2004). Binding personal and extrapersonal space through body shadows. *Nature Neuroscience*; **7**: 14–16.

Poincaré, H. (1907). *La Science et l'hypothèse*. Paris: Flammarion.

Previc, F.H. (1998). The neuropsychology of 3-D space. *Psychological Bulletin*; **124**: 123–64.

Proffitt, D.R. (2006a). Distance perception. *Current Directions in Psychological Science*; **15**: 131–5.

—— (2006b). Embodied perception and the economy of action. *Perspective on Pyschological Science*; **1**: 110–22.

Proffitt, D.R., Stefanucci, J., Banton, T., and Epstein, W. (2003). The role of effort in perceiving distance. *Psychological Science*; **14**: 106–12.

Rand, A.S. (1964). Inverse relationship between temperature and shyness in the lizard *Anolis lineatopus*. *Ecology*; **45**: 863–4.

Rizzolatti, G., Matelli, M., and Pavesi, G. (1983). Deficits in attention and movement following the removal of postarcuate (area 6) and prearcuate (area 8) cortex in macaque monkeys. *Brain*; **106**: 655–73.

Rizzolatti, G., Scandolara, C., Matelli, M., and Gentilucci, M. (1981). Afferent properties of periarcuate neurons in macaque monkeys. II. Visual responses. *Behavioural Brain Research*; **2**: 147–63.

Robinovitch, S.N. (1998). Perception of postural limits during reaching. *Journal of Motor Behavior*; **30**: 352–8.

Robinson, C.J. and Burton, H. (1980). Organization of somatosensory receptive fields in cortical areas 7b, retroinsula, postauditory, and granular insula of *M. fascicularis*. *Journal of Comparative Neurology*; **192**: 69–92.

Rochat, P. (1995). Perceived reachability for self and for others by 3- to 5-year-old children and adults. *Journal of Experimental Child Psychology*; **59**: 317–33.

Rochat, P. and Goubet, N. (1995). Development of sitting and reaching in 5- to 6-month-old infants. *Infant Behavior and Development*; **18**: 53–68.

Rochat, P. and Wraga, M. (1997). An Account of the Systematic Error in Judging What Is Reachable. *Journal of Experimental Psychology: Human Perception and Performance*; **23**: 199–212.

Samson, J.F. and de Groot, L. (2000). The influence of postural control on motility and hand function in a group of 'high risk' preterm infants at 1 year of age. *Early Human Development*; **60**: 101–13.

Saoud, M., Coello, Y., Dumas, P., Franck, N., d'Amato, T., Dalery, J., et al. (2000). Visual pointing and speed/accuracy trade-off in schizophrenia. *Cognitive Neuropsychiatry*; **5**: 123–34.

Sawa, A. and Snyder, S.H. (2002). Schizophrenia: diverse approaches to a complex disease. *Science*; **26**: 692–5.

Schlack, A., Sterbing-D'Angelo, S.J., Hartung, K., Hoffmann, K.P., and Bremmer, F. (2005). Multisensory space representations in the macaque ventral intraparietal area. *Journal of Neuroscience*; **25**: 4616–25.

Schwebel, D.C. and Plumert, J.M. (1999). Longitudinal and concurrent relations among temperament, ability estimation, and injury proneness. *Child Development*; **70**: 700–12.

Shelton P.A., Bowers D., and Heilman K.M. (1990). Peripersonal and vertical neglect. *Brain*; **113**: 191–205.

Shergill, S.S., Samson, G., Bays, P.M., Frith, C.D., and Wolpert, D.M. (2005). Evidence for sensory prediction deficits in schizophrenia. *American Journal of Psychiatry*; **162**: 2384–6.

Smith, D.G. (1997). Ecological factors influencing the antipredator behaviors of the ground skink, *Scincella lateralis*. *Behavioural Ecology*; **8**: 622–9.

Sommer R. (1959). Studies in personal space. *Sociometry*; **22**: 247–260.

Spence, C., Pavani, F., and Driver, J. (2000). Crossmodal links between vision and touch in covert endogenous spatial attention. *Journal of Experimental Psychology: Human Perception and Performance*; **26**: 1298–319.

Treisilian, J.R., Mon-Williams, M., and Kelly, B.M. (1999). Increasing confidence in vergence as a cue to distance. *Proceedings of the Royal Society London B*; **266**: 39–44.

Van de Heide, J.C., Otten, B., van Eykern, L.A., and Hadders-Algra, M. (2003). Development of postural adjustments during reaching in sitting children. *Experimental Brain Research*; **151**: 32–45.

Van der Fits, I.B.M., Klip, A.W.J., Eykern, L.A., and Hadders-Algra, M. (1999). Postural Adjustments during spontaneous and goal-directed arm movements in the first half of life. *Behavioral Brain Research*; **106**: 75–90.

van Hoof JJ. (2003). A motor hypothesis of the origin of schizophrenia. *Schizophrenia Research*; **62**: 183–185.

Walther, F.R. (1969). Flight behaviour and avoidance of predators in Thomson's gazelle. *Behaviour*; **34**: 184–221.

Walton, M. and Spence, C. (2004). Cross-modal congruency and visual capture in a visual elevation discrimination task. *Experimental Brain Research*; **154**: 113–20.

Waszak, F., Wascher, E., Keller, P., Koch, I., Aschersleben, G., Rosenbaum, D.A., and Prinz, W. (2005). Intention-based and stimulus-based mechanisms in action selection. *Experimental Brain Research*; **162**: 346–56.

Weiss, P.H., Marshall, J.C., Zilles, K., and Fink, G.R. (2003). Are action and perception in near and far space additive or interactive factors? *NeuroImage*; **18**: 837–46.

Witt, J.K., Proffitt, D.R., and Epstein, W. (2005). Tool use affects perceived distance but only when you intend to use it. *Journal of Experimental Psychology: Human Perception and Performance*; **31**: 880–8.

Witter, M.S., Cuthill, I.C., and Bonser, R.H.C. (1994). Experimental investigation of mass-dependent predation risk in the European starling, Sturnus vulgaris. *Animal Behaviour*; **48**: 201–22.

Wolpert, D.M., Ghahramani, Z., and Jordan, M.I. (1995). An internal model for sensorimotor integration. *Science*; **269**: 1880–2.

Wolpert, D.M. and Kawato, M. (1998) Multiple paired forward and inverse models for motor control. *Neural Network*; **11**; 1317–29.

Ydenberg, R.C. and Dill, L.M. (1986). The economics of fleeing from predators. *Advances in the Study of Behavior*; **16**: 229–49.

Yonas, A. and Granrud, C.A. (1985). Reaching as a measure of infants' spatial perception. In *Measurement of audition and vision in the first year of postnatal life: A methodological overview*, (ed. Gottlieb, G.K.N.A.), pp. 301–22. Norwood, NJ: Ablex Publishing Corp.

Yonas, A. and Hartman, B. (1993). Perceiving the affordance of contact in 4- and 5-month-old infants. *Child Development*; **64**: 298–308.

CHAPTER 13

Vision without representation

Alva Noë

Abstract

According to Actionism, perceptual consciousness depends constitutively on perceivers' practical grasp of the significance of movement and action for perceptual experience. This position—versions of which have been developed in O'Regan and Noë (2001), Hurley and Noë (2003) and Noë (2004) (with important antecedents in Hurley (1998))—does not identify perception and action, but proposes that a distinct kind of sensorimotor understanding is exercised in perceptual experience. It has been suggested—by Goodale (2001), Block (2005), Jacob and Jeannerod (2003), and Clark (2006), among others—that Actionism runs up against evidence from neuropsychology that demonstrates the insulation of perceptual function from action-related states and processes, and also, that action-related states and processes are insulated from the influence of perceptual consciousness. I argue that this isn't so. I argue that to understand the relation between perception and action, and, in particular, to understand the findings about two-visual systems in question, we need a view such as Actionism.

13.1. Introduction

Movement produces sensory change. When you approach an object, it looms in your visual field. When you move around it, its profile changes. Blinking disrupts your sensory relation to the object. Perceivers have an implicit understanding of these ways sensory change depends on movement. This is revealed by such facts as that, for example, we are not startled by the effects of blinking, or by the way things around us vary in appearance as we move. This implicit understanding is put to work in perception. According to the sensorimotor or, as I shall call it, actionist approach, perceiving is an activity of exploring the environment making use of this kind of knowledge of the sensory effects of movement (O'Regan and Noë, 2001; Hurley and Noë, 2003; Noë, 2004).

Actionism breaks with traditional approaches to perception that take as their starting point the idea that seeing is a process whereby the brain builds up a picture (or model, or representation) of the world. You see the scene before you when the brain has represented it. Psychologists and perceptual neuroscientists labour to understand how the brain does this. An interesting feature of this standard approach is that it sets up a particular conception of the relation between seeing and acting. First we see; then we think and plan; then we act. Susan Hurley (1998) called this conception the 'input–output' conception. Seeing is input from world to mind. Action is output from mind to world. Action, even the body itself, on this conception, is not required for seeing.

According to actionism, perceptual consciousness is skill-based, environmentally-situated activity. Perception, therefore, on this approach, is not something that happens in us (in our brains) and so it is not a process in our brains whereby an internal picture or representation is produced. According to actionism, and in sharp contrast with the input–output picture, perception is related intimately to action (although it does not itself require action).

In the last few years, actionism has come under attack from those who call into question the kind of dependence it posits between perception and action (e.g. Goodale, 2001; Block, 2005; Jacob, 2006; Clark, 2006). In this chapter I respond to these criticisms. I offer a taxonomy of different ways of thinking about the relation between perception and action. I show that none of these, understood correctly, provide grounds for rejecting the claims of actionism. Moreover, I show that one influential line of thinking about the relation between vision and action, a line associated with the two visual systems hypothesis of Milner and Goodale (1995), far from providing resources for rejecting actionism, actually depends on its truth.

13.2. **Actionism** *in action*

To help bring the claims of the actionist, sensorimotor view, into focus, and to get a feel for its significance and reach, let's consider a well-known but poorly understood phenomenon: the effects of inverting or reversing goggles. Normal prescription lenses function by changing the angle and location at which light is brought to a focus in the eye. Experimental lenses of the sort used by Kohler (1951), Taylor (1962), and many others, function the same way. In one type of case, for example, light approaching the eye from the left is refracted so as to stimulate the eye as if the light were coming in from the right (and vice versa). One might have expected that this sort of alteration would bring about a systematic inversion or reversal in the quality of one's experience, e.g. things on the left would now look as though they are on the right, and vice versa. In fact, this is not what happens. Reversal produces not inversion, but rather visual distortion.

Kevin O'Regan and Noë (O'Regan and Noë, 2001; Hurley and Noë, 2003; Noë, 2004) proposed the following to explain this. The glasses do not distort the light; nor do they deprive it of the information that it carries. They do, however, systematically change the way stimulation varies as a result of the perceiver's self-movement. O'Regan and Noë proposed that changing the patterns of sensorimotor contingency in this way—that is, changing the way sensory stimulation varies as a function of movement—even leaving the character of the stimulation itself unchanged, deprives the resulting stimulation of its meaningful content. Further support for this sensorimotor hypothesis is provided, or so we argued, by consideration of the effect of long-term wearing of inverting lenses. Individuals who wear the lenses for lengthy periods of time, and who are made to engage dynamically with the environment around them as they do so, eventually recover normal perceptual experience (Kohler, 1951; Taylor, 1962). Such individuals experience the position and layout of things as they are, even though they continue to wear the reversing goggles, and even though, as a result, they continue to receive inverted patterns of stimulation. Once again, how things look depends less on the discrete, individual, intrinsic character of stimulation, than it does on the way that stimulation is governed by patterns of sensorimotor contingency.

Actionism offers an explanation of the effects of the goggles on perceptual consciousness and it does so by giving up the basic assumptions of the traditional view. What explains the character of our visual experience (e.g. what makes it an experience of 'on the left' as distinct from 'on the right') is not the fact that this or that neural structure or representation is activated in the brain. That is, it is not the intrinsic character of the pattern of stimulation that fixes the character of our visual experience. What fixes experience, rather, is the way that pattern of stimulation varies as a function of the perceiver's movement, together with the perceiver's expectations regarding those very patterns of dependent variation.

13.3. **Actionism criticized**

The actionist approach to perceptual consciousness has been criticized for misrepresenting the relationship between perception and action.

1. One charge, for example, that has been levelled against actionism is that it holds (wrongly) that perception requires movement, but this is not the case. According to actionism, perception requires sensorimotor knowledge, that is, knowledge of the sensory effects of movement. But neither the possession nor the exercise of such knowledge requires movement, at least not as a logical matter. Of course, it's entirely possible that actual movement is required for the development of such knowledge; just as it is possible that paralysis would compromise one's sensorimotor understanding. But these are not matters on which actionism is required to take stand. They are matters for empirical investigation.

Actionism *is* committed to the idea that perception is active, but not in the sense that it requires that one move. What is required is that one understand the relevance of movement to action, and that one knows what would happen if one were to move. Perception is active, according to the actionist, in the same way that thought is active. We exercise our sensorimotor understanding when we see. Surely there is no reason to think that the paralysed lack an appreciation of the sensory upshots of their own possible or actual movements.

Actionism views perception as intrinsically movement-sensitive, but actionism does not hold that seeing requires movement.

It should be noted, as an aside, that the idea that seeing, for example, requires some minimal movement, is not without some basis. For example, as is well known, if images are stabilized on the retina, they fade from view (owing to retinal fatigue), but this is a fairly superficial consideration. And there is good reason to doubt that there is any deeper requirement for movement in order to see. After all, the paralysed can see. And it is possible to see flashes of light in small units of time in which movements would be impossible. Finally, we all know that it is possible to sit still and watch the passing show, just as it is possible to dream.

2. Turning to a second line of criticism: Actionism is sometimes criticized for commitment to the view that seeing is *for* acting, or, put differently, that we only see what we act on, or what we can act on.

On a familiar reading of Gibson (1979), he is said to have held something like this. For example, Campbell (2002) characterizes Gibson as follows:

> … suppose, for example, that an unfamiliar piece of apparatus appears on a workbench. I have no idea what this thing is for. I don't know if I can touch it - maybe I will be electrocuted, or the thing will blind me, if I do that. Or maybe it is simply the latest kind of television, or a paper weight. So I don't see it as affording anything in particular. In that case, by Gibson's theory, the thing should be simply invisible; I should be able to see it only when I am told what it is for. But that is not a persuasive conclusion; it seems perfectly obvious that we can see things without knowing what they can be used for.
>
> (Campbell, 2002, p.143)

As I read Gibson he is not committed to such a conclusion, for it is not Gibson's view that we *only* see affordances, or that we can only see objects in so far as we can see their affordances. Gibson's point comes earlier: that we can see affordances. The significance of his thought is this: for Gibson, perceptual consciousness is not confined to so-called categorical properties of things, such as shape say, or size, or qualities like colour. Gibson is advancing 'the radical hypothesis' that 'the "values", and "meanings" of things in the environment can be perceived directly' (Gibson, 1979, p.127).

The idea that perception is *for* seeing, or that we only see what presents itself to us for purposes of action, has something to recommend it. For one thing, it makes evolutionary sense. We have every reason to believe that sensory systems evolved, in the first instance, out of simple mechanisms for guiding movement to desired goals (nourishment, sexual partners) and also for avoiding dangers. The earliest sensory systems were, in fact, sensorimotor systems—sensors were linked up directly to motor systems, as in the simple bacteria whose sugar detectors are biochemically linked to flagella. The *seeing-for-acting* idea is also a useful antidote to a more extravagant *representationalist* assumption of so many cognitive scientists. If perception is *for action*, then representation-constructing in the nervous system must be supposed only insofar as such representations serve to facilitate and guide behaviour. Robotocists in particular have made productive use of these ideas, seeking to minimize unnecessary and taxing representation-making activity in the design of perceiving robots.

Despite these positives, there is good reason to doubt the seeing-is-for-acting thesis. As Pylyshyn has written:

> Most things we see are things we cannot act upon directly, such as the words in the target article. Of course what we find out through vision may lead to new beliefs and so may eventualy affect what we do, but this is not the sort of behavior that people have in mind when they speak of visually guided action ... Much of what we see guides our action only indirectly by changing what we believe and perhaps what we want.

> (Pylyshyn, 2001, p.999)

Pylyshyn is right. It is dogmatic and implausible to insist that the only aim of vision is action (just as it would be dogmatic to suppose that the only aim of vision is the production of representations). Pylyshyn's observation, however, was actually offered as a criticism on our 2001 BBS target article in which O'Regan and Noë first laid out the basic elements of the sensorimotor view. But this rests on a misunderstanding. Actionism does not rest on or imply a thesis about the aims or functional value of vision. In particular, it is no part of actionism to hold that perception is for action, or for the guidance of action. Nor does actionism hold that we only see what we can act on. Rather, Actionism, as I have tried to explain, is committed to the view that seeing, and perception in other modalities, depends on the perceiver's possession and exercise of knowledge of the sensory effects of movement. For something to be visible, then, is for it to show up as standing to us in a relation of, as I will put it, sensorimotor perturbability. If you see something, then movements of your eyes or body will affect the way you experience it. This is of course no less true of words in an article or the clouds in the sky than it is true of hammers and pencils.

To repeat, actionism is not committed to the perception is for action thesis and it is therefore not vulerable to this sort of criticism.

I want to mention a more subtle development of the seeing-is-for-acting idea in the recent work of Tom Roberts, James Ward, and some others working with Andy Clark in Edinburgh. This proposal, which Roberts calls the Action Space view, builds on ideas first put forward by Philip Pettit. Pettit (2003) had proposed what he called a 'powers' view of colours, according to which the experience of a colour is understood in terms of the perceiver's being manifestly empowered to sift and sort and track. Roberts stresses that such mental acts as sifting, sorting, and tracking, are actions, and he then suggests that seeing (and other modalities of perceptual awareness) can be taken to be, basically, for the performance of these actions. Ward, Roberts, and Clark (ms) argue that perceptual experience is a special kind of poise over a space of possible actions. Objects of conscious experience enable us to achieve poise over an action-space.

A further advantage of a view of this kind, it has been suggested, is that it does not rely on the idea that experience is related to action at the level of granularity of individual movements. Clark and others think that such a commitment (a commitment they think actionism is wedded to) leads to sensorimotor chauvinism: only creatures whose bodies and sensorimotor repertoires match those of ourselves, can have experience like ourselves. In contrast, for the Action Space theory, action gets into the story at a more abstract functional level, the level of (at least) epistemic actions such as sifting, tracking, and sorting. In effect, Clark and colleagues defend a seeing-is-for-action proposal by modifying it in the light of the claim that conscious vision doesn't govern our low-level movements. It serves a more executive function than that. And they offer this 'action-space' view as an empirically more robust alternative to actionism. They do not, however, give any convincing argument that we need the alternative. For actionism is not committed to the problematic conception of seeing as for action.

Actionism, it should be noticed, allows that radically different kinds of physical systems can support seeing. According to Actionism, for example, the human visual system and the artificial Tactile Visual Substitution System of Paul Bach-y-Rita (1983) can both count as visual. They are visual because there is sensorimotor isomorphism between them, but only at the right high level of abstraction. So it is difficult to see how the charge of chauvinism can be made to stick.

I won't venture detailed criticism of the Action Space idea here. One concern is worth mentioning, however. My experience of the difference between red and green, say, is the basis of my ability to sift and sort them. It gets things backwards to say that the difference consists in my ability to sift, sort, and track them. The Actionism view is intended to get explanatory purchase precisely at this more fundamental level.

3. In recent visual neuroscience it is now accepted widely that there are two distinct visual capacities: conscious seeing, on the one hand, and vision for the guidance of action, on the other, each of which is subserved by anatomically distinct neural structures (the ventral and dorsal streams, respectively). Milner and Goodale, in a series of writings over twenty years or so (e.g. 1995), have argued that ventral and dorsal seeing are doubly dissociatiable. In *optic ataxia*, a condition produced by dorsal stream damage, normal visual consciousness is preserved even though perceivers are impaired in their ability to use what they see to guide action. In *visual agnosia*, the capacity to make use of what you see to guide action is intact even though normal visual consciousness entirely disrupted. The two visual systems approach thus grants that there is an important relation between vision and action, but it is one that requires us radically to rethink what seeing is. The vision that guides action is unconscious, subserved by neural processes in the dorsal stream. The vision that generates conscious visual representations of the world is immune to action-directed considerations.

The two visual systems view would seem to be incompatible with the claims of actionism. This is certainly what influential scientists and philosophers have written repeatedly. Goodale makes this claim in his commentary on our target article. He stresses that D.F. (a much studied visusal agnosic) 'shows nearly perfect visuomotor control in the absence of any evidence that she actually "sees" the form of the object she is grasping' (Goodale 2001, p.984). D.F. lacks normal perceptual consciousness even though she is normal in visuomotor terms. But then visuomotor skill can't be the basis of normal perceptual consciousness. In a similar vein, Block, in his 2005 review of *Action in Perception*, draws on work by Goodale and others to argue that a proper appreciation of the dorsal/ventral story undercuts the actionist view. The dorsal stream, he reasons, is the basis of visuomotor know-how. A distinctive feature of this know-how is that it is effective in peripheral as well as in central vision. In contrast, conscious vision seems to be only effective in central vision. But if visual activity includes dorsally based visual know-how, then visual activity 'simply doesn't reflect the phenomenology of conscious vision' (Block, 2005, p.260). And Block adds that 'It is hard to see how skilled activity of exploring the environment could fail to involve visually guided action' (Block, 2005, p.269).

These critics misunderstand the claims of actionism. Crucially, *pace* Block, actionism does not claim that visual awareness depends on visuomotor skill, if by 'visuomotor skill' one means the ability to make use of vision to reach out and manipulate or grasp. Our claim is that seeing depends on an appreciation of the sensory effects of movement (not, as it were, on the practical significance of sensation). That is, as we have already seen, actionism is not committed to the general claim that seeing is a matter of knowing how to act on or in respect of or relation to the things we see. *Pace* Goodale, the fact that visuomotor skill—in the sense of the ability to use sight to give reaching and grasping—is intact, does *not* give the actionist reason to expect that visual consciousness should also be intact. For, again, that is not the kind of sensorimotor understanding that Actionism claims is constitutive of perceptual consciousness.

13.4. A taxonomy of theories of action in vision

It is useful to summarize the discussion so far. At least four distinct types of view about the vision/ action relationship are now on the table.

1. Actionism

   This is the view that seeing requires the possession and exercise of knowledge of the sensory effects of movement (sensorimotor understanding, in other words).

2. The Movement View

   On this view, actual physical movement is necessary for seeing.

3. Seeing is for acting

   We only see what we act on; or alternatively, all seeing serves to guide, or influence, or enable, movement.

4. The two visual systems view.

   Dorsal vision is unconscious and for the guidance of action. Ventral vision—conscious seeing— is independent of action. These are two autonomous capacities only one of which is in any interesting way action-directed.

   I have sought to make the following points.

   Actionism is not committed to the second and/or third type of view, that is, to the idea that seeing requires movement or that it is always for action.

   The two visual systems view does not provide a counterexample to the Actionism view.

I now want to show that far from it being the case that the two visual systems view provides the reason to reject Actionism (on the grounds that it misrepresents the relation between perception and action), it turns out that the two systems view faces problems that Actionism can help us appreciate. The two visual systems view, I will suggest, takes an implausible conception of visual experience for granted. Actionism can help us frame a superior one.

13.5. Bringing the two visual systems into focus

I begin with a question that comes into focus when we take seriously the central idea of the version of the two visual-systems hypothesis that has been championed by Milner and Goodale (1995). The idea is that there are two distinct visual capacities: conscious seeing, on the one hand, and vision for the guidance of action, on the other, each of which is subserved by anatomically distinct neural structures (the ventral and dorsal streams, respectively).

The question I want to pose is this: how do these distinct visual capacities interact? How are they able jointly to operate in normal vision? That they do jointly operate is beyond doubt.

Consider what happens when you drop your purse and coins scatter across the floor. You look around and spot them, one by one. You find them with your eyes and pick them up. Vision guides you to them. You couldn't pick them up in anything like the way you do if did not see them. Or consider D.F., who has residual visual consciousness—she sees colours, and they show up for her, as belonging to objects, as opposed to being free-floating or unattached. D.F. is able to reach for and succeed in grasping objects of various shapes and sizes (a fork, say, or a screwdriver), moulding her fingers and hand correctly to reflect the visible size and shape of the object. What she cannot do, or rather, what she is unlikely to do, is to grasp these items in ways that are appropriate to their use or function, for she cannot identify what she sees, and so she is not visually sensitive to the function or meaning of what she sees.

What D.F. is unable to do on the basis of what she sees helps us mark out the role performed by normal visual experience in guiding action.

(As an aside: the fact that D.F. is not visually sensitive to what things are for (to what Gibson called their affordances) should put to rest the suggestion that the dorsal stream subserves the perception of affordances, a claim made, for example, by Jacob and Jeannerod [2003, p.181].)

We can appreciate more fully the point that visual guidance of action (even visually guided reaching and grasping) can rely on visual consciousness by recalling that in daily life, optic ataxia seems to be a fairly minor impairment. (1) Most optic ataxics do not complain of action deficits in daily life. In Vighetto and Perenin's 1981 group study, half the patients complained of mild sensory difficulties and half seem not to have noticed any impairment at all, prior to their participation in systematic experimental investigation. (2) It is not generally the case that optic ataxia is a deficit in visual guidance of action. Consider, for example, the following: '…most patients with optic ataxia are able to guide accurate actions toward objects in central vision' (Rossetti et al., 2003, p.173). Again, 'Out of ten patients studied by Vighetto (1980; Perenin and Vighetto 1983 and 1988), only three had a deficit in central vision' (Rossetti et al., 2003, p.173). Even patients with bilateral optic ataxia 'exhibit normal visuomotor performance in central vision in many experimental conditions' involving a grasping response. Problems show up when reaching into the periphery of the visual field or (3) when there is a requirement for fast, online modifications of reaching in response to the displacement of a target object. (4) Performance in reaching and grasping is much improved for familiar objects even when they are in the periphery of the visual field (Jeannerod et al., 1994; Milner et al., 2001). And of course most of the objects that we reach out and grasp in daily life are likely to be familiar.

Now these considerations have several upshots:

First, we can rule out that the dorsal stream is the only support of visually guided action. The ventral stream supports action in a broad range of cases. Neither the phenomenon of visual form agnosia, nor that of optic ataxia, give us reasons to doubt that seeing plays a basic role in the guidance of action; in particular, there is no challenge to the idea that what we see causally influences our reaching and grasping, even if it is also true that we don't need conscious visual attention to help us decide how to move our fingers when reaching for something.

Second, we can see that it is misleading to suggest that there is, globally, a double dissociation of seeing and visually guided action. What is dissociable, rather, is visual consciousness, on the one hand, subserved by the ventral stream perhaps, and something like vision for the setting of some (size- and shape-based) parameters for reaching and grasping, as well as for making rapid, quick responses to objects and events around one. This dissociation is pronounced. Interestingly, it isn't very surprising either. Every typist knows that paying close visual attention to your fingers will disrupt rather than improve performance; and psychologists have shown experimentally that expert performance is impaired when the performer attends to the mechanics of execution. The opposite is the case with novices; performance improves when they pay attention to the mechanics of what they're doing.

These conclusions help us take a first step towards answering the question I have posed: how does conscious seeing influence the mechanisms (in the dorsal stream, say) that are responsible for setting the parameters for reaching and grasping?

To a first approximation, the answer would seem to be that the ventral stream enables us to see objects of interest, and so to select them as targets for reaching and grasping; the information about the selected objects represented in an experience is then passed on to the dorsal stream. Visual experience gives us the world as present; with the world made present in experience, we can act on it.

On this way of thinking, the dorsal stream is analogous to the autofocus on a camera. The autofocus is not controlled by the photographer; it responds automatically to the situation. But you need a photographer to find objects worth taking pictures of and to aim the camera in the right direction. For ease of reference, I am going to refer to this simple picture of how seeing and dorsal visuomotor guidance are related as the Autofocus Conception. The Autofocus conception has two parts: (1) the ventral stream selects objects of interest; (2) the dorsal stream is then able automatically to target and calibrate itself appropriately to the represented objects.

The Autofocus conception faces a problem. Let's call this the commensurability problem. It is widely appreciated and has been stated nicely by Bridgeman (1999): 'It is not clear how the cognitive system [the ventral stream] communicates a particular object as a target, to a system [the dorsal stream] that cannot distinguish different targets.' The problem is this: the ventral stream builds up a representation of the object in object-centred coordinates, but the dorsal stream is a kind of robotic zombie that is built to detect and respond to the true size and shape of things; whatever the dorsal robot represents, it represents it in egocentric, not object-centred, terms. So we can ask, how is it that the dorsal system ever manages to pick up the very thing the ventral system is looking at? Suppose, to use Jeannerod's example (Jeannerod, 1997, p.80), that we want to eat the lone red apple among the many green ones. We see the red one; we want it; and we manage to reach precisely for it. How do we carry this off?

A suggestion made by Jeannerod (1997, p.80) and endorsed by Campbell (2002), and I think by Goodale and Milner (2004) too, is that what the ventral stream needs to do is to tell the dorsal stream the location of the object on which it is to act. The ventral stream passes along the object's coordinates to the visuomotor system. The dorsal stream doesn't need to be sensitive to the object itself, merely to its location.

This proposal raises two issues, one merely technical and one more substantive. The technical issue is this: how does the dorsal stream get the real-world, egocentric location information from the allocentric visual representation of the object made available by the visual consciousness module? Goodale and Milner address this issue when they point out that the dorsal and ventral stream share a common retinotopic base camp in primary visual cortex; they suggest that 'Once a target has been highlighted on a retinal map [thanks to back-projections from the ventral stream], it can be converted into any other coordinate system that the dorsal stream might need to use' (Goodale and Milner, 2004, p.102). This seems right, as far as it goes.

But this proposal to the technical problem doesn't address the more substantive issue. The substantive problem, or question, is this: how should we think (or better: how can we think) of conscious seeing such that it is able to discharge this role of enabling the dorsal stream to target the objects that it has selected? What I will show is that proponents of the two systems idea don't have the resources to frame a conception of seeing that will do this job.

Most researchers working in this framework suppose what I will call the picture theory of seeing. They suppose that when we see we have picture-like, allocentric representations of the scene in consciousness. The ventral system produces pictures similar to what the Mars rover sends back to earth.

Consider how Jacob and Jeannerod describe conscious visual experience; they write (2003, p.197):

Consider a visual representation of a mug to the left of a telephone. In the visual percept, the location of the mug relative to the location of the telephone is coded in allocentric coordinates. The percept has an iconic or pictoral content that is both informationally richer and more fine grained than any conceptual representation of that state of affairs. For example, it cannot depict the mug as being to the left of the telephone without depicting how far the former is from the latter. Nor can it depict the relative distance of the mug from the telephone without depicting the orientation, shape, texture, size, and content (if any) of the mug, the orientation, shape, size, and colour of the telephone.

Here, Jacob and Jeannerod describe the content of visual experience as allocentric or object-centred and as pictorial. Their idea seems to be that we encounter the world in our experience as, so to speak, a tableau or composition of elements, rather as we might encounter the world in a still life on the wall of a museum. There is a certain amount of backsliding in this characterization. As Bermudez has remarked, talk of 'left' and 'right' already suggests an egocentric perspective. Tellingly, Jacob and Jeannerod use distinctively non-allocentric descriptive resources to describe the content of what we see. We can rephrase the autofocus conception in terms of Jacob and Jeannerod's picture theory of experience: according to the autofocus conception, seeing (subserved by the ventral stream) produces picture-like, allocentric representations along the lines of *there is a cup to the left of a telephone*; the dorsal stream is then able automatically to target and calibrate itself appropriately to the represented objects.

The problem with the picture theory, it seems to me, is that it doesn't seem to be able to do the job we need it to do, that, namely, of telling us where things are so that we can, among other things, reach out and grab them. Just as looking through binoculars won't tell you how far away a thing is, so an allocentric, picture-like representation won't tell you where things are in relation to you. Indeed, the problem is deeper than that. The picture theory tells us that what we see is that an object satisfying such and such a description stands in such-and-such relations to other things at a certain place in the environment; or, to use Jacob and Jeannerod's example, an experience has a content like this: *a mug is to the left of a telephone*. But how can knowing that a cup is to the left of a telephone tell me where the cup is in relation to me, or to my hand, so that I can reach out and grab it?

In a way, the problem with the picture theory is more basic than this. Although it is true that you can see a cup, or a 'phone, that you can see a thing as falling under this or that description, that is never all you see. When you see a cup and 'phone, say, you see this particular cup here and you see it in relation to that particular 'phone; and you see them both as located not only in relation to each other but also in relation to you, as here or there, as within reach or just out of reach. Objects and properties show up in experience—experience teaches us about them—but they always show up in relation to us, that is, they show up as located in an egocentric and not merely an allocentric space. Experience teaches us not only that there is a cup to the left of a 'phone, but that this cup and that 'phone stand in a certain relation to me.

So the picture theory distorts what seeing is like in an important way. Not only does the picture theory leave it mysterious as to how we can reach out and pick up the things we see, it leaves it mysterious how we can ever manage to see anything or in perception to come into contact with anything. So it makes it mysterious how we ever see particular things as present in relation to ourselves. And so it leaves unaddressed how we ever manage to even think about or identify the things we see.

The picture theory of visual experience doesn't seem to be able to do justice to the role that experience actually needs to play for us, that of selecting targets which we can then grasp, or pick up, or which we can identify, or about which we can think and talk. But now we come to the crux of the problem. What we need is a conception of experience according to which we can think of the experience as presenting the perceiver with the object as standing in a relation to him or herself. That's just to say that we need a conception of conscious seeing which is already imbued with immediate pertinence to the perceiver's space of possible actions. This is precisely the sort of conception of experience that actionism provides. According to actionism, the visual world always shows up in such a way that our relation to what we see is always already perturbable by movements.

13.6. **Biting the bullet or spitting it out**

Now, it might be objected: precisely what makes the research of Goodale and Milner so astonishing, and so important, is that it requires us to accept the consequence that the dorsal stream succeeds in targeting its object even though, as it turns out, visual experience *does not* lock onto the object in particular. Dorsal-based adjustments of grip aperture, for example, are simply autonomous in respect of what we see. Seeing may not deliver reference to the object of sight. But that's just so much the worse for seeing; it's no skin off the dorsal stream's nose, for the dorsal stream can get the job done its own way.

In fact, so the defender of the picture theory will continue, what the data shows us is not only that we do not need to experience the presence of particular things in order to reach out and grasp them, but further, that the feeling of visual presence itself is nothing but an illusion. Indeed, perhaps it is an illusion generated by the very fact that we can reach out and pick things up!

If the picture theory is right, then the structure of visually guided action in normal vision is identical to that of visually guided reaching and grasping in blindsight. In blindsight the patient does not see or consciously experience that for which he reaches. He reaches not on the basis of what he sees, but rather on the basis of what the experimenter instructs him to do. He relies on the experimenter's description of what is there. The blindsight patient lacks a sense of the presence of what he sees, and so he is not guided by that presence. On the picture of experience, it would seem, visual experience stands in just the same relation to our reaching and grasping as the instructions of the experimenter stand in relation to the blindsight patient's visuomotor system—the ventral stream of the normal and the experimenter each offer the visuomotor system (or, for that matter, the reasoning thinking system) a more or less useful description of what is there. On this approach, what differentiates the normal seeing case from that of blindsight, is that in the former there is an accompanying (probably illusory) feeling of presence! Blindsight, on this way of thinking, would be a less confused state than normal vision.

One reason for rejecting this defense of the picture theory is that it now carries the burden of making intelligible the claim that you can factor experience into a representational content, on the one hand, and a dissociable feeling of presence, on the other. Mohan Matthen (2005) suggests that we are all familiar with cases of visual experience minus the normally associated feelings of perceptual presence. This is what happens when we visually imagine a couch that is not before us, say. The content of our experience—that there is a couch with such and such qualities in such and such relation to a background—may be exactly the same as that of the corresponding experience of seeing the couch. In the latter case, however, but not the former, we typically have the added feeling of the presence of the particular couch. Pictures provide Matthen's second example. When you see a picture you have a visual experience with the content that is depicted in the picture, but you don't have a sense of the presence of that which is thus depicted. For example, when you see picture of the Eiffel Tower you have an experience that represents it thus, but you don't have a sense of its actual presence.

What supplies representational content with presence, according to Matthen? The dorsal stream. Motion guiding vision, Matthen argues, is nondescriptive and deictic. It secures reference to particulars and makes it the case that that which is represented is made to feel vividly present. A consequence of Matthen's view is that damage to the dorsal stream would in fact alter visual consciousness by making it more like picture-consciousness or like the visual imagination. However, this is not tenable. Optic ataxics sometimes fail to know that they have any impairment whatsoever, let alone an impairment in their visual consciousness of this order of magnitude.

What we need, I think, is a conception of seeing whereby it can enable us to encounter present particulars and their properties. We don't have visual impressions and then, subsequently, acquire a feeling of presence. Things show up in experience always already as present.

Here is another problem with the picture theory. If it is right, then we ought to find, but we do not find, that there is a kind of visual analogue of Capgras syndrome (Hirstein and Ramachandran, 1997). In Capgras syndrome, a patient might come to be convinced that his wife is an imposter. He grants that she looks exactly like his wife, but he is convinced it's not really her but a look-alike. According to Ramachandran, patients with Capgras' are perceptually normal; for some reason they are missing the feeling of familiarity that usually accompanies our perceptual judgments. Dennett (1996) has speculated along similar lines about some kinds of obsessive/compulsive disorder. The obsessive/compulsives checks the door, establishes that it's locked, but finds that he must check again and again, not because he hasn't confirmed that the door is locked but because, for some reason, he isn't getting the familiar feeling of having confirmed it. Well, if the way of thinking about experience that we are considering is right, then we ought to find patients in whom, as a result of lesion, presence and representational content are in fact dissociated.

So it seems that we need a different conception of visual experience, one that does justice to the fact that experience does not merely yield information to the effect that there is an x of such and such a kind at a certain place in an allocentric frame. We need an account of seeing according to which what we see shows up from the start not only as a thing of a such and such a kind, bearing relations to other elements in a scene, but also as standing in a definite relation to us.

Now I submit (and this now is meant to be a positive claim) that any conception of experience that meets this explanatory demand will be a conception that treats seeing as related intimately to action in at least this way: it belongs to the very character of seeing, to the way things show up for us in visual consciousness, that how what is seen shows up for us is poised to be affected by our movements. Seeing something is standing in a movement and action-sensitive relation to it. Only such an active, or action-oriented conception of seeing can capture the ways in which seeing is responsive now only to how things are, but also to our dynamic relation to how things are.

This is the central idea behind the sort of Actionist or sensorimotor approach to vision that has been advanced by Kevin O'Regan and myself. Movement produces sensory change and visual content—what we see when we see—depends on and incorporates a sensitivity to or understanding of the ways in which sensory stimulation varies in relation to movement. Seeing does yield information about how things are in themselves around us, but it does so only by allowing us access to how things are in relation to us. For example, seeing something whose visible profile is elliptical (e.g. a coin held away at an angle) can be, for a suitably skilful perceiver, that is, for a perceiver with the right sort of sensorimotor understanding, a visual experience of something precisely circular.

Against this background, we can say: instead of thinking of the ventral stream as delivering picture-like visual experiences that are useless for the purposes of telling us where things are or whether they are there, let us suppose that seeing is a way of being in touch with particular things. The content of a visual experience is not: a cup is to the left of a telephone; rather, it will be something more like, this cup here is to the left of that telephone. Seeing is a way of locking onto things; it is a way of being related to them.

If visual experience is in this way non-descriptive and so non-representational, it becomes immediately clear why blindsight feels so different from normal visually guided action. It isn't that in normal seeing we have an associated (illusory) feeling of presence that we misguidedly think makes a difference to how we act. It is that in normal seeing we act on the basis of the presence of particular objects or situations, whereas in blindsight we act only on the basis of general descriptions, descriptions that leaves our relation to what is described unspecified and indeterminate. What makes healthy intact vision different from blindsight is that vision results in contact with objects themselves, but blindsight is forced to make do with mere descriptions.

This way of thinking about seeing also helps us see how to solve the commensurability problem. When we act on what we see, we aren't in the position of needing to convert one kind of description of where a thing is into another. Our predicament is not like that at all. That framing of the problem presupposes the standard view of experience that we are giving up. Think of seeing the object as like pointing to it with the eyes. The dorsal stream doesn't need to be told where to reach; it already knows that it needs to reach where you are looking, to reach for what you are looking at. Here we take a leaf from the page of the roboticist Dana Ballard. Metaphorically, it is as if visual consciousness takes us by the hand and leads us to the object.

13.7. **Summary**

I have been advancing a theory of seeing that makes seeing depend crucially on the understanding of action-related patterns and also on our dynamic relation to the objects around us. I hope it will be clear that there is no conflict between this proposal and facts about the existence of a strong dissociation between visual consciousness and the adjustment of low-level parameters of reaching and grasping. Given an active, perceptual encounter with the world, low-level adjustments can take place without the help of seeing. Indeed, far from its being the case that an actionist proposal is in conflict or disagreement with the basic facts on which the two-visual systems hypothesis rests, if I am right, the two-visual systems view actual needs an actionist account if it is to offer any account of conscious seeing and its relation to visually guided action.

References

Bach-y-Rita, P. (1983). Tactile vision substitution: past and future. *International Journal of Neuroscience*; **19**(1–4): 29–36.

Block, N. (2005). Review of action in perception. *Journal of Philosophy*; **102**: 259–72.

Bridgeman, B. (1999). Two visual brains in action. *Psyche*; **5**(18).

Campbell, J. (2002). *Reference and consciousness*. Oxford: Oxford University Press.

Clark, A. (2006). Vision as dance? Three challenges for sensorimotor contingency theory. *Psyche*; **12**(1): 1–10.

Dennett, D. (1996). *Kinds of minds. Toward an understanding of consciousness*. New York: Basic Books.

Gibson, J.J. (1979). *The ecological approach to visual perception*. Hillsdale, NJ: Lawrence Erlbaum.

Goodale, M.A. (2001). Different spaces and different times for perception and action. *Progress in Brain Research*; **134**: 313–31.

Goodale, M.A. and Milner, A.D. (2004). *Sight unseen: an exploration of conscious and unconscious vision*. Oxford: Oxford University Press.

Hirstein, W, and Ramachandran, V.S. (1997). Capgras syndrome: a novel probe for understanding the neural representation and familiarity of persons. *Proceedings of the Royal Society of London*; **264**: 437–44.

Hurley, S. (1998). *Consciousness in action*. Cambridge, MA: Harvard University Press.

Hurley, S. and Noë, A. (2003). Neural plasticity and consciousness. *Biology and Philosophy*; **18**: 131–68.

Jacob, P. and Jeannerod, M. (2003). *Ways of seeing: the scope and limits of visual cognition*. Oxford: Oxford University Press.

Jacob, P. (2006). Why visual experience is likely to resist being enacted, *Psyche*; **12**: 1–11.

Jeannerod, M., Decety, J., and Michel, F. (1994). Impairment of grasping movements following a bilateral posterior parietal lesion. *Neuropsychologia*; **32**: 369–80.

Jeannrod, M. (1997). *The cognitive neuroscience of action*. Oxford: Blackwell.

Kohler, I. (1951). *ÜberAufbau und Wandlungen der Wahrnehmungswelt*. Vienna: Rohrer.

Matthen, M. (2005). *Seeing, doing, and knowing: a philosophical theory of sense perception*. Oxford: Clarendon Press.

Milner, A.D. and Goodale, M.A. (1995). *The visual brain in action*. Oxford: Oxford University Press.

Milner, A.D., Dijkerman, H.C., Pisella, L., McIntosh, R.D., Tilikete, C., Vighetto, A., et al. (2001). Grasping the past: delay can improve visuomotor performance. *Current Biology*; **11**: 1896–901.

Noë, A. (2004). *Action in perception*. Cambridge, MA: MIT Press.

O'Regan, K. and Noë, A. (2001). A sensorimotor account of vision and visual consciousness. *Behavioral and Brain Sciences*; **24**(5): 883–917.

Pettit, P. (2003). Looks red. *Philosophical Issues*; **13**(1): 221–52.

Pylyshyn, Z.W. (2001). Seeing, acting and knowing: commentary on O'Regan and Noë 2001. *Behavioral and Brain Sciences*; **24**(5): 999.

Rossetti, Y., Pisella, L., and Vighetto, A. (2003). Optic ataxia revisited: visually guided action versus immediate visuo-motor control. *Expimental Brain Research*; **153**: 171–9.

Taylor, J.G. (1962). *The behavioral basis of perception*. New Haven, CT: Yale University Press.

Vighetto, A. and Perenin, M.T. (1981). Optic ataxia: analysis of eye and hand responses in pointing at visual targets. *Revue Neurologique;* **137**: 357–72.

Ward, D., Roberts, T., and Clark, A. (ms.). Knowing what we can do: actions, intentions and the construction of phenomenal experience.

CHAPTER 14

Sensorimotor knowledge and the contents of experience

Julian Kiverstein

Abstract

I take up an argument that has been advanced recently by Andy Clark according to which one lesson of research that purports to establish the existence of two-visual systems is that the content of experience must abstract away from the details of our sensorimotor engagement with the world. I argue for two ways in which sensorimotor knowledge might contribute to the contents of experience. Both contributions, however, are based on the assumption that our spatial point of view is reflected in the content of experience. I suggest that it is the denial of this assumption that might be the basis of Clark's argument. His argument rests on the claim that, if visual experiences are to play the functional role assigned to the vision-for-perception system, the contents of those experiences must be independent of any spatial point of view. I argue that experiences can be from a spatial point of view and play the functional role Clark assigns to them precisely because the contents of experience depend on a perceiver's sensorimotor knowledge.

14.1. Introduction

Perhaps the defining feature of perceptual experience is its intentionality or directedness upon the world. As I look about my office I can see pictures on the wall, my houseplant, and the books and papers scattered around my messy desk. My visual experience is of, or about, these things by virtue of its intentional content, but when do two perceptual experiences have the same or different intentional contents, and what is it that explains this sameness or difference? I will argue that at least some aspects of the intentional content of experience depend on a perceiver's *sensorimotor knowledge*; hence, I will be defending a version of the sensorimotor theory of consciousness.[1] Sensorimotor knowledge is an implicit or practical form of knowledge. What the perceiver knows are the *sensorimotor contingencies* that govern his experience. Sensorimotor contingencies are law-like relationships that hold between sensory input and motor output. Previous sensorimotor theories have made the

---

[1] See Merleau-Ponty (1962); Hurley (1998); O'Regan and Noë (2001); Noë (2004); Siewert (2005); and Thompson (2007), for different versions of this idea. The sensorimotor theory is also known as the 'enactive' theory of perception (Noë, 2004; Thompson, 2007) and actionism (Noë, 2007, this volume).

strong claim that the exercise of sensorimotor knowledge can explain fully the content and character of our experiences. They have defended the hypothesis that patterns of interdependence between sensory input and motor output can explain both *intermodal* qualitative differences in experience (e.g. the difference between sight and touch), and *intramodal* qualitative differences in experience (e.g. the difference between seeing red rather than green).[2] I will label this the 'strong sensorimotor hypothesis' (SSH). I will not attempt a defence of SSH. Instead I will describe two ways in which sensorimotor knowledge might be thought to contribute to the contents of experience.

Andy Clark (2006b and 2008, ch.8) has argued that SSH is inconsistent with what we have learned about visual experience from work on the two visual systems. The two visual systems hypothesis claims that the brains of humans and primates comprise two functionally dissociable visual systems: a phylogenetically ancient system subserving visually based action, and a more recent system subserving conscious visual awareness (Milner and Goodale, 1995/2006).[3] Clark suggests that work on two visual systems seems to establish that the contents of *conscious* vision are 'tweaked and optimised' in ways that do not 'march in step' with sensory stimulation (2008, p.179). The contents of conscious experience are suited to tasks like planning and selecting types of action, or identifying and discriminating an object's properties. These tasks do not require representations that are sensitive to every nuance in sensory stimulation and its modulation by movement. What will prove important for success in these tasks is locking on to features such as rough spatial location, colour, size, shape and so on, information that is useful for selecting targets for action and types of action. This conclusion is, he argues, incompatible with SSH, which seeks to explain qualitative differences of experience in terms of the ways in which sensory stimulation varies with movement.

Suppose Clark is right and conscious experiences are optimized in ways that make them fit to play a role in reason, recall, and planning. Must our experiences have contents that abstract away from sensorimotor knowledge? I defend a negative answer to this question in what follows. In section 14.2, I set out the account of sensorimotor knowledge I will operate with in this chapter. In sections 14.3 and 14.4, I describe two ways in which sensorimotor knowledge might contribute to the contents of visual experience. In section 14.5, I look at an argument that has been made by Jacob and Jeannerod (2003), according to which visual experiences must represent space using allocentric coordinates. This argument, if correct, would seem to provide further support for Clark's conclusion. I will suggest however that their argument fails. I end by suggesting tentatively that conscious vision may depend on sensorimotor knowledge if it is to do the functional work Clark assigns to it.

14.2. **Sensorimotor knowledge: some clarifications**

I have defined 'sensorimotor knowledge' as a perceiver's implicit understanding of sensorimotor contingencies, the laws that determine how sensory stimulation varies with motor output. As it stands, however, this definition is subject to a number of ambiguities. Clark (2006a) has, for instance, pointed out that 'sensory stimulation' as it figures in this definition can be understood in at least two ways. According to the first interpretation, sensory stimulation refers to raw, unprocessed sensory

---

[2] See, for instance, O'Regan and Noë (2001) and Hurley and Noë (2003).

[3] This is to say that the underlying brain systems differ when we perceive and recognize an object such as a cup, and when we make use of visual information to reach and grasp for the very same cup. Reporting and describing a visual stimulus are said to be under the control of the vision for perception system, subserved by the ventral visual pathway that travels from primary visual cortex (V1) to inferotemporal cortex. The performance of simple automatic motor responses based on information about a visual stimulus is, by contrast, said to be under the control of the dorsal visual pathway that travels from primary visual cortex to posterior parietal cortex. Jacob and Jeannerod (2003, part II) offer a nuanced and balanced discussion of a wide range of evidence for the two visual systems hypothesis. For a different take on the neurological evidence, see Rossetti et al., this volume.

input such as light received at the retina. On the second interpretation 'sensory 'stimulation' refers to conscious sensations—states that there is something it is like for a perceiving animal to undergo.

Briscoe (2008, p.461) identifies a related ambiguity in Noë's (2004) account of sensorimotor contingencies.[4] Frequently, Noë glosses sensorimotor knowledge as implicit understanding of the way 'sensory stimulation varies as you move' (op cit. p.78). In this reading, sensorimotor contingencies are defined as laws relating changes in sub-personal, proximal sensory stimulations with types of movement. Noë also describes sensorimotor contingencies in distal terms as changes in the 'perspectival properties' an object instantiates as the perceiver varies his relation to an object. Noë tells us that perspectival properties are mind-independent, relational properties of objects; they are 'relations among objects, the location of the perceiver's body, and illumination' Noë (2004, p. 85). As the perceiver varies his relation to an object, so the perspectival properties an object instantiates will vary. Your sensorimotor knowledge, on this second interpretation of sensorimotor contingencies, is an understanding of how an object's perspectival properties (construed distally) change when you move. Moreover, sensorimotor contingencies on this second reading need not be construed as laws relating sub-personal vehicles of visual perception with movement, as in the first reading. Perspectival properties are visible: they are properties of objects we experience. Thus sensorimotor contingencies can be described as relations of dependence that hold between properties of objects we experience, and movement.

We can combine Clark and Briscoe's objections to raise the following two questions:

1. Are sensorimotor contingencies best understood proximally (in terms of sub-personal, vehicles of visual perception), or distally (in terms of properties of objects we see)?
2. Is sensorimotor knowledge accessible to the perceiving organism or is it rather a property of the bearers or vehicles of content, and hence not consciously accessible to you or me?

This second question asks whether sensorimotor knowledge is something to be attributed to persons (and animals), or to sub-personal information processing machinery. Sub-personal explanations describe functional or neural mechanisms that carry content and can be appealed to in causal explanations of behaviour. Personal- or animal-level explanations, by contrast, posit content-bearing representational states that enter into normative and rational relations with other representational states. These normative and rational relations determine how the representational state figures in rational explanations of behaviour. We can therefore paraphrase this second question as asking whether sensorimotor knowledge is a concept to be deployed in explaining representational vehicles or in explaining the contents of those vehicles.

I will begin with the first question. The sensory stimulation appealed to in the description of sensorimotor contingencies can of course be understood proximally in terms of the changes taking place at the sense organ. However, to understand changes in sensory input purely in proximal terms is, at best, only partially correct. This we can see by reminding ourselves of a distinction J.J. Gibson (1972) made between 'optical stimulation' and 'optical information'. Optical stimulation occurs when the photoreceptors in the eye receive light, but this light carries no information about the layout of the environment. This occurs when, for instance, the perceiver is immersed in a dense fog, or when the perceiver wears plastic diffusing eye-caps that cause him to see nothing but a homogenous field of whiteness, a *Ganzfeld*. Optical information is, by contrast, what the perceiver receives normally as sensory input. It is light that has reflected off the surfaces in a perceiver's surrounding environment and converged on a point of observation, which Gibson called an 'ambient optic array'. The light converging on a point of view stands in a relation of 'specifying' the substances and surfaces around the perceiver. According to Gibson, and those that have followed him, the eye does not just receive optical stimulation; it receives *optical information* by virtue of which the perceiving organism is able to perceive its surrounding environment directly. Thus, the sensory stimulation impacting the eyes

---

[4] Noë (2004) employs the expression 'sensorimotor dependencies' rather than 'contingencies'. I will assume that nothing turns on this difference in terminology.

and other sense organs should not be understood in purely proximal terms. It must also be understood distally in relation to the substances and surfaces in the environment that the sensory stimulation specifies.

The idea that optical information could 'specify' or uniquely correspond to properties in the environment might give the impression that Gibson means to attribute magical powers to sensory systems. Famously, Marr (1982, pp. 29–30) responded to Gibson that the enormity of the task of extracting information about environmental invariants from sensory stimulation should not be underestimated. The information available in sensory stimulation, Marr argued, underdetermines the visual scene massively.[5] I suggest that it is, in part, the acquisition of sensorimotor knowledge by our sensory systems that may explain how they come to have this seemingly magical power. Sensory systems learn to associate movements with changes in sensory stimulation they receive. Acquiring familiarity with the ways in which sensory stimulation is correlated with movement is what enables the perceiving animal to extract information about environmental invariants. It is the possession of sensorimotor knowledge that explains how sensory stimulation comes to carry information that specifies the layout of the environment.

We can see how this might work by thinking briefly about the problem of categorization. A sensory state *specifies* the layout of the distal environment when it has a content that could serve as the ground for categorizing the items that make up a perceptual scene informing the perceiver of what is where. Categorization requires the identification or recognition of environmental invariants, and it is supposedly these invariants that optical information enables the organism to detect. Thus if we can explain how sensory systems learn to categorize stimuli, this would go a long way in explaining how the states of such systems come to carry optical information. I will argue that sensorimotor knowledge holds the solution to both these problems.

Categorization is a tricky problem for sensory systems since one and the same object can lead to a very large number of different sensory inputs, depending on the angle from which the object is viewed, lighting conditions, sensory noise, and many other contextual factors. Given this large input space, it is difficult for a sensory system to learn how to categorize stimuli by learning how to map sensory inputs onto exemplars stored by category. Movement can make all the difference in overcoming this problem; by actively moving, and the perceiving agent can structure its own sensory input, transforming the input space so that categories can be learned. Movement can allow the agent to pick up on the invariants in a flow of information. Consider for instance how infants move objects in front of their faces at a fixed distance (Bushnell and Boudreau, 1993, cited by Pfeifer and Scheier, 1999, p. 396). The object is thereby always viewed from the same distance, allowing the infant to pick up on correlations that it can exploit for learning.

Consider as a second example the following simple control system described in Nolfi and Marocco (2002). The artificial agent had the task of classifying objects with different shapes based on tactile information. They describe how the agent learned to select a sequence of behaviours that allowed for the easy discrimination of sensory states, arising from interaction with particular objects. The robot moved its arm, for instance, in such a way as to follow the curvilinear surface of the sphere, or so as to make contact with one of the angles of the cubic object. Moreover, the robot terminated its movement with its arm fully extended in the case of its interaction with spherical objects. When interacting with cubic objects its movement ended with the arm in a bent position. The robot learned to use the position of its arm at the end of its interaction with an object as an indicator of the category of the object it was interacting with. Crucially, this strategy depended on the temporally extended interaction of the robot with its environment in which the robot created multiple, temporally correlated flows of sensory and motor information. One lesson we can draw from this study and many others like it (see e.g., Lungarella and Pfeifer, 2001; Pfeifer and Scheier, 1997; Te Boekhorst et al., 2003; Thelen and Smith, 1994) is that the temporal correlation of sensory and motor information

---

[5] Also see Fodor and Pylyshyn's (1981) critique of Gibsonian theories.

can allow a perceiving organism to lock on to environmental invariants or regularities that would be hard, if not impossible, for a passive, immobile perceiver to detect.[6]

Let us now return to the two questions I posed above, beginning with our first question. Sensorimotor contingencies as I shall understand them are the correlations the infant discovers between time-locked multimodal sensory information and its own movements, which I have just argued play a crucial role in categorization. Should such sensory information be understood proximally or distally? I have just argued that it is the acquisition of sensorimotor knowledge by an organism that enables its perceptual states to carry optical information. It would seem to follow that the sensory input the organism receives prior to the acquisition of sensorimotor knowledge does not tell the organism anything about the layout of its environment. It is only when the organism has learned something of the regular ways in which movement generates sensory consequences that it can begin to be informed about its environment.

Consider in this light the experiments of Paul Bach-y-Rita (1983) with tactile-visual sensory substitution (TVSS) devices. Bach-y-Rita equipped blind subjects with an array of tactile stimulators positioned on their back or abdomen and wired up to a video camera. Visual information presented to the camera produced a range of tactile stimulation on the subject's skin. Some of the subjects had the video camera mounted on their head or shoulder allowing them to generate tactile stimulation that was contingent on their movements. After a few hours of getting used to the device these subjects were able to reach out and pick up objects, and even participate in games of ping-pong. They were also able to make judgements about the size, shape and number of objects placed on the other side of the room, objects with which they were not in tactile contact. However, prior to familiarizing themselves with the regular ways in which tactile stimulation varied with movement, these subjects experienced nothing but a variety of tactile stimulations. Perhaps every organism is in an analogous position prior to the acquisition of sensorimotor knowledge. They have not yet learned the regular ways in which modality-specific sensory stimulation is related to simultaneously occurring flows of sensory information, and to their own movements. For this reason, the sensory stimulation they undergo does not bear any meaningful relation to their distal environment.

Sensory stimulation taken on its own, in isolation from its relationship to movement and the other sense-modalities, can be described properly in terms of the proximal changes occurring at the sense organ. However it does not follow that sensory stimulation as it figures in laws of sensorimotor contingency should also be understood solely in proximal terms. On the contrary, we have seen how modality-specific sensory information stands in relationships with movement and other types of sensory information that allow the organism to pick up information about the layout of its surrounding environment. It is precisely these relationships that seem to make the difference in determining whether the organism can pick up information about its environment or not. For this reason, I suggest that in the context of sensorimotor contingencies, it would be a mistake to understand sensory stimulation solely in proximal terms. The sensory stimulation that enters into law-like relationships with movement and other types of sensory stimulation should be understood in relation to the information it carries about distal environment.

Should sensorimotor knowledge be understood as a property of contents or of vehicles? I have argued that sensorimotor knowledge should be understood as a property that explains how sensory states can be taken up by an organism in classifying and categorizing the objects in its environment. As such, sensorimotor knowledge is viewed as part of the sub-personal machinery that explains how perceiving animals come to be in touch with their environments.

Sensorimotor knowledge can, however, make a contribution to the contents of experience in the formation of what I will call sensorimotor expectations. Sensorimotor expectations have as their representational content the sensory consequences of movement. Many such expectations never

---

[6] Pfeifer and Scheier (1999, p.403) cite Edelman's (1987) theory of neuronal group selection in support of this claim. According to Edelman's theory, categorization depends on the interplay of multiple sensory and motor maps related by recurrent anatomical connections (Edelman 1987, p.210).

make it into the contents of conscious experience. One such example might be the emulator circuits which Clark and Grush (1999) appeal to in order to explain smooth reaching. Emulators 'anticipate' or model the sensory feedback generated by movement. Visual cortex takes up to 150 ms to process sensory feedback, a delay that could prove costly in the course of fast, online action. The motor system's solution to this problem, Clark and Grush hypothesize, is to use knowledge of the sensory consequences of movement to produce mock feedback that can then be used to test out and fine tune movements in advance of trying them out in the world. However, emulation does not exhaust the ways in which sensorimotor knowledge can be deployed to form sensorimotor expectations. I will argue in the next two sections for two ways in which sensorimotor expectations may also contribute to the contents of experience.

14.3. **Experience, attention, and the background**

Our eyes are constantly in motion as we experience the world visually with gaze redirection taking place three to four times per second (Findlay and Gilchrist, 2003, p. 4). This continuous movement of the eye is no coincidence. As Findlay and Gilchrist (2003, p. 5) have pointed out, bodily movements enable the visual system to combine a restricted (foveal) area of high-resolution processing with an ability to monitor the entire visual field. The retinal image is not homogenous; the retina is, for instance, nearly colour blind outside the high-resolution foveal region. Moreover, projections to the retina away from the central foveal area are given decreased weighting in the processing of visual information. This has the consequence that visual acuity decreases for every degree we move out into peripheral vision, and certain discriminations become impossible (Findlay and Gilchrist, 2003, §2.2.3).[7] Yet despite this non-homogeneity of visual processing, we do not experience the periphery of our visual field as out of focus and monochrome. We have the impression of seeing a uniformly coloured and detailed visual field, from the centre right out to the periphery.

In order for us to have an awareness of this kind, must our experiences actually represent all of this detail? We need not have densely detailed experiences in order to experience dense detail in the environment. Much of this detail could instead figure in our experiences only potentially, and whenever we have a question about some unseen detail, we could find out the answer by looking.[8] The easy access to such information might give rise to the illusion that we are already in possession of a richly detailed representation of our environment. Consider in this light some experiments by McConkie and colleagues (McConkie and Rayner, 1975; McConkie and Zola, 1979) in which subjects were asked to read from a screen of text, only a small area of which was normal (a few letters to the left of, and 15 to the right of the subject's fixation point). The remainder of the letters on display were continuously perturbed. Subjects reported having the impression of seeing a page of normal text because this is what they accessed from moment to moment. Their perceptual contact with a small but moving area of normal text sufficed to give them the impression that the page as a whole contained normal text.

How much of the phenomenology of our experience is explicable in this way, in terms of potential access to the things around us, and their qualities? A surprising amount of what we experience might be explained in this way. Take my messy desk: much of the clutter is outside of the central area of my visual field, but what I see is not confined to what is currently occupying the centre of my visual field. I see mess extending around me. We also see the occluded parts of an object. We see a cat strolling

---

[7] In order to demonstrate this progressive decline of acuity, Dennett (1991, p.53) invites us to try to tell the colour of a playing card held at arms length in the periphery of the visual field. He points out that we would not be able to tell if the card is black, red, or a face card.

[8] O'Regan (1992) has made this point in arguing for the 'world as outside memory hypothesis' (WOM). WOM claims that visual processing takes place in the world rather than inside the head. Our impression of seeing everything derives from the fact that 'if we so much as faintly ask ourselves some question about the environment, an answer is immediately provided by the sensory information on the retina' (p.484).

behind a picket fence, and not only the visible parts of the cat. Finally, consider our visual experiences as whole, three-dimensional, solid, opaque objects such as apple, tables, and books. We always see such objects from a particular perspective or point of view, and not all the parts of such objects are visible to a perceiver from the point of view they occupy at a given time. Yet we undergo experiences that present us with whole, three-dimensional, solid, opaque objects. All of these examples are aspects of what I will call the *background* to an experience. Everything in this background forms a part of experience insofar as we have a sense of it being potentially available to be accessed.

Noë (2004, § 2.5 and pp. 193 and 216–17; 2008) argues that there is no aspect of the phenomenology of our experience that is not explicable in this way in terms of potential access. We might think that the facing surfaces of objects, such as the screen and keyboard of my laptop, are immediately given to us in experience. But, says Noë, 'crucially, in an important sense, *nothing* is given. The most that we can have is skill-based access to what is there' (2008, p. 697). The very same phenomenology attaches to our experience of a particular's facing sides as holds of our experience of the particular as a whole. There is no way, claims Noë, a token experience can take in all the details of an object's facing side, any more than an experience can encompass all aspects of the object we see. As I look at the label on a bottle, for instance, I can pay attention to some properties of the label only by ignoring others. There will always be a subset of the visible aspects of an object that do not currently figure in my attention. Noë accepts that there are phenomenological differences between what is currently visible to me from the point of view I occupy, and what is hidden or out of view. However, he claims that the difference between that which is open to view and that which is not, is simply a matter of the ease with which we can access that which is open to view. In exploring an object perceptually we have to do less to access those parts of an object that are visible, and work comparatively harder to gain access to the hidden aspects of an object.

However, Noë's framing of this argument presupposes that there is a phenomenological difference between the parts of a scene that are currently focally attended, and those parts which are experienced as available to be accessed. I agree with Noë that there is always more to the visible parts of an object than we can experience in a single glance. Conceding this point, we can still make a distinction at any given moment between those items that form a part of an experience's background and those that occupy its foreground. An experience's foreground will comprise whatever objects and properties are, at the time, the targets of a perceiver's focal attention. It is only the background to experience, which I will seek to explain in terms of potential access. Whatever is in the foreground to experience is already accessed.

I have been assuming that items that are not attended focally can nevertheless enter the contents of experience. This, however, is controversial. Rensink (2000a, 2000b) has for instance developed an account of visual processing which seems to imply that only those items that are attended focally ever make it into the contents of experience. Why then do we have the sense of experiencing all the objects in our surroundings simultaneously? We have this sense of seeing all the detail in our surrounding environment because this detail is made available to us whenever it is requested. Pre-attentive processing provides information about the spatial arrangement or layout of the objects in a scene together with the 'gist' of the scene (i.e. whether it is a city, country, home, or work scene). This information is used to guide attention speedily and effortlessly to whatever object in a scene the perceiver is interested in. The effective management of attention then generates the illusion that we see all the detail in a visual scene. If Rensink is right, our experience is confined to what is attended focally and attention, even when spread diffusely, is limited in the detail it can deliver. Thus, at any given moment there will a large part of a visual scene that we are not experiencing. It may seem to us as if we see all the detail in a scene, but Rensink explains this appearance away in terms of the easy access we have to any of the items in a scene as and when such access is needed.

Rensink's model of visual processing is elegant but it cannot be the whole story. We experience the detail in a visual scene as *present* and we do so in a visual way. The same is true of the other illustrations of the background I gave above, such as our experience of the parts of an object that are out of view (e.g. the back of the screen of my laptop), or the occluded parts of an object (e.g. the non-visible parts of a cat walking behind a picket fence). In all of these cases we have a visual experience of the presence of something that is not visible to us at the time. It is this presence of the background in experience that I suggest may be explicable in terms of sensorimotor expectations. Since this presence of the background is an aspect of the contents of our conscious experience, it follows that sensorimotor expectations can figure in the contents of experience.

My sense of the presence of detail in a visual scene, for instance, partly consists in my expectation that if I were to move this will bring into view parts of a scene, and details that were previously not visible. We know how to move our bodies in such a way as to orient our attention to different parts of the scene than those we are currently in contact with. This know-how partly consists in our expecting our movements to have particular sensory consequences. Something analogous holds for the occluded or currently out of view parts of an object. In both cases, I experience the parts of an object that are not visible to me as present, insofar as I expect that my movements would bring into view those parts of an object that are currently hidden.[9] The sensory consequences I anticipate are determined by the sensorimotor contingencies characteristic of vision. It is for this reason that the unseen parts of a scene are present in my experience in a visual way. If, for instance, I move my eyes or head or get up from my chair and start walking, I expect those movements to have an immediate effect on the parts of the scene that are currently visible to me and the parts that are not. Moreover, the effects of my movements will be different for the different senses. Moving my eyes will have no effect on what I can hear or smell but it will have a more or less predictable effect on what I can see.

So far, I have argued that sensorimotor knowledge might be employed to form conscious sensorimotor expectations that account for the presence of the background in a subject's experience. In the next section, I will argue that an object's intrinsic properties[10] may also be thought of as forming a part of the background to experience. We experience the presence of these properties only to the extent that the background is present in our experience. I will suggest again that our experience of the presence of the background in experience is to be explained in terms of sensorimotor expectations. Hence our experience of the presence of an object's intrinsic properties is likewise to be explained in these terms.

14.4. The phenomenological problem of constancy

All of our perceptual experiences take place from a particular spatial location, under particular viewing conditions that determine the way an object and its properties show up for us in experience. Nevertheless, we succeed in seeing the intrinsic properties of things. We can see, for instance, two trees of the same size that are located at different distances from us, to be trees of the same size.[11] We can see an object's shape, although only the facing side is visible to us. We can see the uniform colour of the wall despite the fact that some parts of the wall are better illuminated than others. How do we

---

[9] Block (2005) has made a similar suggestion in his review of Noë (2004) and he attributes a related proposal to Sean Kelly. Block suggests that the background 'may be a matter of multi-modal or amodal spatial imagery, and that imagery may in part be motor imagery—since its brain basis appears to overlap with motor guidance systems in the dorsal visual system' (p.271). What I am calling 'sensorimotor expectations' might be thought of in terms of amodal spatial imagery. Sensorimotor expectations could be understood as the perceiver's simulating movements and their sensory consequences. The latter imagery could secure for us an experience of the object's hidden parts. It is an interesting empirical prediction that the dorsal stream might be making this kind of contribution to the contents of visual experience, but I wish to leave it as a question for further investigation whether this is the right way to think about sensorimotor expectations.

[10] I take a property p to be an 'intrinsic' property of an object o if p's identity does not depend on o's relation to other objects. As David Lewis (1983) puts it: 'A thing has its intrinsic properties in virtue of the way that thing itself, and nothing else, is' (p.111). For further discussion of the distinction between 'intrinsic' and 'extrinsic' properties see Weatherson (2006).

[11] I have borrowed this familiar example from Peacocke (1983). Tye also discusses this example in his (1996) and (2000), on which more later.

come to experience the intrinsic properties of things, and not only the properties that things appear to have when seen from a particular place and in a particular context? The way things appear when viewed from a particular place and in different contexts is something that varies. To experience the intrinsic properties of things, our experiences must somehow represent something that remains constant, the thing's intrinsic properties, across these variations in experience. How do we get to experience a thing's intrinsic properties, given that a thing's intrinsic properties are always present to us in experience from a particular spatial point of view? I will call this the *phenomenological problem of constancy*.

The problem of constancy as I have just described might seem like a problem that arises because experiences present us with conflicting appearances. The way a property looks to a perceiver is something that varies as we move. As we vary the distance from which we are viewing an object, for instance, the size a given object appears to have when compared with other objects will appear to vary. The further we move away from the object, for instance, the smaller it will look as compared with objects that are nearer to us. Our experiences also represent the intrinsic size of objects we see, and to succeed in doing so they must represent something that remains the same as we vary the distance from which the object is viewed. Thus it would seem that our experiences must have conflicting contents. How can one and the same experience represent a property such as size both as varying with our point of view on an object, and as staying the same across such variations?

This way of presenting the problem of constancy is, however, the result of conflating an epistemic sense of 'looks' with a comparative or phenomenological sense of 'looks'.[12] If we use 'looks' in the epistemic sense, it is not the case that the size of the object looks to vary as we vary our distance from an object. We are not, for instance, in the least bit inclined to judge that the object is getting smaller as we move away from it. We judge that the object remains the same size. If we use 'looks' in the comparative or phenomenological sense, it may well be right to say the size the object looks to have, as compared with other objects in a scene, is something that varies as we move closer to or away from an object. However, we would not be similarly inclined to say that when compared with other objects the object's size appears to stay the same as we vary our distance from the object. Once we are careful to distinguish the comparative from the epistemic senses of 'looks' or 'appears', we see that in fact there is no problem of conflicting appearances.

While I agree that our experiences do not present us with conflicting appearances, the phenomenological problem of constancy nevertheless remains. My experiences always take place from a particular spatial point of view that is determined by the location of my body. The foreground to an experience represents the properties of an object as they are presented from this location. As I vary my spatial point of view of an object, the way the properties of this object are presented to me will also vary. Within experience we can therefore make a distinction between the property that is presented, and the way in which a property is presented. The properties that are presented in experience are an object's intrinsic properties. Yet these properties always show up in an experience in a particular way from a spatial point of view, and under very particular viewing conditions. The phenomenological problem of constancy is the problem of explaining how it is that our experience can represent an object's intrinsic properties, and not only an object's properties as presented from a perspective that varies with our movements. This is a *phenomenological* problem insofar as it arises in the context of describing what appears to us in experience. Intrinsic properties appear to us in experience, but they always show up in a particular way. The problem is therefore to explain how both these descriptions can be true of experience.

Tye (1996 and 2000, chapter 4) argues for a distinction between what he calls *viewpoint-relative* and *viewpoint-independent* content. Perceptual experiences, he claims, have both kinds of content. It might seem as if we can appeal to this distinction to resolve the phenomenological problem of constancy. Viewpoint-independent content carries information about an object's intrinsic properties, while viewpoint-relative content carries information about an object and its properties relative to

---

[12] My thanks to Matt Nudds for pressing this objection.

some coordinate system centred on the perceiver's body. Consider again our experience of two trees of the same size, one of which is twice as near to us as the other. The tree that is closer subtends a larger visual angle relative to the eyes of the viewer as compared with the tree that is further away. This difference is reflected in the viewpoint-relative content of our experience that represents the nearer tree as having a facing surface that looks larger from here than the facing surface of the tree that is further away. Our experience also has a viewpoint-independent content that represents the two trees as being the same size. Thus there is no problem about how our experiences can represent both the properties of an object from a spatial point of view, and the intrinsic properties of an object. This is something our experiences achieve by means of distinct layers of content.

Tye also argues that we should think of viewpoint-relative properties and viewpoint-independent properties as distinct properties. An object's viewpoint-relative size will depend on the angle the object subtends relative to the eyes of the perceiver, and this is no part of an object's viewpoint-independent size. However, if Tye's two layers of representational content are to represent distinct properties, the success conditions for the one layer of content must be conditions that can be satisfied independently of the success conditions for the other layer of content. In order for this to be the case, one of two possibilities must obtain. It must either be possible for an experience to represent a property such as size correctly whilst misrepresenting size from a particular viewpoint or it must be possible for an experience to represent size from a particular location correctly whilst misrepresenting an object's intrinsic size. I take it that the failure of either of these possibilities would cast doubt on the claim that the two layers of content represent distinct properties.

Consider now an Ames room in which two identically sized adult twins are standing. This, as we will see, is an example of a case in which viewpoint-relative content is nonveridical. Do our visual experiences of an Ames room nevertheless have veridical viewpoint-independent contents? I will argue that they do not. Thus the Ames room looks to be a possible counterexample to Tye's proposal.

Ames rooms appear to be cubical when viewed from a particular vantage point. In fact the true shape of the room is distorted cleverly; the floor, ceiling, some of the walls and the windows are all trapezoidal. Although the floor appears level it is really at an incline: the far left corner is much lower than the near right corner. The walls appear perpendicular to the floor when they are actually slanted outwards. When seen from a particular vantage point the two visible corners of the room subtend the same visual angle to the eye, and thus appear the same size and distance away from the perceiver. The experience's viewpoint-relative content is incorrect in this case. It represents the room as looking cubical from the perceiver's vantage point, when it is in fact distorted cleverly in the ways just described.

Now consider what we see when two twins of identical size stand in the two corners. The twin in the left corner (the corner that is actually further away) shrinks in size to appear smaller than a child, while the twin in the right corner looks comparatively much taller. Thus, size constancy fails, and two twins of the same size are represented as being very different sizes, contrary to what Tye's theory would predict: we do not find veridical viewpoint-independent content and non-veridical viewpoint-relative content. Both layers of content are illusory.

Size constancy fails in Ames rooms because our visual experience has illusory viewpoint-relative content.[13] Our experience has a viewpoint-relative content that misrepresents the shape of the room, and thus the twins are seen as located at an equal distance away from the viewer. Yet because the two twins are located at different distances from the perceiver they project different retinal sizes. On the basis of viewpoint-relative representation of size and distance, the visual system arrives at viewpoint-independent representation of the twins as different sizes. The viewpoint-independent size is computed on the basis of viewpoint-relative information. Can we conclude anything more general about the relation between these layers of content on the basis of this case?

---

[13] See Palmer (1999, pp. 247–248) for an explanation along these lines.

One conclusion that seems to follow is that it is only if a property is represented in the right way at the level of viewpoint-relative content that it can be represented correctly at the level of viewpoint-independent content. This, however, would seem to challenge Tye's claim that the different layers of content represent distinct properties. It would suggest that the two layers of content represent one and the same property in distinct ways. Viewpoint-relative content represents a property from a spatial point of view, while viewpoint-independent content does not. If this is right, we have not yet escaped the phenomenological problem of constancy. We still want to know how experiences can have both kinds of content.

The solution to the phenomenological problem lies in distinguishing the background to an experience from its foreground. An experience's foreground represents a property from a spatial point of view and under particular viewing conditions. Recall how with each shift of focal attention the foreground to experience changes. What we attend focally will be determined by what falls within the foveal area of visual processing, and this will always be an object and its properties as presented from a perspective. We saw that in the case of opaque, three-dimensional objects there is always more detail to such objects than we can represent in a single encounter. The very same claim can be made for the intrinsic properties of those objects. Intrinsic properties, in common with whole three-dimensional objects, have aspects that exceed what we can perceive in a single encounter. We cannot see at a single glance the wall's colour, as it would appear under every illumination, any more than we can see at a single glance every part of the wall. Nevertheless, we experience in a visual way the presence of the wall's uniform whiteness, just as we experience the presence of the currently out of view parts of the wall. We do so because both the uniform whiteness of the wall and the currently out of view aspects of the wall form a part of the background to our experience.

I argued in the previous section that we experience the items that make up the background as present by means of our sensorimotor expectations. This account can be extended to explain the sense in which our experiences represent an object's intrinsic properties. We experience the cube's intrinsic shape because we expect our movements to bring into view the sides of the cube that are currently hidden. Each movement results in our representing the cube from a different spatial point of view, and thus from a different perspective. We nevertheless see the cube's shape because we expect our movements to alter our perspective on the cube in certain predictable ways.[14] Moreover, we do not actually have to move in order to see an object's intrinsic shape. We can see its intrinsic shape just by being presented with it from a spatial point of view, and by forming a set of sensorimotor expectations about the ways in which the cube's shape will be presented to us as we vary our point of view on it. Both an object and its intrinsic properties have details that exceed what the foreground to experience can encompass at any single instant. It is our sensorimotor expectations that give us a sense of the presence of this detail.

I have claimed that the foreground to experience presents us with intrinsic properties as presented from a perspective. It follows that at least part of what we are aware of at any moment will be an object and its properties as they are presented from a point of view. Since the foreground will change each time we vary our point of view (even when we are attending focally to one and the same property)

---

[14] Noë (2004, ch.3) introduces the concept of perspectival properties (p-properties) to capture the way in which a property is presented from a point of view. It is an object's p-properties that vary as we move. He characterizes perspectival properties in terms of the patch we would need to draw on a flat surface perpendicular to the line of sight in order to occlude the object (*op cit*, p.83). Thus it looks like Noë is committed to describing the way objects and their properties appear from a perspective in terms of two-dimensional coloured surfaces. I reject this way of characterizing the foreground to experience, which is why I have talked instead of the foreground being occupied by intrinsic properties as presented from a particular perspective. The foreground is not made up of two-dimensional coloured surfaces. Rather our perspective on an object includes the object's orientation in depth just as much as its colour or texture. This is a point that is rightly emphasized by Briscoe (2008, §3). Insisting on this point does not however deprive us of a distinction between the property that is presented in experience and the way this property is presented.

it would seem to follow that we are always aware of something that is varying in experience. This latter claim is, however, controversial. Some philosophers might be willing to concede that if we turn our attention to experience by introspecting, we can become aware of this constantly varying foreground to our experience. However they would deny this is something we are aware of ordinarily, prior to introspecting. Normally they would insist our experience is of objects and their intrinsic properties.[15]

There is a sense in which I am happy to concede this point, and a sense in which I am not. Let us begin with what I take to be uncontroversial. Stephen Palmer (1999, pp. 313–14) makes a distinction between *proximal* and *distal* modes of perception. The proximal mode 'reflects mainly the properties of the retinal image, or proximal stimulus', while the distal mode 'reflects mainly the properties of the environmental object or distal stimulus' (p. 313). Palmer goes on to suggest that perceptual experience is normally a blend of these two modes, but that sometimes one mode can dominate the other. The distal mode dominates in much of our everyday experience, which is to say that normally we experience an object's intrinsic properties, and not the ways in which a property is presented from a perspective. However Palmer acknowledges that under certain circumstances the proximal mode can dominate. He gives as an example a painter attempting to recreate perspective in a painting.

I agree with Palmer that ordinary experience is a blend of what he calls the proximal and distal modes of perception. What he calls the *proximal* mode of perception lines up roughly with what I have been calling the foreground (though I would not characterize this aspect of our experiences in proximal terms). Palmer's distal mode of perception, which he takes to dominate our ordinary experience, is a compound of a more-or-less constantly varying foreground and a background or set of sensorimotor expectations. I agree that this is the form that our awareness takes for the most part. Normally our experience is composed of a foreground and background, and our awareness is made up of both. Moreover, we can, if we choose, attend to the foreground in isolation from the background.

However, I am committed to a further claim that all that is actually present in our experience is the object and its intrinsic properties as they are accessed from a point of view. An object's intrinsic properties are present in our experience, but as something potentially available to us to access through further exploration. I am making a distinction between what is present in experience because it is actually accessed, and what is present in experience as potentially accessible. I suspect that when philosophers say we are normally aware of an object and its intrinsic properties, they mean to claim that this is what is *actually* present to us in experience at any instant. We do not experience an object and its properties as presented from a point of view. Rather what we experience are objects and their properties independent of the spatial point of view from which they are encountered. In the final section, I will show how proponents of the two visual systems hypothesis are committed to a view of experience along these lines. I will argue that this commitment generates a genuine conflict with the sensorimotor theory.

14.5. Are the contents of experience egocentric or allocentric?

Jacob and Jeannerod (2003) have argued that any perceptual state must satisfy what they label *the constraint of contrastive identification* if it is to qualify as a perceptual experience. Following Evans (1982),

---

[15] Sean Kelly (2008) has argued that we can become aware of the way a property is presented, such as the colour of the differently illuminated parts of a wall, only by adopting a detached and reflective attitude towards our experience. This is a fundamentally different mode of awareness from ordinary experience, which is engaged with, and immersed in the world. Schellenberg (2008, p.78) has suggested that properties as presented from a point of view may form a part of the background that is ordinarily recessive in our experience. Briscoe (2008) takes what is perhaps the hardest line on this issue in arguing that while we can notice the way an object appears we do so by engaging in an 'exercise of visual imagination guided by seeing' (p.479). We are never literally aware of the ways in which properties appear. This is something we can bring ourselves to experience by engaging in acts of what Briscoe describes as 'make-perceive'.

they claim that it is definitive of perceptual experience that it puts subjects in an epistemic position to recognize and re-identify or keep track of objects in space and time. Recognition or re-identification of a property F 'requires the ability to contrast and compare different instantiations of property F, either by different objects or items at the same time or by the same object at different times' (Jacob and Jeannerod 2003, p. 193). They then proceed to argue that only an allocentric frame of reference allows for the representation of the relative locations of two or more items. They deny that representations that code for spatial location egocentrically can represent more than one item at a time. Since no comparison of features can be carried out unless two or more items are represented, it follows that the constraint of contrastive identification is not satisfied by visual representations that code for spatial location using an egocentric frame of reference. It is satisfied only by states that represent space using an allocentric frame of reference. Thus, perceptual experiences must code for the spatial location of features using an allocentric frame of reference, not an egocentric frame of reference.[16]

This looks to be in conflict with my claim that the foreground to experience is made up of objects and properties as presented from a particular spatial point of view. If objects and properties are represented in experience using a scene-based or allocentric frame of reference, it follows that they must be represented independently of any spatial point of view. Goodale and Milner (2004, chapter 6) offer a useful comparison of visual experiences with the way in which television or film represents the world. Television does not provide us with information about the size, distance, or position in relation to us the viewer. Yet we have no trouble segregating the shifting and changing patterns of light, shade, and colour into meaning objects and complex events. Crucially when we make sense of what we are seeing on television we do so using the same mechanisms that allow us to see and make sense of a scene in the real world. In both cases, we rely on scene-based information about the relative size, shape, orientation, and position of objects. Moreover these features are not represented as they are presented from the perceiver's point of view. Rather they are represented in a way that allows for comparison at a time or over time, and so in a way that is not tied to any particular spatial standpoint.

However, such an account of the spatial content of experience does face a difficulty (set out nicely by Noë in this volume). When we use a visual experience to select an object such as a coffee mug as the target of an action, such as reaching and grasping the cup to take a drink, our motor system needs to know where this object is located relative to our hand. The motor system needs visual information that codes for the location of the object using egocentric coordinates. Moreover, if it is to reach and grasp the cup successfully it requires visual information about an object's absolute size and shape, not its size and shape relative to other objects. Let us suppose the vision for perception system and the vision for action are distinct visual systems. The two systems use fundamentally different codes to represent objects and their properties. If this is right, we face the difficulty of accounting for the interactions between the two systems. If the two systems code for information about the same object using what are fundamentally different languages, how do they ever succeed in communicating with each other? I will call this the *communication problem*.[17]

According to my view, the communication problem does not arise as objects and properties are always represented from a spatial point of view centred on the subject's body. Perceptual experiences do not just inform us of the spatial relations objects stand in to each other, but they also inform us of the relations objects stand in to us.[18] Jacob and Jeannerod argue that no single visual representation

---

[16] Jacob and de Vignemont (this volume, §2.2) run an argument along the same lines.

[17] Goodale and Milner (2004) have what looks like a good answer to this objection. They appeal to back-projections to primary visual cortex where a common retinotopic representation of an object's spatial location can be found. The target of an action can then be flagged or highlighted on this retinotopic representation allowing the vision for action system to compute its location relative to an effector and launch an action. Their proposal however faces a number of technical difficulties nicely set out in Briscoe (forthcoming, §7). I lack the space to rehearse these difficulties here.

[18] This is a point Noë also emphasizes in his contribution to this volume.

can carry both these types of spatial information, since a visual representation with egocentric spatial content cannot represent more than one object. Bermúdez (2007) has made a useful distinction between what he calls *focused* perception and *relational* perception. Focused perception represents a single object in relation to the perceiver, while relational perception represents an object in the context of a scene. Relational perception, he points out, can be either allocentric or egocentric. An object can be represented in the context of a scene centred on a perceiver.[19] Thus consider Jacob and Jeannerod's example of a representation of a bottle to the left of a glass. This location of the bottle can be represented egocentrically if the bottle is represented as to the left of the glass relative to me. If an object of relational perception can be localized using egocentric coordinates as seems plausible, it follows that states with egocentric content can satisfy the constraint of contrastive identification. It is not necessary for a state to code for spatial location using allocentric coordinates in order to satisfy this condition. Visual representations with egocentric spatial content can meet the conditions required for qualifying as an experience.[20]

Jacob and Jeannerod seem to assume that it is only if experiences represent objects independent of any particular spatial point of view that experiences can be used to make the kinds of comparisons required for recognition, recall, and planning. Perhaps they suppose that experiences tied to a particular spatial point of view would not allow a perceiver to re-identify objects and properties at different times. Insofar as the object's property is represented from distinct spatial points of view at different times there will be nothing that stays the same that we might be said to track over time. Recognition and recall require that we keep track of the same property over time. Thus, both these capacities would seem to require us to represent a property independent of any spatial point of view. Perhaps something like this reasoning is also behind Clark's argument that perceptual experience must abstract away from our sensorimotor engagement with the world. The latter seems to involve a constantly changing point of view on the world. It is only if our experiences abstract away from this changing point of view to find something constant that they will be suited to play the role they do in reasoning, recall, and planning.

I have argued, however, that experiences can represent properties from a particular point of view, and also represent properties independently of a spatial point of view through the contribution of sensorimotor expectations. The foreground to an experience represents properties from a spatial point of view. By means of our sensorimotor expectations we are able to go beyond the foreground to access an object's intrinsic properties that form a part of the background to our experience. It is by means of our sensorimotor expectations that we can represent one and the same object and its properties over time. In addition, I have appealed to Bermúdez's notion of relational perception to argue that an experience can represent more than one object simultaneously from a subject's point of view. Thus, there is no problem in understanding how an experience can be from a subject's point of view and allow for comparisons at the same time.

---

[19] Jacob and de Vignemont (this volume) seem to concede this point when they write of the flexibility of perceptual judgement and how 'some perceptual judgements use an egocentric frame of reference; others use an allocentric frame of reference' (ms, p.9). If perceptual judgements can use an egocentric frame of reference it seems to follow that states with egocentric content can after all satisfy the constraint of contrastive identification.

[20] Jacob and Jeannerod (2007) in their reply to Bermúdez take his notion of relational perception to be a kind of fact perception: we see *that* the glass is to the left of the bottle. They go on to argue that to see that *p* is to have a perceptual belief that *p* where such beliefs have conceptual content. Thus they take Bermúdez to be making a claim about our spatial *concepts* according to which in order to see that one object is to the left of another, one must have an explicit conceptualized representation of the two objects and oneself as standing in a particular spatial relationship. It is not obvious to me, however, why Bermúdez must be read as making a claim about perceptual belief or epistemic-seeing rather than non-epistemic seeing. (For evidence that he should not be read in this way see his (1995) and (1998).) Jacob and Jeannerod's response loses its force if we read Bermúdez as making a claim about non-epistemic-seeing, as I think we should.

I conclude then that there is no need for experience to abstract away from sensorimotor knowledge in order to play a role in recognition, recall, and planning. On the contrary, experiences that represent the world from a point of view require sensorimotor knowledge in order to play this role. It is only if experiences have purely allocentric spatial content that they would need to abstract away from our sensorimotor engagement with things. However, I see no reason to grant that experiences have spatial content of this kind.

14.6. Conclusion

I have defended a weak version of the sensorimotor theory, according to which sensorimotor knowledge may make two kinds of contribution to the contents of experience. I have suggested that sensorimotor knowledge is exercised in the formation of sensorimotor expectations, some of which contribute to our experience of objects and their properties. Sensorimotor expectations give us a sense of the presence of whole, three-dimensional objects and the detail in a visual scene that exceeds what is made available to us by focal attention at any given moment in time. Sensorimotor expectations also give us a sense of the presence of an object's intrinsic properties. We cannot perceive an object's intrinsic properties in any single encounter with an object any more than we can perceive an object in its entirety. An object as a whole and its properties form a part of the background to experience, which is present in an experience thanks to our sensorimotor expectations.

We began with Clark's argument that perceptual experiences have contents that abstract away from the fine details of our sensorimotor engagement with the world. However, we have seen (in section 14.5) that if perceptual experiences have egocentric spatial content they can play a role in recognition, recall, and planning only by means of our sensorimotor expectations. I concede this argument would fail if it should turn out that perceptual experiences have spatial content that is purely allocentric in the way proponents of the two-visual systems hypothesis have argued. I have attempted to show, however, that such a claim faces difficulties, which are avoided if we allow that perceptual experiences can code for spatial location using egocentric coordinates. I conclude then that there is no incompatibility between the sensorimotor theory and two visual systems hypothesis. On the contrary, visual experience must be informed by sensorimotor knowledge if it is to succeed in carrying out its functions.

Acknowledgements

Thanks to Kevin O'Regan, Ron Rensink, Andy Clark, Matt Nudds, Erik Rietveld, Dave Ward, and to participants in the MINDMAP seminar at Edinburgh for very helpful discussion of the ideas in this paper. Any remaining errors are of course down to me. Many thanks also to the editors for their excellent and insightful criticisms, which led me substantially to revise my arguments in countless places. This chapter also owes a large debt to Susan Hurley. I learned a great deal about the sensorimotor theory from discussions with her. She might not have agreed with all my conclusions but hopefully she would have recognized her influence in what I have written.

References

Bach-y-Rita, P. (1983). Tactile-vision substitution: past and future. *International Journal of Neuroscience*; **19**(1–4): 29–36.
Bermúdez, J.L. (2007). From two visual systems to two forms of content? *Psyche*; **132** (April).
—— (1998). *The paradox of self-consciousness*. MIT Press, Cambridge, MA.
—— (1995). Ecological perception and the notion of nonconceptual point of view. In *The body and the self*, (ed. Bermúdez, J.L., Marcel, A.J., and Eilan, N.), Cambridge, MA: MIT Press.
Block, N. (2005). Review of *Action in Perception. Journal of Philosophy*; **CII** (5): 259–72.
Briscoe, R. (2009). Egocentric spatial representation in action and perception. *Philosophy and Phenomenological Research*; **79**(2): 423–460.
Briscoe, R. (2008). Vision, action and make-perceive. *Mind and Language*; **23**: 457–96.

Bushnell, E. and Boudreau, J. (1983). Motor development in the mind: the potential role of motor abilities as a determinant of perceptual development. *Child Development*; **64**: 1005–21.

Clark, A. (2008). *Supersizing the mind: embodiment, action and cognitive extension.* Oxford: Oxford University Press.

—— (2006a). Vision as dance: three challenges for sensorimotor contingency theory. *Psyche*; **12**(1): (downloaded from: http://psyche.cs.monash.edu.au/).

—— (2006b). Cognitive complexity and the sensorimotor frontier. *Aristotelian Society: Supplementary*; **80**(1): 43–65.

Clark, A. and Grush, R. (1999). Towards a cognitive robotics. *Adaptive Behaviour*; **7**(1): 5–16.

Dennett, D.C. (1991). *Consciousness explained.* London: Penguin.

Edelman, G. (1987). *Neural Darwinism: the theory of neural group selection.* New York: Basic Books.

Evans, G. (1982). *Varieties of reference*, (ed. McDowell, J.) Oxford: Clarendon Press.

Findlay, J.M. and Gilchrist, I.D. (2003). *Active vision: the psychology of looking and seeing.* Oxford: Oxford University Press.

Fodor, J. and Pylyshyn, Z. (1981). How direct is visual perception? Some reflections on Gibson's 'ecological approach'. *Cognition*; **9**: 139–96.

Gibson, J.J. (1972). A theory of direct perception. In *The psychology of knowing* (ed. Royce, J.R. and Rozeboom, W.W), pp. 215–40. New York: Gordon & Breach.

Goodale, M.A. and Milner, A.D. (2004). *Sight unseen: an exploration of conscious and unconscious vision.* Oxford: Oxford University Press.

Hurley, S.L. (1998). *Consciousness in action.* Cambridge, MA: Harvard University Press.

Hurley, S.L. and Noë, A. (2003). Neural plasticity and consciousness. *Biology and Philosophy*; **18**; 131–68.

Jacob, P. and de Vignemont, F. (Chapter 8, this volume). Spatial coordinates and phenomenology in the two-visual systems model.

Jacob, P. and Jeannerod, M. (2007). Replies to our critics. *Psyche*; **13**(2), April.

—— (2003). *Ways of seeing: the scope and limits of visual cognition.* Oxford: Oxford University Press.

Kelly, S.D. (2008). Content and constancy: phenomenology, psychology and the content of perception. *Philosophy and Phenomenological Research*; **76**(3): 682–90.

Lewis, D. (1983). Extrinsic properties. *Philosophical Studies*; **44**: 197–200.

Lungarella, M. and Pfeifer, R. (2001). Robots as cognitive tools: an information-theoretic analysis of sensorimotor data. *Proceedings of the 2nd IEEE-RAS International Conference on Humanoid Robotics*, pp. 245–52.

Marr, D. (1982). *Vision.* New York: W.H. Freeman and Sons.

McConkie, G.W. and Rayner, K. (1979). Is visual information integrated across successive fixations in reading? *Perception and Psychophysics*; **25**: 221–4.

McConkie, G.W. and Rayner, K. (1975). The span of the effective stimulus during a fixation in reading. *Perception and Psychophysics*; **17**: 578–86.

Merleau-Ponty, M. (1945/1962). *The phenomenology of perception,* (trans. Smith, Co.). London: Routledge.

Milner, D. and Goodale, M. (1995/2006). *The visual brain in action.* 2nd edn. Oxford: Oxford University Press.

Noë, A. (Chapter 13, this volume). Vision without representation.

—— (2008). Reply to Campbell, Martin & Kelly. *Philosophy and Phenomenological Research*; **76**(3): 691–706.

—— (2007). Real presence. *Philosophical Topics*; **33**(1): 235–64.

—— (2004). *Action in perception.* Cambridge, MA: MIT Press.

Nolfi, S. and Marocco, D. (2002). Active perception: a sensorimotor account of object categorisation. *Proceedings of the seventh international conference on simulation of adaptive behaviour: from animals to animats*, pp. 266–71.

O'Regan, J.K. (1992). Solving the 'real' mysteries of visual perception: the world as an outside memory. *Canadian Journal of Psychology*; **46**(3): 461–88.

O'Regan, J.K. and Noë, A. (2001). A sensorimotor approach to vision and visual consciousness. *Behavioural and Brain Sciences*; **24**: 883–975.

Palmer, S.E. (1999). *Vision science: from photons to phenomenology.* Cambridge, MA: MIT Press.

Peacocke, C. (1983). *Sense and content: experience, thought and their relations.* Oxford: Oxford University Press.

Pfeifer, R. and Scheier, C. (1999). *Understanding intelligence.* Cambridge, MA: MIT Press.

—— (1997). Sensorimotor coordination: the metaphor and beyond. *Robotics and Autonomous Systems*; **20**: 157–78.

Rensink, R.A. (2000a). Seeing, sensing and scrutinising. *Vision Research*; 40: 1469–87.

Rensink, R.A. (2000b). The dynamic representation of scenes. *Visual Cognition*; **7**: 17–42.

Rossetti, Y., Ota, H., Blangero, A., Vighetto, A., and Pisella, L. (Chapter 10, this volume). Why does the perception-action functional dichotomy not match the ventral-dorsal streams anatomical segregation: optic ataxia and the function of the dorsal stream.

Schellenberg, S. (2008). The situation-dependency of perception. *The Journal of Philosophy*; **CV**(2): 55–84.

Schwitzgebel, E. (2007). Do you have constant tactile experience of your feet in your shoes? *Journal of Consciousness Studies*; **14**(3): 5–35.

Siewert, C. (2005). Attention and sensorimotor intentionality, In *Phenomenology and philosophy of mind*, (ed. Woodruff-Smith, D. and Thomasson, A.L.), pp. 270–94. Oxford: Oxford University Press.

Te Boekhorst, R., Lungarella, M., and Pfeifer, R. (2003). Dimensionality reduction through sensorimotor coordination. In *Proceedings of the Joint International Conference ICANN/ICONIP*, LNCS 2714. (ed. Kaynak, O., Alpaydin, E., Oja, E., and Xu, L.) pp. 496–503.

Thelen, E. and Smith, L. (1994). *A dynamic system approach to the development of cognition and action.* Cambridge, MA: MIT Press.

Thompson, E. (2007). *Mind in life.* Cambridge, MA: Harvard University Press.

Tye, M. (2000). *Consciousness, colour and content.* Cambridge, MA: MIT Press.

—— (1996). Perceptual experience is a many-layered thing. *Philosophical Issues 7, Perception.* Atascadero, CA: Ridgeview Publishing Company.

Weatherson, B. (2006). Intrinsic vs. Extrinsic Properties. In *The Stanford encyclopedia of philosophy,* (ed. Zalta, E.): (downloaded from: http://plato.stanford.edu/archives/fall2008/entries/intrinsic-extrinsic/>).

PART 6

Boundaries of the agent

CHAPTER 15

Extended vision

Robert A. Wilson

Abstract

Vision constitutes an interesting domain, or range of domains, for debate over the extended mind thesis: the idea that minds extend physically beyond the boundaries of the body. In part this is because vision (and visual experience more particularly) are sometimes presented as a kind of line in the sand for what we might call *externalist creep* about the mind: once all reasonable concessions have been made to externalists about the mind, visual experience marks a line beyond which lies a safe haven for individualists. Here I want to put a little more pressure on such a view of visual experience, as well as to offer a more constructive, positive argument in defence of the idea of extended vision.

15.1. Vision, visual experience, and the extended mind

Vision is a domain in which two sets of competing considerations clash. On the one hand, the notion of a perceptual *system* is relatively well entrenched in the cognitive sciences, and even some of the most trenchant critics of the extended mind thesis (e.g. Adams and Aizawa, 2008, 2009) are prepared to allow that cognitive systems may be extended. Since the version of the extended mind thesis I favour is most naturally expressed in terms of the extension of cognitive systems beyond bodily boundaries (Wilson, 1994, 2004, chapters 4–8), perceptual domains in general seem to be pre-adapted (as it were) as likely domains for which the extended mind thesis is defensible. On the other hand, not every aspect of cognition and cognitive processing is extended. Perceptual *phenomenology* in general, and the phenomenology of visual experience in particular, has been the first port of call for those with individualistic intuitions about the mind (*sensu* Burge, 1979, 1986). The idea that my perception of the world, *how the world seems to me from the inside*, might be *exactly as it is*, even were I not the embodied, world-enmeshed being that I actually am, but merely a brain in a vat (or were Descartes' evil demon hypothesis true), has both motivated and sustained individualistic thinking about the mind since before the time that there were individualists as such (see also Wilson, 2010).

I have argued previously (Wilson, 2004, chapter 9) that at least some of the various phenomena collected under the rubric of consciousness (higher order thought, introspection, and some aspects of attention) fall under the umbrella of the extended mind thesis, and that at least some aspects of visual experience should be viewed likewise (ibid., 232–38). There I also resisted what I called *global externalism*, the view that the extended mind thesis is true across the board for all mental phenomena, opting for a kind of pluralistic view of the mind vis-à-vis the debate over individualism, whereby individualistic and externalist views of cognition divide the mind between them. This moderate externalist view allows that some cognitive systems are individualistic; I have suggested previously (ibid., pp. 238–40) that the nociceptive system that realizes pain is a likely example.

In this chapter, I want to reconsider such pluralism, and to put a little more pressure in particular on an individualistic treatment of visual systems and visual experience in light of that reconsideration. I shall offer a more constructive, positive argument in defence of the idea that vision is extended, aiming to shift the balance of power in any pluralistic coalition further towards externalism. As part of this discussion of the question of whether visual systems and the experiences they generate are extended, I will also take up the question of whether they are embodied (see also Wilson and Foglia, 2010). Some individualists about visual experience (e.g. Block, 2005; Aizawa, 2007) have denied the embodiment of vision in anything but a fairly weak sense, e.g., we happen to have bodies that are causally important to vision in the actual world.

I have indicated that visual experience has been a sort of first port of call for individualists. More recently, however, visual experience has become the last refuge for individualism about the mind: visual experience has been taken to be a phenomenon that, after all reasonable concessions have been made to externalists, remains a safe haven for individualists. Ned Block captures this individualistic view of visual experience neatly in a recent, prominent review of Alva Noë's *Action in Perception* in considering the claim that perceptual experience is essentially embodied. Block denies this claim, saying that 'the minimal constitutive supervenience base for perceptual experience is the brain and does not include the rest of the body' (Block, 2005, p. 271). The intuition that Block's own claim about perceptual experience draws on is: that whatever the precise material realization of perceptual experience consists in, it does not extend beyond the brain. This intuition expresses a widely accepted 'embrained view' of the mind, and such *embrainment* is incompatible with the *embodiment* of the mind. Moreover, if perceptual experience is not embodied because its material realization does not extend beyond the brain into the body, then it would also seem that the mind is not extended for that very same reason.

I will try to show not only why I think that Block's claim here is false, but why this, in turn, provides reason to view perception not only as embodied but also as extended. In short, rather than argue (along with Block) that the failure of perceptual experience to be embodied implies that it is not extended, I will argue that precisely because perceptual experience is embodied, it is also extended. In fact, if the line of argument that I am developing is on track, then the physical embodiment and physical extension of at least some forms of perception are tightly entwined facts about how the corresponding perceptual systems operate (cf. Gallagher, 2005; Myin and O'Regan, 2009; Noë, 2009).

Whether this is true *only* of perception because of specific ways in which perception is embodied, or true more generally (e.g. of consciousness; cf. Prinz, 2009; Clark, 2009), is something that I leave open here. In fact, my concern will be almost exclusively with *visual perception* and *visual experience*, bringing in other perceptual modalities only insofar as they shed light on vision. Discussions of vision that are partially cast in terms of broader notions, such as perception or even consciousness, can sometimes be misleading, especially when probing into what it is that vision *requires* or what it is that is necessary or sufficient for *visual* experience.

15.2. **Loosening the skullcap**

In order to loosen the screws on the individualistic skullcap about perception, consider two kinds of cases, one concerning perceptual *systems*, the other perceptual *experience*.

The first are cases in which organisms generate a sensory field that they then move through in order to achieve basic biological goals, such as mating and prey-detection. Bats and electric fish are two of the better-known examples of such creatures. Where is the boundary of *their* sensory systems, given that their self-generated sensory fields are located beyond their bodily boundaries? At first glance, their sensory systems, and indeed the sensory processing they engage in, do not begin and end at their bodily boundaries, since they use their bodies to generate electromagnetic or sonic fields beyond those bodies. In any case, exploring just how such creatures function successfully in the world is relevant to answering this question. Attention to the mechanistic and computational details of that functioning push against, I shall later argue, at least some of the individualistic intuitions behind Block's claim (Section 15.5). What they suggest specifically about perceptual *experience* is something I will return to.

The second are cases that are more directly relevant for thinking about perceptual experience, and they help to frame issues about *visual* experience in a particular way. Consider not perceptual experience in general but *tactile* experience in particular. Does the minimal constitutive supervenience base for tactile experience include only the brain and exclude the rest of the body? Precisely the same question could be asked of *orgasmal experience* or the experience of *physical pain* (e.g. that associated with breaking one's leg). All three kinds of experience seem to be more intimately related to the body than are visual, auditory, and olfactory experience, as reflected in common reference to them as *bodily* experiences. The experience, in each case, is *felt in the body*, and the material realization of the experience as it actually occurs involves sensors in, on, and nerves that run through, the body. (Whether the appearances in ordinary cases are merely apparent, or this is true of *all* bodily experience, such as in cases of pain felt in phantom limbs, I leave aside here.) If at least some kinds of perceptual experiences are bodily experiences, in this sense, then the embodiment of perceptual experience more generally, and of visual experience in particular, is cast in a new light (see section 15.7).

These cases are introduced here as suggestive screw-looseners, but it is worth saying a little more about which screws on the individualistic skullcap about perception they aim to loosen. I take the first kind of case, involving apparently extended sensory fields, to suggest that whether the corresponding perceptual system ends at the body is in part an empirical question, and the second kind of case, involving bodily experience, to suggest the same about the issue of whether *all* experience supervenes only on the brain to the exclusion of the rest of the body. Ultimately, I shall argue that such suggestions not only loosen the skullcap on thinking about perception and perceptual experience; they also provide the bases for an argument for the extended vision thesis. The full defence of that argument will require showing how it avoids some of the now-standard objections to arguments for the extended mind thesis, or their analogues for perception, such as a putative 'coupling/ constitution fallacy', and a failure to consider the significance of the distinction between cognitive *systems* and cognitive *processes* (Adams and Aizawa, 2008, 2009; Block, 2005). For now, it is enough if these suggestions challenge non-externalists to entertain the prospect that individualism about perception and perceptual experience is not as secure a position as is often assumed. This is a kind of *externalist creep* (I've been called worse). I want to turn next to briefly recount a broader and perhaps more familiar externalist creep in philosophy of mind over the past 35 years or so, primarily for those unfamiliar with the trajectory of the debate over individualism and externalism in the philosophy of mind.

15.3. **Externalist creep**

Contemporary externalist thinking about the mind originates in the work of Hilary Putnam (1975) and Tyler Burge (1979). The arguments of Putnam and Burge appeal, respectively, to the attribution of 'meaning' or belief in counterfactual circumstances. Both Putnam and Burge acknowledge the debt of their views to earlier works, including their own, on the causal theory of reference, particularly as it applied to both proper names and natural kind terms in natural languages. Here we have our first instance of externalist creep: from the philosophy of language to the philosophy of mind. Given this starting point, two individualistic responses which concede that the Putnam-Burge thought experiments show some form of externalism about mental representation to be true, are natural.

The first kind of individualistic response (Field, 1978; Loar, 1981; McGinn, 1982) was to argue for 'two factor' theories of mental content, where one factor is externalist (or 'wide'), the other individualistic (or 'narrow'). The most common ways to develop an account of narrow content have been either as a form of conceptual role semantics, or by analogy with David Kaplan's notion of *character* in his semantics (see Wilson, 1995, chapter 9 for discussion).

The second kind of individualistic response (Fodor, 1982) was to argue that while conceptual content is externalist, *non-conceptual* content, as exemplified in unarticulated perceptual experience, is individualistic. As philosophical attention shifted its focus from the problem of intentionality to the problem of consciousness during the 1990s, more sophisticated defences of the idea that phenomenology (especially *visual* phenomenology) was individualistic have appeared (e.g. Loar, 2002, 2003; Horgan and Tienson, 2002). While the focus here is squarely on the first-person phenomenology of our mental states, these efforts are an attempt to reinvigorate the narrow content programme about intentionality by arguing that 'phenomenal intentionality' is individualistic. The basic idea of these views is that there is a kind of intentionality, phenomenal intentionality, determined by one's phenomenology (how the world seems to one at a given time) that is individualistic. Although the view is intended to apply to mental states more generally, sensory experience has been presented as a paradigm of where one could locate phenomenal intentionality (see Wilson, 2003, 2004, chapter 10 for discussion).

This section has reprised briefly a central strand to the individualist–externalist debate, one that has focused on mental representation, intentionality, and content. The central question here, as it pertains to vision, has been something like this: is the content of visual experience, or our visual phenomenology, individuated individualistically? Aficionados of the individualism–externalism debate will have followed discussions of this kind of question in the context of Marr's theory of vision, where there has been sustained attention to the question of whether Marr's theory was externalist (Burge, 1986; Shapiro, 1997) or individualistic (Segal, 1989) or neither (Egan, 1992; Chomsky, 1995) about content. Here we can note another kind of externalist creep: from externalist claims about folk psychology (e.g. belief) to externalist claims about cognitive science (e.g. zero-point crossings and 2.5 D sketches in Marr's theory; see also Wilson, 2004, chapter 7). Yet none of these views have considered the question that is now at the forefront of contemporary debate between individualists and externalists: does the mind itself extend physically beyond the physical boundary of the body? Those who answer affirmatively (Clark and Chalmers, 1998; Clark, 2007, 2008, 2010; Hurley, 1998; Wilson, 2000, 2004, 2010; Wilson and Clark, 2009) defend the *extended mind thesis*. Those who answer negatively (Adams and Aizawa, 2001, 2008, 2009; Rupert, 2004; Prinz, 2009) view that thesis as resting on one or more errors. They hold, instead, that the 'vehicles' of cognition are bound by the head. The *extended vision thesis* is an instance of the extended mind thesis that applies to vision; an early version of it was defended in my 'Wide Computationalism'"through discussion of the multispatial channels theory of form perception and of work on animal navigation systems (Wilson, 1994. See also Wilson, 1995, chapter 3). It is to an argument for this thesis that I now turn.

15.4. **An argument for the extended vision thesis**

One general consideration that opens up ground for taking the extended vision thesis seriously is that cognitive systems that have evolved through world-mind constancies are good candidates for extended cognition (Clark, 1989, 1993, chapter 6; Wilson, 1995, chapter 4). Together with what Andy Clark (1989, p.64) has called the *007 Principle* for organisms engaged in costly internal processing—'know only as much as you need to know to get the job done'—this consideration suggests that we should expect to find cognitive systems designed to rely on world-mind constancies to perform their function, rather than form and compute complex internal representations, when such constancies are there to exploit. Visual systems are often in just this position.

Over the past 15 years, a number of new accounts of visual processing have taken up a question that is very much in the background of such general considerations, and in so doing, have made the extended vision thesis more plausible. That question concerns the global function of vision: what it is that vision, as a whole, *is for*. Answering questions about the global function of any biological structure, capacity, or behaviour are far from straightforward, turning at least in part on organismal and lineage history, current utility, and the relationship between them. But at least one defensible epistemic handle on this question is to ask what it is that vision allows organisms who have it to do that those without it either cannot do, or at best do in a much more constrained and cumbersome way. The particular argument for the extended vision thesis that I shall discuss appeals, in the first instance, to the global function of visual systems.

To a large extent, the question 'What is vision for?' has not been centre-stage in traditional theories of perceptual processing. When it has been asked, the answer given has been something like this: vision is for recording some kind of raw imprint of the world, which then gets processed 'down-stream' to arrive at a reconstruction of the world in terms of concepts and categories (in organisms that have such tools) that are employed either consciously or unconsciously. Human vision in partic-ular, and human perception more generally, is 'for' cognition: vision extracts information from the world to deliver inputs to various cognitive processes. Insofar as access to visual information results in a massively enriched database on which cognitive processes can operate, vision is for the enhance-ment of cognition and, eventually, action.

A range of recent theories of vision—including O'Regan and Noë's [2001] sensorimotor theory of perception, Ballard's [Ballard et al., 1997] animate vision programme, Milner and Goodale's [1998] dual systems account of visual perception, and Matthen's [2005] action-oriented account of percep-tion as sensory sorting—have provided variants of a different answer to this question (see Wilson, 2006). They all hold that *vision is for guiding action*. While this is not the only function performed by every visual system, including those that humans have, it is the 'big thing' that vision is for. The global function of vision is to allow individuals to get around in the world. Only mobile organisms have vision, and the visual systems that organisms are equipped with, when those systems are work-ing as they ought to, ultimately guide their action. More specifically, the overarching function of vision is to guide action via the processing of a certain kind of information: visual information.

If the guidance of action is the ultimate function of visual systems, then what follows? To answer this question, consider another: how is it that visual systems achieve this function of guiding action through distal visual information? One way to do so would be to make an internal, encoded repre-sentation of what is in the world, and then, combining this with other internal representations, use internally stored computational rules to deliver outputs that serve as inputs to internal motor programmes that, in turn, generate action. This presents what we might call a *flow through* model of visual representation and visually guided action, whereby visual representations are formed inter-nally and flow through the agent's cognitive system to generate, eventually, actions and behaviours.

Such flow through models have dominated how visual representation has been conceptualized, perhaps because such models fit so tidily with the conception of vision as a feeder process that delivers raw 'sensation-like' representations to cognition central and with standard computational views of vision (Marr, 1982). They also instantiate what Susan Hurley has called the *Input-Output* picture of perception and action, which 'conceives of perception as input from the world to the mind and action as output from the mind to the world' (1998, p. 288). To be sure, flow through models have not been articulated with the conception of visual systems as being for the guidance of action in mind, but instead within a framework that holds that what vision is for is the provisioning of cogni-tive processing. Perhaps not surprisingly then, on these models, most attention has been focused on the nature of the encoding from world to mind, and to the character of the resulting internal repre-sentations. However, flow through models are not the only way to think about how visual systems operate, and they are not all that plausible as general models of how visual systems achieve their goal of guiding action. In part, this is because in the absence of basic bodily actions, such as physiological nystagmus and saccadic eye movement, many visual systems do not operate at all, or do so only in degraded or radically modified ways. As Steve Palmer notes with regard to the absence of the former, '[I]f a patterned stimulus is presented to the eyes without any retinal motion whatsoever for more than a few seconds, the pattern completely disappears!' (Palmer 1999, p. 521). Moreover, in part, this is because the kinds of rich, internal structures that flow through models require do not seem to be as ubiquitous in vision as researchers had assumed they were. On flow through models, all that bodily actions can do is to re-position the organism to produce novel inputs, or stabilize the perceiver so that inputs remain fixed over time. On these models, representations themselves cannot be enriched through later stage processes, such as motor output, except in such 'indirect' ways.

The chief alternative to viewing visual information as flowing through from perceptual to cognitive (then to motor) systems is to take the systems that process such information as *feedback systems*. In such systems, information is fed back *to the very same system in completing that system's task processing.* Such feedback can take place entirely at the level of encoding, but it can also involve feedback that does not form such an internal loop. The kind of representation that such boundary-crossing feedback systems traffic in can be partial and improvisational, including cases in which visual representation is a form of what I have elsewhere (Wilson, 2004, chapter. 8) called *exploitative representation* (see also Shapiro, 1997). Rather than taking a representational fix on the world, and then having those representations transformed internally as they flow through the organism to generate visually guided action, in exploitative visual representation the activity of representing exploits whatever resources it can to generate the appropriate action. Importantly, exploitative representation can rely on *the body's own structures and behaviours* in its activity of representing, with relevant bodily actions (in the first instance, eye-movements of various kinds, foveation, head-turning, squinting)constituting, and not simply causing, a key part of an overall perception–action cycle that manifests not informational flow through, but informational feedback.

To summarize this point: I have been drawing a contrast between two views of vision that give different answers to two questions. Concerning the question *what is vision for?*, the traditional view holds that vision is for encoding information from the world for downstream cognitive processing, while recent views that cluster under the heading of embodied approaches hold that vision is for guiding action via visual information. Concerning the question *how does vision operate?*, traditional views offer what I called flow through models, while embodied views suggest that vision functions via boundary-crossing feedback mechanisms that link perception to action. As I have indicated, traditional encoding, flow through views of vision can adapt in the direction of action-oriented views of the function of vision, but there is somewhat of an awkward fit here with the overall separability of perception and action. Likewise, such views could attempt to incorporate feedback as part of how visual systems operate, but again this adjustment to traditional views leads to positions with some instability to them. Either kind of move pushes one from separating perception and action as distinct, determinable, cognitive natural kinds towards the view that perception and action are more intimately related than such a view allows.

Susan Hurley's *Consciousness in Action* was a watershed in breaking the grip that the flow through view of perceptual representation has had on philosophers and cognitive scientists alike. One of its important contributions was in arguing against individualists about perception on very much their own turf. In doing so, Hurley provided at times a painstaking critical review of thought experiments (e.g. Twin Earth, Inverted Earth) that had been used in support of individualistic conclusions about perceptual content, and introduced discussion of actual experiments (e.g. work with inverted lenses by Ivo Kohler and by James Taylor; Paul Bach-y-Rita's development of tactile-visual substitution systems). While the negative point of Hurley's discussion was to call into question some of the large-scale frameworks in terms of which perception (and consciousness) had been conceptualized, the alternative, positive perspective on vision as involving dynamic perception-action cycles suggests a view of perception and action as being integrated much more tightly than often depicted by both philosophers and cognitive scientists. On the view that Hurley shares with many others who take the function of vision to be the guidance of organismic action, it is not simply that our visual systems are causally hooked up to (the rest of) our brains/bodies, or that these systems deliver sensory outputs to (the rest of) the brain/body, which then executes motor routines. Rather, what is usually thought of as the human visual system (starting at the retina and terminating in one or another area of visual cortex) is *coupled integratively* with the non-neural body via a sequence of bodily actions. This use of the body, this body-in-action, creates and stabilizes a chain of representations tied directly to actions.

Although I have said that visual systems are embodied 'in a fairly strong sense', it is important to note that this is not the strongest possible sense in which one might speak of the embodiment of vision. The claim is not that visual systems are *necessarily* parts of bodies, or that it is impossible to have functioning visual systems that are removed from, or even temporarily causally disengaged from, the rest of the body. Both of these stronger claims seem to me to be clearly false. This is not, however, because the body merely provides causal inputs to perception through its actions, nor because bodies (for some reason) fail to realize visual processing. Rather, it is chiefly because of general facts about how complex, modularly decomposable systems operate. Such systems in general do not have *any* parts that are strictly necessary, since one can substitute functionally equivalent parts for any given part. That, I think, is one of the implications of functional decomposition, however constrained actual substitutions might be given actual circumstances. Yet since this is true as much of 'brain parts' as of 'bodily parts', it does little to soften the claim that vision is embodied. Physical bodily parts need not be subject to theses that are stronger than those that hold true of physical neural parts; neural parts are, after all, just body parts with a particular location, composition, and range of functions.

I hope to have said enough about the starting points of the argument for extended vision that I am making now to lay out the whole argument more explicitly. The argument runs as follows:

1. The function of some visual processes is to guide action via visual information.

2. A primary way to achieve that function is through the active embodiment of visual processing (in a fairly strong sense).

3. Visual processes are actively embodied (in that same fairly strong sense) just if in their normal operation in natural environments, these processes are *coupled* with bodily activities so as to form an *integrated system* with *functional gain*. But

4. Visual processes that are actively embodied, in this sense, are also extended. Therefore,

5. Some visual processes, and the visual systems those processes physically constitute, are extended.

The argument begins, at (1), with a claim about the function of some visual processes, and is based on my discussion of the more general global function of vision. Premise (2) purports to identify the active embodiment of visual processing as *one way*, albeit an important way, in which this function is achieved, at least in human beings and other mobile material beasts with which we are familiar. The 3 makes more precise what I mean by the active embodiment of vision, while the 4 draws a link between active embodiment and extended vision. Yet (3) requires further explication, not least of all because it is cast in terms of a notion that I have mentioned but not explained so far, that of *functionally gainful, integrative coupling*. And (4) has not been discussed at all. To work!

15.5. **External sensory systems: back to bats and electric fish**

Let us return first to some of the cases mentioned in section 15.2: those of organisms, such as bats, which use self-generated sonic fields for navigation and prey detection, and electric fish, which generate weak electric fields for the same purposes. Just as the examples of inverting lenses and tactile visual substitution systems provide the basis for viewing perception as embodied in a fairly strong sense, these examples provide grounds for taking perception to be *extended* in that same fairly strong sense. In such cases, organisms expend energy in creating a field (acoustic or electric in these cases) that they then interact with through motion in order to hunt, feed, mate, or navigate. I suspect that it would be at best very strained to argue that these fields do not physically constitute part of the sensory system of these organisms (and are, instead, say, simply resources used by, or inputs to, bodily-bounded sensory systems) as a broader consideration of their sensory ecology and evolution implies. These sensory systems are, in Richard Dawkins's (1982) terms, *extended phenotypes* of the organism; they are adaptations that have been selected for, much as their *internal* sensory physiology has. In at least these cases, sensory systems are extended, and they provide examples of a fairly radical form of 'vehicle externalism' about the mind, one that does not appeal to intuitions about mental content, or claims about what happens on Twin Earth (or if there is an evil demon). In such cases, a slab of sensory processing, some of which is almost certainly computational, takes place outside of the body of the organism, as MacIver (2009) has argued recently. Still, might all the computation that underpins bat echolocation be going on solely in the bat's brain?

One function of such extended sensory systems is to ease the 'in-the-head' computational and representational load, much as is the case of sensory off-loading where *non-sensory* body parts, such as the forelimbs of the legs of crickets, are recruited as part of an overall sensory function (in this case, phonotaxis). By redistributing computation beyond the nervous system, adaptive behaviour is clearly facilitated, as a closer look at any of the above examples reveals. Moreover, in all of these cases, it is not just aspects of the self-generated environment that are recruited as sensory resources, but parts of the organism's own body. In many cases, and in more distinctly philosophical terms, the body becomes part of the *realization base* for the computations that allow the organism to perform its cognitive functions. MacIver (2009) refers to such computation as *morphological computation*: computation that uses the organism's own morphology as part of computing machinery in play (see also Paul, 2004; Pfeifer and Bongard, 2006). This recruitment of one's own body as a computational resource can make itself visible over evolutionary time, as the variation one finds in bat pinnea implies, as MacIver also suggests. The shape and character of the ear itself is a morphological adaptation that forms part of the more complex behavioural adaptation of the echolocatory and visual-motor systems, both of which have been the object of natural selection over many generations. As MacIver says, the 'conformation of skin and supporting tissue of the ear in the bat forms a computational device that solves a key problem in the localization of prey in three-dimensional space' (2009, p. 488).

To take an example closer to home ground, consider optic flow, the pattern of apparent motion of objects and features in a visual scene that is created when an organism, such as a vertebrate, moves through space. When the optic field flow expands, it indicates, in conjunction with the organism's movement, that it is approaching some fixed point, while contracting optic flows indicate a growing gap between organism and object (Gibson, 1979, p. 227). Optic flow also crosses the divide between vertebrates and invertebrates. Recent research in invertebrate neuroethology on the visual systems of flies has focused on ways in which flies detect self-propulsion in order to stabilize their flight pattern. Facts about the geometry and physiological wiring of the fly's photoreceptors simplify the computation of optic flow (see Egelhaaf et al., 2002). For example, the dendrite of a tangential cell (VS6) likely integrates the input from sensors that detect optic flow patterns. The sensors (the ommatidia) that feed the neuron detecting a fly's rolling motion (as when it tips to one side) are located in a row that lies parallel to the pattern of optic flow. Given that the change in optic flow characteristic of rolling is typically caused in the fly's usual environment by the fly's own motion, activity in this neuron indicates self-motion to the fly. Both of these physiological set-ups contribute to simplifying the neural computation of optic flow in ways that connect the fly's visual system more effectively to action. They do so by distributing the overall computation over brain and body, not brain alone.

This kind of example provides the connection between what we might regard as the exotic cases of paradigmatic extended sensory systems (the echolocating bat, the electrically sensing fish) and more familiar and mundane examples of sensory systems. For *lots of creatures, including us,* operate visually in part through optic flow, and through a variety of other means whereby aspects of the organism's environment and their interaction with and manipulation of it are crucial to the visual tasks that they undertake. This is just what we should expect if sensing is a kind of doing, a kind of activity, a way in which organisms extract and exploit information from their environments through their bodily interactions with it. To connect this up directly with the earlier discussion of the embodiment of human vision: eye movements, foveation, saccading, head-turning and other forms of head movement, and even squinting are all familiar ways in which organisms like us adjust their bodies with respect to their environments in order to improve their visual performance. Once sensory systems are conceptualized in dynamic terms, such that we consider not only their in-the-head functional decomposition but also their in-the-world functional role, there is pressure to see more and more of their activity as extending beyond the brain into the body and, as I shall argue, into the world. More externalist creep.

One natural response to this point is to acknowledge a role for both body and world in easing perceptual computation and generating perception, but dispute that either body or world have a *constitutive* role in perception. To counter such a response, and to respond in turn to related objections to premises in the argument, I shall elaborate on the notion of active embodiment and its relation to extended vision.

15.6. **Integrative coupling, embodiment, and extended vision**

I have been arguing that vision is embodied in a fairly strong sense (section 15.4), a conclusion reinforced and connected to the extended vision thesis by consideration of the active, extended sensory systems of creatures like bats and electric fish, and reflection on the connection between such exotic cases and those that are more familiar (section 15.5). However, more needs to be said about the notion of embodiment itself in play, which brings us back to Premise (3):

> (3) Visual processes are actively embodied (in a strong sense) just if in their normal operation in natural environments, these processes are *coupled* with bodily activities to form an *integrated system* with *functional gain*.

I introduce *functionally gainful, integrative coupling* as a technical notion that can be explained in terms of the three component notions that it contains.

First, two processes are *coupled* just if there are reliable causal connections between them. Since reliable causal connections between x and y entail a strong correlation between the presence of x and the presence of y, but (notoriously) correlation does not entail causation: coupling is a *stronger* notion than mere correlation. The processes leading to the growth in height of the summer annuals planted in various parts of my garden are correlated but not coupled. Second, two processes form an *integrated system* just if there are contexts in which they operate as one, as a whole, in the causal nexus, with causes affecting the resultant system as a whole, and the activities of that system as a whole producing certain effects. Although causal coupling need not produce an integrative system (two annuals planted very close together in my garden might have processes that are reliably coupled without those processes forming an integrative system), integrative systems result typically from causal coupling, and when they do, we have *integrative coupling*. What bridges the gap between mere reliable coupling and the formation of integrative systems is the sharing of parts and activities. Third, an integratively coupled system shows *functional gain* just when it either enhances the existing functions of its coupled components, or manifests novel functions relative to those of any functions possessed by those components.

Before considering special features of the active embodiment of visual processing, note that functionally gainful, integrative coupling is a general phenomenon that is commonplace in biological and social processes (see Wilson, 2005, chapters 3–4 and 6–7). Consider human digestion, which involves the causal coupling of the activities of human body parts, such as the stomach, and the activities of microorganisms, like *Escherichia coli*, that find a useful habitat in those parts. The resultant, integratively coupled system, the human digestive system, has evolved over time to process foods more effectively than do any of its constituent processes alone, and so that system shows functional gain. Although the process of human digestion incorporates non-human components, such as those processes undertaken by *E. coli*, note that these still take place in the digestive system *of a human being* whose trajectory in the world is affected by these processes. The relevant processes (and, I think, systems) here are one kind of entity; the human being whose behaviour is governed, in part, by those processes, is another.

To take an example from the social domain, consider the process of pairwise cooperation as facilitated through explicit agreements to cooperate. I say 'I'll scratch your back, if you scratch mine' and you say 'Sure'. Here such agreements causally couple the activities of distinct individuals, who thus come to engage in pairwise cooperation. When things go well, this results in a dyadic cooperative system, one sustained by internalized and externally imposed sanctions, that shows functional gains in terms of problem-solving and desire satisfaction in certain contexts (e.g. those in which a pair of backs are to be scratched), as classic discussions of prisoner's dilemma and other game-theoretic scenarios indicate. The fact that there is a functionally gainful, integratively coupled system is compatible with the existence of identifiable parts, each with its own integrity and functions, and with the decomposition of that integrative system into those functional parts.

As these examples perhaps suggest, functionally gainful, integrative coupling can result in systems of various levels of durability and robustness over time and circumstance (cf. Wilson and Clark, 2009, pp. 64–68). It does not require any form of lawful or other necessary connection between the constituent components to the integrated system, or at least none more than reliable causation itself requires. For this reason, it is irrelevant to whether there is integrative coupling that there are possible (even actual) circumstances in which the constituent processes come apart, or in which there can be (or are) alternative constituent processes. For example, that bacteria other than *E.coli* might play the role in digestion that *E.coli* actually play does nothing to undermine the claim that stomachs and *E.coli* are (together with much else) integratively coupled in the process of digestion as it actually occurs. Likewise, the vulnerability of an integratively coupled system to dissolution—as is pairwise cooperation through cheating and external threat—does not itself call into question whether there is integrative coupling when those threats are absent or non-effective.

Returning to visual processing and bodily activities, it seems that *everyone* who is party to the debate over the embodiment of vision grants that there is causal coupling between (some aspects of) vision and (some aspects of) action, just as everyone who is party to the debate over the extended mind thesis grants that there is causal coupling between (some aspects of) cognition and (some aspects of) the beyond-the-skin environment. The real question, in both cases, is of the significance of such causal coupling. In the case of the active embodiment of visual processing, this is of significance just when such coupling between visual processing and bodily activity produces integratively coupled systems and those systems manifest functional gain, in the senses just explained, through their normal operation in their natural environments. Such systems are often called *visuo-motor systems* or *modules* (e.g. Ballard, 1996; Milner and Goodale, 1998a and 1998b). If the overarching function of vision is the guidance of action through visual information, then such systems or modules have functional gain with respect to the functions of the constituent processes in such systems.

Of what sorts of visual process might this be true? Some might suggest, following Milner and Goodale (1998a and 1998b), that such processes are restricted to those subserved by the dorsal stream of visual processing, the *where system* in primate visual systems, including motion perception and spatial orientation. This would leave those subserved by the ventral stream, the *what system*, such as object recognition, beyond the reach of the kind of active embodiment thesis being used here to defend extended vision. While the distinction between dorsal and ventral streams of visual processing has been articulated both functionally and anatomically in increasing detail over the past 40 years since Schneider (1969) first postulated the distinction based on work with hamsters, and Ungerleider and Mishkin (1982) developed it further on the basis of work with primates, I am sceptical that the distinction can serve adequately to demarcate (or contain) actively embodied visual processing in the manner suggested here. Many of the common types of visual processes that are invoked in theories of vision (visual attention, depth perception, shape perception, image change detection, even motion perception and objection recognition themselves) involve aspects or dimensions that fall under *both* kinds of system. Accounts of these processes that approach empirical adequacy for the range of phenomena that each encompasses will almost certainly appeal to *both* what and where systems (cf. also Hurley, 1998, pp. 180–183). All require eye movements and associated bodily adjustments, for example in how they normally operate in natural environments.

To say that visual processes are actively embodied, then, is to say much more than that they are causally coupled, or to infer directly from the causal coupling of vision and action to their active embodiment, committing what some, following Adams and Aizawa (2001, 2008, 2009), call the *coupling-constitution fallacy* (e.g. Block, 2005; Prinz, 2009). To elaborate on this second point, we need to be more explicit about precisely what this fallacy is. Often when Adams and Aizawa (2008, pp. 93–99; 2009, pp. 81–83) ascribe this fallacy, they attribute to proponents of the extended mind thesis the following inference pattern:

a. Y is a cognitive process

b. X is causally coupled to Y; therefore

c. X is part of a cognitive process

where X = activities involving some environmental structure, such as a notebook, and Y = some specific in-the-head processing, such as memory retrieval. Whatever one thinks of Adams and Aizawa's claim to find such an inference pattern almost ubiquitously in the work of those defending the extended mind thesis, the preceding argument contains no inference of this form, modified so that X = bodily actions or activities and Y = some specific in-the-head visual processing, such as the computation of depth from disparity or shading in visual cortex. Rather, the claim is that the causal coupling between visual processing and bodily activities *builds an integratively coupled system that is a causal entity in its own right, both subject to, and an agent of, causal influence.* This is parallel to the way in which the causal coupling between body parts (like stomachs) and bacteria (like *E. coli*) builds an integratively coupled system that digests, and that between individuals, facilitated by explicit agreements, builds a dyadic group that cooperates pairwise to achieve particular goals. My view is that only by denying integrative coupling as a general phenomenon, or that it is a phenomenon that one finds in perception, can one challenge Premise (2) in the argument I have offered. But that would be to make something other than the charge that the argument trades on a 'coupling/constitution fallacy'.

Although Adams and Aizawa sometimes identify that fallacy as I have above, they also employ that term more broadly to pick out a larger family of faulty inferences that they believe proponents of extended cognition make. Prominent amongst these are defences of the extended mind thesis that involve an inference from claims about extended *systems* to conclusions about extended *processes* (e.g., Adams and Aizawa, 2008. chapter 7; 2009, pp. 83–5). One might think that this is precisely the form that the coupling-constitution fallacy takes in the argument I have offered for the extended vision thesis, since that argument is cast explicitly in terms of the notion of integrated *systems*. To link this transparently to the preceding schema, we might characterize this version of the putative fallacy as follows:

A. Y is a cognitive (perceptual) process

B1. X is causally coupled to Y

B2. X and Y form an integrated system (with functional gain), therefore

C. X is part of a cognitive (perceptual) process.

However, there are two reasons why my argument does not instantiate this fallacious pattern of inference. The first is that it does not begin with a premise like (A); in fact, it does not even contain a premise like (A); cf. my premises (1)–(4). The second is that it does not conclude with a conclusion like (C). Rather, it begins with a claim about a function of vision and how that function is achieved, and concludes with a claim about not the character of any component of the resulting system but with a claim about the character of that system itself. In offering a conception of visual processes as actively embodied, it depicts visual processing as a kind of *building* or *construction*, whereby bodily resources are recruited to enhance and even create visual functioning of various kinds.

Having spent some time articulating and defending (3) (and (2)) in the argument for extended vision, which takes us only to the claim that vision is actively embodied, not extended, what of the remaining premise, (4), that completes the argument?

(4) Visual systems that are embodied, in this sense, are also extended.

Given the conception of active embodiment that I have defended, (4) is less of a leap than it may sound initially, since the resultant integratively coupled system is one tracing an arc that reaches beyond the body of the organism. While proprioception and kinesthesia provide two sources for causal couplings between visual processing and bodily activities that remain within the bodily envelope, simple visual observation of one's own body and its movements over time provides a kind of feedback from vision to action that goes beyond that boundary. Much like the extended sensory systems of bats and electric fish, the visuo-motor systems with which we explore our visual world are not contained fully within the bodily boundary. While their extended sensory systems are realized, in part, by sonic and electromagnetic fields that they generate through their bodily movements, our extended visual systems are realized, in part, by optic flow fields that we generate through *our* bodily movements. Neither the sonic, nor electromagnetic, nor optic flow fields that are used in perceptual processing, respectively, by bats, electric fish, or human beings, exist simply in the world independently of these organisms. Rather, they are created and sustained by the ongoing, active bodily engagement of those organisms with their environments. Since this form of embodiment involves causal integration between organisms and physical structures that lie beyond the physical boundaries of those organisms, it is a kind of extended perception. In the case of human (and much other animal) vision, it is a kind of extended vision.

Perhaps this becomes clearer once we consider more explicitly the *dynamic* dimension to visual processing (Hurley, 1998, Chapter 10), acknowledging the fact that it is only through bodily movement over time, especially of the eyes through physiological nystagmus, saccadic eye movements, and smooth pursuit and vergence movements (Palmer, 1999, pp. 519–25), that there is a visual field with anything like the richness of our actual visual field at all. Visual representational cascades are built up dynamically over time, with repetitive feedback loops building the information that fills visual pathways, and that makes visual experience possible. Vision is a hungry constructive process, one that needs to be fed continually over time if it is to function as it is supposed to. While it feeds on inputs and produces outputs, those outputs themselves feed back over time into the system that produces them. The 'it' here is not a system that begins and ends in a part of the brain, nor even in the body. It involves a body that moves over time, and through a particular environment. Vision is extended.

15.7. **What of visual experience?**

This brings me back, finally, to visual experience, and the role that it has come to play as a last refuge for individualistic intuitions. Recall Block's claim that 'the minimal constitutive supervenience base for perceptual experience is the brain and does not include the rest of the body' (Block, 2005, p. 271). Even putting aside (4) in the argument for extended vision, if the premises (1)–(3) in that argument are true, then we can see why this claim is false, at least of much perceptual experience. Moreover, it is false for much the reason that the corresponding claim is false of tactile and orgasmal experience: the visual processing that underlies visual experience, like the sensory processing that underlies these paradigmatic forms of bodily experience, is coupled integratively with bodily activity.

Strictly speaking, what (1)–(3) imply most directly is the falsity of the claim that the minimal constitutive supervenience base for perceptual *systems* is the brain and does not include the rest of the body. Could one not concede that point, but insist, with Block, that perceptual *experience* is located firmly within the neural fold, inside not just the body, but the head, much in the way that one might allow that an air-conditioning *system* extends throughout a house but insist that *the air-conditioning itself* is localized *right here* in a particular unit within that system, such as the compressor (cf. Adams and Aizawa, 2009)? *That's* where the air-conditioning is taking place, just as all of the computing in a computational system (which might include screens, printers, hard drives, wireless signals, and more) takes place in the *central processing unit*. In short, does not the explicit appeal in (1)–(3) in the argument to visual systems, an appeal that is then used to reach a conclusion about visual *experience*, commit a fallacy that falls under the broad head of the coupling-constitution fallacy?

To be clear on this: no, it does not. While there is an inference being made from a claim about the visual system to a claim about visual processing *and so visual experience*, the visual system just is the system in which visual processing takes place. Certainly, the neural pathways that subserve many aspects of vision are located in the head, and they will have some properties that are unique (and so not shared by other parts of the visual system) and not possessed by the system as a whole. Neurons fire; visual systems do so at best metaphorically or in some other sense. My claim is that *having visual experience* and *being the place where visual experience happens* are not amongst such properties. What is at issue is whether any amount or form of activity just in those pathways themselves is metaphysically sufficient for the full range of visual experience, or something suitably like our actual visual experience. For this reason, reports of some kind of experience or other in cases of partial paralysis of the body, or even of the more extensive paralysis brought on by the neuromuscular blockade of receptors for the transmitter acetylcholine (Adams and Aizawa, 2008, pp.166–72), offer no challenge to the argument I have offered, which is specifically about everyday vision and visual experience. The same is true of appeals to other cases, such as dreams, TMS stimulation to orgasm, or pain in phantom limbs, in which experience of some kind is putatively divorced from the kind of active embodiment that is extended. Whether a modification of the argument offered here can be defended for the full range of experience is an issue I leave for further discussion (see also Wilson, 2004, Chapter 9).

In fact, if visual processing itself is actively embodied in the way I have defined that notion here, it is hard to see how a feature generated by that processing in toto, visual experience, could fail to be actively embodied as well. To look to identify the realization base for visual experience in the brain would be more like aiming to locate digestion solely in the stomach, or fitness solely in the organism. Stomachs digest, and organisms have fitness, but at best they realize these properties partially. Sometimes we look inside organisms and their parts to identify what is metaphysically sufficient for the properties they possess, but sometimes we need to look to what those organisms, and those parts, in turn form a part of, as I have argued at length elsewhere (Wilson, 2004, Chapters 5–6). Visual experience, I am claiming, is a property that falls into this latter category.

Since I have argued that visual processing is not simply actively embodied but also, in light of that, extended, I think that the same reasoning above implies that visual experience, as an outcome of some forms of extended visual processing, is also extended. At the outset I noted that I have previously argued that at least some of the various phenomena that fall under the rubric of consciousness—higher order thought, introspection, and some aspects of attention—fall under the umbrella of the extended mind thesis, and that at least some aspects of visual experience should be viewed likewise (Wilson, 2004, chapters 9–10). In appealing to the active embodiment of visual processing, and the link between that and extended vision, I have sought a way to reinforce that conclusion. Visual experience thus joins these other aspects of consciousness, processes of awareness, in further extending externalist creep from the intentional into the phenomenal. Thus, the space for individualistic refuge is smaller than many individualists have thought it is.

Acknowledgements

This paper is dedicated to the memory of Susan Hurley, and owes much (though, no doubt, not enough) to her *Consciousness in Action*. I would like to thank the audience at the Bristol workshop on vision organized by Susan in July 2007 for constructive feedback on the first airing of the main argument that the paper contains, and Andy Clark and Malcolm MacIver for 'collaboration interrupted' that has proven relevant to this chapter. Thanks also to Larry Shapiro, Fred Adams, Ken Aizawa, Rob Rupert, Matt Barker, and Ned Block for perceptive comments on the full draft, even if they feel that their hard work has not been embodied (in a fairly strong sense) in the final version.

References

Adams, F. and Aizawa, K. (2001). The bounds of cognition. *Philosophical Psychology*; **14**: 43–64.
—— (2008). *The bounds of cognition*. Oxford: Blackwell.
—— (2009). Why the mind is still in the head. In *The Cambridge handbook of situated cognition*, (ed. Robbins, P. and Aydede, M.), pp.78–95. New York: Cambridge University Press.
Aizawa, K. (2007). Understanding the embodiment of perception. *Journal of Philosophy*; **104**: 5–25.
Ballard, D.H. (1996). On the function of visual representation. In *Perception*, (ed. Akins, K.A.). New York: Oxford University Press.
Ballard, D., Hayhoe, M.M., Pook, P.K., and Rao, R.P.N. (1997). Deictic codes for the embodiment of cognition. *Behavioral and Brain Sciences*; **20**: 723–67.
Block, N. (2005). Review of Alva Noë, action in perception. *Journal of Philosophy*; **102**: 259–72.
Burge, T. (1979). Individualism and the mental. In *Midwest Studies in Philosophy*, (ed. French, P., Uehling Jr., T., and Wettstein, H.), Vol. 4, pp. 73–121. Minneapolis: University of Minnesota Press.
—— (1986). Individualism and psychology. *Philosophical Review*; **95**: 3–45.
Chomsky, N. (1995). Language and nature. *Mind*; **104**: 1–61.
Clark, A. (1989). *Microcognition: philosophy, cognitive science, and parallel distributed processing*. Cambridge, MA: MIT Press.
—— (1993). *Associative engines*. Cambridge, MA: MIT Press.
—— (2007). Curing cognitive hiccups: a defense of the extended mind. *Journal of Philosophy*; **104**: 163–92.
—— (2008). *Supersizing the mind: embodiment, action, and cognitive extension*. New York: Oxford University Press.
—— (2009). Spreading the joy: why the machinery of consciousness is (probably) still in the head. *Mind*; **118**: 963–993.
—— (2010). Coupling, constitution and the cognitive kind: a reply to Adams and Aizawa. In *The extended mind*, (ed. Menary, R.). Cambridge, MA: MIT Press.

Clark, A. and Chalmers, D. (1998). The extended mind. *Analysis*; **58**: 10–23.

Dawkins, R. (1982). *The extended phenotype*. Oxford: Oxford University Press.

Egan, F. (1992). Individualism, computation, and perceptual content. *Mind*; **101**: 443–59.

Egelhaaf, M., Kern R., Krapp H.G., Kretzberg J., Kurtz R., and Warzecha A.K. (2002). Neural encoding of behaviorally relevant visual-motion information in the fly. *Trends in Neurosciences*; **25**(2): 96–102.

Field, H. (1978). Mental representation. *Erkenntniss*; **13**: 9–61.

Fodor, J.A. (1982). Cognitive science and the Twin-Earth problem. *Notre Dame Journal of Formal Logic*; **23**: 98–118.

Gallagher, S. (2005). *How the body shapes the mind*. New York: Oxford University Press.

Gibson, J.J. (1979). *The ecological approach to perceptual systems*. Boston, MA: Houghton Mifflin.

Horgan, T. and Tienson J. (2002). The intentionality of phenomenology and the phenomenology of intentionality. In *Philosophy of mind: classical and contemporary readings*, (ed. Chalmers, D.J.), pp. 520–32. New York: Oxford University Press.

Hurley, S. (1998). *Consciousness in action*. Cambridge, MA: Harvard University Press.

Loar, B. (1981). *Meaning in mind*. Cambridge: Cambridge University Press.

—— (2002). Transparent experience and the availability of qualia. In *Consciousness: New Essays*, (ed. Smith, Q. and Jokic, A.), pp.77–96. New York: Oxford University Press.

Loar, B. (2003). Phenomenal intentionality as the basis of mental content. In *Reflections and replies: essays on the philosophy of Tyler Burge*, (ed. Hahn, M. and Ramberg, B.), pp. 229–58. Cambridge, MA: MIT Press.

MacIver, M. (2009). Neuroethology: from morphological computing to planning. In *The Cambridge handbook of situated cognition*, (ed. Robbins, P. and Aydede, M.), pp. 480–504. New York: Cambridge University Press.

Matthen, M. (2005). *Seeing, doing, and knowing: a philosophical theory of sense perception*. New York: Oxford University Press.

McGinn, C. (1982). The structure of content. In *Thought and object: essays on intentionality*, (ed. Woodfield, A.), pp. 206–58. Oxford: Oxford University Press.

Milner, D. and Goodale M. (1998a). The visual brain in action. *Psyche*; 4(12): (http://psyche.cs.monash.edu.au/v4/psyche-4-12-milner.html).

—— (1998b). *The visual brain in action*. Oxford: Oxford University Press.

Myin, E. and O'Regan, J.K. (2009). Situated perception and sensation in vision and other modalities: a sensorimotor approach. In *The Cambridge handbook of situated cognition*, (ed. Robbins, P. and Aydede, M.), pp.185–200. New York: Cambridge University Press.

Noë, A. (2004). *Action in perception*. Cambridge, MA: MIT Press.

—— (2009). *Out of our heads: why you are not your brain, and other lessons from the biology of consciousness*. New York: Hill and Wang.

O'Regan, J.K. and No A. (2001). A sensorimotor account of vision and visual consciousness. *Behavioral and Brain Sciences*; **24** (5), 883–917.

Palmer, S. (1999). *Vision science*. Cambridge, MA: MIT Press.

Paul, C. (2004). Morphology and computation. In *Proceedings of the Eighth International Conference on the Simulation of Adaptive Behaviour*, (ed. Schaal, S., Ijspeert, A.J., Billard, A., and Meyer, J-A.), pp. 33–38. Cambridge MA: MIT Press.

Pfeifer, R. and Bongard J.C. (2006). *How the body shapes the way we think: a new view of intelligence*. Cambridge, MA: MIT Press.

Prinz, J. (2009). Is consciousness embodied. In *The Cambridge handbook of situated cognition*, (ed. Robbins, P. and Aydede, M.), pp. 419–36. New York: Cambridge University Press.

Putnam, H. (1975). The meaning of 'meaning'. In *Language, mind and knowledge*, (ed. Gunderson, K.), pp.131–93. Minneapolis: University of Minnesota Press.

Rupert, R. (2004). Challenges to the hypothesis of extended cognition. *Journal of Philosophy*; **101**: 389–428.

Schneider, G.E. (1969). Two visual systems. *Science*; **163**: 895–902.

Segal, G. (1989). Seeing what is not there. *Philosophical Review*; **98**: 189–214.

Shapiro, L. (1997). A clearer vision. *Philosophy of Science*; **64**: 131–53.

Ungerleider, L.G. and Mishkin M. (1982). Two cortical visual systems. In *Analysis of Visual Behavior*, (ed. Ingle, D.J., Goodale, M.A., and Mansfield, R.J.W.), pp.549–86. Cambridge, MA: The MIT Press.

Wilson, R.A. (1994). Wide computationalism. *Mind*; **101**: 351–72.

—— (1995). *Cartesian psychology and physical minds: individualism and the sciences of the mind*. New York: Cambridge University Press.

—— (2000). The mind beyond itself. In *Metarepresentations: A multidisciplinary perspective*, (ed. Sperber, D.), pp. 31–52. New York: Oxford University Press.

—— (2003). Individualism. In *The Blackwell companion to philosophy of mind*, (ed. Stich, S. and Warfield, T.A.), pp. 256–87 New York: Blackwell.

—— (2004). *Boundaries of the mind: the individual in the fragile sciences: cognition*. New York: Cambridge University Press.

—— (2005). *Genes and the agents of life: the individual in the fragile sciences: biology*. New York: Cambridge University Press.

—— (2006). Critical notice of Mohan Matthen's *Seeing, knowing, and doing: a philosophical theory of sense perception*. *Canadian Journal of Philosophy*; **36**: 117–32.

Wilson and Foglia (2010). Embodied cognition, *Stanford encyclopedia of philosophy*.

—— (in press). Meaning making and the mind of the externalist. In *The Extended Mind*, (ed. Menary, R.). Cambridge, MA: MIT Press.

Wilson, R.A. and Clark A. (2009). How to situate the mind: letting nature take its course. In *The Cambridge handbook of situated cognition*, (ed. Robbins, P. and Aydede, M.), pp. 55–77. New York: Cambridge University Press.

Author Index

Subject Index

Note: 'n.' after a page reference indicates the number of a note on that page.